HANDBOOK
on
THE LAW OF SMALL BUSINESS ENTERPRISES

JOHN H. WILLIAMSON
Attorney at Law

ARGYLE PUBLISHING COMPANY
Lakewood, Colorado

Other law books published by Argyle Publishing Company:

The Wills, Trusts and Estate Planning Handbook

The Attorney's Handbook on Consumer Bankruptcy and Chapter 13

The Bankruptcy Issues Handbook

The Attorney's Handbook on Small Business Reorganization Under Chapter 11

The Attorney's Handbook on Drinking Driving Defense

The Attorney's Handbook on Qualified Domestic Relations Orders

Sixth Edition, 1999

ISBN 1-880730-24-3

Published and Distributed by

ARGYLE PUBLISHING COMPANY

10395 West Colfax Avenue
Lakewood, Colorado 80215
(Telephone: 1-800-955-4569)
(Fax: 303-237-2617)

Printed in the United States of America
on elemental chlorine-free paper

CONTENTS

CHAPTER FOUR

LIMITED LIABILITY COMPANIES

EXHIBITS FOR CHAPTER FOUR

CHAPTER FIVE

ORGANIZING A SMALL BUSINESS CORPORATION

EXHIBITS FOR CHAPTER FIVE

CHAPTER SIX

OPERATING A SMALL BUSINESS CORPORATION

EXHIBITS FOR CHAPTER SIX

CHAPTER SEVEN

TERMINATING A SMALL BUSINESS CORPORATION

APPENDIXES

INDEX

INTRODUCTION

The Handbook on the Law of Small Business Enterprises is designed to serve as a ready reference for advising small businesses and as a guide in the organization of small business enterprises. To this end, this handbook contains, in addition to the text, checklists for organizing partnerships, limited liability companies and corporations and samples of documents typically needed to organize and operate these entities. This handbook also contains, in Appendix I, summaries of the business organization laws of each state. Included here are summaries of and citations to the partnership, limited liability company, and corporation laws of each state.

Chapter one of this handbook covers the legal, practical, and tax aspects of selecting a business entity for a small business enterprise. Discussed here are the advantages and disadvantages of limited liability companies, limited liability, general, and limited partnerships, corporations and sole proprietorships. Chapter two covers the organization and use of sole proprietorships. Chapter three covers the organization and use of general, limited, and limited liability partnerships. Included in this chapter are extensive checklists for use in organizing partnerships. Sample partnership agreements are set forth in the exhibits at the end of this chapter. This chapter also contains a section on the organization and use of joint ventures.

Chapter four covers the organization and use of limited liability companies. Included here is a section on the tax status of limited liability companies and a section on converting existing partnerships and corporations to limited liability companies. Section 4.04 contains a Limited Liability Company Checklist and Guide for use in organizing a limited liability company. Included in the exhibits at the end of chapter four are sample articles of organization for a limited liability company and sample operating agreements for both member-managed and manager-managed limited liability companies.

Chapter five covers the organization and use of small business corporations. Included in this chapter are sections on the tax aspects of incorporating a small business, the use of preincorporation agreements, the use of shareholder agreements, preparing and filing articles of incorporation, the special problems of incorporating an existing business, the capital structure of a small business corporation, controlling the transfer of stock, and the Subchapter S election. Section 5.21 contains a list of the documents needed to organize a small business corporation and an extensive checklist setting forth the matters that should be taken into account when organizing a small business corporation.

Chapter six covers the legal aspects of operating and managing small business corporations. Included in this chapter are sections on employee compensation, handling corporate meetings, handling internal disputes, the personal liability of corporate officers and directors, and the purchase of a business by a corporation. Chapter 7 deals with the termination of small business corporations. Included in this chapter are sections dealing with the alternatives available to a failing business and the sale of a small business corporation.

In using this handbook the reader is encouraged to refer to the summaries of state business organization laws set forth in Appendix I in the back of this book. A separate summary is set forth for each state. Each summary contains much of the information needed to organize a small business enterprise in that state, together with citations to the appropriate sections of the state corporation, partnership, and limited liability company laws. The reader is also encouraged to use the subject index in the back of this book. The subject index will refer the reader to the appropriate page of text and the paragraph notes in the margin of each page of text will refer the reader to the exact location of the desired subject in the text. The corporate, limited liability company, and partnership documents that appear in the exhibits of this handbook are available on a computer diskette, which may be purchased from the publisher at the address shown in the front of this book.

CHAPTER ONE

SELECTING THE BUSINESS ENTITY

1.01 The Entities Available to a Small Business Enterprise

small businesses, available entities

For purposes of selecting a business entity, one-person businesses should be distinguished from multi-person businesses. The business entities available to a one-person business are a sole proprietorship, a corporation, and, in most states, a limited liability company. The corporation may be a C corporation or an S corporation and in some states may be a close corporation. The business entities available to a multi-person business include a corporation, a limited liability company, a general partnership, a limited partnership, a joint venture, and, in most states, a limited liability partnership. Again, the corporation may be a C corporation or an S corporation and in some states may be a close corporation.

small business, entities, brief descriptions of

An S corporation is a small business corporation qualified under Subchapter S of the Internal Revenue Code. A C corporation is a nonSubchapter S corporation; that is, a corporation for which a Subchapter S election is not in effect (such a corporation is referred to as a C corporation in the Internal Revenue Code). A close corporation, which is provided for in the corporation laws of several states, may be a C corporation or an S corporation, but must be organized under a close corporation statute or code. A limited liability company (LLC) must be organized in accordance with the state Limited Liability Company Act and in most states may consist of one or more members. A general partnership consists of two or more general partners and may be created formally or informally. A limited partnership consists of one or more general partners and one or more limited partners and may be formed only by complying with the requirements of the state limited partnership act. A limited liability partnership (LLP) is a general partnership that has registered as a limited liability partnership under the state limited liability partnership statutes. In some states a limited partnership may also register as an LLP. Joint ventures have most of the legal characteristics of general partnerships except that the scope or purpose of the enterprise is narrower, and must be formed pursuant to a written or verbal agreement between the persons involved. A sole proprietorship is a business that is owned and managed by one person and is usually formed informally by the person involved. Joint stock companies, cooperatives, business trusts, and other seldom-used entities are not covered in this handbook.

alternatives to business entities

In certain situations additional options, in the nature of relationships not usually thought of as forms of business entities, may be used by the persons involved. Included here are such relationships as lender and creditor, lessor and lessee, and principal and agent. For example, if one person supplies most of the capital for a business enterprise, a promissory note coupled with an agreement creating a security interest in the business property or proceeds or an agreement to share the business profits in certain proportions may be preferable to the establishment of a partnership or joint venture. A retired participant or other person who desires a stable income from a family business may find it advantageous to lease the business assets to the successor in the business rather than being an associate in the business. Co-owners of income-producing property often need only be joint owners of the property, supplemented by a power of attorney, if necessary. Simple forms of relationships such as these may sometimes be used in lieu of traditional business entities if the circumstances of the parties so permit.

1.02 Selecting an Entity for a Small Business Enterprise

selecting proper business entity, importance of

For tax, legal and practical reasons, it is highly important to select a business entity that suits the needs of both the business and its owners. Selecting an improper business entity can result in the assessment of unnecessary taxes against the business or its owners, either during the course of operating the business or upon its sale or termination. Selecting an improper entity can also result in management difficulties and the needless exposure of one or more of the business owners to personal liability for the debts and liabilities of the business. In addition, an improper business entity may result in the imposition of management or organizational structures that do not fit the needs of the business and may stifle its growth or give rise to unnecessary conflicts among the business owners. Especially with the newly available options of the limited liability company (LLC) and the limited liability partnership (LLP), it is important to take the time necessary to select a business entity that fits the needs of the business as well as the needs of the business owners.

selecting business entity, needs of minority owners

The first step in the process of selecting a business entity is to ascertain the needs of the business and needs and desires of the business owners. In most cases this can be accomplished only by interviewing all of the business owners and key participants. If there will be minority owners in the business enterprise, it is important to interview the minority owners as well as the controlling owners. It often happens that the business needs and desires of the minority owners differ from those of the majority. Even if the attorney is well acquainted with the business needs and desires of the majority owners, it is ethically important to separately ascertain the business needs and desires of the minority owners because in representing the business the attorney is in effect representing all of owners, including the minority.

In selecting an entity for a small business enterprise, there are several factors that should be considered. The relative importance of each factor varies with the business setting. The factors that should be considered include the following:

selecting business entity, factors to consider

(1) The type of business owners. Will the business be owned by individuals, corporations, trusts, U.S. residents, foreign residents, or other entities? This factor is important because certain types of business entities (primarily S corporations) are not available to certain types of owners.

(2) The number of business owners. Will there be one owner, a few owners, or numerous owners. This factor is important because certain types of business entities are not available to one-owner businesses and other types of entities are either not available or not practicable if the number of owners is too high.

(3) The primary purpose of the business venture. Is the primary purpose of the business to provide employment for the business owners or is investment the primary purpose? Is the primary purpose of the business the same for each owner or are some of the owners involved primarily for employment purposes and others primarily for investment or other purposes? This is important because the business entity must be capable of being structured so as to accomplish the purposes of all of the owners.

(4) Whether the business is startup or existing. If the business is already in existence, certain entities might not be feasible because of the impracticality of reorganizing the business into those entities. For example, if an existing business is being operated as a corporation, it may not be practicable taxwise to reorganize the business into an LLC or partnership.

(5) How the business will be capitalized? Will it be capitalized primarily by debt or equity? If it will be capitalized primarily by debt, an LLC, partnership, or S corporation might be preferable to a C corporation because a portion of the debt may be includible in the tax basis of the owners' interest in the business.

(6) The importance to the owners of pass-through taxation. If this is important, a C corporation should not be used. If the owners anticipate net losses in the business operation during its early years and if it is important to the owners that these losses be passed directly to them in the year of incurrence, then a C corporation should not be used. An LLC, partnership or S corporation will clearly be preferable in this instance.

(7) The importance to the business owners of personal liability protection. If it is important to the owner or owners that they not be personally liable for the unassumed debts and liabilities of the business, then a sole proprietorship or general partnership should not be used unless the partnership is a limited liability partnership.

(8) The extent to which the owners wish to have personal control over important business functions, such as the admission of new owners, a change in the type of business conducted, the transfer of ownership interests, or the discontinuance of the business. While controls over these functions are possible under any type of entity, they are most easily imposed in a general partnership or LLC.

(9) Do the owners wish to distribute profits not in proportion to equity ownership or capital contribution? If so, this can most easily be accomplished in a partnership or LLC.

(10) The importance of being able to retain earnings in the business for purposes of expansion or other future capital needs without it being reportable as income by the business owners. If this is important, a C corporation should be used.

(11) The importance to the business owners of being able to participate in the employee benefit plans of the business. If this is important to the owners, a C corporation offers significant advantages because of the restrictions imposed on partners, LLC members, and shareholders of S corporations who own 2 percent or more of its stock.

(12) The importance of being able to raise capital or expand the business by selling ownership interests to large numbers of outsiders or to the public. If this is important, a C corporation is usually preferable because of the universal recognition of corporate stock as an indicia of ownership. However, the sale of ownership interests may also be feasible in an LLC or limited partnership.

(13) The limitation imposed by the owners on the amount of initial organizational expenses that they wish or can afford to incur. If this factor is important, a sole proprietorship, partnership or LLC should be used because they are usually easier and less expensive to organize and set up than C or S corporations.

selecting business entity, general procedure

In selecting a business entity it is important to weigh the needs and desires of the business and each of its owners against the advantages and disadvantages of each available type of business entity. The advantages and disadvantages of each type of business entity are discussed below; first for one-person businesses and then for multiperson businesses.

one-person business, definition of

One-Person Businesses. A one-person business is a business that is owned and managed by one person. There may be other persons involved in the business, but they must be employees or agents of the owner and, while the owner may delegate certain management or supervisory powers to employees or agents, the source of all delegated authority must be the owner.

one-person business, available entities

The entities available to a one-person business include a sole proprietorship, an S corporation, a C corporation, and in most states a limited liability company. The advantages and disadvantages to a one-person business of each of these entities are summarized in the following paragraphs.

sole proprietorship, advantages and disadvantages for one-person business

Sole proprietorship. The advantages of a sole proprietorship are: (1) there are few, if any, organizational expenses, (2) for income tax purposes the profits and losses of the business are those of the owner, which means that business losses are deductible by the owner in the year they are incurred and the business profits are not taxed twice, (3) the owner can organize and manage the business without statutory restriction, and (4) the owner is not required to register the business with any public official or file any reports or pay any annual fees and may conduct business in any state without registration or qualification. The disadvantages of a sole proprietorship are: (1) the owner is personally liable for all debts and obligations of the business, (2) it is impossible to add additional owners or partners to the business without changing the business entity, (3) it is impossible to retain earnings for future capital needs without being reportable as income by the owner, and (4) the availability to the owner of employee benefit plans is limited.

S corporation, advantages and disadvantages for one-person business

S corporation. The advantages of an S corporation to a one-person business are: (1) the business owner is shielded from personal liability for the unassumed debts and obligations of the business, (2) because the profits and losses of the business are passed through to the owner, there is no danger of a double tax and most business losses are deductible by the owner in the year of the loss, and (3) additional owners or partners (up to 75 in number) may be added to the business without changing the business entity. The disadvantages of an S corporation to a one-person business are: (1) management and organizational flexibility is limited by the requirements of subchapter S of the Internal Revenue Code and, unless a close corporation code or statute is applicable, by the state corporation laws, (2) the business must be registered with the state filing official in each state where it conducts significant business and periodic reports and fees must be filed and paid, (3) the organizational expenses may be substantial, depending on the complexity of the business, (4) it is impossible to retain earnings for future capital needs without being reportable as income by the owner, and (5) the availability to the owner of employee benefit plans of the business is limited.

C corporation, advantages and disadvantages for one-person business

C corporation. The advantages of a C corporation to a one-person business are: (1) the business owner is shielded from personal liability for the general debts and obligations of the business, (2) additional owners or partners may be added to the business without changing the business entity, (3) earnings may be retained by the corporation (up to certain amounts) for future capital needs without being taxable to the business owner, and (4) it is easier for the owner to participate in the employee benefit plans of the business. The disadvantages of a C corporation to a one-person business are: (1) because a C corporation is a separate taxable entity, there is a danger of a double tax (i.e., a tax at both the corporate and the shareholder level) being imposed and because there is no pass-through tax treatment business losses may not be personally deductible to the business owner in the year of the loss, (2) unless a close corporation code or statute is applicable, management and organizational flexibility is limited by the requirements of the state corporation laws, (3) the business must be registered with the state filing official in each state where it conducts significant business and periodic reports and fees must be filed and paid, and (4) the organizational expenses may be substantial, depending on the complexity of the business.

limited liability company, advantages and disadvantages for one-person business

Limited liability company (LLC). An LLC is not available to a one-person business in a few states because of the two-or-more member requirement for LLCs in those states. In most states, however, only one member is required of an LLC. The LLC membership requirement in each state is set forth in Appendix I in the back of this book under the heading of "Limited Liability Company Laws, General LLC Requirements." A single-member LLC can elect to be disregarded as an entity for federal income tax purposes; which means that it is treated as a sole proprietorship for tax purposes (see section 4.02, infra). The advantages of an LLC for a one-person business are: (1) the business owner is shielded from personal liability for the unassumed debts and obligations of the business, (2) because the profits and losses of the business are those of the owner, there is no danger of a double tax and business losses are deductible by the owner in the year of the loss, (3) additional owners or partners may be added to the business without changing the business entity, and (4) because there are few, if any, statutory organizational or management requirements, the owner can organize and manage the business as he or she sees fit. The disadvantages of an LLC for a one-person business are: (1) the business must be registered with the state filing official in each state where it conducts significant business and periodic reports and fees must be filed and paid, (2) there may be significant organizational expenses, although if the LLC is member-managed the organizational expenses can usually be kept to a minimum, (3) it is impossible to retain earnings for future capital needs without them being reportable as income by the owner, and (4) the availability to the owner of employee benefit plans of the business is limited.

multiperson business, available entities

Multiperson Businesses. A multiperson business is a business that is owned and managed to some degree by two or more persons. The entities available to a multiperson business include a general partnership, a limited partnership, a limited liability company, a joint venture, an S corporation, a C corporation, and in most states a limited liability partnership. The advantages and disadvantages of each of these entities to a multiperson business are summarized in the paragraphs below.

General Partnership. The advantages of a general partnership to a multi-person small business enterprise include the following: (1) flexibility of management and organizational allowing the partners to organize and manage the business without significant statutory restriction, (2) organizational control whereby each partner has control over important partnership matters such as the admission of new partners and acts in contravention of the partnership agreement, (3) control of the business can be maintained even if a partner leaves the business because a partner's management rights cannot be transferred without the consent of the other partners, (4) pass-through taxation whereby the profits and losses of the business are attributed directly to the partners thus avoiding a double tax and rendering business losses deductible by the partners in the year of the loss, (5) ease of equitable withdrawal whereby each partner can withdraw from the business and obtain equitable compensation for his or her interest in the business, (6) it is not necessary to register the business with the state filing official and periodic reports and fees are not required, (7) ease of convertibility in that it is not difficult to convert a general partnership to a corporation, a limited liability company, or a limited liability partnership, and (8) the organizational expenses are usually less than for other entities. The disadvantages of general partnerships are: (1) each partner is personally liable without limitation for all partnership debts and liabilities, including those incurred by other partners in the course of partnership business, (2) interests in the business are not readily transferable, (3) it is difficult to raise capital by selling ownership interests in the business to the public, (4) it is impossible to retain earnings in the business for future capital needs without being reportable as income by the owners, and (5) the availability to the owners of employee benefit plans is limited.

general partnership, advantages and disadvantages of as business entity

Limited liability partnership. Virtually every state has enacted limited liability partnership laws so as to provide for the registration of limited liability partnerships (LLPs). The existence or nonexistence of such laws in each state is shown in Appendix I, infra. The advantages and disadvantages of LLPs are those listed above for general partnerships except that an LLP must be registered and must file reports and pay fees in each state where it conducts significant business. Also, a general partner of an LLP is shielded from personal liability for some or all of the partnership debts and obligations, depending on the degree of liability protection given in the LLP statutes of a particular state. In some states LLPs may be used only by professionals and in several states financial responsibility requirements are imposed on LLPs. See section 3.11, infra, for further reading on limited liability partnerships. See sections 3.11 and 4.01, infra, for a further discussion of the advantages and disadvantages of limited liability partnerships.

limited liability partnership, advantages and disadvantages of

Limited Partnership. The advantages of a limited partnership to a multi-person small business enterprise include the following: (1) pass-through taxation in the manner described above for a general partnership, (2) personal liability protection for limited partners who do not participate in the control of the partnership business, (3) management and organizational flexibility, (4) interests in business are readily transferable, and (5) capital can be raised by selling interests in the business (usually limited partnership interests) to outsiders or the public. The disadvantages of limited partnerships are: (1) there is no personal liability protection for general partners or for limited partners who participate in the control of the partnership business, (2) limited partners may not participate in the control of the partnership business without becoming liable for the partnership debts, which usually means that one or more of the business owners may not participate in the control of the business, (3) the business must be registered with the state filing official in every state where significant business is conducted and periodic reports and fees must be filed and paid, (4) it is impossible to retain earnings in the business for future capital needs without being reportable as income by the owners, (5) the availability to the owners of employee benefit plans is limited, and (6) the organizational expenses may be substantial.

limited partnership, advantages and disadvantages of as business entity

limited liability company, advantages and disadvantages of as multiperson business entity

Limited liability company. The advantages of a limited liability company to a multi-person small business enterprise include the following: (1) all of the business owners are shielded from personal liability for the unassumed debts and obligations of the business, (2) an LLC is entitled to pass-through partnership taxation in the manner described above for a general partnership, (3) organizational and management flexibility is available because few significant statutory restrictions are imposed, (4) methods of equitable withdrawal are easily imposed whereby a withdrawing or deceased participant can obtain equitable compensation for his or her interest in the business, (5) it is not difficult to convert an LLC to another entity, and (6) the organizational expenses are usually less than for a corporation or limited partnership. The disadvantages of limited liability companies are: (1) the business must be registered with the state filing official in every state where significant business is conducted and periodic reports and fees must be filed and paid, (2) because there is no universally recognized indicia of ownership, it may be difficult to sell interests in the business to outsiders or the public, (3) unless an LLC elects to be taxed as a corporation, it is impossible to retain earnings in the business for future capital needs without being reportable as income by the owners, and (4) the availability to the owners of employee benefit plans is limited. The reader is referred to section 4.01, infra, for a further discussion of the advantages and disadvantages of limited liability companies as compared to partnerships and corporations.

joint venture, advantages and disadvantages of

Joint venture. The advantages and disadvantages of a joint venture are generally those described above for a general partnership. An additional disadvantage of a joint venture for most small businesses is that because a joint venture terminates upon the completion of the venture for which it was formed, it is not usually a suitable entity for a continuing business.

S corporation, advantages and disadvantages as multiperson business entity

S corporation. The advantages of an S corporation to a multi-person small business enterprise include the following: (1) the business owners are shielded from personal liability for the unassumed debts and obligations of the business, and (2) the benefits of pass-through taxation in the manner described above for a general partnership. The disadvantages of an S corporation are: (1) membership and organizational restrictions are imposed by Subchapter S of the Internal Revenue (75 or fewer shareholders, one class of stock, etc.), (2) the business must be registered with the state filing official in every state where significant business is conducted and periodic reports and fees must be filed and paid, (3) management and organizational flexibility is restricted by the requirements of the state corporation laws and by the Subchapter S restrictions, (4) unless elaborate provisions are made, it may be difficult for a deceased or withdrawing participant to obtain fair compensation for his or her interest in the business, (5) it is difficult to convert an S corporation to another entity other than a C corporation, (6) it is impossible to retain earnings in the business for future capital needs without being reportable as income by the owners, (7) the availability to the owners of employee benefit plans is limited, and (8) the organizational expenses may be substantial.

C corporation, advantages and disadvantages of as multiperson business entity

C corporation. The advantages of a C corporation to a multi-person small business enterprise include the following: (1) the business participants are protected from personal liability for the unassumed debts and obligations of the business, (2) the business can be expanded indefinitely without the necessity of changing the business entity, (3) if desired, interests in the business can easily and effectively be sold or transferred to outsiders or the public, (4) the status of a corporation as a business entity is universally recognized, (5) most employee benefit plans of the business are available to the business owners, and (6) business earnings may be retained in the business for expansion or other purposes up to certain limits without being taxable to the business owners. The disadvantages of a C corporation are: (1) because a C corporation is a separate taxable entity, there is a danger of a double tax (i.e., an income tax being assessed on the same funds at both the corporate and the shareholder level), especially if the business is highly profitable, (2) management and organizational flexibility is limited by the requirements of the Internal Revenue Code and the state corporation laws, (3) the business must be registered with the state filing official in every state where significant business is conducted and periodic reports and fees must be filed and paid, (4) unless elaborate provisions are made, it may be difficult for a deceased or withdrawing participant to obtain fair compensation for his or her interest in the business, (5) it is difficult to convert a C corporation to another entity, and (6) the organizational expenses may be substantial.

In selecting a business entity there are no infallible general rules that are applicable to every small business. Each situation is unique and must be dealt with separately. In selecting the entity best suited to a particular business enterprise, the various factors listed above in this section should be applied, considering both the business itself and personal situations of the owners. The owners may disagree among themselves on the choice of a business entity, usually because of differing personal or financial situations. Obviously, such disagreements must be resolved before the organization of the business enterprise can proceed. It may be possible to accommodate the disagreeing parties by using more than one entity in organizing the business, such as a partnership containing an LLC or corporate general partner. selection of business entity, general considerations

Many times the business owners will have decided in advance on the type of business entity, either on their own or on the advice of an acquaintance. In such cases, they should at least be made aware of the advantages, if any, offered by other types of business entities, and, more importantly, advised of any pitfalls or disadvantages inherent in the entity they have chosen. In the final analysis, of course, the decision on the choice of business entity must be made by the business owners, but it is important that the decision be an informed one. selection of entity, advising owners

CHAPTER TWO

SOLE PROPRIETORSHIPS

sole proprietorship, popularity

The sole (or individual) proprietorship is the oldest, simplest, and most widely used business form. There are approximately 15 million nonfarm sole proprietorships in the United States, making it, numerically, far and away the most popular form of doing business. The reasons for its popularity are obvious: it is easily formed, the individual proprietor may operate the business as he or she sees fit, and the proprietor does not have to share his or her profits with others.

2.01 Sole Proprietorships - An Introduction

sole proprietorship, definition

A sole proprietorship is a business that it is owned and managed by one person. If more than one person becomes involved in the ownership and management of the business, it ceases to be a sole proprietorship and becomes either a partnership or a joint venture, depending on the nature of the enterprise. This does not mean, however, that a sole proprietorship business cannot involve other persons. The proprietor may seek assistance in the running of the business by hiring others, but the relationship must be that of either master and servant or principal and agent. The proprietor may delegate authority to others, but the source of the authority must be the proprietor. In theory, there is no limit to the size of a sole proprietorship, but in practice it is usually a small business with limited capital.

sole proprietorship, general aspects

A sole proprietorship is an extension of the individual owner. The assets and liabilities of the business are the proprietor's assets and liabilities. The taxes of the business are the proprietor's taxes. The profits and losses of the business are the proprietor's profits and losses, and the capital invested in the business is the proprietor's. The credit of the business is the proprietor's credit, and the good will of the business is normally that of the proprietor. The torts and breaches of trust of the business are those of the proprietor. And when the proprietor dies, the business normally ceases to exist. In short, the proprietor is the business and the business is the proprietor.

sole proprietorship, how to organize

There are few, if any, legal formalities involved in organizing a typical sole proprietorship. Because there is only a single owner, an agreement is seldom needed to create the entity. However, written instruments such as leases, notes, mortgages, and the like may be necessary to commence the business of the enterprise. The only expenses involved are the capital requirements of the business, and the only organizing is that of organizing the business itself. The business may be conducted anywhere in any state, or in any number of states, without registration or qualification, unless the business is a licensed or registered trade or profession, in which case the licensing or registration requirements must be complied with.

sole proprietorship, fictitious name registration

A sole proprietorship may conduct business under any name, provided that the name is not the same as or deceptively similar to the name of another firm doing business in the area or another registered or well-known name. If a proprietor wishes to conduct business under an assumed name (e.g., John Doe d/b/a Worldwide Plumbing), the name may have to be registered under a fictitious name statute. Some states prohibit the use of the words "& Co." and the like when there are no associates in the business. Some states also require the publication of fictitious names for certain periods. The fictitious name registration requirements for a sole proprietorship are usually the same as those for a general partnership. The fictitious name registration requirements in each state are set forth in Appendix I in the back of this book under the heading of Partnership Laws, Name Registration.

personal liability of proprietor for business debts

In a sole proprietorship, the proprietor is personally liable for all of the debts and liabilities of the business. The financial risk of the proprietor is not limited to his or her investment in the business; the liability extends to all nonexempt property and assets owned by the proprietor. The personal liability of the proprietor may be diminished somewhat by the purchase of liability insurance to cover specified risks and through contractual arrangements whereby those doing business with the firm agree to satisfy their claims only from business assets. The overall and long-term risk, however, is on the proprietor.

sole proprietorships, transferability

With only limited exceptions, the interest of a sole proprietor is freely transferable. The exceptions arise from the rights, if any, of the proprietor's spouse under dower, curtesy, or community property statutes, and from the application of bulk transfer or fraudulent conveyance statutes. See section 5.13, infra, for a discussion of bulk transfer and fraudulent conveyance laws. See section 2.03, infra, for a discussion of the sale of a sole proprietorship business.

sole proprietorships, continuity of existence, death of owner

There is usually no continuity of existence of a sole proprietorship business upon the death of the proprietor. If the proprietor has delegated extensive authority in the running of the business to others, the authority of the agents terminates upon the death of the proprietor, even if a written instrument provides to the contrary. See 3 Am. Jur. 2d, Agency, sec. 51. If the business is not overly dependent on the personal skills or efforts of the individual proprietor, some degree of business continuity upon the death of the proprietor may be obtained through the proprietor's will. This is generally accomplished by vesting authority in the proprietor's executor or personal representative to continue the business so that it may be sold as a going concern or so that a legatee may receive a going business. Because in most states a sole proprietorship terminates as a matter of law upon the death of the proprietor, when the business is continued by the proprietor's executor or personal representative a new proprietorship is technically created. In New York, and possibly a few other states, the continuity of sole proprietorships is covered by a statute that permits the proprietor's executor or personal representative to continue the business if authorized by the probate court.

2.02 The Tax Aspects of Sole Proprietorships; Retirement Plans

sole proprietorships, tax rules and forms

The business income and losses of a sole proprietorship business are taxed as the personal income and losses of the proprietor. See 26 U.S.C. 61(a)(2), 165(c)(1). Also, the tax deductions, credits, gains, losses, and other tax items of the business are those of the proprietor. See 26 U.S.C. 162(a). Of course, the proprietor is personally liable for all taxes and penalties assessed on account of the business. In practice, the proprietor must attach a Schedule C, entitled "Profit or (Loss) From Business or Profession," to his or her federal income tax return, showing the income and deductible expenses of the sole proprietorship business for the proprietor's personal tax year, which is also the tax year of the business. It should be noted that a one-person business may elect to be taxed as a corporation, if desired. See Treasury Reg. 301.7701-2. See section 4.02, infra, for further reading on this election

election to be taxed as corporation

tax-qualified employee benefit plans, use of

An important tax-related aspect of sole proprietorships is the availability of tax-qualified employee benefit and retirement plans for both the proprietor and the proprietor's employees. If a proprietor wishes to establish tax-qualified employee benefit and retirement plans for the employees only, he or she may do so to the same extent as any other employer, corporate or noncorporate. See section 6.01, infra, for further reading. However, if, as is usually the case, the proprietor wishes to be included under such plans, the options are restricted, because a sole proprietor is not considered to be an employee of his or her own business for purposes of most tax-qualified employee benefit plans. See 26 U.S.C. 105(g) and Revenue Ruling 72-596, 1972-2 C.B. 395. A tax-qualified plan is one where the contributions to the plan are deductible by the employer but are not currently taxable to the employee.

owner-employee, benefits available

The only tax-qualified employee benefit plans available to owner-employees of sole proprietorships and partnerships are plans providing lump sum death benefit payments of up to $5,000, group legal services plans, educational assistance plans, and dependent care assistance plans. See 26 U.S.C. 101(b)(2), 120(d)(1),(2), 127(c)(2),(3), and 129(e)(3),(4). Qualified employee benefit plans providing disability and health benefits, group life insurance benefits, and room and board benefits are not available to owner-employees of unincorporated businesses.

Simplified Employee Benefit Plan, use of

Owner-employees of unincorporated businesses, including sole proprietorships and partnerships, are treated as self-employed individuals for purposes of tax-qualified retirement plans. Since 1984, self-employed individuals have enjoyed substantially the same retirement benefits as corporate employees, although they must use different types of retirement plans and, of course, they must fund the plan themselves. A self-employed individual may provide for his or her retirement needs, and for those of the employees of the business, by establishing a tax-qualified Simplified Employee Pension Plan. Under a Simplified Employee Pension Plan an individual retirement account (an IRA) is established for each participating employee (including owner-employees) and the employer simply contributes specified amounts to the accounts. The annual contribution limits are the lesser of $22,500 or 15 percent of an employee's annual compensation. A lengthier discussion of Simplified Employee Pension Plans may be found in section 6.01, infra.

Keogh plans, use of

A sole proprietorship or a partnership may provide for the retirement need of its owners and its employees by establishing a tax-qualified self-employed retirement plan. These plans are often referred to as Keogh plans or HR-10 plans. They will be referred to in this section as Keogh plans.

Keogh plans, contribution and benefit limits

Keogh plans were first established under the Self-Employed Individuals Retirement Act of 1962. Amendments in 1966, 1974, 1976, 1981, and 1982 liberalized the benefits available under Keogh plans. Since 1984, Keogh plans have been subject to the same benefit and contribution limitations as qualified corporate plans. The annual contribution limits are the lesser of $30,000 or 15 percent of compensation for a single defined contribution Keogh plan, and the lesser of $30,000 or 25 percent of compensation for any combination of defined contribution Keogh plans, which may include profit-sharing plans. For defined benefit Keogh plans, which include pension plans, the annual benefit limits are the lesser of $90,000 (plus annual cost of living increases since 1986 - it was $130,000 in 1998) or 100 percent of compensation. The annual contributions to a defined benefit plan are the amounts calculated to produce the prescribed benefits at retirement. See section 6.01, infra, for a definition of defined benefit and defined contribution plans.

Keogh plans, deductibility of contributions

As in all qualified retirement plans, the contributed amounts, up to the statutory limits, are not includible as current income by the person for whom they are contributed, and earnings on the contributions accumulate tax-free until distribution. If paid for the benefit of an employee, the contributed amounts are currently deductible as a business expense by the employer.

Keogh plans, covered employees

A Keogh plan must be established by an unincorporated employer for the exclusive benefit of its employees and their beneficiaries. See 26 U.S.C. 401(a)(2). A sole proprietor is considered to be an employee for purposes of a Keogh plan, and a partnership is treated as the employer of each partner. See 26 U.S.C. 401(c)(4). All full time employees over 25 years of age with at least one year of service must be included under the plan, except that employees covered by a collective bargaining agreement may be excluded, if the agreement was a product of good-faith bargaining.

Keogh plans, includible income

Only earned income is counted in determining the contribution and benefit limits of Keogh plans. Earned income includes net earnings from self-employment, including professional fees, and compensation for personal services actually rendered to the employer sponsoring the plan. See 26 U.S.C. 401(c)(2)(A). Interest and dividend income, wages from outside employment, and income from nonbusiness-related sales or exchanges of capital assets are not includible. Under "top heavy" Keogh plans (see below), only the first $200,000 of compensation is counted in determining benefit and contribution limits.

top heavy Keogh plans, special rules

Special contribution, vesting, and distribution rules are applied to so-called "top heavy" plans, which are defined as plans that provide more than 60 percent of their benefits to "key employees." See 26 U.S.C. 416(g). Key employees include the top 10 owners, the officers, all more-than-five-percent owners, and all more-than-one-percent owners earning more than $150,000 per year. See 26 U.S.C. 416(i)(1).

Keogh plans, general requirements

While Keogh plans are not required to have banks or other approved financial institutions as trustees or custodians, the fiduciary requirements imposed on those dealing with contributed funds may necessitate the use of such institutions in many cases. Loans to plan participants are permitted, within certain limits, except that loans are not permitted to participants with a 10 percent or more interest in the profits or capital of the sponsoring employer. Certain Keogh plans may be integrated with Social Security so as to reduce contributions and benefits for lower-paid employees. All Keogh plans, or masters or prototypes thereof, must be approved in advance by the Internal Revenue Service.

Keogh plans, distribution and benefit requirements

Distributions under ordinary Keogh plans may begin at any age up to age 70 1/2. Under "top heavy" plans, distributions to "key employees" may not begin until age 59 1/2, except in cases of disability or death. Distributions to plan participants under all Keogh plans must begin by age 70 1/2, and distribution must be such as to be completed by the end of the participant's life expectancy. Lump sum distributions are also permitted. Both lump sum and periodic distributions are fully taxable as received.

2.03 The Purchase or Sale of a Sole Proprietorship Business

sole proprietorships, sale of business tax treatment

As between the buyer and the seller, a sole proprietorship business may be sold as a going business or its assets may be sold separately. For tax purposes, however, the sale of a sole proprietorship business is always treated as an asset sale and not as the sale of a single entity, even if it is sold as a going business. For tax purposes, a sole proprietorship business must be broken down into its component assets to determine the gain or loss from the sale. For federal income tax purposes, the assets of a sole proprietorship business are classified as (1) capital assets, (2) noncapital assets, and (3) Section 1231 assets. The best practice is to allocate the sales price among the various business assets in the sales contract, rather than leaving the allocation to the discretion of the Internal Revenue Service. A good-faith allocation of the sales price by the parties to a sale will be honored by the Internal Revenue Service as long as it can be supported by some basis in fact or business reality.

allocation of sales price, seller's priorities

For tax purposes, it is usually in the best interest of the seller to allocate the sales price of a sole proprietorship business in accordance with the following priorities:

(1) First, to capital assets (including good will) and Section 1231 assets not subject to recapture provisions.

(2) Second, to depreciable assets and assets upon which a capital gain subject to recapture provisions will be realized.

(3) Third, to noncapital assets and covenants not to compete.

capital assets, definition

section 1231 assets, definition

Capital assets include any business property other than noncapital assets. Noncapital assets include stock in trade, inventory, depreciable and real property used in the business, certain copyrights, accounts or notes receivable in the ordinary course of business, and assets purchased with a substantial investment purpose. See 26 U.S.C. 1221. Section 1231 assets include depreciable personal property and real property, if used in the business and held by the business for more than a year. See 26 U.S.C. 1231(b)(1). The depreciation and other recapture provisions applicable to the sale of a business are discussed in section 7.02, infra.

good will, covenants not to compete

If a business is sold as a going concern, a portion of the sales price may be allocated to good will and to covenants by the seller not to compete against the business after the sale. Because the good will of a sole proprietorship business is normally the personal good will of the proprietor, to preserve as much of the good will of the business as possible for the purchaser, it is important to the purchaser that the seller agree not to compete against the business after the sale. In this respect, the good will of the business and covenants by the seller not to compete against the business are closely related and difficult to value separately.

good will, covenants not to compete, tax treatment, allocation in sales contract

Good will is a capital asset and any gain resulting from the portion of the sales price allocated to good will is taxable to the seller as a capital gain. See Comm. v. Killian, 314 F. 2nd 852 (CA 5, 1963). However, good will has no ascertainable life and, therefore, may not be depreciated or amortized by the purchaser. See Treasury Reg. 1.167(a)-3. On the other hand, the portion of the sales price allocated to a covenant not to compete constitutes ordinary income to the seller and, because it has an ascertainable life, is amortizable by the purchaser. See Yandell v. U.S., 315 F. 2nd 141 (CA 9, 1963). If the sales contract lumps good will and a covenant not to compete together, making no separate allocation for each item, the covenant not to compete is normally considered ancillary to the good will, and the entire allocation will usually be credited to good will, thus avoiding the assessment of ordinary income to the seller and depriving the purchaser of an amortizable asset. See Dixie Finance Co. v. U.S., 474 F. 2nd 501 (CA 5, 1973). Therefore, it is usually in the best interest of the seller not to allocate the two items separately in the sales contract, or, if the items are allocated separately (as most knowledgeable purchasers insist), to allocate as much of the purchase price as possible to good will and as little as possible to the covenant not to compete.

CHAPTER THREE

PARTNERSHIPS

Partnerships, types of

A partnership is the simplest and most flexible form of conducting a multiperson business. Partnerships also enjoy significant income tax advantages over corporations for most small business participants. There are four types of partnerships: general partnerships, limited liability partnerships, limited partnerships, and in a few states limited liability limited partnerships. General partnerships are used by a wide variety of businesses and are the most common and widely used type of partnership. Limited liability partnerships, which are provided for in the partnership laws of virtually every state, are used most often by professionals but in most states may be used by other types of multiperson businesses. Limited partnerships and limited liability limited partnerships are used primarily in investment enterprises.

3.01 General Partnerships - An Introduction

general partnerships, a description

A general partnership is an association of two or more persons for the purpose of carrying on a business for profit as co-owners It may consist of any number of partners, but there must be at least two. It may be formed under a written agreement, under a verbal agreement, or under an agreement or understanding that is implied from the conduct of the persons involved. A general partnership may carry on any type of lawful business except a nonprofit business and businesses such as banks and insurance companies that are governed by special statutes.

general partnerships, distinguishing aspects vs. other partnerships

General partnerships should be distinguished from limited partnerships and limited liability partnerships. A general partnership consists of two or more partners, all of whom are general partners with full rights of managerial control over partnership affairs and unlimited personal liability for partnership debts. A limited partnership consists of one or more general partners and one or more limited partners. Limited partners are primarily investors and have little managerial control over partnership affairs and only a limited liability for partnership debts. Limited liability partnerships are general partnerships wherein the liability of the individual partners for the debts and obligations of the partnership is limited. Even though they are now governed by statute, general partnerships are a product of the common law and may be formed informally under a verbal or implied agreement. Limited partnerships and limited liability partnerships are the products of statute and may be formed only by complying with the requirements of the authorizing statute. Limited partnerships are discussed in sections 3.05 to 3.07 of this chapter and limited liability partnerships are discussed in section 3.11 of this chapter.

general partnerships, recognition as separate entity

Under the common law, general partnerships were not recognized as legal entities apart from their members. Under modern statutes, however, general partnerships are recognized as separate entities for most purposes. For example, a general partnership may conduct business under a name that is separate and distinct from the name of its partners, and it may own and convey property, enter into contracts, and engage in litigation, all in its own name and stead. However, a partnership is not recognized as a separate entity for purposes of federal income tax liability (see section 3.02, infra).

uniform partnership act, adoption of, where to find

Every state except Louisiana has adopted the Uniform Partnership Act (the U.P.A.) as its basic law governing the legal aspects of general partnerships. This uniform act, with only minor local modifications, governs the organization, conduct, and termination of general partnerships in the United States. It will be repeatedly cited in this chapter. The provisions of the local Act that correspond to the cited sections of the Uniform Partnership Act are not difficult to find. The statutory citation to the Uniform Partnership Act in each state is set forth in Appendix I in the back of this book under the heading of Partnership Laws, General Partnerships.

A general partnership has many of the legal characteristics of a sole proprietorship and a few corporate characteristics. The distinguishing characteristics of a general partnership include the following:

general partnerships, distinguishing characteristics

(1) Every partner is a general agent for purposes of acting on behalf of the partnership business. See U.P.A. § 9.

(2) No one may become a partner without the consent of all existing partners. See U.P.A. § 18(g).

(3) Partners are accountable as trustees to the partnership and high standards of conduct are imposed on partners in their dealings with one another. See U.P.A. § 21.

(4) Each partner is personally liable to outsiders for all partnership obligations, including those resulting from the wrongful acts of other partners committed in the course of partnership business. See U.P.A. §§ 13, 14, 15. It should be noted that the liability of partners for the wrongful acts of other partners can be limited by qualifying the partnership as a registered limited liability partnership in states where such partnerships are recognized by statute. See section 3.11, infra, for further reading on limited liability partnerships.

(5) A partnership is dissolved upon the death, bankruptcy, or withdrawal of a partner, although if so agreed, the partnership business may be continued without interruption by the remaining partners. See U.P.A. § 31(2),(4),(5).

general partnership, elements of

For a general partnership to exist, the following five elements must be present: There must be (1) an association, (2) of two or more persons, (3) for the purpose of carrying on a business, (4) as co-owners, (5) for profit. See U.P.A. § 6(1). To be "associated" for purposes of forming a partnership, the persons involved must intend to associate together for a business purpose. See Chariton Feed & Grain, Inc. v. Harder, 369 N.W. 2d 777 (Ia., 1985). The association must consist of two or more individuals or other entities with the legal capacity to act as partners. The business to be carried on may include every trade, occupation, or profession. See U.P.A. § 2. It should be noted, however, that some courts have refused to recognize a single venture (as opposed to a continuing business) as a partnership. See section 3.10, infra, for a discussion of joint ventures. The persons involved must, to some extent at least, be co-owners of the business, which means that there must be co-ownership of the partnership property and a sharing of profits. One person cannot simply be an employee, creditor, or tenant of the other. Finally, the business must be for profit, which means that it cannot be a charitable, religious, or fraternal organization.

In determining whether a general partnership exists, the following rules of construction are applied:

general partnerships, rules of construction

(1) Persons who are not partners as to each other are not partners as to third parties, except when partnership by estoppel is established.

(2) Joint ownership of property, without more, does not establish the existence of a partnership, even if the joint owners share the profits from the property.

(3) The sharing of gross returns does not in itself establish the existence of a partnership.

(4) The receipt of profits from a business is prima facie evidence that the recipient is a partner in the business, unless the receipts constitute debt repayments, wages, rent, annuity payments, interest, or proceeds from the sale of a business. See U.P.A. § 7.

partner, legal requirements

Persons with the legal capacity to become partners in a general partnership include individuals, partnerships, corporations, and other associations including limited liability companies. See U.P.A. § 2. Because the contracts of certain individuals (e.g., minors, legal incompetents, etc.) are voidable, their capacity to serve as partners may be restricted, although it is common for minors to become partners for tax and other reasons. The ability of a trustee to become a partner may be governed by the agreement or document creating the trust. The legal capacity of a corporation to serve as a partner is governed by its articles of incorporation and the corporation laws of its state of incorporation. The corporation laws of virtually every state grant corporations the power to serve as partners in a partnership. The capacity of a limited liability company to serve as a partner is governed by its articles of organization or operating agreement and by the limited liability company laws of its home state.

A written agreement or contract is not required for the formation of a general partnership. See U.P.A. § 6. Therefore, a general partnership may arise informally through the association and conduct of the persons involved. In such cases the terms of the relationship between the partners are either implied from their actions or established by statute. In practice, many general partnerships are formed when two or more persons simply begin doing business together and share the profits of the business.

general partnership, formation of without agreemen

The partners of a general partnership are subject to unlimited personal liability for the debts and obligations of the partnership. See U.P.A. § 15. Accordingly, if another partner or a partnership employee commits a tort or a breach of contract or trust while acting within the scope of partnership business, every partner may be held personally liable to the damaged party to the full extent of any damages incurred. However, absent an agreement to the contrary, a partner who pays off or satisfies a partnership claim or judgment is entitled to contribution from the other partners, unless he or she committed the act that gave rise to the claim or judgment. See U.P.A. § 18(b).

partnership debts, liability of general partners

A personal creditor of an individual partner may not attach property that belongs to the partnership because specific partnership property is exempt from execution, except on claims against the partnership. See U.P.A. § 25(2)(c). The personal creditor of a partner may, however, obtain a charging order from the court ordering the partnership to pay over to the creditor, or to a receiver, any partnership profits or other money otherwise payable to the debtor-partner. See U.P.A. § 28.

creditor of general partner, rights against partnership

A new or incoming partner is personally liable only for partnership obligations incurred after becoming a partner, unless the incoming partner contractually or voluntarily assumes earlier liabilities, such as those of a retiring partner. However, prior partnership obligations may be satisfied out of an incoming partner's share of the partnership property. See U.P.A. § 17.

new general partner, liability for prior partnership debts

Absent a release or novation from the partnership creditors, a retiring or withdrawing partner remains personally liable for partnership debts and obligations incurred while that person was a partner. See U.P.A. § 36. Unless an outgoing partner gives actual or published notice of withdrawal from the partnership to creditors who had done business with the partnership while that person was a partner, the outgoing partner may be personally liable to those creditors for debts incurred after withdrawal. See U.P.A. § 35.

withdrawing general partner, liability for partnership debts

The separate property of a deceased partner is liable for partnership obligations incurred while he or she was a partner, but such obligations are subordinated to the deceased partner's personal debts. See U.P.A. § 36(4). In some states partnership creditors are barred from pursuing this remedy unless remedies against the surviving partners have been exhausted or are of no value. It should be noted that upon the death of a partner, the partner's estate does not become a partner unless so provided in the partnership agreement. See U.P.A. § 25(d). Also, the use by partnership of a deceased partner's name does not make the individual property of the deceased partner liable for partnership debts. See U.P.A. § 41(10).

deceased general partner, liability for partnership debts

Partners have three kinds of rights in connection with their ownership interests in a general partnership. See U.P.A. § 24. These rights are:

(1) Rights in specific partnership property. Specific partnership property may be property contributed to the partnership by a partner or, absent an agreement to the contrary, property purchased with partnership funds or credit. See U.P.A. § 8. The legal nature of a partner's interest in specific partnership property is described as a tenancy in partnership. Absent an agreement to the contrary, a tenancy in partnership - (a) gives the holder an equal right with the other partners to possession of the property for partnership purposes, (b) is not assignable unless all parties assign their rights in the property, (c) is exempt from execution except on claims against the partnership, (d) vests in the surviving partners upon the death of a partner, and (e) is not subject to dower, curtesy, or widow's allowances. See U.P.A. § 25.

general partner, rights in partnership property

general partner, rights to partnership profits

assignee of general partner, rights to partnership profits

(2) The right to a share of the profits and business of the partnership. This right, which is deemed to be personal property, entitles a partner to a share of partnership profits and surplus. See U.P.A. § 26. Unless forbidden by the partnership agreement, this right may be transferred or assigned by a partner without causing dissolution of the partnership. The transferee or assignee, however, does not become a partner and is not entitled to participate in the management of the partnership. The transferee or assignee is entitled only to the transferor's profits, and, in the event of dissolution, to the transferor's share of any distributions. See U.P.A. § 27. A partner's right to share in partnership profits and surplus may also be subjected to a charging order by a court upon the request of a judgment creditor of a partner. See U.P.A. § 28. Further, an assignee of this right or a foreclosing creditor of a partner, may obtain a judicial dissolution of the partnership at the end of its term of existence, or at any time if the term of the partnership was at the will of a partner when the assignee's interest was acquired. See U.P.A. § 32(2).

general partner, management rights

(3) The right to participate in the management of the partnership. This right is nonattachable, and, in the absence of an agreement to the contrary, is nonassignable and is shared equally with all other partners. See U.P.A. §§ 27(1), 18(e). This does not mean that all partners must have equal management powers, for it is a common practice for general partnerships to delegate management functions to particular partners or to outsiders. An agreement to share management functions or powers unequally does not have to be in writing and may be established by practice or custom. See U.P.A. § 18.]

authority of partner to bind partnership

Every partner of a general partnership is deemed to be a general agent of the partnership in the conduct of its usual course of business. A partner's agreements and contracts bind the partnership unless the partner has no authority to bind the partnership on a particular matter and the person with whom the partner is dealing has knowledge of that fact. See U.P.A. § 9(1). An act for which a partner has no apparent authority in connection with the partnership business does not bind the partnership unless it was actually authorized by the other partners. See U.P.A. § 9(2).

limitations on authority of partner

Unless authorized to do so by the other partners or unless the other partners have abandoned the business, a partner has no authority to:

(1) assign partnership property in trust for creditors,

(2) dispose of the good will of the partnership business,

(3) perform any act that would make it impossible to carry on ordinary partnership business,

(4) confess a judgment against the partnership, or

(5) submit a partnership claim or liability to arbitration or reference. See U.P.A. § 9(3).

liability of partnership for acts of partners

The general agency that exists among partners renders a general partnership liable for the wrongful acts and omissions of a partner acting in the ordinary course of partnership business and for breaches of trust committed by a partner while acting within the scope of his or her apparent authority. See U.P.A. §§ 13, 14. Similarly, admissions and representations made by a partner concerning partnership affairs within the scope of the partner's legal authority is binding on the partnership. See U.P.A. § 11. Also, notice to a partner on partnership matters constitutes notice to the partnership, and the knowledge of a partner acting on a particular partnership matter constitutes knowledge of the partnership, except in cases of fraud on the partnership committed by or with the consent of a partner. See U.P.A. § 12.

general partners, duties of good faith and accountability

Because of the ability of one partner to bind the other partners, the following duties of good faith and accountability are imposed on partners in the course of their conduct of partnership business and affairs:

(1) A partner must account to the partnership for any benefit or profit derived without the consent of the other partners from any partnership transaction or from the use of partnership property. See U.P.A. § 21.

(2) A partner must render on demand to any other partner a true and full account of all matters affecting the partnership. See U.P.A. § 20.

(3) A partner who is wrongfully excluded from the partnership business or from the possession of partnership property has the right to a formal accounting as to partnership affairs if such right exists under the terms of any agreement, if another partner refuses to render a true and full account on a partnership matter, or if a formal accounting is just and reasonable under the circumstances. See U.P.A. § 22.

(4) A partner at all times has access to the partnership books and may inspect and copy any of them, and the books must be kept at the partnership's principal place of business unless an agreement between the partners provides otherwise. See U.P.A. § 19.

3.02 The Tax Aspects of Partnerships

general & limited partnerships, tax treatment

The Internal Revenue Code does not distinguish between general partnerships, limited partnerships, and limited liability partnerships. Accordingly, they are treated substantially the same for tax purposes and are discussed together in this section. Unless otherwise noted, the term partnership in this section includes all types of partnerships. The provisions dealing with the taxation of partnerships are found in Subchapter K of the Internal Revenue Code (26 U.S.C. 701-761). It should be understood that the tax aspects of partnerships can be extremely complicated and that this section is intended only to give the reader a general understanding of the subject.

partnership tax status, election of, procedure

Under the so-called "check the box" tax regulations that became effective on January 1, 1997 a domestic business with 2 or more members that is not a corporation may elect to be classified as either a partnership or a corporation for federal income tax purposes. See Treasury Reg. 301.7701-3. This means that a newly formed general or limited partnership may elect to be classified as either a partnership or a corporation for federal income tax purposes. While there may be instances when a partnership would desire corporate tax status (see section 4.02, infra, for examples), in almost every instance partnership tax status should be elected.

partnership tax status, necessity of filing election

A tax status election is made by filing IRS Form 8832 (with the appropriate box checked) with the IRS in the manner described in section 4.02, infra. However, if partnership tax status is desired, it is not necessary to file Form 8832 because under the default rules in the regulations a non-corporate multiperson entity that does not file an election will automatically be classified as a partnership for federal income tax purposes. See Treasury Reg. 301.7701-3(b)(1). This default classification can be changed, if desired, by filing a subsequent election to be taxed as a corporation. Partnerships that were in existence prior to January 1, 1997 automatically retain their existing tax classification unless they file an election to change the classification. See section 4.02, infra, for further reading on this matter.

partnerships, tax reporting responsibilities

liability of partner for partnership taxes

partnership as tax shelter

A partnership is a tax-reporting entity under the Internal Revenue Code, but is not a tax-paying entity. Therefore, a partnership is not itself directly liable for the payment of income taxes. See 26 U.S.C. 701. However, a partnership is required to file an annual informational tax return (on I.R.S. Form 1065) disclosing the particulars of its income, deductions, and other tax items for the tax year and indicating how the various items are allocated among the partners. See 26 U.S.C. 6031 and Treasury Reg. 1.6031-1. Each partner is deemed to be a self-employed individual and must include on his or her individual income tax return the share of the various items of income, gain, loss, credits, deductions, and other items allocated on the partnership return. See 26 U.S.C. 702. These items retain their character when allocated to the individual partners and are treated for tax purposes as though incurred by the partner personally. The pass-through feature of such items as accelerated real estate depreciation, oil and gas depletion allowances, and other types of business deductions enables individual partners, including limited partners, to use their allocated shares of such deductions to "shelter" other income from tax liability. This is a principal reason for the popularity of the limited partnerships as an investment entity.

partnership income, losses, etc., allocation to partners

A partner's allocated share of the various partnership items of income, gain, loss, deduction, and credit is normally determined by the partnership agreement, if one exists. See 26 U.S.C. 704(a). If there is no definitive partnership agreement or if the agreement is silent on the subject, each partner's allocated share of the various tax items is determined in accordance with the partner's interest in the partnership, taking into account all of the facts and circumstances. See 26 U.S.C. 704(b). Regardless of how a partner's allocated share of partnership income is determined, it is taxable to the partner whether or not it is distributed to the partner during the tax year. A partner's allocated share of partnership losses (including capital losses) in any tax year may not exceed the adjusted basis of the partner's capital interest in the partnership at the end of the partnership's tax year. See 26 U.S.C. 704(d).

partner's capital contribution, tax treatment

When a partner contributes property to a partnership in exchange for a partnership interest, gain or loss is not recognized in the transaction. See 26 U.S.C. 721(a). Thus, the partner's basis in the property is carried over to the partnership and determines the tax basis of the partner's capital interest in the partnership. See 26 U.S.C. 722, 723. A partner's capital interest in the partnership is distinct from, and should not be confused with, the partner's interest in partnership profits.

Inequities may occur if the tax basis of contributed property differs from its market value. Suppose, for example, that partner A contributes property with a value and a tax basis of $10,000 to the partnership and partner B contributes property also valued at $10,000, but with a tax basis of only $5,000. Suppose, further, that A and B have equal interests in partnership profits and other tax items, including depreciation. If both properties are fully depreciated by the partnership, each partner will be allocated depreciation deductions totalling $7,500, thus penalizing A (who contributed $10,000 worth of depreciation) and benefiting B. Similarly, if both properties are sold by the partnership in the year of contribution for their actual values, each partner will be charged with a $2,500 gain, again penalizing A and benefitting B.

contributed property, differing tax basis, consequences

To compensate for such inequities, the Internal Revenue Code permits partners to agree to share depreciation, depletion, or gain or loss with respect to contributed property in such a manner as to take into account any variations between the tax basis of contributed property and its fair market value at the time of contribution. See 26 U.S.C. 704(c)(1). In the example of the previous paragraph, if A and B had provided in their partnership agreement that any depreciation or gain or loss with respect to contributed properties shall be allocated in the same manner as though the properties were separately owned by the contributing partners, the inequities would have been eliminated. The drafting of such provisions may be difficult, however, especially if numerous partners and several kinds of property are involved.

same, permitted tax treatment

Other methods of avoiding tax inequities resulting from contributions of property with a tax basis that differs from its fair market value are: (1) each partner contributes only the use of the property to the partnership, with the contributing partner retaining title to the property, or (2) the partnership purchases the property from the contributing partner, in which case the tax basis will be equal to the purchase price. The first alternative has the advantage of being simple, but problems may arise in valuing the basis of the partners' capital interest in the partnership, and any rents paid for the use of the property will constitute ordinary income to the contributing partner. The second alternative may result in the recognition of gain (or loss) by the contributing partner in the year of contribution, and if the contributing partner owns, directly or indirectly, more than 50 percent of the capital interest in the partnership, any losses incurred in such a transaction will not be recognized. See 26 U.S.C. 707(b).

same, other methods of handling

If a partner contributes personal services to the partnership in return for his or her capital interest, the receipt of the capital interest constitutes ordinary income to the contributing partner in the amount of the fair market value of the interest received. See Treasury Reg. 1.721-1(b)(1). The other partners are entitled to a deduction in the same amount in the same tax year. Valuation problems and questions as to when the contributions were made are likely to arise when capital interests are conveyed for personal services in the absence of an agreement as to the terms of the arrangement.

personal services as capital contribution, tax treatment

Even though a partnership is not a taxable entity, because it is a tax-reporting entity it must have a tax year. With only limited exceptions, a partnership must use a "required tax year," which must conform to the tax year of its majority partners, or, if no such year exists, to the tax year of its principal partners, or, if no such year exists, to the calendar year unless the Treasury Regulations prescribe another period. See 26 U.S.C. 706(b)(1). If a partnership is unable to determine its tax year by reference to either majority or principal partners, it must use the tax year that results in the least aggregate deferral of income to its partners. A partnership may adopt a tax year other than a "required tax year" either by establishing a valid business purpose for doing so or by filing and obtaining approval of a "Section 444 election," whereunder a different tax year may be elected if the new tax year results in a deferral period of three months or less. See 26 U.S.C. 444.

partnership tax year, rules

Perhaps the most complicated tax aspects of partnerships are those dealing with the disposition of a partnership interest upon a partner's death or withdrawal from the partnership. There are several methods of compensating a deceased or withdrawing partner for his or her partnership interest, and each method is treated differently for federal income tax purposes.

deceased or withdrawing partner, methods of compensating for partnership interest

For federal income tax purposes, a deceased or withdrawing partner may be compensated for his or her partnership interest through any of the following methods:

compensation provided by liquidation of partnership

(1) The dissolution and complete liquidation of the partnership, accompanied by the distribution of each partner's share of partnership assets. In such an event the partners (including the successors of deceased partners) continue to be treated as partners for tax purposes until the liquidation of the partnership is completed. See Treasury Reg. 1.708-1(b)(1)(i). This method of compensation is viable only when the partnership business will not be continued after the death or withdrawal of a partner or when the partnership business is sold by means of an asset sale (see section 3.07, infra). The tax aspects of the complete liquidation of a partnership are discussed in section 3.08, infra.

compensation provided by sale of partnership interest

basis of partnership interest, how determined

tax basis of acquired partnership interest

(2) The sale of a deceased or withdrawing partner's interest in the partnership to another partner or to an outsider. Any gain realized by the selling partner upon the sale or exchange of his or her partnership interest is treated for tax purposes as a capital gain or loss, except for gain realized from Section 751 assets (i.e., the selling partner's interest in unrealized receivables and substantially appreciated inventory - see section 3.07, infra), which is taxed as ordinary income. See 26 U.S.C. 741, 751. The gain realized by the selling partner is equal to the amount realized from the sale, less the basis of his or her partnership interest. The amount realized from the sale of a partnership interest is the amount of money (or the fair market value of any property) received for the interest, plus the selling partner's share of partnership liabilities. See 26 U.S.C. 752(d), 1001(b). The basis of the selling partner's interest in the partnership is usually the aggregate of such partner's basis in the partnership assets adjusted to take into account the partner's share of undistributed partnership income and loss for the current tax year. See 26 U.S.C. 705(a). In special situations more complicated rules are applied in determining the basis of the partnership interest, and the advice of tax counsel should be sought. See 26 U.S.C. 705(a)(1),(2),(3), (b). The remaining partners are not generally affected by the transfer of the selling partner's interest to a third party unless the transfer involves 50 percent or more of the total interest in the partnership capital and profits, in which case the partnership is deemed to be terminated under 26 U.S.C. 708(b). Whether a partnership interest is purchased by a third party of by another partner, the tax basis of the acquired partnership interest in the hands of the purchaser is equal to the amount paid for the interest plus the share of partnership liabilities assumed in the transaction. See 26 U.S.C. 742, 752.

compensation provided by liquidation of partnership interest

valuation of partnership interest

(3) The liquidation of the partnership interest of a deceased or withdrawing partner in exchange for partnership distributions, with the partnership business continuing. In essence, this transaction amounts to the purchase of the former partner's interest by the partnership. In such a transaction the payments made by the partnership in liquidating the former partner's interest are divided, for tax purposes, into two categories: (a) payments for the former partner's interest in partnership property, and (b) all other payments. See 26 U.S.C. 736. Payments under (a) above include all payments for the former partner's interest in partnership property other than for unrealized receivables and goodwill. Payments for goodwill may also be included in this category if so provided in the partnership agreement. Payments in this category are treated as partnership distributions and constitute gain to the recipient (except for Section 751 assets, upon which any gain is taxed as ordinary income - see 26 U.S.C. 751(b)), and are not deductible by the partnership. See 26 U.S.C. 736(b). The value of a former partner's interest in partnership property agreed to by the parties to the transaction will usually be accepted by the Internal Revenue Service. See Treasury Reg. 1.736-1(b)(1). All other payments made by the partnership in liquidation of a former partner's interest (i.e., the payments under (b) above) are considered as either distributive shares of partnership income (if determined with regard to partnership income) or as guaranteed payments under 26 U.S.C. 707(c). See 26 U.S.C. 736(a). These payments normally constitute ordinary income to the recipient and are deductible by the partnership.

It is not uncommon for the owner of a successful unincorporated business to form a family partnership. Family partnership are usually formed to allocate a portion of the business income to children or other family members in lower income brackets and to encourage family members to enter or continue the business. Family partnerships are recognized in the Internal Revenue Code. See 26 U.S.C. 704(e). Generally, a family member will be recognized as a partner if he or she owns a capital interest in the partnership, provided that capital is an income-producing factor in the business. The family member's partnership interest may be acquired by purchase or by gift, and he or she need not contribute services to the partnership. See 26 U.S.C. 704(e)(1). Whether capital is a material income-producing factor is a question of fact. See Treasury Reg. 1.704-1(e)(1)(iv). family partnerships, recognition, tax treatment

Family members include the spouse, ancestors, and lineal descendants of an individual, and any trusts primarily benefitting such persons. See 26 U.S.C. 704(e)(3). Especially when minor children are involved, family partnership agreements must be carefully drafted with profits clearly allocated in proportion to capital interests and with reasonable compensation made for the personal services of the active partners. The minor children should have complete control over their interests, with independent trustees or custodians appointed, if necessary. See Treasury Reg. 1.704-1(e)(2)(viii). family member, what constitutes; family partnerships, minors as partners

3.03 Organizing a General Partnership

organizing partnership, preliminary aspects

Normally the first task in organizing a general partnership is to meet with the prospective partners and ascertain their wishes and objectives with respect to the business. It is important to determine, first of all, whether a general partnership is the best form of entity for the business. The issue of selecting the business entity is dealt with in chapter one of this handbook and the reader is referred to that chapter for further reading on the matter.

organizing partnership, informing prospective partners

Once it is determined that the business can best be conducted, initially at least, as a general partnership, it is a good practice to explain the general concepts of partnership law and operation to the prospective partners. This will better enable the prospective partners to understand the nature of a partnership and will help them to make informed decisions on the issues that must be determined in the course of organizing the partnership.

written partnership agreement, reasons for

A threshold matter to consider in organizing a general partnership is the necessity of a written agreement defining the relationship among the partners. While a general partnership may arise informally without a written, or even an express, agreement among the partners, the best practice, of course, is to define their relationship in a written instrument. Sometimes called "articles of partnership," written agreements among partners will be referred to in this handbook simply as partnership agreements. A written partnership agreement is needed for the following reasons:

(1) To establish the existence of the partnership for legal and tax purposes.

(2) To attain flexibility in the handling of partnership matters and to clarify the rights and duties of the partners among themselves. This is especially important if the interests of the partners are to be unequal as to any aspect of the partnership.

(3) To establish each partner's share of partnership profits for income tax and other purposes. This is especially important if the partners make unequal capital contributions to the partnership or wish to divide partnership profits and losses unequally.

(4) To insure continuation of the partnership business upon the death, bankruptcy, or withdrawal of a partner.

(5) To avoid statute of frauds and other problems in the event of assignments of interests in the partnership or conveyances of real property by the partnership.

limited liability partnership, desirability of registering partnership as

Another threshold matter to consider in many states is whether the partners wish to qualify and register the partnership as a limited liability partnership. If so, the requirements of the limited liability partnership statutes in the partnership's home state and in each state where the partnership will be conducting significant business will have to be complied with. Registering the partnership as a limited liability partnership serves to limit the liability of the general partners for all or certain partnership debts, depending on the degree of liability protection provided by the limited liability partnership statutes of the partnership's home state. Limited liability partnerships are discussed in sections 3.11 to 3.13 of this handbook and the reader is referred to those sections for further reading on limited liability partnerships.

partnership name, requirements

Another early issue in organizing a general partnership is likely to be that of selecting the partnership name. A general partnership may operate under any name it chooses, provided the name is not the same as or deceptively similar to the name of another firm doing business in the area or a name that is well known or registered with the state filing official. A general partnership with a fictitious name must, in most states, register the name, usually with the county clerk under a fictitious name statute. Any general partnership name that does not include the surname of each partner is usually considered fictitious and must be registered. In some states publication of the fictitious name is also required. In a few states all general partnerships must be registered. In any event, name registration is a matter that should be checked on, and carried out if necessary, in the course of organizing a general partnership. The general partnership name registration requirements in each state are set forth in Appendix I in the back of this book under the heading of "Partnership Laws, Name Registration."

fictitious name statutes, when applicable

In organizing a general partnership, the following major partnership functions should be considered by the prospective partners and dealt with in the partnership agreement: (1) the management and control of the partnership and its business, (2) the capitalization of the partnership, (3) the division of partnership profits and losses, (4) the admission of new or substituted members into the partnership, (5) the treatment of the partnership interests of withdrawing or deceased partners, and (6) the termination of the partnership. Both the Uniform Partnership Act and the Internal Revenue Code permit considerable flexibility in dealing with each of these functions in partnership agreements. In the absence of a partnership agreement, or should the agreement fail to deal with one or more of these functions, the legal and tax aspects of the omitted functions are governed by the applicable provisions of the Uniform Partnership Act and the Internal Revenue Code, respectively.

partnership agreement, functions dealt with in

Depending on the number of partners and their relationship with one another, the allocation of partnership management responsibilities can be simple, complex, or somewhere in between. In the absence of an agreement to the contrary, all partners have an equal voice in the management and control of a general partnership. See U.P.A. § 18(e). In many partnerships this is the desired form of management, especially if the partners make equal contributions to the partnership and are few in number, are all active in the business, and are on good terms with one another. However, if so desired the partnership agreement can provide for the management of the partnership to be delegated to a single partner (the managing partner), or to a committee or group of partners (the management committee), or the various management functions can be divided among the partners or assigned to outsiders. See section 3.04, infra, for a list of commonly used partnership management methods.

partnership management rights

The management of the general affairs of a partnership is normally controlled by a majority vote of the partners, or of the managing partners. However, the partnership agreement may provide for higher voting requirements, either for all partnership matters (not usually a good practice) or on specified matters or issues. It should be understood that acts in contravention of the partnership agreement are not permitted without the consent of all the partners. See U.P.A. § 18(h).

partnership management, general requirements

To avoid misunderstandings, it is a good practice to include in the partnership agreement provisions dealing with the amount of time that a partner must devote to the partnership business and the permissible scope of a partner's nonpartnership activities. Such provisions are especially important if any of the partners will be devoting only a portion of their time to the partnership business. In the absence of a provision to the contrary in the partnership agreement, a partner may not engage in any activity that in any way competes with the partnership business. See 60 Am. Jur. 2d, Partnership, § 128.

nonpartnership activities of partners

If a partnership business is to continue, it sometimes becomes necessary for the partners to expel one or more of their members. The expulsion of a partner for cause in accordance with the provisions of the partnership agreement is a cause of dissolution that is not in violation of the partnership agreement. See U.P.A. § 31(1)(d). This means that the remaining partners have the right to continue the partnership business, provided that the expelled partner is discharged from partnership liabilities and compensated in cash for the net value of his or her partnership interest. See U.P.A. §§ 38(1), 41(6). The partnership agreement should set forth the grounds and circumstances justifying expulsion, together with the voting requirements for expulsion. The agreement should also provide a reasonable opportunity for the partner being expelled to present a defense and be heard. If the partnership agreement does not provide for the expulsion of a partner, such an expulsion will be in contravention of the partnership agreement and will likely result in the termination of the partnership business.

expulsion of a partner, effect of

In arranging the capitalization of a general partnership, it should be understood that there are no statutory or other legal requirements as to either the amount or the type of capital that may be contributed to a partnership, either prior to the commencement of partnership business or thereafter. Partnership capital contributions may be in the form of cash, property of any type, or personal services. If desired, partners with otherwise equal partnership rights may contribute unequal amounts of capital or different forms of capital to the partnership without altering their partnership status. Partners may contribute property or money to the partnership, loan money or property to the partnership, or contribute the use of property to the partnership.

capital contributions to partnership, general aspects

unequal capital contributions

While great flexibility is permitted in capitalizing general partnerships, the capitalization should be organized so as to prevent inequities and future disputes, especially if equal partners contribute unequal amounts of capital or if personal services are contributed. The central concept should be one of general financial and tax fairness so as to prevent future disputes should the personal relationships among the partners change. If equal partners contribute unequal amounts of capital, it may be advisable to provide for the payment by the partnership of interest on cash contributions and rent on property contributions. Provision should also be made in the partnership agreement for the sharing of depreciation, depletion, and gains and losses on contributed property in such a manner as to take into account any variation between the value and the tax basis of contributed property. See section 3.02, supra, for further reading on this matter.

contribution of services as capital

When a partner contributes services in return for a partnership interest, care should be taken to value the services contributed and to specify in the agreement as to when and how the services are to be (or have been) rendered. Such a practice will avoid confusion over the value of the contributed services for both partnership and tax purposes. It may be desirable to provide in the partnership agreement that a partner who contributes services is entitled to cash distributions from partnership profits only up to a certain annual or monthly amount, with the balance retained by the partnership and credited as capital contributions by the partner until the services have been rendered in full. In this way, a partner without initial capital can, in effect, earn his or her capital contribution while in the employ of the partnership.

contribution of property as capital

It is important that any property, or interest in property, contributed by a partner be accurately described in the partnership agreement. If property is loaned or leased to the partnership by a partner, the terms and duration of the arrangement should be fully spelled out in the agreement. If special assets (e.g., licenses, special permits, copyrights, etc.) are contributed to the partnership, the treatment of such assets, both during the course of partnership business and upon dissolution of the partnership or withdrawal from the partnership by the contributing partner, should be specified in the agreement.

withdrawal of capital

The partnership agreement should include provisions for the withdrawal of capital by the partners. In the absence of such provisions there is no right of withdrawal of capital until the end of the partnership term or its earlier dissolution, unless all partners consent to such a withdrawal. See U.P.A. § 18(a). The withdrawal of capital by a partner, it should be noted, does not affect the partner's management rights or the partner's liability to partnership creditors. See U.P.A. §§ 15, 18(e).

partnership profits and losses, sharing of by partners

In the division of partnership profits and losses, the general rule is that in the absence of an agreement to the contrary, partnership profits and losses are shared equally by all partners, regardless of the amounts of their respective capital contributions to the partnership. See U.P.A. sec. 18(a). Accordingly, one of the most important functions of a partnership agreement is to specify the respective rights of the partners to the profits of the partnership and how its losses shall be shared or contributed to. Both the U.P.A. and the Internal Revenue Code permit partners to allocate partnership profits as they see fit, provided that the terms are specified in the partnership agreement and provided, for tax purposes, that the allocations have substantial economic effect. See U.P.A. § 18, and 26 U.S.C. 704(a),(b). See section 3.04, infra, for a list of common methods of allocating partnership profits, losses and other tax items.

partners' salaries, when permitted

While partners have no statutory right to a salary from the partnership, a salary may be provided for in the partnership agreement. See U.P.A. § 18(f). If the partnership agreement provides for the payment of a salary to one or more of the partners, the salaries are treated as partnership expenses in determining partnership profits. Thus, in effect, a partner drawing a salary pays a portion of his or her own salary in the form of a reduction in the partner's distributive share of partnership profits.

retirement and fringe benefits of partners

An important aspect of partnership compensation may be the providing by the partnership of tax-qualified retirement or other employee benefit plans. If so, the funding and scope of any such plans should be fully described in the partnership agreement. Because a partner is deemed to be a self-employed individual for federal income tax purposes, the tax-qualified retirement and fringe benefit plans available to general partners and their employees are the same as those available to sole proprietors and their employees. These plans and benefits are described and discussed in section 2.02, supra.

In dealing with the admission of new partners to a general partnership, the basic rule is that a new partner may not be admitted without the consent of all existing partners unless the partnership agreement provides otherwise. See U.P.A. § 18(g). For most small partnerships the best practice is to employ the statutory rule of unanimous consent and incorporate it into the partnership agreement. In larger partnerships (i.e., partnerships of, say, six or more partners) this rule may become unworkable and the admission of new partners should be contingent upon a less than unanimous vote of the existing partners. Admitting new partners on a vote of 75 percent of the existing partners is often a satisfactory arrangement, but any voting requirement (including requiring the consent of certain specified partners) may be incorporated into the partnership agreement. If the parties so desire, a distinction can be made in the partnership agreement between new and substituted partners, with different voting requirements imposed for the admission of each type of incoming partner. Lower voting requirements are typically imposed for the admission of a substituted partner. A substituted partner is a partner who is replacing a deceased, withdrawing, or expelled partner.

admission of new partners, general rules

substituted partner, what constitutes

When a general partnership increases its membership by admitting one or more new partners, it usually becomes necessary for the existing partners to relinquish a portion of their interest in partnership profits. For example, if a partnership with four equal partners admits a new equal partner, the interest of the existing partners in partnership profits will decrease from 25 percent to 20 percent. The matter can become complicated in partnerships composed of many partners with unequal interests, especially if several new partners are admitted at the same time. Disputes may arise among the existing partners as to the interest that each shall relinquish in such situations.

adjustment of partnership interests, admission of new partner

A method of simplifying the redistribution of partnership interests upon the admission of new partners is to describe the partnership interest of each partner in terms of units instead of a percentage. Then, when a new partner is admitted the total number of partnership units is simply increased instead of mathematically recalculating the interest of each existing partner. Suppose, for example, that a partnership composed of four partners sharing profits on a 40-percent, 30-percent, 20 percent, and 10-percent basis, takes in a new 5-percent partner. Rather than readjust the partnership percentage of each existing partner, it is usually easier to describe the interest of each in terms of units (e.g., 4,000 units, 3,000 units, 2,000 units, and 1,000 units, for a total of 10,000 units) and then simply add the interest, in terms of units, of the incoming partner to the previous partnership total (500 units for the incoming partner, which would bring the total for the partnership to 10,500 in the example). The unit method also makes it easier to readjust the partnership interest of existing partners when a junior partner is promoted or when a partner withdraws from the partnership. See Reed, Why Units Instead of Partnership Percentages?, 58 A.B.A. Journal 80 (1972).

same, use of partnership units

Perhaps the most difficult aspect of organizing a general partnership is that of determining the method of dealing with partnership interests of deceased or withdrawing partners. About half of the Uniform Partnership Act is devoted to this complicated aspect of partnership law. The basic rule is that unless the partnership agreement provides otherwise, a withdrawing partner (other than a wrongfully withdrawing partner) or the successor in interest of a deceased partner can force the dissolution and liquidation of the partnership. See U.P.A. §§ 29, 38(1). If it is desired that the partnership be dissolved and its business terminated upon the death or withdrawal of a partner, the interest of a deceased or withdrawing partner can normally be satisfied through liquidating distributions by the partnership. While the contractual provisions implementing this method of dealing with such interests are relatively simple, the tax consequences of distributions in the complete liquidation of a partnership can be complicated. See section 3.09, infra, for further reading on the dissolution and liquidation of partnerships. The tax aspects of partnership liquidation and distributions are also discussed in section 3.02, supra.

deceased or withdrawing partners, rights of

In most cases it is desirable to continue the partnership business, or at least give the remaining partners the option of continuing the business, upon the death or withdrawal of a partner, and most partnership agreements contain provisions to that effect. In such cases, the partnership interest of a deceased or withdrawing partner may be dealt with in any of the following manners:

deceased or withdrawing partners, continuation of business, methods of handling

(1) Give the remaining partners the option to either liquidate the partnership business or continue the business by purchasing the interest of the former partner at a fixed or determinable price.

(2) Obligate the surviving partners to continue the partnership business and pay the former partner, or the estate thereof, a fixed or determinable price for his or her partnership interest.

(3) In the case of a deceased partner, give the executor or personal representative of such partner the option (or the obligation) of continuing in the business as a partner, either indefinitely or for a specified period of time.

(4) In the case of a deceased partner, provide that the partners own the partnership business (or certain aspects of the business, such as its property or good will) as joint tenants with rights of survivorship so that upon the death of a partner the surviving partners become the owners of the deceased partner's interest. The payment of a fixed or determinable amount of compensation to the estate of a deceased partner may also be provided.

same, tax treatment

In methods (1) and (2) above, the interests of a deceased or withdrawing partner may be purchased by any or all of the remaining partners individually, by the partnership, or by one or more outsiders or substituted partners. There may be substantially different tax consequences, however, if a former partner's interest is purchased by the partners individually as opposed to its being purchased (or liquidated) by the partnership. See section 3.02 supra, and 3.09, infra, for further reading on the tax consequences of compensating deceased or withdrawing partners.

valuation of partnership good will

It is important to select a method of valuing the partnership interest of a deceased or withdrawing partner that will be fair to both the former partner and the remaining partners. See sections 5.17 and 7.02, infra, for further reading on the methods and techniques of valuing businesses and interests therein. It is particularly important to deal specifically with the compensation, if any, to be paid for the former partner's share of partnership good will. Unless the agreement provides that good will shall be treated as partnership property, payments for good will are treated as distributive shares of partnership income and constitute ordinary income to the recipient (see section 3.02, supra).

partnership interest, use of life insurance to purchase

Life insurance is often used to provide the funds for purchasing the partnership interest of a deceased partner. If this method of funding is desired, the specific obligations of each partner with respect to the purchase of life insurance should be carefully and fully spelled out in the partnership agreement. See section 5.17 infra, for further reading on the use of life insurance to fund buy-out agreements.

liquidation of partnership, inclusion in partnership agreement

While many prospective partners do not like to talk about the termination and liquidation of their business when the partnership is being organized, provisions for these matters should be made in the partnership agreement. Otherwise, costly tax consequences may result, disputes over who is to conduct the liquidation may arise, and the partners will be limited to the default distribution priorities set forth in the U.P.A. The U.P.A. permits a partnership agreement to provide for the winding up of the partnership business and to establish distribution priorities in settling accounts among the partners. See U.P.A. §§37, 40. The partnership agreement should provide for the appointment of one or more liquidating partners to handle the winding up of the partnership business and should set forth the desired liquidation distribution priorities among the partners. See section 3.09, infra, for further reading on the termination and liquidation of general partnerships. If the prospective partners contemplate the future incorporation of the business, a provision to the effect should be included in the partnership agreement (see section 3.04, infra).

3.04 Drafting a General Partnership Agreement - A Checklist

A primary function in the organization of a general partnership is the drafting of a general partnership agreement. The principal purpose of the agreement, of course, is to define the relationship among the partners, and to this end the Uniform Partnership Act permits great latitude and flexibility. The partnership profits and losses, for example, may be divided among the partners in any desired proportions. Capital contributions in any form or amount and in any proportions may be provided for in the partnership agreement, and the partnership may be managed in the manner and by the persons agreed upon by the partners. drafting partnership agreements, permitted flexibility

A partnership agreement must also deal effectively with the tax-related aspects of partnerships, including: (1) the allocation of the various partnership items of income, gain, loss, deductions and credits among the partners, (2) the allocation among the partners of depreciation, depletion, and gain or loss with respect to contributed property, and (3) the method, if any, used to compensate deceased or withdrawing partners for their interest in the partnership and whether good will shall be treated as partnership property in the compensation arrangement. partnership agreements, tax aspects

Functionally, a general partnership agreement should deal with the three major aspects of a partnership arrangement: (1) the organization of the partnership, (2) the operation of the partnership, and (3) the dissolution and termination of the partnership. The organizational provisions are usually fairly simple and not difficult to draft. The operational provisions are more involved and are many in number. The dissolution and termination provisions are often the most complicated and the most difficult to draft, especially in situations where the partnership is likely to be highly profitable or will possess substantial assets. partnership agreements, parts of

The organizational portion of a general partnership agreement should set forth or deal with the following matters:

(1) the names of the partners; partnership agreement, organizational matters

(2) the name of the partnership;

(3) the purposes of the partnership and a description of its business;

(4) the location of the partnership business;

(5) the term or duration of the partnership;

(6) if the partnership will be a limited liability partnership, the matters related thereto; and

(7) a description of the capital contributed to the partnership by each partner and the tax treatment to be accorded the contributed property.

The operational portion of a general partnership agreement should deal with the following matters:

(1) the allocation of partnership profits, losses, deductions and other tax-related items among the partners; partnership agreement, operational matters

(2) the timing and form of the distribution of profits by the partnership;

(3) the fiscal (or tax) year of the partnership;

(4) the partnership books and records, including a description thereof, where they are to be kept, who is responsible for their upkeep, and the bookkeeping and accounting methods to be used by the partnership;

(5) the management of the partnership and its business, including the resolution of disputes;

(6) where the partnership shall bank and who shall perform this function;

(7) whether a bond shall be required of any of the partners, and if so, for whom and in what amount;

(8) when and where partnership meetings shall be held;

(9) the limitations, if any, to be imposed on the authority of any partner to represent or obligate the partnership;

(10) the admission of new or substituted partners and the requirements for their admission; and

(11) the requirements for amending the partnership agreement.

partnership agreement, termination matters

The dissolution and termination portion of a general partnership agreement should deal with the following matters:

(1) the disability or bankruptcy of a partner, including the obligations, if any, of the remaining partners to acquire the interest of a disabled or bankrupt partner;

(2) the expulsion of a partner, including the grounds for expulsion, the methods of effecting expulsion, and the rights and limitations imposed on expelled partners;

(3) the withdrawal of a partner, including the notice requirements, penalties, compensation, and restrictions against competing with the partnership business after withdrawal;

(4) the obligation, if any, of the remaining partners to continue the partnership business upon the death or withdrawal of a partner;

(5) the obligation of the remaining partners or of the partnership to purchase the interest of a deceased or withdrawing partner, including whether the buy-out obligations are to be optional or mandatory, the methods of valuation to be used, how the payments are to be made, and the treatment of good will; and

(6) the liquidation, winding up, and termination of the partnership following dissolution when the business will not be continued.

partnership agreements, suggested drafting procedures

sample partnership agreement

The best practice, of course, is for the partners to meet, consider the available options, and agree on the details of their undertaking and relationship before the partnership agreement is drafted. To accommodate this practice and to insure that no aspect of the undertaking is overlooked during such a meeting, it is suggested that the General Partnership Checklist and Guide shown on the following pages be used as a guide when meeting with the partners, as well as in the drafting of a general partnership agreement. Not all partnership agreements will need provisions on every matter set forth in the Checklist and Guide, but every matter should be considered before drafting an agreement. A sample General Partnership Agreement is set forth in Exhibit 3-A at the end of this chapter.

GENERAL PARTNERSHIP CHECKLIST AND GUIDE

The following matters should be considered when organizing a general partnership and in the preparation and drafting of a general partnership agreement.

ORGANIZATIONAL MATTERS

1. **The names and addresses of the partners.** Persons who may legally become partners include individuals, partnerships, corporations, limited liability companies, and other associations. See section 3.01, supra, for further reading.

2. **The name of the partnership.** Generally, any name that is not the same as or deceptively similar to the name of another business in the area may be used. Registration of the name may be required if it does not contain the surname of every partner. See section 3.03, supra, for further reading.

3. **The business and purposes of the partnership.** The partnership business must be for profit. The partners may restrict the business or purposes of the partnership if they wish to do so. See section 3.01, supra, for further reading.

4. **The place or places of business of the partnership.** The address of the principal place of the partnership business should be shown, along with the locations of any separate or branch offices, if established.

5. **The term or duration of the partnership.** The term or duration of a partnership may be established by any of the following methods, or by any combination of the following methods:

   (a) A fixed or definite term, usually by establishing a finite period of existence or by setting a specific date when the term of the partnership will expire unless the date is earlier extended by a specified vote of the partners.
   (b) Termination at the will of any partner, usually following a specified period of advanced notice.
   (c) Termination by unanimous agreement of the partners or by the affirmative vote of a specified percentage of the partners; or
   (d) termination upon the completion of the partnership purpose or upon the happening or nonhappening of a future event or condition.

   partnership term, methods of establishing

   If no term is specified in the partnership agreement or if the partnership business is continued after the expiration of its period of existence, the partnership is terminable at the will of any partner with no specific notice requirements. See U.P.A. § 23.

   partnership term when none specified

6. **Whether the partnership will be a limited liability partnership.** It should be decided whether the partners wish to register the partnership as a limited liability partnership. If so, the limited liability partnership statutes of the partnership's home state and of each state where the partnership will be conducting significant business must be complied with. See sections 3.11-3.13, infra, for further reading on limited liability partnerships. See Exhibit 3-B at the end of this chapter for additional provisions to be included in a partnership agreement for a limited liability partnership.

   limited liability partnership, matters to cover if partnership is to be registered as capital contributions, methods

7. **Capital contributions to the partnership.** Capital contributions may be in the form of cash, property, or services, or any combination of these. Cash may be contributed or loaned to the partnership, and property may be contributed, loaned, or leased to the partnership. Cash or property contributed to the partnership becomes partnership property. Cash or property loaned or leased to the partnership remains the separate property of the individual partner. It is important that the value of all contributions of whatever form or type, as well as the type and length of all service contributions, be agreed to and specified in the agreement. If unequal capital contributions are made by otherwise equal partners, provisions for interest or rental payments should be made. If property contributions of unequal values or tax bases are made, provisions for the allocation among the partners of depreciation, depletion, and gain or loss with respect to the contributed property should be made. If profit distributions are to be withheld from partners contributing services, the details of the arrangement should be set forth. If additional capital contributions may be required in the future, the conditions and requirements thereof should be stated. If desired, provisions should be made for the withdrawal of capital, or its cash equivalent, by the partners. See sections 3.02 and 3.03, supra, for further reading.

OPERATIONAL MATTERS

8. **Salaries and expenses of partners.** Unless provided for in the partnership agreement, partners are not entitled to salaries. Salaries provided for in the agreement may be fixed, contingent upon profits, or based on other considerations, such as sales. The establishment of expense accounts or other methods of reimbursing partners for partnership expenses may also be provided for in the agreement. See section 3.03, supra, for further reading.

partnership tax items, unequal sharing of

partnership profits and losses, methods of allocating

9. **The sharing of partnership profits and other tax items.** The method of sharing partnership profits and losses should be established in the agreement. If there are to be unequal partners, the use of partnership units rather than percentages may be more practical. See section 3.03, supra. For income tax purposes, profits, losses, gains, deductions, credits, and other tax items must normally be shared in the same proportions by all partners, but different proportions of each may be allocated if the allocations are not primarily for the purpose of avoiding taxes and have substantial economic reality. See 26 U.S.C. 704(b) and section 3.02, supra. Extraordinary expenses may be shared differently by the partners if economically justifiable. Common methods of sharing or allocating partnership profits, losses, and other tax items include:

   (a) equal sharing by all partners;
   (b) sharing in proportion to capital contributions;
   (c) sharing in accordance to specified standards, such as seniority or productivity;
   (d) allocating tax deductions, credits, and gains and losses with respect to certain assets to the partners who contributed the assets;
   (e) the guaranteeing of certain profit distributions to certain partners, often with contribution requirements from other partners if the guaranteed payments cannot be met by the partnership; and
   (f) allocating any losses caused by the willful misdeed or default of any partner to that partner.

disposable cash, distribution of

10. **Cash distributions to partners.** Because it is possible for a partnership to produce paper losses (usually through depletion, depreciation, or other deductions) and have disposable cash, provisions should be made for the distribution of cash. Such distributions may be in the same method and proportions as for profit distributions, or a different arrangement may be implemented, such as distributions in accordance to the individual partners' need for cash.

11. **The partnership's fiscal (or tax) year and method of accounting.** Because a partnership is a tax-reporting entity, it must have a tax year. The partnership's tax year must usually conform to the tax years of its partners. See section 3:02, supra, for further reading. The accounting practices of the partnership should also be established, including its tax reporting methods.

12. **The books and records of the partnership.** The official books and records of the partnership business should be identified, and provisions made for their upkeep, custody, audit, and inspection. Provisions should also be made for the rendering of periodic reports to the partners on the financial status of the partnership.

13. **The partnership's banking arrangements.** The bank (or banks) to be used for the deposit of partnership funds should be established, and the persons authorized to sign checks and otherwise deal with the funds identified.

14. **Partnership meetings.** Provisions should be made for periodic meetings of the partners, usually at specified times and places or upon the giving of specified notices.

management of partnership business, permitted methods

15. **The management of the partnership business.** Unless the partnership agreement provides to the contrary, all partners share equally in the management of the partnership business and the majority vote of the partners controls. See U.P.A. § 18(e), (h). Different methods of management may be imposed by the agreement, however. See section 3.03, supra, for further reading. If certain partners are to be designated as the managing partners, their duties and limitations should be specified. The desired management arrangement should be clearly spelled out in the agreement, and a method of resolving disputes or deadlocks should be provided. Common methods of partnership management include:

    (a) equal sharing of management responsibilities by all partners;
    (b) unequal sharing of management responsibilities, usually in accordance with seniority, the sharing of profits, or capital contributions;
    (c) delegation of all or certain management functions to either a committee of partners or a managing partner;
    (d) the removal of all management responsibilities from certain partners (i.e., silent partners), with the management functions vested in the remaining partners; and
    (e) the division of management functions and responsibilities among all or certain partners, usually in accordance to their special skills, often with requirements of periodic reports from those partners responsible for major partnership functions.

16. **Limitations on partners' authority.** If limitations on the authority of partners to represent or obligate the partnership, other than those imposed by law, are to be imposed on all or certain partners, the limitations should be specified. See section 3.01, supra, for further reading.

17. **Outside activities of partners.** If any partner will be devoting less than full time to the partnership business, the permitted (or forbidden) outside activities should be specified, with special attention given those activities that may be viewed as conflicting or competing with the partnership business. See section 3.03, supra, for further reading.

18. **Fidelity bonds.** If any partner is to be required to obtain a fidelity bond for the faithful performance of his or her duties, the partner should be identified and the amount of the bond specified.

19. **Restrictions on transfers of partnership interests.** If desired, the rights of partners to transfer their interest in partnership profits and surplus may be restricted in the partnership agreement. Common types of restrictions include consent restrictions that require the consent of the other partners prior to any transfer, and option restrictions that give the other partners a right of first refusal to purchase the interest sought to be transferred at a fixed or determinable price. See section 3.01, supra, for further reading.

20. **Partnership property.** The name in which the partnership property is to be titled should be specified, and all partnership property should be clearly identified. Any property leased or loaned to the partnership by any of the partners should be separately identified, and the terms and duration of the partnership's right to the use of the property specified. Accounting procedures for the treatment of depreciation, depletion, repairs, taxes, and other expenses of all property owned or used by the partnership should be established.

21. **The admission of new or substituted partners.** Unless the partnership agreement provides otherwise, a new partner may be admitted to the partnership only with the consent of all existing partners. See U.P.A. § 18(g). However, the partnership agreement may provide for other voting requirements or conditions of admissions. If desirable, a different voting requirement can be imposed for the admission of a substituted partner (i.e., a partner replacing a deceased or withdrawing partner) than for the admission of an additional partner. Provisions should be made for the reallocation of the partnership interest of each existing partner should additional partners be admitted. See section 3.03, supra, for further reading.

amending partnership agreement, provisions for

22. **Amending the partnership agreement.** Provisions should be made for amending the partnership agreement, should the need or desire to do so arise in the future. In most cases the best practice is to provide that the agreement may be amended by majority vote of the partners except that any provision in the agreement that requires the vote, consent or approval of more than a simple majority of the partners may be amended only by a partnership vote that is equal to that called for in the provision sought to be amended. Any amendment restrictions or procedures desired by the partners may be inserted, however, including requiring the consent of all or specified partners.

DISSOLUTION AND TERMINATION MATTERS

continuation of partnership business upon death or withdrawal of partner, provisions for

23. **Death or withdrawal of a partner.** The grounds for the retirement or withdrawal of a partner should be specified, together with a requirement of reasonable advance notice to the other partners. If the remaining partners are to have the option or obligation of continuing the business after the death or withdrawal of a partner, as is usually the case, their rights and obligations in this regard should be fully spelled out. The giving of notice to the withdrawing partner, or to the estate of a deceased partner, of an intention to continue the business is often required. The method and procedures for compensating deceased or withdrawing partners for their interest in the partnership should be established (see paragraph 26 below). If the estate or personal representative of a deceased partner is to continue as a partner or share in partnership profits, such rights and the duration thereof should be specified. Any penalties to be imposed for the wrongful withdrawal from the partnership should also be specified, and if the remaining partners elect to continue the business after a wrongful withdrawal, provisions should be made for indemnifying the withdrawing partner against partnership liabilities and compensating the partner for his or her partnership interest. It is common to include covenants by the partners not to compete against the partnership business after withdrawal. See section 3.03, supra, and section 3.09, infra, for further reading.

expulsion of partner, provisions for

24. **Expulsion of a partner.** The grounds and circumstances justifying the expulsion of a partner should be specified, together with a method of deciding on expulsion and a procedure for effecting the expulsion, which should include reasonable notice and an opportunity for the partner being expelled to be heard. The method of compensating an expelled partner should also be set forth in the agreement. See section 3.03, supra, for further reading.

25. **Disability or bankruptcy of a partner.** A definition of disability should be established, together with a method of determining when a disability exists and the permitted length of any compensible disability. A method of compensating a disabled partner during the period of disability should also be established. Provisions should be made for the purchase of the partnership interest of a disabled partner and for the continuation of the partnership business, should the disability continue for a specified period. Provisions should also be made for the continuation of the partnership business in the event of the personal bankruptcy of a partner, together with the terms and conditions for the purchase of the partnership interest of a bankrupt partner.

disability of partner, provisions for

26. **Compensating deceased or withdrawing partners.** If the partnership business is not to be continued after the death or withdrawal of a partner, the deceased or withdrawing partner is normally compensated in the course of liquidating and terminating the partnership. If the partnership business is to be continued after the death or withdrawal of a partner, the interest of the former partner may be purchased individually by the remaining partners in specified proportions, by the remaining partners jointly, by the partnership, or by an incoming partner. The tax aspects of the method of purchase should be thoroughly examined. The method of funding the purchase should be established. Such funding may be through the personal funds of the existing or incoming partners, by a special fund established by the partnership, or by the purchase of life insurance, either by the partners individually or by the partnership. A method of valuing the former partner's interest should be established. Common methods include a sum stipulated in the agreement (with periodic revisions if desired), the use of a formula based on partnership earnings or on the value of partnership assets, or by a return of capital plus interest. The terms of any required payments should be specified in the agreement, as should the treatment of partnership good will. See sections 3.02 and 3.03, supra, and section 3.09, infra, for further reading on the matters discussed in this paragraph.

compensating deceased or withdrawing partners, provisions for

27. **Liquidation and termination of the partnership.** Provisions should be included dealing with the liquidation, winding up, and termination of the partnership business when the partnership is dissolved and its business discontinued. If desired, a liquidating partner or committee may be designated, and their compensation established. If distribution priorities are to be other than as provided by statute, they must be specified. If additional contributions are to be required to cover partnership losses or obligations, the terms and requirements thereof should be specified. See section 3.03, supra, and section 3.09, infra, for further reading.

liquidation of partnership business, provisions for

28. **Incorporating the partnership.** If the partners contemplate incorporating the business or forming a limited liability company upon the happening of certain events (e.g., the death or withdrawal of a certain partner, the attainment of certain profit levels, etc.), upon a certain vote of the partners, or otherwise, provisions governing the organization and formation of the corporation or limited liability company should be included in the partnership agreement. This is a good practice for a start-up business whose participants have expressed an interest in forming a corporation or limited liability company if the business prospers.

incorporation of partnership business, provisions for

3.05 Limited Partnerships - An Introduction

limited partnership, general aspects

A limited partnership is a partnership having one or more general partners and one or more limited partners. A general partner in a limited partnership is substantially the same as a general partner in a general partnership (i.e., full management rights and unlimited personal liability), while a limited partner is primarily an investor with little voice in the management of the partnership and only limited personal liability for partnership debts.

limited partnership, how created

Limited partnerships are the creation of a statute and were not recognized under the common law. Accordingly, a limited partnership can be created only under a written agreement that complies with the requirements of a statute and that is filed with a designated filing official. Unlike a general partnership, a limited partnership cannot arise informally. Limited partnerships should not be confused with limited liability partnerships, which are general partnerships wherein the liability of the partners for the debts of the partnership is limited (see section 3.11, infra).

limited partnership, laws governing

Like general partnerships, the legal aspects of limited partnerships are governed by a uniform law that has been adopted in every state except two. The Revised Uniform Limited Partnership Act has been adopted with only minor local variations in every state except Vermont and Louisiana. It is this act that governs the creation, operation, and termination of limited partnerships in the United States. The Revised Uniform Limited Partnership Act (R.U.L.P.A.) will be cited repeatedly in this handbook. The statutory citation to the R.U.L.P.A. in each state is set forth in Appendix I in the back of this book under the heading of Partnerships, Limited Partnerships. The provisions of the local Act correspond generally to the sections of the R.U.L.P.A. that are cited in this book.

limited partnerships, distinguishing characteristics

The distinguishing characteristics of a limited partnership include the following:

(1) Its creation is dependent upon the existence of a signed written agreement. See R.U.L.P.A. § 201.

(2) There must be at least one general partner and one limited partner. See R.U.L.P.A. § 101(7).

(3) Under most circumstances, the personal liability of a limited partner for partnership debts is limited to the amount of capital that the partner has contributed to the partnership. See R.U.L.P.A. § 303(a).

(4) A limited partner may not participate in the control of the partnership business without incurring extended liability for partnership debts. See R.U.L.P.A. § 303(a),(b).

(5) The death, withdrawal, or assignment of a partnership interest by a limited partner does not cause the dissolution of the partnership. See R.U.L.P.A. § 702, 801.

limited partnership, who may be partner, filing requirements

A natural person, a corporation, a limited liability company, a trust, an estate, an association, a general partnership or another limited partnership may be a general or limited partner in a limited partnership. See R.U.L.P.A. § 101(5), (6), (11). As indicated above, a limited partnership may not arise informally. It is created only when a properly signed certificate of limited partnership is filed with the state filing official (usually the Secretary of State) and the filing fee paid. See R.U.L.P.A. §§ 201, 206. In a few states certain other recording functions must be performed before the partnership comes into existence.

limited partner, personal liability

In the absence of extenuating circumstances, the liability of a limited partner is limited to the amount of capital that the partner contributed or agreed to contribute to the partnership. See R.U.L.P.A. § 303(a). A limited partner is not liable to partnership creditors beyond the amount of the partner's capital contribution unless the partner either takes part in the control of the partnership business or permits his or her name to be improperly included in the partnership name. See R.U.L.P.A. § 303(a),(d). A limited partner who permits his or her name to be used in the partnership name is personally liable to partnership creditors who extend credit to the partnership without actual knowledge that he or she is not a general partner. See R.U.L.P.A. § 303(d). A limited partner may also be liable for misrepresentation in the filed certificate of limited partnership. See R.U.L.P.A. § 207. Also, if a limited partnership is defectively formed, a limited partner may be liable for partnership debts as a general partner unless the limited partner either corrects the defect or promptly withdraws from the partnership. See R.U.L.P.A. § 304.

A limited partner who participates in the control of the partnership business is liable to persons transacting business with the partnership who reasonably believe the limited partner to be a general partner. See R.U.L.P.A. § 303(a). While it is not totally clear as to exactly what constitutes participation in the control of a business, guidance may be found in section 303(b) of the R.U.L.P.A., which sets forth a nonexclusive list of permitted activities which if performed by a limited partner do not constitute participation in the control of the business. These permitted activities include: limited partner, personal liability

(1) being a contractor for or an agent or employee of the limited partnership or of a general partner of the limited partnership, or being an officer, director, or shareholder of a corporate general partner of the limited partnership;

(2) consulting with and advising a general partner with respect to the business of the limited partnership; control of business, acts not constituting

(3) acting as surety for the limited partnership or guaranteeing or assuming one or more specific obligations of the limited partnership;

(4) taking any action required or permitted by law to maintain a derivative action on behalf of the limited partnership;

(5) requesting or attending a meeting of the partners;

(6) proposing, approving, or disapproving, by voting or otherwise, one or more of the following matters:

(a) the dissolution and winding up of the limited partnership;

(b) the sale, exchange, lease, mortgage, pledge, or other transfer of all or substantially all of the assets of the limited partnership;

(c) the incurrence of indebtedness by the limited partnership other than in the ordinary course of its business;

(d) a change in the nature of the partnership business;

(e) the admission or removal of a general or limited partner in the partnership;

(f) a transaction involving an actual or potential conflict of interest between a general partner and the limited partnership or the limited partners;

(g) an amendment to the partnership agreement or to the certificate of limited partnership; or

(h) other matters related to the limited partnership business not listed herein, which, under the partnership agreement, are subject to the approval or disapproval of the limited partners;

(7) winding up the limited partnership upon termination; and

(8) exercising any other right or power granted to limited partners in the R.U.L.P.A.

The rights and interests of a general partner in a limited partnership are substantially the same as those of a general partner in a general partnership, except that in a limited partnership the assignee of a general partner may become a limited partner. See R.U.L.P.A. §§ 402, 403. See section 3.01, supra, for a discussion of the rights and interests of general partners. general partner, rights and interests of

The interest of a limited partner in a limited partnership constitutes personal property and is assignable unless otherwise provided in the partnership agreement. See R.U.L.P.A. §§ 701, 702. The assignee of a limited partner becomes a substituted limited partner with all of the rights and powers of a limited partner, unless otherwise provided in the partnership agreement. See R.U.L.P.A. § 704. The partnership interest of a limited partner may be subjected to a charging order by a court, and, unless otherwise exempt, may be attached or executed upon by the judgment creditor of a limited partner. See R.U.L.P.A. § 703. limited partner, assignment of partnership interest

limited partners, rights of

Limited partners have certain basic rights in regard to partnership matters, whether or not these rights are set forth in the partnership agreement. For example, a limited partner has the right to inspect and copy the partnership's required records and to be fully informed as to partnership affairs. See R.U.L.P.A. § 105. See section 3.06, infra, for a list of the records that a limited partnership is required to keep and make available to the limited partners. A limited partner also has the right to obtain a copy of the partnership's most recent tax return and such other information regarding partnership affairs as is reasonable and just. See R.U.L.P.A. § 305. In addition, a limited partner has the right to file and maintain a derivative action on behalf of the partnership against any general partner who has wronged or damaged the partnership. See R.U.L.P.A. §§ 1001-1004. It should be noted that the rights of a limited partner may be enforced by the partner's personal representative should the partner die or be adjudicated incompetent. See R.U.L.P.A. § 705.

deceased limited partner, rights of

limited partnership, doing business in other states, registration requirements

A limited partnership may conduct business in states other than the state where it was organized. However, if sufficient business is transacted in a foreign state, the partnership must be registered with the Secretary of State (or other specified recording official) in the foreign state as a foreign limited partnership. See R.U.L.P.A. § 902. The R.U.L.P.A. does not specify the activities that constitute (or that do not constitute) the transaction of business in a foreign state sufficient to require registration. Presumably the rules applicable to the transaction of business by foreign corporations are also applicable to foreign limited partnerships. These rules are discussed in section 6.08, infra. The specific registration requirements for foreign limited partnerships are set forth in section 902 of the R.U.L.P.A. The name registration requirements for a foreign limited partnership are the same as those described in section 3.06, infra, for a domestic limited partnership. See R.U.L.P.A. § 904. It should be noted that a limited partnership that transacts business in a foreign state is denied access to the courts in the foreign state until it has registered in that state as a foreign limited partnership. See R.U.L.P.A. § 907.

3.06 Organizing a Limited Partnership

Because a limited partnership can be lawfully formed only by the proper filing of a certificate of limited partnership, the preparation of a written document defining at least a portion of the relationship among the partners is always necessary. The best practice in most cases is to prepare a limited partnership agreement defining the complete relationship among the partners, together with a certificate of limited partnership containing only the statutorily-required information. Because limited partnerships are usually formed for purposes of investment by the limited partners in a specific business venture, it will usually be necessary to prepare the documents that will enable the limited partnership to conduct the business for which it is being formed. The required documents may include deeds, mortgages, trust agreements, and other instruments conveying interests in real estate, or similar documents conveying or creating interests in other properties forming the subject of the investment or venture. limited partnerships, necessary documents

While a written agreement separate and apart from the certificate of limited partnership is not legally required, the use of such an agreement will serve to shield many of the aspects and terms of the partners' relationship and business operations from public disclosure. However, if the business undertaking of the limited partnership is simple, if the relationship among the partners is uncomplicated, and if the partners do not object to the public disclosure of their entire agreement, then it may be practicable to organize and establish a limited partnership under a certificate of limited partnership only. To this end, it is permissible to include in the certificate of limited partnership matters other than those specifically required by statute to be included. See R.U.L.P.A. § 201(a)(5). limited partnerships, separate written agreement, necessity of certificate of limited partnership as agreement

Because a limited partnership must have a name, one of the first matters to resolve in the organization of a limited partnership is that of the partnership name. See R.U.L.P.A. § 201(a)(1). The name of a limited partnership - (1) must contain the words "limited partnership" without abbreviation, or, in some states, the abbreviation "L.P.", or, in a few states, other specified words or abbreviations, (2) may not contain the name of a limited partner unless the limited partner is also a general partner or was not a limited partner when the name was adopted, and (3) may not be the same as, or deceptively similar to, the name of any other registered corporation, limited partnership, or limited liability company. In addition, the R.U.L.P.A. as adopted in many states contains a list of prohibited words (usually words implying the existence of a corporation, a bank, or an insurance company). See R.U.L.P.A. § 102. The precise phraseology used in implementing the above requirements varies from state to state. If desired, a partnership name may be reserved for a specified period (usually 120 days) by filing a name reservation application with the Secretary of State and paying the required fee. See R.U.L.P.A. § 103. name of limited partnership, requirements

The inclusion of the name of an existing limited partner in the partnership name may subject the limited partner to extended personal liability to partnership creditors. See R.U.L.P.A. § 303(d) and section 3.05, supra. The use of a name that is the same as or deceptively similar to that of another business will probably result in the refusal of the filing official to file the certificate of limited partnership and may constitute an unfair or deceptive trade practice. See R.U.L.P.A. § 102(3), and David B. Findlay, Inc. v. Findlay, 18 N.Y. 2nd 12, 271 N.Y.S. 2nd 652, 218 N.E. 2nd 531 (1966). It should be noted that the partnership name requirements in the R.U.L.P.A. are similar in many respects to the corporate name requirements in the corporation laws. improper partnership name, effect of

In organizing a limited partnership the following major partnership functions should be considered and dealt with: (1) the management and control of the partnership, (2) the capitalization of the partnership, (3) the allocation of partnership profits, losses, depreciation, and other tax items, (4) the admission of new general and limited partners, (5) the treatment of partnership interests of deceased or withdrawing partners, and (6) the dissolution and termination of the partnership. limited partnership, major functions

The normal management functions of a limited partnership must be performed by the general partner(s). A general partner in a limited partnership, it should be noted, has essentially the same rights and powers as a general partner in a general partnership. See R.U.L.P.A. § 403. See sections 3.01 and 3.03, supra, for a discussion of the rights and powers of general partners. If there is more than one general partner, it may be necessary to provide in the partnership agreement for a division of managerial responsibilities and specify the voting requirements on partnership matters. See R.U.L.P.A. § 405. limited partnership, management functions

removal of general partner

Provisions should be made in a limited partnership agreement for the removal of a general partner because in the absence of such a provision there is no statutory right to remove a general partner. If the partnership agreement so provides, a general partner may be removed and such a removal is treated as a withdrawal of the general partner for partnership purposes. See R.U.L.P.A. § 402(3). The partnership agreement should specify the grounds for removal, the voting requirements for removal, and a method of replacing the removed general partner.

limited partners, permitted management functions

While limited partners may not participate in the control of the partnership business without exposing themselves to extended personal liability, they do have rights in this regard, including the right to vote on any matter specified in the partnership agreement. See R.U.L.P.A. § 302. In addition, a limited partner may consult with and advise a general partner with regard to the partnership business and may request or attend a meeting of the partners without incurring extended personal liability. See R.U.L.P.A. § 303(b)(2), (5). A limited partner may exercise certain voting rights without incurring personal liability, whether or not the voting rights are specified in the partnership agreement, and may participate in certain other partnership activities without incurring extended personal liability for partnership debts. See R.U.L.P.A. § 303(b). See section 3.05, supra, for a nonexclusive list of activities in which a limited partner may engage without incurring extended personal liability. These matters should be considered when organizing the management and control structure of a limited partnership.

capital contributions, forms of

Most limited partnerships are formed for purposes of investment. Therefore, the capitalization of the partnership is usually a matter of much concern to the parties involved. The R.U.L.P.A. permits great flexibility in capitalizing a limited partnership. For example, the capital contributions of either a general or a limited partner may be in the form of cash, property, services rendered, promissory notes, or obligations to contribute cash, property or services in the future. See R.U.L.P.A. § 501. The capital contributions, or commitments for future contributions, of any partner, general or limited, need not be shown on the certificate of limited partnership. See R.U.L.P.A. § 201(a). However, a promise by a limited partner to contribute to the partnership is enforceable only if the promise is in a writing signed by the limited partner. See R.U.L.P.A. § 502(a). In addition, both general and limited partners may loan money to the partnership and may become secured or unsecured creditors of the partnership with the same rights and obligations as nonpartner creditors, unless otherwise provided in the partnership agreement. See R.U.L.P.A. § 107.

partners as creditors, rights of

partnership profits and losses, allocation of

In the allocation of partnership profits, losses and other tax items, both the R.U.L.P.A. and The Internal Revenue Code permit great flexibility. Under the R.U.L.P.A., partnership profits and losses may be allocated among the partners, general and limited, in the manner provided for in the partnership agreement. If the agreement is silent on the subject, profits and losses are allocated among the partners on the basis of the values of their respective capital contributions as shown in the partnership records, less any returned contributions. See R.U.L.P.A. § 503. The Internal Revenue Code provides that a partner's share of the partnership's income, gain, loss, deduction, and credit is determined by the partnership agreement. See 26 U.S.C. 704(a). Therefore, it is important that the partnership agreement fully spell out the rights of all partners in this regard. A partner's allocated share of income, loss and other tax items is normally based on the amount of the partner's capital contribution, but other methods may be used as long as they have substantial economic effect. See 26 U.S.C. 704(a), (b). See section 3.02, supra, for further reading on the tax aspects of partnership allocations.

additional general partners, admission of

After a limited partnership has been formed, additional general partners may be admitted in the manner provided for in the partnership agreement. If the partnership agreement is silent on the matter, additional general partners may be admitted only on the written consent of all partners, general and limited. See R.U.L.P.A. § 401. It is important, therefore, to provide for the admission (or nonadmission, if desired) of additional or substituted general partners in the partnership agreement. The necessary voting standards and other admission requirements, if any, should be specified.

new limited partners, admission of

Additional limited partners may be admitted after the formation of a limited partnership either directly by the limited partnership (i.e., a new limited partner) or as an assignee of an existing general or limited partner (i.e., a substituted limited partner). It should be noted that the assignee of the partnership interest of a general partner may become a substituted limited partner.. See R.U.L.P.A. § 704(a). A new limited partner may be admitted only upon compliance with the admission requirements set forth in the partnership agreement or, if the agreement makes no provision therefor, upon the written consent of all partners, general and limited. See R.U.L.P.A. § 301. The partnership agreement should specify the admission requirements for new limited partners.

substituted limited partners, admission of

The assignee of the partnership interest of a general or limited partner may become a substituted limited partner if and to the extent that the assignor partner gives the assignee that right in accordance with the authority contained in the partnership agreement. A substituted limited partner may also be admitted upon the consent of all other partners, general and limited. See R.U.L.P.A. § 704(a). It should be noted that a substituted limited partner must assume the known liabilities of the assignor partner and that the assignor partner is not released from certain partnership liabilities. See R.U.L.P.A. § 704(b), (c). The partnership agreement should specify the assignment rights of both general and limited partners and establish the admission requirements for substituted limited partners.

withdrawal of general partner

A general partner may, without causing dissolution, withdraw from a limited partnership at any time by giving notice of withdrawal to the other partners, provided that if the withdrawal violates the partnership agreement the withdrawing partner may be liable in damages to the partnership. These damages may be deducted from any amounts otherwise distributable by the partnership to the withdrawing partner. See R.U.L.P.A. § 602.

withdrawal of limited partner

A limited partner may withdraw from the partnership upon a date specified in the partnership agreement or upon the happening of an event specified in the partnership agreement. If no date or event is specified in the partnership agreement, a limited partner may withdraw from the partnership only upon its dissolution or upon the giving of six months advance written notice to the partnership. See R.U.L.P.A. § 603. However, unless the partnership agreement provides otherwise, a limited partner may assign his or her partnership interest and be replaced by a substituted limited partner. See R.U.L.P.A. §§ 702, 704.

distribution rights of withdrawing partners

Unless otherwise provided in the partnership agreement, a withdrawing partner, general or limited, is entitled to receive, within a reasonable time after withdrawal, the fair value of his or her partnership interest as of the date of withdrawal, based on the partner's right to share in partnership distributions, less any amounts owed to the partnership by reason of the withdrawal or otherwise. See R.U.L.P.A. § 604. Unless the partnership agreement provides otherwise, all distributions to withdrawing partners must be in cash. See R.U.L.P.A. § 605. A withdrawing partner has the status of a creditor of the limited partnership with respect to the partner's distribution. See R.U.L.P.A. § 606. A partner is not entitled to a distribution that would render the partnership insolvent. See R.U.L.P.A. § 607.

dissolution of limited partnership, causes of

Because limited partnerships are usually formed for a specific venture or investment, they do not normally exist indefinitely. Therefore, it is important to provide for the dissolution of the partnership in the partnership agreement. A limited partnership may be dissolved at a time specified in the certificate of limited partnership, upon the happening of an event specified in the partnership agreement, upon the written consent of all partners, upon the withdrawal of the only limited partner, or upon a court decree of dissolution. See R.U.L.P.A. § 801. See section 3.09, infra, for further reading on the dissolution of limited partnerships. The partnership agreement should specify the date, event, or other happening upon which the partnership is to be dissolved.

winding up of limited partnership, distribution priorities

Upon dissolution and winding up, the partnership assets must be distributed first to the partnership creditors, including partners who are creditors. Unless the partnership agreement provides otherwise, the remaining funds must be distributed to the partners, first as interim distributions, then as a return of contribution, and finally as liquidation distributions. See R.U.L.P.A. § 804. See section 3.09, infra, for further reading on the liquidation and termination of limited partnerships. The agreement should specify the distribution priorities among the partners if they are to be other than as provided by law.

certificate of limited partnership, preparation of

Another function that must be performed in the organization of a limited partnership is that of preparing and filing the certificate of limited partnership. Unless the certificate of limited partnership will also serve as the partnership agreement, it is not necessary to prepare an elaborate or lengthy certificate. A sample certificate of limited partnership is set forth in Exhibit 3-D at the end of this chapter. It should be noted that a stamped copy of the filed certificate of limited partnership must be delivered to each limited partner unless the partnership agreement provides otherwise. See R.U.L.P.A. § 209.

A certificate of limited partnership must set forth the following matters:

certificate of limited partnership, required provisions

(1) the name of the limited partnership,

(2) the address of the partnership's registered office and the name and address of its registered agent for service of process,

(3) the name and business address of each general partner,

(4) the latest date upon which the limited partnership will be dissolved, and

(5) any other matters which the general partners choose to include. See R.U.L.P.A. § 201(a).

certificate of limited partnership, execution and filing requirements

The original copy or copies of the certificate of limited partnership must be signed under penalty of perjury by each general partner or by a general partner's attorney in fact. See R.U.L.P.A. § 204. For a limited partnership to come into existence, the certificate of limited partnership must be filed with the filing official designated in the statute (usually the Secretary of State) and the required filing fee paid. See R.U.L.P.A. §§ 201, 206. A few states impose additional recording requirements.

local registered office and agent, requirements

A limited partnership is required to continuously maintain in the state a registered office and a registered agent for service of process. See R.U.L.P.A. § 104. The initial registered office and agent must be specified in the certificate of limited partnership. See R.U.L.P.A. § 201(a)(2). The local registered agent of the partnership may be an individual resident of the state or a corporation authorized to do business in the state. The local registered office may, but need not be, a place of business of the partnership. In any event, the statutorily-required records of the partnership must be kept at the local registered office. See R.U.L.P.A. § 104. Care should be taken to insure that these office and agent requirements are fulfilled during the course of organizing a limited partnership.

A limited partnership is required under section 105(a) of the R.U.L.P.A. to keep and maintain the following records at its local registered office:

limited partnership, required records

(1) a current alphabetical list of the names and addresses of its general partners and a current alphabetical list of the names and addresses of its limited partners,

(2) a copy of the partnership's certificate of limited partnership and all certificates of amendment and powers of attorney,

(3) copies of the partnership's federal, state and local income tax returns for the last three years,

(4) copies of any written partnership agreements currently in effect,

(5) copies of all partnership financial statements for the last three years, and

(6) unless contained in the partnership agreement, a written record of all partnership contributions, agreements for contributions, distributions, and dissolution-causing events.

The preparation and maintenance of the records described above should be provided for during the course of organizing a limited partnership. These records may be inspected and copied by any partner during ordinary business hours. See R.U.L.P.A. § 105(b).

certificate of limited partnership, filing of in foreign states

If the partnership will be conducting business in more than one state, registration of the partnership in other states may be required. The filing requirements of all other states where the partnership will be conducting business should be ascertained and complied with. The provisions dealing with foreign limited partnerships are contained in article 9 of the R.U.L.P.A. The transaction of business by a limited partnership in other states is discussed in section 3.05, supra.

amendments to certificate of limited partnership

Amendments to the certificate of limited partnership must be filed upon the happening of specified events, including the admission or withdrawal of a general partner. See R.U.L.P.A. § 202. An amendment to a certificate of limited partnership is subject to essentially the same execution and filing requirements as an original certificate. See R.U.L.P.A. §§ 204, 206.

sale of limited partnership interests, S.E.C. requirements

If a limited partnership is formed for the purpose of selling limited partnership interests to a substantial number of persons or to the public generally, registration with Securities and Exchange Commission and the state securities commissioner may be required. The S.E.C. has ruled that a limited partnership interest constitutes a security (an investment contract) under the Securities Act of 1933. See S.E.C. Release No. 4877, August 6, 1967. See also, S.E.C. v. W.J. Howey Co., 328 U.S. 293, 66 S.Ct. 1100, 90 L.Ed. 1244 (1946). Exemptions from S.E.C. registration for limited partnership interests may be available under S.E.C. Rules 147, 504, 505 and 506, and under S.E.C. Regulation A. See section 5.16, infra, for further reading on federal and state securities laws.

3.07 Drafting a Limited Partnership Agreement - A Checklist

limited partnership agreement, purpose

A principal function in the organization and formation of a limited partnership is the drafting of a limited partnership agreement and a certificate of limited partnership. While a written limited partnership agreement separate and apart from the certificate of limited partnership is not legally required, the use of such an agreement is clearly the better practice (see section 3.06, supra). The purpose of a limited partnership agreement, it should be remembered, is to establish the relationship among the partners and govern the conduct of partnership affairs, including the tax considerations.

certificate of limited partnership, preparation and filing of

The purpose of a certificate of limited partnership is to establish the legal existence of the partnership, which means that it must contain the information required by statute and be properly signed and filed. See R.U.L.P.A. § 201. Under most circumstances, the preparation of a certificate of limited partnership is a simple matter. However, if a separate limited partnership agreement is not used, the certificate of limited partnership should be expanded so that it can also serve as an effective partnership agreement. The preparation, execution, and filing of the certificate of limited partnership is covered in section 3.06, supra. A sample certificate of limited partnership is set forth in Exhibit 3-D at the end of this chapter.

limited partnership agreement, matters to cover

A limited partnership agreement should deal with the following major aspects of the partnership arrangement: (1) the organization of the partnership, including the initial number of general and limited partners, (2) the operation of the partnership, and (3) the withdrawal of partners and the termination of the partnership. The legal, practical, and tax aspects of the undertaking should be set forth in a manner and in words that are understandable to the persons involved. It is suggested that the Limited Partnership Checklist and Guide set forth below be used in both organizing the partnership and drafting the limited partnership agreement. A sample limited partnership agreement is set forth in Exhibit 3-C at the end of this chapter.

LIMITED PARTNERSHIP CHECKLIST AND GUIDE

The following matters should be considered in organizing a limited partnership and in the preparation and drafting of a limited partnership agreement:

ORGANIZATIONAL MATTERS

1. **Name of partnership.** The statutory partnership name requirements are set forth in § 102 of the R.U.L.P.A. See section 3.06, supra, for a discussion of the partnership name requirements. See R.U.L.P.A. § 103 for the name reservation requirements.

2. **Names and addresses of general partners.** The name and address of each general partner must be set forth in the certificate of general partnership and should also be contained in the partnership agreement.

3. **Names and addresses of limited partners.** The names and addresses of the limited partners should be set forth in the partnership agreement.

4. **Partnership business and purpose.** The purpose for which the partnership is formed and the nature of the partnership business should be specified in the partnership agreement. A limited partnership may engage in any lawful business except a nonprofit business and any business specially prohibited to limited partnerships under local law. See R.U.L.P.A. § 106.

5. **Place of business.** The address of the partnership's registered office must appear on the certificate of limited partnership and its place or places of business should be set forth in the partnership agreement.

6. **Duration of partnership.** The latest date upon which the partnership is to dissolve must appear on the certificate of limited partnership. See R.U.L.P.A. § 201. The events causing or the time of dissolution, if any, should be set forth in the partnership agreement. See R.U.L.P.A. § 801 for the causes of dissolution. See section 3.06, supra, and 3.09, infra, for further reading on the dissolution of limited partnerships.

7. **Capital contributions of general and limited partners.** Capital contributions may be in the form of cash, property, services rendered, promissory notes, or obligations for future contributions of cash, property, or services. See R.U.L.P.A. § 501. See section 3.06, supra, for further reading on capital contributions. The capital contributions of each general and limited partner should be fully spelled out in the partnership agreement.

OPERATIONAL MATTERS

8. **Compensation of general partners.** If the general partners are to draw a salary or be compensated other than from a share of the partnership profits, the amount and times of payment thereof should be specified in the agreement, together with the requirements for any changes in the amount of compensation.

9. **Management duties of general partners.** These duties should be specified either generally or specifically, if necessary, in the partnership agreement. If there is more than one general partner, the voting requirements for deciding partnership matters should be specified. Matters of specific concern to the particular business or undertaking should be dealt with, as well as general matters, such as the borrowing of money, the sale or mortgaging of partnership property, and the disposition of partnership funds. The extent to which the general partners may delegate their management functions should also be specified. See section 3.06, supra, for further reading on the management functions of general partners.

10. **Restrictions on powers of general partners.** Any acts or functions that the general partners are to be prohibited from performing, either absolutely or without the consent of the limited partners, should be specified.

11. **Limited partners' role in control of partnership business.** Remembering that limited partners may incur extended personal liability if they participate in the control of the partnership business, the role of the limited partners in the operation of the partnership business should be described. It is permissible to give limited partners voting rights and veto powers over certain major partnership transactions (such as the sale of its assets) by requiring their prior approval of such transactions. See R.U.L.P.A. § 302. All voting requirements should be fully spelled out. See sections 3.05 and 3.06, supra, for further reading on this matter.

12. **Rights of limited partners.** The specific rights, if any, of the limited partners should be enumerated, consistent, of course, with their passive role in the management of the partnership business. Specific statutory rights are customarily listed, but special rights unique to the particular business setting may also be included. See section 3.05, supra, for further reading on the rights of limited partners.

13. **Allocation among partners of partnership profits, losses and other tax items.** The method of allocating these items among the partners should be set forth in the partnership agreement. Any method may be used, but the tax aspects of the allocation should be considered. See R.U.L.P.A. § 503 and 26 U.S.C. 704. See sections 3.02 and 3.06, supra, for further reading on this matter.

14. **The partnership's fiscal year and method of accounting.** These matters should be dealt with in the partnership agreement. See section 3.02, supra, for further reading on the fiscal year requirements for partnerships.

15. **The partnership's books and records and banking arrangements.** The official books and records and the banking arrangements of the partnership should be specified in the partnership agreement. The limited partners' rights of inspection of these books should also be set forth. See R.U.L.P.A. § 105 and section 3.06, supra, for a list of the required books and records.

16. **Restrictions on the transfer of partnership interests.** The restrictions, if any, to be imposed on the transferability of partnership interests should be specified. Partnership interests are fully assignable by both general and limited partners unless the partnership agreement provides otherwise. See R.U.L.P.A. § 702. Consent or options restrictions may be used, if desired. See section 3.06, supra, for further reading on this matter.

17. **Admission of new or substituted partners.** The conditions and procedures necessary for the admission of new or substituted general or limited partners in the future should be specified. If none are to be admitted, it should be so stated. See R.U.L.P.A. § § 301, 401, 704. See section 3.06, supra, for further reading on this matter.

18. **Amending the limited partnership agreement.** Provisions should be made for amending the limited partnership agreement should the need or desire to do so arise in the future. In most cases the best practice is to provide that the agreement may be amended by majority vote of the limited partners and the general partners, except that any provision in the agreement that requires the vote, consent or approval of more than a majority of the limited or general partners may be amended only by a vote equal to that provided for in the provision being amended. Any amendment procedures or restrictions desired by the partners may be inserted, however, including requiring the consent of all partners or of certain specified partners.

WITHDRAWAL AND TERMINATION MATTERS

19. **Death or withdrawal of general partner.** The grounds, if any, for the withdrawal of a general partner should be specified in the partnership agreement, together with the notice requirements. Provisions should also be made in the agreement for compensating a deceased or withdrawing general partner. See R.U.L.P.A. § § 402, 602. See section 3.06, supra, for further reading on the withdrawal of a general partner.

20. **Removal of general partner.** The rights, if any, of the limited partners to remove and replace a general partner should be specified. The causes for removal, if any, should be stated, as well as the voting requirements necessary for removal. The method of replacing a general partner should also be specified, together with a requirement of forced dissolution should all of the general partners be removed without replacement.

21. **Withdrawal of limited partner.** The events permitting, or the time of withdrawal by, a limited partner should be specified in the partnership agreement. See R.U.L.P.A. § 603. The notice requirements and the method of compensating withdrawing limited partners should also be set forth in the agreement. See section 3.06, supra, for further reading on the withdrawal of a limited partner.

22. **Liquidation and termination of partnership.** Provisions should be made in the partnership agreement for the winding up of the partnership upon dissolution. See R.U.L.P.A. § § 801-804 for the statutory dissolution and distribution requirements. The distributions priorities among the partners should be specified in the partnership agreement if they are to be other than as provided by statute. See sections 3.06, supra, and 3.09, infra, for further reading on these matters.

3.08 Selling a Partnership Business

The sale of a partnership business may take one of two basic forms: (1) an interest sale, which is the sale of individual partnership interests by the partners, or (2) an asset sale, which is the sale of the partnership assets by the partnership. It may also be possible to liquidate the partnership prior to the sale, distribute the partnership assets to the partners, and have the partners individually sell the distributed assets to the purchaser. However, such a transaction is essentially an asset sale and will not be treated separately in this section. sale of partnership business, basic forms

Depending on the type and tax status of the partnership assets, the form of the sale may substantially affect the tax liability of the selling partners. Not surprisingly, then, the reason for selecting one form of sale over the other is usually tax related. It should be noted that because the Internal Revenue Code does not distinguish between general and limited partnerships, the tax aspects of the sale of either type of partnership are substantially the same. form of sale, tax aspects

The sale or exchange of a partnership interest (i.e., an interest sale) is treated for tax purposes as a sale or exchange of a capital asset, with certain limited exceptions. See 26 U.S.C. 741. This rule is followed whether or not the sale terminates the partnership. See Treasury Reg. 1.741-1(b). Thus, with the exceptions noted below, a selling partner will recognize capital gain or loss on the transfer of a partnership interest to the extent of the difference between the sales price and the basis of his or her partnership interest. See Pollock v. Comm., 69 T.C. 142. The basis of a partnership interest is usually the aggregate of a partner's basis in the partnership assets adjusted to take into account the partner's share of undistributed partnership income and loss for the current tax year (see section 3.02, supra). sale of partnership interest, tax treatment basis of partnership interest, what constitutes

The exceptions to the above rule relate only to the portion of the sales price allocated to a selling partner's interest in unrealized receivables and substantially appreciated inventory. Any gain realized from the amounts allocated to these assets, which are referred to as Section 751 assets, constitutes ordinary income to a selling partner. See 26 U.S.C. 741, 751(a). when gain taxable as ordinary income

Unrealized receivables are accounts receivable from the sale of goods or services, to the extent not previously included as income under the partnership's method of accounting. See 26 U.S.C. 751(c). An account receivable is includible in the sale if the partnership's right to receive the account had arisen under an agreement in existence at the time of the sale, even if payment could not be enforced until a later date. See Treasury Reg. 1.751-1(c). If an account receivable is from the sale of property subject to depreciation or other recapture provisions, the recapture provisions apply and the recapture amounts allocable to a selling partner constitute ordinary income. See 26 U.S.C. 751(c) and Treasury Reg. 1.751-1(c)(4). unrealized receivables, what constitutes

Inventory items include stock in trade, property held for sale in the ordinary course of business, and any property that would not have been treated as a capital asset if sold by the partnership or a selling partner. See 26 U.S.C. 751(d)(2) and Treasury Reg. 1.751-1(d)(2). Inventory items are considered to be substantially appreciated only if their fair market value exceeds 120 percent of their adjusted partnership basis and 10 percent of the fair market value of all partnership property other than money. See 26 U.S.C. 751(d)(1). substantially appreciated inventory, what constitutes

In determining the portion of the sales price allocable to Section 751 assets, the allocation made by the parties to the sale in an arm's length transaction will normally be accepted by the Internal Revenue Service. See Treasury Reg. 1.751-1(a)(2). In this regard, it is usually in the best interest of the seller to allocate as little of the sales price as possible to Section 751 assets. section 751 assets, treatment asset sale, tax treatment

In an asset sale by a partnership, the particular items of income, gain, loss, and other tax items are passed directly through the partnership to the partners in proportion to their respective interests in the particular assets, which interests are normally established in the partnership agreement (see section 3.02, supra). In an asset sale, of course, any gain attributed to noncapital assets (e.g., inventory, accounts receivable, covenants not to compete, etc.) is reportable by the partners as ordinary income. Also, the depreciation and other recapture provisions of 26 U.S.C. 1245 and 1250 are applicable to asset sales, and each partner must report his or her allocable share of recapture income. In an asset sale, it is especially important that the parties to the sale allocate the sales price among the assets being sold. See section 7.02, infra, for a discussion of the allocation priorities in the sale of a business from the viewpoint of the seller.

sale of partnership interest, when preferable

asset sale, when preferable

In many cases it will make little difference, taxwise, whether the sale of a partnership business is an asset sale or an interest sale. However, if a partnership has inventory assets that are not substantially appreciated or other noncapital assets which, if transferred in an asset sale, would result in reportable ordinary income, an interest sale may be to the tax advantage of the partners. The gains attributable to these items are not reportable separately in interest sales, and are therefore taxable only as capital gains. However, if the sale of noncapital assets (or of Section 1231 assets - see section 7.02, infra) will result in a reportable loss, an asset sale might be preferable so as to permit the partners to report their distributive shares of the loss as an ordinary loss. In any case, it is important that the contract of sale clearly specify the form of the sale, because otherwise it may be difficult to determine the form of sale and unfavorable tax consequences may result.

good will and covenants not to compete, tax treatment

If the sale of a partnership interest includes both good will and covenants by the seller not to compete against the purchaser, it will normally be in the interest of a selling partner not to allocate or treat the items separately in the sales contract. If the items are not treated separately in the sales contract they are usually lumped together and treated as good will, which means that any reportable gain will be taxed as a capital gain to the seller and that the purchaser will acquire a nonamortizable asset. However, if the items are treated separately in the sales contract (as knowledgeable purchasers usually insist), recognition is normally given to the separate allocations and the seller will have reportable ordinary income (and the purchaser an amortizable asset) in the amount allocated to the covenant not to compete. See Yandell v. U.S., 315 F. 2nd 141 (CA 9, 1963).

installments sales, use of in partnership, sale

It should be noted that the installment sale provisions of 26 U.S.C. 453 apply to both asset sales and interest sales, except for amounts allocated to inventory and to property customarily sold on the installment plan. An installment sale can be advantageous to the sellers of a partnership business because it is usually possible to spread most of the reportable gain from the sale over several tax years, thus reducing both the initial and the overall tax burden from the sale. To qualify as an installment sale at least one payment must be received by the seller after the tax year of the sale. See section 7.02, infra, for further reading on installment sales.

like-kind exchanges, use of in partnership sales

It is sometimes possible to utilize the like-kind exchange provisions of 26 U.S.C. 1031 in connection with the sale of a partnership business. While a like-kind exchange may be permissible in asset sales (depending, of course, on the similarity of the assets being exchanged), like-kind exchanges of partnership interests (i.e., exchanging one partnership interest for another) are generally not recognized by the Internal Revenue Service. See Revenue Ruling 78-135, 1978-2 C.B. 256.

3.09 The Dissolution, Liquidation and Termination of Partnerships

scope of section

The Uniform Partnership Act and the Revised Uniform Limited Partnership Act contain substantially different provisions dealing with the dissolution, liquidation, and termination of partnerships. Therefore, the dissolution, liquidation and termination of general and limited partnerships are discussed separately in this section. The dissolution, liquidation, and termination of general partnerships is discussed first, followed by a discussion of these aspects of limited partnerships.

dissolution of general partnership, definition.

Dissolution of general partnership. The dissolution of a general partnership is defined by statute as the change in the relation of the parties caused by any partner ceasing to be associated in the carrying on of the partnership business. See U.P.A. sec. 29. The Uniform Partnership Act further provides that upon dissolution the partnership continues until the winding up of partnership affairs is completed. See U.P.A. sec. 30. While it might appear from the foregoing that whenever a partner leaves a general partnership for any reason, the partnership must be dissolved, liquidated, and terminated, in practice this does not usually happen.

death or withdrawal of partner, continuation of business

There are two major exceptions to the rule requiring the liquidation and termination of a general partnership upon a dissolution caused by the death or withdrawal of a partner. These exceptions permit the continuation of the partnership business (1) if the withdrawal was wrongful (i.e., in violation of the partnership agreement), or (2) if the partners agree to continue the partnership business upon the death or withdrawal of a partner. See U.P.A. sec. 38.

withdrawal of partner, right to continue partnership business

The right to continue the partnership business upon the wrongful withdrawal of a partner exists only if the remaining partners unanimously agree to its continuation and if the wrongfully withdrawing partner is paid for the value of his or her partnership interest (less any damages caused by the wrongful withdrawal) and is indemnified against present and future partnership liabilities. See U.P.A. sec. 38(2)(b). The right to provide in the partnership agreement for the continuation of the partnership business upon the death or withdrawal of a partner is granted by permitting any partner to liquidate a dissolved partnership "unless otherwise agreed." See U.P.A. sec. 38(1). Most partnership agreements contain express provisions permitting or compelling the remaining partners to continue the partnership business upon the death or withdrawal of a partner, usually with provisions for compensating the former partner for his or her partnership interest.

withdrawal of partner, right to continue partnership business

If, under the partnership agreement, the remaining partners have the right to continue the partnership business upon the death or withdrawal of a partner, the business may be continued essentially without interruption following a death or withdrawal, with the withdrawing or deceased partner dealt with in the manner specified in the agreement. It should be noted that even if the partnership agreement does not provide for the continuation of the partnership business upon the death or withdrawal of a partner, the remaining partners may agree among themselves to continue the business, provided that the partnership is not insolvent and the withdrawing partner is justly compensated for his or her partnership interest. See U.P.A. sec. 38(1).

dissolution of general partnership, grounds for

Under sections 31 and 32 of the U.P.A., any of the following events may result in the terminating dissolution of a general partnership:

(1) The expiration of the term or undertaking specified in the partnership agreement, or the happening or nonhappening of an event specified in the agreement. This is, perhaps, the most common cause of dissolution, and provisions of this kind are often contained in partnership agreements, usually to prevent the partnership from being terminable at the will of any partner.

(2) The will of any partner, if the partnership agreement so provides or if the partnership agreement is silent as to the duration of the partnership.

(3) The express agreement at any time of all partners who have not assigned or otherwise relinquished their rights to partnership profits.

(4) The expulsion of a partner from the partnership pursuant to expulsion provisions in the partnership agreement. If the expelled partner is discharged from partnership liabilities, he or she is entitled only to a cash payment for his or her net partnership interest, which means that an expelled partner cannot force the liquidation of the partnership and that the remaining partners, if they so agree, may continue the partnership business. See U.P.A. sec. 38(1).

(5) The wrongful act (including the wrongful withdrawal) of a partner or the expulsion of a partner in violation of the partnership agreement. In the event of a wrongful withdrawal by a partner, the remaining partners may seek damages from the withdrawing partner and, if they properly indemnify and compensate the withdrawing partner, may agree among themselves to continue the partnership business.

(6) Any event which makes it unlawful to carry on either the partnership business or the partnership arrangement.

(7) The death or bankruptcy of a partner, unless the partnership agreement provides for the continuation of the partnership business by the remaining partners in such events.

(8) The bankruptcy of the partnership.

judicial dissolution of partnership, grounds for

(9) A lawful court decree entered upon the application of a partner and the establishment of any of the following grounds:

(a) the legal incapacity of a partner,

(b) the inability of a partner to perform his or her partnership obligations,

(c) conduct by a partner that is prejudicial to the carrying on of the partnership business,

(d) the willful breach of the partnership agreement by a partner or other misconduct making it impractical to carry on the partnership with such person,

(e) a showing that the partnership business can only be carried on at a loss, or

(f) a showing that dissolution of the partnership is equitable under the circumstances.

(10) A lawful court decree entered upon the application of the purchaser or assignee of a partner's interest in partnership profits and distributions upon the expiration of the partnership's term, or at any time if the partnership was at will when the interest was acquired.

termination of partnership, winding up affairs

Liquidation of general partnership. When a general partnership is dissolved, the partnership continues until the winding up of partnership affairs is completed. See U.P.A. sec. 30. The remaining partners have the legal right to complete any pending partnership business, collect and dispose of the partnership assets, pay the partnership obligations, and distribute the balance of the partnership property and funds to the remaining partners in accordance with the partnership agreement or as provided by law.

liquidation of partnership, by whom conducted

It is often desirable to appoint, either in the partnership agreement or otherwise, a liquidating partner to handle the function of winding up the partnership business and affairs. Unless otherwise agreed, any partner who has not wrongfully caused the partnership to be dissolved may wind up its affairs. Any partner, or a partner's legal representative or assignee, may, upon a showing of good cause, file a court proceeding and obtain a judicially-supervised winding up of the partnership business and affairs. See U.P.A. sec. 37. It should be noted that the authority and power of the partners to act for or obligate the partnership are severely restricted after dissolution. See U.P.A. secs. 33, 35.

general partnership, distribution priorities

Certain priorities are established by the U.P.A. in connection with the distribution of partnership assets upon the liquidation of a general partnership. The first rule is that the claims of nonpartner-creditors of the partnership must be satisfied first. See U.P.A. § 40. If there are insufficient assets or funds with which to satisfy the claims of partnership creditors (including partner creditors), the partners must make contributions to the partnership, in proportion to their allocated shares of partnership profits, sufficient to satisfy the claims. See U.P.A. § 40(a),(d). Once the partnership creditors have been paid, the applicable provisions, if any, of the partnership agreement control the distribution priorities among the partners. If the partnership agreement is silent on the matter, the following priorities are established in section 40(b) of the U.P.A.:

(1) First, the claims of nonpartner creditors.
(2) Second, the claims of partners who are creditors.
(3) Third, the claims of partners in respect of capital.
(4) Fourth, the claims of partners in respect of profits.

partnership liquidations, tax aspects

The federal income tax aspects of partnership liquidations are often complex and may require the assistance of a tax adviser. Only the general rules applicable to liquidating distributions are discussed in this section. Distributions in the complete liquidation and termination of partnerships are covered in 26 U.S.C. 731-735, while distributions by a continuing partnership in the liquidation (i.e., the purchase) of the partnership interest of a deceased or withdrawing partner are covered in 26 U.S.C. 736 (see section 3.02, supra).

complete liquidation of partnership, tax aspects

The general rule is that distributions made in the complete liquidation and termination of a partnership result in neither gain nor loss to either the partnership or the partners. With the exceptions shown below, the distribution transaction is essentially tax-free. See 26 U.S.C. 731(a), (b). The exceptions are: (1) a distributee partner must recognize gain to the extent that the value of the money or property received exceeds the basis of such partner's interest in the partnership, and (2) if the liquidating distribution consists only of money, unrealized receivables, or inventory, a distributee partner may recognize a loss to the extent that the basis of his or her partnership interest exceeds the total value of the money or property received plus the distributee's basis in any unrealized receivables or inventory. See 26 U.S.C. 731(a). If the property distributed is subject to depreciation or other recapture provisions, special rules are applied to their subsequent resale or transfer. See 26 U.S.C. 751(c). The resale of inventory items and unrealized receivables is governed by 26 U.S.C. 735.

tax basis of distributed partnership property

A distributee partner's total basis in any property received in a liquidating distribution is generally equal to the adjusted basis of his or her partnership interest reduced by the amount of any money distributed in the same transaction. See 26 U.S.C. 732(b). See section 3.02, supra, for a discussion of the method of determining the basis of a partnership interest. A distributee partner's basis in distributed properties must be determined in accordance with 26 U.S.C. 732(c), (d). The basis of undistributed partnership assets is not affected by liquidating distributions of other property to partners unless an election under 26 U.S.C. 754 is in effect, in which case special rules apply. See 26 U.S.C. 734.

limited partnership, grounds for dissolution

Dissolution and liquidation of limited partnership. Section 801 and 802 of the R.U.L.P.A. provide that a limited partnership shall be dissolved and its affairs wound up upon the first to occur of any of the following:

(1) a time specified in the certificate of limited partnership,

(2) the happening of an event specified in the partnership agreement,

(3) the written consent of all partners, general and limited,

(4) the withdrawal of the only general partner (or the withdrawal of any general partner if the partnership agreement does not permit the business to be carried on by the remaining general partners) unless within 90 days all partners agree to continue the business and to the appointment of another general partner, if necessary, or

(5) the entry of a decree of judicial dissolution upon the application of a general or limited partner upon the grounds that it is not reasonably practicable to continue the partnership business in conformity with the partnership agreement.

limited partnerships, winding up

The winding up of a limited partnership may be in the manner provided for in the partnership agreement, or, if no provisions are made, by the general partners who have not wrongfully dissolved the partnership, or, if none exist, by the limited partners. However, any partner, or the successor in interest of any partner, may obtain a judicial liquidation and winding up of a limited partnership. See R.U.L.P.A. § 803.

liquidation of limited partnerships, distribution priorities

The distribution of assets upon the winding up and termination of a limited partnership may be as specified in the partnership agreement, provided that the claims of nonpartner creditors must be satisfied first. See R.U.L.P.A. § 804. If no provisions are made for the distribution of assets, the priorities are as follows:

(1) First, to creditors (including, to the extent otherwise permitted by law, partners who are creditors) in satisfaction of partnership liabilities, other than liabilities for distributions to partners.

(2) Second, to partners in satisfaction of liabilities for interim and withdrawal distributions.

(3) Third, to partners, in proportion to their share in distributions, first for the return of their capital contributions and then in respect to their partnership interests. See R.U.L.P.A. § 804.

limited partnerships, tax aspects of liquidation

Because the Internal Revenue Code does not distinguish between general and limited partnerships, the tax aspects of the liquidation of a limited partnership are substantially the same as in the liquidation of a general partnership. The tax aspects of partnership liquidation are discussed above in this section and in section 3.02, supra.

limited partnership, certificate of cancellation

The certificate of limited partnership must be cancelled upon the commencement of the winding up of a dissolved limited partnership, or at any time when there are no limited partners. See R.U.L.P.A. § 203. A certificate of cancellation must be filed with the Secretary of State or other designated recording official. The certificate of cancellation must set forth (1) the name of the limited partnership, (2) the date of filing of the certificate of limited partnership, (3) the reason for filing the certificate of cancellation, and (4) the effective date of the cancellation. It may contain other information, if desired. See R.U.L.P.A. § 203.

3.10 Joint Ventures

Sometimes referred to as syndicates, groups, joint enterprises, joint undertakings, joint adventures, or coadventures, joint ventures have most of the legal characteristics of general partnerships. Indeed, joint ventures are distinguishable from partnerships, if at all, only by the narrowness of their purpose or scope of business. They are usually formed not to carry on a continuing business, but to carry out a particular venture or enterprise, dissolving and terminating upon its completion. Joint ventures are typically formed to construct a building, subdivide and sell a tract of real estate, produce a play or movie, or drill and operate an oil or gas well. The number of parties to a joint venture may vary from two to a hundred or more, and the parties may be natural persons, partnerships, corporations, limited liability companies, or (as in partnerships) any other entity legally capable of entering into a contractual relationship. Joint ventures, general aspects

There are no uniform laws dealing exclusively with joint ventures and there is a lack of uniformity among the courts in their treatment of joint ventures. There is not even a precise, generally-accepted definition of what constitutes a joint venture. However, most courts apply the general partnership laws (the U.P.A.) to most aspects of joint ventures. The reported cases in the local state should be checked whenever a question involving the existence of a joint ventures arises. Joint ventures, applicable law

It is generally held that a joint venture cannot exist in the absence of an agreement showing a joint intention to carry on the venture. See Legum Furniture Corp. v. Levine, 217 Va. 782, 232 S.E. 2nd 782(1977). The agreement may be express or implied, and does not have to be in writing. See Institutional Management Corp. v. Translation Systems, Inc., 456 F. Supp. 661 (DC MD, 1978). However, certain aspects of the relationship between the parties must be dealt with in an agreement or understanding of some kind in order for a joint venture to exist. Provisions for the sharing of profits and losses from the venture must be included in the agreement or understanding, along with provisions for the contribution of the money, property, or services used in the venture and the management of the venture. See Modern Air Conditioning, Inc. v. Cinderella Homes, Inc., 226 Kan. 70, 596 P. 2nd 816 (1979), and Crest Construction Co. v. Ins. Co. of No. America, 417 F. Supp. 564 (DC OK, 1976). Joint venture agreement, requirements

As with partnerships, the parties to a joint venture are accorded great flexibility in defining the relationship among themselves in a joint venture agreement. The parties to a joint venture may, by express agreement, establish the rights and liabilities among themselves in any proportion. See Goodwin v. S. A. Healy Co., 383 Mich. 300, 174 N.W. 2nd 755(1970). For example, the parties may divide the profits (or losses) unevenly or as they choose, and unequal contributions may be made to the venture by the parties. Provisions for continuing the venture after dissolution may be included, if desired, and the management duties of the parties may be delegated to certain parties or to outsiders. The rights of the parties in either the profits or the property of the venture may be assignable or nonassignable, as desired. Sample joint venture agreements may be found in 10 Am. Jur. Legal Forms 2d, chapter 155, and 2 West's Legal Forms, 2nd Edition, chapter 26. Joint venture agreements, general rules

Once a joint venture is found to exist, certain rules of law govern the conduct, duties, and liabilities of the parties to the venture. Most courts apply the rules of law governing the conduct of general partners to the conduct of the parties to a joint venture. For example, the parties to a joint venture have a fiduciary obligation to each other to account for the profits and joint property of the venture and not to compete against the venture. See R.C. Gluck & Co. v. Tankel, 24 Misc. 2nd 841, 199 N.Y.S. 2nd 12 (1970). Joint ventures, applicable law

Unless otherwise provided in an agreement, each party to the venture is a general agent with the power to bind the other parties and subject them to liability on matters within the scope of the venture. See Wenzel Mach. Co. v. Adkins, 189 Kan. 435, 370 P. 2nd 141(1962). Accordingly, each party to a joint venture has unlimited personal liability to outsiders for the debts, liabilities, and obligations of the venture, including liability for the actions of the other parties while acting within the scope of the venture. See Pritchett v. Kimberling Cove, Inc., 568 F. 2nd 570(CA 8, 1977). One party to a joint venture may not substitute another to replace him or her in the venture without the consent of all parties to the venture. See Polikoff v. Levy, 55 Ill App. 2nd 229, 204 N.E. 2nd 807(1965). And, a party to a joint venture may not assign or transfer his or her interest in joint-venture property without the consent of the other parties. See Terminable Shares v. Chicago, B. & Q. Ry. Co., 65 F. Supp. 678(DC MO, 1946). Joint ventures, general rules

joint venture to form business enterprise, general rules

It is common for the parties to a joint venture to change the form of the enterprise at some point in its existence. For example, the promoters of a corporation usually constitute a joint venture, at least until the corporation is formed. Once the new corporation (or other organization) is formed, it is important to determine and make clear whether the new organization is intended to supersede or supplement the joint venture. Some courts have held that a joint venture relationship may not legally continue after the parties to the venture have formed a new organization with which to conduct the enterprise for which the joint venture was created.

joint ventures, termination

Once formed, a joint venture continues until the completion of its purpose or until the termination date specified in an agreement, except that it may be terminated at any time by the mutual agreement of all parties to the venture or by any of the parties for good cause. As with general partnerships, a joint venture is usually dissolved as a matter of law upon the death, bankruptcy, or withdrawal of a party, unless the parties have otherwise agreed. See 46 Am. Jur. 2d, Joint Ventures, sec. 4.

joint ventures, tax aspects

A joint venture is normally taxed as a partnership. See 26 U.S.C. 761(a). However, if the venture has the characteristics of an association, it may be taxed as a corporation. See Treasury Reg. 301.7701-2, and section 3.02, supra. If the venture constitutes an association and is otherwise eligible, it may elect to be taxed under Subchapter S of the Internal Revenue Code (see section 5.18, infra). See Treasury Reg. 1.1371-1(b).

3.11 Limited Liability Partnerships - An Introduction

LLP, definition and description of

A limited liability partnership (an LLP) is a partnership wherein the liability of the general partners for the debts and obligations of the partnership is limited by state law. In most states only a general partnership may become an LLP. In a few states, however, a limited partnership may become an LLP. To become an LLP a partnership must file a registration statement with the state filing official in the partnership's home state. If the registration statement is approved by the state filing official, the partnership is accorded limited liability status under state law. It should be noted that because of the registration requirement, LLPs are often referred to in LLP statutes as registered limited liability partnerships

state filing official, where to find

In most states the state filing official is the Secretary of State. The identity, address and telephone number of the state filing official in each state is listed in Appendix I in the back of this book under the heading of State Filing Official.

LLP statutes, location of, citations to

Every state has enacted LLP statutes that provide for the creation of limited liability partnerships. The LLP statutes in most states consist of amendments or additions to the general partnership laws (the U.P.A.). Unlike Limited Liability Company Acts, LLP statutes are not normally set forth in a separate chapter of the state code. In most states the LLP provisions are interspersed throughout the general partnership laws, but the LLP registration provisions are usually set forth in separate sections of the U.P.A. Citations to the LLP registration provisions in each state are set forth in Appendix I in the back of this book under the heading of Partnership Laws, Limited Liability Partnerships.

LLPs, need for, history of

LLPs evolved in response to the vicarious liability concerns of professionals. The proliferation of malpractice and other awards against professionals caused individual partners in professional partnerships to seek protection from liability for the misconduct of other partners. This need was especially acute in large accounting and law firms with offices in many states, where many of the partners did not know one another, had little control over either the admission of other partners or the performance of their partnership functions, but were nevertheless personally liable for their professional malpractice and other misconduct. The result was the LLP, the first of which was registered under a Texas LLP statute in 1991. Because of the background of their development, LLPs are used primarily by professionals. In a few states, including California, New York, and Oregon, LLPs are limited to certain professionals. In most states, however, an LLP may be organized and registered by any type of business. Several states, it should be noted, impose financial responsibility requirements on LLPs, usually in the form of liability insurance or security deposit requirements.

LLP statutes, degree of liability protection offered by, generally

The most common reason for converting a general partnership to an LLP is to obtain liability protection for the partners. In this regard, it should be noted that LLP statutes differ among the states as to the extent and nature of the liability protection that is accorded to partners of LLPs. The LLP statutes in all states provide liability protection for partnership liabilities created vicariously by the torts or misconduct of other partners. However, most LLP statutes do not provide liability protection to individual partners for other partnership liabilities, including commercial and contractual obligations such as partnership trade accounts and partnership lease and credit obligations.

3rd generation LLP statutes, degree of liability protection offered by

In a growing number of states, however, a greater degree of liability protection is given to LLP partners. In those states liability protection is extended to include normal commercial and contractual obligations of the partnership. The liability of LLP partners for partnership debts in those states is similar to the liability of LLC members for LLC debts. Presently included among the states where this expanded liability protection is given to LLP partners are the following: California, Colorado, Georgia, Hawaii, Idaho, Indiana, Maryland, Massachusetts, Minnesota, Missouri, Montana, New York, North Dakota, Ohio, Oregon, South Dakota and Virginia. These are to so-called third-generation LLP statutes. The trend in LLP liability protection is in this direction and the list of states with third-generation LLP statutes is growing yearly. In some states, it should be noted, the degree of liability protection provided by the LLP statutes is unclear because of vaguely-worded statutory provisions.

LLP statutes, acts not covered by

It should be understood, however, that no LLP statute provides liability protection to a partner for his or her own torts or misconduct. It is not possible in any state to shield a partner from personal liability for his or her own misconduct. Further, under most statutes a partner remains liable for the misconduct of those acting under his or her direct supervision and control. However, the degree of supervision and control necessary to impose personal liability on a partner is often unclear. It should also be understood that liability protection is given only for acts that were committed and obligations that were incurred while the partnership is a registered LLP. Partners remain jointly and severally (and vicariously) liable for acts that were committed and for debts and obligations that were incurred before the partnership became an LLP.

LLP statutes, types of partnerships applicable to

limited partnerships, registration of as LLPs or LLLPs

Most LLP statutes apply only to general partnerships and are not applicable to limited partnerships. The LLP statutes of several states are expressly limited to "partnerships other than limited partnerships" or "partnerships without limited partners." The LLP statutes of most states, however, are silent with respect to the registration of limited partnerships as LLPs. In those states it may be possible for a limited partnership to register as an LLP if, under state law, the general partnership laws are applicable to the general partners of a limited partnership. It should be noted that the LLP statutes in some states expressly include limited partnerships and that a few states have enacted limited liability limited partnership statutes that expressly provide for the registration of "limited liability limited partnerships."

LLP, tax classification of

Unless it elects to be classified as a corporation for federal income tax purposes, an LLP is treated as a partnership for state and federal tax purposes. The fact that the partners are shielded from personal liability for certain partnership obligations does not change a partnership's tax classification. However, if an LLP desires to be classified as a corporation for federal income tax purposes, it may do so by filing IRS Form 8832 and checking the appropriate box thereon. See section 4.02, infra, for further reading on the 1997 "check the box" federal income tax regulations.

3.12 Organizing a Limited Liability Partnership for a New Business

A limited liability partnership (an LLP) is not subject to the organizational requirements of a corporation or limited liability company. It is not required to be organized under a separate code or set of statutes. For the most part an LLP is organized under the informal requirements of the Uniform Partnership Act. To qualify as an LLP it need only register with the state filing official as an LLP. There is no requirement, for example, that its partnership agreement be in writing. However, to properly organize an LLP for a new or startup business, a general partnership should be organized in the manner described in section 3.03, supra. In addition, the name, registration and other requirements of the home state LLP statutes must be complied with. LLP organizational requirements

The first order of business in organizing an LLP for a new or startup business is to organize a general partnership in the manner described in sections 3.03 and 3.04 of this handbook. In addition to the matters listed and discussed in sections 3.03 and 3.04, supra, the following matters must be dealt with if the partnership is to qualify and be registered as an LLP:

organizing new business as LLP, matters to provide for

(1) The home state of the LLP should be determined and each state where the LLP will be required to register as a foreign LLP should be identified.

(2) The partnership name must conform to the requirements of the LLP statutes in each state where it will be registered.

(3) Provisions dealing with the following matters should be included in the partnership agreement:

   (a) The vote of the partners that is required to authorize the partnership to register an LLP should be established.
   (b) The person who is to be responsible for registering the partnership as an LLP should be identified and authorized to prepare and file the initial LLP registration statement and take the steps necessary to continuously maintain the partnership's status as an LLP.
   (c) The vote of the partners that is necessary to terminate and withdraw LLP status for the partnership should be established.
   (d) The effect of an LLP statute on any inconsistent provision in the partnership agreement should be clarified (i.e., in most cases the inconsistent provision should be inoperative).

(4) Provisions in the partnership agreement, if one exists, that are incompatible with limited liability should be amended or excluded from the agreement.

(5) If liability insurance or a security deposit is required of LLPs in any state where LLP registration will be made, provisions should be made to satisfy those requirements.

Samples of the above-described partnership agreement provisions for LLPs are set forth in Exhibit 3-B at the end of this chapter. LLP provisions in partnership agreement, samples of

One of the first functions to perform in organizing an LLP is that of determining the LLP's home state. If partnership business will be conducted in more than one state, the degree of personal liability protection offered by the LLP statutes in each state where significant partnership business will be conducted should be considered in choosing the home state for the LLP. As indicated above, the degree of personal liability protection offered by LLP statutes varies among the states, but the degree of protection provided by the home state is almost universally recognized by other states. selection of LLP home state, factors to consider

If all of the partners reside in the local state and if the LLP statutes in the local state offer sufficient liability protection for the partners, then the LLP should be registered as a domestic LLP in the local state. In other words, the local state should be the home state for the LLP. However, if the LLP will be conducting significant business in another state and if the LLP statutes of the other state offer a greater degree of liability protection, then consideration should be given to making the other state the LLP's home state. Similarly, if one or more of the partners reside in a state whose LLP statutes offer a greater degree of liability protection for the partners than is available in the local state, then consideration should be given to making the non-local state the LLP's home state for purposes of LLP registration. Selecting a proper home state is important because the internal affairs of an LLP, including the degree of liability protection, is governed by the laws of the home state even with respect to business that is conducted in a foreign state. selection of LLP home state, importance of registration as foreign LLP, advantages and disadvantages

If the LLP will be conducting significant business in one or more states other than the home state, it will probably be necessary to register the LLP as a foreign LLP in the other states. The LLP statutes of most states require the registration of foreign LLPs as a condition of transacting business in that state. A significant benefit of registering an LLP in a foreign state is that in most states the liability protection of the partners and the internal affairs of a registered foreign LLP are governed by the laws of the LLP's home state. It is not clear whether this rule is applicable to non-registered foreign LLPs. Another benefit of registering as a foreign LLP in most states is access to the foreign state courts. Non-registration may also result in liability for fines and penalties that are applicable to non-registered foreign LLPs in many states. The detriments of registering as a foreign LLP include the requirements of paying fees, filing registration statements and filing annual or periodic reports.

registration as foreign LLP, when required

foreign LLP, limitation on business of

In determining whether registration in a foreign state is required, it should be noted that the LLP statutes in many states contain a list of activities that do not constitute transacting business in the state for purposes of LLP registration. It should be understood, however, that registering as a foreign LLP does not permit a foreign LLP to engage in a business that local LLPs are not permitted to engage in. This in an important consideration if the foreign state is a state like California, New York and Oregon that limits LLPs to certain professionals.

LLP name, suffix requirements

Most LLP statutes contain name requirements for registered LLPs. These requirements typically include a requirement that the LLP name end with a prescribed designation, such as "limited liability partnership," "registered limited liability partnership," "L.L.P.," or "R.L.L.P." The specific name designation requirements vary somewhat from state to state, so the specific requirements in each state where the LLP will be registered should be checked.

LLP name, general statutory requirements

In addition to the suffix requirements described above, many states preclude the use of LLP names that are the same as or deceptively similar to the name of another entity that is registered in the state. Many states will deny registration to an LLP unless its name is distinguishable from the names of all other registered entities. Registered entities usually include corporations, limited liability companies, limited partnerships, and other registered LLPs. The requirements of each state where the LLP will be registered should be checked in this regard. The availability of the desired LLP name should be checked with the state filing official in each state where the LLP will be registered.

LLP registration, authorization of, voting requirements

To be effective the registration of an LLP must be approved by the partners in the style and manner specified in the home state LLP statute. Some LLP statutes require a specified vote of the partners in order to register a partnership as an LLP. However, the authorization requirements for LLP registration vary from state to state. California, for example, requires the affirmative vote of the partners possessing a majority of the interests in current partnership profits, unless a different vote is specified in the partnership agreement. Colorado requires the unanimous consent of all partners, unless the partnership agreement provides otherwise. Some states require approval by the vote necessary to amend the partnership agreement. In any event, the authorization requirements of the home state should be ascertained and complied with. The vote of the partners necessary to authorize LLP registration should be specified in the partnership agreement.

filing of registration statement, effective date of

To avoid uncertainty, the person or persons who are authorized to sign the LLP registration document in the home state should be specified in the partnership agreement. The person responsible for filing the registration statement and paying the required fees should also be specified. The effective date of the LLP status should also be specified if it is to be other than the date of filing of the registration document. In most states LLP status is effective upon the filing of the registration document and the payment of the required fees. However, most states permit a partnership to elect to have LLP status become effective at a future date specified in the registration document. If this is desired, the applicable provisions of the LLP statutes in the home state should be checked in this regard.

In most states LLP status, once effective, continues until the LLP withdraws or cancels the registration or until the state filing official revokes the registration for failure to renew the registration or file a post registration report. In some states a termination date for LLP status may be specified in the registration document, if desired. It is important to maintain LLP status for a partnership because if the status is allowed to lapse liability protection will be lost. Most LLP statutes contain "savings clauses" which require the state filing official to notify a partnership that its LLP status will be lost unless the required reports and fees are submitted by a specified date.

LLP status, continuance of, requirements for

It is important to include a provision in the partnership agreement dealing with the termination or withdrawal of LLP status for the partnership. Most LLP statutes provide that a partnership that has registered as an LLP may voluntarily withdraw its registration by filing a statement of withdrawal with the state filing official. The filing of a withdrawal statement is usually subject to the same statutory partnership voting requirements as the filing of an LLP registration document. The withdrawal statement, if filed, should state that the partnership is withdrawing its LLP registration and acknowledge that the withdrawal will terminate the partnership's LLP status. Some state filing officials have a form for a withdrawal statement.

withdrawal of LLP status, requirements, procedure for

If either the home state or any state where the LLP will be registered as a foreign LLP requires financial responsibility in the form of liability insurance or a security deposit as a condition of conferring LLP status to a partnership, steps must be taken to satisfy these requirements. Proof that the required amount of insurance has been obtained or that a deposit in the required amount has been made with the required person or office must usually accompany the registration statement, if either of these items are required. The applicable LLP statutes should be examined for requirements of this nature. Most states have no such requirements, but several states, including California and Delaware, impose these requirements.

financial responsibility requirements for LLPs, existence of

A necessary and important function in organizing an LLP is the preparation and filing of an LLP registration document with the state filing official in each state where LLP registration is required. Because of its importance, the best practice is to provide for the carrying out of this function in the partnership agreement. The LLP registration document has various names in various state LLP statutes. In several states it is referred to as an "LLP Registration Statement," while in other states it is variously called an LLP Certificate, an LLP Application, an LLP Registration Application, or an LLP Statement of Qualification. The designation given the LLP registration document in each state is noted in Appendix I in the back of this book under the heading of State Filing Official. State filing officials often have forms that may be used for this purpose. If a prescribed form is not available, the sample LLP Registration Statement set forth in Exhibit 3-E at the end of this chapter may be used as a guide in the preparation of an LLP registration document.

LLP registration document, preparation of

The required contents of an LLP registration document for domestic or foreign LLPs are usually set forth in the LLP statutes. Typically, provisions dealing with the following matters must be included in an LLP registration document for either a domestic or a foreign LLP:

LLP registration document, contents of

(1) the name of the LLP;
(2) a statement that the partners have approved the registration statement in the manner required by the applicable statute;
(3) the address of the partnership's principal office;
(4) the address of an office of the partnership in the local state or, if none exists, the name and address of the partnership's agent for service of process in the local state;
(5) the state under whose laws the LLP was formed;
(6) a brief description of the partnership business;
(7) a statement that the partnership is applying for LLP status;
(8) the effective date of LLP status if later than the filing date, and
(9) the signatures of the person or persons who are authorized to sign the document.

Not every state requires all of these items in the LLP registration document, so the specific requirements of the state in question should be checked. Some states require slightly different information from a foreign partnership than from a domestic partnership. In any event, an LLP registration document is not difficult to prepare. After it has been prepared and signed, the required number of copies of the document should be filed with the state filing official. In most states LLP status becomes effective when the registration document is filed with the state filing official, unless a deferred effective date is set forth in the registration document.

LLP registration document, general requirements, effective date of

3.13 Converting an Existing Business to a Limited Liability Partnership

converting business to LLP, degree of difficulty

The degree of difficulty in converting an existing business entity to a limited liability partnership (an LLP) depends primarily on the type of entity that is being converted. If the existing entity is a partnership, the conversion is normally a relatively simple affair unless there are partners who are actively opposed to the conversion. If the existing entity is a corporation, the conversion will be more complicated, both legally and taxwise. While it is possible to convert a limited liability company (an LLC) to an LLP, there is usually little to be gained by such a conversion and such conversions are not discussed in this handbook.

existing business, LLP vs. LLC, advantages and disadvantages

If the existing business is a general partnership that is seeking liability protection for its partners, it should first be determined whether an LLP is preferable to an LLC for the business. The principal advantage of an LLP over an LLC for an existing partnership business is that because an LLP is a partnership it is not necessary to convert the partnership to another entity in order to obtain personal liability protection for the partners. In some states franchise taxes that are assessed against LLCs are not assessed against LLPs. The principal disadvantages of an LLP are that in many states a lesser degree of personal liability protection is provided by an LLP and in some states the types of businesses that may register as an LLP are limited and liability insurance or security deposit requirements are imposed on LLPs. Generally, however, if the LLP can be organized under a third-generation LLP statute and if the LLP statute does not require liability insurance or a security deposit and does not prohibit the business in question from registering as an LLP, then an LLP will provide personal liability protection that is substantially equal to that offered by an LLC.

converting existing business to LLP, general factors

As indicated above, there are two factors to consider in determining whether an existing business should be converted to an LLP. One factor concerns the legal requirements of the conversion. What must be done from a legal standpoint to convert the existing business from its present form to an LLP? The other factor involves the income tax aspects of the conversion. What are the tax consequences of converting the business from its present form to an LLP?

converting partnership to LLP, degree of difficulty, factors

If the existing business is a general partnership, the degree of difficulty in converting the business to an LLP from a legal standpoint depends on three factors: (1) whether there are partners who oppose the conversion, (2) whether there are provisions in the existing partnership agreement that must be changed in order for the partnership to function as an LLP, and (3) whether there are liability insurance or security deposit requirements for LLPs in the home state or in a foreign state where the partnership will be conducting sufficient business to require registration as a foreign LLP.

converting partnership to LLP, general requirements

If there are no partners who oppose converting the partnership to an LLP, the mechanics of the conversion will normally consist of (1) drafting the necessary amendments to the existing partnership agreement (or drafting a written partnership agreement if one does not exist), and (2) preparing and filing a registration statement with the state filing official in the home state and in each state where the LLP will have to register as a foreign LLP. If liability insurance or security deposits are required of LLPs in the home state or in a foreign state when the LLP will have to register as a foreign LLP, then these requirements must also be taken care of.

existing partnership agreement, provisions to be amended for LLP conversion

The existing partnership agreement should be reviewed to ascertain whether it must be amended before converting the partnership to an LLP. Provisions in the partnership agreement requiring the partners to make contributions to the partnership in order to satisfy partnership obligations should either be removed from the agreement or amended so as to conform to the limited liability provisions of the LLP statutes. Provisions in the partnership agreement that deal with the liability of partners for partnership debts should also be amended so as to conform to the limited liability provisions of the home state LLP statutes. In addition, a clause should be added to the partnership agreement providing that the limited liability provisions of the home state LLP statutes shall take precedence over and render inoperative any inconsistent provisions that may exist in the partnership agreement.

A provision requiring the registration of the partnership as an LLP in the home state and in any designated foreign states should be added to the partnership agreement. Provisions delineating the person or persons who are authorized to sign and file LLP registration statements should also be added to the partnership agreement, as should provisions specifying the partnership voting requirements for LLP registrations and withdrawals. The reader is referred to section 3.12, supra, for further reading on these matters.

existing partnership agreement, provisions to be added for LLP conversion

The home state for the LLP should be chosen in the manner described in section 3.12, supra. The available state offering the greatest degree of personal liability protection for the partners should normally be chosen as the home state for the LLP. If the home state LLP statutes impose liability insurance or security deposit requirements for LLPs, then these requirements must be complied with prior to filing the LLP registration statement. The LLP registration statement should be prepared and filed in the manner described in section 3.12, supra.

LLP, selection of home state, factors

If there are partners who oppose the conversion of the partnership to an LLP, the ability of the partnership to register as an LLP will depend on two factors: (1) the partnership voting requirements for LLP registration imposed by the home state LLP statute, and (2) the provisions of the existing partnership agreement, including the voting requirements for amending the partnership agreement.

LLP conversion with opposition, feasibility

The LLP statutes in every state contain partnership voting requirements for LLP registration. These requirements are discussed generally in section 3.12, supra. The LLP statutes in some states require a specified vote of the partners for LLP registration unless the partnership agreement provides for a different voting requirement, in which case the voting requirement in the partnership agreement governs. Other states require the vote of the partners that is necessary to amend the partnership agreement or, if the partnership agreement contains no provisions as to its amendment, the unanimous vote of the partners. In any event, it is important to ascertain the partnership voting requirements for LLP registration in each state where the partnership will be required to be registered as an LLP.

LLP registration, statutory voting requirements

If the LLP statutes of the local state contain partnership voting requirements that cannot be met because of the opposition of one or more partners, then it will not be possible to register the existing partnership as an LLP in that state. If LLP status is desired, it will be necessary to either register the partnership in a state with less stringent voting requirements or dissolve the existing partnership and form a new partnership consisting of the partners who are in favor of the LLP conversion. Upon dissolution of the existing partnership the favoring partners can transfer their partnership interests in the dissolved partnership to the new LLP. If this is done, it may be necessary to compensate the omitted partner or partners for their interests in the dissolved partnership. Unfavorable tax consequences may also result from a conversion of this type. See section 3.09 for further reading on the dissolution and liquidation of partnerships.

LLP conversion when voting requirement cannot be met, methods

It is important to review the existing partnership agreement to ascertain whether provisions exist in the agreement that are incompatible with LLP status and to ascertain the voting requirements for amending the agreement. If there are partners who oppose the conversion, if the existing partnership agreement must be amended to permit the partnership to function as an LLP, and if the partnership agreement requires a unanimous or other unobtainable vote of the partners for its amendment, then it may not be feasible to register the partnership as an LLP, even if the statutory voting requirements for LLP registration can be complied with.

review of partnership agreement, importance of

The conversion of a general partnership to an LLP is usually tax free if the partners of the LLP continue to own the same percentage interests in the partnership after the conversion. In Revenue Ruling 95-55, 1955-35 I.R.B. 13, the IRS ruled that a conversion from a general partnership to an LLP is treated as a partnership-to-partnership conversion and that a termination under 26 U.S.C. 708 does not occur as a result of an LLP registration. The IRS has also ruled that because the partnership remains in existence, the LLP may continue to use the same federal tax identification number that was used by the partnership. See Private Letter Ruling 9325043 (March 29, 1993) and Revenue Ruling 95-37, 1995-17 I.R.B. 10.

LLP, use of partnership tax ID number

partnership-LLP conversion, requirements for tax free conversion

In Revenue Ruling 95-55, supra, the IRS also ruled that a partnership-LLP conversion is subject to the requirements of Revenue Rule 84-52, 1984-1 C.B. 157. This means that for a partnership-LLP conversion to be tax free the partners' respective ownership interests in the partnership business must not be changed in the conversion and that the partnership business must be continued by the LLP after the conversion. Revenue Ruling 84-52 is discussed in section 4.05, infra, and is set forth in its entirety in Exhibit 4-D at the end of chapter 4, infra.

partnership-LLP conversion, section 752 gain, rules governing

An exception to the tax-free conversion rule occurs when a partner's share of the partnership debt is reduced by the conversion. Under 26 U.S.C. 752(b), a decrease in a partner's share of partnership liabilities is considered for tax purposes to be a distribution of money by the partnership to the partner. Such a distribution, which is referred to as Section 752 gain, reduces the partner's basis in his or her partnership interest. See 26 U.S.C. 733. If the amount of the Section 752 gain exceeds the basis of the partner's partnership interest, the partner will incur a tax liability for the amount of the excess.

section 752 gain, recognition of in partnership-LLP conversions, general rules

A partner's share of partnership liabilities is measured by determining the extent to which a partner bears the economic risk of loss or the ultimate burden of paying the partnership liabilities. See Treasury Reg. 1-752-2. Because the liability for partnership debts of a partner in an LLP is more limited than the liability of a partner in a general partnership, the possibility of incurring Section 752 gain in a partnership-LLP conversion is a real one. However, the fact that an LLP partner is not shielded from liability for pre-conversion partnership debts mitigates against the incurrence of Section 752 gain. Consequently, Section 752 gain is not ordinarily assessed in a partnership-LLP conversion if the partners retain the same share of profits and other tax items in the LLP and if the partnership debt-sharing arrangement between the partners is not changed in the conversion.

corporation-LLP conversions, general aspects

Converting an existing corporate business to an LLP requires the formation of an LLP in the manner described in section 3.12, supra, and a transfer of assets from the corporation to the newly-formed LLP. This can be an involved process, both legally and taxwise. The conversion procedures and tax consequences of corporation-LLP conversions are essentially the same as those described in section 4.05, infra, for corporation-LLC conversions. The reader is referred to section 4.05, infra, for further reading on the subject.

GENERAL PARTNERSHIP AGREEMENT

THIS AGREEMENT, dated _______________, by and among the parties set forth below, who covenant and agree as follows:

1. **Name of Business.** The parties do hereby form a general partnership which shall transact business under the name of _________________________.

2. **Partnership Business.** The partnership shall engage in the business of _________________ and in such other businesses of a similar or related nature as may be determined by the Managing Partners.

3. **Place of Business.** The place of business of the partnership shall be located at _________________ or at such other location or locations as the Managing Partners may from time to time designate.

4. **Term.** The term of the partnership shall begin on _______________, and shall continue until _______________, unless sooner terminated as provided in this agreement.

5. **Capital.** The capital of the partnership shall be ___________ dollars. The following persons shall be Partners and shall contribute to the capital of the partnership the cash, property, or services indicated below, in the amounts or values set opposite their names below, and shall receive the interest or use payments on such contributions indicated below:

Name	Form of Contribution	Value	Percentage of Total	Interest or Use Payment

An individual capital account shall be established for each Partner. The initial capital accounts of the Partners shall be equivalent to their respective contributions of the capital of the partnership as set forth above. If at any time or times hereafter the Managing Partners should unanimously determine that further capital is required in the interests of the partnership, and that the capital of the partnership should be increased, the additional capital shall be contributed by the Partners in the respective percentages set forth above. Interest or use payments on contributed capital shall be paid on the initial and any subsequent contributions to the capital of the partnership only as set forth above in this Section 5. Except by the unanimous written consent of all Partners, or upon dissolution, the capital contributions of the Partners shall not be subject to withdrawal. For income tax purposes, depreciation, depletion, and gains or losses with respect to contributed property shall be allocated among the Partners in the same manner as though the contributed properties were owned separately by each contributing Partner.

6. **Salaries and Expenses.** Each Partner shall be entitled to receive such salary as may be determined by the Managing Partners under Section 14 of this agreement, but the payment of salaries shall be an obligation of the partnership only to the extent that there are partnership assets available for them, and shall not be an obligation of the Partners individually. All salaries paid shall be treated as expenses of the partnership in determining net profits and losses. Expense accounts and drawing accounts may be established by the Managing Partners for any Partner or employee.

7. **Partnership Profits and Losses.** The net profits of the partnership shall be divided among the Partners, and the net losses of the partnership shall be borne by the Partners, in proportion to their respective capital contributions as set forth in Section 5 of this agreement. For income tax purposes, all gains, losses, credits, and depreciation deductions on partnership property shall be allocated among the Partners in proportion to their capital contributions, except as provided in Section 5 of this agreement.

8. **Distribution of Disposable Cash.** Should the partnership have disposable cash, whether through the refinancing of a mortgage, depletion or depreciation deductions, or otherwise, such cash shall be contributed to the Partners in proportion to their respective capital contributions.

9. **Fiscal Year.** The fiscal year of the partnership shall commence on _______________ and shall end on _______________.

10. **Accounting Procedures.** The method of accounting of the partnership shall be _______________. As of the last day of each fiscal year during the continuance of the partnership, a full, true and accurate account shall be made in writing of all of the assets and liabilities of the partnership, and of all of its receipts and disbursements, and the assets, liabilities and income, both gross and net, shall be ascertained, and the net profits or net losses shall be fixed and determined; and the account of each Partner shall thereupon be credited or debited, as the case may be, with his or her share of such net profits or losses. In preparing such account, there shall be charged all expenses of the partnership, and also, all losses and other charges incident or necessary to the carrying on of the purpose of the partnership.

Any Partner may withdraw his or her share of the net profits (less his or her share of principal payments on any notes or mortgages) at the end of each fiscal year. If any Partner shall not withdraw all or any portion of his or her share of the net profits, such Partner shall not be entitled to receive interest upon any undrawn profits, nor shall any undrawn profits be deemed an increase of his or her capital, or entitle such party to an increase in the share of the profits of the partnership, without the express written consent of all other Partners.

11. **Book and Records.** The partnership shall maintain full and accurate books of account, which shall be kept at the principal partnership office. The Managing Partners shall cause to be entered in such books all transactions of or relating to the partnership. Each Partner shall have access to and the right to inspect and copy such books and all other partnership records during normal business hours. The official books and records of the partnership shall consist of ________________ . The Managing Partners shall be responsible for their upkeep, custody and audit. Reports on the financial status of the partnership shall be rendered annually.

12. **Bank Accounts.** The partnership shall maintain such bank accounts as the Managing Partners shall determine. Checks shall be drawn for partnership purposes only, and may be signed only by the person or persons designated by the Managing Partners. All moneys received by the partnership shall be deposited in such accounts.

13. **Meetings.** Meetings of the Partners shall be held at ____________ on the ________ day of each month, at ________ o'clock, commencing ____________________ .

14. **Management Duties and Restrictions.** ______________________ shall be the Managing Partners. Except as otherwise provided in this agreement, the Managing Partners shall have full charge of the management, conduct and operation of the partnership in all respects and in all matters, including, but not limited to, the power to purchase, sell or convey personal and real property on such terms as they may determine but subject to the provisions of Section 15 of this agreement, to lease such property or any part thereof on such terms and for such period as they may determine, to borrow money on behalf of the partnership to the extent authorized under Section 15, and, to the extent permitted under Section 15, to mortgage personal and real property and to make agreements modifying any contract, lease, note or mortgage.

Except as otherwise provided in this agreement, a majority of the Managing Partners shall be authorized and empowered to determine all questions relating to the conduct and management of the partnership business, and the determination by a majority of the Managing Partners on any such question shall be binding on all Partners.

15. **Matters Requiring Unanimity.** No Managing Partner shall, without the consent of all other Partners (which consent shall not be unreasonably withheld), do any of the following:

(a) Assign the partnership property in trust for creditors or on the assignee's promise to pay the debts of the partnership.

(b) Dispose of the good will of the partnership business.

(c) Do any other act which would make it impossible to carry on the ordinary business of the partnership.

(d) Confess a judgment against the partnership.

(e) Submit a partnership claim or liability to arbitration or reference.

(f) Make, execute or deliver for the partnership any bond, mortgage, deed of trust, guarantee, indemnity bond, surety bond or accommodation paper or accommodation endorsement.

(g) Borrow money in the partnership name or use partnership property as collateral.

(h) Assign, transfer, pledge, compromise or release any claim of or debt owing to the partnership except upon payment in full.

(i) Convey any partnership real property.

(j) Pledge or transfer in any manner his or her interest in the partnership except to another Partner.

(k) Any other act for which unanimity is required under other Sections of this Agreement.

16. **Activities.** Each Managing Partner shall each devote his or her entire time and attention to the business of the partnership, except that a Managing Partner may devote reasonable time to civic, family, and personal affairs. Other Partners may devote their time and attention to other business matters, except those that in any way conflict with or compete against the business of the partnership.

17. **Fidelity Bonds.** ____________________ shall be required to obtain a fidelity bond in the amount of $ ________ for the faithful performance of his or her partnership duties. The expense of the bond shall be borne by the partnership.

18. **Transferability of Partnership Interests.** Except as otherwise provided in this agreement with respect to withdrawing or decreased partners, the interest of any Partner in the partnership, or in the profits, assets, property, receivables, records, files, or clientele of the partnership, should not be sold, assigned, pledged, mortgaged, or transferred in any manner by a Partner unless the written consent to do so is first obtained from every other Partner.

19. **Partnership Property.** Partnership property, personal and real, shall be acquired, held, and conveyed in the name of the partnership, except that upon the unanimous consent of the Partners, partnership property may be acquired, held, or conveyed in the name of any Partner or other person as nominee for the partnership. Property acquired, held, or conveyed by a nominee shall be recorded as partnership property in the partnership books and records.

20. Admission of New or Substituted Partners. A new Partner may be admitted to the partnership only upon the written consent of all existing Partners. A substituted Partner may be admitted to the partnership only upon the written consent of two-thirds of the existing Partners and only if the substituted Partner purchases the partnership interest of a deceased or withdrawing Partner. Upon the admission of a new Partner, the name and capital contribution of the new Partner shall be added to Section 5 of this agreement and Section 7 of this agreement (and any other applicable section) shall be construed so as to take into account the modification of Section 5 caused by the addition of the new Partner. The name of a substituted Partner shall be substituted in Section 5 of this agreement for the name of the deceased or withdrawing Partner whose partnership interest was purchased by the substituted Partner, and the substituted Partner shall assume the capital account of the deceased or withdrawing Partner.

21. Withdrawal of a Partner. Any Partner shall have the right to withdraw from the partnership at the end of any fiscal year. Written notice of intention to withdraw shall be served upon the other partners at the office of the partnership at least three months before the end of the fiscal year. The withdrawal of any Partner shall have no effect upon the continuance of the partnership business. The remaining Partners shall have the right either to purchase the withdrawing Partner's entire interest in the partnership or to terminate and liquidate the partnership business, or the partnership interest of a withdrawing Partner may be purchased by a substituted Partner as provided in Section 20 of this agreement. If the remaining Partners elect to purchase the interest of the withdrawing Partner, they shall serve notice in writing of such election upon the withdrawing Partner at the office of the partnership within two months after receipt of the notice of intention to withdraw. If a remaining Partner shall not elect to participate in the purchase of the withdrawing Partner's interest, he or she shall serve written notice of his or her intention not to participate upon the other Partners at the office of the partnership within one month after the service of the voluntarily withdrawing Partner's notice of intention to withdraw. Such nonparticipation notice shall be deemed to be an irrevocable notice of intention to withdraw by the nonelecting Partner and a tender by the nonelecting Partner to the other Partners of his or her entire partnership interest which shall be subject to purchase by the other Partners upon the same terms and conditions applicable to the interest of the Partner giving voluntary notice of intention to withdraw.

(a) If the remaining Partners elect to purchase a withdrawing Partner's interest in the partnership, the percentages of purchase of the withdrawing Partner's interest, the purchase price, and the method of payment shall be as provided in Section 25 of this agreement.

(b) If the remaining Partners do not elect to purchase a withdrawing Partner's interest in the partnership, the Managing Partners shall proceed with reasonable promptness to liquidate the business of the partnership. The procedure as to liquidation and distribution of the assets of the partnership business shall be as provided in Section 26 of this agreement.

(c) A withdrawing Partner shall not engage in the business of ____________ or otherwise compete against the business of the partnership within a radius of 100 miles from the partnership office for a period of 5 years after withdrawal.

22. Death of a Partner. Upon the death of any Partner, the surviving Partners shall have the right either to purchase the decedent's entire interest in the partnership or to terminate and liquidate the partnership business. If the surviving Partners elect to purchase the decedent's interest, they shall serve notice in writing of such election, within three months after the death of the decedent, upon the executor or administrator of the decedent, or, if none, upon any one of the known legal heirs of the decedent at the last known address of such heir. If a surviving Partner shall not elect to participate in the purchase of the decedent's interest, the Partner shall serve written notice of his or her intention not to participate upon the other surviving Partners at the office of the partnership within one month after the death of the decedent. Such nonparticipation notice shall be deemed to be an irrevocable notice of intention by the nonelecting Partner to withdraw from the partnership and a tender by the Partner to the other Partners of his or her entire partnership interest, which shall be subject to purchase by the other Partners upon the same terms and conditions applicable to the interest of the deceased Partner.

(a) If the remaining partners elect to purchase a deceased Partner's interest in the partnership, the percentages of purchase of the deceased Partner's interest, the purchase price, and the method of payment shall be as stated in Section 25 of this agreement.

(b) If the remaining Partners do not elect to purchase a deceased Partner's interest in the partnership, the Managing Partners shall proceed with reasonable promptness to liquidate the business of the partnership. The procedure as to liquidation and distribution of the assets of the partnership business shall be as stated in Section 26 of this agreement.

23. Expulsion of a Partner. A Partner may at any time be expelled from the partnership by the unanimous vote or consent of the Managing Partners, or of the other Managing Partners if the Partner being expelled is a Managing Partner, for: (a) professional misconduct or disqualification, (b) willful and continued breach of this agreement, or (c) conduct prejudicial to the carrying out of the business and affairs of the partnership. Prior to expulsion, a Partner for whom expulsion is contemplated shall be entitled to appear before the Managing Partners for the purpose of refuting the charges. An expelled Partner shall be compensated in cash for his or her partnership interest in the amount provided in Section 25 of this agreement.

24. **Disability or Bankruptcy of a Partner.** The partnership shall not be dissolved by the disability or the bankruptcy of a Partner. Disability shall mean physical or mental disability which has continued for six months and which the Managing Partners determine to be permanent. A Partner whose disability is under consideration shall submit to reasonable examinations by qualified physicians if requested by the Managing Partners. Bankruptcy shall include the filing of a voluntary petition by a Partner under any Chapter of Title 11, United States Code, the entering of an order for relief upon the filing of an involuntary petition with respect to a Partner under any Chapter of Title 11, United States Code, and an adjudication of insolvency of a Partner under the insolvency laws of any state. The disabled or bankrupt Partner, or his successor in interest, shall be compensated for his or her partnership interest as provided in Section 25 of this agreement.

25. **Compensating Deceased or Withdrawing Partners.** If the surviving or remaining Partners elect to purchase the partnership interest of a deceased or withdrawing Partner, the purchase price shall be equal to the capital account of the deceased or withdrawing Partner as shown on the partnership books, increased by his or her share of partnership profits or decreased by his or her share of partnership losses (plus interest or use payments on capital in accordance with the provisions of Section 5) for the period from the beginning of the fiscal year in which the death or withdrawal occurred until the date of the death or withdrawal, and decreased by withdrawals during such period. No allowance shall be made for goodwill, trade name, patents, or other intangible assets, except as those assets have been reflected on the partnership books immediately prior to the death or withdrawal. Each of the surviving or remaining Partners shall have the right to purchase a portion of the partnership interest of the deceased or withdrawing Partner in the proportion which his or her interest in the profits of the partnership bears to the interest of the other surviving or remaining Partners in the profits of the partnership. The purchase price shall be paid with interest at the rate of 6% per annum in four semiannual installments beginning six months after the date of death or withdrawal. In the event of the purchase of the interest of the deceased or withdrawing Partner, the continuing partnership shall have the right to use the firm name of the partnership.

26. **Liquidation and Termination of Partnership.** If the surviving partners do not elect to purchase the partnership interest of a deceased or withdrawing Partner, or if the partnership is otherwise dissolved without a continuation of the partnership business, the surviving or remaining Managing Partners shall proceed with reasonable promptness to liquidate the business of the partnership. The partnership name shall be sold with the other assets of the business and each Partner shall, if requested, covenant with the purchaser not to compete in the ________________ business under a similar name within a radius of 300 miles from the principal place of business of the partnership for a period of 5 years after the sale. The surviving or remaining Partners and the deceased or withdrawing Partner, if any, shall share in the profits and losses of the business during the period of liquidation in the same proportions in which they shared such profits and losses immediately prior to the dissolution, except that a deceased or withdrawing Partner shall not be liable for losses in excess of such Partner's interest in the partnership at the time of the death or withdrawal. So long as any surviving Partner shall devote his or her full time to the liquidation of the partnership business, the Partner shall receive a salary at the same rate as immediately prior to the commencement of liquidation. After the payment of partnership debts, the proceeds of liquidation shall be distributed as realized, first in discharge of the undrawn partnership profits of the deceased or withdrawing Partner prior to death or withdrawal and the undrawn partnership profits of such Partner's liquidation, then in such manner as to make the capital accounts of the Partners proportionate to the capital accounts in the partnership as of the date of its organization, and then proportionately in discharge of the respective capital accounts.

27. **Incorporation of Partnership Business.** Upon the affirmative vote or written consent of _____ percent of the Partners, a corporation shall be formed to conduct the business of the partnership. The common stock of the corporation shall be distributed to the Partners in proportion to their respective capital interests in the partnership at the time of the vote or consent to incorporate. The Managing Partners shall execute the documents and take all steps necessary to carry out the formation of the corporation and the transfer of the partnership property and assets to the corporation. The name of the corporation shall be ________________________.

28. **Amendment.** This agreement, or any provision thereof, may be amended at any time by a majority vote of the partners, except that any provision of this agreement that provides for a vote, approval or consent of more than a majority of the partners may be amended only by a vote of the partners that is equal to that specified in the provision sought to be amended.

29. **Binding Effect.** This agreement shall bind the Partners, their heirs, personal representatives, and assignees.

IN WITNESS WHEREOF, the parties have executed this agreement as of the date first above appearing.

________________________ ________________________ ________________________

Name, Partner Name, Partner Name, Partner

ADDITIONAL PROVISIONS FOR PARTNERSHIP AGREEMENT OF LIMITED LIABILITY PARTNERSHIP

Note - These provisions should be added to the partnership agreement of a general partnership that is to be registered as a limited liability partnership in any state.

Registration as Limited Liability Partnership. The partners may elect to have the partnership registered as a domestic registered limited liability partnership under the partnership laws of the state of ______________________ only upon the affirmative vote of ________ percent or more of the partners. The partners may elect to register the partnership as a foreign registered limited liability partnership in any state where the partnership conducts business only upon the affirmative vote of ________ percent or more of the partners. If the partners affirmatively vote to register the partnership as a domestic or foreign registered limited liability partnership in any state, the managing partners are authorized and directed to sign and file with the appropriate state official any application or registration statement that is required to register the partnership as a registered limited liability partnership in that state. The managing partners are also empowered and directed to pay the fees necessary to register the partnership as a registered limited liability partnership in any state where registration has been affirmatively voted for and thereafter to perform all acts and functions that are necessary to continuously maintain the registration of the partnership as a registered limited liability partnership in any such state, including the filing of renewal applications or periodic reports and the payment of any required fees and behalf of the partnership. The registration shall continue until such time as the partners vote to withdraw the partnership's registration as a registered limited liability partnership in the manner described in paragraph 31 of this agreement or until the partnership is liquidated and terminated in the manner described in paragraph 26 of this agreement.

Withdrawal of Registration as Limited Liability Partnership. The partners may elect to withdraw the registration of the partnership as a domestic registered limited liability partnership in the state of ______________________ only upon the affirmative vote of ________ percent or more of the partners. The partners may elect to withdraw the registration of the partnership as a foreign registered limited liability partnership in any state where it is so registered only upon the vote of ________ percent or more of the partners. If the partners affirmatively vote to withdraw the registration of the partnership as a registered limited liability partnership in any state, the managing partners are directed and empowered to promptly prepare, sign and file with the appropriate state official the documents necessary to effect the withdrawal.

Effect of Statute on Inconsistent Provision. If any provision in this agreement is in conflict or inconsistent with a provision of an applicable statute that limits the liability of a partner in any state where the partnership is registered or operates as a domestic or foreign registered limited liability partnership, the provision of this agreement shall be inoperative and of no effect insofar as it is inconsistent with the statute.

LIMITED PARTNERSHIP AGREEMENT

THIS AGREEMENT OF LIMITED PARTNERSHIP dated ______________________, by and among the persons set forth below, all of whom agree as follows:

ARTICLE 1

Formation of Limited Partnership

1.01. The parties hereby form a limited partnership under the Revised Uniform Limited Partnership Act of the State of ______________.

1.02. The names and addresses of the general partners are: ____.

103. The names and addresses of the limited partners are: ____.

1.04. The general partners shall forthwith prepare and execute a Certificate of Limited Partnership, which shall be duly filed in the office of the Secretary of State of the State of ______________, in accordance with the provisions of the Revised Uniform Limited Partnership Act of said state. A true copy of the filed Certificate of Limited Partnership shall be delivered to each limited partner.

ARTICLE 2

Partnership Business and Term

2.01. The business of the partnership shall be conducted under the name of ______________.

2.02. The purpose of the partnership shall be to engage in the business of ______________.

2.03. The principal place of business of the partnership shall be at ______________, but additional places of business may be conducted at such locations as may from time to time be agreed upon by the general partners.

2.04. The partnership shall commence on ______________, and shall continue until ______________.

ARTICLE 3

Capital Contributions and Withdrawals

3.01. Each partner shall make the contribution to the capital of the partnership shown below:

Name	Form of Contribution	Value of Contribution	Percentage of Total

3.02. Each partner may make additional contributions to the capital of the partnership in the amounts agreed upon by the general partners.

3.03. A partner may not withdraw any portion of his or her capital contribution without the written consent of all of the general partners, except that a limited partner may withdraw all or a portion of his or her capital contribution upon giving six months' notice in writing to all other partners.

3.04. An individual capital account shall be maintained for each partner, to which shall be credited or debited his or her contributions or withdrawals, as the case may be.

3.05. No partner shall assign such partner's rights to the partner's capital account without the prior written consent of the general partners.

ARTICLE 4

Profits and Losses

4.01. The fiscal year of the partnership shall start on ____________________ and shall end on ____________________. The net profits or losses of the partnership shall be determined in accordance with generally accepted accounting practices as soon as possible after the close of each fiscal year.

4.02. The net profits or losses of the partnership during each fiscal year shall be credited or debited as of the close of the fiscal year to the capital accounts of the partners in proportion to the capital contributions of the partners as shown in Section 3.01 of this agreement.

4.03. Any accumulated net profits contained in the capital account of a partner shall be delivered to the partner within 30 days after a written demand therefor is delivered by the partner to the general partners.

4.04. No partner shall assign such partner's rights to partnership profits to another person without the prior written consent of the general partners.

ARTICLE 5

Management and Records

5.01. The partnership shall be managed by the general partners, who shall devote their full time and best efforts to the conduct of the partnership business. Each general partner shall have an equal voice in the management and conduct of the partnership business. Except as otherwise provided in this agreement, questions related to the conduct and management of the partnership business shall be determined by a majority vote of the general partners.

5.02. Checks drawn on partnership bank accounts shall be signed by the following general partners: ____________________.

5.03. The general partners shall receive the salaries set forth below. Such salaries shall not be increased without the written consent of all limited partners. The payment of salaries shall be an obligation of the partnership only to the extent that partnership assets available for them and shall not be a personal obligation of any partner. Salary payments shall be treated as partnership expenses in determining the net profits or losses of the partnership.

Name of General Partner	Salary

5.04. Except as otherwise provided in this agreement, the limited partners shall not take part in the management of the partnership business or transact any business for the partnership, and they shall have no power to obligate the partnership. No salary shall be paid to a limited partner.

5.05. Proper and complete records and books of account of the business of the partnership shall be kept by or under the supervision of the general partners at the principal place of business of the partnership and shall be open to inspection by any partner, or by the representative of a partner, at any reasonable time during business hours. The books and records of account of the partnership shall be examined and reviewed at the close of each fiscal year by an independent certified public accountant chosen by the general partners, and the accountant shall issue a report thereon, a copy of which shall be promptly sent to each limited partner. The records kept by the partnership shall include the following:

(a) a current list of the full name and last known business address of each partner, separately identifying the general partners (in alphabetical order) and the limited partners (in alphabetical order);

(b) a copy of the certificate of limited partnership and all certificates of amendment thereto, together with executed copies of any powers of attorney pursuant to which any certificate has been executed;

(c) copies of the partnership's federal, state and local income tax returns and reports, if any, for the three most recent years;

(d) copies of any then effective written partnership agreements and of any financial statements of the partnership for the three most recent years; and

(e) records setting out:

(i) the amount of cash and a description and statement of the agreed value of the other property or services contributed by each partner and which each partner has agreed to contribute;

(ii) the times at which or events on the happening of which any additional contributions agreed to be made by each partner are to be made;

(iii) any right of a partner to receive, or of a general partner to make, distributions to a partner which include a return of all or any part of the partner's contribution; and

(iv) any events upon the happening of which the limited partnership is to be dissolved and its affairs wound up.

ARTICLE 6

General Partners

6.01. A general partner may not, without the consent of all partners:

(a) Assign, transfer, or pledge a partnership claim except upon payment in full.

(b) Make, execute, or deliver an assignment for the benefit of creditors or a bond, confession of judgment, lease, mortgage, deed, guarantee, or other contract involving the transfer of an interest in all or substantially all of the partnership property.

(c) Lease, mortgage, or transfer of any of the partnership property, other than in the normal course of partnership business.

6.02. A general partner may withdraw from the partnership by giving 90 days' notice thereof in writing to each partner. A withdrawing general partner shall be compensated for his or her partnership interest as provided in Section 6.05 of this agreement.

6.03. A general partner may be removed from the partnership upon the unanimous vote of the limited partners for (a) professional misconduct or disqualification, (b) willful and continued breach of this agreement, or (c) conduct prejudicial to the carrying out of the business and affairs of the partnership. Prior to expulsion, a general partner for whom expulsion is contemplated shall be entitled to appear before the limited partners for the purpose of refuting the charges. A removed partner shall be compensated in cash for his or her partnership interest as provided in Section 6.05 of this agreement.

6.04. In the event of the withdrawal, removal, death, or legal incompetency of a general partner, the remaining partners, provided that there is within 90 days thereafter at least one remaining general partner, shall have the right to continue the business of the partnership under its present name by themselves, or in conjunction with any other person or persons whom they may select, but they shall pay to the departing general partner, or to the legal representatives of a deceased or legally incompetent general partner, as the case may be, the value of such partner's interest in the partnership, as provided in Section 6.05 of this agreement.

6.05. The value of the partnership interest of a withdrawing, removed, deceased, or legally incompetent general partner, as of the date of the exercise of the option given in Section 6.05 of this agreement, shall be the sum of such partner's capital account plus the partner's proportionate share of accrued net partnership profits. If a net loss has been incurred to the date of dissolution, the partner's shares of such loss shall be deducted from the partner's capital account. The assets of the partnership shall be valued at book value for purposes of this Section. In computing the value of a partnership interest under this Section, no value shall be attributed to goodwill.

6.06. A new or substituted general partner may be admitted to the partnership only with the unanimous written consent of the limited partners.

ARTICLE 7

Limited Partners

7.01. A limited partner shall have the following rights:

(a) The right to vote on partnership matters as otherwise provided in this agreement.

(b) The right to inspect and copy the partnership records and to promptly obtain copies of the partnership's income tax returns.

(c) The right to obtain from the general partners upon reasonable demand true and complete information regarding the financial condition of the partnership and the state of its business, and other reasonable information regarding the affairs of the partnership.

(d) The right to consult with and advise a general partner regarding the partnership business.

(e) The right to bring a derivative action in the right of the partnership.

(f) The right to request or attend a meeting of the partners.

(g) The right to wind up the limited partnership as provided by law, to the extent permitted under this agreement.

(h) The right to propose, approve, or disapprove, by voting or otherwise, any of the following matters:

(i) the dissolution and winding up of the partnership,

(ii) the sale, exchange, lease, mortgage, pledge, or other transfer of all or substantially all of the assets of the partnership,

(iii) the incurrence of indebtedness by the partnership other than in the ordinary course of its business,

(iv) a change in the nature of the partnership business,

(v) the admission or removal of a general partner or a limited partner,

(vi) a transaction involving an actual or potential conflict of interest between a general partner and the partnership or a general partner and the limited partners, and

(vii) an amendment to the partnership agreement or to the certificate of limited partnership; and

(i) The right to exercise any other power or right permitted to limited partners by applicable law.

7.02. A new or substituted limited partner may be admitted to the partnership only upon the majority vote of all partners, except as provided in Section 7.06 of this agreement.

7.03. A limited partner may be removed from the partnership only upon the unanimous vote of all partners for: (a) willful and continued breach of this agreement, or (b) conduct prejudicial to the carrying out of the business and affairs of the partnership. Prior to expulsion, a limited partner for whom expulsion is contemplated shall be entitled to appear before the partners for the purpose of refuting the charges. An expelled limited partner shall be compensated for his or her partnership interest as provided in Section 7.05 of this agreement.

7.04. A limited partner may withdraw from the partnership by giving 60 days notice thereof to each partner. A withdrawing limited partner shall be compensated for his or her partnership interest as provided in Section 7.05 of this agreement.

7.05. The value of the partnership interest of a withdrawing or removed limited partner shall be the sum of such partner's capital account plus the partner's proportionate share of accrued net partnership profits. If a net loss has been incurred to the date of dissolution, the partner's shares of such loss shall be deducted from the capital account. The assets of the partnership shall be valued at book value for purposes of this Section. In computing the value of a partnership interest under this Section, no value shall be attributed to goodwill.

7.06. In the event of the death of a limited partner, the partner's personal representative during the period of administration of the estate shall succeed to the deceased partner's rights hereunder, and that interest may be assigned to any member of the family of the deceased limited partner in distribution of the partner's estate, or to any person in pursuance of a bequest in the last will and testament of such partner, and the family member or person shall thereupon succeed to the deceased partner's interest as a limited partner and have all the rights of a substituted limited partner.

ARTICLE 8

Termination

8.01. The partnership shall be dissolved upon the occurrence of any of the following events:

(a) The time specified in Section 2.04 of this agreement or in the Certificate of Limited Partnership.

(b) The time specified in a written consent to dissolve the partnership signed by all partners.

(c) Ninety days after the death, withdrawal, removal, or legal incompetence of the last remaining general partner if at that time a new general partner has not been appointed.

(d) Two consecutive fiscal years without net profits by the partnership business followed within 120 days thereafter by a majority vote of limited partners to dissolve the partnership.

(e) The entry of a decree of judicial dissolution by a court of competent jurisdiction.

8.02. Upon the dissolution of the partnership, the remaining general partners, or, if there are no remaining general partners, the limited partners, or a person appointed by a majority of the limited partners, shall wind up the business and affairs of the partnership.

8.03. Upon the winding up of the partnership and its business and affairs, the assets of the partnership shall be distributed as follows:

(a) First, to the creditors of the partnership, including partners who are creditors, in satisfaction of the liabilities of the partnership other than liabilities for distributions to partners.

(b) Second, proportionately to partners and former partners as distributions owed under Sections 6.05 and 7.05 of this agreement.

(c) Third, proportionately to partners as distributions for the return of their respective capital contributions.

(d) Fourth, to partners as distributions in respect to their partnership interests in proportion to their respective capital contributions.

ARTICLE 9

Amendment and Interpretation

9.01. This agreement may be amended only by the unanimous written consent of all persons who are then partners.

9.02. Any matter not specifically covered by a provision of this agreement shall be governed by the laws of the state of ________________, including the applicable provisions of the Revised Uniform Limited Partnership Act of that state.

9.03. This agreement shall be binding on the partners, their heirs, personal representatives, assignees, and successors in interest.

IN WITNESS WHEREOF, the parties have executed this agreement as of the day and year first above appearing.

________________________	________________________
Name, General Partner	Name, Limited Partner
________________________	________________________
Name, General Partner	Name, Limited Partner

CERTIFICATE OF LIMITED PARTNERSHIP

We, the undersigned general partners, for the purpose of forming a limited partnership under the Revised Uniform Limited Partnership Act as set forth in the Statutes of the State of ______________________, hereby certify and affirm under penalty of perjury as follows:

1. **Name.** The name of the limited partnership is ____________________.

2. **Office.** The address of the office of the limited partnership at which the official records of the limited partnership shall be kept is ____

3. **Agent.** The name and address of the agent for service of process for the limited partnership is ________________________ ____

4. **General Partners.** The name and business address of each general partner of the limited partnership is:

Name	Business Address

5. **Dissolution.** The latest date upon which the limited partnership is to dissolve is ____________________

6. **Other Matters.**

1. The purpose of the limited partnership is to acquire, develop, and sell that parcel of real estate located in the County of Pitkin in the State of Colorado, described as follows:

Lots 10, 11, 12, 13, 14, and 15, Block 4,
Bakers Addition to the City of Aspen.

2. The number of limited partners that may be admitted to the limited partnership shall not exceed ten and the minimum capital contribution for each limited partner shall be $100,000.

Dated this ____________ day of __________________ 19_____ in Aspen, Colorado.

____
General Partner

____
General Partner

____
General Partner

REGISTRATION STATEMENT FOR REGISTRATION OF PARTNERSHIP AS A LIMITED LIABILITY PARTNERSHIP

The partnership hereby applies for limited liability partnership status in this state as a (domestic or foreign) partnership.

The general partners of the partnership have approved this registration statement in the manner provided for in the partnership agreement or, if the agreement has no provisions therefor, this statement has been approved by the partnership in the manner and by the vote of the partners required by section ____________ of the Uniform Partnership Act of this state.

The name of the partnership is ____.

If different, the name by which the partnership proposes to be registered, or, if foreign, the name by which the partnership proposes to transact business in the state is ____.

The state in which the partnership was formed and organized is ____________________.

The street address of the principal office of the partnership is ____.

If the principal office of the partnership is not in this state, the name and street address of the partnership's registered agent for service of process in this state is ____

____.

The partnership is engaged in the business of ____.

The effective date of limited liability partnership status for the partnership, if other than the date of filing of this statement, is (future date).

Date: ________________________ Name of Partnership

by ________________________________
General Partner

CHAPTER FOUR

LIMITED LIABILITY COMPANIES

The popularity of limited liability companies among small business enterprises has increased enormously in recent years. In less than ten years the limited liability company has emerged from virtual obscurity to universal acceptance as an innovative and flexible business entity for small or closely-held businesses. Limited Liability Company Acts have been passed in every state. Thousands of small businesses have been organized as limited liability companies and great numbers of existing partnership and corporate businesses have reorganized into limited liability companies. It is obviously important for an attorney representing a small business enterprise and its participants to be knowledgeable on the subject of limited liability companies.

LLCs, recent emergence of

4.01 An Introduction to Limited Liability Companies

A limited liability company (an LLC) is an unincorporated but registered entity whose members are protected from personal liability for company debts and are allowed to participate in the management of the company business in any desired degree. In addition, a properly organized LLC is normally treated as a partnership for federal income tax purposes. Thus, a properly organized LLC enjoys the limited liability benefits of a corporation together with management flexibility and pass-through tax treatment benefits of a general partnership.

LLC, definition of

Limited liability companies (LLCs) are creatures of statute. They may exist only if authorized by statute and must be organized in the manner set forth in the local LLC Act. Typically an LLC comes into legal existence when "articles of organization" are filed with the state filing official, usually the Secretary of State. The persons who organize an LLC are usually referred to as "organizers" and the owners of an LLC are usually referred to as "members." Under most LLC Acts an LLC may be managed either directly by the members or by persons referred to in the LLC Act as "managers." Member-managed LLCs are managed very much like a general partnership, while manager-managed LLCs are managed more like corporations or limited partnerships than general partnerships. Managers are normally elected by the members and are required to operate an LLC in accordance with rules set forth in a document called an "operating agreement." The articles of organization and the operating agreement are the governing documents for LLCs in most states.

LLC, general aspects of

The fundamental characteristics of LLCs may be summarized as follows:

1. **Limited Liability of LLC members for company debts.** Most LLC Acts expressly provide that LLC members and managers are not liable for company debts solely because they are members or managers of the LLC. In most states the statutory liability of an LLC member for company debts is limited to the member's unfulfilled contractual obligation to contribute capital to the company. In other words, the liability of an LLC member for LLC debts is the same as the liability of a shareholder for debts of a corporation. The liability of an LLC manager for LLC debts is the same as the liability of a corporate officer for debts of the corporation. The limited liability of members and managers for company debts is the single great advantage of an LLC over a general partnership, where each general partner is liable without limitation for all partnership debts.

liability of member for LLC debts, extent of

liability of member for LLC debt, when imposed

It should be understood that despite the limited liability shield, an LLC member or manager may become personally liable for one or more of the company debts. The most common method of incurring personal liability for a company debt is for an LLC member or manager to personally guarantee or otherwise become contractually liable to an LLC creditor for an LLC debt. When dealing with small businesses, creditors and lenders often require personal guarantees from the business participants before credit will be extended to the business. In addition, in most states an LLC member or manager who wrongfully appropriates company funds or otherwise acts to defraud company creditors may be personally liable to company creditors under a doctrine analogous to the corporation law doctrine of piercing the corporate veil.

ownership rights in LLC, treatment of by members

2. **Flexibility of management and capitalization**. The management and capital structure of a multi-member LLC is similar to that of a general partnership. This means that a member's rights to capital, profits and management may be treated separately and without significant statutory restriction. This is an important practical advantage of an LLC over a corporation where a shareholder's rights to capital, profits and management are combined in the form of stock, the issuance of which is often subject to significant statutory restriction.

tax treatment of LLC, general rules

3. **Income tax treatment.** Unless an LLC elects otherwise, it will be treated as a partnership for federal income tax purposes if it is a multi-member LLC and as a sole proprietorship if it is a single-member LLC. This means that the profits and losses of the business are passed directly to the members. For most small businesses, this pass-through tax treatment is a significant advantage of an LLC over a C corporation. In essence, an LLC is taxed in the same manner as an S corporation without the necessity of qualifying the business under Subchapter S of the Internal Revenue Code. The tax status of LLCs is discussed at length in section 4.02, infra.

LLCs, filing and organizational requirements

While considerable informality is permitted in the organization and operation of LLCs under most LLC Acts, some filing and other statutory requirements are imposed. First of all, unlike a sole proprietorship or general partnership, a prescribed document (usually articles of organization) must be filed with the state filing official in order for an LLC to come into legal existence. Some LLC Acts impose disclosure requirements with respect to the names of the members or managers of an LLC, some impose limits with respect to the period of existence of an LLC, some require certain records to be maintained, and periodic reports and fees must be filed with and paid to the state filing official. In addition, LLC name requirements are imposed in all states.

LLC, required number of members

Another important restriction is that some LLC Acts require the existence of two or more members, thus rendering it impossible for a one-person business to operate as an LLC without the addition of a real or dummy business associate. Most LLC Acts, however, permit an LLC to be owned and operated by one person. The number of members required of LLCs in each state is set forth in Appendix I in the back of this book under the heading of "Limited Liability Company Laws, General LLC Requirements."

LLC Act, default provisions of

Most LLC Acts contain default provisions that apply in the event that certain matters are not dealt with in either the articles of organization or the operating agreement of an LLC. For example, most LLC Acts contain a provision vesting management of an LLC in the members unless the articles of organization or operating agreement provide for the management by managers. It is important to be aware of the various default provisions in the local LLC Act.

LLC, advantages of over general partnership

LLCs vs. general partnerships. As indicated above, the great advantage of an LLC over a general partnership as a form of business entity is the limited liability shield of LLC members and managers for company debts. This limited liability shield is especially significant in the case of professional or personal service businesses where a general partner is liable for the torts or other misconduct of the other general partners that were committed or incurred in the course of the partnership business. In an LLC, a member or manager is not personally liable for the torts or other misconduct of the other members or managers, even if the tort or misconduct was committed in the course of company business.

LLCs vs. LLPs, advantages and disadvantages

LLCs vs. limited liability partnerships. The advantages, if any, of an LLC over a limited liability partnership (an LLP) depend primarily on the extent of the liability protection accorded LLP partners under the LLP statutes of the LLP's home state. The main advantage of an LLC over an LLP is that in most states LLC members enjoy a greater degree of personal liability protection than do LLP partners. In some states, however, the degree of liability protection accorded LLP partners is substantially equal to that accorded LLC members. These states are those that have enacted the so-called third-generation LLP statutes that give partners liability protection from virtually all partnership debts (see section 3.11, infra, for a list of these states and for a description of the type and degree of liability protected given thereunder). In a few states, however, LLPs are limited to certain professionals and may not be used by other businesses. Under the new "check the box" tax regulations, the tax aspects of both entities are essentially the same, at least with respect to new or startup businesses. For an existing partnership business, however, an LLP has the significant tax and organizational advantage of being able to continue the existing business entity without the necessity of transferring the business and its assets to a new entity. Therefore, it is usually simpler and less expensive for an existing partnership business to convert to an LLP than to an LLC.

LLC, advantages of over limited partnership

LLCs vs. limited partnerships. The big advantage of an LLC over a limited partnership is that, unlike a limited partner, an LLC member does not risk incurring general liability for company debts by participating in the management of the company business. It should be remembered that in a limited partnership, a limited partner who participates in the management of the partnership business risks the incurrence of unlimited personal liability for partnership debts. See section 3.05, supra. Another significant advantage of an LLC over a limited partnership is that it is not necessary for at least one of the LLC members to be personally liable for the company debts. In a limited partnership, it should be remembered, there must be at least one general partner who is personally liable for the partnership debts. Another practical advantage of an LLC over a limited partnership is that of simplicity of organization: when organizing an LLC it is not necessary to create such entities as corporate general partners in order to shield the active business participants from personal liability for business debts.

self-employment tax, liability of LLC members for

A disadvantage of an LLC vs. a limited partnership is that in an LLC each member is subject to the federal self-employment tax with respect to his or her distributive share of LLC income. However, under Proposed Regulation 1.1402-(a)(18) an LLC member would not be subject to this tax if the member is not a manager of the LLC and could qualify as a limited partner in a limited partnership in the local state. If this proposed regulation is adopted, the liability of LLC members for the federal self-employment tax would be substantially the same as that of partners in a limited partnership. It is not clear when or if this proposed regulation will be adopted because its adoption was postponed by Congress in the Taxpayer's Relief Act of 1997.

LLC, advantages of over C corporation

LLCs vs. C corporations. As indicated above, both a C corporation and an LLC shield individual business participants from personal liability for business debts. The major advantages of an LLC over a C corporation are pass-through taxation, flexibility of management, simplicity of organization, and ease of an equitable withdrawal from the business by a participant.

LLC, tax advantages of over C corporation

Perhaps the most significant advantage of an LLC over a C corporation is that an LLC, if properly organized, is treated as a partnership for federal income tax purposes, which means that the LLC is not taxed and the profits and losses of the business are passed directly to the members for tax purposes. This eliminates the danger of double taxation and most of the other C corporation tax disadvantages. The pass-through nature of partnership taxation also makes it easier for the business participants to deduct business losses in the year of incurrence.

C corporation, difficulty of dealing separately with elements of ownership

The three principal elements of ownership of any business are the owners' rights to profits, capital, and management. In a corporation these ownership rights are combined in the form of stock, which makes these rights difficult to deal with separately. While it is usually possible to separate these corporate rights, such a separation normally requires the issuance of different classes of stock, the preparation of lengthy shareholder agreements, and other cumbersome and expensive undertakings that often invite litigation should the relations between the business participants sour.

ownership rights, LLC vs. C corporation

In an LLC, on the other hand, a member's rights to profits, capital and management may be segregated and dealt with separately by so providing in the operating agreement or articles of organization. In an LLC, unlike a corporation, both the management and the capital structures of a business can be determined by the business participants without significant statutory restriction and can be easily implemented in the operating agreement. For example, in an LLC it is not necessary to create a hierarchy of shareholders, directors, and officers in order to manage the business. Under most LLC statutes, the members can either manage the company themselves (as in a general partnership) or provide for the company to be managed by one or more managers under the rules and conditions set forth in the operating agreement.

LLC ownership rights, dealing with in LLC, illustration

Suppose, for example, that A, B and C desire to conduct a business that will be managed by A, financed by B, and operated on property or equipment owned by C. If an LLC is used, B and C can relinquish their management rights in the company, either absolutely or conditionally, without impairing their rights to profits or capital. Similarly, A and C can relinquish all or a portion of their rights to the company profits without impairing their other ownership rights, and A and B can relinquish all or a portion of their capital rights in the company in order to protect C's rights in the contributed capital. Further, because each owner's rights to profits, capital and management can be dealt with separately, this complicated capital and management structure can be established in a few paragraphs in the operating agreement.

LLC, advantages of for deceased or withdrawing member

Still another advantage of an LLC over a C corporation is that because a deceased or withdrawing member can cause the dissolution of the LLC, it is usually easier for a deceased or withdrawing member to collect his or her interest in the business. Unless advance provisions are made to compensate withdrawing participants in a small business corporation, it is often impossible for the withdrawing participant to obtain compensation for his or her stock. See section 5.17, infra.

LLC, disadvantages of vs. C corporation

The most significant disadvantage of an LLC as compared to a C corporation is that because there is no universally recognized indicia of ownership, it may be difficult to sell ownership interests in the company to outsiders, especially in large numbers. Therefore, if the public sale of ownership interests in the business is contemplated, a C corporation may be preferable to an LLC. Shares of corporate stock are better suited for such purposes than are LLC ownership interests. LLCs are best suited for closely-held businesses of any kind and investment businesses involving only a limited number of investors. Another disadvantage of an LLC in a few states is the two-or-more member requirement which makes it difficult to operate a one-person business as an LLC. In most states, it should be noted, an LLC may be organized and operated by a single member.

LLC, advantages of over S corporation, generally

LLCs vs. S corporations. The LLC advantages of flexibility of management, simplicity of organization and ease of equitable withdrawal described above with respect to C corporations are equally applicable to S corporations. However, because LLCs are taxed in essentially the same manner as S corporations, LLCs do not enjoy significant tax advantages over S corporations in most instances.

LLC, tax advantages of over S corporation

LLCs do enjoy several tax-related advantages over S corporations under certain circumstances. First of all, unlike an S corporation, an LLC is not limited to 75 members and its members are not limited to natural persons, estates and certain trusts. Thus, a corporation, a partnership, another LLC, or a nonresident alien can be a member of an LLC without endangering the LLC's tax status. Secondly, the partnership tax status of an LLC, once established is secure and cannot be endangered by the acts of a member, whereas the acts of a single shareholder can cause an S corporation to become disqualified and lose its tax status. See section 5.18, infra. Therefore, it is not necessary for an LLC to impose stock (or membership) transfer restrictions in order to insure the continued existence of its tax status.

LLC, tax advantages of over S corporation

Another advantage of an LLC over an S corporation is that an LLC is not bound by the one class of stock limitation imposed on S corporations and may have as many classes of members as desired without losing its tax status. This gives an LLC greater flexibility in distributing its profits, surplus, and capital. Also, an LLC, unlike an S corporation, may own more than 80 percent of the stock of another corporation. Unlike a shareholder in an S corporation, an LLC member can contribute property to the LLC in exchange for membership without recognizing a taxable gain even if the member is in "control" of the LLC. Finally, while profits and losses must be allocated on a prorata basis among the shareholders of an S corporation, unequal or nonprorata distributions can be made to LLC members if the allocations have substantial economic effect. See 26 U.S.C. 704(b).

LLCs, use of by professionals

Because of their tax and limited liability features, LLCs are popular with professional businesses. LLCs are widely used by attorneys, physicians, accountants, architects, engineers, dentists, and other professionals who wish to limit their personal liability for the debts of the business. Most LLC Acts either expressly permit professionals to organize as LLCs or are silent on the issue, in which case the use of an LLC by professionals is permitted. The LLC Acts in a few states, including California, Oregon and Rhode Island, expressly prohibit professionals from using LLCs. In addition, a particular profession in a particular state may preclude or impose restrictions on the use of LLCs by the practitioners of that profession in that state. In any event, the availability of an LLC for the professionals in question in the local state should be checked before organizing a professional LLC. It should be noted that limited liability partnerships are often preferable to LLCs for many professionals. See sections 3.11-3.13, supra, for further reading on limited liability partnerships.

4.02 The Tax Status of Limited Liability Companies

federal income tax status of LLCs, general rules

As of January 1, 1997, a limited liability company (an LLC) with two or more members may elect to be classified for federal income tax purposes as either a partnership or a corporation. An LLC with only one member may elect to be classified as a corporation or to have the entity disregarded for federal income tax purposes, in which case it will be treated as a sole proprietorship for federal income tax purposes. See Treasury Reg. 301.7701-3(a). The cumbersome rules set forth in Revenue Procedure 95-10 that formerly governed the tax status of LLCs are no longer applicable. Instead a "check the box" method of establishing the tax classification of LLCs is now used. The appropriate boxes to be checked are found in IRS Form 8832, a copy of which is set forth in Exhibit 4-E at the end of this chapter.

federal income tax classification of LLCs, applicable tax regulations

Under the tax regulations that became effective on January 1, 1997, multiperson business entities that are not automatically classified as corporations may choose to be classified as either a partnership or as an association that is taxable as a corporation. A multiperson business entity is automatically classified as a corporation if it (1) was organized as a corporation or joint stock company or under a state, federal, or American Indian statute, (2) elects to be classified as an association that is taxable as a corporation, (3) is an insurance company or an FDIC-insured bank, (4) is a state-owned business entity, (5) is taxable as a corporation under another provision of the Internal Revenue Code (i.e., a provision other than 26 U.S.C. 7701(a)(3)), or (6) is a foreign business entity as described in Treasury Reg. 301.7701-2(b)(8). See Treasury Reg. 301.7701-2. Because an LLC that has not filed an election to be classified as a corporation does meet any of these criteria, it is not automatically classified as a corporation and therefore may elect to be classified as either a partnership or a corporation for federal income tax purposes.

LLCs in existence prior to 1-1-97, tax status of

As indicated above, beginning on January 1, 1997 the federal income tax status of an LLC may be elected by filing a properly completed election form (which is IRS Form 8832) and checking the appropriate box. LLCs that were in existence prior to January 1, 1997 may change their tax classification by filing an election form and checking the appropriate box. The tax status of LLCs that were in existence prior to January 1, 1997 and who do not file an election form will remain unchanged, except that single-member LLCs that were previously classified as partnerships will be disregarded as an entity for federal income tax purposes (i.e., will be treated as sole proprietorships). See Treasury Reg. 301.7701-3(b)(3)(i).

existing LLC, election to change tax status, effect of

Care should be taken in changing the tax classification of an existing LLC, especially if the change is from corporation to partnership tax status. An election to change the tax classification of an entity is treated as a conversion of the entity from one form of entity to another for tax purposes. For example, if an existing LLC is classified as a corporation and elects to be classified as a partnership, the election will be deemed to effect a taxable conversion of the LLC from a corporation to a partnership. In such a situation the LLC will be deemed to have been liquidated and reorganized as a partnership, usually with unfavorable tax consequences for the business owners in the form of recognizable gain. The LLC would have to file a final income tax return as a corporation and a first-year return as a partnership. See section 4.05, infra, for a discussion of the tax aspects of corporation-LLC conversions. The rules described in that section are applicable to a corporation-partnership conversion following an election to change the tax classification of an LLC from a corporation to a partnership.

LLCs formed after 1-1-97, election of tax status by

LLCs that were organized after January 1, 1997 may elect their initial tax status by filing an election form (IRS Form 8832) and checking the appropriate box. An LLC that is formed after January 1, 1997 and does not file an election form is subject to the default rules of Treasury Reg. 301.7701-3. Under this regulation an LLC that does not file an election form will be classified as a partnership for federal income tax purposes if it has two or more members and will be disregarded as an entity (i.e., treated as a sole proprietorship) for tax purposes if it has only a single member. See Treasury Reg. 301.7701-3(b)(1). Thus, a newly-organized LLC that fails to elect its tax status will automatically be taxed as a partnership if it has two or more members and will be disregarded as a tax entity if it has a single member.

tax classification of LLC, as partnership or sole proprietorship, when preferable

It is usually preferable for a multiperson LLC to be classified as a partnership rather than a corporation. The advantages of pass-through reporting of income, losses, gains, deductions, credits and other tax items and the elimination of the double tax imposed on corporate earnings that are distributed as dividends make partnership tax status favorable to corporate tax status for most multi-member LLCs. The same tax advantages make sole proprietorship tax status preferable to corporate tax status for most single-member LLCs. As indicated above, sole proprietorship tax status is obtained by electing to have a single-member LLC disregarded as a tax entity by the IRS. For further reading on the tax treatment of partnerships, see section 3.02, supra. The tax treatment of corporations is discussed generally in section 5.02, infra. For further reading on the tax treatment of sole proprietorships, see section 2.02, supra.

tax classification of LLC as corporation, when preferable

Generally, an LLC should consider electing to be classified or reclassified as a corporation for federal income tax purposes only if it is necessary to retain earnings for future expansion or if a tax-free reorganization or merger with a publicly-held corporation is contemplated. Such a classification (or reclassification) should be elected and completed well in advance of any reorganization or restructuring, which would be governed by the tax-free incorporation provision of 26 U.S.C. 351. Any reclassification of an LLC as a corporation should not be made in conjunction with the reorganization and should not be a part of an agreement or overall plan because such an agreement or plan would violate the tax-free incorporation requirements of 26 U.S.C. 351.

tax classification election, signature requirements

The Treasury regulations require an LLC to make its tax classification election on IRS Form 8832, a copy of which is set forth in Exhibit 4-E at the end of this chapter. The election form must be signed either by each member of the electing LLC who is an owner at the time the election is filed or by an officer, manager or member of the LLC who is authorized to make the election and who represents such authorization under penalty of perjury. An election form filed by a member-managed LLC should normally be signed by each member, unless the election function has been specifically delegated to an officer. An election form filed by a manager-managed LLC should be signed by its manager or managers. However, if the election is to be effective prior to the date it is filed with the IRS, each person who was a member of the LLC between the effective date of the election and the date of filing and who was not a member on the date of filing must also sign the election form.

tax classification election, effective date of

The tax classification election will be effective on the date specified on the election form or on the date the form is filed if no date is specified. The effective date specified on the form may not be more than 75 days before the date of filing and may not be more than 12 months after the date of filing. See Treasury Reg. 301.7701-3(C)(1).

tax classification election, filing requirements

An LLC must file the election form (Form 8832) with the Internal Revenue Service Center indicated on the form and must attach a copy of the form to its federal income tax or informational return for the tax year of the election. If the LLC elects to be disregarded as a tax entity or is otherwise not required to file a tax or informational return for that year, a copy of the election form must be attached to the federal income tax return of each LLC member for that year. While a failure to attach a copy of the election to the LLC or member's tax or informational return will not invalidate an otherwise valid election, it may result in the assessment of tax penalties against those who failed to do so. See Treasury Reg. 301.7701-3(C)(1)(ii).

changing existing tax classification, time requirement

An LLC may change an existing tax classification by filing a subsequent election, again using IRS Form 8832. However, an LLC that makes an election to change its tax classification is precluded from making another change during the 60-month period after the effective date of the election, except that the IRS may permit an LLC to change its tax classification by election within the 60-month period if more than 50 percent of its members on the effective date of the subsequent election were not members at the time of the prior election. See Treasury Reg. 301.7701-3(C)(1)(iv).

changing existing tax classification, exceptions to time requirement

An exception to the 60-month waiting period for subsequent elections is made for LLCs who wish to change their tax classification that was in effect on the effective date of the adoption of the "check-the-box" regulations (which is January 1, 1997). An election to change a pre-January 1, 1997 classification may be made within 60 months after January 1, 1997, regardless of when the election was made. The 60-month limitation, it should be noted, only applies to previous elections that were affirmatively made by the LLC; it does not apply to tax classifications that occurred by default. Therefore, an LLC that fails to file an election upon its formation and receives a tax classification by default may elect out of the default classification at any time. See Treasury Reg. 301.7701-3(C)(1)(iv).

state tax status of LLCs, general rules

The tax status of an LLC in the local state should also be considered. Most states tax LLCs in the same manner as under federal law. That is, an LLC is classified as either a partnership or a corporation for state tax purposes, depending on the election it files or is defaulted to under federal law. Most states follow the federal rule and do not impose an income or franchise tax on partnerships or LLCs that have elected to be classified as partnerships for tax purposes, but do impose income or franchise taxes on corporations and LLCs that elect to be taxed as corporations. A few states, including Florida, Pennsylvania and Texas, impose an income or franchise tax on all LLCs, regardless of how they elect to be taxed for federal income tax purposes.

4.03 Organizing a Limited Liability Company

determining type of entity best suited for business

The first decision to be made when organizing or reorganizing a small business is whether a limited liability company (LLC) is the entity that best serves the needs of the business and its participants. The subject of determining the type of business entity that best suits the needs of the business participants is discussed in chapter one of this handbook. The advantages and disadvantages of LLCs as compared to partnerships and corporations are also discussed in section 4.01, supra.

LLC Act, default rules in, importance of

Prior to organizing an LLC, it is important to become familiar with the relevant provisions of the local LLC Act and with the relevant provisions of the LLC Act in any other state where the LLC will be transacting sufficient business to require registration as a foreign LLC. It should be understood that all LLC Acts are unique and usually contain several so-called "default rules." Default rules are rules that apply if the organizational documents of an LLC contain no provisions dealing with the subject covered by the rule. For example, most LLC Acts provide that an LLC shall be managed by the members unless otherwise provided in the articles of organization. The default rule of member management applies unless the LLC's articles of organization provide for management by managers. Default rules are typically imposed for such matters as voting and election requirements and distribution requirements. It is important to be aware of the default rules in the local LLC Act when organizing an LLC.

types of businesses permitted to use LLCs

Before organizing an LLC it should be ascertained whether the type of business to be conducted by the LLC is one that is authorized by both the LLC Act and the laws regulating the particular business that is to be conducted by the LLC. Most LLC Acts provide that an LLC may be organized for any lawful purpose. In those states any business which is not prohibited from being conducted in the form of an LLC by another statute or by the rules or regulations governing the business of the LLC may be conducted by an LLC.

LLC, use of by professionals

LLC, use of by farmer or rancher

In some states, it should be noted, the rules or regulations governing certain professions may either prohibit the use of LLCs by the practitioners of that profession or impose conditions or restrictions on LLCs that are engaged in that profession. The LLC Acts in California, Oregon and Rhode Island prohibit the use of an LLC by professionals. It should also be noted that some states have enacted separate LLC statutes for professionals. In a few states special restrictions are imposed on LLCs engaged in certain businesses, usually farming or ranching. In any event, before organizing an LLC it should be ascertained whether the business to be conducted by the LLC is one that is prohibited or restricted under local law. The restrictions, if any, imposed by each state on the types of businesses that an LLC may conduct are summarized in Appendix I, infra, under the heading of Limited Liability Company Laws, General LLC Requirements.

LLC, general organizational aspects

One of the most important functions in organizing an LLC is to devise a capital structure and a management and control structure for the LLC. Most LLC Acts permit considerable flexibility in devising both of these structures. Because fewer statutory limitations and requirements are imposed on LLCs than on corporations, the tasks of devising capital and management and control structures are usually simpler and easier for LLCs than for corporations. In most cases both the capital structure and the management and control structure can be set forth in the operating agreement. In some states it may be necessary to include a few matters dealing with these functions in the articles of organization.

LLC capital contributions, general requirements

Capital Structure. The only statutory limitation on the capital structure of an LLC in most states is the LLC Act provision dealing with capital contributions. Most LLC Acts provide that the contribution of a member to an LLC may be in the form of cash, property or services rendered or a written promise or obligation to provide cash, property or services in the future. LLC Acts vary somewhat, especially with respect to future obligation requirements, so the local Act should be checked in this regard. In a few states the capital contributions of each member must be set forth in the articles of organization. In most states, however, this is not required and they may be set forth in the operating agreement.

LLC capital structure, general aspects

Because of the absence of statutory restrictions, just about any type of capital structure desired by the business participants may be adopted for an LLC. The members can contribute cash, property or services, or promises to provide cash, property or services in the future, in any desired proportion or amount. The only limitations are that in many states promises to provide future contributions must be in writing to be enforceable and capital distributions must usually be in proportion to capital contributions.

LLC ownership interests, general aspects, written instruments, of

Unlike the corporation laws, most LLC Acts do not require or even provide for the issuance of stock or other securities in return for capital contributions. The only type of ownership in an LLC under most Acts is an LLC membership interest, which is similar to a general partnership interest. However, the LLC Acts in some states, including California, provide for the existence of LLC shares or certificates, which are similar to shares of corporate stock. If desired, a certificate or other written instrument evidencing a member's interest in the LLC may be issued by an LLC under most LLC Acts. While in most cases the issuance of such an instrument is neither necessary nor advisable, under certain circumstances the issuance of written instruments of ownership may be appropriate. For example, an LLC engaged in the investment business may wish to issue written instruments of ownership to its investor members.

To protect and safeguard the capital and other interests of LLC members, most LLC Acts contain certain record-keeping requirements. The specific LLC record-keeping requirements vary considerably from state to state and the local requirements should be ascertained and complied with. Typically, an LLC is required to keep the following records:

LLC records, general requirements

(1) a record of the name and address of each member and each manager,
(2) a copy of the articles of organization and all amendments thereto,
(3) a copy of each currently effective operating agreement,
(4) copies of all recent LLC financial statements,
(5) copies of all recent LLC income tax returns, and
(6) a statement describing the capital contributions made or to be made by each member.

management of LLC, first decision

Management Structure. Most LLC Acts permit LLC members to either manage the company themselves or provide for the election or appointment of one or more managers to manage the company. Member-managed LLCs are usually managed like general partnerships, with each member having a direct voice in the management of LLC affairs. Manager-managed LLCs, on the other hand, are managed more like a corporation, with much authority delegated by the members to elected officers. For most LLC's, then, the first management structure decision is whether the LLC is to be member-managed or manager-managed.

member-managed LLC, when advisable

In making the decision on whether an LLC is to be member-managed or manager-managed, much depends upon the nature and size of the business to be conducted by the LLC and the relationship among the LLC members. If the business is small and local, if all of the members will be active participants in the business, and if all of the members wish to participate or have an equal voice in the management of the business, member-management will usually be preferable. There is little to be gained by the use of managers in such situations. Creating a hierarchy of officers that is likely to be ignored in practice by the members will serve no useful purpose. An advantage of a member-managed LLC is that it is usually easier and less expensive to organize than a manager-managed LLC. It should be understood, however, that unless it is otherwise provided in the operating agreement, individual members have only limited management rights in a manager-managed LLC (their status is similar to that of a shareholder of a corporation). Minority members of manager-managed LLCs have virtually no enforceable management rights unless they are provided for in the operating agreement.

manager-managed LLC, when advisable

If the business of the LLC will be widespread geographically or will be of sufficient size to require a hierarchy of officers in order to be properly managed, if the LLC members do not wish to manage the business themselves, or if there will be members who will not be active participants in the business, then it will usually be necessary to provide for one or more managers in the LLC management structure. A significant advantage of a manager-managed LLC in certain situations is that it is easier to limit the ability of the individual members to bind or act on behalf of the LLC. For example, in a manager-managed LLC individual members can more easily be precluded from signing contracts on behalf of the LLC.

A manager-managed LLC is usually preferable in the following situations:

manager-managed LLC, when preferable

(1) Where the LLC has a large number of members or a small number of members who are geographically widespread and not actively involved in the day-to-day business operation.

(2) Where the LLC will be dealing with numerous third parties who may be concerned about the ability of individual members to bind the LLC to important contracts or agreements. If the LLC is not manager-managed third parties frequently require the signature or consent of all members to important contracts and agreements.

(3) Where the LLC has passive or silent members who do not wish to be involved in the day-to-day operation of the LLC business.

(4) Where the LLC is controlled by a dominant person who wishes to maintain overall control of the business but wishes to distribute interests in the business for tax or other purposes to family members or others who will not participate in the control of the business. The manager would be appointed by the dominant member and would be answerable only to that member.

(5) Where the LLC is a joint venture by two or more unaffiliated corporations or investors who have other interests and wish to retain a qualified person to manage the venture on their behalf.

LLC managers, appointment or election of

If managers are to be used by an LLC, the initial managers are usually named in either the articles of organization or the first LLC operating agreement, depending on the requirements of the local LLC Act. In most states the managers named in the initial LLC documents serve until they are replaced by managers elected by the LLC members. Some LLC Acts contain elaborate provisions dealing with the election and removal of managers, while others contain only a few provisions on the subject. The provisions of the local LLC Act should be ascertained before preparing LLC organizational documents and devising a management and control structure for a manager-managed LLC.

LLC membership voting requirements

action-without-meeting statutes for LLCs

All managers other than the initial managers named in the LLC's organizational documents must be elected by the LLC members. Under most LLC Acts, membership voting rights are in proportion to a member's capital contribution unless the articles of organization or operating agreement provide for different voting rights. In some states, however, membership voting is based on the members' rights to profits, unless the articles of organization or operating agreement provide otherwise. Like the corporation laws, many LLC Acts impose unanimous or higher-than-majority voting requirements on certain matters such as dissolution, merger, amending the articles of organization, and the admission of new or substituted LLC members. Quorum requirements are often imposed for the transaction of business at membership meetings and most LLC Acts contain action-without-meeting provisions for both member and manager action. The provisions of the local LLC Act with respect to these matters should be ascertained before devising a management and control structure for an LLC.

LLC managers, general requirements

In most states, managers may be natural or corporate persons and need not be LLC members. In most states, then, an LLC may be managed by a nonmember management company, if desired. In a few states, however, managers are required to be natural persons. The local LLC Act should be checked for the existence of manager qualification requirements. It should be understood, however, that manager qualifications may be imposed, if desired, by providing for them in the articles of organization or operating agreement. It is common, for example, for an LLC to require its managers to be LLC members.

LLC managers, number of

Under most LLC Acts an LLC may have one or more managers with no maximum number. The number of managers must usually be set forth in the articles of organization, although in some states the number may be specified in the operating agreement. The requirements of the local LLC Act in this regard should be ascertained before preparing the organizational documents for an LLC.

LLC managers, authority of

If limitations are to be imposed on the authority of all or certain of the managers, or if each manager is to have specified areas of responsibility, the limitations or responsibilities should be set forth in the operating agreement. To this end, it should be noted that most LLC statutes impose no restrictions on the duties or functions of managers, so any type of management arrangement desired by the members can usually be implemented in the operating agreement.

LLC managers, titles of

Most LLC statutes contain no limitations or requirements as to the titles or offices that managers or their appointees may be given. Therefore, a manager or appointee may usually be given any desired title or office. For example, a manager or an appointee may be given the title of president, if desired. If officers are provided for in the operating agreement, provisions should be made for their election and removal and, if desired, their indemnification. A clear job description for each officer should also be given.

4.04 Preparing Organizational Documents for Limited Liability Companies

LLC organizational documents, use of

Under most LLC Acts two organizational documents are required: (1) articles of organization and (2) an operating agreement. Considerable flexibility and overlap is usually permitted in determining the matters that are to be included in each document. Therefore, one of the issues that should be determined when organizing an LLC is whether a particular matter should be dealt with in the articles of organization or the operating agreement.

articles of organization, function of

In determining whether to deal with a particular matter in the articles of organization or the operating agreement, it should be understood that the function of the articles of organization varies depending on the particular LLC Act. In some states the articles of organization are treated as ministerial documents requiring the inclusion of few, if any, substantive provisions (although such provisions may usually be included in the articles if desired). In other states the LLC Act requires many substantive provisions to be included in the articles of organization (as opposed to the operating agreement) if they are to be effective. It is obviously important, then, to ascertain the article of organization requirements of the local LLC Act before preparing the LLC organizational documents.

articles of organization, statutory requirements

articles of organization, sample of

Articles of Organization. The first document to be prepared when organizing an LLC is usually the articles of organization. In a few states, it should be noted, the formative LLC document is referred to as the "certificate of formation," rather than the articles of organization. Most LLC Acts contain a section dealing explicitly with the required and permitted contents of the articles of organization. Typically, this statute will list the matters that are required to be included in the articles of organization. Most LLC Acts also list or describe the matters that are permitted (but not required) to be included in the articles. Terms such as "any other lawful provision" or "any provision that may be included in an operating agreement" are often used to describe the permitted article provisions. The section or provision of the LLC Act in each state that contains the article of organization content requirements is cited in Appendix I in the back of this book under the heading of Limited Liability Company Laws, Formation of LLC. Sample articles of organization for an LLC are set forth in Exhibit 4-A at the end of this chapter.

articles of organization, matters to include in

Although the specific requirements vary from state to state, the following matters are typically required to be set forth in the articles of organization:

(1) the name of the LLC,
(2) the name and address of the LLC's registered agent and office,
(3) the LLC's period of existence,
(4) the LLC's business purpose, and
(5) the names and addresses of the LLC's initial members and/or managers.

LLC name, statutory requirements

LLC Name Requirements. All LLC Acts contain provisions explicitly setting forth LLC name requirements in the local state. These provisions should, of course, be checked and complied with when choosing a name for an LLC. The LLC name provisions normally contain both inclusive and prohibitive name requirements for LLCs. The inclusive LLC name requirements typically provide that the name of an LLC must include the words "limited liability company" or the abbreviation "LLC." The prohibitive LLC name requirements are usually similar to those for the names of corporations (e.g., may not be the same as or deceptively similar to the name of any registered local or foreign business entity, etc.). Most LLC Acts also contain LLC name reservation provisions which are usually similar to those for corporations. See section 5.05, infra, for further reading on selecting and reserving a name.

LLC registered agent, statutory requirements

Registered Agent and Office. All LLC Acts require each domestic and foreign LLC to maintain an agent for service of process in the local state. The name and address of this agent must normally be set forth in the articles of organization. In some states the registered agent must be a member or manager of the LLC or an attorney admitted to practice in the local state. In some states the agent must accept the appointment and the written acceptance must be filed with the state filing official. The registered agent requirement is usually the same for LLCs as for corporations. Many LLC Acts also require the address of the LLC's initial registered office to be listed in the articles.

LLC period of existence, statutory requirements

Period of Existence. Apparently on the mistaken theory that a limited period of existence helps an LLC qualify for partnership tax status (that this theory is incorrect, see section 4.02, supra), some states impose a maximum period of existence for LLCs (often 30 years) and require the period of existence for an LLC to be set forth in the articles of organization. Several states impose no period of existence limitation but do require a period of existence to be specified in the articles. Other states impose no period of limitation and do not require a period of existence to be specified in the articles of organization. The period of existence requirements, if any, in the local state should be ascertained and complied with when drafting the articles of organization. The LLC period of existence requirements in each state are summarized in Appendix I, infra, under the heading of Limited Liability Company Laws, General LLC Requirements.

business purpose of LLC, statutory requirements

Business Purpose. While most states do not restrict the business that may be conducted by an LLC, several states require the business or business purpose of an LLC to be set forth in the articles of organization. This requirement is similar to the business purpose requirements set forth in the corporation laws. Unless the local LLC Act provides to the contrary, the LLC business purpose requirement can usually be satisfied by stating that the LLC is organized "to conduct any lawful business" or "for all lawful purposes." In a few states it may be necessary to specify the precise business or businesses that will be conducted by the LLC. The wording of the local LLC Act should be examined for such requirements. Special business purpose requirements are sometimes imposed on professional LLCs. If the business participants wish to limit the nature of the company's business, they may usually do so by inserting "self-denying" business purpose clauses in the articles of organization. See sections 5.09 and 5.15, infra, for further reading on the use of self-denying clauses.

self-denying clauses, use of

identification of LLC members and managers, statutory requirements

Member and Manager Identification. The extent to which the initial members and/or managers of an LLC must be identified in the articles of organization varies from state to state. Some LLC Acts require no disclosure of either LLC members or managers, while other Acts require a full disclosure of both. Some states require the names and addresses of the initial members to be listed in the articles of organization if management of the LLC is reserved to the members and the names and addresses of the managers if managers are to manage the LLC. Many Acts also require a statement in the articles of organization indicating whether management of the LLC is vested in the members or in managers. Some states require a statement in the articles stating that the LLC has two or more members. The provisions of the local LLC Act dealing with the contents of the articles of organization should be examined and complied with.

articles of organization, required or permitted matters

Other Required or Permitted Provisions. In a few states, including Wyoming and Florida, detailed financial information regarding the initial capitalization of the LLC must be set forth in the articles of organization. Some LLC Acts require the articles of organization to set forth rules or requirements governing such matters as the admission of new members, the election of managers, and the right of the remaining members to continue the LLC business following the death or disassociation of a member. Most LLC Acts contain a provision expressly permitting the inclusion in the articles of any other lawful provision, in which case just about any desired provision may be included in the articles. Some LLC Acts, however, do not contain a permissive article provision. In such states it may be advisable to check with the state filing official before including article provisions other than those specifically required or permitted by the LLC Act in order to insure that they will be accepted for filing by the state filing official.

LLC organizers, functions of, number of

Organizers. Most LLC Acts require the articles of organization to be signed and filed with the state filing official by persons identified in the Act as organizers. The organizers of an LLC are similar in function to the incorporators of a corporation. In most states the organizers of an LLC need not be members or managers of the LLC. In most states, then, the organizer of an LLC may be a nonmember, including the LLC's attorney or another person. Some states require two or more organizers, while other states require only one. In many states the organizer(s) of an LLC must be a natural person. In a few states, it should be noted, the articles of organization must be executed by the LLC's initial members, which means that in those states the organizers must be LLC members. The number of organizers required in each state is set forth in Appendix I, infra, under the heading of Limited Liability Company Laws, Formation of LLC.

articles of organization, execution and filing requirements and fees

Execution and Filing Requirements. In most states the articles of organization must be executed only by the organizers. As indicated above, a few LLC Acts require the articles to be executed by all or a specified number of the initial LLC members. The executed articles of organization must be filed with the state filing official and the filing fee paid. In some states the written acceptance of the LLC's local agent for service of process must also be filed with the state filing official. The name, address, and telephone number of the state filing official in each state is also set forth in Appendix I in the back of this book under the heading of Corporation Laws, State Filing Official. The filing fee for filing articles of organization in each state is also set forth in Appendix I, infra, under the heading of Limited Liability Company Laws, Formation of LLC.

legal existence of LLC, beginning of

In some states the legal existence of an LLC begins when the articles of organization are accepted for filing by the state filing official. In other states legal existence begins when the state filing official issues a certificate giving notice that the articles of organization have been accepted and filed. The provisions of the local Act should be checked in this regard, if this issue is important. If the articles of organization provide for the legal existence of an LLC to begin at a later date, the date specified in the articles normally governs.

operating agreement, function of

Operating Agreement. The defining and most important document in the organization and operation of most LLCs is the operating agreement. It is the LLC equivalent of a partnership agreement. It should deal with all matters related to the business relationship of the members, the affairs of the LLC, and the conduct of its business.

operating agreement, what constitutes, contents of

An operating agreement is typically defined in LLC Acts to include any valid agreement of the members as to the affairs of the LLC and the conduct of its business. Under most LLC Acts an operating agreement may contain any lawful provision regarding the affairs of the LLC and the conduct of its business. Except as otherwise provided in the LLC Act or in the articles of organization, an operating agreement governs the rights, duties, limitations, qualifications, and relationships among the members and managers of an LLC and their assignees. Of course, an operating agreement may not contravene a right, duty or requirement set forth in the LLC Act. For example an operating agreement may not restrict a member's statutorily-provided right of access to the books and records of the LLC. Many LLC Acts provide that an operating agreement need not be in writing to be valid. However, the matters that may be dealt with in an oral operating agreement are usually restricted. There is seldom a valid reason for having an oral operating agreement. Sample operating agreements for a member-managed LLC and for a manager-managed LLC are set forth in Exhibits 4-B and 4-C, respectively, at the end of this chapter.

operating agreement, samples of

operating agreement, matters dealt with in

Operating agreements vary greatly in format, length and complexity. Much depends on the nature of the business that will be conducted by the LLC, the relationship between the members, and the type of management and control structure that is to be implemented. Generally, however, an operating agreement should deal with the following matters:

(1) The identification and location of the LLC.
(2) The identification of the LLC members and their respective membership interests.
(3) The restrictions or requirements, if any, that are to be imposed on LLC members and managers.
(4) The rights of LLC members, including their voting rights.
(5) The initial and future capital contribution requirements of each member.
(6) The allocation of profits, losses and distributions among the members.
(7) The permitted businesses of the LLC and the management thereof.
(8) The assignability of membership interests, the rights of assignees, and the membership admission requirements of new and substituted members.
(9) The death or disassociation of a member and the rights of the remaining members to continue the LLC business thereafter.
(10) The compensation of deceased or disassociated members for their interests in the LLC.
(11) The accounting, fiscal, and record keeping policies of the LLC.
(12) The liquidation, winding up, and termination of the LLC following dissolution when the business will not be continued.
(13) The requirements for amending the operating agreement.

operating agreement, preparation of

The best practice, of course, is for the members to meet, consider the available alternatives, and agree on the details of the undertaking before the operating agreement is prepared. To accommodate this practice and to ensure that no important aspect of the undertaking is overlooked during such a meeting or during the LLC organization process, some type of checklist or guide should be used. Those without a checklist or guide of their own will find the Limited Liability Company Checklist and Guide set forth below useful in preparing an operating agreement and in organizing an LLC.

LIMITED LIABILITY COMPANY CHECKLIST AND GUIDE

The following matters should be considered and dealt with when organizing an LLC and when preparing an LLC operating agreement:

1. **The name and address of the LLC and its registered agent.** The name of the LLC must meet the requirements of the LLC statute (see, supra, this section). The registered agent should be the agent identified in the articles of organization. The address of the registered office of the LLC should be listed if a registered office is required under the local LLC Act. The principal business address or addresses of the LLC should also be listed.

2. **The name and address of each LLC member.** The operating agreement, or an addendum or attachment thereto, should contain the name and address of each LLC member. In most states a natural person, a corporation, a partnership, another LLC, a trust, an estate, an association, or any other legal entity may be an LLC member. Special restrictions may be imposed upon membership in certain professional LLCs in many states. If a member is not a natural person, the type of entity of the member should be listed.

3. **The LLC interest of each member.** The interest of each member in the LLC should be listed in the operating agreement, usually in terms of a percentage. If the interest of members with respect to capital, profit, and management rights are to be unequal, the interest of each member with respect to each item should be listed, if feasible.

4. **Membership restrictions or conditions.** If restrictions, requirements or conditions are to be imposed on membership in the LLC or on the transferability of membership interests, they should be clearly specified in the operating agreement.

5. **The voting rights of members.** The rights of members to vote on such matters as the election of managers or officers, the admission of new members, a change in the LLC business, the continuation of the business following the death or withdrawal of a member, and the dissolution of the LLC should be clearly provided for. If unanimous or super-majority voting requirements are to be imposed on certain matters, these requirements and the procedures therefor should be clearly set forth.

6. **Capital contributions and accounts.** The capital contribution requirements of each member should be clearly specified. In most states capital contributions may be in the form of cash, property or services or any combination thereof, or a promise to provide cash, property or services in the future. If additional capital contributions may be required in the future, both the conditions giving rise to the future contributions and the obligation of each member with respect thereto should be set forth. A capital account should be established and maintained for each member in accordance with accepted accounting practices.

7. **Allocating profits, losses, and other tax items.** The method of allocating LLC profits, losses and other tax items among the members should be established in the operating agreement. Common methods of sharing LLC profits, losses and other tax items include:

   (a) equal sharing by all members;
   (b) sharing in proportion to capital contributions;
   (c) sharing in accordance to specified standards, such as seniority or productivity;

(d) allocating tax deductions, credits, and gains and losses with respect to certain assets to the members who contributed the assets;
(e) the guaranteeing of certain profit distributions to certain members, often with contribution requirements from other members if the guaranteed payments cannot be met by the company; and
(f) allocating any losses caused by the malpractice, willful misdeed or default of a member to that member.

8. **Allocating capital and other distributions.** Distributions of capital are usually made to members in proportion to their capital contributions. In many states this is required by the LLC Act. Because it is possible for an LLC to produce paper losses (usually through depletion, depreciation or other deductions) and have disposable cash, provisions should also be made for cash distributions. Such distributions may be in the same proportions as either profit distributions or capital distributions, or a different allocation may be made.

9. **Management of business.** The first management decision to be made is whether the LLC shall be member-managed or manager-managed. If the LLC is to be member-managed, it must be decided whether all members are to have equal management rights. If not, the management rights of each member should be specified. If the LLC is to be manager-managed, the membership voting requirements for electing and removing managers should be specified. Also to be specified in the operating agreement are such matters as the rights, powers, and limitations of managers, a description of their duties and titles, the qualifications, if any, for managers, and their compensation.

10. **Assignees and new or substituted members.** Under most LLC Acts a member may freely assign his or her LLC membership interest but the assignee has no management rights in the LLC unless the assignment is consented to by all or a specified portion of the other members. If the assignment is approved by the other members the assignee becomes a substituted member with full management rights. Under most LLC Acts a new member (i.e., one who is not the assignee of an existing member) may be admitted to an LLC only upon the written consent of all or a specified portion of the existing members. Both of these statutory requirements can usually be modified in the operating agreement, if desired. Therefore, the membership consent requirements for admitting new members and substituted members should be determined and set forth in the operating agreement. The rights of assignees to profits and distributions may also be modified in the operating agreement, if desired.

11. **Continuation of business upon the death or disassociation of a member.** The events that constitute disassociation should be listed. Events of disassociation normally include such matters as the assignment of a member's LLC interest, the bankruptcy of a member, the expulsion, withdrawal, or disability of a member, and the dissolution of a corporate member. The rights of the remaining members to continue the business upon the disassociation of a member should be specified. The membership voting requirements for continuing the business should be specified. The time limits within which the remaining members must act should also be specified. If the members are to agree in advance to continue the LLC business after the death or disassociation of a member, that agreement should be set forth in the operating agreement.

12. **Compensating deceased or disassociated members.** If the LLC business is to be continued following the death or disassociation of a member, the methods of compensating deceased or disassociated members should be specified in the operating agreement. Methods of funding such compensation should also be specified. Such funding may be provided personally by the existing or incoming members, by a special fund established by the LLC, or by the purchase of life insurance, either by the members individually or by the LLC. A method of valuing the LLC interest of a deceased or disassociated member should also be set forth in thc operating agreement. The terms of any required payments should be specified, as should the treatment of LLC good will.

13. **Liquidating and terminating the LLC.** Provisions should be included in the operating agreement dealing with the liquidation, winding up, and termination of the LLC business when the LLC is dissolved and its business is not continued.

14. **Method of accounting and fiscal year.** Because an LLC is normally a tax-reporting entity, it must have a tax year, which should be specified in the operating agreement. The general accounting practices and tax-reporting methods of the LLC should also be specified in the operating agreement.

15. **Books and records.** Most LLC Acts require LLCs to keep and maintain certain records. Included here are usually membership records and copies of the articles of organization, all effective operating agreements, minutes of membership meetings, LLC income tax returns, and certain financial information. The location of and the person responsible for maintaining the LLC books and records should be specified in the operating agreement. Provisions may also be made in the operating agreement for the rendering of periodic reports to the members, if desired.

16. **Amending the Operating Agreement.** Provisions should be made in the operating agreement for the amendment of its provisions. The membership voting requirements for amending the agreement should be clearly specified. If desired, different voting majorities may be required to amend different provisions of the agreement.

4.05 Converting Existing Businesses to Limited Liability Companies

A startup business may be organized as a limited liability company (LLC) by simply complying with the organizational requirements of the local LLC Act when the business is organized. An existing sole proprietorship business may also be organized as an LLC by simply complying with the local LLC organizational requirements (which in states that require two or more LLC members may require the addition of a real or dummy associate to the business). However, an existing partnership or corporate business must be converted to an LLC. In most states the conversion of a business to an LLC may be carried out either under a procedure set forth in the LLC Act or under a nonstatutory or common law procedure. The principal complicating factors in most LLC conversions is the necessity of terminating the existing business entity and transferring its assets to the LLC without incurring a tax liability.

start up or sole proprietor business, organizing LLC for

partnership or corporate business, organizing LLC for

There are usually more reasons to convert a partnership to an LLC than to convert a corporation to an LLC. Partnership-LLC conversions are easier to implement and less burdensome taxwise than corporation-LLC conversions. Consequently, there are many more partnership-LLC conversions than corporation-LLC conversions and most of this section is devoted to partnership-LLC conversions.

LLC conversions, partnerships v. corporations

Partnership-LLC Conversions. The most common reason for converting a general partnership to an LLC is to limit the liability of the partners for the partnership debts. Limited partnerships are usually converted to LLCs for two reasons: (1) to permit one or more of the limited partners to engage in the management of the partnership business without the risk of becoming liable for all of the partnership debts, and (2) to limit the liability of the general partners for partnership debts.

partnership-LLC conversions, reasons for

There are several statutory and nonstatutory methods of converting a partnership to an LLC. Each method is discussed separately below in this section. Regardless of the method of conversion used, however, in partnership-LLC conversions legal or practical difficulties are most likely to arise with respect to the following matters:

partnership-LLC conversions, matters of special concern

(1) **Federal income taxes.** Income in the form of actual or imputed gain may be assessed to one or more of the partners by reason of a partnership-LLC conversion. The federal income aspects of partnership-LLC conversions are discussed below in this section. The best practice, of course, is to employ a method of conversion that will result in the least possible actual or imputed taxable gain for the partners.

(2) **Sales and other transfer taxes.** Sales or use taxes and real property transfer taxes may be assessed by reason of the transfer of partnership assets to an LLC. Because of the great variation in the type and applicability of state and local sales and use taxes, it is impossible to treat the subject here with any degree of accuracy other than to say that methods of transfer that are sanctioned by statute, (i.e., statutory conversions and mergers) are less likely to be subject to sales and use taxes than nonstatutory methods of transfer. The provisions of all applicable sales and use tax statutes and ordinances should be examined to determine their applicability to any proposed asset transfer. If real estate is to be transferred, a similar determination should be made with respect to the applicability of any local real estate transfer fees or taxes.

(3) **Obtaining the consent of lenders and secured creditors.** It may be necessary to obtain the consent of certain lenders or creditors who have a mortgage or other security interest in property that is being transferred from the partnership to the LLC during the conversion. In determining whether such a consent is necessary, much depends on the language of the particular security instrument. Generally, however, the consent of lenders and secured creditors is more likely to be necessary under a nonstatutory method of conversion than under a statutory method.

(4) **Federal and state securities laws.** If the existing business is a limited partnership, replacing limited partnership interests with LLC interests may require compliance with federal and state securities laws. See section 5.16, infra, for a brief discussion of federal and state securities laws.

partnership-LLC conversions, tax aspects, importance of

Federal Income Tax Treatment of Partnership-LLC Conversions. It is important to understand the federal income tax aspects of partnership-LLC conversions in order to ensure that the conversion does not result in the incurrence of an unnecessary tax liability by any of the partners. An understanding of the federal income tax aspects of partnership-LLC conversions is also necessary in order to select the method of conversion that will incur the least possible tax liability for the partners.

partnership-LLC conversion, tax rule under §741

There are three income tax rules that apply to partnership-LLC conversions. The first rule is the rule that gain or loss is attributable to a partner in the event of the sale or exchange of his or her partnership interest. See 26 U.S.C. 741. Under this rule it would appear that the exchange of a partnership interest for an LLC interest by a partner would result in the assessment of gain or loss to the partner.

partnership-LLC conversions, tax rule under §721

The second income tax rule is that gain or loss is not recognized when property is contributed to a partnership in exchange for a partnership interest. See 26 U.S.C. 721. This rule is applicable to any LLC that qualifies as a partnership for federal income tax purposes. Therefore, under Section 721 gain or loss may not be attributed to a partner who contributes property to an LLC that qualifies for partnership tax status. Because a partnership interest constitutes property under Section 721, it would appear that a partner who contributes a partnership interest to a qualified LLC in exchange for an LLC interest should not be assessed gain or loss in connection with the transaction.

partnership-LLC conversions, applicable tax rule

The apparent conflict between Section 741 and Section 721 has been resolved in favor of Section 721. In Revenue Ruling 84-52, 1984-1 C.B. 157, it was held that no gain or loss was incurred by the partners when a general partnership was converted to a limited partnership, provided that the partnership interest of each partner is the same after the conversion as before and provided that the business of the partnership is continued by the new partnership. It is important to note that the partnership business must be continued by the LLC in order to avoid the partnership termination tax rules under 26 U.S.C. 706, 708.

partnership-LLC conversions, general tax rules

While Revenue Ruling 84-52 did not involve a partnership-LLC conversion, the I.R.S. applied this ruling to partnership-LLC conversions in Revenue Ruling 95-37, 1995-IRB 10 where the holding of Revenue Ruling 84-52 was applied to the conversion of an interest in a domestic partnership to an interest in a domestic LLC. This means that a partnership-LLC conversion does not cause a termination under 26 U.S.C. 708 and does not cause the tax year of the partnership to close with respect to the partners. It also means that the resulting LLC need not obtain a new taxpayer identification number. See Revenue Ruling 95-37, supra. Therefore, the general rule is that a general or limited partnership may be converted to an LLC without the incurrence of a tax liability (except as provided in the next paragraph) if (1) the partners' ownership interests in the business are not changed in the conversion and (2) the partnership business is continued by the LLC after the conversion. Because of its importance in partnership-LLC conversions, Revenue Ruling 84-52 is set forth in its entirety in Exhibit 4-D at the end of this chapter.

partnership-LLC conversions, deemed distribution under §752

The third, and most troublesome, income tax rule applicable to partnership-LLC conversions is the rule that attributes what is called Section 752 gain to a partner whose share of the partnership debts is reduced by the conversion. See 26 U.S.C. 752(b), which provides that a decrease in a partner's share of partnership liabilities is considered for tax purposes to be a distribution of money by the partnership to the partner. This deemed cash distribution has the effect of reducing a partner's basis in his or her partnership interest. See 26 U.S.C. 733. If the amount of the deemed distribution exceeds a partner's basis in his or her partnership interest, the partner will incur an immediate tax liability for the amount of the excess. The assessment of Section 752 gain is most likely to occur in situations where a partner has previously taken income tax deductions for his or her share of the partnership debts and at the time of the conversion has a negative capital account balance.

A partner's share of partnership liabilities is measured by determining the extent to which a partner bears the economic risk of loss or the ultimate burden of repaying the partnership liabilities. See Treasury Reg. 1-752-2. Because the liability of an LLC member for LLC debts is much more limited then the liability of a general partner for partnership debts, the possibility of a partner being assessed Section 752 gain in a partnership-LLC conversion is a real one. A method of preventing the incurrence of Section 752 gain in a partnership-LLC conversion is to include in the appropriate document a provision stating that after the conversion the LLC members shall remain liable for the debts of the former partnership that existed on the date of the conversion to the same extent as before the conversion and that the LLC shall not relieve them of liability for any of these debts.

deemed distribution under §752, applicability, how to avoid

Methods of Partnership-LLC Conversions. Perhaps the most important decision to be made in the course of converting a partnership to an LLC is that of determining the method of conversion that best suits the needs of the partners. There are at least five methods of converting a partnership (general or limited) to an LLC. These methods are:

(1) **Statutory Conversion Method.** Under this method the partnership is converted directly to an LLC pursuant to an enabling partnership conversion statute in the local LLC Act. Such a provision typically permits an existing general or limited partnership to convert itself directly to an LLC by simply filing articles of organization together with a prescribed statement with the state filing official. The prescribed statement must usually set forth the name of the former partnership and the results of the partnership voting on the issue of the conversion. Typically, the conversion must be approved by all of the partners unless the partnership agreement provides otherwise. A conversion statute of this type ordinarily vests the partnership property in the LLC by operation of law and obligates the LLC for the partnership liabilities by operation of law. The statutes vary, however, and the specific provisions of the local partnership conversion statute, if one exists, should be checked and complied with. The statutory conversion method is the simplest and easiest method of converting a partnership to an LLC. Under this method it is not necessary to prepare deeds or other documents of conveyance in order to transfer the partnership assets to the LLC because the transfer occurs by operation of law. While no I.R.S. rulings are currently available on the precise issue of whether taxable gain may be attributed to the partners under the statutory conversion method, the directness of the transfer makes it clear that § 721 applies and no gain will be recognized. Unfortunately, the LLC Act in many states does not contain a partnership conversion statute. The existence or nonexistence of a partnership conversion statute in each state is shown in Appendix I in the back of this book under the heading of Limited Liability Company Laws, Conversion Statutes.

partnership-LLC conversion, statutory conversion method

(2) **Merger Method.** Under this method a partnership is merged with an LLC pursuant to merger provisions contained in the local LLC Act. In most states the LLC Act contains cross-species merger provisions that permit the merger of a general or limited partnership with an LLC wherein the LLC is the surviving entity. To use this method of conversion it is usually necessary to organize an LLC, prepare a plan of merger, have the plan approved by the appropriate vote of both partnership and the LLC, and file articles or a statement of merger with the state filing official. The specific requirements vary, however, and the merger provisions of the local LLC Act should be checked and complied with. The LLC cross-species merger statute in each state where one exists is cited in Appendix I, infra, under the heading of Limited Liability Laws, Conversion Statutes.

partnership-LLC conversion, statutory merger method

The merger method of converting a partnership to an LLC is considerably more complex than the statutory conversion method. However, in many states the merger method is the only method of conversion provided for by statute. In Private Letter Ruling 9210019, the I.R.S. ruled that the merger of a Texas limited partnership with a Texas LLC did not result in the recognition of gain or loss by any of the partners because there was no change among the partners in the sharing of liabilities after the merger and the partnership business was not terminated by the merger. See section 7.02, infra, for further reading on mergers and the requirements thereof.

partnership-LLC merger, tax consequences of

In most states the statutory methods of conversion described above are not exclusive, which means that the nonstatutory methods described below may also be used to convert a partnership to an LLC. However, before using a nonstatutory method of conversion the exclusivity of the statutory methods of conversion in the local state should be checked. If the applicable statute states or implies that a partnership may be converted to an LLC only under the statutory method, then a nonstatutory method of conversion should not be used.

partnership-LLC conversion, exclusivity of statutory methods partnership-LLC conversion, nonstatutory direct transfer method

(3) **Direct Transfer Method.** Under this method, which is nonstatutory (i.e., not provided for by statute), an LLC is organized and the partners then transfer their individual partnership interests to the LLC in exchange for LLC interests. The partnership is then liquidated and its assets distributed to the LLC. This method is fairly simple to implement and does not usually subject the partners to an income tax liability. In Private Letter Ruling 9226035, the I.R.S. ruled that the contribution of a partnership interest in exchange for an LLC interest was exempt from gain or loss under 26 U.S.C. 721, except for the section 752 gain rules of 26 U.S.C. 752, which are discussed above in this section.

partnership-LLC conversion,t nonstatutory partner contribution method

(4) **Partner Contribution Method.** Under this nonstatutory method an LLC is organized and the partnership is liquidated with the partnership assets distributed to the partners. The partners then individually contribute their interests in the partnership assets to the LLC in exchange for LLC interests. The usefulness of this method depends on the type and tax status of the assets possessed by the partnership. Usually no taxable gain or loss is recognized in partnership-LLC conversions using this method. The first step is tax-free because, except for cash distributions (or deemed cash distributions under § 752), gain or loss is not recognized in partnership liquidating distributions to partners. See 26 U.S.C. 731. The second step is tax-free under 26 U.S.C. 721 because the partnership property is contributed by the partners to the LLC in exchange for LLC interests, which are treated as partnership interests for tax purposes if the LLC qualifies for partnership tax treatment.

partnership-LLC conversion, nonstatutory partnership contribution method

(5) **Partnership Contribution Method.** Under this nonstatutory method an LLC is organized and the partnership contributes its assets to the LLC in exchange for an LLC interest. The partnership is then liquidated and its LLC interest distributed to the partners as a liquidating distribution. The difficulty with this method in states which require two or more LLC members is that there is only one LLC member (the partnership) for the period, however brief, between the time of the contribution of the partnership assets to the LLC and the time of the liquidating distribution by the partnership of the LLC interest to the partners. Another question under this method is whether the contribution by the partnership of its assets to the LLC qualifies as a tax-free exchange under 26 U.S.C. 721 because at the time of the contribution to the LLC it has only one member (the partnership) and is therefore technically not a partnership and section 721 applies only to contributions to partnerships. If this one-member problem can be solved or if the brief technical defect is overlooked by the I.R.S., this method is also tax-free under 26 U.S.C. 721 and 731, except for any deemed distributions under Section 752 (i.e., Section 752 gain).

corporation-LLC conversion, difficulty of

Converting Corporations to LLCs. Converting a corporation to an LLC is usually more complex legally and more burdensome taxwise than converting a partnership to an LLC. Therefore, there should be a strong reason to convert a corporation to an LLC before doing so. As discussed in section 4.01, supra, the principal advantages of LLCs over C corporations are partnership tax treatment and flexibility of management. The principal advantages of LLCs over S corporations are flexibility of management and the fact that LLCs do not have to meet the qualification requirements of Subchapter S.

corporation-LLC conversion, when advisable

As a practical matter, then, it is usually advisable to convert a C corporation to an LLC only if the corporation cannot qualify under Subchapter S and the management flexibility offered by an LLC is important to the business. It is normally advisable to convert an S corporation to an LLC only if the management flexibility offered by an LLC is extremely important to the business or if there is a real danger that the corporation may lose its Subchapter S status either because of the threatened action of a disgruntled shareholder or for other reasons.

corporation-LLC conversion, tax treatment of

Tax Treatment of Corporation-LLC Conversions. As indicated above, the federal income tax consequences of corporation-LLC conversions are usually unfavorable. Regardless of the method of conversion, a corporation-LLC conversion is treated for tax purposes as a liquidation of the corporation followed by a contribution of its assets to the LLC by the shareholders. While the contribution of corporate assets to an LLC will normally be tax-free under 26 U.S.C. 721, the liquidation of the corporation will usually result in the assessment of taxable gain. In the case of a C corporation, taxable gain may be assessed at both the corporate and the shareholder level, with a resulting double tax.

In the liquidation of a C corporation a corporate level tax may be assessed on the difference between the fair market value of the distributed assets and the corporation's tax basis in the assets. See 26 U.S.C. 336. In addition, because distributions in the complete liquidation of a corporation are treated as payment for the shareholder's stock, the shareholders will incur a taxable gain on the difference between the value of the distributed assets and the tax basis of their stock. See 26 U.S.C. 331. See section 7.03, infra, for further reading on corporate liquidations.

C corporation-LLC conversion, tax consequences of

In the liquidation of an S corporation, there is no corporate level tax but the shareholders will incur a taxable gain in the amount of the difference between the fair market value of the corporate property and the corporation's tax basis in the distributed property. In addition, if the S corporation was formerly a C corporation, unrecognized built-in gain may be recognized to the extent of the S corporation's income for its last taxable year.

S corporation-LLC conversion, tax consequences of

From an income tax standpoint, a corporation-LLC conversion is normally advisable only in the following situations:

corporation-LLC conversion, when advisable taxwise

(1) Where the corporation is an S corporation with little or no appreciated property and no built-in gain.

(2) Where the corporation is an S corporation whose shareholders have a tax basis in their stock that exceeds the fair market value of the distributed corporate property by an amount sufficient to offset any gain resulting from the distribution.

(3) Where the corporation is a C corporation with sufficient net operating losses to offset any taxable gain that may be assessed at the corporate level as a result of the liquidation and either (a) the fair market value of the corporate assets does not exceed the tax basis of the shareholders' stock, or (b) the shareholders have capital loss carry forwards sufficient to offset any taxable gain that may be assessed at the shareholder level.

Methods of Corporation-LLC Conversions. Like partnerships, corporations may be converted to LLCs either under an implementing statute or by a nonstatutory method. In the case of corporations, the implementing statute is normally a merger statute that permits cross-species mergers between corporations and LLCs. It should be noted that at least one state (Georgia) has a corporation-LLC direct conversion statute in its LLC Act. The existence of a recently-enacted statute of this type in the local state should be checked for because direct conversions are always easier to implement than mergers. Corporation-LLC merger statutes are usually found in the state's LLC Act, but may be set forth in the corporation laws in some states.

corporation-LLC conversions, statutory methods of

A statutory corporation-LLC conversion must be a cross-species merger between the corporation and the LLC wherein the LLC is the surviving entity. The plan of merger must be approved by both entities and the appropriate documents must be filed with the state filing official. The provisions of the local corporation-LLC merger statute, if one exists (not all states have them), should be checked and strictly complied with. See sections 6.11 and 7.02, infra, for further reading on mergers.

corporation-LLC conversion, statutory merger method

Nonstatutory corporation-LLC conversions may be implemented in states that do not have a corporation-LLC merger statute and in states that have such a statute and the statutory method is nonexclusive. A nonstatutory corporation-LLC conversion may be implemented using any of the following methods:

corporation-LLC conversion, nonstatutory methods

(1) Organize an LLC and have the corporation liquidate and distribute its assets to the shareholders, who then contribute the assets to the LLC in exchange for LLC interests.

(2) Organize an LLC, have the shareholders contribute their stock to the LLC in exchange for LLC interests, and then liquidate the corporation and distribute its assets to the LLC, which will then be its only shareholder.

(3) Organize an LLC, have the corporation contribute its assets to the LLC in exchange for an LLC interest, and then liquidate the corporation and distribute its asset (the LLC interest) to the shareholders. This method may be difficult in states that require LLCs to have two or more members.

corporation-LLC conversions, tax treatment of

As stated above, the federal income tax consequences of all of the above-described methods of conversion are the same. Under each method the conversion is treated for tax purposes as a liquidation of the corporation and a contribution of its assets to the LLC by the shareholders.

4.06 Terminating a Limited Liability Company

scope and purpose of this section

The purpose of this section is to provide the reader with a general, but brief, account of the dissolution, liquidation and termination procedures for limited liability companies. It should be understood that the dissolution and liquidation provisions of LLC Acts vary from state to state and the provisions of the local LLC Act should be consulted for specific information and requirements.

Most LLC Acts provide that an LLC shall be dissolved upon the occurrence of any of the following events:

dissolution of LLC, events causing

(1) The occurrence of a time, circumstance or event specified in the articles of organization or operating agreement. If the articles of organization or operating agreement of an LLC specify a limited period of existence for the LLC or provide that the LLC shall cease to exist upon the happening of an event (such as the completion of a project), the LLC is dissolved by operation of law upon the occurrence of the specified time or event.

(2) The unanimous written consent of all LLC members. Like any other business entity, an LLC may always be dissolved and terminated with the consent of all of its members. In a few states the voting or consent requirement for dissolution is a majority in interest of the LLC members. In many states the membership voting or consent requirements for dissolution may be less than 100% if so specified in the articles of organization or operating agreement.

(3) The death, disassociation, dissolution or bankruptcy of a member, unless the remaining members agree to continue the business. Many LLC Acts provide that the agreement to continue the business must be unanimous and made within 90 days after the occurrence of the terminating event, unless the articles of organization or operating agreement provide otherwise. It is common for operating agreements to contain an advance agreement by the members to continue the LLC business upon the death, disassociation, dissolution or bankruptcy of a member.

(4) The entry of a decree of judicial dissolution by a court of competent jurisdiction. This form of dissolution is involuntary and is most often used when disputes arise among the LLC members over the advisability of continuing the LLC business.

dissolution of LLC, voluntary vs. involuntary

It should be understood that there are two forms of dissolution: voluntary and involuntary. Of the four events of dissolution described above, the first three result in a voluntary dissolution and the fourth results in an involuntary dissolution. Involuntary dissolutions are judicial in nature and are carried out under the supervision of a court. In most states an involuntary dissolution proceeding may be filed by a creditor, the LLC, or the State Attorney General.

statement of intent to dissolve, filing of

Many LLC Acts require the filing of a statement of intent to dissolve the LLC with the state filing official as soon as possible after the occurrence of an event causing a voluntary dissolution. After the filing of a statement of intent to dissolve, an LLC must terminate the carrying on of its business except for such activities as may be necessary for the winding up of its business. However, the LLC remains in existence until articles of dissolution are filed with the state filing official.

winding up LLC affairs, when and by whom

After the filing of a statement of intent to dissolve, or after the occurrence of an event of dissolution if the filing of such a statement is not required under the local LLC Act, the affairs of the LLC must be wound up and its assets distributed to the persons entitled thereto under the LLC Act. In most states the affairs of an LLC may be wound up by the LLC members or managers who have the authority under the operating agreement to manage the LLC, except for members or managers who have engaged in wrongful conduct.

LLC liquidation, distribution priorities

When the affairs of an LLC have been wound up and its business terminated, the LLC's assets must be distributed in the manner and to the persons designated in the local LLC Act. Typically, the assets of a dissolved LLC must be distributed in accordance with the following liquidation priorities:

(1) First, to the creditors of the LLC, including creditors who are LLC members.
(2) Second, to members and former members with respect to their rights to profits.
(3) Third, to members with respect to their rights to capital.

The LLC liquidation distribution priorities vary among the states and the priorities under the local LLC Act should be checked in this regard. In many states, for example, the second and third priorities listed above are reversed.

LLC, termination of existence

When all of the debts of the LLC have been paid or provided for and all of the remaining assets distributed to its members, articles of dissolution must normally be filed with the state filing official. Typically, an LLC's articles of organization are cancelled by the state filling official after the filing of its articles of dissolution. The legal existence of an LLC is terminated by the filing of articles of dissolution. In some states the filing of articles of dissolution with the state filing official is optional, but if articles of dissolution are not filed, unpaid claims against the LLC are not satisfied by the dissolution and creditors are not prevented from later seeking to enforce these claims against the LLC.

ARTICLES OF ORGANIZATION

OF ______(name of LLC)______

The undersigned organizer adopts the following Articles of Organization for the limited liability company named below pursuant to section ____ of the Limited Liability Company Act of the state of ____________ .

ARTICLE 1

Name

1.01. The name of the limited liability company is ______________________ .

ARTICLE 2

Registered Office and Agent

2.01. **Registered Office.** The street address of the initial registered office of the limited liability company is ____________________ .

2.02. **Registered Agent.** The name of the initial registered agent of the limited liability company at the above office is ____________________ .

ARTICLE 3

Period of Existence

3.01. The latest date on which the limited liability company shall be dissolved is __________________ .

ARTICLE 4

Business Purposes

4.01. The limited liability company is organized for the purpose of engaging in the business of ____(describe principal business)____ and for the purpose of transacting any lawful business which may be conducted by a limited liability company.

ARTICLE 5

Management

5.01. **Management.** The property, business and affairs of the limited liability company shall be managed by __(indicate whether members or managers)__ .

5.02. **Names and Addresses.** The names and business addresses of the initial __(indicate whether members or managers)__ of the limited liability company are:

____________________	____________________
name	business address
____________________	____________________
name	business address

IN WITNESS WHEREOF, the organizer, by the signature below, affirms under penalty of perjury the truth of the matters set in these articles of organization on this ____ day of ____________ , 19 ____ .

____

organizer

(For Member-Managed LLC)

OPERATING AGREEMENT

OF

(name of LLC)

THIS OPERATING AGREEMENT is dated and adopted this ____ day of ____________, 19 ____ by the persons whose names are subscribed below, who constitute the members of ____(name of LLC)____, a ____(state)____ Limited Liability Company.

The members agree as follows:

ARTICLE 1

Organization of Company

1.01. **Name.** The name of the limited liability company that is to be formed and operated pursuant to this Operating Agreement is ____(name of LLC)____ (hereinafter "the Company"), which is a limited liability company organized under the Limited Liability Company Act of the State of ____________.

1.02. **Registered Agent and Office.** The Company's registered agent in ____(state)____ is ____(name of agent)____, whose business address is ____(address)____. The Company may designate other registered agents or offices at any time in this state or, if necessary, in other states.

1.03. **Principal Place of Business.** The Company's principal place of business is located at ____(address)____. The Company may establish additional offices at any time.

104. **Term.** The term of existence of the Company shall begin with the filing or acceptance of its articles of organization and shall continue until the dissolution and termination of the Company as provided in Article 8 of this Operating Agreement.

105. **Purpose.** The purpose of the Company is to engage in the business of ____(describe principal business)____ and to engage in any lawful business or activity for which a limited liability company may be organized under the ____(state)____ Limited Liability Company Act.

ARTICLE 2

Membership and Capital

2.01. **Initial Members.** The names and addresses of the initial members of the Company are:

Name	Address

2.02. **New or Substituted Members.** New members shall be admitted to the Company only upon the written consent of ____ percent of the existing members. An assignee of a member's ownership interest in the Company shall be admitted to the Company as a substituted member only upon the written consent of ____ percent of the members. A new or substituted member, as a condition of being admitted to membership in the Company, shall be fully bound by the terms and provisions of this Operating Agreement and all amendments thereto, whether or not the new or substituted member actually signs this agreement or an addendum thereto.

2.03. **Ownership Interests.** The ownership interest of each member of the Company shall be expressed in terms of a percentage. The total ownership interests of all members shall always equal 100 percent. The ownership interests of new members shall be determined prior to admission by the existing members. The ownership interests of the initial members are set forth in section 2.04 of this Operating Agreement.

2.04. Capital Contributions. A member's capital contributions to the Company may consist of cash, property, services rendered, or a written promise to contribute cash, property or services in the future. The value of all capital contributions shall be determined by the members. A member shall not be entitled to withdraw a capital contribution without the consent of all other members. A member shall not be entitled to interest on or with respect to any capital contribution. Additional capital contributions may be made by a member only with the consent of all other members. The capital contributions required of new members shall be determined by the existing members. The initial capital contributions and the initial ownership interests of the initial members of the Company are set forth below:

Name	Type and Value of Capital Contribution	Ownership Interest

2.05. Capital Accounts. The Company shall maintain a capital account for each member. A member's capital account shall consist of the total amount of the member's capital contributions to the Company, plus any net income or gain allocated to the member by the Company, plus the amount of any Company liability assumed or secured by the member, less the value of any money or property distributed to the member by the Company, less any net losses allocated to the member by the Company, less the amount of any liabilities of the member assumed or secured by the Company.

2.06. Resignation of Member. A member may resign, retire or withdraw from the Company at any time by giving ____ days advance written notice thereof to the remaining members. The right of a resigning, retiring or withdrawing member to compensation for the member's ownership interest in the Company shall be governed by the provisions of Article 6 of this Operating Agreement. The resignation, retirement or withdrawal of a member shall terminate the member's membership and voting rights in the Company as of the date of the resignation, retirement or withdrawal.

ARTICLE 3

Management

3.01. Management by Members. The Company shall be managed by the members. The Company shall not have managers within the meaning of the ___(state)___ Limited Liability Company Act. No member shall be entitled to compensation for managing the Company unless otherwise approved in advance by the members.

3.02. Authority of Members. Each member may exercise all powers of the LLC and perform any lawful act or function deemed necessary or appropriate in the ordinary course of the Company business, except as otherwise provided in the Operating Agreement. However, a member may not perform any of the following acts or functions without the written consent of all members:

(1) Dissolve or terminate the Company.
(2) Sell or transfer all or a significant part of the Company assets.
(3) Merge or consolidate the Company with another entity.
(4) Incur a Company liability in excess of $ _________.
(5) Any other act or function which requires the approval or consent of all of the other members by the terms of this Operating Agreement or by the provisions of the ___(state)___ Limited Liability Company Act.

3.03. Voting Requirements. Except as otherwise provided in this Operating Agreement or in the ___(state)___ Limited Liability Company Act, all matters requiring the vote, consent or approval of the members shall require the vote, consent or approval of a majority of the members.

3.04. Membership Meetings. The members may hold regular or special meetings either in the State of ____________ or elsewhere. Regular meetings of the members may be held without notice at such time and place as may be determined by the members. A special meeting of the members may be called by any member by giving ____ days prior written notice of the time, place and purpose of the meeting to the other members. Notice shall be as provided in section 9.03 of this Operating Agreement. Notice of any meeting may be waived by any member.

3.05. Action Without Meeting. Action may be taken by the members without meeting if all members sign a written consent to the action taken or in any other manner provided for in the "Action Without Meeting" provisions of the ___(state)___ Limited Liability Company Act.

3.06. Telephonic Meetings. Members may participate in a meeting by means of conference telephone or other video or audio communications equipment whereby all persons participating in the meeting can simultaneously hear each other. Participation in such a meeting by a member shall constitute the presence of the member at the meeting.

3.07. **Officers.** The required officers of the Company shall be a President and a Secretary. The members may also elect a Treasurer and such other officers as may be deemed necessary by the members. The same person may simultaneously hold any number of offices. Each officer shall be elected by majority vote of the members and shall hold office until a qualified successor has been elected. Any officer may be removed from office by majority vote of the members at a special meeting called for that purpose. The duties of the officers shall be determined by the members. The compensation of the officers, if any, shall be fixed by the members.

ARTICLE 4

Allocations and Distributions

4.01. **Allocation of Income and Loss.** The net income or losses of the Company shall be allocated to the members at the end of each accounting period in proportion to their respective ownership interests in the Company. The gains, losses, deductions and other income tax items of the Company shall be allocated to the members in the same manner, except as otherwise provided in this Article.

4.02. **Partnership Tax Provision.** The members expect and intend that the Company shall elect to be classified as a partnership for federal income tax purposes. The members agree individually that they will do nothing with respect to their individual income tax returns that is inconsistent with or that will otherwise jeopardize the Company's partnership tax status.

4.03. **Special Tax Provision.** The income, gain, loss or deduction with respect to an asset contributed to the capital of the Company by a member shall, in accordance with Section 704(c) of the Internal Revenue Code and solely for tax purposes, be allocated between the members so as to take into account any variation between the adjusted income tax basis of the property to the Company and its actual value when contributed.

4.04. **Allocations Upon Transfer.** If, during an accounting period, a member transfers the member's rights to Company profits, losses and other income tax items to another person, the profits, losses and other tax items that would otherwise have been allocated to the transferring member for the accounting period shall be allocated between the transferor and the transferee pursuant to any method chosen by the member that is permitted under Section 706 of the Internal Revenue Code.

4.05. **Distributions.** All distributions by the Company shall be made to the members in proportion to their respective ownership interests as shown in the books and records of the Company. Distributions shall be made in the amount and at such times as are approved by the members. All distributions shall be by cash or Company check unless the members approve a different form of distribution.

4.06. **Restriction on Distribution.** The Company shall not make a distribution to the members unless immediately after giving effect to the distribution, all liabilities of the Company, other than liabilities to the members on account of their interest in the Company and liabilities as to which recourse of creditors is limited to specified property of the Company, do not exceed the fair value of the Company assets, provided that the fair value of any property that is subject to a liability as to which recourse of creditors is so limited shall be included in the Company assets only to the extent that the fair value of the property exceeds such liability.

ARTICLE 5

Accounting, Books and Records

5.01. **Accounting Practices and Tax Year.** The Company shall keep its books and records and prepare its financial statements in accordance with generally accepted accounting principles and shall prepare its income tax returns using such methods of accounting. The Company tax year shall be the calendar year.

5.02. **Location and Inspection.** Proper and complete books of account and records of the business of the Company shall be kept at the Company's principal office and at such other places as may be designated by the members. Notice shall be given to each member of any changes in the location of the Company books and records. The Company books and records shall be open to inspection, audit and copying by any member, or the designated representative of a member, upon reasonable notice at any time during business hours for any purpose reasonably related to the member's interest in the Company. Any information so obtained or copied shall be kept and maintained in strict confidence except as otherwise required by law.

5.03. **Reliance on Books and Records.** A member shall be fully protected in relying in good faith upon the records and books of account of the Company and upon such information, opinions, reports or statements presented to the member, by the Company or any of its other members, officers, or employees, or by any other person selected by the Company, as to matters which the member reasonably believes are within such other person's field of expertise, including information, opinions, reports or statements as to the value and amount of the assets, liabilities, profits or losses of the Company or any other facts pertinent to the existence and amount of assets from which distributions to members might properly be paid.

5.04. Reports and Tax Returns. A financial statement for the Company shall be made and reported on as of the end of each fiscal year. A copy of the annual financial statement and report shall be transmitted to the members within ninety days after the end of each fiscal year. The Company shall, within ninety days after the end of each fiscal year, file a federal income tax informational return and transmit to each member a schedule showing the member's distributive share of the Company's income, losses, deductions, credits, and other information necessary to enable the members to timely file their federal income tax returns. The Company shall also file, and provide information to the members regarding, all applicable state and local income tax returns. The Company's "Tax Matter Partner" shall be __(name of member)__, who shall have the authority to exercise the functions provided in Sections 6221-6223 of the Internal Revenue Code and the authority to delegate those functions to another person.

ARTICLE 6

Deceased or Disassociated Members

6.01. Disassociation of a Member. The withdrawal, resignation, retirement, expulsion, bankruptcy or dissolution of a member shall terminate the membership of the member in the Company. Such a member shall constitute a "disassociated member."

6.02. Compensation of Deceased or Disassociated Members.

(1) If the death or disassociation of a member causes the dissolution and termination of the Company, a deceased or disassociated member, or the estate or legal representative thereof, shall be entitled to participate in the winding up and liquidation of the Company to the same extent as a member.

(2) If the death or disassociation of a member does not cause the dissolution and termination of the Company, a deceased or disassociated member, or the estate or legal representative thereof, shall be entitled to compensation in an amount equal to the capital account of the deceased or disassociated member as shown on the Company books, increased or decreased, as the case may be by the member's share of Company profits or losses for the portion of the Company's current fiscal year ending on the date of the member's death or disassociation, and decreased by withdrawals made by the member during that fiscal year and decreased by any damages sustained by the Company as a result of any expulsion or wrongful disassociation by the disassociated member. No allowance shall be made for goodwill or other intangible assets except as those assets have been reflected in the Company books immediately prior to the death or disassociation of the member. The amount payable under this section shall be paid by the Company to the deceased or disassociated member, or to the estate or legal representative thereof, in not more than ____ semiannual installments with interest at ____ % per annum beginning not more than ____ months after the date of the death or dissociation.

ARTICLE 7

Indemnification and Limitation of Liability

7.01. Indemnification. A member shall be indemnified for all damages and expenses, including attorneys' fees, and held harmless by the Company from any liability resulting from any act or omission committed by the member on behalf of the Company to the fullest extent permitted under the Limited Liability Company Act and other laws of the state of ____________.

7.02. Exculpation. A member shall not be liable to the Company or to any other member for any act, omission or error committed by the member while acting on behalf of the Company in accordance with the standards of conduct, if any, established in the __(state)__ Limited Liability Company Act.

7.03. Limitation of Liability. No member shall be personally liable for any debt, liability or obligation of the Company solely by reason of being a member of the Company.

ARTICLE 8

Dissolution and Termination

8.01. Dissolution. The Company shall be dissolved upon the first to occur of the following events:

(1) The expiration of the term or period of existence, if any, set forth in its Articles of Organization.
(2) The unanimous written consent of the members to dissolve the Company.
(3) The death, retirement, resignation, withdrawal, expulsion, bankruptcy or dissolution of a member, unless there are at least two remaining members and all of the remaining members consent to continue the Company and its business within ____ days after the occurrence of the event causing the dissolution.
(4) The entry of a decree of judicial dissolution as provided in the __(state)__ Limited Liability Company Act.

8.02. **Winding Up.** The members shall have the power and authority necessary to marshall the Company assets, pay the Company creditors, distribute the Company assets, and otherwise wind up the business and affairs of the Company upon dissolution. The members shall also have the authority to continue to conduct the business and affairs of the Company after dissolution to the extent reasonably necessary to effect an orderly and profitable winding up of the Company's business and affairs.

8.03. **Liquidation and Termination.** After the dissolution of the Company and the winding up of its business and affairs, the Company shall be liquidated by the members, whereupon the assets of the Company shall be distributed in accordance with the distribution priorities set forth in the ________(state)________ Limited Liability Company Act. Immediately following the distribution of the Company's assets, the members shall perform the acts necessary to terminate the existence of the Company.

ARTICLE 9

Miscellaneous

9.01. **Amendment.** This Operating Agreement, or any provision thereof, may be amended at any time by a majority vote of the members at a special meeting duly called for that purpose, except that any provision of this Operating Agreement that provides for a membership vote, approval or consent of greater than a majority may be amended only by a membership vote that is equal to that specified in the provision sought to be amended.

9.02. **Governing Law.** This Operating Agreement shall be governed by the Limited Liability Company Act and other laws of the state of ______________, as such Act and laws may from time to time be amended.

9.03. **Notices.** Any notice given by a member to another member or to the Company, or given by the Company to a member, shall be in writing and shall be deemed effectively given upon personal delivery or upon deposit in the U.S. Mail by registered or certified mail, return receipt requested, or upon confirmed facsimile transmission for delivery to the company or to such member, at the address or facsimile number shown in the records of the Company.

9.04. **Definition.** The term "members" as it appears in this Operating Agreement includes those persons who are members of the Company under the terms of this Operating Agreement at the time in question.

9.05. **Ratification of Organizer.** The acts and deeds of the organizer or organizers performed in the course of organizing the Company are hereby approved and ratified by the members.

9.06. **Entire Agreement.** This Operating Agreement and the amendments thereto, if any, constitute the entire agreement among the parties with respect to the Company and the operation of its business.

9.07. **Binding Effect.** This Operating Agreement and the amendments thereto, if any, shall be binding on, and shall inure to the benefit of, the Company, the members, and their respective transferees, successors, assigns and legal representatives.

IN WITNESS WHEREOF, the members have subscribed their names to this Operating Agreement on or as of the day and year first above written.

______________________________ ______________________________

Member Member

(For Manager-Managed LLC)

OPERATING AGREEMENT

OF

(name of LLC)

THIS OPERATING AGREEMENT is dated and adopted this ____ day of ____________, 19 ____ by the persons whose names are subscribed below, who constitute the Members of ___(name of LLC)___, a ___(state)___ Limited Liability Company.

The Members agree as follows:

ARTICLE 1

Organization of Company

1.01. **Name.** The name of the limited liability company that is to be formed and operated pursuant to this Agreement is ___(name of LLC)___, which is a limited liability company organized under the Act.

1.02. **Registered Agent and Office.** The Company's registered agent in ___(state)___ is ___(name of agent)___, whose business address is ______(address)______. The Company may designate other registered agents or offices at any time in this state or, if necessary, in other states.

1.03. **Principal Place of Business.** The Company's principal place of business is located at ______(address)______. The Company may establish additional offices at any time.

1.04. **Term.** The term of existence of the Company shall begin with the filing or acceptance of its articles of organization and shall continue until the dissolution and termination of the Company as provided in Article 10 of this Agreement.

1.05. **Purpose.** The purpose of the Company is to engage in the___(describe principal business)___ business and to engage in any other lawful business for which a limited liability company may be organized under the Act

ARTICLE 2

Definitions

2.01. **Definitions.** As used in this Agreement, the following terms shall have the meanings set forth below:

(1) "Act" shall mean the Limited Liability Company Act of the State of ____________, as amended from time to time.
(2) "Agreement" means this Operating Agreement, as amended from time to time.
(3) "Capital Account" means, with respect to any Member, the Member's capital contribution to the Company as adjusted pursuant to Article 3 of this Agreement.
(4) "Capital Contribution" means, with respect to any Member, the amount of money and the initial gross asset value of any property other than money contributed to the Company with respect to the Membership Interest held by such Member pursuant to the terms of this Agreement.
(5) "Code" means the Internal Revenue Code of 1986 and all Regulations promulgated thereunder, as amended from time to time, and any successor to the Code.
(6) "Company" means the limited liability company formed or operated pursuant to this Agreement and named in section 1.01 of this Agreement, as it may from time to time be constituted.
(7) "Managers" means the persons named in section 6.01 of this Agreement and any successor or additional Managers elected in accordance with section 6.02 of this Agreement, in their capacities as Managers of the Company.
(8) "Member" means any person whose name is set forth in section 3.01 of this Agreement or who becomes a Member pursuant to section 3.02 of this Agreement. "Members" means all such persons. All references in this Agreement to a majority in interest of the Members shall mean Members holding more than 50 percent of the total Membership Interests then held by Members.
(9) "Membership Interest" means a Member's ownership interest in the Company and such Member's right to participate in the management of the business and affairs of the Company, including, without limitation, the right to vote on, consent to, or otherwise participate in any decision or action of the Members pursuant to this Agreement or the Act. Unless otherwise agreed to in a writing signed by all of the Members and attached to this Agreement, the Members' respective percentage Membership Interests shall be equal to the proportionate values of the capital contributions made by each Member, to the extent that such contributions have been received by the Company and not returned.

(10) "Person" means any individual, partnership, corporation, limited liability company, trust or other lawful entity.

(11) "Transferee" means the owner of an interest in the Company who is not a member, including a person who has acquired an interest in the Company as the assignee of a Member pursuant to section 8.02 of the Agreement or as the successor in interest, personal representative or guardian upon the death, dissolution, bankruptcy or legal incapacity of a Member pursuant to Article 9 of this Agreement.

ARTICLE 3

Members, Interests, and Capital

3.01. Names and Addresses. The names and addresses of the initial Members are as follows:

Name	Address

3.02. Liability of Members. A Member shall not be liable for the debts, liabilities, contracts or other obligations of the Company. Except as otherwise provided by law, a Member shall be liable to the Company only to make any agreed capital contribution and shall not be required to lend or advance money to the Company or make additional capital contributions to the Company.

3.03. Capital Contributions and Membership Interests. Each initial Member shall contribute to the capital of the Company on or before the effective date of this Agreement money or property of the amount or value shown below in this section. Membership interests in the Company shall be expressed in terms of a percentage and shall be in proportion to capital contributions. The initial Membership Interest of each Member in the Company shall be as shown below in this section. The Membership Interests shall be adjusted from time to time to take into account contributions to and distributions by the Company and sales or transfers of Membership Interests. No Member shall be entitled to interest on any capital contribution.

Name	Capital Contribution	Membership Interest

3.04. Capital Accounts. A capital account shall be maintained for each Member. The capital account shall reflect the capital interest of each Member and shall be maintained in accordance with the requirements of the Code. The capital contributions paid to the Company (which for this purpose shall include "deemed" contributions of property to the Company under Code §708) shall be credited to each Member's capital account. The capital account of each Member shall be increased by (1) the amount of money contributed by the Member to the Company, (2) the fair market value of property contributed by the Member to the Company (less the amount of any liabilities secured by such contributed property that the Company is considered to assume or take subject to), and (3) allocations to the Member of Company income and gain including income and gain exempt from tax and income and gain as computed for book purposes. The capital account of each Member shall be decreased by (1) the amount of money distributed to the Member by the Company, (2) the fair market value of property distributed to the Member by the Company (less the amount of any liabilities secured by such distributed property that the Member is considered to assume or take subject to), (3) allocations to the Member of expenditures of the Company described in Code §705(a)(2)(B), and (4) allocations to the Member of Company loss and deduction, including loss and deduction computed for book purposes.

3.05. Distributions of Capital. Except as otherwise provided in this Agreement, a Member may not withdraw a Capital Contribution without the consent of the Managers. Under circumstances requiring a capital distribution to a Member, the Member shall have no right to receive property other than cash except as otherwise provided in this Agreement.

3.06. Loans to Company. If approved by the Managers, Members may make loans or advances to the Company. However, the amount of any such loan or advance shall not be treated as an increase in, or contribution to, the capital account of the lending or advancing Member and shall not entitle the lending or advancing Member to an increase in the Member's share of Company distributions.

ARTICLE 4

Allocations and Distributions

4.01. Allocation of Income and Loss. The net income or losses of the Company shall be allocated among the Members at the end of each accounting period in proportion to their respective Membership Interests. The gains, losses, deductions and other income tax items of the Company shall be allocated to the Members in the same manner, except as otherwise provided in this Article.

4.02. Partnership Tax Provision. The Members expect and intend that the Company shall elect to be classified as a partnership for federal income tax purposes. The Members agree individually that they will do nothing with respect to their individual income tax returns that is inconsistent with or that will otherwise jeopardize the Company's partnership tax status.

4.03. Special Tax Provision. The income, gain, loss or deduction with respect to an asset contributed to the capital of the Company by a Member shall, in accordance with Section 704(c) of the Code and solely for tax purposes, be allocated among the Members so as to take into account any variation between the adjusted income tax basis of the property to the Company and its actual value when contributed.

4.04. Allocations Upon Transfer. If, during an accounting period, a Member transfers the Member's rights to Company profits, losses and other income tax items to another person, the profits, losses and other tax items that would otherwise have been allocated to the transferring Member for the accounting period shall be allocated between the transferor and the transferee pursuant to any method chosen by the Member that is permitted under Section 706 of the Code.

4.05. Distributions. All distributions by the Company shall be made to the Members in proportion to their respective Membership Interests as shown in the books and records of the Company. Distributions shall be made in the amount and at such times as are approved by the Managers. All distributions shall be by cash or Company check unless the Managers approve a different form of distribution. Distributions of capital contributions shall be subject to section 3.05 of this Agreement.

4.06. Restriction on Distribution. The Company shall not make a distribution to the Members unless immediately after giving effect to the distribution, all liabilities of the Company, other than liabilities to the Members on account of their Membership Interests and liabilities as to which recourse of creditors is limited to specified property of the Company, do not exceed the fair value of the Company assets, provided that the fair value of any property that is subject to a liability as to which recourse of creditors is so limited shall be included in the Company assets only to the extent that the fair value of the property exceeds such liability.

ARTICLE 5

Books, Records and Accounting

5.01. Accounting Practices and Tax Year. The Company shall keep its books and records and prepare its financial statements in accordance with generally accepted accounting principles and shall prepare its income tax returns using such methods of accounting. The tax year of the Company shall be the calendar year unless the Managers, with the consent of the Members, select another tax year.

5.02. Location and Inspection. Proper and complete books of account and records of the business of the Company shall be kept at the Company's principal office and at such other places as may be designated by the Managers. Notice shall be given to each Member of any changes in the location of the Company books and records. The Company books and records shall be open to inspection, audit and copying by any Member, or the designated representative of a Member, upon reasonable notice at any time during business hours for any purpose reasonably related to the Member's interest in the Company. Any information so obtained or copied shall be kept and maintained in strict confidence except as otherwise required by law.

5.03. Reliance on Books and Records. A Member shall be fully protected in relying in good faith upon the records and books of account of the Company and upon such information, opinions, reports or statements presented to the Member by the Company or any of its other Members, Managers, officers, or employees, or by any other person selected by the Company, as to matters which the Member reasonably believes are within such other person's field of expertise, including information, opinions, reports or statements as to the value and amount of the assets, liabilities, profits or losses of the Company or any other facts pertinent to the existence and amount of assets from which distributions to Members might properly be paid.

5.04. Reports and Tax Returns. A financial statement for the Company shall be made and reported on as of the end of each fiscal year. A copy of the annual financial statement and report shall be transmitted to the Members within ninety days after the end of each fiscal year. The Company shall, within ninety days after the end of each fiscal year, file a federal income tax informational return and transmit to each Member a schedule showing the Member's distributive share of the Company's income, losses, deductions, credits, and other information necessary to enable the Members to timely file their federal income tax returns. The Company shall also file, and provide information to the Members regarding, all applicable state and local income tax returns.

5.05. Tax Matter Partner. The "Tax Matter Partner" of the Company for purposes of Sections 6221-6223 of the Code shall be _______(name)_______, or such other person as may be designated by the Managers. The "Tax Matter Partner" shall have the authority to exercise all functions described in Sections 6221-6223 of the Code.

ARTICLE 6

Management

6.01. Managers. The Company shall be managed by one or more Managers. The initial Managers of the Company shall be ____________(name(s) of manager(s))____________.

6.02. Number, Election and Removal of Managers. The Company shall initially have ___(number)___ Managers. All managers after the initial Managers shall be elected by the Members at a regular or special meeting of the Members in the manner set forth in Article 7 of this Agreement. The first such election shall be held during the second calendar year after the effective date of this Agreement. Each Manager shall be elected for a term of ____ years. The number of Managers may be changed by the Members at a special meeting of the Members called for that purpose. A Manager may be removed by the Members at a special meeting of the Members called for that purpose.

6.03. Powers and Authority of Managers. Except as otherwise provided in this Agreement or in the Act, the managers shall have the exclusive authority to manage the Company and its business, and to make all decisions regarding the business of the Company, or to delegate these functions to employees or agents of the Company. The Managers shall have the right, power and authority to do, on behalf of and in the name of the Company, all functions, acts and things as are, in the judgment of the Managers, reasonably necessary to carry on the business and purposes of the Company, including the appointment of such officers of the Company as the Managers deem appropriate. The Managers shall have all of the rights and powers which may be granted to Managers under the Act. Any person dealing with the Company may rely on the authority of the Managers to perform any act or function on behalf of the Company that is authorized by this Agreement or by the Act.

6.04. Decisions of Managers. When there is more than one Manager, any Manager may take any action permitted to be taken by the Managers, unless the approval of more than one Manager is required by this Agreement, by the Act, or by other applicable law. Differences between the Managers as to any matter within the authority of the Managers shall be decided by majority vote of the Managers, or, if this is not feasible, by the Members.

6.05. Restrictions on Authority of Managers. The Managers shall not, without the written consent of all Members, have the authority to:

(1) perform any act or function in contravention of this Agreement;
(2) perform any act or function that would make it impossible to carry on the business of the Company, except as otherwise provided in this Agreement;
(3) cause the Company to possess property for other than a Company purpose;
(4) sell or transfer all or a significant part of the Company assets;
(5) dissolve or terminate the Company;
(6) merge or consolidate the Company with another entity; or
(7) incur a Company liability in excess of $________.

6.06. Indemnification of Managers.

(1) The Company shall indemnify, hold harmless, and pay all judgments and claims against a Manager that are related to any liability or damage incurred by reason of any act performed or omitted to be performed by the Manager in connection with the business of the Company, including attorneys' fees incurred by the Manager in connection with the defense of any action based on any such act or omission.
(2) In the event of any action by a Member against a Manager, the Company shall indemnify, hold harmless, and pay all expenses of the Manager, including attorneys' fees, incurred in the defense of such action, if the Manager is successful in the action.
(3) The Company shall indemnify, hold harmless, and pay all expenses, costs or liabilities of a Manager who for the benefit of the Company makes a deposit, acquires an option, or makes any other similar payment or assumes any obligation in connection with any property proposed to be acquired by the Company and who suffers any financial loss as the result of such action.
(4) Notwithstanding the above provisions in this section, no Manager shall be indemnified from any liability for acts or omissions that constitute willful or reckless misconduct.

6.07. Ratification of Actions. All disclosed actions taken by the Managers on behalf of the Company prior to the effective date of this Agreement are hereby ratified and confirmed by the Members.

ARTICLE 7

Membership Meetings and Voting Rights

7.01. Annual Meetings. Annual meetings of the Members shall be held on the ____ day of ___(month)___ each year beginning in the calendar year following the effective date of this Agreement. Written notice of the place, date and time of such meetings shall be delivered by the Managers to all Members who have not waived such notice, either by mail or in person, not less than ____ days nor more than ____ days prior to the meeting. Notice of any annual meeting may be waived by any Member.

7.02. Special Meetings. A special meeting of the Members may be called by the Managers or by Members holding 10 percent or more of the Membership Interests in the Company. Written notice stating the place, date and time of the meeting and the purpose for which the meeting is called shall be delivered to the Managers and to each Member who has not waived such notice, either by mail or in person, not less than ____ days nor more than ____ days prior to the meeting. All special meetings of the Members shall be held at the Company's principal place of business unless a different location is approved by the Managers. Notice of any special meeting may be waived by any Member.

7.03. Voting Requirements. Members may vote in person or by proxy at any annual or special meeting. Except as otherwise provided in this Agreement or in the Act, all matters wherein the vote, consent or approval of the Members is required shall require the vote, consent or approval of a majority in interest of Members to be effective. In such voting, the voting powers of the Members shall be in proportion to their Membership Interests in the Company.

7.04. Action Without Meeting. Action may be taken by the Members without meeting if each Member signs a written consent to the action taken, or in any other manner set forth in the "Action Without Meeting" provisions of the Act.

7.05. Telephonic Meetings. Members may participate in a meeting by means of conference telephone or other video or audio communications equipment whereby all persons participating in the meeting can simultaneously hear each other. Participation in such a meeting by a Member shall constitute the presence of the Member at the meeting.

ARTICLE 8

Transfers of Interests

8.01. General Restriction. Neither a Member nor a Transferee may transfer, whether voluntarily or involuntarily, any portion of the person's Membership or other Interest except as otherwise provided in this Article. For purposes of this Article, a "transfer" includes, but is not limited to, any sale, assignment, gift, devise or other transfer upon death, exchange, hypothecation, collateral assignment or subjection to a security interest.

8.02. Assignment of Membership Interest Without Substitution. Subject to compliance with the conditions of section 8.05 of this Article, a Member shall have the right to transfer all or part of such Member's Membership Interest by a written instrument of assignment, the terms of which are not in contravention of this Agreement. The assigning Member shall deliver to the Managers a written instrument of assignment satisfactory to the Managers, duly executed by the assigning Member or such Member's personal representative or authorized agent. The assignment shall be accompanied by such assurances of genuineness and effectiveness and by such consents or authorizations of governmental or other authorities as may be reasonably required by the Managers. Unless and until admitted as a substitute or new Member in accordance with this Agreement, an assignee shall be deemed a Transferee, who shall be entitled to receive distributions from the Company, and be allocated profits and losses of the Company, attributable to the Membership Interest acquired by reason of such assignment from and after the effective date of the assignment of such Interest, as specified in section 8.07 of this Article. All other Company rights attributable to such transferred Interest, including, the right to inspect Company books and to vote on Company matters, shall terminate with respect to such Membership Interest until or unless the Transferee becomes a substituted or new Member; provided, however, that the Managers and the Company shall be entitled to treat the assignor of such Membership Interest as the owner thereof in all respects and shall incur no liability for distributions made in good faith to such assignor, until such time as both the beneficiary of such assignment has been recognized by the Company as a assignee in accordance with section 8.07 of this Article and the effective date of the assignment has passed.

8.03. Admission of Substituted Members. A Transferee may become a substituted or additional Member in the Company if, in addition to the requirements of section 8.05 of this Article, (1) the Transferee obtains the written consent of the Managers and of Members holding a majority of the Membership Interests, which consent may be withheld for any reason as a matter of discretion; and (2) the parties named in such assignment have executed and acknowledged such other instruments as the Managers may deem necessary or desirable to effect such admission. A Transferee accepted as a substitute or new Member shall have all of the rights and obligations of its predecessor in interest in the Company, to the extent that they relate to the transferred interest. Admission of a substituted or new Member shall be recognized by the Company as provided in section 8.07 of this Article.

8.04. Admission of New Members. Any person acceptable to the Managers and to the Members holding a majority of the Membership Interests may become a new or additional Member in the Company by the issuance of additional Membership Interests in exchange for such consideration as the Managers may require. The person may become a new or additional Member in the Company only if, in addition to the requirements of section 8.05 of this Article, the person executes such instruments as the Managers may deem necessary or desirable to effect such admission. Admission of new or additional Members shall be recognized by the Company as provided in section 8.07 of this Article.

8.05. Conditions on Transfers of Interests. The transfer of a Membership or other interest (including the interest of a Transferee) otherwise permitted by this Article shall be subject to the following additional limitations:

(1) No Membership or other Interest may be transferred or issued if the proposed action, in the opinion of counsel for the Company, would result in the termination of the Company under Section 708 of the Code, would result in the cancellation of the Company's Articles of Organization, or would impair the Company's partnership tax status under the Code.
(2) No Membership or other Interest may be issued by the Company or transferred by a Member unless the transferee confirms in a writing acceptable to the Managers that the transferee has agreed to be bound by the terms and provisions of this Agreement.
(3) No transfer of a Membership or other Interest may be made unless the transferee shall have paid or, at the election of the Managers, becomes obligated to pay all reasonable expenses connected with such transfer, substitution or admission, including but not limited to the cost of preparing and filing any amendment to the Articles of Organization required to effect the transferee's admission as a new or substituted Member pursuant to section 8.07 of this Article.
(4) No Membership or other Interest may be transferred unless, if requested, the Managers receive an opinion of counsel, satisfactory in form and substance to the Company's counsel, to the effect that such transfer will not violate the Federal Securities laws, or any state securities or syndication laws. Such opinion shall, in the case of a transfer by a Member, be furnished at the expense of the Member.

8.06. Withdrawal of Member. Except as otherwise provided in this Article, no Member shall be entitled to withdraw or resign from the Company.

8.07. Recognition of Transferees and Substituted Members. Amendments to the books and records of the Company and, if required by law, amendments to the Articles of Organization, shall be made to recognize assignments of Membership Interests and, if applicable, admission of substituted or new Members. Assignments of Membership Interests and admissions of new Members shall be recognized and effective on and as of the first day of the first month following the date of the satisfaction of the conditions to the transfer and substitution set forth in this Article. Allocation of Company profits, losses and other items upon transfer shall be made as provided in section 4.04 of this Agreement

8.08. Obligations of Transferring Member. Except as otherwise agreed to by the Managers, no transfer by a Member of all or any portion of an interest in the Company shall relieve the transferring Member of any of the Member's obligations to the Company or of any liability as a Member, whether or not the person remains as a Member.

ARTICLE 9

Dissociation of Members

9.01. Dissociation. A person shall cease to be a Member upon the happening of any of the following events:

(1) the transfer by a Member of the Member's entire Membership Interest in accordance with Article 8 of this Agreement;
(2) the death of a Member or the entry of a valid court order adjudicating a Member to be legally incapable of managing the Member's personal affairs;
(3) the bankruptcy of a Member; or
(4) The termination or dissolution of a Member that is a corporation or other separate organization.

9.02. Rights of Dissociating Member. If a Member dissociates prior to the expiration of the term of the Company:

(1) If the dissociation causes a dissolution and winding up of the Company under Article 10 of this Agreement, the Member shall be entitled to participate in the winding up of the Company to the same extent as any other Member except that any distributions to which the Member would have been entitled shall be reduced by any damages sustained by the Company as a result of the dissociation.
(2) If the dissociation does not cause a dissolution and winding up of the Company, the Member who dissociates, or such Member's successor in interest, shall be treated as a Transferee.
(3) If the dissociation does not cause a dissolution and winding up of the Company and occurs by virtue of an assignment of such person's entire Membership Interest in accordance with this Agreement, then the rights of the dissociating Member (and such Member's successor) shall be determined under Article 8 of this Agreement.

ARTICLE 10

Dissolution and Liquidation

10.01. Dissolution. The Company shall be dissolved upon the first to occur of any of the following events:

(1) the expiration of the term or period of existence, if any, set forth in its Articles of Organization;
(2) the unanimous agreement of all of the Members that the Company should be dissolved;
(3) the dissociation of a Member or any other event that causes a Member to cease to be a Member under the Act (other than an assignment of a Member's entire Membership Interest in accordance with the terms of this Agreement), provided that such an event shall not cause the dissolution of the Company if there are at least two remaining Members and the business of the Company is continued by the consent, within 90 days after the dissociation, of the remaining Members holding at least ____ percent of the Membership Interests;
(4) the insolvency or bankruptcy of the Company;
(5) the sale of all or substantially all of the Company assets; or
(6) any event that makes it impossible, unlawful or impractical to carry on the business of the Company.

10.02. Liquidation. Upon dissolution of the Company in accordance with this Article, the Company shall be liquidated. The Managers (or if there are no Managers, the Members holding a majority of the Membership Interests) shall select a Liquidating Manager (who may be any Member or Manager) who shall serve only for purposes of winding up the Company. Unless otherwise provided in the Act, the proceeds of such liquidation shall be applied and distributed in the following order of priority:

(1) First, to the payment of the debts and liabilities of the Company (other than debts or liabilities owing to Members or Transferees) and the expenses of liquidation (including, if applicable, the reasonable fees of the Liquidating Manager), including the setting up of reserves for the payment of such debts and liabilities.
(2) Second, to the repayment of any outstanding advances or loans that may have been made by any of the Members or Transferees to the Company, other than capital contributions, pro rata among them on the basis of such advances and loans to the Company.
(3) Third, to the Members or Transferees in accordance with their respective Capital Accounts, after adjustment for all income, loss, and gain of the Company and after adjustment for all previous contributions to and distributions by the Company.

10.03. Distributions in Kind. The Liquidating Manager may make distributions to the Members and Transferees in cash or in kind, or partly in cash and partly in kind, in divided or undivided interests, and may allocate any property towards the satisfaction of any payment or distribution due to the Members or Transferees in such manner as the Liquidating Manager may determine, whether or not such distributive shares may as a result be composed of differently. Distribution of any asset in kind to a Member shall be considered as a distribution of an amount equal to the asset's fair market value for purposes of this Article.

10.04. Revaluation. If Company assets are distributed in kind, such assets, for purposes of determining the amount to be distributed, shall be revalued on the Company books to reflect their then current fair market value as of a date reasonably close to the date of liquidation. Any unrealized appreciation or depreciation shall be allocated among the Members and taken into account in determining the Capital Accounts of the Members and Transferees as of the date of liquidation.

ARTICLE 11

Miscellaneous

11.01. Amendments Without Consent of Members. Amendments may be made to this Agreement from time to time by the Managers, without the consent of the Members if the amendments (1) do not adversely affect the rights of the Members or their assignees in any material respect; (2) are for the purpose of correcting any error or resolving any ambiguity in or inconsistency among the provisions of this Agreement; (3) are to delete or add a provision to this Agreement that is required to be deleted or added by any federal or state securities commission or other governmental authority; (4) are to amend this Agreement and the Articles of Organization so as to admit new Members in accordance with this Agreement; or (5) is in response to an amendment to the Act that permits or requires an amendment to this Agreement so long as no Member is adversely affected in any material respect by the amendment.

11.02. Amendments Requiring Consent of Affected Members. Anything to the contrary in this Article notwithstanding, this Agreement may not be amended without the consent of the Members affected by the amendment if the amendment (1) modifies the limited liability of a Member; (2) alters the status of the Company as a partnership for federal income tax purposes; (3) modifies the compensation, distributions, or rights of reimbursement to which a Member is entitled, or (4) affects the duties of the Members serving as Managers or the indemnification to which the Members serving as Managers are entitled.

11.03. **Other Amendments.** Except as otherwise provided in this Article, this Agreement may be amended only by an affirmative vote of the Members holding a majority of the aggregate Membership Interests, except that any provision of this Agreement that provides for a membership vote or consent of greater than a majority of the aggregate Membership Interests may be amended only by an affirmative vote of the aggregate Membership Interests that is equal to that specified in the provision sought to be amended.

11.04. **Governing Law.** This Agreement shall be governed by the Act and other laws of the state of ____________ , as such Act and laws may from time to time be amended.

11.05. **Notices.** Except as otherwise provided in this Agreement, any notice required or permitted to be given to a Member or Transferee or to the Company shall be in writing and shall be deemed effectively given upon personal delivery or upon deposit in the U.S. Mail by registered or certified mail, return receipt requested, or upon confirmed facsimile transmission for delivery to the company or to the Member, at the address or facsimile number shown in the records of the Company.

11.06. **Ratification of Organizer.** The acts and deeds of the organizer or organizers performed in the course of organizing the Company are hereby approved and ratified by the Members.

11.07. **Entire Agreement.** This Agreement and the amendments thereto, if any, constitute the entire agreement among the parties with respect to the organization of the Company and the operation of its business.

11.08. **Severability.** The invalidity or unenforceability of a provision of this Agreement shall not affect the validity or enforceability of the remainder of the Agreement.

11.09. **Counterpart Execution.** This Agreement may be executed in any number of counterparts with the same effect as if all of the Members had signed the same document.

11.10. **Binding Effect.** This Agreement and the amendments thereto, if any, shall be binding on, and shall inure to the benefit of, the Company, the Members, and their respective transferees, successors, assigns and legal representatives.

IN WITNESS WHEREOF, the Members have subscribed their names to this Agreement on or as of the day and year first above written.

______________________________	______________________________
Member	Member
______________________________	______________________________
Member	Member

REVENUE RULING 84-52
(1984-1 C.B. 157)

Publication Date: April 6, 1984

What are the federal income tax consequences of the conversion of a general partnership interest into a limited partnership interest in the same partnership?

FACTS

In 1975, X was formed as a general partnership under the Uniform Partnership Act of State M. X is engaged in the business of farming. The partners of X are A, B, C, and D. The partners have equal interest in the partnership.

The partners propose to amend the partnership agreement to convert the general partnership into a limited partnership under the Uniform Limited Partnership Act of State M, a statute that corresponds in all material respects to the Uniform Limited Partnership Act. Under the certificate of limited partnership, A and B will be limited partners, and both C and D will be general partners and limited partners. Each partner's total percent interest in the partnership's profits, losses, and capital will remain the same when the general partnership is converted into a limited partnership. The business of the general partnership will continue to be carried on after the conversion.

LAW AND ANALYSIS

Section 741 of the Internal Revenue Code provides that in the case of a sale or exchange of an interest in a partnership, gain or loss shall be recognized by the transferor partner.

Under section 1001 of the Code, if there is a sale or other disposition of property, the entire amount of the gain or loss realized thereunder will be recognized, unless another section of subtitle A provides for nonrecognition.

Under section 721 of the Code, no gain or loss is recognized by a partnership or any of its partners upon the contribution of property to the partnership in exchange for an interest therein.

Section 708 of the Code provides that a partnership is considered to be continuing if it is not terminated. A partnership is terminated if (1) no part of any business, financial operation, or venture of the partnership continues to be carried on by any of its partners in a partnership, or (2) within a 12-month period there is a sale or exchange of 50 percent or more of the total interest in partnership capital and profits.

CHOOSING THE RIGHT ENTITY

Section 1.708-1(b)(1)(ii) of the Income Tax Regulations provides that a contribution of property to a partnership does not constitute a sale or exchange for purposes of section 708 of the Code.

Section 722 of the Code generally provides that the basis of an interest in a partnership acquired by a contribution of property equals the transferor partner's adjusted basis in the contributed property.

Section 1223(1) of the Code provides that the holding period of property received in exchange for other property includes the holding period of the property exchanged, if the property received has the same basis (in whole or in part) as the property exchanged.

Under section 731 of the Code, if a partnership distributes money to a partner, then that partner will generally recognize gain only to the extent that the amount of money distributed (or deemed distributed) exceeds the adjusted basis of the partner's interest in the partnership immediately before the distribution.

Under section 733 of the Code, if there is a distribution by a partnership to a partner and if there is no liquidation of that partner's interest, then the adjusted basis of that partner's interest in the partnership must be reduced (but not below zero) by the amount of money distributed to the partner.

Section 752(a) of the Code states, in part, that any increase in a partner's share of the partnership's liabilities is considered to be a contribution of money by the partner to the partnership.

Section 752(b) of the Code states, in part, that any decrease in a partner's share of a partnership's liabilities is considered to be a distribution of money by the partnership to the partner.

Section 1.752-1(e) of the regulations provides rules for determining a partner's share of partnership liabilities with respect to both limited partnerships and general partnerships.

Under the facts of this revenue ruling, A, B, C, and D will remain partners in X after X is converted to a limited partnership. Although the partners have exchanged their interests in the general partnership X for interests in the limited partnership X, under section 721 of the Code, gain or loss will not be recognized by any of the partners of X except as provided in section 731 of the Code.

HOLDINGS

(1) Except as provided below, pursuant to section 721 of the Code, no gain or loss will be recognized by A, B, C, or D under section 741 or section 1001 of the Code as a result of the conversion of a general partnership interest in X into a limited partnership in X.

(2) Because the business of X will continue after the conversion and because, under section 1.708-1(b)(1)(ii) of the regulations, a transaction governed by section 721 of the Code is not treated as a sale or exchange for purposes of section 708 of the Code, X will not be terminated under section 708 of the Code.

(3) If, as a result of the conversion, there is no change in the partners' shares of X's liabilities under section 1.752-1(e) of the regulations, there will be no change to the adjusted basis of any partner's interest in X, and C and D will each have a single adjusted basis with respect to each partner's interest in X (both as limited partner and general partner) equal to the adjusted basis of each partner's respective general partner interest in X prior to the conversion. See Rev. Rul. 84-53, this page, this Bulletin.

(4) If, as a result of the conversion, there is a change in the partners' shares of X's liabilities under section 1.752-1(e) of the regulations, and such change causes a deemed contribution of money to X by a partner under section 752(a) of the Code, then the adjusted basis of that partner's interest shall, under section 722 of the Code, be increased by the amount of such deemed contribution. If the change in the partners' shares of X's liabilities causes a deemed distribution of money by X to a partner under section 752(b) of the Code, then the basis of that partner's interest shall, under section 733 of the Code, be reduced (but not below zero) by the amount of such deemed distribution, and gain will be recognized by that partner under section 731 of the Code to the extent the deemed distribution exceeds the adjusted basis of that partner's interest in X.

(5) Pursuant to section 1223(1) of the Code, there will be no change to the holding period of any partner's total interest in X.

The holdings contained herein would apply with equal force if the conversion had been of a limited partnership to a general partnership.

Form **8832**
(December 1996)
Department of the Treasury
Internal Revenue Service

Entity Classification Election

OMB No. 1545-1516

Please Type or Print	Name of entity	Employer identification number (EIN)
	Number, street, and room or suite no. If a P.O. box, see instructions.	
	City or town, state, and ZIP code. If a foreign address, enter city, province or state, postal code and country.	

1 **Type of election** (see instructions):

a ☐ Initial classification by a newly-formed entity (or change in current classification of an existing entity to take effect on January 1, 1997)

b ☐ Change in current classification (to take effect later than January 1, 1997)

2 **Form of entity** (see instructions):

a ☐ A domestic eligible entity electing to be classified as an association taxable as a corporation.

b ☐ A domestic eligible entity electing to be classified as a partnership.

c ☐ A domestic eligible entity with a single owner electing to be disregarded as a separate entity.

d ☐ A foreign eligible entity electing to be classified as an association taxable as a corporation.

e ☐ A foreign eligible entity electing to be classified as a partnership.

f ☐ A foreign eligible entity with a single owner electing to be disregarded as a separate entity.

3 Election is to be effective beginning (month, day, year) (see instructions) . . . . ▶ ___/___/___

4 Name and title of person whom the IRS may call for more information	5 That person's telephone number

Consent Statement and Signature(s) (see instructions)

Under penalties of perjury, I (we) declare that I (we) consent to the election of the above-named entity to be classified as indicated above, and that I (we) have examined this consent statement, and to the best of my (our) knowledge and belief, it is true, correct, and complete. If I am an officer, manager, or member signing for all members of the entity, I further declare that I am authorized to execute this consent statement on their behalf.

Signature(s)	Date	Title

General Instructions

Section references are to the Internal Revenue Code unless otherwise noted.

Paperwork Reduction Act Notice

We ask for the information on this form to carry out the Internal Revenue laws of the United States. You are required to give us the information. We need it to ensure that you are complying with these laws and to allow us to figure and collect the right amount of tax.

You are not required to provide the information requested on a form that is subject to the Paperwork Reduction Act unless the form displays a valid OMB control number. Books or records relating to a form or its instructions must be retained as long as their contents may become material in the administration of any Internal Revenue law. Generally, tax returns and return information are confidential, as required by section 6103.

The time needed to complete and file this form will vary depending on individual circumstances. The estimated average time is:

Recordkeeping . . . 1 hr., 20 min.
Learning about the law or the form . . . 1 hr., 41 min.
Preparing and sending the form to the IRS . . . . 17 min.

If you have comments concerning the accuracy of these time estimates or suggestions for making this form simpler, we would be happy to hear from you. You can write to the Tax Forms Committee, Western Area Distribution Center, Rancho Cordova, CA 95743-0001. **DO NOT** send the form to this address. Instead, see **Where To File** on page 3.

Purpose of Form

For Federal tax purposes, certain business entities automatically are classified as corporations. See items **1** and **3** through **8** under the definition of corporation on this page. Other business entities may choose how they are classified for Federal tax purposes. Except for a business entity automatically classified as a corporation, a members can choose to be classified as either an association taxable as a corporation or a partnership, and a business entity with a single member can choose to be classified as either an association taxable as a corporation or disregarded as an entity separate from its owner.

Generally, an eligible entity that does not file this form will be classified under the default rules described below. An eligible entity that chooses not to be classified under the default rules or that wishes to change its current classification must file Form 8832 to elect a classification. The IRS will use the information entered on this form to establish the entity's filing and reporting requirements for Federal tax purposes.

Default Rules

Existing entity default rule.— Certain domestic and foreign entities that are already in existence before January 1, 1997, and have an established Federal tax classification, generally do not need to make an election to continue that classification. However, for an eligible entity with a single owner that claimed to be a partnership under the law in effect before January 1, 1997, that entity will now be disregarded as an entity separate from its owner. If an existing entity decides to change its classification, it may do so subject to the rules in Regulations section 301.7701-3(c)(1)(iv). A foreign eligible entity is treated as being in existence prior to the effective date of this section only if the entity's classification is relevant at any time during the 60 months prior to January 1, 1997.

Domestic default rule.—Unless an election is made on Form 8832, a domestic eligible entity is:

1. A partnership if it has two or more members.

2. Disregarded as an entity separate from its owner if it has a single owner.

Foreign default rule.—Unless an election is made on Form 8832, a foreign eligible entity is:

1. A partnership if it has two or more members and at least one member does not have limited liability.

2. An association if all members have limited liability.

3. Disregarded as an entity separate from its owner if it has a single owner that does not have limited liability.

Definitions

Business entity.—A business entity is any entity recognized for Federal tax purposes that is not properly classified as a trust under Regulations section 301.7701-4 or otherwise subject to special treatment under the Code. See Regulations section 301.7701-2(a).

Corporation.—For Federal tax purposes, a corporation is any of the following:

1. A business entity organized under a Federal or state statute, or under a statute of a federally recognized Indian tribe, if the statute describes or refers to the entity as incorporated or as a corporation, body corporate, or body politic.

2. An association (as determined under Regulations section 301.7701-3).

3. A business entity organized under a state statute, if the statute describes or refers to the entity as a joint-stock company or joint-stock association.

4. An insurance company.

5. A state-chartered business entity conducting banking activities, if any of its deposits are insured under the Federal Deposit Insurance Act, as amended, 12 U.S.C. 1811 et seq., or a similar Federal statute.

6. A business entity wholly owned by a state or any political subdivision thereof.

7. A business entity that is taxable as a corporation under a provision of the Code other than section 7701(a)(3).

8. A foreign business entity listed in Regulations section 301.7701-2(b)(8). However, a foreign business entity listed in those regulations generally will not be treated as a corporation if all of the following apply:

a. The entity was in existence on May 8, 1996.

b. The entity's classification was relevant (as defined below) on May 8, 1996.

c. No person (including the entity) for whom the entity's classification was relevant on May 8, 1996, treats the entity as a corporation for purposes of filing that person's Federal income tax returns, information returns, and withholding documents for the tax year including May 8, 1996.

d. Any change in the entity's claimed classification within the 60 months prior to May 8, 1996, was a result of a change in the organizational documents of the entity, and the entity and all members of the entity recognized the Federal tax consequences of any change in the entity's classification within the 60 months prior to May 8, 1996.

e. The entity had a reasonable basis (within the meaning of section 6662) for treating the entity as other than a corporation on May 8, 1996.

f. Neither the entity nor any member was notified in writing on or before May 8, 1996, that the classification of the entity was under examination (in which case the entity's classification will be determined in the examination).

Binding contract rule.—If a foreign business entity described in Regulations section 301.7701-2(b)(8)(i) is formed after May 8, 1996, under a written binding contract (including an accepted bid to develop a project) in effect on May 8, 1996, and all times thereafter, in which the parties agreed to engage (directly or indirectly) in an active and substantial business operation in the jurisdiction in which the entity is formed, **8** on page 2 is applied by substituting the date of the entity's formation for May 8, 1996.

Eligible entity.—An eligible entity is a business entity that is not included in items **1** or **3** through **8** under the definition of corporation on page 2.

Limited liability.—A member of a foreign eligible entity has limited liability if the member has no personal liability for any debts of or claims against the entity by reason of being a member. This determination is based solely on the statute or law under which the entity is organized (and, if relevant, the entity's organizational documents). A member has personal liability if the creditors of the entity may seek satisfaction of all or any part of the debts or claims against the entity from the member as such. A member has personal liability even if the member makes an agreement under which another person (whether or not a member of the entity) assumes that liability or agrees to indemnify that member for that liability.

Partnership.—A partnership is a business entity that has **at least** two members and is not a corporation as defined on page 2.

Relevant.—A foreign eligible entity's classification is relevant when its classification affects the liability of any person for Federal tax or information purposes. The date the classification of a foreign eligible entity is relevant is the date an event occurs that creates an obligation to file a Federal tax return, information return, or statement for which the classification of the entity must be determined.

Effect of Election

The resulting tax consequences of a change in classification remain the same no matter how a change in entity classification is achieved. For example, if an organization classified as an association elects to be classified as a partnership, the organization and its owners must recognize gain, if any, under the rules applicable to liquidations of corporations.

Who Must File

File this form for an **eligible entity** that is one of the following:

- A domestic entity electing to be classified as an association taxable as a corporation.
- A domestic entity electing to change its current classification (even if it is currently classified under the default rule).
- A foreign entity that has more than one owner, all owners have limited liability, and it elects to be classified as a partnership.
- A foreign entity that has at least one owner without limited liability, and it elects to be classified as an association taxable as a corporation.
- A foreign entity with a single owner having limited liability, and it elects to have the entity disregarded as an entity separate from its owner.
- A foreign entity electing to change its current classification (even if it is currently classified under the default rule).

Do not file this form for an eligible entity that is:

- Tax-exempt under section 501(a), or
- A real estate investment trust (REIT), as defined in section 856.

When To File

See the instructions for line 3.

Where To File

File Form 8832 with the Internal Revenue Service Center, Philadelphia, PA 19255. Also attach a copy of Form 8832 to the entity's Federal income tax or information return for the tax year of the election. If the entity is not required to file a return for that year, a copy of its Form 8832 must be attached to the Federal income tax or information returns of all direct or indirect owners of the entity for the tax year of the owner that includes the date on which the election took effect. Although failure to attach a copy will not invalidate an otherwise valid election, each member of the entity is required to file returns that are consistent with the entity's election. In addition, penalties may be assessed against persons who are required to, but who do not, attach Form 8832 to their returns. Other penalties may apply for filing Federal income tax or information returns inconsistent with the entity's election.

Specific Instructions

Employer Identification Number (EIN)

Show the correct EIN on Form 8832. If the entity does not have an EIN, it generally must apply for one on **Form SS-4,** Application for Employer Identification Number. If the filing of Form 8832 is the only reason the entity is applying for an EIN, check the "Other" box on line 9 of Form SS-4 and write "Form 8832" to the right of that box. If the entity has not received an EIN by the time Form 8832 is due, write "Applied for" in the space for the EIN. **Do not** apply for a new EIN for an existing entity that is changing its classification. If you are electing to disregard an entity as separate from its owner, enter the owner's EIN.

Address

Include the suite, room, or other unit number after the street address. If the Post Office does not deliver mail to the street address and the entity has a P.O. box, show the box number instead of the street address.

Line 1

Check box 1a if the entity is choosing a classification for the first time **and** the entity does not want to be classified under the applicable default classification. **Do not** file this form if the entity wants to be classified under the default rules.

Check box 1b if the entity is changing its current classification to take effect later than January 1, 1997, whether or not the entity's current classification is the default classification. However, once an eligible entity makes an election to change its classification (other than an election made by an existing entity to change its classification as of January 1, 1997), the entity cannot change its classification by election again during the 60 months after the effective date of the election. However, the IRS may permit (by private letter ruling) the entity to change its classification by election within the 60-month period if more than 50% of the ownership interests in the entity as of the effective date of the election are owned by persons that did not own any interests in the entity on the effective date of the entity's prior election.

Line 2

Check the appropriate box if you are changing a current classification (no matter how achieved), or are electing out of a default classification. **Do not** file this form if you fall within a default classification that is the desired classification for the new entity.

Line 3

Generally, the election will take effect on the date you enter on line 3 of this form or on the date filed if no date is entered on line 3. However, an election specifying an entity's classification for Federal tax purposes can take effect no more than 75 days prior to the date the election is filed, nor can it take effect later than 12 months after the date on which the election is filed. If line 3 shows a date more than 75 days prior to the date on which the election is filed, the election will take effect 75 days before the date it is filed. If line 3 shows an effective date more than 12 months from the filing date, the election will take effect 12 months after the date the election was filed.

Regardless of the date filed, an election will in no event take effect before January 1, 1997.

Consent Statement and Signatures

Form 8832 must be signed by:

1. Each member of the electing entity who is an owner at the time the election is filed; or

2. Any officer, manager, or member of the electing entity who is authorized (under local law or the organizational documents) to make the election and who represents to having such authorization under penalties of perjury.

If an election is to be effective for any period prior to the time it is filed, each person who was an owner between the date the election is to be effective and the date the election is filed, and who is not an owner at the time the election is filed, must also sign.

If you need a continuation sheet or use a separate consent statement, attach it to Form 8832. The separate consent statement must contain the same information as shown on Form 8832.

*U.S. Government Printing Office: 1997 - 417-677/60086

CHAPTER FIVE

ORGANIZING A SMALL BUSINESS CORPORATION

While the advent of the limited liability company and the limited liability partnership has decreased the popularity of the small business corporation among small business owners, the small business corporation remains a viable entity for many small businesses. The availability of superior employee benefit plans, the ability of a corporation to retain earnings for capital expansion without the incurrence of a tax liability for the business owners, the universal recognition of corporate stock as an indicia of ownership, and the prestige of owning or managing a corporation make it the entity of choice for many small business owners. small business corporations, advantages of

5.01 An Introduction to Small Business Corporations

The term "small business corporation" is widely used and variously defined. The term appears twice in the Internal Revenue Code. The terms "close corporation," "closely-held corporation," and "incorporated partnership" are often used by the courts, by other commentators, and in statutes to describe certain classes or types of corporations. These terms are generally synonymous with the term "small business corporation," as that term is used in this handbook. While there is no universally accepted definition of a small business corporation, it may be defined generally as a business in the corporate form that has fewer than 100 employees, 75 or fewer shareholders, and a net worth of less than a million dollars. It is for businesses of this size, desiring the advantages of incorporation, that chapters 5 through 7 of this handbook are intended. small business corporation, definition

The distinguishing characteristics of a typical small business corporation include the following: small business corporations, characteristics

(1) Its stock is not publicly traded in securities markets and usually has no ascertainable market value apart from the transfer of an interest in the assets of the corporation.

(2) Its stock is owned by only a few persons (often only two or three, sometimes only one), or by a few families, and restrictions are usually imposed on the transfer of its stock so as to prevent the intrusion of unwanted business associates.

(3) Most of its stock is owned by persons who know one another, live in the same geographical area, and are active in the conduct of the corporate business. Stated in corporate terms: its controlling shareholders, its directors, and its principal officers are predominantly the same persons.

(4) Its size is such that it meets the size requirements contained in the definitions of "small business corporation" appearing in the Internal Revenue Code. This means that it must have a net worth of one million dollars or less and 75 or fewer shareholders. See 26 U.S.C. 1244(c)(3)(A), 1361(b)(1)(A).

These characteristics are general in nature, and not every small business corporation possesses all of them at all times. However, most small business corporations possess most of them most of the time.

corporate participant, definition

The term "corporate participant" is used in chapters 5, 6 and 7 of this handbook. As the term is used in this handbook, a corporate participant is a person participating in the ownership, management and profits of a small business corporation. A corporate participant is normally a shareholder, a director, and an officer of the corporation. In reality, a person involved in the ownership and management of a small business corporation seldom distinguishes one corporate role from another. Accordingly, it is felt that the term "corporate participant" describes both the role and the status of a typical person involved in the ownership and management of a small business corporation more accurately than any other single term (e.g., shareholder, director, or officer).

corporate participant as shareholder-employee

For most purposes, a corporate participant is the practical equivalent of a general partner in a partnership. For tax purposes, however, a corporate participant is a "shareholder-employee" because that term is used in the Internal Revenue Code. To avoid confusion, the term "shareholder-employee" is used instead of the term "corporate participant" when tax matters are discussed.

small business corporations, similarity to partnerships

In many respects a multi-person small business corporation has more of the characteristics of a general partnership than of a traditional corporation. It is often said that the participants of small business corporations wish to be treated as a corporation by outsiders, but as partners among themselves. Because of their unique characteristics, small business corporations, and their participants, have needs that are quite different from the needs of large or publicly-held corporations.

The distinctive needs of small business corporations include the following:

(1) The need to prevent the intrusion of unwanted associates in the corporate business. This need is often satisfied by restricting the transferability of the corporate stock.

small business corporations, distinctive needs

(2) The need to compensate deceased or departing corporate participants for their stock, the transferability of which is often restricted and for which there is usually no public market. This need may be satisfied through the use of buy-out provisions, whereby the corporation or the other shareholders purchase the stock of a deceased or departing shareholder at a fixed or determinable price.

(3) The need to protect the management, employment, and profit-sharing rights of participants who own less than a controlling interest in the corporation. That is, the need to protect minority participants from being "frozen out" by the majority. Needs of this type are often fulfilled through the use of veto powers, employment contracts, and preemptive rights.

(4) The need to prevent deadlocks and resolve disputes among the participants. This need is difficult to deal with and may be satisfied, in part at least, by including deadlock-prevention procedures in the corporate management and control structure, by employing buy-out provisions requiring one disputant or faction to purchase the stock of the other, and through the use of special dissolution and liquidation provisions.

(5) The need to avoid a double taxation of corporate earnings that are distributed to the participants. This need may be satisfied through the use of the Subchapter S election and by employing compensation arrangements that avoid the payment of stock dividends.

In most states small business corporations must be organized and incorporated under the general corporation laws, which are the same laws that are applicable to publicly-held corporations. The general corporation laws in the various states may be categorized as follows: those that have adopted the Model Business Corporation Act of 1969; those that have adopted the Revised Model Business Corporation Act of 1984; and those that have adopted neither of the Model Acts. Some states that have adopted neither of the Model Acts have patterned their corporation after the Delaware corporation laws. The Model Acts were prepared by the Committee on Corporate Laws of the American Bar Association. The Revised Model Act is generally more flexible and easier to adapt to the needs of a small business corporation than either the Model Act or the Delaware laws. A few states have adopted features of all of these Acts. The type of general corporation laws that exist in each state is indicated in Appendix I in the back of this book under the heading of "Corporation Laws."

small business corporations, general corporation laws

Several states have enacted what are called Close Corporation Codes, which are a special set of corporation laws that are designed to meet the needs of small business corporations. A few other states have enacted one or more statutes (or sections) in their general corporation laws that deal specifically with close corporations. A close corporation is a corporation that has many of the attributes of a partnership, including such features as shareholder management and easy dissolution. Persons organizing a corporation in a state that has a close corporation code may organize the corporation either under the general corporation laws or under the close corporation code. In other states, including several of the states that have adopted the Revised Model Business Corporation Act, a corporation may be organized essentially as a close corporation by means of a shareholders' agreement that complies with a specified provision in the general corporation laws. Under either type of statute, a decision must be made on whether to organize a small business corporation as a traditional corporation or as a close corporation. The close corporation election is discussed in section 5.19, infra. The type of close corporation laws, if any, that exist in each state is set forth in Appendix I, infra, under the heading of "Close Corporation Laws."

small business corporations, special close corporation laws

Even in the absence of close corporation statutes, some courts have imposed rules and standards of conduct on small business corporations and their participants that differ significantly from those applied to publicly-held corporations. These rules and standards of conduct are usually set forth in two types of cases: (1) cases dealing with the rights of minority shareholders, and (2) cases involving the personal liability of corporate participants for corporate obligations and actions. Recognizing that the role of a participant in a small business corporation differs substantially from the role of either an officer, a director, or a shareholder of a publicly-held corporation, the courts often apply what are essentially the rules of partnership law to small business corporations in cases of this type.

small business corporations, treatment by courts

5.02 The Tax Aspects of Incorporating

tax aspects of incorporating, general importance

The tax-related aspects of organizing and incorporating a small business enterprise should always be considered, regardless of the size of the business or the financial status of the business participants. However, special consideration should be given to the tax aspects of incorporating if one or more of the participants is engaged in the business enterprise primarily for purposes of investment rather than the earning of a livelihood, or if the current or anticipated profits of the business will be such as to provide funds beyond the current personal needs of the participants. The tax aspects of incorporating are usually more important to an existing business than to a start-up business, but much obviously depends on the particular financial circumstances of both the business and its participants. Many tax features, it should be noted, are easily applied to businesses of any size or financial condition, and to incorporate a business without considering these features may deprive the participants of an advantage from which they would otherwise benefit.

tax aspects of incorporating, factors

The tax-related matters that should be considered when organizing a small business corporation include the following, each of which is discussed further below:

(1) Avoiding the double taxation of funds distributed by the corporation to its participants.

(2) Establishing a proper debt-to-equity ratio when capitalizing the corporation.

(3) Establishing nontaxable fringe benefits and tax-deferred retirement benefits for the participants and other corporate employees.

(4) Avoiding the special taxes applicable to corporations.

(5) Determining whether the transfer of assets to the corporation should be taxable or nontaxable.

(6) Amortizing the expenses of organizing the corporation.

(7) Selecting an advantageous tax year for the corporation.

(8) Qualifying the corporation's stock under Section 1244 of the Internal Revenue Code.

(9) Qualifying the corporation under Subchapter S of the Internal Revenue Code.

methods of distributing earnings to participants

Double taxation. A typical small business corporation has two principal methods of distributing earnings to corporate participants: (1) compensation for personal services, usually in the form of salaries, commissions, and bonuses, and (2) dividends issued on the corporate stock. Both forms of compensation result in reportable income for the participants. The difference is that funds lawfully distributed as compensation for personal services may be deducted against earnings by the corporation, while funds distributed as dividends may not be so deducted. Because there is no offsetting corporate deduction, funds distributed as dividends are effectively taxed twice; once when the funds are received by the corporation as earnings and again when they are received by the shareholders as dividends. In addition, only amounts distributed as compensation are includable for purposes of determining deductible contributions and benefits under tax-qualified employee benefit plans. For the above reasons, it is almost always preferable to distribute corporate earnings to the participants in a form other than stock dividends.

double taxation of dividends, illustration

compensation for personal services, deductible amount

Limitations are imposed on the amount of deductible compensation that may be paid to a corporate participant by a corporation. The Internal Revenue Code permits a corporation to deduct only "a reasonable allowance for salaries or other compensation for personal services actually rendered" by a shareholder-employee (i.e., a corporate participant). See 26 U.S.C. 162(a)(1). To be deductible by the corporation, payments to shareholder-employees must be solely for services actually rendered to the corporation and must be reasonable in amount. Compensation that fails to meet both of these requirements is treated as a constructive dividend and is not deductible by the corporation, which means that it is effectively taxed twice. See section 6.01, infra, for further reading on this matter.

corporate distributions as lease and debt payments

There are, of course, methods of distributing corporate earnings to the participants other than as compensation for personal services and dividends. Two common methods are distributions in the form of lease or rental payments and debt and interest payments. Lease payments may be arranged by having the corporate participants lease equipment or other assets to the corporation instead of contributing the equipment or assets to the corporation as paid-in capital. Debt and interest payments can be arranged by having the participants capitalize the corporation, in part at least, with debt, as opposed to equity. In both cases the payments made to the participants by the corporation are fully deductible by the corporation, provided that the transactions are made and carried out in good faith and the so-called "thin incorporation" trap is avoided.

debt-to-equity ratio, importance

Debt-to-equity ratio. A so-called "thin incorporation" results when the ratio of debt to equity in the capitalization of a corporation is too high. Obtaining the tax advantages of debt while avoiding a debt-to-equity ratio that is unacceptable to the Internal Revenue Service can be an important tax-related function in the organizing of a small business corporation, especially if the business of the enterprise is highly profitable. This aspect of incorporating is discussed at length in section 5.14 infra, and the reader is referred to that section for further reading.

corporate fringe and retirement benefits

Fringe and retirement benefits. Another important tax-related aspect of organizing a small business corporation is that of determining which, if any, of the various nontaxable or tax-deferred fringe and retirement benefits available to corporate participants and employees should be adopted by the corporation. The benefits available to corporate participants and employees may be divided into three categories:

(1) health and welfare benefits;
(2) retirement and deferred compensation benefits; and
(3) employee stock ownership benefits.

These benefits are described at length in section 6.01, infra. Only a brief description of each type of benefit is given below.

employee health and welfare benefits

Generally, a corporate employer may deduct, without a corresponding inclusion in income by the employee, the cost of payments made to employee disability and health plans, the cost of group life insurance benefits of up to $50,000 per employee, death benefit payments of up to $5,000 per employee, and the cost of an employee's board and lodging under certain circumstances. It should be noted that these benefits (except the $5,000 death benefit) are not available to most participants of S corporations (see section 5.18, infra).

employee retirement benefits

Deferred compensation benefits for corporate participants and employees may be in the form of a tax-qualified corporate employee benefit (or retirement) plan, or in the form of a nonqualified deferred compensation arrangement. The annual contribution limits for tax-qualified profit-sharing and other defined contribution plans are the lesser of $30,000 or 25 percent of compensation, while the annual benefit limits for tax-qualified pension and other defined benefit plans are the lesser of $90,000 or 100 percent of compensation. See section 6.01 infra, for further reading.

employee stock ownership benefits

While not frequently used by small business corporations, employee stock ownership benefits can, under the proper circumstances, be an attractive tax benefit, especially for highly paid employees. A corporation has three basic methods of making its stock available to its employees: employee stock bonus plans, stock option plans, and stock purchase agreements. Each type of plan is discussed in section 6.01, infra.

special taxes, corporations

Special taxes. There are certain taxes, applicable only to small business corporations, which must be avoided if the participants are to take full advantage of doing business in the corporate form. These taxes are:

(1) the personal holding company tax;
(2) the accumulated earnings tax; and
(3) the collapsible corporation tax provisions.

The personal holding company tax and the accumulated earnings tax are designed to force a corporation to distribute its earnings, while the collapsible corporation tax provisions are designed to prohibit the distribution of earnings as capital gains. Each of these taxes is usually avoidable with proper planning.

personal holding company tax

A corporation is deemed to be a personal holding company if: (1) more than 50 percent of its outstanding stock is owned by, or for, not more than five individuals, and (2) at least 60 percent of its adjusted ordinary gross income is derived from dividends, interest, royalties, annuities, trusts, estates, certain personal service contracts, and rents in specified amounts. See 26 U.S.C. 542, 543. If a corporation qualifies as a personal holding company, in addition to its other taxes a penalty tax of 39.6 percent of its undistributed personal holding company income is assessed against the corporation. See 26 U.S.C. 541.

accumulated earnings tax, applicability

A corporation that accumulates earnings and profits in excess of $250,000 for the purpose of avoiding income tax to its shareholders is subject to an accumulated earnings tax of 39.6 percent of its accumulated taxable income. See 26 U.S.C. 531-535. For corporations whose principal business is in the field of health, law, engineering, accounting, architecture, actuarial science, performing arts, or consulting, the dollar limitation on excessive accumulated earnings and profits is only $150,000. See 26 U.S.C. 535. The accumulated earnings tax does not apply to personal holding companies and tax-exempt organizations. See 26 U.S.C. 532(b). It should be noted that the dollar limitation on excessive accumulations is applied collectively to a "controlled group" of corporations. See 26 U.S.C. 535(c)(5), 1551, 1561(a)(2) and 1563(a).

accumulated earnings, needs of business

The accumulation of earnings and profits beyond the reasonable needs of the business is, per se, determinative of the purpose of avoiding income tax to the shareholders, unless the corporation can prove to the contrary. See 26 U.S.C. 533(a). Also, if a corporation is a holding or investment company, that fact alone is prima facie evidence of an intent to avoid income tax to the shareholders. See 26 U.S.C. 533(b).

The accumulation of earnings and profits beyond the dollar limitation is permitted, however, if the accumulation is necessary for the "reasonable needs of the business." See 26 U.S.C. 533, 537. The reasonable needs of the business includes the reasonably anticipated needs of the business and certain stock redemption needs of the business. See 26 U.S.C. 537 for the specific provisions. The criterion for determining the reasonably anticipated needs of the business is that which a prudent business person would consider appropriate for the bona fide needs of the business. See Treasury Reg. 1.537-1(a).

collapsible corporation, illustration

Suppose a corporation is formed for the purpose of constructing an apartment building. Ordinarily, the corporation would realize a profit either from the sale of the building upon completion of construction or from the receipt of rents from the building. These profits would normally be taxed as ordinary income, either at the corporate or the shareholder level. Suppose, however, that immediately upon the completion of construction of the building, the shareholders sold their stock in the corporation to an outsider for a price equal to the fair market value of the building. Absent the collapsible corporation tax provisions, the corporation would pay no tax on the transaction because it realized no income or gain from the sale, and the selling shareholders, assuming that they had held the shares for the required period, would pay only a long term capital gains tax on the gain realized on their stock. What normally would have been ordinary income would thus have been taxed only as a capital gain.

collapsible corporation, definition tax treatment

A collapsible corporation is defined as a corporation formed or used principally for the manufacture, construction or production of property, or for the purchase of certain kinds of properties, for the purpose of (1) the sale or exchange of stock by its shareholders, or a distribution to its shareholders, prior to the realization by the corporation of a substantial portion of the taxable income from such property, and (2) the realization by its shareholders of a gain attributable to such property. See 26 U.S.C. 341(b). With certain exceptions, any gain from the sale, exchange, liquidation or redemption of stock in a collapsible corporation is taxed as ordinary income to its shareholders. See 26 U.S.C. 341(a),(d).

transfer of assets to corporation, tax treatment

The taxability of the incorporation. The transfer of money or property to the corporation can be an important tax aspect of incorporating a small business enterprise. Generally, the transfer of property or money to a corporation by the participants is tax-free if the transfer is solely in exchange for stock in the corporation and if, immediately after the transfer, the transferors own at least 80 percent of the voting stock in the corporation. See 26 U.S.C. 351. This is the so-called tax-free incorporation provision, where no gain or loss is attributable to the transfer. In a tax-free incorporation, the corporation acquires the property at the transferors' tax basis.

tax-free incorporation, how to effect

In the incorporation of a small business it is usually advantageous to maintain the tax-free status of the transfer, and care should be taken to comply with the requirements of 26 U.S.C. 351. This means that stock should not be issued for services and debt instruments should not be issued to the shareholders in exchange for contributed property if the tax-free status of the transfer is to be preserved. See 26 U.S.C. 351, which requires property or money to be transferred to the corporation solely in exchange for stock.

tax-free incorporation, requirements

taxable incorporation, when desirable

If the participants' tax basis in the property to be transferred to the corporation is considerably below its actual or market value, it may be advantageous to both the participants and the corporation for the transfer of the property to the corporation to be taxable. In a taxable transfer (i.e., a taxable incorporation), the participants can usually treat any gain on contributed property as a capital gain, and the corporation will acquire the property at a market-value basis and can depreciate the property from this stepped-up basis, deducting the depreciation against ordinary income. If the participants' basis in the contributed property is considerably above its actual or market value, it may again be advantageous for the transfer of the property to the corporation to be taxable so as to enable the participants to claim a loss on the transfer, either ordinary or capital depending on the status of the property in the hands of the participants.

wholly taxable incorporation how to implement

partly taxable incorporation, definition

Generally, a wholly taxable transfer (i.e., a wholly taxable incorporation) occurs when property is transferred to a corporation in exchange for stock in a transaction that fails to meet the requirements of 26 U.S.C. 351. Therefore, if a taxable incorporation is desired, steps should be taken to insure that the transaction does not meet the requirements of Section 351. A partly taxable transfer (i.e., a partly taxable incorporation) occurs when some assets are transferred to the corporation in exchange for stock and others are sold to the corporation, or when, in connection with an otherwise tax-free transfer, other property (or "boot") is received by the transferor in addition to stock. Special rules apply to transferred property that is subject to a liability such as a mortgage or security interest. See 26 U.S.C. 357. The whole subject of a taxable vs. a tax-free incorporation is complex and may require expert tax guidance to ensure the intended result.

organizational expenses, deductibility

Amortizing organizational expenses. A corporation may amortize its organizational expenses over a period of not less than 60 months, commencing with the month in which it begins doing business. See 26 U.S.C. 248. Amortizable expenses include -

(1) legal and accounting expenses incidental to incorporation;
(2) incorporation or charter fees paid to state and local agencies;
(3) expenses of organizational meetings; and
(4) expenses and fees of incorporators and temporary directors.

organizational expenses, statement of election

To amortize these expenses, a statement of election must be attached to the corporation's tax return for the tax year in which it begins doing business. The statement should show the amount and purpose of the expenditures, the date they were incurred, the month the corporation began doing business, and the number of months over which the expenses are to be ratably deducted. See Treasury Reg. 1.248-1(c). If a corporation does not elect to amortize its organizational expenses, they are deductible as expenses only in the year in which the corporation is liquidated. See Exhibit 5-A at the end of this chapter for a sample statement of election.

new corporation, selection of tax year

Selecting a corporate tax year. Because it is a separate taxable entity, a C corporation (which is a corporation for which a Subchapter S election is not in effect) may select its own tax year. In the case of a newly formed corporation, the selection of the tax year can often be used to the tax advantage of both the corporation and its participants. Any new C corporation may select, without the prior I.R.S. approval, a tax year ending with the close of any of its first 12 months of existence. See 26 U.S.C. 441(f). The tax year, once selected, may not be changed without the approval of the Treasury Secretary until the corporation has maintained the same tax year for at least 10 calendar years. See Treasury Reg. 1.441-1(b). If the corporation fails to affirmatively select a tax year during its first 12 months, or if it keeps no books of account, it must use the calendar year as its tax year. See 26 U.S.C. 441(g). Special rules apply to the selection of a tax year by an S corporation (see section 5.18, infra).

selecting tax year, factors

It may be possible to effect significant corporate or personal tax savings by the judicious selection of the initial corporate tax year. Factors to be considered in selecting the initial tax year for a new corporation include:

(1) the projected income or losses of the corporation, especially in its first year;
(2) the timing of compensation payments to the corporate participants; and
(3) the seasonal aspects of the corporate business, including inventories.

If a corporation expects substantial seasonal fluctuations in income, inventories, or other taxable or tax-related items, these aspects of the business should also be considered in selecting its initial tax year. The selection of a corporation's tax (or fiscal) year is normally a function of the board of directors, and the tax (or fiscal) year should either be set forth in the corporation's bylaws or adopted by a resolution of the board of directors.

section 1244 stock, subchapter S election

Section 1244 stock. If the corporation's stock is qualified under Section 1244 of the Internal Revenue Code, the shareholders may treat their financial investment in the corporate stock as an ordinary loss (as opposed to a capital loss) should the business subsequently fail. To qualify under Section 1244, the stock must be common stock, the capitalization of the corporation must not exceed $1,000,000, the stock must be issued for money or property other than stocks or securities (and not for services), and the corporation may not derive more than half of its income from royalties, rents, dividends, interest, annuities, and sales or exchanges of stocks and securities. See section 5.14, infra, for further reading on Section 1244 stock.

The Subchapter S election. A qualifying small business corporation that elects to be taxed under Subchapter S of the Internal Revenue Code is essentially taxed as a partnership with the corporation paying no taxes (with certain limited exceptions) and the income, losses and other tax features of the business assessed only at the shareholder level. To qualify under Subchapter S a corporation must have 75 or fewer shareholders, have only one class of stock, and have only individuals, estates, or certain trusts as its shareholders. Whether to exercise the Subchapter S election is an important tax decision for many small business corporations. See section 5.18, infra, for further reading on the Subchapter S election, including directions on how and when to exercise the election.

5.03 Preincorporation Agreements

Most small business corporations are organized and incorporated under informal understandings between the persons involved. Because a corporation can ordinarily be organized and incorporated in a matter of days in most states, there is usually no need for a written preincorporation agreement. In most cases, the most efficient practice is to prepare the articles of incorporation, bylaws, minutes, and any related documents or agreements, obtain the necessary signatures, and thereby bind the persons involved.

An agreement binding the persons involved pending the formation of a corporation is most often needed when, for whatever reason, the corporation will not be immediately formed. If a participant will be absent or otherwise unable to sign the required documents for an extended period, or if the state corporation laws require extended publication prior to incorporation, a preincorporation agreement may be in order. Similarly, a preincorporation agreement may be needed if a participant is to be committed to future capital commitments under certain conditions, if a participant has been induced to engage in the business for considerations other than stock (such as employment by the corporation), or if the formation of the corporation is expressly contingent upon the happening or nonhappening of a future event or on the continued profitability of the business for a certain period. A sample preincorporation agreement is set forth in Exhibit 5-B at the end of this chapter. preincorporation agreements, when needed

Preincorporation agreements are also useful in situations where extensive financial commitments prior to incorporation are contemplated, or where the formation of a corporation is expressly contingent upon the obtaining of a certain amount of capital. Preincorporation agreements of this sort, which are often referred to as promoter's contracts or subscription agreements, are usually between the organizers (or promoters) of the corporation, who agree to form the corporation and cause the stock to be issued, and subscribers, who agree to invest money or property in the corporation. It should be noted that the corporation laws of many states provide that subscription agreements must be in writing to be enforceable and that subscribers may not revoke their subscriptions for a certain period (usually six months), unless the agreement provides to the contrary or unless the parties involved so agree. subscription agreements

The promoters of a corporation have fiduciary, as well as contractual, obligations to the subscribers, to other promoters, and to the corporation itself. A promoter must make a full disclosure of his or her proposed relationship and dealings with the corporation to be formed. A promoter must also disclose any financial advantage that he or she may receive as a result of the formation of the corporation, including all transfers of property to or from the corporation. A promoter who obtains a secret advantage over another promoter may be liable to the wronged promoter for damages, for specific performance, or for the imposition of an equitable trust on any wrongfully issued stock. promoters' liability, general aspects

Because promoters are fiduciaries, they may not profit personally at the expense of the corporation to be formed, and may be liable to the corporation for such profits. If promoters expect the corporation to purchase property from them, they must make a full disclosure of all relevant facts surrounding the sale. Any misrepresentation may render a promoter liable to the corporation for either damages or recision. Similarly, promoters may be liable to the corporation and to other investors or subscribers for fraudulently diverting funds and for failing to account for expense moneys advanced to them. promoters' liability to corporation

A corporation, once formed, has no legal obligation to accept contracts made for it prior to its formation. Because it was not in existence, it was incapable of being a principal and the promoter could not have been its agent. Even if some or all of the promoters later become officers or directors of the corporation, if the corporation fails to approve or adopt a promoter's contract, the corporation cannot be held liable thereunder. See Steele v. Litton Industries, Inc., 260 Cal. App. 2nd 157, 68 Cal. Rep. 680 (1968). promoters' contract, acceptance by corporation

If, however, a corporation elects to accept the benefits of a promoter's contract, it may be held to have adopted the contract by implication. See Meyers v. Wells, 252 Wis. 352, 31 N.W. 2nd 512 (1948). And even if a corporation repudiates a promoter's contract, it may be liable for the reasonable value of any services received under the contract. See Ong Hing v. Arizona Harness Raceway, Inc., 10 Ariz. Apps. 380, 459 P. 2nd 107 (1969). promoters' contract, implied acceptance

5.04 Selecting the State of Incorporation

state of incorporation

One of the first steps in organizing a small business corporation is the selection of the state of incorporation. For most small businesses the only practical jurisdiction in which to incorporate is the local state; that is, the home state, the state where all or most of the corporation's business will be conducted. The corporation laws of practically every state permit a corporation to engage in any lawful business or combination of businesses, thus rendering it unnecessary in the vast majority of cases to shop for a state with more permissive corporation laws. Further, a corporation formed in a state other than where it conducts most of its business will have to qualify to do business in the latter state as a foreign corporation, a process that may subject the corporation to fees and expenses sufficient to overcome any savings in this regard that might have been gained by incorporating in another state.

incorporation in foreign state, when desirable

There are, however, certain circumstances under which it may be advantageous for a small business corporation to incorporate under the laws of a state other than its home state. Incorporation in a foreign state may be desirable if any of the following circumstances exist:

(1) The nature of the corporation's business will be such that it will necessarily be conducting business in other states to the extent that it will have to qualify to do business in those states.

(2) While the business is presently local in character, it is believed that in the foreseeable future the business will expand more rapidly in another state.

(3) The features desired for the corporation, including close corporation features, are not permissible under the corporation laws of the local state.

(4) It is anticipated that the corporation may "go public" in the foreseeable future and the securities laws of the local state are too restrictive.

(5) The business participants, for whatever reason, do not wish to make public locally the information required to incorporate the business in the local state.

foreign state, how to select

If the corporation will be conducting business in other states to the extent that qualification as a foreign corporation will be necessary, the corporation laws of each state should be compared so that the incorporation can be made in the most favorable state. In this regard it should be noted that the corporation laws of each state are summarized in Appendix I in the back of this book.

incorporation in foreign state, when necessary

If the management and control structure or the capital structure desired by the business participants calls for devices or procedures not permitted under the local corporation laws, it may be necessary to incorporate in another state. For example, if the business to be incorporated is a one-person business, if the owner insists that he or she be the only director of the corporation, and if the local corporation laws require more than one director, the business may have to be incorporated in another state. If the controlling participants wish to avoid such local requirements as preemptive rights, cumulative voting, or the rights of minority shareholders to approve the extraordinary corporate acts of merger, dissolution, and the sale of assets, the only alternative may be to incorporate in a state where such rights either are less restrictive or can be effectively negated.

5.05 Selecting and Securing a Corporate Name

To the participants of most small business enterprises the selection of a corporate name is a significant event. On the other hand, attorneys incorporating small businesses often treat the selection of a corporate name as an insignificant event and devote little or no time to the matter. Experience has shown, however, that in choosing a corporate name the expenditure of a little time and effort at the outset can prevent the expenditure of much time and effort later on.

selecting corporate name, importance

rules for selecting a corporate name

In selecting a corporate name, the following rules should be followed:

(1) The name of the corporation should be related to the business of the enterprise.

(2) If feasible, the corporate name should relate to a trademark or trade name used by the business.

(3) The name should be adaptable to advertising the business of the corporation; that is, it should be short and easy to pronounce and remember.

(4) The name should be distinguishable from any other registered name and from the name of any other domestic or foreign entity that is authorized to transact business in any state in which the new corporation will be transacting business.

(5) The name should be such that it will not unfairly appropriate the good will of any other entity.

(6) The name must contain the words required by the corporation laws of each state where it will be doing business. These words are usually "corporation," "incorporated," company," "limited," or abbreviations of these words.

(7) The name must not contain any of the words or phrases forbidden by the corporation laws of any state where it will be doing business. These words usually relate to the banking and insurance businesses, but there are other forbidden names in some states.

(8) The name should not imply that the corporation is organized for any purpose not stated in its articles of incorporation.

To ascertain the availability of a particular corporate name in a state it is usually necessary to contact the office of the state filing official. The name and address of the state filing official in each state is set forth in Appendix I in the back of this book under the heading of State Filing Official. In many states this can be done informally by telephone, while in other states a letter or an application is required. If the desired name is not available, another name must be selected and its availability checked. If the checking process is time-consuming, it is a good practice to check more than one name at a time. It is important to remember that the corporate name should be cleared in each state where the corporation will be conducting significant business. Otherwise, it may be necessary to either change the corporate name or conduct business under a fictitious name, a procedure that requires an additional registration in most states (see section 3.03, supra).

corporate name, checking availability

Sources other than the state filing official should be checked with ascertaining the availability of a proposed corporate name. Many states require business name certificates for certain types of businesses to be filed with the county clerk. In such states it is a good practice to check the names listed with the county clerk, along with other available sources such as telephone and business directories, before selecting a name. If the corporation will be doing business in a state that has a fictitious name statute, the names registered thereunder should also be checked. If a corporate name includes a trade name or trademark, the name should be checked against the trademarks registered with the United States Patent Office to insure its availability. See 15 U.S.C. 1051 et seq. If the trademark is available it should be registered with the Patent Office to insure its continued availability.

availability of corporate name, where to check

trademarks, necessity of checking and registering

corporate name, required words

The corporation laws of most states require corporate names to include certain words to identify them as corporations. These words are usually "corporation," "incorporated," "limited," "company," or abbreviations thereof. The exact words vary from state to state, so the requirements in each state where the corporation will be doing business should be checked to insure compliance. If the statutory requirements are not precisely complied with, the proposed corporate name is likely to be rejected by the state filing official.

corporate name, precluded words

To avoid confusing a corporation organized under the general corporation laws with a corporation formed under special statutes (usually the banking and insurance laws), most states preclude the use of corporate names containing words or phrases related to corporations formed under the special statutes (i.e., "bank," "trust," "insurance," etc.). Again, the list of precluded words and phrases varies from state to state, so the requirements in each state where the corporation will be doing business should be checked. The corporate name requirements in each state (except the list of forbidden names) and the name clearance procedures in many states are summarized in Appendix I, infra, under the heading of "Corporate Name."

corporate name, obtaining approval of

Generally, the disapproval of a corporate name on the grounds that it is not distinguishable from or is deceptively similar to an existing name lies within the discretion of the state filing official, whose decision may not be overturned by a reviewing court in the absence of an abuse of discretion. However, most corporation laws provide that the use of an indistinguishable or deceptively similar name may be permitted by the state filing official if the other entity consents to the use of its name in writing and changes its name to one that is acceptable, or if the applicant produces a certified copy of a court decree establishing the applicant's right to use the requested name.

corporate name, effect of approval

It should be understood that the approval of a corporate name by the state filing official is not an adjudication of the legality of the name, and the corporation laws in some states so specify. If the use of the name infringes upon the rights of another corporation or entity, that party may bring an action to enjoin the use of the name and for damages. In this regard, it should be noted that courts are more likely to permit the use of a similar name if the corporate name contains the name of the person or persons conducting or owning the business. See Mozzochi v. Luchs, 35 Conn. Sup. 19, 391 A. 2nd 738 (1977).

reserving corporate name, necessity of

Once a corporate name has been selected and cleared, the next step is to reserve the use of the name, if necessary. It is usually necessary to reserve a corporate name if, for any reason, the corporation will not be immediately organized. If the corporation is to be formed and the articles of incorporation filed within a matter of a few days, it is usually not necessary to formally reserve a name. However, if the business participants wish to make absolutely certain that they can use a specified name, the only safe practice is to reserve the name in advance of incorporation.

reserving corporate name, procedure

The corporation laws of every state permit the reservation of a name for both domestic and foreign corporations for short periods of time ranging from 10 days to 12 months. To reserve a corporate name it is usually necessary to file an application with the state filing official, often on a prescribed form, and pay a modest fee. The name reservation period in each state is set forth in Appendix I, infra, under the heading of "Corporate Name." The name reservation fee in each state is set forth in Appendix I, infra, under the heading of "Fees."

5.06 Shareholders - Rights, Responsibilities and Agreements

shareholders' liability, general rule

One of the most significant advantages of a corporation is the limited liability of its shareholders for the debts of the corporation. Corporation statutes typically provide that a shareholder shall be under no obligation to the corporation or its creditors with respect to his or her stock except for the obligation to pay in full the consideration for which the stock was issued. Therefore, if a corporation is lawfully formed and operated, any shareholder who has rendered full payment for the stock that he or she has agreed to purchase is not personally liable for the debts of the corporation, provided that the shareholder has not become contractually liable for the corporate debts and has not represented himself or herself to be personally doing corporate business. It should be noted, however, that if a shareholder is also an officer or director of the corporation, additional liability for corporate debts may be imposed (see section 6.06, infra).

shareholders' liability for stock

A shareholder is liable to the corporation for failing to pay for any stock received or for any stock that the shareholder has agreed to purchase. Should the corporation become insolvent, a receiver or creditor of the corporation may enforce these obligations against a shareholder. Unless the state corporation laws provide to the contrary, a shareholder's liability for unpaid stock is several and not joint, and each obligated shareholder is liable for his or her pro rata share of any outstanding corporate debt, based on the amount of the unpaid obligation.

defective incorporation, shareholders' liability

If a corporation is defectively incorporated, the shareholders involved in the acts giving rise to the corporate debts, and possibly all shareholders, are liable for the corporate debts. See section 6.06, infra, for further reading on defective incorporation and shareholder liability resulting therefrom. A failure to comply with compulsory statutes requiring the local filing of certain documents or with a minimum capitalization requirement, may also subject certain shareholders and officers to personal liability. If a corporation's charter is forfeited for nonpayment of the franchise tax (a common happening among small business corporations), a shareholder who continues in business under the corporate name is usually personally liable for the debts so incurred, especially if he or she is aware of the forfeiture and is an officer or director of the corporation. See Borbein, Young & Co. v. Cirese, 401 S.W. 2nd 940 (Mo. Apps., 1966), and section 6.06, infra. In New York certain shareholders are personally liable for the payment of wages to corporate employees if the corporation fails to pay them. See Bus. Corp. Law § 630.

defunct corporation, shareholders' liability

shareholders' liability for corporate labor debts

shareholders' S.E.C. registration requirements

If the stock of a corporation is registered with the Securities and Exchange Commission, the holders of more than 10 percent of any class of stock so registered must file statements of ownership with the S.E.C. The failure to file such a statement may subject those shareholders (and the directors) to civil and criminal liabilities, including liability for misuse of insider's information. See 15 U.S.C. 78p and S.E.C. v. Texas Gulf Sulphur Co., 401 F. 2nd 833 (CA 2, 1968).

shareholder's liability, general aspects

In practice it is common for large creditors (especially banks) and major suppliers to require personal guarantees from one or more of the corporate participants before money or credit will be extended to a small business corporation, especially if it is new. The corporate participants who personally guarantee such notes, advances or accounts will, of course, be personally liable for them, and they should be so advised. Also, if a person is employed by the corporation, whether or not he or she is a shareholder, and engages in an act of negligence while performing the corporation's business, both the corporation and the employee may be liable for any injuries or damages resulting from such negligence. If a shareholder leads someone doing business with the corporation to believe that the person is doing business with the shareholder personally, the shareholder may be personally liable for any corporate debts so incurred. See section 6.06, infra for further reading on this issue.

shareholders' agreements, enforceability

A common method of implementing the management and control structure of a small business corporation is through a shareholders' agreement. Shareholder agreements may be entered into for any lawful purpose by any two or more shareholders, regardless of whether the parties to the agreement constitute a minority, a majority, or all of the shareholders of a corporation. Such agreements are expressly recognized by statute in most states, and are generally enforceable in states without statutory recognition, although they may be subjected to some of the limitations applicable to voting trusts if they deal with voting rights and are self-executing. Agreements involving all of the shareholders of a corporation are most likely to be enforced by the courts in cases where the enforceability of an agreement is questionable.

shareholders' agreements, general aspects

The corporation should be made at least a nominal party to a shareholders' agreement for the purpose of enforcing the agreement against the corporation. Also, an endorsement should be placed on any stock certificate representing shares of stock subject to a shareholders' agreement so that a transferee of stock subject to such an agreement will have at least constructive notice of the agreement. Otherwise, a transferee without actual knowledge of the agreement may not be bound by the agreement.

shareholders' agreements, purposes

A shareholders' agreement may be used for any one or more of the following purposes:

(1) the election of directors;

(2) the establishment of corporate policy;

(3) establishing rules on the declaration of dividends;

(4) imposing restrictions on the transfer of stock;

(5) establishing methods of disposing of a shareholder's stock in the event of the shareholder's death or disability;

(6) establishing procedures to be followed in the event of the dissolution of the corporation;

(7) the employment of certain persons by the corporation, as officers or otherwise, and the terms of such employment;

(8) the removal of directors, with or without cause;

(9) establishing methods of resolving corporate disputes or deadlocks;

(10) giving veto powers to certain shareholders under specified circumstances;

(11) insuring shareholder cooperation on Subchapter S matters (see section 5.18, infra), and

(12) providing for the management of the corporation by its shareholders under a special statute (see section 6.19, infra).

control of voting rights by shareholder agreement

The most common function of a shareholders' agreement is to control the voting rights of the parties to the agreement. Such provisions are permissible in every state, usually by express statutory authority. The agreement may provide that the voting rights in the stock held by the parties must be voted as explicitly provided in the agreement (e.g., for director candidates A, B, and C), or as the parties may agree (e.g., for the director candidates backed by the holders of a majority of the shares to the agreement), or as set forth in a procedure contained in the agreement (e.g., for the director candidates endorsed by the incumbent board of directors).

voting trusts, applicability

For small business corporations, the control of shareholder voting rights by shareholder agreement is preferable to control by voting trusts for a number of reasons, including the following: (1) voting trusts usually have a maximum life of only 10 years, which is insufficient in many cases, (2) voting trusts are more complicated and more costly to draft and implement than shareholder agreements, (3) under a voting trust the shareholders must transfer their stock to a trustee, something that many small business participants are reluctant to do and a transaction that may affect their rights as shareholders, and (4) in some states a majority of shares in a voting trust can elect to terminate the trust, thus forfeiting the rights of minority shareholders under the trust. Because of their general inapplicability to small business corporations, voting trusts as devices to control shareholder voting rights are not discussed in this handbook.

If a shareholders' agreement deals with voting rights, the best practice is to make the agreement self-executing, if permitted under local law. This will prevent a shareholder from later thwarting the purpose of the agreement by either refusing to vote or voting other than in accordance with the agreement. Self-execution is accomplished when each party to the agreement grants, in writing, an irrevocable proxy to a specific person (who may be a party to the agreement) or to every other party to the agreement, entitling the holder of the proxy to vote the shares in accordance with the terms of the shareholder agreement. Care should be taken to insure that the proxy provisions in the shareholder agreement meet the requirements of state laws dealing with proxies (see infra, this chapter). In a few states the granting of irrevocable proxies in shareholder agreements is precluded either because irrevocable proxies are void as against public policy or because the courts have held that a self-executing shareholder agreement is, in effect, a voting trust and must comply with the statutory requirements of voting trusts (which is not feasible in most cases). shareholders' agreement, self-executing voting rights; irrevocable proxies, shareholder agreements

It is common for a shareholders' agreement to include provisions dealing with restrictions on the transferability of stock, the disposition of a shareholder's stock in the event of the death or disability of the shareholder, and the removal of directors, with or without cause. Such provisions, if reasonable, are valid and universally enforceable. See section 5.17, infra, for further reading on stock transfer restrictions and the disposition of stock upon the death or disability of a shareholder. See infra, this section and sections 5.15 and 6.05, infra, for further reading on the removal of directors. stock transfer restrictions, use of shareholder agreements

Historically, courts have invalidated shareholder agreements that infringed on the discretion traditionally given to the board of directors in such matters as selecting the corporate officers, declaring dividends, and determining corporate policy. While such cases may still be valid as they relate to publicly-held corporations, modern decisions in many states, as well as statutes in some states, now permit the participants of small business corporations to deal with such matters in shareholder agreements as long as they are reasonable in scope and are not unfair or fraudulent to creditors or shareholders not parties to the agreement. Caution is advised, however, and both the statutory and case law in the applicable state should be examined before including such provisions in a shareholders' agreement. It should be noted that the corporation laws of several states expressly permit certain statutory duties of the board of directors to be reserved to the shareholders, if so provided in the articles of incorporation or in a unanimous shareholders' agreement. shareholder agreements, director functions

In implementing the corporate management and control structure desired by the business participants it is sometimes necessary to give veto powers (i.e., the power to veto or prevent certain acts) over certain corporate acts to one or more of the shareholders. Although veto powers are usually implemented through article of incorporation and bylaw provisions, sometimes the most practical method of implementing a veto power is through a shareholders' agreement. Veto powers are best implemented through a shareholders' agreement when there are only a few shareholders and when only one or two acts, such as the transfer of stock or the election of directors, are to be subjected to a veto power. When implementing veto powers through a shareholders' agreement, it is important that the provisions in the agreement be consistent with the provisions of the articles of incorporation and the bylaws. Finally, if a shareholders' agreement is to contain a veto power it is important that all of the shareholders be parties to the agreement; otherwise it is not likely to be sustained if challenged by a non-party shareholder. See section 5.15, infra, for further reading on veto powers. shareholder agreements, veto powers

In exceptional cases provisions dealing with the breaking of corporate deadlocks and the resolution of corporate disputes may be included in a shareholders' agreement. Such provisions, if reasonable, are usually valid. See section 5.15, infra, for further reading on the resolution of corporate disputes and deadlocks. In exceptional cases, specific provisions dealing with procedures to be followed in the event of the dissolution of the corporation may be included in a shareholders' agreement. As long as the provisions in the agreement do not conflict with statutory dissolution procedures and are not forbidden by the statute, they are usually valid. See section 7.03, infra, for further reading on corporate dissolutions. A sample shareholders' agreement is set forth in Exhibit 5-C at the end of this chapter. shareholder agreements, deadlocks and dissolution

majority shareholders, fiduciary duties to minority

An obligation that is often misunderstood or unrecognized by the participants of small business corporations is the fiduciary obligation of controlling shareholders to minority shareholders. Majority shareholders often assume that because they control the corporation they can operate it solely for their own benefit. Such is not the case. The courts often impose a higher standard of fiduciary responsibility on the controlling shareholders of small or closely held corporations than on the controlling shareholders of publicly held corporations. The shareholders of a small business corporation should treat each other essentially as partners. See Donahue v. Rodd Electrotype Co., 367 Mass. 578, 328 N.E. 2nd 505, 512-515 (1975). It is generally held that the controlling shareholders of a small business corporation bear a fiduciary duty to deal fairly, honestly, and openly with minority shareholders and to disclose all essential information to them. See Helms v. Duckworth, 249 F. 2nd 482, 487(CADC, 1957).

controlling shareholders, dealing with corporation

Questions of fiduciary responsibility often arise when a controlling shareholder sells supplies, materials, or services to the corporation, or when a controlling shareholder also controls another entity with whom the corporation does business. In each case the controlling shareholder (or shareholders) must act fairly and the prices, fees, or contracts charged or entered into with the corporation must be reasonable and competitive. See Gottesman v. General Motors Corp., 279 F. Supp. 361, 385 (SDNY, 1967).

controlling shareholders, duties to minority shareholders

Questions of fiduciary responsibility may also arise when controlling shareholders decide to sell their stock. They must be diligent in not selling to irresponsible or disreputable outsiders whom they have reason to believe may loot the corporation or cause it to fail. See DeBaun v. First Western Bank & Trust Co., 46 Cal. App. 3rd 686, 120 Cal. Rpt. 354 (1975). If the controlling shareholders receive a premium for the sale of their stock because of the control that goes with it, the offer must not be concealed from the minority shareholders. See Thompson v. Hambrick, 508 S.W. 2nd 949, 954 (Tex. Civ. Apps., 1974). Also, if a corporation redeems the stock of a controlling shareholder, a similar opportunity must be offered to the minority shareholders. See Donahue v. Rodd Electrotype Co., 367 Mass. 578, 328 N.E. 2nd 505 (1975). Finally, the controlling shareholders may not unreasonably deny employment to a minority shareholder, because the opportunity for employment is often the principal return on the investment of a minority shareholder in a small business corporation. See Wilkes v. Springside Nursing Home, Inc., 370 Mass. 842, 353 N.E. 2nd 657 (1976). See sections 6.05 and 6.06, infra, for further reading on the fiduciary duties of majority shareholders.

rights of shareholders as owners of corporation

Certain rights are conferred upon shareholders by virtue of the fact that they are the owners of the corporation. These rights, some of which are statutory, include -

(1) the right to exercise the voting rights that accompany the stock, either in person or by proxy;

(2) the right to receive their pro-rata share of any dividends issued by the corporation to their class of stock;

(3) the right to attend shareholder meetings, either in person or by proxy;

(4) the right to amend the bylaws of the corporation;

(5) the right to remove directors for cause;

(6) the right to approve (or disapprove) extraordinary corporate matters such as amending the articles of incorporation, the sale or lease of corporate assets not in the ordinary course of business, mergers, consolidations, and the dissolution of the corporation;

(7) the right of dissenting shareholders to have their stock appraised and redeemed under certain extraordinary circumstances;

(8) the right to inspect the books of the corporation;

(9) the right to have their stock, and the transfer thereof, recorded on the books of the corporation;

(10) the right to sell, bequeath, or otherwise transfer their stock, unless that right has been waived or reasonably conditioned; and

(11) the right to bring an action, either directly against the corporation to enforce an individual right or derivatively on behalf of the corporation against persons who have wronged the corporation.

In the absence of provisions to the contrary in the articles of incorporation, each share of stock is normally entitled to one vote, regardless of whether the vote is to elect the board of directors or to approve a corporate matter requiring shareholder ratification or approval. This is commonly referred to as straight voting. In most states, however, voting may also be cumulative, by class, or disproportionate, if provisions for same are contained in the articles of incorporation. shareholder voting, general rules

Under straight voting the holders of a majority of the shares can elect the entire board of directors if they choose to do so, leaving the minority shareholders unrepresented on the board. To give minority shareholders a chance to be represented on the board of directors, a system of voting commonly referred to as cumulative voting has been devised. Under cumulative voting a shareholder may cast as many votes as are equal to the number of his or her voting shares multiplied by the number of directors to be elected in the election at hand. The votes may then be accumulated and cast for any one or more candidates, rather than cast equally or ratably for each office to be filled. For example, if three persons are to be elected to the board of directors in a certain election, a shareholder who has 100 voting shares may cast 300 votes for one candidate rather than casting 100 votes for each of three separate candidates, as he or she would have to do under straight voting. cumulative voting, general description

Under cumulative voting it is easier for minority shareholders to elect at least one member of the board of directors, but they can never elect a majority. To ascertain the number of voting shares a shareholder must hold in order to elect a specific number of directors under cumulative voting, the following formula may be used: cumulative voting, a formula

$$X = \frac{T \times D}{N + 1} + 1$$

X = the number of shares needed
T = total number of shares voting
D = number of directors desired to elect
N = total number of directors to be elected

Thus, if there are 1800 total voting shares outstanding in the corporation and if five directors are to be elected in the election, a shareholder would need 301 voting shares to elect one director and 601 voting shares to elect two directors under cumulative voting. To elect all of the directors a shareholder would need 1501 voting shares.

Cumulative voting is mandatory in several states, either by constitutional or statutory requirement. In most states cumulative voting is permissible if provided for in the articles of incorporation. In some states cumulative voting is required unless it is denied in the articles of incorporation. In several states the statute requires any shareholder intending to vote cumulatively to give prior notice of an intention of doing so. In any event, it is important to check the corporation laws of the state of incorporation with respect to cumulative voting, regardless of whether the corporate participants desire to utilize it. The statutory cumulative voting provisions in each state are cited and summarized in Appendix I, infra, under the heading of "Cumulative Voting." cumulative voting, when required

Class voting occurs when different classes of stock are issued and each class of stock votes separately for directors and on other designated corporate matters. The most common example of class voting occurs when the board of directors is classified and each class of stock elects a designated number of directors to the board. Classified voting can often dilute the effects of cumulative voting and is sometimes used by majority shareholders for that purpose in states where cumulative voting is mandatory. Disproportionate voting occurs when one class of stock has greater or fewer votes per share than another class of stock. See section 5.07, infra, for further reading on classified voting. class voting, general aspects disproportionate voting

proxies, general aspects

Most corporation laws provide that a shareholder may vote his or her shares either in person or by proxy. Most statutes require a proxy to be in writing and provide that it shall expire in 11 months unless it is otherwise stated in the proxy instrument. The term "proxy" is customarily applied to both the instrument that conveys the authority to vote a shareholder's stock and the person holding the proxy instrument and representing the shareholder at the shareholders' meeting. The relationship between the shareholder and the proxy is generally one of principal and agent, and the laws thereof apply. It is generally against public policy, and a crime in some states, for a shareholder to sell his or her proxy. See Chew v. Inverness Management Corp., 352 A. 2nd 426(Del. Ch., 1976). A proxy is usually revocable at the will of the shareholder unless it is coupled with an interest or given as security. A sample proxy is set forth in Exhibit 4-D at the end of this chapter.

shareholder meetings, requirements

shareholders, action without meeting

Shareholders of record are entitled to receive notice of, and to be represented either in person or by proxy at, both annual and special meetings of the shareholders. See section 6.04, infra, for further reading on shareholder meetings. Most corporation laws provide that any shareholder action that could be taken at a shareholders' meeting may be taken without a meeting if a written consent to the action is signed by all of the shareholders entitled to vote on the matter. See sections 5.11 and 6.04, infra, for further reading on action-without-meeting statutes.

shareholders, right to amend bylaws

shareholders, right to remove directors

Even if the articles of incorporation or the bylaws lawfully confer the right to amend the corporate bylaws to the board of directors, it seems to be settled law that the shareholders, as the owners of the corporation, retain the inherent power to amend them. See Rogers v. Hill, 289 U.S. 582, 53 S.Ct. 731, 77 L.Ed. 1385 (1933). See section 5.10, infra, for further reading on amending the bylaws. Also, even in the absence of statutory authority, it seems to be settled law that the shareholders who are empowered to elect directors have the inherent power to remove them for cause, subject to adequate notice and an opportunity for the directors to be heard. See Auer v. Dressel, 306 N.Y. 427, 118 N.E. 2nd 590, 48 A.L.R. 2nd 604 (1954). See section 6.05, infra, for further reading on the removal of directors.

shareholders, approval of corporate acts

Most corporation laws provide, as does the common law in the absence of statute, that shareholder approval is required for certain extraordinary corporate matters. Such matters usually include amending the articles of incorporation, the sale or transfer of all or substantially all of the corporate assets not in the ordinary course of business, mergers, consolidations, and share exchanges, and the voluntary dissolution of the corporation. The corporate acts that require shareholder approval in each state are summarized in Appendix I, infra, under the heading of "Acts Requiring Shareholder Approval."

dissenting shareholders, appraisal rights

Under most corporation laws shareholders who dissent from certain mergers, consolidations or share exchanges, from the sale or transfer of all or substantially all of the corporate assets not in the usual course of business, or from article of incorporation amendments that eliminate the preferential, redemption, or preemptive rights of a shareholder are entitled to have their stock appraised and purchased by the corporation. The procedure for enforcing appraisal rights is usually set forth in the corporation laws.

shareholders, right to inspect corporate books

shareholders, rights with respect to stock

Shareholders, usually either in person or by agent or attorney, have a statutory right to inspect, and make copies of the corporation's list of shareholders and the corporate books and records for proper purposes and at specified times. This right exists under the common law if no statutory provision for it. See Tucson Gas & Electric Co. v. Schantz, 5 Ariz. Apps. 511, 428 P. 2nd 686 (1967). Shareholders also have a statutory right to have their stock, and the transfer thereof, recorded in the corporation's record of shareholders and, subject to reasonable restrictions, the right to sell, bequeath, or otherwise transfer their stock.

shareholders, right to sue corporation

If a corporation refuses to treat a person holding stock as a shareholder, or if the corporation otherwise wrongs a shareholder in his or her individual capacity, the shareholder may sue the corporation directly to enforce his or her rights as a shareholder. If the corporation has been wronged and if the management of the corporation refuses to bring an action or otherwise act to rectify or seek compensation for the wrong (usually because management has perpetrated the wrong), a shareholder may bring an action, called a shareholder's derivative action, against the alleged wrongdoers. This right of action is recognized by statute in most states and has long been recognized by the common law in the absence of statute. See section 6.05, infra, for further reading on shareholder's derivative actions.

5.07 The Board of Directors

It is the function of the board of directors to manage the affairs of the corporation; that is, to set corporate policy and oversee its execution. Even though the directors are elected by the shareholders and removable by them for cause, the directors are not, in theory at least, agents of the shareholders. The powers of the directors are derived from the state, not delegated by the shareholders, and their principal duties, fiduciary and otherwise, run to the corporation and not to the individual shareholders, although they must treat all shareholders fairly and evenly and may not favor one shareholder or group of shareholders over another. It should be noted that in several states a corporation may, in its articles of incorporation, dispense with the board of directors and permit the shareholders to manage the corporation.

board of directors, functions and powers

In most states there are no statutorily-imposed qualifications for directors, other than a requirement that they be natural persons and, in some states, of lawful age. Most corporation laws permit the articles of incorporation or bylaws to prescribe qualifications for directors, and provide that a director need not be a state resident or a shareholder of the corporation unless the articles of incorporation or bylaws so require.

qualification of directors

The number of directors that a corporation may, or must, have is regulated by statute. While some states require a minimum of three directors, in most states only one director is required. In most of the states that require a minimum of three directors, corporations with fewer than three shareholders may have the same number of directors as shareholders. Usually there are no statutory limits on the maximum number of directors that a corporation may have. Some states, in establishing the number of directors, employ a sliding scale whereby the articles of incorporation or the bylaws establish the minimum and maximum number of directors, with the exact number at any particular time set by a board of director or shareholder resolution, or, if the limits are established in the articles of incorporation, by a bylaw provision. This sliding scale provision can adversely affect the cumulative voting rights of minority shareholders and any such provision should not be in conflict with any statutory or article of incorporation cumulative voting requirements. In any event, it is important to check the appropriate corporation statutes to ascertain the required number of directors and whether the number of directors should be set forth in the articles of incorporation or the bylaws. The laws of each state in this regard are summarized in Appendix I, infra, under the heading of "Board of Directors."

number of directors, general aspects

In many states the initial board of directors of the corporation must be named in the articles of incorporation. In other states the initial board of directors may be named in the articles of incorporation if desired. In either event, the initial board of directors must serve until their successors are elected and qualified. All subsequent directors must be elected by the shareholders.

initial board of directors

The corporation laws of virtually every state require that an organizational meeting be held. The organizational meeting is normally held by the initial board of directors, if they are named in the articles of incorporation. If initial directors are not named in the articles of incorporation, the incorporators are usually required to hold the organizational meeting. A few states require the shareholders to hold the meeting and some states permit either the board of directors or the incorporators to hold the meeting. Many states have an action-without-meeting statute that is applicable to incorporators. The organizational meeting requirements in each state and the existence in a state of an action-without-meeting statute for incorporators are set forth in Appendix I, infra, under the heading of "Organizational Meeting."

organizational meeting, requirements

The business conducted at the organizational meeting, if one is held, may include the following:

organizational meeting, business conducted

(1) The election of a chairman and a secretary, who normally takes the minutes of the meeting.

(2) The recognition of proper notice of the meeting or of the waiver thereof.

(3) The presentation and adoption of the articles of incorporation and bylaws for the corporation.

(4) The adoption of the corporate seal, if the corporation is to have one.

(5) The approval of the form of stock certificate (or certificates) for the corporation.

(6) The authorization for the corporate officers to issue shares of stock to designated persons in designated amounts and the consideration to be received by the corporation for the shares of stock so issued.

(7) The acceptance of transfers of stock subscriptions from the incorporators, if required by local law.

(8) The acceptance of stock subscriptions, if any, procured by the incorporators or promoters.

(9) The authorization for the corporation to reimburse the incorporators or others for fees and expenses incurred in organizing the corporation.

(10) The adoption (or rejection) by the corporation of preincorporation agreements, if any exist.

(11) The election of the officers of the corporation.

(12) The adoption of a banking resolution, usually on a form provided by the bank.

(13) The appointment of a resident corporate agent and office, usually those designated in the articles of incorporation.

(14) The designation, if desired, of the corporation's legal counsel, accountant, engineer, and other professional advisers.

(15) The approval of action taken at previous meetings of directors or incorporators.

(16) The resignation of dummy directors, if any, and the selection of actual directors.

(17) The approval of employment contracts, if any, between the corporation and its employees or officers.

See section 5.21, infra, for further reading on the preparation of the documents and the performance of the functions described above. See Exhibit 5-E at the end of this chapter for sample minutes of an organizational meeting. See Exhibit 5-H at the end of this chapter for a sample Waiver of Notice of Organizational Meeting.

organizational meeting, when not held, minutes

Because the participants of small business corporations often agree on all substantive matters in advance, many times a formal organizational meeting is considered a waste of time and is not actually held. In such event, the minutes of an organizational meeting should still appear in the corporate records so as to clarify the agreement and comply with statutory requirements, if any exist. Consequently, a set of minutes reflecting the meeting, along with notice waivers, should be prepared and signed by the participants. As a practical matter, it is often more convenient to handle the organizational meeting by preparing a memorandum under an action-without-meeting statute, if one is applicable in the local state.

classification of directors, general aspects

Most states permit the classification of directors, although conditions requiring certain numbers of directors, numbers of classes, and frequency of elections are often imposed. The classification of directors simply means that the directors are divided into classes, with a single class of directors elected each year, often by a designated class of shareholders. For example, if a corporation has six directors it would be possible under most classification statutes to divide the directors into three classes each consisting of two directors, with one class of directors elected each year and each director serving a three-year term, except for the first year when one class of directors would be elected for one year, one class for two years, and one class for three years.

directors, term of office

filling vacancies on board of directors

Normally, directors of small business corporations are elected annually for a one-year term, which is the legally required term in most states in the absence of classification. In any case, a director serves until a successor has been elected and qualified. A director elected to fill a vacancy serves the balance of the predecessor's term. In many states the board of directors is empowered to fill a vacancy on the board, unless precluded from doing so by the articles of incorporation or bylaws. In other states, vacancies on the board may be filled by either the shareholders or the board of directors, unless the articles of incorporation provide otherwise.

As stated above, the primary function of the board of directors is to establish policy and manage the affairs of the corporation. The normal management functions of the board of directors of a small business corporation may include the following: management functions of board of directors

(1) The making and implementing of policy determinations regarding the business affairs of the corporation, including products, services, prices, and compensation.

(2) The selection, supervision, and removal of officers and executive personnel.

(3) Setting the salaries of officers and other employees.

(4) The fixing and declaration of dividends.

(5) Adopting and amending the corporate bylaws.

(6) Issuing, purchasing, and redeeming shares of the corporate stock and determining the amount and form of the consideration therefor.

(7) Calling meetings of shareholders.

(8) Approving the appointment of outside advisors such as attorneys and accountants.

(9) Recommending the submission to shareholders of important corporate matters such as mergers, consolidations, amendments to the articles of incorporation, dissolution, and the sale or lease of assets.

(10) Approving the issuing or procuring of corporate loans.

(11) Approving the payment of taxes incurred and owed by the corporation.

(12) The making of political or charitable contributions, if any.

(13) Electing the chairman of the board of directors.

Traditionally, directors must direct and may not be deprived of the exercise of their judgment in managing corporate affairs by agreements that unduly deprive them of their discretion. See Burnett v. Word, Inc., 412 S.W. 2nd 792 (Tex. Civ. Apps., 1967). However, because the directors and shareholders are essentially the same persons modern decisions in many states, as well as statutes in several states, permit the participants of small business corporations to enter into agreements dealing with matters reserved to director discretion in larger corporations, as long as the agreements are not fraudulent or unfair to creditors or other shareholders. See section 5.06, supra, for further reading on this matter. director discretion, effect of agreement

Directors must be reasonably diligent in the management and supervision of corporate affairs and may be held liable in negligence if they are not. Fiduciary duties to minority or outside shareholders are often imposed by the courts on directors, especially those elected by majority shareholders, and directors breaching such duties may be held personally liable. In addition, directors are personally liable by statute in most states for the illegal distribution of dividends and redemption of stock. The corporation laws of many states contain standards of conduct for directors, sometimes relieving them of personal liability if they comply with such standards. See section 6.06, infra, for further reading on the personal liability of directors of small business corporations. personal liability of directors

Of course, the board of directors is not required to pass on every issue or matter that confronts the corporation. Directors have the right to delegate to officers, agents, or committees the authority to carry out the policies and decisions of the board and to transact the day-to-day affairs of the corporation. Other acts, like the 13 functions listed above, cannot normally be delegated to officers. In some states, however, certain functions normally conferred on the board of directors, including the election of officers and the issuance of dividends, may be specifically reserved to the shareholders in the articles of incorporation. board of directors, delegation of authority functions reserved to shareholders

executive committees, authority

Different rules are normally applied to the delegation of authority to executive committees, which are specifically dealt with by statute in most states. An executive committee, which must be composed of directors, may normally deal with any matter except those listed in the statute as being nondelegable. Absent statutory authority, the delegation of authority to executive committees is usually strictly construed, and the delegation of authority to outsiders (consultants, management companies, etc.) is even more strictly construed. The delegation of authority to committees, officers, or agents does not relieve the board of directors of their overall responsibility of managing the corporation.

directors, necessity of meeting

Directors must act as a body. The vesting of management responsibilities is with the board of directors, not with the directors individually. Therefore, the directors must be duly convened as a board before they can legally carry out the corporation's business. Unlike shareholders, directors must always vote per capita, and they may not vote by proxy. An exception to the rule requiring directors to meet are action-without-meeting statutes that expressly permit directors to act without a meeting if a written consent setting forth the action so taken is signed by all or a specified percentage of the directors. Action-without-meeting statutes are discussed in sections 5.11 and 6.04, infra.

directors, necessity of meeting, exceptions

director meetings, use of conference telephone

Even without statutory authority, courts sometimes uphold exceptions to board of director meetings requirements in cases involving small business corporations, especially if the practice is a custom of long duration within the corporation. See Remillong v. Schneider, 185 N.W. 2nd 493 (ND, 1971). It should be noted that in most states the board of directors, or a committee thereof, is legally convened if they can hear each other's voices at the same time by means of a conference telephone or similar communications equipment, provided that such meetings are not precluded by the articles of incorporation or bylaws. The existence of such a statute in each is set forth in Appendix I, infra, under the heading of "Action Without Meeting."

directors' compensation, how established

The corporation laws of most states permit the board of directors to establish their own compensation, unless the articles of incorporation or the bylaws provide otherwise. In some states the amount of director compensation must be set forth in the bylaws, the articles of incorporation, or in a shareholder resolution. If the corporation laws are silent on the subject, the common law rule of treating directors as trustees serving without compensation is likely to be applied, unless a provision expressly permitting and regulating director compensation is contained in the articles of incorporation or bylaws. Even if it is permissible to compensate directors, fixing the amount of compensation in the absence of a statute on the matter may be a problem because of the general rule precluding a director from voting on his or her own compensation (see infra, this section). The best practice in such instances is to establish the amount and form of a director's compensation before the director takes office.

directors, compensation for other services

It is common in small business corporations for the same person to occupy several positions within the corporation. The same person might be a shareholder, a director, and an officer, as well as the corporation's engineer, accountant, or attorney. In most cases the person is entitled to be directly compensated for his or her services in each capacity (except shareholder), provided that the compensation is reasonable in amount. The statutory or corporate authority allowing directors to set their own compensation does not include the right to award unreasonable amounts. See Goldman v. Jameson, 290 Ala. 160, 275 S. 2nd 108 (1973).

directors, amount of compensation

In practice, the compensation of directors of small business corporations varies, depending on the amount and type of actual involvement a director has with the corporation. If a director is also a full-time executive officer with the corporation or serves the corporation professionally as an attorney, engineer, or accountant, his or her fee as a director is likely to be nominal or none at all, especially if the entire board is composed of persons in the same position. The same is usually true if the director, while not actively involved as an officer or agent of the corporation, is a majority or significant shareholder in the corporation. However, a director who is an outsider with no other direct interest or involvement with the corporation usually expects to be compensated for his or her services, either through an annual fee or by a fixed fee for each meeting attended. The actual amount of compensation usually depends on the status of the director, the amount of time devoted to the corporation's affairs, and the size and financial condition of the corporation.

officer-director compensation for extraordinary services

It is not uncommon for a director or an officer of a small business corporation to render extraordinary services to the corporation; that is, services that are outside the scope and beyond the call of his or her normal duties. In such cases it is usually permissible for the corporation to grant additional compensation to the director or officer for the extraordinary services, especially if the corporation has benefitted substantially therefrom. The foregoing rule has been applied even where the director or officer had an employment contract with the corporation couched in broad, general language. See Barnett v. International Tennis Corp., 80 Mich. Apps. 396, 263 N.W. 2nd 908 (1978). The safest practice is for the corporation to agree in advance to compensate a director or officer for extraordinary services, provided that the services result in a substantial benefit to the corporation.

directors, contracts with corporation

In small business corporations it is often necessary or desirable for a corporate participant to enter into a contract with the corporation. The contract may be to loan money to the corporation, to lease property or equipment to or from the corporation, to furnish supplies or services to the corporation, to purchase or sell stock in the corporation, or for any other lawful purpose. Whatever the purpose of the contract, the general rule is that a director or officer may enter into a binding contract with the corporation only if he or she deals openly and fairly with the corporation. See Talbot v. James, 259 S.C. 73, 190 S.E. 2nd 759 (1972). Fiduciary duties of full disclosure and fair dealing are imposed on any director or officer contracting with the corporation. See Underwood v. Stafford, 270 N.C. 700, 155 S.E. 2nd 211 (1967).

directors, conflicts of interest, loans to

directors, corporate loans to

The corporation laws of most states contain provisions dealing with director conflicts of interest. These statutes typically provide that a transaction between a director and the corporation is not voidable by the corporation if a full disclosure of all of the material facts was made to the governing body of the corporation or if the transaction was fair to the corporation. It should be noted that it is provided by statute in most states that a corporation may not lend money to or guarantee the obligation of a director unless the transaction is either approved by a majority vote of the shareholders or approved by the board of directors as benefitting the corporation.

authority of corporation to contract with director

directors, contracts with corporation, voidability

Another requirement of any contract between a director and the corporation is that the corporation be properly authorized to enter into the contract. This requirement is closely scrutinized by the courts because of the obvious opportunity for self dealing present in such situations. To be valid the contract must normally be approved by the board of directors. In submitting the contract to the board, the best practice is for the interested director to refrain from voting on the matter, for if he or she does vote and if the vote is necessary to carry the resolution, the contract may be voidable at the option of the corporation, regardless of its fairness. See Dowdle v. Texas Am. Oil Co., 503 S.W. 2nd 647 (Tex. Civ. Apps., 1973) and Knutson v. Mueller, 68 Wis. 2nd 199, 228 N.W. 2nd 342 (1975). In general, however, if a contract between a corporation and one of its directors is approved by a disinterested majority of directors, it is voidable only on the grounds of unfairness or fraud. See Lipkins v. Jacoby, 42 Del.Ch. 1, 202 A. 2nd 572 (1964). The same general rules are applied to contracts between corporations with common directors. See Murphy v. Washington Am. League Baseball Club, Inc., 324 F. 2nd 394 (CADC, 1963).

directors, suggested rules of conduct

The following rules of conduct are suggested for directors of small business corporations:

(1) Attend all board of director meetings if at all possible. If it is impossible to attend a certain meeting, find out what transpired at the meeting by reading the minutes of the meeting and talking to other directors who were in attendance.

(2) If it is impossible to attend board of director meetings on a regular basis, consider resigning because the constant failure to attend the meetings for any reason (even illness) is a breach of duty and may result in personal liability.

(3) Take notes at all board of director meetings attended and keep a personal record of them.

(4) Read the minutes of all meetings, including those not attended, and insure that the minutes contain an accurate record of such meetings, including the voting records of the directors.

(5) Become familiar with financial reports and legal opinions prepared by the corporation's accountants and attorneys. Don't take someone else's word for their content.

(6) Don't vote, or even participate in discussions, on matters of personal interest, especially if it relates to compensation or employment, unless such voting is specifically authorized by a statute or a valid article of incorporation or bylaw provision. Even then, refrain from voting if possible.

(7) Don't enter into agreements that could compromise the ability to exercise independent judgment on behalf of the corporation unless it is clear that the agreement is legally valid and in the best interest of the corporation.

attorney as director, advisability

It frequently happens that the participants of a small business corporation invite their attorney to serve as a director. The circumstances of the invitation often make it difficult for the attorney to refuse to serve. Before accepting, however, the attorney should consider the situation seriously. First of all, because of an attorney's specialized training and knowledge, he or she may be held by the courts to a higher standard of care in making judgments as a director, especially those having legal implications. See Escott v. BarChris Construction Corp., 283 F. Supp. 643, 690 (SDNY, 1968). Also, an attorney who is both a director and the corporation's legal counsel may encounter conflict of interest problems, as well as the risk of being ethically unable to represent the corporation in litigation where the directors are likely to be called as witnesses. Further, an attorney whose primary interest is his or her law practice is not usually abreast of the day-to-day workings of the corporate business and may not be aware of the manner in which the business is being conducted, a situation that could result in either professional embarrassment or personal liability. Finally, the attorney who serves as a director could be placed in the difficult position of having to choose between opposing directors or factions should corporate disputes arise. In most instances the attorney is best advised to decline the invitation.

attorney as director, rules of conduct

An attorney who chooses to serve as a director should take steps to protect himself or herself from personal liability resulting from the nonpayment of federal withholding taxes by declining the right to sign checks or disburse funds on behalf of the corporation (see section 6.06, infra). The attorney should insist that board of director meetings be held and that accurate minutes be kept. The attorney should also adhere closely to the suggested rules of conduct for directors listed above in this section. Finally, should the attorney disapprove of any corporate action approved by the board of directors, he or she should have the dissent recorded and, at this point, consider resigning.

5.08 The Corporate Officers - Employment Contracts

The corporation laws of most states require corporations to create and fill certain offices, usually the offices of president, secretary, and treasurer. The same statutes typically permit a corporation to create additional offices by providing for them in the articles of incorporation or bylaws. The offices needed by a corporation depend on the particular needs of the business and the desires of the corporate participants. A construction company, for example, would normally require different officers than, say, a dental office. Similarly, a thirty-person corporation is likely to require different officers than a one-person corporation. A well drafted set of bylaws should not only designate the desired corporate officers, but also describe in some detail the functions to be fulfilled by each officer. The corporate officers required or permitted by the corporation laws of each state are listed in Appendix I, infra, under the heading of "Officers."

corporate officers, required and permitted

The manner of electing or appointing corporate officers is also governed by statute in most states. Usually the officers are elected or appointed by the board of directors. However, in a growing number of states the shareholders may elect all or certain of the corporate officers if the articles of incorporation or bylaws so provide. Most corporation laws give a corporation considerable latitude in establishing qualifications for its officers, but many states prohibit dual office holding for certain offices (usually president and secretary). A few states require that oaths be taken by certain officers, usually the secretary and treasurer. Among small business corporations, shareholder agreements calling for the election of certain persons as officers of the corporation are common, and are usually enforceable as long as the officers are competent in the performance of their duties. See section 5.06, supra for further reading on shareholder agreements.

corporate officers, appointment, qualifications

Occasionally it happens that a corporation is formed and commences to do business without having elected or appointed any officers. In such cases the person or persons who hold themselves out to be the corporate representatives are usually held to be defacto officers of the corporation, thus giving legality to the transactions conducted.

corporation without officers, legality of action

The term of office, if any, of an officer is usually established in the bylaws or articles of incorporation. Most corporation laws do not require specific terms of office, and in many cases the best practice is to specify none in the articles or bylaws, thereby gaining flexibility by permitting the officers to serve at the pleasure of the board of directors. It is customary for inferior or assistant officers to be appointed by the senior officers, and the bylaws may so state if desired.

corporate officers, term of office

An officer may, of course, resign at any time, even if he or she has an employment contract calling for a specific term that has not expired. Most corporation laws permit bylaw provisions dealing with the filling of vacancies in offices, and it is a good practice to include such a provision in the bylaws. Absent such a provision, the board of directors has the inherent power to fill vacancies occurring in offices that they fill.

corporate offices, filling vacancies

In the absence of proof to the contrary, it is normally presumed that the president of a corporation is its business head with the power to perform any act that the board of directors could authorize or ratify. See Mo. Valley Steel Co. v. New Amsterdam Co., 275 Minn. 433, 148 N.W. 2nd 126 (1966). If, however, a particular transaction is not in the ordinary course of business, then the authority of the president to bind the corporation must be shown by express authorization. See In Re Lee Ready Mix & Supply Co., 437 F. 2nd 497 (CA 6, 1971). In general, courts are more likely to bind a small corporation on the actions and contracts of its president than a large corporation, especially if the president is also a substantial owner of the corporation.

president, authority to act for corporation

The vice president, the secretary, and the treasurer of a corporation do not customarily have the authority by virtue of their office to bind the corporation in the ordinary course of business. Frequently, however, the power to bind the corporation is delegated to one or more of these officers by the bylaws or by a board of director resolution. In any event, the duties of these officers should be explicitly set forth in the bylaws. Many corporations have a controller, either in addition to or instead of the treasurer. It is also common, especially in small corporations, to combine these offices (e.g., secretary-treasurer), except for the offices of president and secretary, which cannot be combined in some states.

ministerial officers, authority

general managers, authority

It is common for a small business corporation to have a general manager. Usually the general manager ranks below the president and above all other officers. The general manager, like the president, has the authority by virtue of his or her office to bind the corporation in the ordinary course of business. Many times the office of general manager is combined with that of president, and sometimes with that of vice president.

corporate officers, sources of authority

An officer derives the authority to act on behalf of the corporation from one or more of the following sources:

(1) Authority that is inherent in the nature of the office (i.e., inherent authority).

(2) Authority that is set forth in a statute, bylaw, or article of incorporation provision (i.e., express authority).

(3) Authority that is delegated from the board of directors or from a senior officer (i.e., delegated authority).

(4) Authority that is ordinarily implied from, or incidental to, express authority (i.e., implied authority).

(5) Authority that others reasonably believe the person to possess by reason of his or her office (i.e., apparent authority).

corporate contracts, how to sign

A common practical question that arises in many small business corporations, especially early in their existence, is the question of how to sign documents (e.g., notes, contracts, etc.) so as to bind the corporation but not the signer individually. To accomplish this result, a corporate document should be signed in the following manner -

SMITH SUPPLY COMPANY, INC.

by ______________________
John B. Smith, President

corporate contracts, personal liability of signer

It is important that the title or office of the person appear with the name in the signature block. Officers have been held personally liable on notes where only a signature appears beneath the company name on the document. See Medley Harwoods, Inc. v. Novy, 346 S. 2nd 1224 (Fla. Apps., 1977). It is also important to sign a document only in the signature block because officers who have signed a document twice have been held individually liable on the document, even when the officer's title or office appeared on the document. See Rotuba Extruders, Inc. v. Ceppos, 46 N.Y. 2nd 223, 385 N.E. 2nd 1068 (1978).

corporate contracts, validity of signature

A related problem is that posed by a signature that does not bind the corporation. This problem is usually caused by the signing of a document by an officer who does not have the authority to bind the corporation. If the signature on a corporate document is not valid, the corporation is not bound thereby and the contract may be unenforceable by the corporation because of a lack of mutuality. Again, it is important that the title or office of the person signing the document appear on the document as shown above. The addition of the words "authorized signature" or similar words does not establish the signer's authorization to sign the document if the signer's title or office does not appear thereon. In some states the presence of a corporate seal on a written instrument constitutes prima facie evidence that it was executed by a person of authority.

corporate contracts, use of seal

ministerial officers, fixing compensation

The compensation of corporate officers is customarily fixed by the board of directors. Distinctions should be made, however, between ministerial officers and managing officers, and between managing officers who are directors and those who are not. Ministerial officers (e.g., secretary, treasurer, cashier, etc.) have no discretionary control over the management of corporate assets and affairs, and, therefore, do not stand in a fiduciary relationship with the corporation. Their right to compensation is governed by the same rules that apply to employees generally. This is true even if the ministerial officer is also a minority shareholder in the corporation.

Because a managing officer stands in a fiduciary relationship with the corporation and its shareholders, and because his or her compensation is usually substantially greater than the compensation of ministerial officers, the compensation of a managing officer is subject to scrutiny, regardless of whether he or she is a director. Particularly suspicious are attempts to retroactively compensate managing officers, usually in the form of bonuses, for services performed in the past. Such retroactive compensation is often regarded as a gift of the corporate assets and may be voidable if challenged by a shareholder or other interested party, including a creditor. However, if the additional compensation is provided for in an employment contract and if the amount is reasonable, it is usually permissible. The safest practice is for the corporation and the officer to agree on the amount and form of the officer's compensation in advance, including procedures for modifying the amount of compensation in the future. non-director managing officers, fixing compensation

The compensation most likely to be challenged by a shareholder or creditor is the compensation of a managing officer who is a director of the corporation. A common problem for director-officers in small business corporations is the problem of self-dealing; that is, the voting by a director for his or her own compensation. The general rule, in the absence of a statute or article of incorporation provision to the contrary, is that a director may not vote on matters of personal interest, which, of course, means that a director may not vote for his or her own compensation as an officer. And, it should be noted, cross-voting among interested directors (you vote for my compensation and I'll vote for yours) is the equivalent of self-dealing. See Stoiber v. Miller Brewing Co., 257 Wis. 13, 42 N.W. 2nd 144 (1950). The usual consequence of self-dealing by director-officers is that the transaction voted upon is voidable unless a provision to the contrary appears in the corporation laws or in the articles of incorporation or bylaws, or unless the transaction is ratified by all of the shareholders. Even then, the transaction may be voidable, especially by a creditor of an insolvent corporation, on the grounds of fraud or unfairness. See Remillard Brick Co. v. Remillard-Dandini Co., 109 Cal. App. 2nd 405, 241 P. 2nd 66 (1952). See section 5.07, supra, for further reading on director conflicts of interest. director-officers, fixing compensation

A key factor in the legality (or voidability) of any transaction awarding compensation to director-officers is the reasonableness of the amount of compensation awarded. Reasonableness is construed to include not only reasonableness in regard to what other officers in comparable corporations are paid, but also in regard to what the corporation can afford to pay. See Glenmore Distilleries Co. v. Seideman, 267 F. Supp. 915 (EDNY, 1967). Unreasonable compensation awarded to director-officers of an insolvent corporation may be attached and recovered from the officers by creditors of the corporation. See Glenmore Distilleries Co. v. Seideman, supra. See section 6.06, infra, for further reading on the personal liability of corporate officers and directors. director-officers, reasonableness of compensation

A useful technique for small business corporations is to seek shareholder ratification of the compensation of officer-directors. In practice, this may entail shareholder ratification of an officer's employment contract. While this does not necessarily alleviate a subsequent challenge of the transaction by creditors of the corporation, it does prevent (usually by estoppel) ratifying shareholders from later challenging the transaction. In any event, it reduces the burden on the board of directors should the compensation or employment contract be challenged. See Alcott v. Hyman, 42 Del. Ch. 233, 208 A. 2nd 501 (1965). director-officers, compensation, shareholder ratification

The best practice, of course, is to fix the amount and form of an officer-director's compensation before he or she takes office as a director. In many small business corporations, however, this is impossible because the person is more often than not a founder or organizer of the corporation. In such cases the best practice is to include provisions in the articles of incorporation and bylaws permitting directors to vote on matters related to their own compensation, if such is permitted under local law. If such provisions are not includable in the articles or bylaws, the interested director should refrain from voting on transactions related to his or her own compensation (see section 5.07, supra). In any case, it is important to insure that the compensation awarded is reasonable, both as to that of comparable officers in similar corporations and as to the corporation's ability to pay. Shareholder ratification should also be sought, especially if there are shareholders not represented on the board of directors. director-officers, fixing compensation, methods

employment contracts, use of

It often happens that a person is involved in a small business corporation primarily because of the prospect or promise of employment in the business. Such a person may have been a founder of the business or may have joined the business after it was established, often leaving a well-paid, secure position with another employer to do so. Regardless of how or when a person joins a business, such a person typically desires an assurance of meaningful employment for a substantial period of time, usually as an officer with a voice in the management of the business. A common method of insuring such employment is through an employment contract.

employment status, methods of insuring

It should be noted that there are other, often more effective, methods of insuring the tenure and status of corporate officers and employees than the use of an employment contract. The alternate methods include veto powers and other control devices, all of which are discussed in section 5.15, infra. However, if an employee is not a shareholder of the corporation, an employment contract may be the only practicable method of insuring the tenure and status of his or her employment. If an employee is also a shareholder of the corporation, an employment contract may be used in conjunction with veto powers and other control devices to insure his or her continued employment by the corporation.

employment contract, necessity of writing

Although it may seem needless to mention, it is important that employment contracts be reduced to writing. Otherwise, they are at best difficult to enforce, and often not enforceable at all. This matter is raised only because in many small business corporations matters involving employment relationships, and the terms thereof, are thought to be understood verbally and later become the subject of business-wrecking disputes, usually because of misunderstandings.

employment contracts, limitations

It is important to understand at the outset that employment contracts have definite limitations as devices for protecting the tenure and status of corporate officers and employees. Because of these limitations, such contracts are often better suited for use by outside or non-shareholder officers or employees, whose anticipated tenure and involvement in corporate affairs are generally not as extensive as those of a substantial shareholder.

long-term employment contracts, validity

A major detriment to the use of long-term employment contracts by corporate participants is the general uncertainty in the law as to the permitted term of such contracts. Contracts for lifetime employment, perpetual employment, or employment for long or indefinite periods are likely to be held invalid, usually on the grounds that they unduly limit future boards of directors in the management of corporate affairs. Long-term contracts are sometimes upheld by the courts, however, usually on the grounds that the contract was in the best interest of the corporation. Generally, however, the shorter the term of an employment contract, the greater are the chances of its being upheld if challenged.

employment contracts, disadvantages

Another disadvantage of an employment contract, regardless of its term, is that it is impossible, in practice, to protect an employee from being discriminated against should the relationship between the employee and the employer sour during the term of the contract. Such actions as transfers to undesirable offices, changes in duties and responsibilities, lack of cooperation, and other inconveniences designed to make employment difficult are practically impossible to anticipate and prevent contractually. While this disadvantage applies to all employment contracts, it obviously is more likely to occur under a long-term contract.

employment contracts, enforceability, remedies

Another disadvantage of an employment contract is that it ordinarily cannot be specifically enforced by either party. See Burns v. Gould, 172 Conn. 210, 374 A. 2nd 193, 197 (1977). While an employer can usually enforce certain provisions of the contract (usually those restricting the employee's other employment and those protecting the employer's trade secrets, see section 6.05, infra), there is usually no remedy should the employee terminate the contract by leaving the company. Likewise, the employee's remedies are generally limited to monetary damages for the compensation provided in the contract, a remedy that may be inadequate if the employee has staked his or her future on the success of the corporation or if the corporation becomes insolvent or lacking in funds.

employment contracts, elected officers

Even though employment contracts, particularly the long-term variety, are often used by elected officers of the corporation, it is preferable that employment under such contracts be couched in terms of non-elective offices. Even if the person is, say, a vice president of the corporation, his or her employment as described in the employment contract should be as a general manager, production supervisor, sales manager, or the like, rather than as a vice president. The reason for this is to avoid running afoul of statutes that require elected officers to serve specific terms of office or to serve at the pleasure of the board of directors. Employment contracts, especially those covering extended periods, that describe employment in terms of an elected office are more likely to be declared invalid if challenged in the courts.

employment contracts, authority of corporation

Another common cause of unenforceability of employment contracts is the lack of clear authority to enter into the contract on the part of either the corporation or the person signing the contract for the corporation. It is important that both the corporation and the officer signing the contract on behalf of the corporation have the express authority to do so, preferably in the form of a board of director resolution authorizing both the employment contract and the officer's signature thereon. As an additional safeguard, it is a good practice, when feasible, to have important employment contracts ratified (preferably unanimously) by the shareholders.

employment contracts, suggested provisions

Despite their limitations, employment contracts are widely used by participants and employees of small business corporations, mainly because they are easily prepared and provide a workable basis for establishing business relationships between the corporation and its officers and employees. An employment contract, regardless of its duration, should contain provisions dealing with the following matters:

(1) The title and duties of the employee, and where the duties are to be performed.

(2) The term of the employment, including options to renew.

(3) The amount and form of the employee's compensation, including death, disability, retirement, and fringe benefits.

(4) The amount of time the employee is to devote to the employment, including any restrictions on other employment during the term of the contract.

(5) The protection of the employer's trade secrets, confidential information, good will, and employee work product.

(6) The limitations, if any, on the employee's future employment upon the termination of his or her present employment (i.e., covenants not to compete against the employer, etc.).

(7) The effect of the employee's future disability on the contract and the standards for determining disability.

(8) The effect on the contract of the dissolution, merger, or consolidation of the corporation, and of the discontinuance of the activity or function for which the employee was engaged.

(9) Liquidated damages in the event of breach, or severance pay if the contract is not renewed.

(10) The handling of disputes arising under the contract.

(11) The buying or repurchasing by the employer upon termination of the contract, of any stock in the corporation owned or acquired by the employee, and the terms thereof.

See section 6.05, infra, for further reading on covenants not to compete and the protection of trade secrets, confidential information, and employee work product. A sample employment contract is set forth in Exhibit 5-L at the end of this chapter.

5.09 Preparing and Filing Articles of Incorporation

corporate charter, what constitutes

The articles of incorporation, as modified or supplemented by applicable statutory and constitutional provisions, constitute the charter of a corporation. In some states the articles of incorporation are referred to as the articles of association or the certificate of incorporation (which should not be confused with the certificate of incorporation issued by the state filing official in many states evidencing the proper filing of the articles of incorporation). In some states the state filing official supplies official forms that may (or sometimes must) be used in the preparation of articles of incorporation. In some states, also, the state filing official has adopted regulations dealing with the form or contents of articles of incorporation, which must be complied with. A telephone call or letter to the office of the state filing official will usually provide the answers to any questions that might arise as to the existence of either forms or regulations. Copies of both forms and regulations are normally provided free of charge.

articles of incorporation, forms and regulations

state filing official

The state filing official is the state officer in charge of registering and regulating corporations and other entities that must be registered on a statewide basis. In most states the state filing official is the Secretary of State. The name, address, and telephone number of the state filing official in each state is set forth in Appendix I, infra, under the heading of "State Filing Official."

articles of incorporation, general aspects

Because the articles of incorporation are, in effect, the constitution of a corporation, special care should be taken in their preparation. "Boiler plate" clauses taken from form books should be carefully checked to insure that they are consistent with both the business bargain of the participants and the applicable corporation laws. Some of the article provisions, such as those dealing with the corporation's registered agent or the names and addresses of the incorporators, are stock and simple to draft. Other provisions, particularly those dealing with the corporate management and capital structures, lend themselves to considerable discretion in the moulding of a corporation.

articles of incorporation, importance of correctness

It is important that the articles of incorporation be drafted correctly as to both form and content before they are filed, as it is always burdensome, and sometimes embarrassing, to have to file amended articles of incorporation. More importantly, if shares of stock have been issued or contracted to be issued, it may be difficult or impossible to implement a required change in the articles without buying out the stock of, or making concessions to, minority shareholders.

articles of incorporation, types of provisions

While the precise form and content of the articles of incorporation vary from state to state and, of course, from corporation to corporation, their provisions may be divided into two categories: (1) those that are required by statute, and (2) those that are optional or permitted under the local corporation laws. The required provisions are usually explicitly set forth in the corporation laws. These provisions should be drafted so as to comply with the statute. Much latitude is normally given in the drafting of optional or permitted provisions, and in most states virtually any lawful, relevant provision may be included as an optional provision. However, care should be taken that such provisions are not drafted so as to conflict with any of the required provisions.

articles of incorporation, required provisions

The matters that are required to be set forth in the articles of incorporation (i.e., the required provisions) vary considerably from state to state. In many states, including those that have adopted the Revised Model Business Corporation Act, the only required provisions are those dealing with the name of the corporation, the number of shares the corporation is authorized to issue, the name and address of the corporation's initial registered agent and office, and the name and address of each incorporator. In other states, other matters are required to be set forth in the articles. Included here are such matters as the corporation's period of existence, the purpose for which the corporation is organized, provisions granting or denying preemptive rights, the number of initial directors and the names and addresses of the initial board of directors, and provisions dealing with the classification, issuance, and par value of stock. The section(s) of the corporation laws containing the required and optional articles of incorporation content requirements in each state are cited in Appendix I, infra, under the heading of "Articles of Incorporation: Contents."

The provisions that may be included in the articles of incorporation (i.e., the optional provisions) typically include lawful bylaw provisions, lawful provisions regarding the management and regulation of the business and affairs of the corporation, lawful provisions defining, limiting, or regulating the powers of the corporation and its shareholders and board of directors, lawful provisions eliminating or limiting the personal liability of directors, provisions imposing personal liability upon all or specified shareholders for certain corporate debts, and provisions restricting the transfer of stock. In states where they are not listed as required provisions, provisions dealing with such matters as the purpose and period of existence of the corporation, preemptive rights, the par value and classification of stock, and the names and addresses of the initial board of directors are typically listed as optional provisions. articles of incorporation, optional provisions

The matters typically dealt with in the articles of incorporation include the following: articles of incorporation, typical provisions

(1) The name of the corporation. The corporate name must satisfy the requirements of the applicable statute. See section 5.05, supra, for further reading on corporate name requirements, and see Appendix I, infra, for the requirements in each state. name of corporation

(2) The aggregate number of shares that the corporation shall have the authority to issue. If the shares are to consist of a single class, the par value of the shares should be indicated, or it should be stated that the shares are without par value. If the shares are to be divided into classes, the number of shares of each class and the par value of the shares in each class should be indicated, or it should be stated that the shares are without par value. See section 5.14, infra, for further reading on the authorization and issuance of shares. number of authorized shares

(3) The address of the initial registered office of the corporation and the name of its initial registered agent at that address. This requirement is traditionally for purposes of service of process and the mailing of notices by the state filing official. If the corporation has a business address, that address may be used. Otherwise, the address of one of the corporate participants or that of the corporation's attorney or accountant may be used. The name and address of the registered agent can usually be changed without formally amending the articles of incorporation. initial registered agent and office

(4) The name and address of each incorporator. One or more incorporators is usually required. In most states an incorporator may be a natural person or a corporation. The statutory requirements for incorporators in each state are set forth in Appendix I, infra, under the heading of "Incorporators." incorporator qualifications

(5) The number of persons constituting the initial board of directors of the corporation, and the name and address of each. Care should be taken here to comply with any article of incorporation or bylaw requirement that directors be shareholders, residents, citizens, etc. This clause should also be consistent with any article of incorporation or bylaw provision relating to the size of the board of directors. Traditionally, the initial board of directors serves until the first annual meeting of shareholders or until their successors are elected and qualify. See section 5.07, supra, for further reading on the board of directors. initial board of directors

(6) The period of duration of the corporation. In most instances the period of duration will be perpetual, but in some situations perpetual existence may not be desirable. See section 5.15, infra, for further reading on this matter. period of duration

(7) The purpose or purposes for which the corporation is organized. In most states where such a provision is required it is only necessary to state that the purpose of the corporation is to engage in any lawful act or activity for which a corporation may be organized. In a few states the specific purpose or purposes of the corporation must be specified. It is usually possible in such states to word the purpose clause so that the net effect will be to enable the corporation to carry on any lawful business or activity. See below in this section for further reading on purpose clauses. purpose of corporation

classification of stock

(8) If the shares are to be divided into classes, the designation of each class and a statement of the preferences, limitations, and relative rights of the shares of each class. This provision is required in many states and is necessary if more than one class of stock will be issued.

preferred stock, designation of

(9) If the corporation is to issue shares of any preferred or special class in series, the designation of each series and a statement of the variations in the relative rights and preferences as between series, insofar as the same are to be fixed in the articles of incorporation, and a statement of any authority to be vested in the board of directors to establish such series and to fix and determine the variations in the relative rights and preferences as between series. This provision is required in several states, although it is not usually applicable to a small business corporation.

preemptive rights

(10) Provisions dealing with the preemptive rights of shareholders. If preemptive rights are to be granted, the full extent of the rights should be set forth in the articles of incorporation. If they are to be denied, state law often requires a statement to that effect in the articles of incorporation. See section 5.12, infra, for further reading on preemptive rights and see Appendix I, infra, for the requirements in each state.

cumulative voting

(11) Provisions dealing with cumulative voting by shareholders. Depending on local law, it is often necessary to either permit or deny cumulative voting in the articles of incorporation. See section 5.06, supra, for further reading on cumulative voting and see Appendix I, infra, for the requirements in each state.

minimum capitalization requirements

(12) If required by state law, a statement showing compliance with any minimum initial capitalization requirements that must be met before the commencement of corporate business. See section 5.14, infra, for further reading on minimum capitalization requirements and see Appendix I, infra, for the requirements in each state.

stock transfer restrictions and buy outs

(13) Provisions dealing with stock transfer restrictions and the mandatory or optional purchase of a shareholder's stock under certain circumstances, such as the shareholder's death or disability. Provisions of this type are often needed in small business corporations. See section 5.17, infra, for further reading on stock transfer restrictions and buy out provisions.

amending the articles of incorporation

(14) The procedures and requirements for amending the articles of incorporation or any part thereof. These provisions must be consistent with the statutory provisions governing article amendments. Unless a statute provides otherwise, shareholder voting requirements for amending the articles may not be less restrictive than those set forth in the statute. Provisions requiring high shareholder voting requirements to amend specific article provisions are often used to implement shareholder veto powers and other control devices. See sections 5.15 and 6.07, infra, for further reading on amending the articles of incorporation. See Appendix I, infra, for the shareholder voting requirements for amending the articles of incorporation in each state.

close corporation election

(15) The provisions necessary to implement a close corporation election, if such an election is permitted under local law. In most states that have close corporation laws, certain provisions are required to be included in the articles of incorporation if the corporation is to be organized as a statutory close corporation. See section 5.19, infra, for further reading on the close corporation election, and see Appendix I, infra, for a reference to such laws, if any, in the local state.

veto powers

(16) Provisions granting veto powers to certain shareholders under certain conditions. Veto powers usually take the form of high voting requirements for either shareholder or director action on specified matters. See section 5.15, infra, for further reading on the use of veto powers.

removal of directors

(17) Provisions granting the shareholders, or certain shareholders, the power to remove the board of directors at any time without cause, except for the directors, if any, elected by minority shareholders under cumulative voting. See sections 5.15 and 6.05, infra, for further reading on the removal of directors.

action-without-meeting, authorization of

(18) Provisions dealing with action by the shareholders or the board of directors without a meeting. The authorization of such action, if required under local law, usually takes the form of allowing action to be taken without a shareholder or board of director meeting if a written consent to the action is signed by each person entitled to vote on the matter, or, if permitted by statute, by a majority of those entitled to vote. In many states a denial of this right in the articles of incorporation or bylaws is required if the right to act without meeting is to be denied to either the shareholders or the board of directors. See sections 5.11 and 6.04, infra, for further reading on action-without-meeting requirements. See Appendix I, infra, for a description of the statutory action-without-meeting requirements in each state.

right of shareholder to examine corporate books

(19) Provisions dealing with the rights of shareholders to examine the corporate books and records. Generally, any shareholder of a small business corporation should have the unqualified right at any reasonable time during the corporate existence and after dissolution, either in person or by representative, to examine all corporate books, contracts, correspondence, accounts, and other records, and to make copies thereof. See sections 5.06, supra, and 5.11, infra, for further reading on this matter.

corporate dissention and deadlock

(20) Provisions dealing with corporate dissention and deadlock. Such provisions may be needed in a two-person corporation or in any corporation where dissention is likely to arise. See sections 5.15 and 6.05, infra, for further reading on corporate dissention and deadlock.

director conflicts of interest

(21) Provisions validating the acts of interested directors and officers. Clauses of this type usually validate contracts and other transactions between the corporation and its directors and officers or other entities in which a participating director or officer has an interest. See sections 5.07 and 5.08, supra, and 6.05, infra, for further reading on this matter.

indemnification of officers and directors

(22) Provisions permitting the indemnification of corporate officers and directors for expenses and liabilities, including legal expenses, incurred while acting in their corporate capacities, including the purchase of insurance by the corporation to cover such liabilities.

limiting director liability

(23) Provisions providing protection from liability for directors who rely in good faith on corporate records. Such provisions are authorized by statute in many states and are commonly used. See section 6.06, infra, for further reading on director liability.

director conflicts of interest

(24) Provisions authorizing directors to determine their own compensation as officers and directors, and to serve the corporation in other capacities. These provisions, if permitted under local law, are useful to small business corporations. See sections 5.07 and 5.08, supra, for further reading.

dispensing with board of directors

(25) If permitted under local law provisions, dispensing with the board of directors or reserving to the shareholders (under certain conditions, if desired) the right to declare dividends, elect corporate officers, manage the corporation, or perform other functions normally performed by the board of directors. Provisions such as these are permitted in several states. See sections 5.07, supra, and 5.15, infra, for further reading on this matter.

bylaw provisions in articles

(26) Any other provisions, consistent with local law, that deal with the regulation of internal corporate affairs and that are required or permitted to be set forth in the corporate bylaws. In other words, the making of an article provision out of what would normally be a bylaw provision. Veto powers over certain corporate acts may be implemented in this manner.

Most of the above article of incorporation provisions may be used in most states. However, care should be taken that each provision employed is compatible with local law. Samples of many of the above provisions may be found in the sample articles of incorporation that are set forth in Exhibit 5-G at the end of this chapter. See Appendix I, infra, for a summary of the corporation laws of each state.

articles of incorporation, purpose clause

It occasionally happens that the corporate participants wish to specifically limit the activities of the corporation to a particular field or business, in which case the purpose clause in the articles of incorporation should be worded so as to restrict the activities of the corporation. This is most effectively accomplished by inserting "self-denying" clauses in the articles (e.g., The corporation shall not engage in the business of bootlegging.) The insertion of such clauses will enable the shareholders to later enjoin the corporation from expanding into prohibited fields or businesses. See section 5.15, infra, for further reading on this matter.

articles of incorporation, powers clause

Because the powers of a corporation are specifically enumerated in the corporation laws, it normally serves no purpose to repeat them in the articles of incorporation. The corporation laws of most states specifically provide that it is not necessary to set forth the statutory corporate powers in the articles of incorporation. However, if, for any reason, it is necessary to list the corporate powers, the clause containing them should be prefaced as follows: "In furtherance of and not in limitation of the powers conferred by the state of _______ and of the purposes and objects stated herein, the corporation shall have the following powers..."

articles of incorporation, signing and filing requirements

Once the articles of incorporation have been drafted, they must be properly executed and filed in order to become effective. The articles must be signed by the incorporators (or incorporator) and, in many states, the signatures must be either verified or acknowledged. Many states require the filing of duplicate originals (which means that two copies of the articles must be signed and, if necessary, verified), but the required number varies from state to state. Many states require the filing of certain other documents with the articles of incorporation, including an affidavit of acceptance signed by the registered agent. The required filing fees and franchise taxes must also be paid, usually when the articles are filed. The filing fees and the incorporation or franchise taxes that must be paid in each state are listed in Appendix I, infra, under the heading of "Fees."

articles of incorporation, filing, recording, and publishing requirements

In most states the articles of incorporation must be filed with the state filing official. A few states require additional filings with designated county offices or a probate judge. A few states have publication requirements that must be complied with if the corporation is to be effective. In other states there are additional recording requirements that must be complied with. The particular filing, recording, and publication requirements in the state of incorporation must be strictly complied with in order to prevent a defective incorporation. The article of incorporation filing, recording, and publication requirements, if any, in each state are summarized in Appendix I, infra, under the heading of "Articles of Incorporation: Filing and Recording."

articles of incorporation, review of by filing officer, remedies for refusal to accept

Once the filing requirements have been ascertained, the act of filing the articles of incorporation is often perfunctory, provided that the articles do not contain any unusual or legally-questionable provisions. Because articles of incorporation are reviewed by the state filing official prior to acceptance and approval, articles that contain legally-questionable provisions may be rejected by the filing official, a procedure that can delay the proposed incorporation and cause the expenditure of additional time. If legally-questionable article provisions are to be employed, the best practice is to check with the state filing official and attempt to informally submit the questionable article provisions for clearance in advance of filing. A telephone or personal consultation with the state filing official may also be helpful, because sometimes the changing of a few inconsequential words in a questionable article provision will clear the way for its approval. If the filing officer persists in rejecting an article provision, and if the provision is important, most corporation laws contain provisions for appealing a refusal of the state filing official to accept a document for filing. A petition to compel the filing of the document by the state filing official must usually be filed in a designated court.

corporation, beginning of legal existence

In most states the legal existence of a corporation begins when the articles of incorporation are accepted for filing by the state filing official. In some states corporate existence begins when the state filing official issues a certificate of incorporation. The beginning of corporate existence can be important for purposes of taxation and participant liability. The act upon which corporate existence begins in each state is set forth in Appendix I, infra, under the heading of "Articles of Incorporation: Filing and Recording."

5.10 Preparing Corporate Bylaws

Corporate bylaws are a set of rules and regulations designed to govern the internal affairs of a corporation. Unlike articles of incorporation, bylaws are not public documents and copies of them are not filed with any public officer. The bylaws, once adopted, are legally binding on the officers, directors, and shareholders of a corporation, all of whom are conclusively presumed to have knowledge of their contents. See Gwin v. Thunderbird Motor Hotels, 216 Ga. 652, 119 S.E. 2nd 14 (1961). The bylaws are not generally binding on third parties dealing with the corporation unless the third party had actual knowledge of the particular bylaw provision relied upon. See 18 Am. Jur. 2d, Corporations, sec. 169.

corporate bylaws, general aspects

The corporation laws in most states provide that the bylaws of a corporation may contain any provision for managing the business and regulating the affairs of the corporation that is not inconsistent with law or the articles of incorporation. Bylaw provisions that conflict with either the articles of incorporation or a state statute are invalid. Bylaw provisions may also be invalid if they conflict with generally accepted corporate norms.

corporate bylaws, permitted provisions

The bylaws should contain rules and regulations dealing with the powers, duties, and responsibilities of shareholders, directors, executive committees, and officers, the location of the corporate offices, the signing of contracts, the issuance of stock, the fiscal year, the corporate seal, amending the bylaws, the handling of corporate books and accounts, the indemnification of officers, and any other matters of specific interest to the business or its participants. A sample set of corporate bylaws is set forth in Exhibit 5-F at the end of this chapter.

corporate bylaws, contents of

In most states the power to adopt corporate bylaws rests with the board of directors, unless the articles of incorporation provide otherwise. In some states, however, the power rests with the shareholders, or, occasionally, with the original incorporators, although the power can usually be delegated to the board of directors. It is important to insure, when organizing a corporation, that the bylaws are adopted by the proper corporate body, for if they are adopted by an improper body they may be invalid, even if the shareholders and directors are the same persons. See Avant v. Sandersville Production Credit Ass'n, 243 Ga. 173, 253 S.E. 2nd 176, 181 (1979). However, illegally adopted bylaws have been held to constitute an enforceable contract between shareholders. See Palmer v. Chamberlin, 191 F. 2nd 532 (CA 5, 1951). The bylaw adoption requirements in each state are summarized in Appendix I, infra, under the heading of "Bylaws."

corporate bylaws, adoption of

The bylaw amendment provisions are usually set forth in the bylaws. When drafting the bylaws it is important to insure that the amendment provisions in the bylaws conform to the requirements of the applicable statute. While the statutory bylaw amendment provisions vary somewhat from state to state, they typically provide that the bylaws may be amended by the board of directors unless that power is reserved to the shareholders in the articles of incorporation. A majority vote is normally required to amend the bylaws unless a greater vote is required by the articles of incorporation or bylaws. It seems to be settled law that the shareholders, as the owners of the corporation, retain the inherent right to amend the bylaws even if the articles of incorporation confer that right upon the board of directors. See Rogers v. Hill, 289 U.S. 582, 53 S. Ct. 731, 77 L. Ed. 1385 (1933). The statutory bylaw amendment provisions in each state are summarized in Appendix I, infra, under the heading of "Bylaws."

corporate bylaws amendment

In implementing veto powers and other methods of control over corporate activity, it is often necessary to require a higher percentage vote to amend the bylaws (or certain sections of them) than to adopt them (see section 5.15, infra). While the requirements for amending the bylaws are usually set forth in the bylaws themselves, they can, in most states, be set forth in the articles of incorporation, if desired. It should be noted that authority exists for the proposition that a bylaw can be amended by custom or by a course of conduct inconsistent therewith. See Belle Isle Corp. v. Mac Bean, 29 Del. Ch. 261, 49 A. 2nd 5 (1946).

corporate bylaws, methods of amendment

corporate bylaws. suggested inclusions

The bylaws should be prepared (and worded) in such a manner that they can and will be used by the corporate participants on a regular basis. Because corporate participants and employees often find it more convenient if all of their rules and regulations are contained in a single document, it may be helpful to paraphrase and include in the bylaws important or useful provisions of the articles of incorporation and relevant statutes.

corporate bylaws. distinguished from resolutions

It is important to understand that corporate bylaws differ from corporate resolutions. While a bylaw or a set of bylaws may be adopted by a resolution, a resolution is not a bylaw. A resolution generally deals with a single corporate act or event and may be passed at any lawful meeting of the directors or shareholders. A resolution can change or rescind a previous resolution, provided that vested rights have not attached. Bylaws, on the other hand, are continuing rules covering a wide range of matters that remain in effect until they are amended in the manner provided by law. If a resolution conflicts with a bylaw, the bylaw prevails.

5.11 The Corporate Books and Records

In most small business corporations the shareholders, directors, and officers are the same persons, and more often than not there is no day-to-day differentiation between what they do in their different capacities. In many such corporations formal meetings are not held, bylaw requirements are ignored (if, indeed, they even exist), and only fragmentary records are kept. While such practices may have no adverse affect on the corporation or its participants early in the life of the corporation, in the long run they can lead only to problems, even for a one-person corporation.

corporate record keeping, general practices

A disregard of the distinctions between shareholders and directors or officers may result in the participants being personally liable for corporate debts (see section 6.06, infra). Without adequate records, it may be difficult for the corporation to obtain financing in its own name, and an Internal Revenue Service audit could result in disaster. Should disputes later arise, either between the individual corporate participants or between the corporation and others, the lack of formal records and a failure to follow the required corporate rituals may again result in needless confusion and expense. If the business participants wish to form a corporation, it is important that they observe, on paper at least, the traditional corporate distinctions between shareholders, directors, and officers, and that they maintain records sufficient to sustain the corporation's account on matters of importance.

corporate records, consequences of failure to keep

In most states a corporation is required by law to keep as permanent records minutes of all shareholder and board of director meetings, including committee meetings, a record of all shareholder and board of director action taken without a meeting, a record of its shareholders, and appropriate accounting records. In addition, in many states a corporation is required to keep at its principal office copies of its articles of incorporation (including all amendments), bylaws (including all amendments), all board of director resolutions creating classes or series of stock, all written communications to shareholders made within the last three years, a list of the names and addresses of its directors and officers, and the most recent annual report filed with the state filing official. The corporate records are required to be kept in a written form or in a form capable of conversion into written form within a reasonable time. In addition, a corporation that files a federal tax or informational return is required by the tax laws to maintain permanent books and records establishing the income, deductions, credits, and other matters reported in a federal tax return. See Treasury Reg. 1.6001-1(a).

corporate books and records, general requirements

In practice, the books and records of most small business corporations include a minute book, a stock book, the books and records of account, and the corporation's tax records. The corporate books and records are customarily maintained by the secretary of the corporation, although in most states this is not required by statute.

customary corporate books and records

The corporate minute book should contain a complete and correct set of minutes of each corporate meeting, and memoranda of all corporate action taken without a meeting. Corporate meetings include shareholders' meetings, directors' meetings, committee meetings, and incorporators' meetings. In most small business corporations, especially after the initial legalities of incorporating, corporate and business affairs tend to be handled informally, with little time or effort spent on record-keeping. It is important, therefore, that the minutes of the initial corporate meetings be properly drafted, both as to form and content, so that those drafting minutes of future meetings will at least have an example to follow.

corporate minute book, contents

The minutes of corporate meetings constitute what is, in most cases, the only written history of the corporation and its activities. While the task of taking notes and drafting minutes often seems trivial to the person to whom the task is assigned, it is not uncommon for the outcome of corporate disputes or law suits, often decades in the future, to hinge upon the accuracy or clarity of the minutes of a particular meeting. It is settled law that the corporate minutes, if properly prepared and preserved, are the best evidence of the matters covered therein. See Malone v. Melnick, 378 Pa. 483, 106 A. 2nd 806, 48 A.L.R. 2nd 1254 (1954).

minutes of corporate meetings, importance

minutes of corporate meetings, handling notice requirements

The first requirement of corporate minutes is to show that the meeting was lawfully called and held. It is necessary, therefore, to show that all statutory, article of incorporation, or bylaw requirements applicable to the meeting were complied with, including the notice requirements of the meeting. If there is no dispute as to who is permitted or required to attend the meeting, the notice requirements can often be satisfied by the use of waivers of notice signed by the persons required or permitted to attend the meeting. If notice waivers cannot be obtained from certain persons, the minutes should reflect the date and method of the sending or delivery of notice of the meeting, and a copy of the notice should be attached to the minutes. Sample notices and notice waivers are set forth in Exhibit 5-H at the end of this chapter.

minutes of corporate meetings, suggested form and contents

The taker of the minutes has considerable discretion as to the form and content of the minutes, provided that they are accurate and complete. It is suggested that each set of corporate minutes should include the following:

(1) The date and place of the meeting.

(2) The name of the corporation and a description of the type of meeting being held (e.g., annual meeting of shareholders, special meeting of the board of directors, etc.).

(3) The authority under which the meeting is being held. This is normally the statutory, bylaw, or article of incorporation provision calling for or authorizing the meeting.

(4) A showing of compliance with any applicable notice requirement. This may be accomplished by describing the notice given or by waiver of notice, if feasible. Copies of the notice or the signed waivers should be attached to the minutes.

(5) The names of those who are present at the meeting and the names of those who are absent, unless the group is too large. If the meeting is a shareholder meeting, the shareholders represented by proxies should be identified and the proxies, if any, described.

(6) An approval of the minutes of the previous meeting of the same group, with any changes noted.

(7) A description of each substantive issue or matter presented or discussed at the meeting, and the name of the person who presented or raised it.

(8) A complete accounting of all votes taken at the meeting, including a record of how each person voted on each issue, unless the group is too large.

(9) A description of each resolution voted on at the meeting and the results of the voting.

(10) A description of all reports and presentations tendered at the meeting and by whom given. Copies of written reports should be attached to the minutes and summaries of oral reports should be included in the minutes.

(11) A summary of all other business brought before the meeting and any action taken thereon.

(12) A recitation of adjournment and the signature of the taker of the minutes. If only a few persons attended the meeting, it is a good practice to obtain their signatures on the minutes, also.

minutes of directors' meetings, contents

In the case of board of director meetings, it is particularly important to note how or if each director voted. If a particular director has a financial or other personal interest in a matter being considered by the board, it is important that the minutes reflect his or her conduct at the meeting (e.g., whether he or she left the meeting, took part in the discussion, voted, refused to vote, etc.). On matters related to the issuance of dividends or distributions, it is also important to note each director's vote and position on the issue because of the possibility of future personal liability if the dividends or distributions were unlawfully issued. Sample corporate minutes are set forth in Exhibit 5-E at the end of this chapter.

action without meeting statutes, general requirements

The corporation laws of many states provide that action may be taken by directors or shareholders without a meeting, provided that the written consent of all persons entitled to vote on the matter is obtained. The applicable statute should be checked before proceeding, however, because the specific requirements vary. Some statutes permit action to be taken without a meeting if a consent to the action is signed by shareholders or directors, as the case may be, sufficient to carry the action at a meeting, provided that notice of the action is promptly given to all other shareholders or directors. The action without meeting statutes of each state are summarized in Appendix I, infra, under the heading of "Action Without Meeting."

action without meeting, preparation of memoranda

Each time that corporate action is taken without a meeting, a memorandum describing the action taken should be prepared and signed by each person entitled to vote on the matter. It is important to show in the written memorandum that all statutory notice requirements were complied with because under some statutes, usually those requiring less than unanimous consent, the action is not effective unless the required notices were given. Because the potential for future disputes over such matters is probably greater due to the absence of a meeting, it is important that the description of the corporate action taken be complete and accurate. The memoranda of corporate action without meeting, properly signed, should be kept in the corporate minute book in chronological order with the other minutes. Samples of memoranda of corporate action without meeting are set forth in Exhibit 5-I at the end of this chapter.

stock certificates, requirements

An event that occurs early in the life of most small business corporations is the issuance of stock. This is accomplished (usually at the organizational meeting of the board of directors or shortly thereafter) by the issuance of stock certificates to the persons entitled to the stock. A stock certificate should show - (1) the name of the corporation, (2) the state of incorporation, (3) the name of the shareholder, (4) the par value, if any, of the shares represented by the certificate, (5) the number and class of any shares represented by the certificate, and (6) if the corporation is authorized to issue more than one class of stock, a full statement of the rights of each class or a statement that the corporation will furnish such information free of charge upon request. In most states stock may also be issued without a certificate, if desired, in which case a written informational statement containing the information normally contained in the certificate must be sent to the shareholder within a reasonable time after the issuance of the shares. Whether the issuance of uncertified shares is permitted in a particular state is indicated in Appendix I, infra, under the heading of "Stock Certificates."

uncertified shares, issuance of

stock certificates, preparation of

In most states stock certificates must be signed by two corporate officers, usually the president and the secretary. State statutes vary on these requirements, however, so the appropriate statute should be checked before preparing the certificates. Facsimile signatures are usually permitted, although they are not normally needed by small business corporations. The stock certificate signature requirements for each state are set forth in Appendix I, infra, under the heading of "Stock Certificates."

stock certificates, consideration requirements

Many states prohibit the issuance of a stock certificate until the shares represented thereby have been paid for in full. This requirement, if applicable in the local state, must be fulfilled before the issuance of either a stock certificate or uncertified shares. See section 5.14, infra, for further reading on consideration for shares. The consideration requirements for the issuance of shares in each state are set forth in Appendix I, infra, under the heading of "Consideration For Shares." If transfer or other restrictions are to be imposed on the shares of stock represented by the certificate, notice of such restrictions should conspicuously appear on the certificate. A sample stock certificate is set forth in Exhibit 5-J at the end of this chapter.

stock certificates, forms of

stock record and transfer book, necessity of

There are no statutorially-required forms of stock certificates, although most of the major stock exchanges have their own requirements for stock certificates. Stock certificates can be found in a variety of sizes, shapes, and forms, any one of which will usually suffice. Most stock certificates are attached to a stub wherein the name of the shareholder, the dates of issuance and transfer, and the number of shares represented by the certificate can be recorded. If there are only a few shareholders in the corporation, the stubs in the stock certificate book can serve as the stock record and transfer book of the corporation, especially if transfers of the shares are not anticipated. A separate page or two in the corporate minute book may also be used for this purpose. If a large number of stock certificates are to be issued, or if frequent transfers of the shares are anticipated, a separate stock transfer and record book (or ledger) should be obtained and used. In any event, it is important to keep a record of these matters because the corporation laws require a corporation to maintain a current record of the names and addresses of its shareholders and the number of shares held by each.

corporate seal, necessity, form

The necessity of maintaining a corporate seal has been abolished by statute in every state. Many participants in small business corporations, however, find it convenient or desirable to have a seal for their corporation, the use of which is always permissible. The seal is usually circular and contains the name of the corporation, its state and year of incorporation, and the words "Corporate Seal." The cost of a seal varies with the type, but an acceptable seal can usually be purchased for less than ten dollars.

corporate books and forms, types and cost

Corporate minute books, books of stock certificates, and corporate seals may be purchased at legal stationery stores and from lawyers' service organizations. Simple forms and books, as well as elaborate, personalized stock certificates, seals, and minute books, may be purchased. Costs may vary from under twenty to several hundred dollars. The loose-leaf type of minute book is usually preferable because the pages can be removed for typing and it is easier to include such miscellaneous, but important, documents as contracts, bank resolutions, and insurance papers in them. It is important to realize that in many small business corporations the corporate minute book is the keeping place of all corporate documents and any other papers deemed "legal" in nature.

corporate financial books and records, requirements

The financial, business, and tax records of a corporation should be maintained in accordance with good accounting and bookkeeping practices. No particular type or form of such records is normally required, but the records should be reasonably accurate and current because in many states a corporation is required to mail annual financial statements to its shareholders and to make financial statements and other information available to its shareholders upon request. If a corporation files federal income tax returns or, in the case of an S corporation, informational returns, it is required to keep permanent books and records (including inventories) establishing the income, deductions, credits, and other matters contained in any return. Again, the records do not have to be in any particular form, but they must be accurate and should be maintained by the appropriate corporate official.

corporate employment and tax records, requirements

A corporation should retain copies of all tax returns and other matters filed with any taxing or regulatory authority, and all tax returns, books, and records must be available for inspection by the Internal Revenue Service. See 26 U.S.C. 6001 and Treasury Reg. secs. 1.6001-1 and 31.6001-1. Also, the Social Security and Wage-Hour laws require that employment records be kept for a period of four years. It is a good practice to consult an experienced accountant when setting up the financial, business, and tax books and records of a corporation.

5.12 Handling Preemptive Rights

The participants of most small business corporations expect their fortunes to grow with the business. Many times it is the main reason they are in the business. If the business prospers, it is usually a direct result of their energy and skills. It only stands to reason, then, that such participants should be given the right to acquire additional stock issued by the corporation and thereby share in its growth and prosperity. The alternative is to see the results of years of hard work and deprivation result in shares of stock in the hands of others, whose contribution to the success of the business has been much less.

preemptive rights, need for

Most participants in small business corporations wish to maintain their proportionate ownership of the corporation. Should additional shares of stock be issued to outsiders, or to some shareholders and not to others, those not issued additional stock, who are most likely to be minority shareholders to begin with, stand to lose all or a portion of their control over important corporate activities. And, the loss of control often means the loss of income, either through the loss of employment by the corporation or the loss of control over the issuance of dividends. Without preemptive rights or other controls over the issuance of stock, even the most carefully formulated corporate management and control structure can be irreparably disrupted simply by the issuance of additional stock. If properly implemented, preemptive rights can play an important role in the management and control structure of a small business corporation.

preemptive rights, usefulness, importance

A shareholder's preemptive right is the right to purchase newly issued stock of the corporation in the same proportion as the shareholder's existing stock holdings before it is offered to others. While preemptive rights are a nuisance to publicly-held corporations and are invariably denied to their shareholders, in small business corporations such rights are important facets of both control and growth. Preemptive rights are especially important to minority shareholders.

preemptive rights, definition

The corporation laws of every state deal with preemptive rights in one way or another. In many states preemptive rights exist unless they are denied in the articles of incorporation. A preemptive rights statute in such a state typically provides that the shareholders of a corporation have a right to be provided with a reasonable, fair and uniform opportunity to exercise their preemptive rights. In other states preemptive rights do not exist unless they are conferred in the articles of incorporation. The rule on the existence of preemptive rights that is followed in each state is set forth in Appendix I, infra, under the heading of "Preemptive Rights."

preemptive rights, statutory provisions

Even when preemptive rights are granted, there are several instances where they may not be exercised. For example, unless such rights are specifically granted in the articles of incorporation, preemptive rights do not usually exist in stock that is issued for property or as compensation for services (a common happening in small business corporations), in treasury stock, or in preferred stock. Because the extent of the preemptive rights granted by most statutes is limited or, in many cases, unclear, if preemptive rights are to be granted, they should be explicitly set forth in the articles of incorporation. It is not a good practice to rely on a statute which may be amended and which the participants will probably never read or even be aware of. Article of incorporation provisions dealing with preemptive rights are valid as long as they do not conflict with the mandatory provisions of the applicable statute. See section 6.05, infra, for a discussion of the strengths and weaknesses of preemptive rights as devices to protect the rights of minority shareholders.

preemptive rights, extent of, how to implement

In drafting article of incorporation provisions dealing with preemptive rights, the rights and interests of the individual corporate participants, especially the minority participants, must be balanced against the anticipated need of the corporation for flexibility in managing its financial affairs. Also, the danger of minority participants being later frozen or squeezed out by the majority must be weighed against the possibility of participants who contribute little or nothing to the success of the business later demanding an equal share of the rewards should the business prosper. Sometimes the balancing problem can be solved by issuing different classes of stock, some of which carry preemptive rights and some of which do not.

preemptive rights, balancing interests

preemptive rights, article provisions, drafting considerations

The following matters should be considered when drafting article of incorporation provisions granting preemptive rights:

(1) If more than one class of stock is to be issued, identify the classes of stock, and the issues in each class, that will carry preemptive rights.

(2) Identify the classes of stock, and issues thereof, that the holders of preemptive rights shall be permitted to acquire when exercising their preemptive rights.

(3) State whether preemptive rights shall apply to stock issued for property or services, to stock issued under employee stock programs or plans, to treasury stock, to stock issued to discharge corporate debts, to stock issued upon corporate reorganizations or mergers, to stock issued as dividends, or to stock issued under options or convertible debentures.

(4) Describe how the preemptive rights may be exercised, who may exercise them, the type of notice required, and the time period during which the rights may be exercised.

(5) Describe the method of establishing the price and the method of payment for any stock issued subject to preemptive rights. It is important here to consider the relative financial situations of the various participants; otherwise a participant without ready funds may be prevented from exercising a preemptive right by the establishment of a high price for the stock.

(6) Describe the authority necessary to issue additional stock that is subject to preemptive rights (e.g., majority vote of the board of directors, unanimous vote of the shareholders, etc.).

(7) Describe the shareholder vote necessary to amend the article of incorporation provisions dealing with preemptive rights (e.g., two-thirds vote, unanimous vote, etc.).

preemptive rights, article amendments, effect of

Under (7) above, minority corporate participants will be fully protected only if very high or unanimous shareholder voting requirements are imposed. It is important to understand that even if the articles of incorporation may otherwise be amended by, say, a majority vote of the shareholders, it is permissible to require a higher voting percentage to amend a specific provision in the articles, in this case the provision dealing with preemptive rights. See section 4.15, infra, for further reading on amending the articles of incorporation. It should be noted that in many states article of incorporation amendments abolishing preemptive rights entitle affected shareholders to appraisement rights (i.e., the right to obtain payment for the fair value of their stock).

denial of preemptive rights, remedies

A shareholder who has been denied a preemptive right by the corporation has a choice of remedies. The shareholder may seek injunctive relief against the corporation and its participants, either to prevent the issuance of the contested shares to another or to compel their issuance to the shareholder. The shareholder may also seek specific performance of his or her preemptive right. If the stock has already been issued, the shareholder may seek to rescind the sale if the purchaser was not an innocent third party. In the alternative, the shareholder may seek compensatory (and perhaps punitive) damages, the measure of which would be the difference between the sales price of the stock and its market value or value to the shareholder, or, in some cases, the anticipated loss of future income or profit from the stock or from the corporation, if the issuance resulted in the shareholder's loss of control of or employment by the corporation.

5.13 Incorporating a Going Business - Special Problems

Unique problems may be encountered when incorporating a going or existing business. The type and extent of these problems usually depends on the type of business being conducted, the organizational form of the business prior to incorporation, and the length of time the business has been in existence. Generally, special problems involving one or more of the following matters can be anticipated: (1.) obtaining the legal authority to incorporate the business, (2) the legal and tax aspects of transferring the assets of the business to the new corporation, and (3) the liability of the new corporation for the debts of the predecessor business. incorporating going business, typical problems

The type and form of authority needed to incorporate a going or existing business depends on both the legal structure of the business prior to incorporation and the relationship among the business participants. If the business is a sole proprietorship, a simple statement or letter from the proprietor requesting that the business be incorporated will normally suffice (in most cases a verbal statement to the proprietor's attorney is all that is needed). If the business is multi-person, much will depend on the relationship among the business participants. The number of business participants can also be an important factor. If there are only a few participants and if they are all on friendly terms and actively involved in the conduct of the business, a simple statement or letter to the attorney requesting that the business be incorporated will suffice in most cases. However, the attorney should be certain that incorporation is desired by each participant before proceeding. If there is any doubt on the matter, a statement conferring the authority to incorporate and setting forth any special conditions related to the incorporation should be prepared for the signature of each participant. incorporating going business, necessary authority

If there are participants in the business, whether as investors, small percentage owners, or otherwise, who are not actively involved in the day-to-day conduct of the business, it is important that their consent to the incorporation be obtained, preferably in writing. If there are numerous participants in the business, written authority to incorporate the business should be obtained from each of the participants. If the incorporation process will be extended or if there are absentee owners, the best practice is to prepare a preincorporation agreement setting forth both the authority to incorporate the business and the specifics of the proposed incorporation. The incorporation process should not be commenced until each participant or owner has signed the agreement. See section 5.03, supra, for further reading on preincorporation agreements. minority owners of business, necessity of consent to incorporation

Difficulty in obtaining the authority to incorporate a going or existing business can be expected when less than all of the participants in the existing business will be participants in the successor corporation. Similar difficulties may also be encountered when the attempted incorporation follows the death or disability of a participant in the business, especially if the person was an active participant. And, of course, if one or more of the participants is opposed to incorporation, complications will almost certainly arise. consent to incorporation, difficulty in obtaining

As a practical matter, the successful incorporation of an existing business is usually impossible without the consent of each of the business participants. First of all, a person cannot be forced to become a shareholder in a corporation. Secondly, a partnership or association is not bound by an agreement on a matter that is not in the normal course of business, such as the transfer of all its assets to a corporation, unless all of the partners or associates consent to the agreement. See section 3.01, supra. incorporation of business, objecting owner

If a business participant is adamantly opposed to incorporation, the only procedure in most cases is to dissolve the existing partnership and form a corporation to take over the share of the business distributed to the participants desiring to incorporate. If the entire business, or 100 percent of its assets, must be transferred to the new corporation in order for the business to function, it will be necessary for the incorporating participants to compensate the discontinuing participants for their interests in the dissolved entity. See sections 3.08 and 3.09, supra, for further reading on the sale and dissolution of partnerships. A well-drafted partnership agreement should contain a clause dealing with the procedures to be followed should the partners, or a specified percentage of them, decide to incorporate. incorporation of partnership business incorporation of business, transferring assets

The formation of a corporation for a business does not, in itself, vest the property and assets of the business in the corporation. There must be an actual conveyance of the business assets to the corporation. The conveyance may take the form of a lease where the corporation is the lessee, a sale from the previous owner to the corporation, or a transfer to the corporation in consideration for the issuance of stock. It should be understood that a corporation acquires only the title in the business property held by its predecessor.

transfer of assets, fraudulent conveyance acts

Not only must the transfer of business assets to a new corporation be valid among the parties involved, the transfer must not be fraudulent as to the creditors of the predecessor business. Accordingly, the provisions of any applicable fraudulent conveyances act should be checked and complied with. A transfer may be fraudulent if the predecessor business or its owners receive inadequate consideration for the transfer of the business assets to the corporation. The issue of adequate consideration, which is often complicated by valuation problems to begin with, is further complicated when the predecessor business or its owners receive stock in the new corporation as consideration for the transfer of the business assets.

transfer of assets for stock, fraudulent conveyance acts

Whether a transfer for stock is fraudulent often depends on whether the predecessor business was solvent at the time of the transfer. If the predecessor business was solvent at the time of the transfer, a transfer for stock is likely to be upheld as against an objecting creditor. However, if the predecessor business was insolvent at the time of the transfer, the transfer is likely to be deemed fraudulent, especially if stock manipulations occur that result in the stock of the new corporation being placed beyond the reach of the creditors of the predecessor business.

transfer of assets, bulk sales acts

The transfer of assets from a predecessor business to a new corporation may also have to meet the requirements of the state Bulk Sales Act. This act is set forth in Article 6 of the Uniform Commercial Code in most states. If the predecessor entity is subject to this act (most bulk sales acts cover only those enterprises engaged in the sale of merchandise), and if the particular transfer is covered by the act (generally, to be covered the transfer must constitute a major part of the merchandise or materials of the transferor and must not be in the ordinary course of business), it must comply with the notice requirements of the act. If the bulk sales act provisions are applicable to the transfer and are not complied with, the objecting creditors of the predecessor business may either set the conveyance aside or disregard both the conveyance and the corporate entity and treat the assets as if no conveyance had occurred.

transfer of assets, tax aspects

Tax considerations often play an important role in the transfer of assets from an existing business to a new corporation. Generally, the transfer will be tax-free (i.e., no gain or loss to the transferors) if the transferors receive as consideration only stock in the new corporation, provided that they own at least 80 percent of the voting stock in the corporation immediately after the transfer. See 26 U.S.C. 351. In such a transfer the corporation acquires the property at the tax basis of the transferor. If the tax basis of the property to be transferred to the corporation is substantially below its market value it may be advantageous for the corporation to acquire the property at the higher basis. In such cases care must be taken to insure that the transfer to the corporation is taxable. See section 5.02, supra, for further reading on this and other tax-related matters relevant to the incorporation of a business.

liability of corporation for debts of predecessor

As a general rule a successor corporation is liable for the debts of the predecessor business only if: (1) it expressly assumes liability for them, (2) there is a fraudulent transfer as described above, or (3) a presumed or implied liability for them arises. See Annotation: Liability of Corporation for Debts of Predecessor, 149 A.L.R. 787, 797. If the successor corporation continues to conduct the business in the same manner as its predecessor, it may be held implicitly liable for its predecessor's debts. Also, if the successor corporation accepts the benefits of a contract made by its predecessor, it will be liable for its predecessor's obligations under the contract. See Mechanical Constructors, Inc. v. B-W Acceptance Corp., 412 P.2nd 957 (Okla., 1966). However, the assumption of liability for certain of its predecessor's debts does not, without more, render the new corporation liable for all of the predecessor's debts and obligations. See section 6.11, infra, for further reading on the liability of a purchasing corporation for the debts of an acquired corporation or business.

5.14 Arranging the Capital Structure of a Corporation

The capital structure of a corporation consists of all securities issued, or authorized to be issued, by the corporation. Included in the capital structure are common stock, preferred stock, and long-term debt instruments such as debentures and bonds. Short-term debt instruments are not normally considered to be a part of the corporate capital structure. The capital structure may be designed and used to raise funds for the operation and growth of the corporation, to allocate corporate profits, to spread the risk of loss should the corporation fail, and to allocate the ownership and control of the corporation. capital structure, definition, purpose

The issuance of stock. For many small business corporations, a capital structure consisting of a single class of voting common stock will suffice. This is especially true in the case of a new business with a small number of equal participants, all of whom are active in the business. Unless the business shows an unusual promise of success, it will make little sense for the participants of such a business to spend several hundred dollars setting up an extensive capital structure. Similarly, a simple capital structure will usually suffice for a one-person corporation and for most family corporations. However, the needs and purposes of small business corporations vary considerably, so each business should be examined in its own setting before deciding on the capital structure to be used. simple capital structure, when sufficient

The net equity of a corporation is represented by its common stock, which is ordinarily issued for money, property, or services. Great flexibility is usually permitted in establishing the rights, powers, and preferences among the holders of common stock. Should the corporation fail, however, the holders of common stock will bear the greatest risk of loss because their stock is junior to all other securities issued by the corporation. common stock, general aspects

Even if the capital structure of a corporation is to consist of only a single class of voting common stock, a few matters will require some decision-making and planning. These matters are: (1) Should the stock have a par value, and, if so, what should the value be? (2) How many shares of stock shall be authorized and issued, and in what proportions? (3) What type of consideration should be given for the stock and in what amounts? and (4) Should the stock issued by the corporation be qualified under section 1244 of the Internal Revenue Code? issuance of common stock, matter to resolve

The easiest and most convenient method of capitalizing a simple corporation (i.e., one with a single class of voting common stock) is to issue stock that does not have a par value. Before proceeding, however, the corporation laws of the state of incorporation should be checked to insure that the franchise tax on no-par-value stock is not unreasonably high. Many states base their corporate franchise taxes on the par value of the issued or authorized stock of a corporation and assign an arbitrary value to stock without par value. If this arbitrary value is high and if it is necessary to issue a large number of shares, it may be advisable to issue par value stock. The stock transfer tax in some states is based on a similar formula, so if the participants anticipate selling or transferring substantial amounts of stock in the foreseeable future, this tax should also be considered. stock without par value, when desirable

The concept of "par value" for stock originated under the early corporation laws when stock had to be sold for the par value set forth in the corporation's charter. This concept is retained in a watered-down form in the corporation laws of most states, which typically prohibit the issuance of par value stock for consideration that is less than par in value. This rule can be a problem when stock is issued for services or property without an ascertainable market value, such as used property or equipment, promotional endeavors, or general unspecified services. Challenges to the issuance of par value stock for such consideration usually arise when a corporation fails and its creditors attempt to hold the participants personally liable for the corporate debts under the doctrine of piercing the corporate veil (see section 6.06, infra). par value stock, consideration for stock, determining par value

The best practice, if par value stock is to be issued, is to assign a relatively low par value to the stock and issue it for consideration that is well above that in value. A low par value will also enable a corporation to issue stock in the desired proportional denominations without resorting to fractional shares. Fractional shares should be avoided if at all possible because they are clumsy to work with and because it is not clear in many states whether fractional shares carry voting rights. See Annotation: Voting of Jointly Held or Fractional Shares, 98 A.L.R. 2nd 357 (1964). On the other hand, if the par value of stock is too low (e.g., penny stock), it may frighten away potential future investors who may view the corporation's stock as speculative because of its low par value. A par value in the one-dollar to ten-dollar range is reasonable for most small business corporations.

issuance of stock, consideration for

The corporation laws of many states provide that stock may be issued for money, property, or services rendered, but not for future services or promissory notes. In other states, including most of the states that have adopted the Revised Model Business Corporation Act, stock may be issued for any tangible or intangible property or benefit to the corporation, including promissory notes and future services. The consideration requirements for the issuance of stock in each state are summarized in Appendix I, infra, under the heading of "Consideration For Stock."

stock, issuance of for services

Small business corporations frequently issue stock for services. The local corporation laws should be checked before doing so, however, because while stock may be issued for services previously rendered to the corporation, in many states it may not be issued for services that are to be rendered in the future. Also, if the corporation's stock is to qualify as Section 1244 stock (see, infra, this section), it may not be issued for services, and if stock is to be issued in exchange for property, it may not be issued for services if the tax-free status of the transaction is to be preserved. See 26 U.S.C. 351. See section 5.02, supra, for further reading on these matters.

common stock, valuation of consideration

The judgment of a corporation's board of directors as to the value of property or services received as consideration for the issuance of stock is usually conclusive in the absence of fraud. In other words, as long as the directors act in good faith in valuing the property or services, the transaction will usually be upheld. It should be noted, however, that a court is likely to scrutinize the directors' assessment of value in a small business corporation because of the obvious self-dealing aspects of the transaction (they are usually setting the value of their own consideration). The corporation laws of some states specifically require property received for stock to be given its actual or fair value. In any case, the corporate minutes should contain a board of director resolution accurately describing and realistically valuing any property or services received as payment for stock.

watered stock, liability for

Stock issued for legally prohibited or intentionally overvalued property or services is commonly referred to as "watered stock." Generally, directors who intentionally issue watered stock are liable to the corporation and its creditors for the amount of any overvaluation. See 18A Am Jur. 2d, Corporations, § 515. Also, the watered shares may be cancelled or assessed for the deficiency in payment if they have not been transferred to third parties without knowledge of the fraud. See 18A Am Jur. 2d, Corporations, § § 505, 506.

Section 1244 stock, general considerations, deductible amounts

Section 1244 stock. Statistically, most small business corporations fail. Common sense and sound business judgment dictate that this risk should be considered in arranging the capital structure of a corporation. Section 1244 of the Internal Revenue Code (26 U.S.C. 1244) contains a special tax benefit applicable only to the original shareholders of small business corporations whose stock later becomes worthless or is sold at a loss. If a corporation fails and if the stock qualifies under Section 1244, the shareholder will be permitted to treat his or her loss on the stock as an ordinary loss, deductible against ordinary income, up to the applicable limits, which are $50,000 for an individual and $100,000 for a husband and wife filing jointly in any tax year, with overall limits of $500,000 and $1,000,000, respectively. Only individual or partnership shareholders may use Section 1244, as it does not apply to corporate, trust, or estate shareholders, and it does not apply to transferees of the original shareholders, including their heirs and legatees.

Ordinarily, it should be noted, stock losses are treated as capital losses, which are deductible only against capital gains. Under Section 1244, however, the stock loss is treated as an ordinary loss as described in the previous paragraph. Therefore, when a small business corporation fails and its stock becomes worthless, its shareholders may take advantage of the Section 1244 ordinary tax loss up to the amount of their investment or the statutory limit described above, whichever is less. section 1244, advantages of

For the stock of a corporation to qualify under Section 1244, each of the following requirements must be satisfied: section 1244 stock, requirements

(1) The stock issued must be common stock (voting or nonvoting) of a domestic corporation.

(2) At the time the stock is issued the corporation must qualify as a "small business corporation" under 26 U.S.C. 1244(c)(3), which means that the total amount of money and property received by the corporation in exchange for stock must not exceed $1,000,000.

(3) The stock must be issued for money or for property other than stocks or securities, and must not be issued for services.

(4) At the time the loss is sustained the corporation must have derived not more than 50 percent of its income from royalties, rents, dividends, interest, annuities, and sales and exchanges of stocks and securities during the preceding five years or during the life of the corporation if it was in existence for less than five years. This condition is inapplicable if the total income of the corporation was less than its total deductions less deductions for loss carryovers and dividends received.

Classes of stock. In arranging the capital structure of a small business corporation, it may be necessary to provide for the issuance of more than one class of stock. Different classes of stock are most often needed when there are shareholders who are involved in the enterprise primarily for purposes of investment and are not active in the day-to-day management of the corporate business. Different classes of stock may also be needed for the estate planning purposes of the participants and for various other reasons. different classes of stock, when necessary

The first requirement for the issuance of differing classes of stock is that the authorization to do so be set forth in the articles of incorporation. If the articles so authorize, a board of director resolution will normally permit the corporation to issue the desired classes of stock, whether they be common stock, preferred stock, or a combination of both. If a particular class of stock is to be treated substantially different from the other classes, the applicable corporation laws should be checked to assure the legality of the treatment. classes of common stock, how to issue

Preferred stock is a hybrid security, a cross between a common stock and a bond, although a preferred stockholder is still a stockholder and not a creditor of the corporation. Preferred stockholders typically are given preferences in corporate earnings or in the distribution of corporate assets in the event of liquidation, or a combination of both. While preferred stock does not customarily have voting rights, it often has conditional voting rights such as voting rights in the event of nonpayment of dividends for a specified period. If preferred stock is to be issued, it should, if feasible, be stipulated in the issuing resolution that additional issues of preferred stock may be created and sold without the consent of the outstanding holders of preferred stock. Otherwise, it may be necessary to redeem the outstanding shares of preferred stock in order to issue additional shares of preferred stock. preferred stock, general aspects preferred stock, issuing resolution

While preferred stock is not customarily issued by small business corporations because of the tax advantages of issuing debt securities (see infra, this section), it may, on occasion, be used to accomplish the goals of the business participants. For example, nonvoting preferred stock may be issued to various members of the participants' families and thereby shift some of the business income and profits to those in lower income brackets while maintaining control of the corporation in the original or active participants. preferred stock, use of to shift income

preferred stock, use of to transfer control of corporation

Preferred stock may, in the proper situation, be used to transfer control of a corporation. A participant who wishes to transfer his or her voting rights in the corporation to another person, but who wants to retain his or her financial interest in the business, may do so through the issuance of preferred stock. This may be accomplished by recapitalizing the corporation and issuing to the participant, in exchange for his or her common stock, a comparable amount of nonvoting preferred stock, while conveying the voting common stock to the other person for services or other nominal consideration. By so doing the participant will retain most of the present value of the corporation (the value of the preferred stock should be roughly equal to the value of the corporation), while the future growth of the corporation will accrue to the other person (who is typically a son or daughter or a key employee). If the proper financial arrangements have been made, the corporation can, upon the death of the participant, redeem all or a portion of the preferred stock without altering the management and control structure of the corporation. See sections 5.17 and 6.02, infra, for further reading on buy-out provisions and stock redemptions.

preferred stock, use of in estate planning

Preferred stock may also be used, again in the proper situation, to permit the heirs or the estate of a deceased participant to retain control of the corporation and still raise the funds required to pay the taxes and administration expenses brought about by the death of the participant. By issuing preferred stock to the participant during his or her lifetime and arranging for the corporation to redeem this stock upon the participant's death, the funds necessary to pay death taxes and estate administrative expenses may be obtained while preserving the common stock of the corporation for distribution in accordance with the will or trust of the deceased participant. It should be noted, however, that the retirement or redemption of preferred stock by a holder of common stock is risky taxwise because the retirement or redemption proceeds are likely to be treated as constructive dividends on the common stock for federal income tax purposes. See 26 U.S.C. 302, 316. See section 6.02, infra, for further reading on this matter.

corporation, minimum capital requirements

Consideration for stock. When arranging the capital structure of a corporation, it should be noted that in a few states there is a minimum capitalization requirement (usually of $1,000) that must be complied with before a corporation can lawfully commence business. It is important that any such requirement be ascertained and complied with before the corporation commences business because personal liability is usually imposed on the directors or officers of the corporation if the requirement is not met. The minimum capitalization requirement in each state where such a requirement exists is set forth in Appendix I, infra, under the heading of "Minimum Capitalization Requirement."

consideration for stock, capital vs. surplus

Once the minimum capitalization requirement, if any, has been satisfied, it is not necessary to treat all of the consideration received by a corporation from the issuance of stock as capital. Except for consideration equal to the par value of par-value stock, which must normally be treated as capital, the board of directors usually has the authority to designate the balance of any consideration received for par-value stock and all of the consideration received for stock without par value as either capital or surplus. If the board of directors makes no designation between capital and surplus, the entire consideration is normally treated as capital, especially if the stock is without par value.

consideration for stock, advantages of surplus

It is usually advantageous for a corporation to maintain a surplus from the beginning because the corporation laws of most states place restrictions on the use of a corporation's capital that are not imposed on funds designated as surplus. Designating a portion of the consideration received for the issuance of stock as surplus, therefore, permits greater flexibility in dealing with corporate funds and assets. See section 6.02, infra, for further reading on the necessity of a surplus for the issuance of dividends.

capital structure, debt vs. equity, importance of planning

Debt-to-equity ratio. An important determination to be made when organizing a small business corporation is that of the debt-to-equity ratio. That is, how much of the capital made available to the corporation shall be in the form of debt and how much shall be in the form of equity (i.e., stock). It is important to note at the outset that if debt is to be used in the capitalization of a corporation, it should be implemented when the corporation is formed. Any attempt to recapitalize a corporation by replacing equity securities with debt after a corporation has commenced business is very likely to be ignored for purposes of federal income taxes. It should be understood that this discussion (i.e., debt vs. equity) applies only to C corporations and is not applicable to S corporations, whose income is attributed for tax purposes to its shareholders regardless of how or whether it is distributed to them.

For federal income tax purposes, a capital structure that is heavy with debt is preferable for the following reasons:

capital structure, advantages of debt

(1) Corporate distributions to shareholders in the form of interest on bonds, notes, or other debt instruments are deductible by the corporation against gross income, while distributions to shareholders in the form of stock dividends are not deductible by the corporation.

(2) If the business prospers, the repayment of the debt principle by the corporation permits excess funds to be transferred from the corporation to the participants in a tax-free transaction.

(3) The risk of an accumulated earnings surtax being assessed against the corporation is reduced because a corporation is allowed to retain earnings for the purpose of paying off its debts.

(4) A high debt-to-equity ratio gives a successful corporation greater financial flexibility because debt can be converted into equity without unfavorable tax consequences, but it is very difficult, taxwise, to convert equity to debt.

debt capital, how to create

debt capital, tax-free incorporation

It is usually to the tax advantage of a corporation to maintain a high debt-to-equity ratio. One method of effecting a high debt-to-equity ratio is for the participants to transfer to the corporation in exchange for stock only a portion of the assets needed to operate the business, with the balance of the assets either leased to the corporation by the participants or, preferably from a tax standpoint, purchased by the corporation from the participants with funds borrowed from third parties. In the alternative, the corporation can issue bonds, notes, or other debt instruments to the participants in exchange for the assets. It should be noted, however, that if debt instruments are issued the tax-free status of the incorporation will be lost. See 26 U.S.C. 351 and section 5.02, supra.

high debt-to-equity ratio, dangers

The overriding danger of a high debt-to-equity capital structure (the so-called thin incorporation) is that for purposes of federal income taxes and insolvency, a creditor-shareholder may be treated as a shareholder only. If a corporation's debt-to-equity ratio is too high, the debt instruments may, for tax purposes, be treated as equity securities at risk in the business and the interest and principle payments made thereon taxed as corporate dividends.

safe debt-to-equity ratio, how to determine

What constitutes a safe debt-to-equity ratio for a small business corporation? Unfortunately there is no definitive answer to this question. Much depends upon the intent of the corporate participants as evidenced by their treatment of the debt instruments. If, for example, they neglect to make the required principal or interest payments, or otherwise treat debt instruments as equity, the chances of the instruments being treated as equity will be greatly enhanced. In this regard, the book and record keeping practices of both the participant and the corporation are important. Other factors that influence the treatment of debt instruments are the custom or practices of the particular industry or business of the corporation (some industries or businesses are traditionally more debt intensive than others), and whether the debt instruments were issued for assets needed to get the corporate business started (if so, they are more likely to be treated as equity). See Henderson v. U.S., 245 F. Supp. 782 (MDAL, 1965).

debt, when treated as equity, factors

Section 385 of the Internal Revenue Code (26 U.S.C. 385) and the regulations issued thereunder set forth the following factors to be used in determining whether an interest in a corporation shall be treated for tax purposes as equity or indebtedness:

(1) Whether there is a written unconditional promise to pay on demand, or on a specified date, a sum certain in money in return for an adequate consideration in money or money's worth, and to pay a fixed rate of interest.

(2) Whether there is subordination to or preference over any other indebtedness of the corporation.

(3) The ratio of debt to equity of the corporation.

(4) Whether there is convertibility of the interest into the stock of the corporation.

(5) The relationship between the person's stock holdings in the corporation and the holdings in question.

safe debt-to-equity ratio, what constitutes

It seems to be generally agreed that a debt-to-equity ratio of 2 to 1 or less is usually safe, whereas the tax advantages of a ratio greater than 4 to 1 probably do not justify the risk of thinning beyond that point. Again, much depends on the intent of the participants, both at the time of the creation of the instruments and during the period of their existence. If the apparent intent of the participants is to advance funds at the risk of the business, they are likely to be viewed as capital advances regardless of the form of the instruments. See Arlington Park Jockey Club, Inc. v. Sauber, 262 F. 2nd 902 (CA7, 1959). Even loans by nonshareholders may constitute equity contributions if the corporation is thinly incorporated and if the lender is closely associated with the corporation. See Foresun v. Comm., 348 F. 2nd 1006 (CA 6, 1965).

third-party loans, when treated as equity

thin incorporation, disadvantages

Should a corporation fail, a thin incorporation (i.e., a high debt-to-equity ratio) is likely to work against its shareholders, for tax purposes and otherwise. Regardless of the form of the security (i.e., stock, bond, note, etc.), when it becomes worthless, the loss will be a capital loss (unless the security is a stock that qualifies under Section 1244; see supra, this section). See 26 U.S.C. 165(g). The bad debt of the shareholder-creditor is treated as a nonbusiness bad debt and thus a short-term capital loss. See 26 U.S.C. 166(d). The thinner the incorporation, of course, the smaller the percentage of the participant's investment that will qualify as an ordinary loss if the stock is qualified under Section 1244.

thin incorporation, treatment in bankruptcy, shareholder liability

In the event of insolvency or bankruptcy proceedings, a shareholder-creditor of a thin corporation is likely to be treated as a shareholder only. The debt claims against the corporation of such a shareholder are likely to be subordinated to the claims of third-party creditors. See Arnold v. Phillips, 117 F. 2nd 497 (CA 5, 1941). Also, the participant of a thin corporation is more likely to be held personally liable for corporate debts under the doctrine of piercing the corporate veil (see section 6.06, infra).

high debt-to-equity ratio, suggested rules of conduct

In practice, the following rules should be followed whenever the debt-to-equity ratio of a corporation approaches 1 to 1:

(1) Debt instruments should contain an unqualified obligation to pay both the principal and the interest on fixed dates or intervals.

(2) The holder of each debt instrument should have the power to enforce payment.

(3) A debt instrument should not contain voting rights.

(4) The shareholders should treat their advances to the corporation as representing real obligations.

(5) Advances by a shareholder to the corporation should be evidenced by properly drawn up and executed corporate notes or bonds.

(6) Debts owed to shareholders should appear on the books, records, and financial statements of the corporation as debts.

(7) The corporate minutes should clearly reflect the incurrence by the corporation of a debt when funds are advanced by a shareholder.

(8) If at all possible, the skipping of interest payments and the extension of maturity dates by the corporation should be avoided, but if avoidance is impossible the transaction should be handled formally and should appear in the corporate records and minutes.

(9) If possible, debts owed to the shareholders should be secured by mortgages or security interests on corporate property and if the corporation should have to pledge or mortgage this property to borrow money or obtain other credit, the shareholder-creditors should not subordinate their claims to that of a subsequent creditor.

(10) If feasible, debt instruments should not be issued to shareholders in the same proportions as their stock holdings.

(11) Debt money should be advanced by the shareholders to the corporation in separate transactions as it is needed, and not in one lump sum.

A guaranteed loan, whereby a lender loans funds to the corporation upon the personal guarantees of the shareholders, may strengthen the position of the shareholders on the thin incorporation issue. See Murphy Logging Co. v. U.S., 378 F. 2nd 222 (CA 9, 1967). However, the Treasury Regulations provide that if it is not reasonable at the time of the guarantee to expect the loan to be collected from the corporation according to its terms, the loan will be treated as being made by the shareholder and the shareholder will be treated as having made a capital contribution to the corporation in the amount of the loan. See Treasury Reg. 1.385-9(a). guaranteed loans to corporation, use of

Another tactic frequently used by small business corporations is that of leasing property from the participants. Instead of contributing all of the necessary property or equipment to the corporation as consideration for stock or debt, the participants may withhold certain properties or equipment and lease them to the corporation. This technique is particularly effective if the corporation is profitable and methods are needed to transfer corporate profits to the participants in a form other than dividends. The lease payments should be realistic in amounts and terms and should be regularly paid and treated as a real obligations by the corporation. corporate assets, leasing from participants

5.15 Planning the Corporate Management and Control Structure

management and control structure, purpose, definition

The active participants of most small business corporations wish to have a say in the management and control of their corporation that is at least equal to their degree of ownership. The purpose of the management and control structure of a corporation, therefore, is to vest the management of the corporation in the desired persons and to insure that the control of the corporation is vested in the desired persons in the desired proportions. The management and control structure of a corporation consists of those provisions in the articles of incorporation, the bylaws and any applicable shareholder agreements that deal with the management of the corporation or with the control of important corporate acts or functions, including the election of directors, the election or appointment of officers and the fixing of their compensation, the authorization, issuance and transfer of stock, the issuance of dividends, the borrowing or lending of money, and the extraordinary corporate acts of dissolution, merger, sales or transfers of assets not in the usual course of business, and amending the articles of incorporation.

categories of corporations

For purposes of management and control, there are four types of small business corporations: (1) a one-person corporation, (2) a corporation with several participants, but with one dominant participant, (3) a two-equal-persons corporation, where both participants own or control equal amounts of stock in the corporation, and (4) a multiperson corporation with control distributed to a significant number of participants. Substantially different approaches and techniques are needed for each type of corporation to insure that the intended management and control of the corporation is properly vested in the desired persons and remains so vested in the future. Each type of corporation is discussed separately below in this section.

one-person corporation, control of

The one-person corporation. If, under state law, the same person is permitted to serve as the only director of the corporation and to hold every required corporate office, then the ownership of all of the corporate stock will give that person absolute control of the corporation. The corporation laws of most states permit the sole shareholder of a corporation to serve as the only required director and to personally hold every corporate office. In those states nothing else is normally needed to give the sole shareholder of a corporation absolute control of the corporation. The minimum number of directors required in each state and whether the same person may hold every required corporate office is indicated in Appendix I, infra, under the headings of "Board of Directors" and "Officers."

one-person corporation, removal of officers

In some states, however, such an arrangement is impossible, usually because the corporation laws prohibit the same person from holding every required corporate office. In order to vest absolute control of the corporation in the sole shareholder in such a state it will be necessary to include in the bylaws, or in the articles of incorporation if necessary, provisions enabling the board of directors (or the shareholder, if permissible) to preemptorily remove any corporate officer at any time without cause. Similar provisions may be needed in any state if the sole shareholder wishes to have other persons serve as officers of the corporation.

dominant-person corporation, types of

The dominant-person corporation. It often happens that while there are several participants in a small business enterprise, for one reason or another one person is clearly dominant and it is desired by all of the participants that the dominant person remain in control of the business. Other times the sole shareholder of a business, often for estate planning or tax purposes or in connection with the raising of additional capital, may wish to divest a substantial equity in the business to others without relinquishing control. Whatever the situation, the idea is to vest control of the corporation in the dominant participant while vesting substantial equity in the other participants or shareholders.

dominant-person corporation, statutes to check

Two aspects of the state corporation laws should be checked before organizing the management and control structure of a dominant-person corporation. These are - (1) whether cumulative voting for directors is required under state law, and (2) the statutory voting requirements for the extraordinary corporate acts of dissolution, merger, sales or transfers of assets not in the regular course of business, and amending the articles of incorporation. The amendment of the articles of incorporation is the extraordinary corporate act that is usually of most concern in this type of corporation. The laws of each state dealing with the above-described matters are summarized in Appendix I, infra, under the headings of "Cumulative Voting" and "Acts Requiring Shareholder Approval."

dominant-person corporation, requirements for control

If cumulative voting is not required and if a shareholder vote of more than a simple majority is not required for any relevant extraordinary corporate act, then the dominant shareholder can maintain control of the corporation by owning 50 percent of each class of outstanding voting stock plus one share. The dominant shareholder will then be able to elect the entire board of directors and the other shareholders will be unable to prevent any legally permissible corporate action. At the same time it will vest in the other shareholders considerable (but less than 50 percent) equity in the corporation.

dominant-person corporation, effect of cumulative voting

If cumulative voting is statutorily required, it may be necessary to substantially increase the percentage of shares owned by the dominant participant in order to enable the participant to control (i.e., to elect a majority of) the board of directors. See section 5.06, supra, for further reading on cumulative voting and for a formula for determining the number or percentage of shares needed by the dominate participant to control the board of directors. If greater-than-majority shareholder voting requirements are statutorily mandated by the corporation laws for any relevant extraordinary corporate act, then the dominant participant must own or control the required percentage of outstanding shares to order to maintain control.

dominant-person corporation, checks on control

Not every group of corporate participants wishes to vest absolute control of the corporation in the dominant participant under all circumstances. Minority participants often wish to have some representation on the board of directors, in which case cumulative voting might be necessary to insure them representation. A similar result may also be achieved through classified voting for the board of directors (see section 5.07, supra). It may be the desire of the participants that, while the dominant participant should run the corporation on a day-to-day basis, he or she should not be permitted to take extraordinary corporate action without the approval of all or a certain percentage of the other participants. If such is the case, it may be necessary to include in the articles of incorporation provisions for greater shareholder voting requirements on such matters.

dominant-person corporation, use of nonvoting stock

There are other, more involved, methods of maintaining substantial control of the corporation in the dominant participant while vesting substantial equity in the other participants. One method is to issue all or most of the voting stock to the dominant participant, while issuing nonvoting stock to the others. The nonvoting stock may be preferred or common, depending on the desires of the persons involved. This method is complicated by the necessity of protecting the dividend and other rights of the holders of the nonvoting stock. It should be noted here that the corporation laws of some states require that the holders of all shares of stock, voting and nonvoting, be permitted to vote on certain extraordinary corporate actions, especially dissolution.

nonvoting stock, protection of shareholders' rights

The overriding danger of issuing nonvoting stock is that the voting shareholders will use their voting rights to deprive the nonvoting shareholders of their share of the corporate profits or assets. If it is the intent of the participants that a certain percentage or amount of corporate profits be distributed to the nonvoting shareholders, whether as dividends, compensation for personal services, or otherwise, it is important that appropriate provisions insuring such distribution be made prior to the issuance of the stock. Shareholder agreements, employment contracts, and article of incorporation provisions may all be used in the proper situation to implement such provisions. See, infra, this section and section 6.02, infra, for further reading on the protection of dividend and distribution rights in small business corporations.

dominant-person corporation, contingent control

Occasionally it is the desire of the corporate participants to vest control of the corporation in the dominant (or active) participant as long as certain profit or dividend levels are maintained. If the required levels are not maintained, usually for a specified period of time, then control of the corporation is to be turned over to the other participants. This is often the case where outside participants supply most of the business capital. It is important to note that the active participant in this type of arrangement is not necessarily the dominant participant in the sense of owning most of the stock in the corporation.

dominant-person corporation, control devices

Perhaps the simplest method of implementing the type of control device needed in the previous paragraph is through the use of an employment contract employing the active participant as the president or general manager of the corporation with the express powers to run the corporation for so long as the desired profit or dividend levels are maintained. See section 5.08, supra, for further reading on employment contracts. This type of control device may also be implemented by issuing to the inactive participants stock with conditional voting rights that become effective if the required profit or dividend levels are not maintained. A shareholder agreement may also be used to implement this type of control device. See section 5.06, supra, for further reading on shareholder agreements.

two-equal-persons corporation, management objectives

The two-equal-persons corporation. The two main objectives in organizing the management and control structure of a two-equal-persons corporation are to provide a management structure that will accommodate the desires of both participants and to devise a control structure that will prevent, or provide a solution for, corporate deadlock should the participants be unable to agree on important corporate matters. The first objective can usually be achieved without undue difficulty. The deficiency inherent in this type of corporation makes the second objective difficult to achieve in any meaningful way.

two-equal-persons corporation, officers of

While there can usually be only one president of a corporation, most corporation laws are sufficiently flexible to permit the creation of one or more other offices that will satisfy the participants in this regard. One practical solution is to make one participant the president and the other the chairman of the board. Another possible solution may be to rotate the presidency of the corporation between the participants on an annual or other regular basis.

two-equal-persons corporation, deadlock prevention devices

The overriding danger in a two-equal-persons corporation is corporate deadlock brought about by disagreements between the two participants. This danger can be mitigated against somewhat by allocating in advance, usually by means of a shareholders' agreement, the handling of specified corporate functions by one or the other (but not both) of the participants. A practical method of preventing deadlock in a two-equal-person corporation is to provide for an odd number of directors, requiring the participants to elect at least one outside director (presumably when they are on friendly terms), and then making it difficult or impossible to remove the outside director once a deadlock is threatened.

two-equal-persons corporation, deadlock solution devices

Once a deadlock has occurred, a possible solution is to give each participant the right to state a price for either the sale of his or her stock or the purchase of the other participant's stock, giving the other participant the choice of either buying or selling at that price. Another solution is to permit or require each participant to submit a sealed bid for the purchase of the other participant's stock, with the high bid prevailing and the low bidder being obligated to sell. Still another solution is to give either participant the power to dissolve the corporation, but first requiring the participant to offer his or her stock to the other participant at a price that is either fixed or determined by specified formula.

two-equal-persons corporation, veto powers

In a two-equal-persons corporation, the creation of veto powers is usually unnecessary. (For the definition of a veto power, see the second paragraph below.) Unless provisions are made to the contrary, each participant will have a veto power over practically every significant corporate act simply by virtue of his or her one-half ownership of the corporation. Veto powers or control over practical and monetary matters can be implemented by adopting a bylaw provision requiring the signature of both participants on all corporate contracts and on checks of over a specified amount.

multiperson corporation, control of, general aspects

The multiperson corporation. The management and control structure of a multiperson corporation with several active participants is, understandably, more involved than in a corporation where control is concentrated in one or two persons. In a multiperson corporation it is often necessary to determine which of the corporate acts or functions are to be decided by majority vote, which, if any, are to require greater-than-majority vote, and which, if any, are to be permitted only with the consent of all the participants. It may also be necessary to implement safeguards to protect individual or minority participants from later being squeezed or frozen out of the management and control of the corporation by the majority. Finally, it may be necessary to include methods or procedures to prevent and deal with corporate deadlocks.

Most participants of multiperson small business corporations wish to be able to prevent the other participants from banding together and depriving a participant of any voice whatsoever in the running of the corporation. Also, while the participants are usually willing to submit most matters of corporate management to the wishes of the majority or controlling interests, there are often certain corporate functions or acts that each participant wishes to be able to prevent from occurring without his or her consent. The ability of a participant in a corporate enterprise to prohibit the happening of a corporate act or function is commonly referred to as a veto power. Not surprisingly, veto powers often play an important role in the management and control structure of a multiperson small business corporation. Veto powers are seldom needed or used in a one or two-person corporation. They are sometimes used in a dominant person corporation.

multiperson corporation, typical powers of participants

veto power, definition

Veto Powers. In determining whether veto powers should be created in a particular business setting, it is important to understand the drawbacks as well as the advantages of veto powers. First of all, veto powers do not, by themselves, enable individual corporate participants to affirmatively determine and carry out corporate policy. They are essentially negative in character and can normally be used only to prevent others from implementing unwanted corporate policies or actions. Accordingly, the biggest disadvantage of veto powers is that they can lead to corporate deadlock and can deprive a corporation of the flexibility needed to adjust to changing business conditions. In an extreme case, the existence of veto powers might enable an unscrupulous participant to extort unfair concessions from the other participants as the price of not exercising a veto power. It is important, therefore, to balance the needs and interests of the individual participants against those of the business itself when deciding whether veto powers should be granted to individual corporate participants.

veto powers, disadvantages, limitations

veto powers, balancing of interests

Veto powers should not be granted unless all of the corporate participants agree to them in advance. As a practical matter, the corporate participants are most likely to unanimously agree on such matters when the corporation is being organized, usually as a part of their original business bargain. Accordingly, the most appropriate time to insert veto powers into the corporate management and control structure is when the corporation is being organized.

veto powers, when to insert

The use of veto powers in the management and control structure of a small business corporation may be broad or narrow. That is, they can be extended to cover virtually every corporate act or restricted to certain basic corporate acts, such as changing the nature of the corporate business or the addition of new participants. If extensive veto powers are to be employed, the use of a statutory close corporation should be seriously considered in states that have a close corporation code or statute. Veto powers are generally easier to implement and enforce in close corporations. See section 5.19, infra, for further reading on the close corporation election. The close corporation laws, if any, in each state are cited in Appendix I, infra, under the heading of "Close Corporation Laws."

veto powers, scope of, use of close corporation

Determining the corporate acts, if any, that shall be subjected to the veto power of an individual participant is one of the most difficult decisions to be made in the course of incorporating a multiperson business, especially a successful one. More often than not, the participants will not have considered this aspect of the business in striking their original business bargain. Further, the participants are likely to possess little or no knowledge as to which corporate acts can or should be subjected to veto powers, or of the ramifications of subjecting particular acts to veto powers. In such instances, the advantages and disadvantages of employing veto powers should be explained to the participants to the extent that each participant is capable of making an informed decision on this important matter.

veto powers, determining acts subject to

veto powers over basic corporate acts

Most informed corporate participants want veto powers over basic corporate functions and little else. For example, most participants of small business corporations expect to be on the board of directors, and it is common for them to wish to be able to prevent the other participants from joining together and denying a particular participant a position on the board. The same is usually true with respect to the employment of a participant by the corporation, his or her salary, and the holding of a particular office in the corporation. Most participants also wish to be able to prevent the dilution of their equity in the corporation by the issuance of additional stock, and veto powers over such matters are common. Similarly, participants typically wish to have a direct voice in the choice of future business participants. Many participants wish to have control over the creation of corporate debts and the distribution or allocation of corporate profits and assets. Finally, participants often wish to have the power to prevent drastic or extraordinary corporate acts, such as dissolving the corporation, merging or consolidating the corporation with another corporation, acquiring another business, or the transfer of substantial corporate assets.

veto powers, typical acts subject to

In practice, the corporate acts and functions that are most often subjected to participant veto powers in a multiperson small business corporation include -

(1) changing the corporate business;

(2) the election and removal of directors;

(3) the employment and compensation of key employees, including the participants;

(4) the holding or filling of certain corporate offices, either by a certain participant or otherwise;

(5) the borrowing or lending of money by the corporation;

(6) the issuance of dividends and other corporate distributions;

(7) the authorization or issuance of additional stock;

(8) the transfer of stock; and

(9) the extraordinary corporate acts of dissolution, merger, sales or transfer of substantial assets, and amending the articles of incorporation.

broad veto powers, desirability

Occasionally a participant will want to have a veto power over practically every corporate act, even such day-to-day functions as the signing of checks, the purchase of supplies, and the salaries of clerical employees. Normally, such broad veto powers should be discouraged because they are likely to result in disputes and deadlocks over insignificant matters and weak corporate management. However, if the participants insist on broad veto powers and if they have demonstrated an ability to work together in the past, a corporate management structure can usually be set up so as to accommodate their wishes, especially if only one or two participants desire such veto powers.

veto powers, methods of implementing

Once the corporate acts and functions that are to be subjected to veto powers have been established, the methods of implementing the veto powers must be determined. In making such a determination, much depends on the nature of the particular acts or functions that are to be subjected to veto powers, exactly who is to be given the veto powers, and the circumstances under which the powers may be exercised. Generally, veto powers may be implemented by any combination of the following methods:

(1) By requiring unanimous consent or high shareholder or director voting and quorum requirements for certain corporate acts.

(2) By issuing different classes of stock, with the holders of each class having the right to fill certain directorships or approve certain corporate acts.

(3) By inserting provisions in a shareholders agreement requiring the prior approval of certain shareholders for the performance of certain corporate acts.

(4) By requiring mandatory cumulative voting for directors.

(5) By creating preemptive rights in stock.

(6) By the use of voting trusts and irrevocable proxies.

practical veto powers, how to implement

If a corporation has only a few participants, certain practical veto powers can be implemented by requiring the signatures of all participants on all or specified corporate contracts and on checks of over a certain amount. Requirements such as these may be implemented through a bylaw provision coupled with an article or bylaw provision requiring a unanimous vote of the participants to amend the bylaw provision.

veto powers, use of cumulative voting

If each participant wishes only to be assured a position on the board of directors, the simplest method may be to include a requirement for cumulative voting for directors in the articles of incorporation. Care must be taken, however, to insure that a majority of the shareholders cannot dilute another shareholder's stock to the extent that he or she cannot elect a representative to the board. It should also be insured that the articles of incorporation cannot be amended so as to eliminate the cumulative voting requirement.

veto powers, implementing by high voting requirements

The imposition of high or unanimous voting requirements for certain specific corporate acts is probably the most common method of implementing veto powers. Suppose, for example, that the five equal participants of Corporation Y wish to limit the business of the corporation to its present field unless they all agree otherwise. A veto power preventing a change in the corporate business may be established by inserting a purpose clause in the articles of incorporation containing self-denying language preventing the corporation from engaging in any other than its present business and requiring a shareholder vote of, say, 90 percent to amend the purpose clause. The corporation would then be limited to its present business unless each participant voted affirmatively to amend the purpose clause and permit it to engage in another business. In this manner, each participant would effectively have the power to veto any unwanted change in the corporate business.

veto powers, common methods of implementing

High voting requirements are most often imposed on corporate participants in their role as shareholders. This is because the action through which a veto power is sought to be implemented is usually deemed a shareholder function under the state corporation laws. The shareholder action most often used to implement veto powers is that of amending the articles of incorporation. If, however, the action over which a veto power is desired is a board of director function (e.g., the election or removal of an officer, the issuance of dividends, etc.), high voting requirements may also be imposed on the board of directors.

veto powers implemented by shareholder voting, illustration

Suppose that each of the five equal participants of Corporation Y wishes to be able to prevent the corporation from issuing additional stock without his or her consent. In most states the issuing of stock is a function of the board of directors, provided that there are authorized shares available for issuance. The authorization of shares for issuance is normally a function of the articles of incorporation. One method of creating a veto power for each participant would be to limit the number of authorized shares to that already issued, thus requiring an amendment to the articles of incorporation before additional stock could be issued. An article provision requiring an affirmative shareholder vote of, say, 90 percent to amend the provision in the articles dealing with authorized shares would effectively create a veto power for each participant. In several states, it should be noted, the corporation laws specifically permit functions such as the issuance of stock to be delegated to the shareholders by so providing in the articles of incorporation. In such states a veto power can be created by imposing high shareholder voting requirements for the issuance of stock.

veto powers, alternative methods of implementing

The five participants of Corporation Y might decide that it is too bothersome or expensive to amend the articles of incorporation every time they want to issue additional stock. In that case, the articles of incorporation of Corporation Y could be drafted so as to require a five-man board of directors and provisions could be made, either through cumulative voting, a shareholders agreement, or classified voting, to permit each participant to elect one director. The inclusion in the articles of incorporation and the bylaws of provisions requiring the unanimous vote of the board of directors for the issuance of stock would create the desired veto power for each participant. As always, care must be taken to prevent the elimination of the veto power by amendment or otherwise. As shown by this example, it is often possible to implement a desired veto power by different methods and at different levels. Obviously, it is important to choose the method best suited for the business situation at hand.

veto powers, use of article amendment

As indicated above, the power of the shareholders to amend the articles of incorporation can be used to implement veto powers over a wide range of corporate activities. Any activity that can be limited or controlled by provisions in the articles of incorporation can be the subject of a shareholder veto power by this method. Sometimes it is possible to give shareholders a direct veto power over what would otherwise be a director function by inserting in the articles of incorporation a provision dealing specifically with that function. The applicable state corporation laws should be checked before doing so, however, because if the statute specifically designates a function as a director function, an article provision dealing with that function may be invalid.

veto powers at shareholder level, advantages

As a general rule, it is preferable to implement veto powers through shareholder action rather than through director action. Veto powers at the shareholder level are usually less complicated, easier to enforce, and more difficult to evade than veto powers at any other level. Also, there are generally more methods available for implementing veto powers at the shareholder level (e.g., by shareholder agreement, by classified voting, by article of incorporation amendment, through preemptive rights, etc.).

veto powers, shareholder approval, required percentage

Whenever possible it is a good practice to avoid unanimous voting requirements for shareholder action (as opposed to director action, where it is usually appropriate). If even a single share of stock winds up in the hands of an outsider, by whatever means, the outsider may have a veto power equal to that of the participants if unanimous shareholder voting requirements are imposed. As a practical matter, a 90 or 95 percent shareholder voting requirement is as effective for veto power purposes as a unanimous shareholder voting requirement in most instances. Whenever less than unanimous voting requirements are called for, however, care must be taken to insure that a participant's veto power is not lost by the issuance of additional stock.

veto powers, use of shareholder agreements

A shareholders' agreement is a common method of implementing veto powers at the shareholder level, especially in situations where there are only a few shareholders and only one or two acts to be subjected to the veto power. Veto powers over such matters as the transfer of stock and the election of directors are relatively easy to deal with in shareholder agreements. See section 5.06, supra, for further reading on shareholder agreements. See section 5.17, infra, for further reading on stock transfer restrictions.

veto powers, use of voting trust

Voting trusts and irrevocable proxies may also be used to implement veto powers at the shareholder level. These devices are most useful when there are opposing factions each consisting of numerous, small-percentage shareholders who wish to band together to effect a veto power over certain specified corporate activities, usually the election of directors. Such devices, especially voting trusts, tend to be expensive and difficult to implement and administer and are not often used to implement veto powers in small business corporations.

veto powers, use of class voting for directors

Another method of insuring representation on the board of directors and of implementing veto powers at the shareholder level is class voting. The most common use of this method is to require class voting for directors, which is simple to implement and has the advantage of being specifically authorized by statute in most states. Class voting for directors is accomplished by establishing as many classes of stock as there are shareholders, or factions thereof, and permitting each class of stock to elect a fixed, and usually equal, number of directors. The stock should be otherwise equal in every respect. This technique assures each shareholder, or faction of shareholders, a fixed representation on the board of directors. See sections 5.06 and 5.07, supra, for further reading on classified voting for directors.

veto powers, use of class voting, generally

The class voting method may also be used to implement veto powers over a wide range of corporate functions. The technique here is to delegate the control of the function over which there is to be a veto power directly to a specified class or classes of shareholders. This can usually be accomplished by inserting clauses in the articles of incorporation dealing directly with that function and then requiring the affirmative vote of the holders of each specified class of stock in order to carry out or change the function.

Veto powers may also be implemented by the issuance of voting and nonvoting stock in various ratios. This technique is useful if the strength of the veto powers is not necessarily proportional to equity. Because the issuance of stock with unequal voting rights is permissible under Subchapter S of the Internal Revenue Code, this technique, unlike the class voting technique, may be used in an S corporation.

veto powers, use of stock with unequal voting rights

For reasons of either convenience or necessity, activities such as the election of officers, the declaration of dividends, the issuing of stock, the compensation of employees, and the borrowing or lending of money may require a veto power at the director level. Because agreements affecting director discretion and voting are of questionable validity in some states, it is usually preferable to implement veto powers at the director level by the imposition of high or unanimous voting requirements, rather than through voting agreements. Director voting requirements can normally be imposed by article of incorporation and bylaw provisions. Care should be taken, however, that high director voting requirements are not circumvented by low quorum requirements.

veto powers at director level, how to implement

When providing veto powers for corporate participants it is obviously important to insure that the veto powers cannot later, without the consent of the holders, be avoided or taken away by amendment of the articles of incorporation, by the issuance of additional stock, by low quorum requirements, or otherwise. It would make little sense, say, to insert an article provision requiring cumulative voting for directors in order to give the participants a veto power against being frozen out of the board of directors, if the articles of incorporation could later be amended so as to eliminate the cumulative voting requirement by a simple majority vote of the participants. A veto power would also be meaningless if it could be circumvented by the issuance of stock in quantities sufficient to permit the majority shareholders to simply outvote the minority's cumulative vote.

veto powers, protection from circumvention

The usual, and best, practice is to require the same voting requirements for amending the substantive provision in the articles of incorporation as is required to approve the corporate act or function dealt with in the substantive provision. For example, if an article provision calls for a vote of, say, 90 percent of the outstanding shares to remove a director from office, a vote of 90 percent of the outstanding shares should also be required to amend that article provision. While the imposition of high voting requirements to amend specific article of incorporation provisions is generally permissible, often by express statutory authority, the law on the issue in the local state should be checked. See Annotation: Validity of Supermajority Voting Requirements, 80 ALR 4th 667 (1990).

veto powers, preventing loss of by article amendment

It is also important to provide that directors elected by either cumulative or class voting cannot be removed from office other than by those who elected them. Similarly, care should be taken to insure that a veto power is not lost through the death or resignation of a director. The articles of incorporation or bylaws (whichever is used to create the veto power) should provide that any vacancy created by the death or resignation of a director can be filled only by those who had elected the deceased or resigned director. If veto powers are implemented in whole or in part by bylaw provisions, it is important to prevent circumvention of the veto powers by amendment of the bylaws. The same voting standards set forth in the substantive bylaw provision should be required to amend the bylaw provision. Finally, it is important not to permit high voting requirements to be circumvented by low quorum requirements.

veto powers through director election or bylaw provision, protection of

If a veto power is implemented by a high, but less than unanimous, shareholder voting requirement or by cumulative voting for directors, care must be taken to prevent circumvention of the veto power by the issuance of additional stock (i.e., circumvention by dilution). Otherwise, the majority owners could simply issue themselves, usually for services or property, a sufficient number of shares to permit them to outvote the veto holder. This type of circumvention can best be prevented through article of incorporation provisions controlling the issuance of stock (see supra, this section). The granting of preemptive rights will, to a lesser degree, also serve to protect against circumvention by dilution. The main detriment to the use of preemptive rights to preserve veto powers is that stock can be offered to a veto holder at such a time or in such a manner that he or she may be financially unable to exercise the preemptive right. See section 5.12 supra and section 6.05, infra, for further reading on preemptive rights and on their strengths and weaknesses as control devices.

veto power, loss of through issuance of stock

veto power, loss of through merger, etc.

Veto powers implemented by high shareholder voting requirements may also be lost through merger or consolidation, by the dissolution and reincorporation of the business, and by the transfer of the corporate assets to another entity. Extraordinary corporate actions such as these should always be made subject to the approval of the holders of the veto powers in order to prevent circumvention. This is easily accomplished by simply making the extraordinary corporate acts of merger, consolidation, dissolution, and the sale or transfer of assets subject to the same shareholder voting requirement as that required to implement the veto power.

veto powers, necessity of planning

It is apparent from the preceding discussion that veto powers are not matters to be dealt with summarily. Each business situation is unique and requires study, analysis, and research in order to determine, first, whether veto powers should be implemented, and, second, the most effective and enforceable method of implementing the desired veto powers. The use of stock provisions in their entirety is seldom advisable. Individualized and careful drafting is usually required.

veto powers, construction of by courts

veto powers, dispositive provisions, where to insert

It should be kept in mind that provisions granting veto powers, because they depart from the corporate norm of majority rule, are likely to be strictly construed by the courts, should they later be challenged. It is important, therefore, that veto provisions be worded clearly and unambiguously, and that the various provisions be consistent with one another, leaving no loopholes or means of circumvention. It is a good practice to include the dispositive veto provisions in both the articles of incorporation and the bylaws, even if they are not legally required in the bylaws to be enforceable. It is also a good practice to insert a notice of any applicable veto provisions on each stock certificate representing shares affected by veto powers.

employment contracts, use of in management structure

An employment contract is a device frequently used in the management and control structure of small business corporations. Because small business corporations usually distribute most of their profits in the form of compensation for personal services and because the participants typically devote their full time to the corporate business, it is important that the participants assure themselves of continued employment by the corporation. An employment contract is often the most practical method of satisfying the specific employment demands of a participant, especially a minority participant. It is common for employment contracts to contain specific guarantees as to job descriptions and management responsibilities of the employees. In this regard, it may be possible to substitute an employment contract for a veto power in the corporate management and control structure. However, the unavailability of specific performance as a remedy for the breach of an employment contract weakens it effectiveness. See section 5.08, supra, for further reading on the use of employment contracts and the drafting thereof.

corporate participants, similarity to partners

Dealing with dissention. In many ways a small business corporation is more of a partnership than a corporation in the traditional sense. It is said that the participants of small business corporations wish to be treated as a corporation by outsiders, but as partners among themselves. Because of the closeness of their business relationship, it is imperative that a high degree of good faith, fair dealing, and mutual respect exist among the participants. Once dissatisfaction and distrust develops, friction, dissention, and deadlock are likely to follow.

dissatisfied participants, remedies

A dissatisfied participant of a small business corporation is faced with severe problems. Unlike a dissatisfied partner in a partnership, he or she normally does not have the power to dissolve the corporation and get out with his or her share of the business assets. Unlike a dissatisfied shareholder in a publicly-held corporation, such a participant cannot normally sell his or her stock without incurring a substantial financial loss, and if the participant remains in the business, he or she is likely to be relegated to a minor role in the corporation.

participant dissention, corporate deadlock

Dissention among the participants of a small business corporation is, perhaps, the most difficult aspect of the management and control structure to anticipate and deal with. When dissention is coupled with veto powers or high voting requirements for corporate action, the result is often a deadlock, paralyzing the corporation and preventing it from carrying out the functions for which it was formed. While it is impossible to grant veto powers to the participants and not increase the chances of corporate deadlock, certain provisions can be made for the prevention and breaking of at least some forms of deadlock. It is important that the management and control structure of a small business corporation be devised so as to minimize both the likelihood and the effects of corporate deadlock.

participant dissention, typical causes

Participant dissatisfaction and dissention in small business corporations can result from any number of causes. The most common causes include - (1) disagreements among the active participants as to the financial goals and general policies of the business; (2) disagreements between active participants and participants who are not active in the management of the business, (3) dissention resulting from struggles for control of the business, and (4) dissention resulting from personality conflicts among the participants. All categories of dissatisfaction and dissent except the last can be anticipated and mitigated against in planning the corporate management and control structure. Dissention resulting from the personal dislike of one participant by another is virtually impossible to prevent and provide for in any meaningful way.

participant dissention, methods of dealing with

Methods of dealing with participant dissatisfaction and dissention include:

(1) Providing for the purchase of the stock of, or otherwise compensating or buying out, a dissatisfied participant.

(2) Providing for the arbitration of participant disputes.

(3) Providing practical provisions designed to reduce the likelihood of corporate deadlock.

(4) Providing for the dissolution of the corporation under certain circumstances.

dissention provisions, how to implement

A practical rule to keep in mind when implementing dissent and dissatisfaction provisions is that a solution that preserves the corporation as a going business is normally preferable to one that results in its dissolution or extinction. It should also be remembered that the best, and often the only feasible, time to include such provisions in the corporate management and control structure is when the corporation is being organized. It is then that the participants, as a part of their overall business bargain, will be most likely to agree on such matters.

participant dissention, use of buy-out provisions

When organizing a small business corporation it is common to provide for the buying out of the shares of certain shareholders under certain circumstances. The buy-out provisions can be optional or mandatory. The general subject of buy-out agreements is discussed at length in section 5.17, infra, and the reader should examine the relevant portions of that section.

dissident buy-outs, required provisions

To provide for the buying out of the shares of a dissatisfied corporate participant, it will be necessary to include provisions for such in the triggering mechanism of the buy-out provisions. For example, a buy-out provision could be implemented if the board of directors remains deadlocked for a specified period of time, if a specified period of time passes after the expiration of the term of the directors without the shareholders being able to elect a new board, or if a participant receives less than a specified amount of compensation from the corporation over a certain period.

dissident buy-outs, advantages and disadvantage

The advantages of dissident buy-out provisions are that they preserve the corporate business as a going concern and they compensate dissatisfied participants for their stock in the corporation. The disadvantages are the disadvantages of buy-out agreements generally (valuation and funding) and the fact that they tend not to fairly compensate the participant (usually a minority participant) whose principal benefit from the corporation is employment. Dissident buy-out provisions tend to give a significant advantage to participants with ample and available funds.

participant dissention, use of arbitration

The use of arbitration as a solution to the dissident or dissatisfied participant problem is limited primarily to the resolving of deadlocks, and not to the prevention of deadlocks. In this regard it has the advantages of being quicker and less expensive that traditional litigation. Its principal disadvantage is that, like traditional litigation, it is more of a dispute-settling than a policy-formulating proceeding, and is not readily adaptable to many kinds of dissent and dissatisfaction situations. The use of arbitration as a method of breaking corporate deadlocks requires a thorough study of local law and careful drafting of the arbitration provisions to insure compliance. A detailed account of the enforceability and drafting of arbitration provisions is beyond the scope of this handbook.

corporate deadlock, use of directors to resolve

Certain practical methods or safeguards can be inserted in the corporate management and control structure to reduce the likelihood of corporate deadlock. One safeguard is simply to provide for an odd number of directors whenever possible. If this is not feasible, usually because there are an even number of participants and outside directors are not wanted, provisions can sometimes be made for the appointment of a provisional director for the purpose of breaking a board of director deadlock. The provisional director could be appointed by the existing directors, by the shareholders generally, by a special class of shareholders, by a disinterested third party, or by a court in a special proceeding, if permitted under local law.

corporate deadlock, other methods of resolving

Another practical method is to provide for the retirement of certain participants at a stated pension or salary in the event of deadlocks that last for specified periods. If the business lends itself to such divisions, it may be possible to devise a procedure for dividing up the business whereby certain lines or assets are parcelled out to certain participants, either by spinning off new corporations or otherwise. Another device to prevent future deadlocks is to provide for a fixed corporate existence (as opposed to perpetual existence) in the articles of incorporation, thereby requiring the participants to periodically reexamine the desirability of continuing the corporation. A failure to extend the life of the corporation would automatically result in its dissolution.

participant dissention, dissolution of corporation

The dissolution of a corporation is normally the last resort in resolving differences between corporate participants. Because the remedy is so drastic, many courts are reluctant to order the dissolution of a corporation, especially a profitable one. Also, the liquidation of a dissolved corporation is normally a taxable transaction to the shareholders and usually results in the sale of the business or its assets under unfavorable circumstances.

forced dissolution, easy vs. difficult

A matter of corporate policy that should be resolved before inserting dissolution provisions in the management and control structure is whether to make the dissolution of the corporation by the participants easy or difficult. A difficult dissolution (i.e., one requiring a unanimous or high percentage shareholder approval) generally favors the interests of controlling participants, while an easy dissolution (i.e., one at the will of each shareholder or one requiring a low percentage shareholder vote) usually favors the interests of minority participants. Because most small business corporations are akin to general partnerships, where each partner can normally dissolve the partnership, easy dissolution, within reasonable limits, is usually preferable. Many close corporation codes, it should be noted, specifically permit dissolution at the will of a shareholder.

forced dissolution, factors to consider

The nature and type of business conducted by the corporation should be considered when resolving the easy-vs.-difficult dissolution issue, because some businesses lend themselves more readily to being divided up or liquidated than others. The tax consequences of any liquidation should also be considered. In any event, the best practice in most cases is to combine compulsory dissolution with buy-out provisions, giving the corporation or the other participants the right to purchase the stock of the dissident participants prior to forced dissolution.

forced dissolution, legality

Provisions in shareholder agreements and in the articles of incorporation and bylaws dealing with forced or mandatory dissolution upon the occurrence of certain events (director deadlock, failure to purchase a dissident participant's stock, etc.) are enforceable in most states, either by specific statutory provision or by case law. See section 7.03, infra, for further reading on the dissolution and liquidation of small business corporations.

5.16 Complying With Federal and State Securities Laws

Unless a small business corporation has an unusually large number of shareholders or seeks to raise capital by publicly selling its stock, it will not normally be necessary for the corporation to register its stock. In almost every instance the stock of a typical small business corporation will be exempt from the registration requirements of the federal and state securities laws. Occasionally, however, a particular stock transaction, or series of transactions, will create a question as to the applicability of the securities laws. Or, the participants of a corporation might wish to examine the feasibility of adding a substantial number of new shareholders or selling a substantial number of additional shares of stock without running afoul of the securities laws. It is to questions such as these that this section is addressed. securities laws, applicability to small business corporations

An extended discussion of securities regulation is beyond the scope of this handbook. Only a general and brief outline of the scope of the federal securities laws and their possible effect on a small business corporation is given. The various federal registration exemptions are described and a brief description of state securities laws is given. scope of section

The basic requirement of the Securities Act of 1933, which, with the Securities Exchange Act of 1934, constitutes the heart of the federal securities laws, is that a full and accurate disclosure of all relevant information must be made before the securities of a corporation can be sold. The use of false, misleading, or incomplete statements in connection with the offer and sale of securities may result in - (1) the delay or prevention of a public offering of the securities, (2) the recovery by the purchasers of the securities of monetary damages from the responsible parties, and (3) the imposition of criminal penalties against the persons responsible for the misstatements. See 15 U.S.C. 77h, 77l, 77x. It should be noted that the civil and criminal liability sanctions apply whether or not a security is exempt from registration. Securities Act of 1933, general features

The Securities Act of 1933 requires that all securities offered or sold to the public in interstate commerce or through the mails be registered with the Securities and Exchange Commission (the S.E.C.) by the filing of a registration statement, unless either the security to be issued or the transaction in which the securities are to be sold is exempt. Unless an exemption is available, the securities may not be offered for sale until the registration statement has been filed and may not be sold until the registration statement has been declared effective by the S.E.C. Helpful in the preparation of a Registration Statement is S.E.C. Securities Act Release no. 4936, entitled "Guides for Preparation and Filing of Registration Statements." This release was issued in 1968 (33 Fed. Register 18,617) and has been periodically updated. The requirements in time, money and resources necessary to obtain S.E.C. approval of a registration statement make it very difficult in practice for a typical small business corporation to sell its stock to outsiders other than under one or more of the registration exemptions set forth below. Securities Act of 1933, registration requirements; registration statement, preparation of

The registration exemption most widely used by small business corporations is the so-called private offering exemption. See 15 U.S.C. 77d(2). Under most circumstances, an offering to 25 or fewer persons is not considered a public offering, and registration is not required. The rule is not hard and fast, however, and much depends upon the size of the offering, the need of the offerees for the type of protection offered by registration, and the offerees' access to sufficient information upon which to make an informed investment judgment. See S.E.C. v. Ralston Purina Co., 346 U.S. 119, 97 L.Ed. 1494, 73 S.Ct. 981 (1953). The S.E.C. has adopted a rule (S.E.C. Rule 146) establishing objective, but nonexclusive, standards for the application of the private offering exemption. securities registration, private offering exemption

The private offering exemption may be lost if even one person buys the stock for purposes of resale to the general public. If stock is to be issued to an outsider or to a person who may be purchasing the stock for resale, the stock certificate should contain a legend stating that the stock is not registered with the S.E.C. and that it should not be offered for resale unless either a registration statement is filed or an opinion of counsel satisfactory to the corporation is produced stating that registration is not required. It is also a good practice, in the appropriate situation, to obtain an investment letter from each purchaser stating that the stock is being purchased for purposes of investment and not for resale. private offering exemption, loss of securities registration, intrastate exemption

Another exemption used by small business corporations is the intrastate exemption, wherein the offer and sale of securities solely to persons residing within a single state by a corporation incorporated and doing significant business in that state is exempt from registration. See 15 U.S.C. 77c(a)(11). Objective standards for this exemption are set forth in S.E.C. Rule 147. This exemption, too, may be lost if even a single purchaser resells the stock within a short period to a nonresident. To guard against this in the appropriate situation, the purchasers should be required to sign statements to the effect that they are actual residents of the state and are not purchasing the stock for purposes of resale to nonresidents. Any advertising of the offering should also state that sales will be made only to bona fide residents of the state.

securities registration, Regulation A exemption

An exemption designed almost exclusively for small business corporations is the so-called Regulation A offering. See 15 U.S.C. 77c(b) and S.E.C. Regulation A, which includes S.E.C. Rules 251-264. Under this exemption a public offering not exceeding $1,500,000 in amount (which amount includes certain other sales within the last 12 months) is exempt from registration if the corporation obtains the approval of the S.E.C. Regional Office by the filing of an offering statement and certain other documents.

Regulation A exemption, requirements

To qualify for a Regulation A offering, five copies of an offering statement must be filed with the appropriate Regional Office of the S.E.C. at least ten days prior to the offering or sale of the Regulation A securities. The offering statement must contain current financial statements and certain other information related to the corporation, its predecessors, principals, creditors, criminal and civil actions, and other activities. Special limitations are imposed on corporations that have been incorporated for less than a year or that have had no net income in at least one of its last two fiscal years. In all offerings exceeding $100,000 an offering circular containing basic disclosure information, including the proposed use by the issuer of the proceeds of the Regulation A securities, must be given to the offerees prior to sale. If the securities are to be offered prior to S.E.C. approval of the offering statement, a preliminary offering circular must be provided to the offerees.

securities registration, Rule 240 exemption

Another registration exemption available to small business corporations is the S.E.C. Rule 240 exemption. Under this exemption the sale of up to $100,000 worth of stock during a 12-month period by a corporation beneficially owned by 100 or fewer persons is exempt from registration. This exemption applies to the transaction and not to the security, so that securities issued thereunder may not be resold without either registration or the application of another registration exemption. No commissions may be paid on sales under this exemption and the securities may not be publicly advertised.

securities registration, Rule 242 exemption

The final registration exemption available to a typical small business corporation is the S.E.C. Rule 242 exemption. This exemption permits a corporation to offer and sell an aggregate of $2,000,000 worth of securities over a six-month period to an unlimited number of accredited persons plus 35 other (non-accredited) purchasers. Accredited persons include financial institutions, purchasers of $100,000 worth or more of the securities, and officers or directors of the issuing corporation. General advertising of the stock offering is prohibited and sales within six months before or after the offering must be included in the $2,000,000 limit. The issuing corporation must provide non-accredited purchasers with certain financial information regarding the offering, including a certified financial statement. Securities purchased under the Rule 242 exemption are unregistered and have the same status as those sold under the private offering exemption described above. Notices of Rule 242 sales must be filed with the S.E.C. on prescribed forms.

state securities laws, general requirements, applicability

Every state has a securities (or blue sky) law that applies to offers and sales of securities within, or to residents of, that state. While the laws differ widely, most of them contain anti-fraud provisions and require, with certain exemptions, the registration of stock prior to its sale. Many provide for alternative types of registration, including registration by notification (which is the simplest), registration by coordination (usually with federal registration), and registration by qualification. The only safe practice is to check the securities laws of the applicable state before offering or issuing any stock that might be subject thereto, for even if a federal exemption is applicable to either the stock or the transaction, registration with the state securities administrator might still be necessary. Pertinent materials related to securities registration, including any applicable regulations, can usually be obtained from the state securities administrator. State registration is usually easier and less costly than federal registration.

5.17 Controlling the Transfer of Stock - Options and Buy-outs

In a typical small business corporation the participants are the shareholders. They manage and run the business on a day-to-day basis. They are in close and constant contact with one another and business decisions are routinely made without formality. Often, the main reasons they are in business together is their ability to work well together and the complimentary nature of their skills and abilities. Not surprisingly, one of the most important requirements of a typical small business enterprise is the preservation by the participants of the right to choose their associates in the business. Most participants have little desire to share their business with strangers, should one or more of their associates decide to sell out, or with the spouse or heirs of a fellow participant, should the participant die.

participants' right to choose associates in the business

On the other hand, one of the main reasons for the existence of a business enterprise is to enhance the value of one's investment in the business. In a corporation the value of a participant's investment is normally measured by the value of his or her stock. If, instead of selling to the highest bidder, a participant is forced to sell his or her stock to the other participants at a price determined or substantially influenced by the other participants, or at a fixed price that is unrealistically low because the other participants do not have the resources to pay more, then the value of that stock will probably not fairly reflect the real worth of the participant's investment in the business.

participants' investment in business, fairness of compensation

The only proven method of prohibiting the transfer of stock to unwanted persons while providing for the payment of a fair price to departing or deceased shareholders is to impose restrictions on the transfer of the stocks and give the other shareholders or the corporation the option or obligation of purchasing the stock at a price that is fair to all parties. The object, then, is to devise stock transfer restrictions that protect the right of the remaining participants to choose their associates in the business and yet do not unfairly deprive a departing or deceased participant of the value of his or her investment in the business.

stock transfer restriction, general objectives

The preservation of the right to choose one's associates in the business and compensating deceased or departing participants for their interest in the business, while important, are not the only reasons for imposing transfer restrictions on the stock of a small business corporation. Stock transfer restrictions may also be imposed for the following purposes:

stock transfer restrictions, reasons for imposing

(1) To prevent the transfer of stock to business competitors who might use the stock (even if only a share or two) as a means of gaining access to the corporate books and records for purposes of acquiring trade secrets or confidential business information.

(2) To prevent a shareholder, or group of shareholders, from acquiring enough shares to gain absolute control of the corporation.

(3) To prevent stock from being transferred from one class of shareholders to another (e.g., from employee-shareholders to nonemployee-shareholders).

(4) To preserve an exemption for the stock under the Securities Act of 1933 or under a state securities law (see section 5.16, supra).

(5) To preserve the corporation's eligibility as an S corporation under Subchapter S of the Internal Revenue Code (see section 5.18, infra).

(6) To prevent the transfer of stock to any identifiable person or class of persons who might be detrimental to the business of the corporation.

(7) To enable the corporation or its shareholders to value the stock for estate tax or other purposes.

The legality of transfer restrictions. The first requirement of a stock transfer restriction is that it be for a lawful purpose. Otherwise, it is unenforceable. If the purpose of a restriction is, say, to prohibit members of certain races or creeds from becoming shareholders, then the restriction would be invalid. The purposes listed or described above are generally held to constitute lawful purposes for the imposition of stock transfer restrictions in small business corporations. The corporation laws of many states contain provisions dealing with stock transfer restrictions. These statutes typically provide that a restriction on the transfer of stock is lawful if the purpose of the restriction is to control the number or identity of a corporation's shareholders, to preserve an exemption under a federal or state securities law, or any other reasonable purpose.

stock transfer restrictions, lawful purpose

stock transfer restrictions, restraint on alienation

The second, and more difficult, requirement is that a stock transfer restriction, to be enforceable, must not constitute an unreasonable restraint on alienation. An absolute restriction on alienation (one that prohibits any transfer of the stock at any time) is universally unenforceable. See Greene v. E.H. Rollins & Sons, 22 Del. Ch. 394, 2 A. 2nd 249 (1938). The corporation laws of many states contain provisions dealing with the validity of stock transfer restrictions. These statutes typically provide that stock transfer restrictions that prohibit the transfer of the restricted shares to designated persons or classes of persons are lawful if the prohibition is not manifestly unreasonable.

stock transfer restrictions, reasonableness, factors

The courts generally consider the following factors in determining whether restrictions on the transfer of stock are reasonable:

(1) The number of shareholders in the corporation. The fewer the number of shareholders, the more likely it is that the restriction will be deemed reasonable.

(2) The degree of the restraint on transferability and the length of time the restraint is to run. The lesser the degree of restraint and the shorter the period of the restraint, the more likely it is that the restriction will be deemed reasonable.

(3) The method, if any, used to determine the price of the stock upon which the restrictions are imposed. The fairer the method of valuation, the more likely it is that the restriction will be deemed reasonable.

(4) The objective or business purpose of the restrictions. Transfer restrictions with a valid business purpose are more likely to be deemed reasonable.

(5) The likelihood that the restrictions will accomplish the objectives and purposes for which they were intended. Transfer restrictions that appear to accomplish the purpose for which they were imposed are more likely to be deemed reasonable.

In a sentence, the basic test is whether the transfer restrictions are sufficiently necessary to the business enterprise and its participants to justify overriding the general policy against restraints on alienation. See 18A Am. Jur. 2d, Corporations, sec. 683. It should be noted that more restrictive stock transfer restrictions are usually permitted in a statutory close corporation in states that have a close corporation code or statute. See section 5.19, infra, for further reading on the close corporation election.

stock transfer restrictions, types

Types of transfer restrictions. Several types of stock transfer restrictions are used by participants of small business corporations. Many of these restrictions are specifically authorized by statute in many states. The most common types of enforceable restrictions include the following:

(1) Absolute prohibitions against transfer for a very limited period.

(2) Consent restrictions, requiring the consent of someone (usually the other shareholders or the corporation) prior to transfer.

(3) Right of first refusal option restrictions granting someone (usually the corporation or the other shareholders) the first right to purchase, at a fixed or determinable price, the stock sought to be transferred.

(4) Conditional option restrictions giving someone (again, usually the corporation or the other shareholders) the right to purchase the stock upon the happening of an event (e.g., the shareholder's death, leaving the employ of the corporation, etc.) at a fixed or determinable price.

(5) Buy-out provisions requiring the corporation or the other shareholders to purchase a shareholder's stock upon the happening of a specified event (usually the shareholder's death or disability) at a fixed or determinable price.

(6) Provisions limiting transfers to certain classes of persons (employees, family members, etc.) or prohibiting transfers to certain persons or classes of persons (business competitors, etc.).

The type of transfer restrictions needed in a particular business setting usually depends on such factors as the number of shareholders and their respective ages, abilities, and financial positions,. the value of the business, the size of the business enterprise, the type of business conducted, whether the business is new or established, the relative importance of a particular shareholder to the success of the business, and the personal needs and wishes of the individual shareholders. In practice, transfer restrictions are usually adopted for a number of purposes and it is common to employ two or more types of restrictions in a single agreement. It is common, for example, to employ an option or consent restriction during a shareholder's lifetime, with a mandatory buy-out provision effective upon the death or disability of the shareholder. stock transfer restrictions, general considerations

The preparation of agreements or other documents containing stock transfer restrictions is not a matter to be taken lightly. The first step is to ascertain the thoughts and wishes of the business participants on the matter. When conferring with the participants, the following matters should be determined: stock transfer restrictions, matters to determine

(1) the types of restrictions to be employed,

(2) who, if anyone, should buy the stock,

(3) the method of determining the price of the stock,

(4) the source of funds for purchasing the stock, and

(5) the methods of enforcing the transfer restrictions and related obligations.

Option restrictions. The type of transfer restriction most commonly used in small business corporations is the option restriction, which has the advantage of being universally enforceable, either by statute or court decision. The most common form of option restriction is the desire-to-sell option in which the option mechanism is triggered by the expressed desire of the shareholder to sell his or her stock, either to an outsider or to another shareholder. The selling shareholder is normally obligated to offer the stock to the optionees (usually either the corporation or the other shareholders) at a fixed or determinable price before it can be transferred to the proposed purchaser. Typically, the optionees will then have a certain period of time in which to exercise the option, and upon their failure to do so the stock may be transferred to the proposed purchaser. stock transfer restrictions, desire-to-sell options

Options may also be given to purchase a shareholder's stock upon the death or disability of the shareholder, upon the shareholder's leaving the employ of the corporation or bringing discredit to the corporation, or upon any other reasonable contingency. While most of these options are not as court-tested as the desire-to-sell option, they are generally enforceable if reasonable in scope. Options such as these may be, and often are, combined with a desire-to-sell option, with the same option-exercising mechanisms applied to both options. stock transfer restrictions, other options

The first task in implementing any form of option restriction is to determine who the optionees shall be. Normally, the best practice is to have the option to purchase run first to the corporation and then to the other shareholders in proportion to their existing stockholdings. The main reason for giving the corporation the first option to purchase the stock is to prevent a change in the proportional ownership interests of the remaining shareholders should one or more of them be unable or unwilling to exercise the option. Making the corporation the sole optionee is not usually a good practice for the reason that it may not have funds legally available with which to purchase or redeem its own stock when the option is to be exercised. The corporation laws of most states restrict the right of a corporation to purchase its own stock, usually by requiring that the stock be purchased by funds from some form of unrestricted surplus (see section 6.02, infra). Of course, the remaining shareholders could contribute capital to the corporation to enable it to purchase the stock, but such a method is sometimes difficult to enforce and could result in unfavorable tax consequences for the shareholders. option restrictions, corporation as optionee option restrictions, shareholders as optionees

Making the option run to the other shareholders in proportion to their existing holdings has the advantage of precluding a few shareholders from increasing their percentage of corporate ownership at the expense of the others. Difficulties may arise, however, if one or more of the remaining shareholders are unable or unwilling to purchase their portions of the optioned stock. Cross options are normally given to the other shareholders to purchase the stock not purchased by an optionee shareholder, but this results in a change in the relative ownership interests of the remaining shareholders. Optionee shareholders without the necessary funds can sometimes be accommodated by providing for installment payments to the optioner.

option restrictions, disadvantages

The biggest detriment of the option type of stock transfer restriction, as used in most small business corporations, is that in situations where a shareholder is forced to sell his or her stock, the shareholder normally has little leverage to force the optionees to exercise the option and purchase the stock. The problem is particularly acute when minority shareholders are forced to sell because their holdings don't represent control of the corporation and are much more likely to be unmarketable to outsiders. A possible solution to this problem is to include a buy-out provision in the agreement obligating the corporation or the remaining shareholders to purchase the stock at a fixed or determinable price. Other possible solutions include giving the selling shareholder the right to purchase the stock of the other shareholders at the price established in the option, or the right to force the liquidation of the corporation if the option is not timely exercised.

option restrictions, necessity of valuation

Another important task in the preparation of option restrictions is that of determining the price of the stock subject to the option. It is important, first of all, to select a method of valuing the stock when the option is drawn up, rather than leaving it to be decided when the attempted transfer occurs. It is always easier to reach an agreement on such matters before the particular buyers and sellers (or the optionees and optioners) become identified. Also, an agreement merely to agree later on the price of the stock may render the option unenforceable. See Hardin v. Rosenthal, 213 Ga. 319, 98 S.E. 2nd 901 (1957). The method of valuation agreed upon should be explicitly set forth in the agreement and each shareholder should be aware of how the valuation process operates. It should be noted that the method of valuation employed may also have estate tax significance.

option restrictions, methods of valuation

Methods of valuing stock. There are numerous methods of valuing the stock of a small business corporation. The most common methods of valuation include:

(1) Using the book value of the stock as shown on the books and records of the corporation.

(2) Setting a fixed value on the stock by mutual agreement of the shareholders, with or without periodic redeterminations.

(3) Capitalizing the earnings of the corporation over a specified period.

(4) Using the best bona fide offer for the stock made by an outsider.

(5) Using a value fixed by the board of directors or the other shareholders.

(6) Using the value established by the estate or inheritance tax authorities.

(7) Setting the value by independent appraisal.

method of valuation, use of book value

The book value of a corporation's stock is the total value of the corporate assets, as shown in the books of the corporation, divided by the number of outstanding shares of stock. Using the book value of the stock as the transfer or option price is probably the most common method of valuing stock in small business corporations. The reason for its popularity is that it appears to be a simple method that is easy to both draft into an agreement and calculate when the time comes to use it.

book value method of valuation, disadvantages

Despite its popularity, however, in many ways the book value method is an unsatisfactory method of valuing stock. First of all, the book value of corporate assets is more often than not an unreliable standard for determining their worth. Corporate balance sheets, even those using generally accepted accounting practices, are basically historical records which show the purchase price of tangible assets less their accumulated depreciation. The values shown often have little resemblance to actual or market values. The depreciation shown is usually the maximum allowed for tax purposes and not necessarily the actual depreciation. The value of intangibles, such as good will, are almost never accurately shown on the corporate books, and complications in allocating the value of the assets can arise when there is more than one class of stock. Finally, corporate management usually has considerable control over the values assigned to assets on the corporate books, and can thus influence the value assigned to the stock, usually to the detriment of a selling shareholder.

book value method of valuation, suggested safeguards

If the book value method of valuation is used, the following safeguards should be implemented:

(1) Book value should be determined as of the end of an accounting period, and the value of inventories, supplies, and the like should be made current.

(2) It should be specified as to whether intangibles are to be treated as assets, and, if so, a guide should be set forth for determining their value. It may be preferable to eliminate good will as an asset in instances where the selling shareholder is a key person who may take a portion of the corporate good will when departing.

(3) The book value should be determined by an independent accountant or auditor using standard accounting procedures augmented only by the particular requirements of the agreement at hand.

valuation of stock by mutual agreement

Another commonly-used method of valuing the stock of a small business corporation is by mutual agreement of the shareholders. Usually it is easy to agree on an initial value for the stock. The par value of the stock is often used. However, after the corporation has been in business for some time this initial estimate usually becomes meaningless as an indicator of actual value (which is presumably what the parties want the valuation to reflect). Therefore, to be at all meaningful and fair, the agreed-upon estimate of value must be periodically revised. Periodic revisions are often easier said than done, however, because the shareholders often neglect to revise the estimate either because they overlook it or because they sense that they will be unable to agree and don't want to create unnecessary friction. In addition, it often happens that the shareholders are simply unable to agree on a revised estimate of value for the stock.

valuation of stock by mutual agreement, procedure when unable to agree

In the event of a transfer under the mutual agreement method, the last value agreed upon in writing by the parties usually becomes the transfer price, unless the parties have been unable to agree for a prolonged or specified period, in which case the best practice is to utilize an alternative method of valuation. Another possible approach in the event of such a deadlock is to use the last figure agreed upon by the parties as adjusted by the change in book value of the stock since the time the figure was agreed upon.

valuation of stock by capitalization of earnings, disadvantages

In theory, capitalizing a corporation's earnings to determine the value of its stock makes sense. The average annual earnings of a corporation are simply capitalized, using a reasonable capitalization rate, to show what a prudent investor would pay for the stock on the open market. In practice, however, this method is difficult to implement. First of all, the corporation has to have been in business for a sufficient period (at least three to five years, and preferably ten) to establish its earning capacity. Secondly, it is very difficult to derive a capitalization rate (especially in an agreement drawn up when the corporation is formed) that will fairly represent the future earning capacity of a particular business. Capitalization rates are very dependent upon such intangibles as the state of the economy, the rates of both interest and inflation, and the economic condition of the particular industry that the business is either in or dependent upon. See Arneson, Capitalization Rates for Valuing Closely Held Corporations, 59 Taxes 310. Thirdly, the earnings of a small business corporation are very dependent upon such factors as nonrecurring items of profit or loss, the role of management in the earnings of the business, how that role might be affected by the departure of a key participant, and the chances of such a departure occurring.

valuation of stock by capitalization of earnings, when advisable

An additional complication is that in most small business corporations a great deal of the profits are absorbed by the participants in the form of compensation for personal services, thus rendering the corporate books unreflective of the real earnings of the corporation. In summary, if a corporation has an established earnings record, if it is in an established trade or industry, if the national and local economies are reasonably stable, and if the success of the business is not overly dependent on one or two key persons, then the capitalization of earnings method can be a fair and accurate indicator of value. Otherwise, it is best avoided.

valuation of stock by best offer of outsider, procedure

Another method of valuation popular with small business corporations is to use the best bona fide offer by an outsider as the value of the optioned or transferred stock. Under this method the shareholder who wishes to sell all or a portion of his or her stock is required to notify the optionees (normally the corporation and the other shareholders) of the terms of the outsider's offer, whereupon the optionees have a stated period in which to purchase the stock on those terms. If the optionees fail to purchase the stock within the required time, the stock may then be sold to the outsider.

same, advantages and disadvantages

A weakness of this method of valuation is that it can only be applied to desire-to-sell options with any degree of reliability. The lack of a market for the stock of most small business corporations, especially the stock of minority shareholders, makes it impossible in most instances to obtain a bona fide outside offer. If this method of valuation was applied, say, to an option triggered by the death of a shareholder, the unfairness of the situation would be apparent. Another weakness of this method is that prospective buyers, especially those acquainted with the shareholders, tend to be reluctant to make meaningful offers if they are aware that their offer will set the price of the stock for the other shareholders. Despite its shortcomings, this method of valuation can, if the stock is at all salable to outsiders, be reasonably reliable for the desire-to-sell option. It is often a good practice to use this method of valuation for a desire-to-sell option and alternative methods of valuation for other types of options and for buy-out provisions.

other methods of valuing stock

The drawbacks of having the board of directors or the other shareholders fix the value of optioned or transferred stock are obvious. Even if they are required to act in good faith, as they are under most such arrangements and under the law, letting a direct or indirect party to the sale set the price of the property being sold is of dubious logic. Letting the estate or inheritance tax authorities set the price of the stock is usually unsatisfactory, even for transfers triggered by the death of a shareholder (which are normally the only types of transfers that could be so valued with any degree of reliability), because of the time delays involved and because of the loss of possible tax advantages that may be obtained under other methods of valuation. See section 6.02, infra, for further reading on the tax aspects of stock redemptions.

valuation of stock by independent appraisal, matters to cover

If the appraisal method of valuing stock is used, either as the primary or a secondary method of valuation, the following matters should be covered in the agreement:

(1) Either the names of the appraisers or a procedure for choosing them should be provided. For example, each side could choose one appraiser and the appraisers so chosen select a third; or an independent party, such as a bank, could choose the third appraiser.

(2) Standards to guide the appraisers should be established. The method of valuation should be established for each class of stock and for each type of property (e.g., real estate, inventory, good will, accounts receivable, etc.).

(3) The source of funds for compensating the appraisers should be established.

unfair methods of valuation, legality

Whatever the method of valuation, it occasionally happens that a shareholder receives compensation amounting to only a fraction of the actual value of his or her stock. The courts, in such instances, generally uphold the legality of the transaction and refuse to substitute their judgment for that of the parties who agreed to the transaction in advance. See Allen v. Biltmore Tissue Corp., 2 N.Y. 2nd 534, 141 N.E. 2nd 812, 61 A.L.R. 2nd 1309 (1957). Despite the refusal of most courts to set aside financially one-sided option restrictions, the best practice is to employ methods of valuation that are as fair as possible to all shareholders, as it is usually impossible to foresee which of them will later be seeking compensation for his or her stock. Also, some courts construe transfer restrictions with unfair methods of valuation as unreasonable restraints on alienation, especially if an applicable statute requires that a fair price be paid for the stock. See Systematics, Inc. v. Mitchell, 253 Ark. 848, 491 S.W. 2nd 40 (1973).

consent stock transfer restrictions, when useful

Consent restrictions. Consent stock transfer restrictions, whereby the consent of a party (usually the corporation or the other shareholders) is required before a transfer can occur, are usually valid if the power to permit or deny the transfer is exercised reasonably and in good faith. A consent restriction has the advantage of being easy to draft and impose, and it is not burdened with valuation problems. It is useful in situations where the existing shareholders wish to prevent the stock of the corporation from being transferred to certain persons, but not necessarily to all outsiders.

consent transfer restrictions, disadvantages

The disadvantages of consent restrictions are that they are often unfair to shareholders who wish to sell their stock and to the estates of deceased shareholders, and their legality may be questionable in some states because their enforceability usually depends on the reasonableness and fairness of the exercise of the restriction. It is a good practice to impose limitations or guidelines on the granting or withholding of a consent to transfer, and to state that a consent to transfer will not be unreasonably or arbitrarily withheld. A consent restriction, for example, could be combined with a provision limiting transfers to certain classes of persons (e.g., prohibiting transfers to anyone other than employees of the corporation unless approved by the other shareholders).

absolute restrictions against transfer, legality, usefulness

Absolute prohibitions against transfer should be avoided because many courts will not enforce them. See Annotation: Transfer of Stock - Restrictions, 61 A.L.R. 2nd 1318 (1957). However, an absolute prohibition against transfer for a very limited time might be enforceable if a strong business necessity for the prohibition could be shown. If a prohibition against transfer is to be used, the best practice is to prohibit the transfer of stock only to certain persons or classes of persons, or to anyone except certain classes of persons. As always, there should be a legitimate business purpose for imposing the transfer restriction. Even then, a consent restriction is usually preferable.

stock of deceased participant, disposition

Buy-out agreements. A typical participant of a successful small business corporation devotes most of his or her time to the business of the corporation and in return receives liberal compensation, mostly in the form of salary and bonuses. The participant's stock in the corporation often comprises the participant's most valuable single asset. When the participant dies, his or her salary ceases and the participant's heirs must pay death taxes on the stock, which is often valuable for death tax purposes but which earns little, if any, dividend income and is often unsaleable because of transfer restrictions or the lack of a public market.

stock of disabled or departing participant, disposition

Should such a participant become disabled, he or she may or may not continue to receive a salary, depending on the participant's contractual and personal relationships with the other participants and the corporation. Because the disabled participant can no longer contribute to the operation of the business, the participant's relationships with the other participants may become strained, or disputes may arise between the participants making it impossible for them to continue working together. In either event, it often becomes impossible for a disabled or departing participant to leave the business without incurring a tremendous financial loss unless some provision is made for the purchase of his or her stock.

mandatory buy-outs, when desirable

In the situations described above, consent restrictions are useless to the participant, and option restrictions do not adequately protect the interests of a deceased or disabled participant. The best method of adequately protecting the investment of a deceased, disabled, or departing participant is to include a buy-out provision in the stock restriction arrangement obligating the remaining participants or the corporation to purchase the participant's stock at a fixed or determinable price.

buy-out agreements, general types

There are two basic types of buy-out agreements: stock-purchase agreements, where the corporation agrees to purchase the stock of a deceased, disabled or departing shareholder; and buy-and-sell agreements (or cross-purchase agreements), where the remaining shareholders agree to purchase the stock of a deceased, disabled or departing shareholder. Combinations of the two types of agreements are possible, wherein the corporation and the remaining shareholders each purchase a portion of the selling shareholder's stock, but for tax reasons they are seldom used (see section 6.02, infra). It should be remembered in this discussion that in small business corporations the shareholders are usually the business participants.

stock purchase agreements, legal requirements

Before preparing a stock-purchase agreement, it should be ascertained whether the corporation will legally be able to purchase the stock at the required time. See section 6.02, infra, for further reading on the legal requirements for stock redemptions. It is usually possible, with careful planning, to devise a lawful method of purchasing the stock, either directly by the corporation, through a third party controlled by the corporation, or through the purchase of life insurance. The provisions empowering the corporation to purchase its own stock should be included in the articles of incorporation and bylaws, if necessary.

buy-out agreements, valuation of stock

A major task in drafting any type of buy-out agreement is that of determining the price to be paid for the stock being purchased or redeemed. The valuation requirements in buy-out agreements are similar to those described above in connection with option restrictions, and the reader is referred to that discussion. An important additional factor to consider in selecting a valuation method for use in a buy-out agreement funded by life insurance is that of matching the amount of the insurance with the value of the stock. In buy-out agreements valuation methods that establish the value of the stock during the lifetime of the shareholders when the amount of insurance can be adjusted to fit the value of the stock are preferable over methods that determine the value of the stock after the death of the shareholder.

buy-and-sell agreements, general provisions

Most buy-and-sell agreements provide that upon the death of a shareholder (or other specified contingency), the remaining shareholders shall be obligated, in proportion to their holdings, to purchase the stock of the deceased shareholder at a fixed or determinable price. If the agreement is not funded by life insurance or otherwise (see infra, this section), problems may arise when one or more of the remaining shareholders is unable to pay for the stock that he or she is obligated to purchase under the agreement. The problem may be alleviated somewhat by providing for cross-options to the other remaining shareholders to purchase any unpurchased shares, by permitting the corporation to purchase them, or by permitting the obligated shareholder to pay for the shares in installments.

buy-and-sell agreements, death of two shareholders

Provisions should be made in a buy-and-sell agreement for the deaths of more than one shareholder within a short period of time, especially if the agreement is not funded by life insurance. Otherwise, the estate of a shareholder may find itself obligated to purchase the stock of another shareholder who died a few days or weeks earlier. Typical provisions in this regard state that if the deaths occur within a specified period of time of one another, the deceased parties are released from their obligations to purchase the stock, or that the surviving parties shall be obligated to purchase the stock, but on extended payment terms.

buy-out agreements, methods of funding

It is important that the source of the funds with which to purchase the stock be provided for in a buy-out agreement, regardless of whether the agreement is a stock purchase agreement or a buy-and-sell agreement. Methods of funding buy-out agreements include: (1) life insurance; (2) savings, either individually by the shareholders or by the corporation; (3) shareholders' contributions to capital; and (4) making the required payments in extended installments.

buy-and-sell agreements, funding by life insurance

The purchase of life insurance on the lives of the individual shareholders is a common method of funding both types of buy-out agreements. In a typical buy-and-sell agreement funded by life insurance, each shareholder purchases (and pays for) an insurance policy on the life of every other shareholder in amounts that are as nearly as possible equal to the amounts that the shareholder will owe to each of the other shareholders upon their death. This method works reasonably well if there are only a few shareholders (say, three or fewer), if all of the shareholders are equally insurable, and if the shareholders own roughly equal interests in the corporation.

buy-and-sell agreements, methods of funding

If there are two shareholders, each shareholder will, initially at least, have to purchase only one insurance policy. If there are three shareholders, each shareholder will have to purchase two policies, for a total of six policies among them. If there are four shareholders, each shareholder will have to purchase three policies for a total of 12 among them, which may become unwieldy, especially if other policies are purchased over the years to cover increases in the value of the stock.

buy-and-sell agreements, funding by life insurance, inequities

If a shareholder is young and in good health, the cost of his or her life insurance will be considerably less than the cost of the same insurance on a shareholder who is older and in poor health. Because a young shareholder in good health often pays for insurance on the life of an older shareholder in poor health, the unfairness is obvious. If shareholder A owns 80 percent of the stock of a $100,000 corporation and shareholder B owns the remaining 20 percent, shareholder A (the 80 percent holder) will pay for $20,000 worth of insurance, while shareholder B (the 20 percent holder) will pay for $80,000 worth. While such inequities may be alleviated through corporate compensation, the burden of the additional insurance on a minority owner cannot always be offset by additional compensation because of the limitations on compensation for personal services of shareholder-employees imposed by the Internal Revenue Service (see section 6.01, infra).

buy-and-sell agreements, funding by life insurance, drawbacks

Another drawback of funding buy-and-sell agreements with life insurance when there are more than two shareholders is that when the first shareholder dies the proportionate ownership interests of the remaining shareholders are increased with no increase in the amount of insurance coverage. The remaining shareholders then have the problem of purchasing additional insurance, which may then be impossible or impractical because of age and insurability problems. It may be possible to transfer the policies held by the deceased shareholder on the lives of the other shareholders to the remaining shareholders. However, unless the policies are transferred to the respective insureds or to the corporation, such a transfer may create tax problems later on because a portion of the transferred policy may be treated as taxable income to the beneficiary upon the death of the insured. See 26 U.S.C. 101(a)(2)(B).

stock purchase agreements, funding by life insurance

In a stock purchase agreement funded by life insurance, the corporation normally purchases (and pays for) an insurance policy on the life of each shareholder in an amount that is as nearly as possible equal to the value of the stock held by that shareholder. Therefore, regardless of the number of shareholders, there is, initially at least, only one policy per shareholder. The beneficiary of the policies can be the corporation, the estate of the deceased shareholder, or a trustee, depending on the type of arrangement that is decided upon. Because corporate funds are used to purchase the insurance, the majority owners, whose estates will receive the lion's share of the insurance proceeds, will indirectly pay for their proportionate share of the cost of the insurance, assuming, of course, that the shareholders are compensated roughly in proportion to their equity.

stock purchase agreements funding by life insurance, advantages

In a stock purchase agreement, the inequities of unequal insurability among the shareholders and unequal costs of insurance can be taken into account in their respective salaries or bonuses, with the shareholder who is costly to insure receiving less. Because there are fewer policies with greater amounts of insurance, the corporation may be able to purchase the insurance more cheaply than could the individual shareholders under a buy-and-sell agreement. Also, under a stock-purchase agreement the accumulation of assets in the form of the cash surrender values of the insurance policies can be accomplished without subjecting the earnings of the invested funds to income taxes, an advantage that can lessen the cost of funding the agreement. This advantage is offset somewhat by the risk of exposing the corporation to a possible accumulated earnings penalty tax if the cash surrender values exceed $150,000 (see section 5.02, supra).

buy-out agreements, income tax considerations

Income tax considerations can be an important factor in determining the type of buy-out agreement best suited to a particular corporation. Since neither the corporation nor the individual shareholders may deduct the expenses of life insurance premiums used to fund buy-out agreements (see Novelart Mfg. Co. v. Comm., 434 F. 2nd 1011 (CA 6, 1970)), a stock-purchase agreement, where the corporation pays the premium, is advantageous if the corporation is, or will be, in a lower income tax bracket than the individual shareholders. Conversely, if the shareholders are in lower tax brackets than the corporation, then a buy-and-sell agreement with the individual shareholders paying the premiums may be advantageous. The current income tax rates for individuals and corporations are set forth in section 1.02, supra.

same, advantages of stock purchase agreements

If the shareholders receive, or will receive, substantial dividend income from the corporation, either actual or constructive, then a stock-purchase agreement is clearly preferable because the funds used by the shareholders to pay the insurance premiums funding a buy-and-sell agreement will have been taxed twice (see section 5.02, supra). If the corporation is an S corporation, it will make little difference, taxwise, whether the insurance premiums are paid by the shareholders or the corporation.

buy-and-sell agreements, tax treatment of stock purchases

The purchase of stock (including that of a deceased shareholder) by the remaining shareholders under a buy-and-sell agreement is treated as a sale or exchange of stock for federal income tax purposes. If the stock qualifies as a capital asset, the excess of the net sales price over the adjusted basis of the stock will be taxed as a capital gain. The basis of the stock after acquisition by the remaining shareholders will be the per-share purchase price of the stock.

stock purchase agreements, tax treatment of stock redemptions

The purchase or redemption of stock by a corporation under a stock-purchase agreement is treated differently for tax purposes. First of all, regardless of the price paid by the corporation for a deceased or selling shareholder's stock, the basis of the stock remains unchanged. See 26 U.S.C. 1032. In most cases, however, this is not an important consideration. Secondly, and more importantly, unless the transaction meets one of the exceptions of 26 U.S.C. 302(b), the transaction will be treated as a corporate distribution for tax purposes and most of the payment received for the stock will be taxed as ordinary income to the seller (see Section 6.02, infra). However, if the interest of the seller in the corporation is completely terminated by the transaction, as it usually is under a stock-purchase agreement, one of the exceptions will have been met and the transaction will be treated for tax purposes as a sale or exchange of stock, which means that the sales proceeds will be taxed as a capital gain. If the seller is so related to the other shareholders (by family, partnership, trusts, etc.) that their shares are attributable to him, the exemption may be lost. See 26 U.S.C. 318 and Section 6.02, infra.

buy-out agreements, financial considerations

Before attempting to fund a buy-out agreement with life insurance, the ability of the corporation or the shareholders to bear the cost of the insurance, both at present and in the future, should be considered. It will make little sense to incur the expense of several years' premiums if the insurance is dropped before any of the shareholders die. Also, if the chances are good that the business enterprise will not survive any of the shareholders, it may not be advisable to fund a buy-out agreement with life insurance.

buy-out agreements, expert assistance

There are an almost infinite number of insurance schemes available and most life insurance companies are more than willing to share their information with corporate participants. Estate tax problems may also be created (or prevented) by the use of business life insurance, and this matter should be examined before proceeding. If the corporate participants are, or expect to become, reasonably wealthy, a tax specialist, a knowledgeable insurance underwriter, and possibly a trust officer should be consulted before drafting and funding an extensive buy-out agreement with life insurance.

buy-out agreements, use of sinking fund

Many times it happens that neither the corporation nor the participants can, in the beginning at least, afford the additional expense of the life insurance needed to fund a buy-out agreement. Or it may be that one or more of the participants is uninsurable. In such cases the use of life insurance to fund a buy-out agreement will probably not be practicable, and the possibility of establishing a sinking fund with which to fund the agreement should be considered. The corporation is usually in a better position to establish such a fund than each of the participants individually, especially if there are more than two or three participants. Therefore, a stock-purchase agreement is usually preferable to a buy-and-sell agreement in this situation.

same, accumulated earning tax

If the sinking fund becomes substantial (over $150,000) the corporation may run the risk of being assessed a penalty tax on the accumulated earnings. See 26 U.S.C. 531-537 and section 5.02, supra. This surtax is avoidable, however, if the corporation can show a legitimate business need for the retained earnings, and, in most cases the redemption of a deceased or disabled shareholder's stock is considered to be a legitimate business need. See 26 U.S.C. 537. If there are several participants and only one of them is uninsurable, it may be feasible to carry life insurance on the insurable shareholders and establish a reserve fund, funded by periodic payments in lieu of insurance payments, for the uninsurable participant.

stock purchase agreements, funding by capital contributions

If it is otherwise desirable to have a stock-purchase agreement, as opposed to a buy-and-sell agreement, and if the participants will have the personal funds necessary to fund the agreement, it may be feasible to provide in the agreement that the surviving participants will, when the occasion arises, make contributions to the capital of the corporation sufficient for it to redeem or repurchase any stock called for in the stock-purchase agreement. The obligations of each party should be fully spelled out in the agreement and, if necessary, collateral should be given to insure the availability of the funds when needed.

buy-out agreements, installment payments under

It often happens, especially with new businesses, that the only practical method of funding (if that is the proper term in this instance) a buy-out agreement is by providing for extended installment payments to be made by those purchasing the stock under the agreement. In such cases provisions should be made in the buy-out agreement for the amount or percentage of the down payment, the signing of promissory notes for the balance of the amount due, the interest rate to be charged, the type and amount of collateral or security to be given (the purchased stock itself, sometimes supplemented by the purchaser's other stock in the corporation, is often used), and who shall hold, receive dividends from, and vote the stock during the installment period. Often the stock, endorsed in blank by the seller, is deposited with an escrow agent until the payments have been completed. Special problems may be encountered when the stock being purchased constitutes a majority or controlling interest in the corporation. In such cases it may be advisable to protect the seller by depositing the appropriate corporate books, records, and documents with the escrow agent so that the seller will not be prevented from retaking control of the corporation should the purchaser default.

buy-out agreements, shareholder's disability

The funding of buy-out agreements providing for the purchase of a disabled participant's stock presents unique problems, primarily because it is usually impossible to purchase disability insurance that provides for a lump sum payment. Therefore, the funding must usually be by another method. If the installment payment method is used, it can be funded, in part at least, by periodic payments made under a disability insurance policy, if one was purchased for the disabled participant under the buy-out agreement. The purchase of disability insurance on each participant in addition to life insurance can be expensive, however, and sometimes a scheme can be devised to use the cash surrender values of the life insurance policies to purchase the stock of a disabled participant.

advantages of stock purchase agreements

In practice, stock-purchase agreements are more widely used than buy-and-sell agreements. The reasons for the preference of stock-purchase agreements are:

(1) Funding the agreement is more manageable and easier to control if done by the corporation, especially if there are more than two participants.

(2) Participants with high salaries fear that increases in their salaries to cover the costs of funding a buy-and-sell agreement will be treated as constructive dividends for income tax purposes.

(3) It is administratively easier for the corporation to fund and oversee the agreement.

(4) Any estate tax disadvantage of a stock-purchase agreement can usually be overcome by making certain that the purchase terminates the seller's interest in the corporation.

buy-out agreements, valuation of stock, estate tax, I.R.S. criterion

A major advantage of a buy-out agreement, especially for older or wealthier participants, is that it can be used to establish a value of the stock for estate tax purposes. If the stock does not have a market, the Internal Revenue Service will value the stock for estate tax purposes based on the corporation's net worth, dividend-paying capacity, earning power, and other relevant factors. See Treasury Reg. 20.2031-2(f). If a valid buy-out agreement exists and meets Internal Revenue Service criteria, the value established by the agreement will usually be accepted for federal estate tax purposes. See Roth v. U.S., 511 F. Supp. 653 (EDMO, 1981). To meet Internal Revenue Service criteria, a buy-out agreement must -

(1) prohibit or substantially restrict the transfer of the stock during the lifetime of the shareholder,

(2) be a binding obligation to sell on the part of both the decedent and the estate,

(3) be a bona fide business arrangement and not a device for passing assets to the decedent's heirs for less than adequate consideration,

(4) provide for a fixed or determinable price for the stock, and

(5) be sufficiently current so as to reasonably reflect the recent fortunes of the business.

stock transfer restrictions, how to implement

Implementing stock transfer restrictions and buy-out provisions. A final, but important, matter to be determined is where in the corporate documents to insert the stock transfer restrictions and buy-out provisions. They may be inserted in the articles of incorporation, in the bylaws, in a separate shareholders' agreement, or in a combination of the foregoing. Generally, the best practice is to include the stock transfer restrictions and buy-out provisions in a shareholders' agreement, and to include the same provisions in more impersonal language, in the articles of incorporation and the bylaws. A notice of the transfer restrictions should also appear on each stock certificate representing stock that is subject to the restrictions so as to prevent its transfer to third parties without notice. These practices are specifically authorized by statute in most states. The statutory provisions in each state dealing with stock transfer restrictions are summarized and cited in Appendix I, infra, under the heading of "Stock Transfer Restrictions."

stock transfer restrictions, advantages of shareholders' agreement

Many times, especially in complex or involved restrictive stock arrangements, it simply is not legally or administratively possible to include all of the desired provisions in the articles of incorporation. For example, it is often difficult to draft article provisions requiring the shareholders to purchase life insurance in the required amounts. Also, it is usually possible to be more personal and explicit and to cover more detail in a shareholders agreement than in the articles of incorporation, which should be worded in impersonal and objective language. It is especially important to use a shareholders agreement when mandatory buy-out provisions are to be included in the restrictive arrangement so as to personally obligate each shareholder to perform the required functions.

stock transfer restrictions, inclusion in articles

Conversely, to include a restrictive stock arrangement only in a shareholders agreement may make enforcing the restrictions difficult, especially against subsequent shareholders who are not parties to the agreement, and against minors. To insure the enforceability of the transfer restrictions and related obligations, and to provide an adequate remedy to non-breaching parties, the restrictive provisions should also be included in the articles of incorporation. Including the restrictive provisions in the articles of incorporation will also make a later attack on the provisions by a shareholder or the shareholder's successor more difficult to sustain.

stock transfer restrictions, inclusion in bylaws

The main reason for including stock transfer restrictions in the bylaws is the practical reason of keeping the directors and officers informed of such provisions and to assist them in implementing the provisions and any related obligations, especially those of the corporation. Once the wording of the transfer restrictions has been devised for the articles of incorporation, it is usually a simple matter to include them in the bylaws.

stock transfer restrictions and buy-outs, importance of

Shareholder agreements containing restrictive stock arrangements, especially those containing buy-out provisions and extensive funding arrangements, are expected to remain in effect for many years. Money and property rights accumulated over a lifetime are often dependent upon the enforceability of such agreements many years after they have been drawn up and executed. Often, because of changes in ownership or personal relationships, it becomes impossible to amend or change the agreement. It is extremely important, therefore, that the agreement be drafted correctly at the outset, which is often at the very birth of the business enterprise.

It is suggested that the following rules be followed when preparing a shareholders' agreement containing stock transfer restrictions, buy-out provisions, and related matters:

stock transfer restrictions and buy-outs, suggested rules

(1) The parties to the agreement should be explicitly identified and should include the corporation. To render the agreement enforceable against the corporation, it is important to include it as a party, even if it has no options to exercise or explicit duties to perform. The successors in interest of the participants and the corporation should also be included as parties.

(2) The business purpose of the agreement should be explicitly set forth.

(3) The consideration for the agreement should be explicitly described. This rule should be followed even if, as is often the case, the consideration consists of the mutual obligations and promises of the parties.

(4) Both the restrictions imposed and the types of transfer of the stock to which the restrictions apply should be clearly and unambiguously described. In defining the types of transfers to which the restrictions apply, it is important to state whether the restrictions apply to pledges or other security-type transfers, transfers by operations of law, gifts, and transfers by reason of death or incompetency.

(5) The valuation figure or formula should be given or described in detail.

(6) Any buy-out or option provisions should be thoroughly described, and the duties of all parties with respect to such provisions should be clearly delineated.

(7) Any funding provisions included in the arrangement should be set forth, together with the duties and obligations of all parties with respect to these provisions. A list of all life insurance policies provided under the agreement should be included.

(8) Provisions should be made for the amendment and termination of the agreement.

(9) If the agreement is to provide disability buy-outs for disabled participants, a definition of disability and the amount and source of any disability insurance should be set forth.

(10) The state whose laws are to govern the agreement should be stated.

(11) Especially in community property states, the written consent of the participants' spouses to the agreement should be obtained. This is particularly necessary in agreements containing buy-out provisions in the event of the death or disability of a participant.

(12) The stock certificates of all stock subject to the agreement should contain an appropriate notice of the transfer restrictions.

(13) The participants should be required to take the steps necessary to reconcile their personal estate documents (wills, trusts, etc.) with the provisions of the agreement.

5.18 The Subchapter S Election

Subchapter S election, advantages and disadvantages

A decision that should be made early in the life of a small business corporation is whether to exercise the Subchapter S election: that is, whether to qualify the corporation for pass-through (i.e., partnership) taxation under Subchapter S of the Internal Revenue Code. Like a partnership, a Subchapter S corporation is a tax-reporting entity and not a tax-paying entity. The advantages of Subchapter S tax treatment are: (1) because a Subchapter S corporation is not taxed, the danger of double taxation of corporate earnings is eliminated, which means that dividends and excessive or irregular compensation may be paid to the participants without adverse tax consequences, (2) most business losses are deductible by the participants in the year of the loss, and (3) the tax reporting and accounting duties of the business are usually simplified. The disadvantages of Subchapter S tax treatment are: (1) it is impossible to retain undistributed profits in the corporation for expansion or other purposes without the earnings being taxed to the participants, (2) because there is no tax at the corporate level, it is impossible to take advantage of low corporate income tax rates at the lower income levels (15% on the first $50,000 and 25% on the next $25,000); and (3) the organization and management of the corporation may be stymied by the Subchapter S qualification requirements, which are listed below on this page.

Subchapter S status, general aspects

Subchapter S of the Internal Revenue Code (26 U.S.C. 1361-1379) was substantially revised in the Small Business Job Protection Act of 1996. Most of the revisions became effective on January 1, 1997. Basically, Subchapter S permits qualifying small business corporations to elect to be exempted from federal income taxes and yet retain most of the advantages of doing business in the corporate form. A corporation that elects (and qualifies) to be taxed under Subchapter S is referred to as an S corporation. See 26 U.S.C. 1361(a)(1). An S corporation is taxed essentially as a partnership, with the corporation paying no taxes (except on passive investment income and certain capital gains) and its income, losses, and other tax features assessed only at the shareholder level. In other words, the income, losses, and other tax features of an S corporation are treated for tax purposes as being those of the shareholders individually.

S corporation, definition

Subchapter S election, corporation requirements

To be eligible for a Subchapter S election and to qualify as an S corporation, a corporation must satisfy all of the following requirements:

(1) It must be a domestic corporation with not more than 75 shareholders.

(2) Its shareholders must be individuals, estates, certain permitted trusts (see below) or certain charitable organizations (see below).

(3) It may not have a nonresident alien as a shareholder.

(4) It may have only one class of stock.

(5) It may not be an insurance company, a financial institution that uses the reserve method of accounting for bad debts, or a present or former Domestic International Sales Corporation. See 26 U.S.C. 1361(b).

S corporation, shareholder requirements, qualifying trusts

In determining the number of shareholders in an S corporation, husband and wife shareholders (and their estates) are treated as a single shareholder. See 26 U.S.C. 1361(c). An estate includes the estate of a deceased individual and the estate of an individual in a Bankruptcy case. See 26 U.S.C. 1361(C)(3). An organization that is described in 26 U.S.C. 401(a) or 501(c) and that is exempt from taxation under 26 U.S.C. 501(a) may be a shareholder of an S corporation. See 26 U.S.C. 501(a). This means that such entities as charitable organizations and qualified retirement plans (including qualified pension plans, profit-sharing plans, 401(k) plans, and employee stock ownership plans) may be shareholders of S corporations. Each qualified tax-exempt shareholder counts as one shareholder for purposes of the 75 shareholder limit. The following trusts qualify as shareholders of S corporations: (1) grantor trusts during the life of the grantor and for 2 years after the death of the grantor, (2) voting trusts, (3) testamentary trusts for a period of 2 years after the date the stock is transferred to the trust, (4) an electing small business trust, and (5) qualified Subchapter S trusts. If a trust other than one of the above owns or acquires stock in the corporation, the corporation will not qualify under Subchapter S and, if previously qualified, will cause the termination of its Subchapter S status.

grantor trust, definition, Subchapter S treatment

A grantor trust is a trust that is deemed for income tax purposes to be owned by a citizen or resident of the United States. When a grantor trust is a shareholder of an S corporation, the owner of the trust, rather than the trust, is treated as the shareholder during his or her lifetime for purposes of Subchapter S. Upon the death of the owner, the estate of the owner is a permitted shareholder for two years. A voting trust is defined as a trust created primarily to exercise the voting power of the stock transferred to it, and each beneficiary of the trust is treated as a separate shareholder for purposes of Subchapter S. See 26 U.S.C. 1361(c)(2).

voting trust, Subchapter S treatment

electing small business trust, requirements

For a trust to qualify as an electing small business trust, all of the beneficiaries of the trust must be individuals or estates who would themselves qualify as S corporation shareholders, except that a contingent remainder beneficiary interest in the trust may be held by a charitable organization. The interest of each beneficiary in the trust must have been acquired by gift, bequest or inheritance and not by purchase. Certain trusts may not become electing small business trusts. Included here are (1) qualified Subchapter S trusts that have filed an election, (2) tax-exempt trusts, (3) charitable remainder annuity trusts, and (4) charitable remainder unitrusts. See 26 U.S.C. 1361(e)(1). Each potential current beneficiary of an electing small business trust is treated as a separate shareholder, except that if for any period there is no potential current beneficiary the trust is treated as the shareholder for that period. See 26 U.S.C. 1361(c)(2)(B)(v). A potential current beneficiary is a person who is entitled to receive mandatory or discretionary distribution from the principal or income of the trust during the period in question. See 26 U.S.C. 1361(e)(2). As the name implies, an election must be filed by the trustee in order for a trust to be treated as an electing small business trust. Once made, the election applies to the current tax year and all subsequent tax years of the trust unless revoked with the consent of the I.R.S. See 26 U.S.C. 1361(e)(3).

qualified Subchapter S trust, requirements, election

To qualify as a Subchapter S trust, a trust must meet the following requirements: (1) it must own stock in one or more S corporations, (2) all of its income must be distributed currently to one individual, who must be a citizen or resident of the United States, and (3) the terms of the trust must require that there be only one income beneficiary at a time, that any corpus distributed during the term of the trust be distributed to the current income beneficiary, and that the trust terminates not later than the death of the last income beneficiary with the trust corpus being distributed to the beneficiary. See 26 U.S.C. 1361(d)(3). The beneficiary of such a trust, who is treated as the owner, must file an election to have the trust treated by the I.R.S. as a qualifying Subchapter S trust. See 26 U.S.C. 1361(d)(2).

S corporation, stock with differing voting rights

To qualify under Subchapter S, a corporation must have only one class of stock outstanding. However, different voting rights may be allocated among the holders of the stock. See 26 U.S.C. 1361(c)(4). Thus, the exclusion or limitation of voting rights for specified holders of a single class of stock will not cause a corporation to lose its Subchapter S status. All other rights in the stock must be the same for all shareholders, however.

S corporation, debt instruments, safe debt harbor provisions

To preserve a Subchapter S election, care should be taken to insure that any debt instruments issued by the corporation comply with the safe debt harbor requirements of 26 U.S.C. 1361(c)(5). This statute provides that straight debt instruments shall not be treated as a separate (or second) class of stock. To constitute straight debt, an instrument must - (1) contain a written unconditional promise to pay a sum certain either upon demand or on a specified date, (2) specify an interest rate and interest payment dates that not contingent upon profits, borrower's discretion, or similar factors, (3) not be convertible, directly or indirectly, into stock, and (4) specify as the creditor either an individual (except a nonresident alien), an estate, a trust that qualifies as an S corporation shareholder, or a person who is actively and regularly engaged in the business of lending money (i.e., a financial institution). If these requirements are not complied with and if the debt instruments are found to constitute equity, another class of stock will have been created and the corporation will lose its Subchapter S status. It is important to note that a bank or other financial institution may now be the creditor of an S corporation debt instrument for purposes of the safe debt harbor requirements.

S corporation, tax treatment

passive investment income

If a corporation qualifies as an S corporation, its earnings and profits are not taxable to the corporation, except as provided below in this paragraph. See 26 U.S.C. 1363(a), 1371(c). Generally, an S corporation is not taxed on its capital gains. However, if the Subchapter S election has not been in effect for each of the corporation's tax years, the corporation may be liable for certain capital gains taxes. See 26 U.S.C. 1374. If an S corporation has passive investment income exceeding 25 percent of its gross receipts, it may be subject to a tax at the highest corporate rate on the lesser of its excess net passive income or its taxable income. See 26 U.S.C. 1375(a). Passive investment income includes gross receipts from royalties, rents, dividends, interest, annuities, and sales and exchanges of stocks and securities. See 26 U.S.C. 1362(d)(3)(D).

Subchapter S election, how to make, consent of shareholders

A Subchapter S election may be made by any qualifying small business corporation, except one whose Subchapter S election has been terminated within the last five years, except that terminations of S status that were in effect on the date of enactment of the Small Business Job Protection Act, of 1996 are not taken into account. The election is made by filing an election and consent with the regional office of the Internal Revenue Service. I.R.S. Form 2553 is normally used for this purpose, although the form is not required as long as the required information is provided. All persons who are shareholders of the corporation on the day that the election is made must sign a written consent to the election, and the consent must be filed with the election. See 26 U.S.C. 1362(a)(2). Even though a husband and wife are treated as a single shareholder for purposes of determining the number of shareholders, both must sign the consent for it to be effective. See Clemens v. Comm., 453 F. 2nd 869 (CA 9, 1971). If the election is timely filed during the current tax year, all persons who were shareholders at any time during the current tax year, even if they are not shareholders on the day the election is made, must sign the consent if the election is to be valid for the current tax year (see next paragraph). See Exhibit 5-K at the end of this chapter for a sample Subchapter S Election and Consent.

Subchapter S election, filing requirements, current tax year

The election and consent must be filed either during the preceding tax year or on or before the 15th day of the third month (i.e., during the first 2 1/2 months) of the current tax year in order to be effective for the current tax year. See 26 U.S.C. 1362 (b)(1). However, if the election is filed during the first 2 1/2 months of the current tax year and if the corporation did not qualify as a small business corporation on one or more days during that period or if one or more of the persons who held stock in the corporation during that 2 1/2-month period failed to sign the consent to the Subchapter S election, then the election will be valid only for the following tax year. See 26 U.S.C. 1362(b)(2).

Subchapter S election, how terminated

Once a Subchapter S election has been made and accepted by the Internal Revenue Service, it automatically remains in effect for all succeeding tax years of the corporation until the election is terminated, even if new shareholders are added (provided the total number of shareholders does not exceed 75). See 26 U.S.C. 1362(c). A Subchapter S election may be terminated in the following manners: (1) voluntarily by filing a revocation of the election, or (2) involuntarily by operation of law if the corporation ceases to qualify as a small business corporation under Subchapter S or if the corporation's passive investment income exceeds 25 percent of its gross receipts for three consecutive tax years during each of which the corporation would have had earnings and profits had it not been an S corporation. See 26 U.S.C. 1362(d).

Subchapter S election, voluntary revocation

The voluntary revocation of a Subchapter S election by a corporation can occur only with the written consent of the shareholders holding more than one-half of the stock of the corporation on the day in which the revocation is made. The revocation may be effective for the current tax year if made on or before the 15th day of the third month of the current tax year. Otherwise, it will be effective beginning the first day of the following tax year. However, if the revocation specifies a later date for revocation, the revocation will be effective as of the later date. See 26 U.S.C. 1362(d)(1).

Subchapter S election, termination by disqualification

Subchapter S election, inadvertent termination

If a corporation ceases to qualify as a small business corporation under Subchapter S, the election is deemed to be terminated as of the date of disqualification. See 26 U.S.C. 1362 (d)(2). For example, if a corporation acquires more than 75 shareholders, its Subchapter S election is deemed terminated as of the date of the acquisition of stock by the 76th shareholder. The termination is effective for the current and succeeding tax years. If, however, the termination was inadvertent, as determined by the I.R.S., the Subchapter S election may be continued subject to any adjustments required by the I.R.S., provided that the corporation and all of its shareholders agree to the adjustments. See 26 U.S.C. 1362(f).

Subchapter S election, passive investment income, termination by

If a corporation has passive investment income that, for three consecutive tax years, exceeds 25 percent of its gross receipts, and if the corporation, had it not been an S corporation, would have had earnings and profits during those three years, its Subchapter S election will be terminated. The definitions of passive investment income, gross receipts, and nonSubchapter S earnings and profits are too lengthy to be included here, and the reader is referred to 26 U.S.C. 1362(d)(3) for the specifics.

Subchapter S election, termination of, when effective

S termination year, definition

If the termination of a Subchapter S election is effective on any day of a corporation's tax year other than the first day, the tax year is termed an "S termination year." The portion of the S termination year ending with the termination is called the "S short year," and the balance of the tax year is called the "C short year." See 26 U.S.C. 1362(e)(1),(4). For example, if a corporation's tax year is the calendar year and if its Subchapter S election is terminated as of May 31, the period from January 1 to May 31 is the S short year and the period from June 1 to December 31 is the C short year.

S termination year, prorating income and losses

Generally, in an S termination year a corporation is required to allocate items of income and loss between the two tax years (the S short year and the C short year) on the basis of a daily proration. See 26 U.S.C. 1362(e)(2). However, if a corporation so elects and if the written consent of all affected shareholders is obtained, an alternative method of proration may be applied whereby the income or loss attributable to the affected shareholders is prorated as shown on the books of the corporation. Several special rules, too lengthy to include here, are applicable to this elective proration. See 26 U.S.C. 1362(e)(3),(4),(5) for the specifics.

Subchapter S election, eligibility of corporation after termination

Once a Subchapter S election has been terminated, the corporation (and any successor corporation) is not eligible for another Subchapter S election in any tax year before the fifth tax year beginning after the first tax year in which the termination is effective unless the I.R.S. consents to an earlier election. See 26 U.S.C. 1362(g). However, under the Small Business Job Protection Act of 1996, any corporation that had terminated its S status within the 5-year period prior to the date of enactment of the Act can reelect its S status without the consent of the I.R.S.

S corporation, tax year, requirements

Even though an S corporation normally pays no taxes, because it files a tax return it must have a tax year. An S corporation must adopt a "permitted year" as its tax year regardless of when the corporation filed its Subchapter S election. A "permitted year" is defined as either the calendar year or any other accounting period for which the corporation establishes a business purpose to the satisfaction of the Treasury Secretary. See 26 U.S.C. 1378. Generally, an S corporation must conform its tax year to that of a majority of its shareholders. However, an S corporation may elect a different tax year by filing what is called a "Section 444 election," but the tax year elected must result in a deferral period of three months or less. See 26 U.S.C. 444.

Shareholders of corporation, tax treatment

The shareholders of an S corporation are taxed on their pro rata share of - (1) the corporation's separate items of income, loss, deduction, or credit, if the separate treatment of these items will affect the shareholder's tax liability, and (2) the corporation's nonseparately computed income or loss. The corporation's nonseparately computed income or loss is its gross income less its applicable deductions as determined by excluding the separate items of income, loss, deduction and credit affecting the shareholders' individual tax liability. See 26 U.S.C. 1366(a).

S corporation, allocation of tax items to shareholders

Generally, any item of income, loss, deduction, or credit that may affect the individual income tax liability of a shareholder must be stated separately by the corporation and may be treated by the shareholder as if he or she had personally received that item directly from the source. See 26 U.S.C. 1366(b). For example, if the corporation has tax exempt income, that income may be passed directly to the shareholders, in proportion to their stock holdings, as tax-exempt income without being offset against any ordinary losses of the corporation. It should be noted that a shareholder of an S corporation is taxed on the shareholder's pro rata share of the corporation's nonseparately computed income, whether or not it is actually distributed to the shareholder. Also, the amount of deductions or losses that may be attributed to a shareholder in any tax year is limited to the basis of the shareholder's stock plus the basis of any debt owed by the corporation to the shareholder. See 26 U.S.C. 1366(d)(1).

S corporation, shareholders' family members, tax treatment

If a member of the family of a shareholder of an S corporation renders services or furnishes capital to the corporation without receiving reasonable compensation in return, the Treasury Secretary may make adjustments in the applicable items of income, loss, deduction or credit of both the family member and the shareholder so as to reflect the value of the services or capital. See 26 U.S.C. 1366(e). This rule applies even if the family member is not a shareholder, and the term "family member" includes spouses, ancestors and lineal descendents. This rule makes it difficult for a family S corporation to defer taxable income to family members in lower income tax brackets by issuing stock to them for services or nominal consideration.

S corporation, transfer of stock, allocation of tax items

If a shareholder transfers or acquires stock in an S corporation during the tax year, the shareholder's pro rata share of the various items of income, loss, deduction, credit, and nonseparately computed income or loss is determined on a per-share, per-day basis. See 26 U.S.C. 1377(a)(1). If, for example, an S corporation had 100 shares outstanding and had $36,500 of nonseparately computed income for the entire tax year, a shareholder who held 20 shares of its stock for 100 days during the tax year would be allocated $2,000 of the income for the tax year ($36,500 x 100/365 x 20/100 = $2,000). However, if a shareholder terminates his or her interest in the corporation during the tax year and if all persons who were shareholders at any time during the tax year consent, the termination tax year may be treated as two separate years, the first of which ends with the shareholder's termination. See 26 U.S.C. 1377(a)(2). In other words, the books of the corporation can be closed for the tax year as of the date of the termination, if all shareholders agree.

S corporation, distribution of property, tax treatment

If an S corporation distributes property to its shareholders, the distribution is tax-free unless the actual value of the property distributed exceeds the basis of the property in the hands of the corporation, in which case a gain must be realized. See 26 U.S.C. 1368. Property distributed to its shareholders by an S corporation is valued at the greater of its market value or its tax basis on the books of the corporation.

S corporation, fringe benefits, general aspects

In determining the treatment of shareholder and employee fringe benefits, an S corporation is treated as a partnership and any two-percent shareholder of the corporation is treated as a partner. See 26 U.S.C. 1372(a). A two-percent shareholder is any person who owns on any day during the tax year, either in fact or constructively through family members or trusts, more than two-percent of the outstanding stock of the corporation or stock containing more than two-percent of the total combined voting power of all stock in the corporation. See 26 U.S.C. 1372(b). Thus, a person can be a two-percent shareholder without owning any stock in the corporation if more than two-percent of the stock is owned by a family member or by a trust attributable to the person. See 26 U.S.C. 318. As a practical matter, most shareholders (and shareholder family members) of S corporations are two-percent shareholders.

two-percent shareholder, definition

S corporations, fringe benefits, two-percent shareholders

The following fringe benefits, which are available to other shareholders and employees of S corporations and to shareholder-employees of C corporations, are not available to two-percent shareholders of S corporations:

(1) accident and health benefit plans,
(2) $50,000 of group-term life insurance, and
(3) payments to employees for meals or lodging furnished for the convenience of the employer. See 26 U.S.C. 101(b)(3).

S corporations, retirement benefits

The pension, profit-sharing, and other retirement or deferred compensation plans of S corporations are subject to essentially the same rules and limitations as comparable plans of C corporations. See section 6.01, infra, for further reading on the retirement and other fringe benefits available to employees and shareholder-employees of corporations.

Subchapter S election, effect on state taxes

A factor to consider when making a Subchapter S election is the effect of the election on state and local income taxes. Many states follow the federal rule and do not tax S corporations. Other states, however, have no such rule and impose a regular corporate income tax on S corporations. In such cases a Subchapter S election could result in substantially increased state and local income taxes. The rule followed in the local state should be ascertained before making a Subchapter S election.

It is not uncommon for Subchapter S status to be financially beneficial for some shareholders and not for others. Because the Subchapter S election requires the unanimous consent of all shareholders, a single non-consenting shareholder can, in effect, deny the Subchapter S benefits to all other shareholders. Once a Subchapter S election has been made, a single shareholder can cause the election to be terminated by transferring his or her stock to a nonqualifying purchaser or by dividing up the shares so as to create a total number of shareholders in excess of 75. subchapter s election, shareholder disputes

On the other hand, the majority or controlling shareholders can force the termination of a Subchapter S election against the will of the minority by simply revoking the election. Also, because corporate income is taxed against the shareholders whether or not it is distributed to them, majority shareholders can penalize minority holders by terminating their employment and by refusing to distribute accumulated earnings, thus subjecting them to income tax liability on funds they have yet to receive. subchapter s election, control of by majority shareholders

As indicated above, the Subchapter S election can be the source of substantial conflicts among shareholders. The most effective method of preventing or resolving such conflicts is through a shareholders' agreement that deals with the problems in advance. Such an agreement should set forth the voting requirements to both elect and revoke Subchapter S status for the corporation, and should require all shareholders to sign the election consent if a Subchapter S election is voted for by the required number of shareholders. The agreement should prevent any shareholders from signing a consent revoking the Subchapter S election unless revocation has been voted for as provided in the agreement. The agreement should also prevent the unfair withholding of corporate distributions or termination of employment. Finally, the loss of a Subchapter S election through the transfer of stock should be prevented by prohibiting the transfer of the stock in a manner or to persons that will cause the Subchapter S election to be terminated. See section 5.06, supra, for further reading on shareholder agreements, and see section 5.17, supra, for further reading on stock transfer restrictions. A sample Subchapter S provision in a shareholders agreement is set forth in Exhibit 5-C at the end of this chapter. Also, if necessary the wills and other estate documents of the shareholders should be reviewed to insure that the Subchapter S election will not be forfeited upon their death by passing the stock to unqualified or numerous persons. subchapter s election, use of shareholders' agreement

Prior to January 1, 1997, an S corporation was not permitted to own a subsidiary corporation. Now, under the provisions of the Small Business Job Protection Act of 1996, an S corporation is permitted to own 80 percent or more of the stock of a C corporation. In addition, an S corporation is also allowed to own a "qualified Subchapter S subsidiary," which is defined to mean a Subchapter S eligible domestic corporation of which 100 percent of the stock is held by the parent S corporation and the parent elects to treat the subsidiary as a qualified Subchapter S subsidiary. If such an election is made, the subsidiary is not treated for tax purposes as a separate corporation and all of its assets, liabilities and items of income, deduction and credit are treated as those of the parent. See 26 U.S.C. 1361(b)(3). S corporation, eligibility to own subsidiary corporations qualified Subchapter S subsidiary, definition of

5.19 The Close Corporation Election

close corporation election, types of

There are two types of close corporation elections: declared elections and undeclared elections. The type of election, if any, that is permitted or required in a particular state is determined by the type of close corporation laws that exist in the state. A declared close corporation election is normally required if a corporation is being organized (or reorganized in the case of an existing corporation) as a statutory close corporation under a designated close corporation code or statute. An undeclared close corporation election is permitted if a corporation is being organized or reorganized under a statutorily-authorized shareholder agreement that, in effect, permits a corporation to be organized and operated in the manner of a close corporation. A corporation that is organized under a declared close corporation election is usually referred to in the close corporation code or statute as a statutory close corporation. A close corporation organized under a statutorily-authorized shareholder agreement (i.e., under an undeclared election) usually has no special name or designation.

close corporation laws, types of, where to find

Before a close corporation election can be exercised, the type of close corporations laws, if any, that exist in the local state must be ascertained. Fifteen states have enacted a close corporation code that is separate and distinct from the general corporation laws. A close corporation code normally requires a declared close corporation election wherein a separate statement or heading must be included in the articles of incorporation declaring the corporation to be a statutory close corporation formed under the close corporation code. A few states have enacted a designated close corporation statute that is included in the general corporation laws. A statute of this type may or may not require a declared close corporation election, depending on the language of the statute.

close corporation shareholder agreement, where permitted

In a few states, including some of the states that have adopted the Revised Model Business Corporation Act, the general corporation laws (i.e., the business corporation act) contain provisions that permit the shareholders of a corporation to enter into an agreement that, in effect, permits a corporation to be organized and operated as a close corporation. These statutes, which are usually similar to sections 7.32 and 8.01(c) of The Revised Model Business Corporation Act, are not specifically designated as close corporation statutes. In states with this type of statute the corporation is organized under the general corporation laws (as opposed to a close corporation code) and becomes the equivalent of a close corporation by virtue of a close corporation shareholders' agreement that complies with the specified statute. A few states have both a close corporation code and provisions in the general corporation laws permitting a close corporation shareholders' agreement. In these states, a close corporation may be organized (or reorganized) under either the close corporation code or a close corporation shareholders' agreement. The close corporation laws, if any, that exist in each state are designated and cited in Appendix I in the back of this book under the heading of "Close Corporation Laws."

close corporation codes, types of

Several states adopted the Close Corporation Supplement to the Revised Model Business Corporation Act before the American Bar Association Committee on Corporate Laws withdrew its recommendation of the Supplement in favor of the adoption of sections 7.32 and 8.01(c) of the Revised Model Act. The close corporation code in other states bears little resemblance to the model code. While most close corporation codes provide essentially the same features, the methods of adopting these features differ significantly from state to state. It is important, therefore, to examine the local close corporation code, if one exists, before organizing a corporation thereunder or rendering legal advice thereon.

close corporation election, effect of

A declared close corporation election under a close corporation code is a declaration, usually in the articles of incorporation, that the corporation is being organized (or reorganized) as a statutory close corporation under the local close corporation code or statute. If a valid close corporation election is made in such a state, certain specified corporate functions are governed by the close corporation code and not by the general corporation laws. The corporate functions and matters that are not covered in the close corporation code are governed by the general corporation laws.

Close corporation codes and statutes that require a declared election usually set forth requirements and qualifications that must be complied with if a corporation is to qualify as a statutory close corporation. The articles of incorporation of a newly organized corporation must contain these required provisions. An existing corporation may become a statutory close corporation by amending its articles of incorporation so as to include the required provisions. A unanimous vote of the shareholders is usually required for article of incorporation amendments of this type. The statutory close corporation requirements and qualifications typically include the following: close corporation election, requirements

close corporation requirements

(1) The articles of incorporation must contain a heading or statement that the corporation is a statutory close corporation organized under a specified close corporation statute or code.

(2) All of the issued and outstanding stock of the corporation must be subject to specified transfer restrictions, unless otherwise provided in the articles of incorporation.

(3) All of the issued and outstanding stock of the corporation must be held by not more than a specified number of persons. In some states the number of shareholders in a close corporation is not limited.

(4) The election to organize or reorganize the corporation as a statutory close corporation must be approved by all, or a statutorily-specified percentage, of the existing shareholders or subscribers.

(5) Each stock certificate (or information statement if uncertified shares are issued) issued by the corporation must conspicuously state that the corporation is a statutory close corporation and that its shares of stock are subject to specified transfer restrictions.

Once attained, statutory close corporation status normally continues as long as the corporation and its shareholders continue to meet the above requirements. If desired, however, close corporation status may be terminated upon a specified vote of the shareholders. The termination is effected by amending the articles of incorporation so as to delete the required close corporation provisions. Typically, a close corporation code specifies a minimum shareholder voting requirement for terminating close corporation status, but permits a corporation to adopt a greater voting requirement, if desired. close corporation status, termination of

A statutory close corporation, after meeting the requirements and qualifications listed above, is typically permitted to provide for the following functions:

statutory close corporations, permitted functions

(1) It may adopt qualifications for its shareholders by specifying who may or who may not become a shareholder. Some statutes require shareholder qualifications to be set forth in the articles of incorporation, while other statutes permit them to be contained in a shareholders' agreement.

(2) It may dispense with, or limit the authority of, the board of directors and permit the shareholders to either manage the corporation themselves or provide for the management of the corporation in a shareholders' agreement.

(3) It may provide for the dissolution of the corporation upon the will of a shareholder, upon a specified vote of the shareholders, or upon the occurrence or nonoccurrence of a specified event or contingency. Dissolution provisions of this type must normally be set forth in the articles of incorporation to be effective.

(4) It may provide for the appointment of a custodian or provisional director in the event of a deadlock among the shareholders or directors.

In a state where a close corporation (or the equivalent thereof) can be organized under a shareholders' agreement that complies with a specified statute in the general corporation laws, a formal or declared close corporation election is not required. All that is usually required in such a state is the adoption of a shareholders' agreement that meets the requirements of the specified statute. Such a statute typically states that a shareholders' agreement that complies with the statute is effective even though it is inconsistent with one or more provisions of the business corporation act. To be effective, such an agreement is usually required to be either set forth in the articles of incorporation or bylaws and approved by all or a specified percentage of the existing shareholders or set forth in a written agreement signed by all or a specified percentage of the existing shareholders and made known to the corporation. close corporation shareholder agreement, requirements

Typically, a close corporation shareholders' agreement of the type described in the preceding paragraph may provide for some or all of the following functions.

close corporation shareholders agreement, permitted functions

(1) It may dispense with or restrict the authority of the board of directors.

(2) It may authorize the making of corporate distributions that are not in proportion to the ownership of shares.

(3) It may name or specify the directors and officers of the corporation, their terms of office, and the manner of their selection and removal.

(4) It may provide for the methods and manner of voting by shareholders and directors.

(5) It may establish the terms of any agreement between the corporation and any shareholder, director, officer, or employee for the transfer or use of property or for the provision of services.

(6) It may permit one or more of the shareholders or other persons to manage the corporation and its business.

(7) It may provide for the dissolution of the corporation upon the request of one or more of the shareholders or upon the occurrence of a specified event or contingency.

(8) It may otherwise provide for the exercise of corporate powers, the management of the corporate business and affairs, and the relationship among the shareholders, the directors, and the corporation in any manner that is not contrary to public policy.

close corporation shareholders agreement, effect of

In most states where a close corporation shareholders' agreement of the type described above is permitted, the agreement may be amended only by a unanimous vote of the shareholders, unless the agreement provides otherwise. Such agreements are normally valid for only a specified period (usually 10 years), unless the agreement provides otherwise. The existence of such an agreement must be conspicuously noted on each stock certificate or on each information statement if uncertified shares are issued. If such an agreement limits the discretion or powers of the board of directors, it also relieves the directors of liability for acts and omissions and imposes that liability upon the persons to whom the discretion and powers are granted. Such an agreement does not impose personal liability upon the shareholders for corporate debts, even if the agreement treats the corporation as if it were a partnership. If the agreement ceases to be effective for any reason, the board of directors may amend the articles of incorporation or bylaws without shareholder approval so as to delete any reference to the agreement.

close corporation, necessity of

It is evident from the above discussion that essentially the same results can be obtained under either a close corporation shareholders' agreement or a declared close corporation election under a close corporation code or statute. The question, then, is under what conditions or circumstances is it advisable to form a close corporation? While there is no definitive answer to this question, close corporation status, either under a close corporation code or through a close corporation shareholders' agreement, should be considered whenever any of the following requirements or conditions exist:

shareholder management, when needed

(1) When direct shareholder management of the corporation is desired. If the business participants are all active in the business and are used to working together as partners, shareholder management may be desirable, especially if the election of directors may cause dissention or if it is felt that the participants will not in the future perform the corporate functions of electing directors and officers. Direct shareholder management may also be desirable in the case of an incorporated joint venture, especially if one or more of the joint venturers is a corporation.

easy dissolution, when needed

(2) When easy dissolution of the corporation is desired. Because most small business corporations are closely akin to general partnerships where each partner can effect a dissolution of the partnership by withdrawing, easy dissolution is usually favored by the participants of small business corporations. Easy dissolution (i.e., dissolution of the will of a shareholder or upon a specified less-than-majority vote of the shareholders) is especially useful if there is a good chance of shareholder dissention or of one or more of the participants leaving the business for any reason. Easy dissolution may also be advisable if the business is owned by two equal shareholders.

(3) When severe or unusually restrictive stock transfer restrictions are needed. If the type of stock transfer restrictions needed to insure the continued control of the corporate stock are of questionable legality, the enforceability of the restrictions can usually be shored up by organizing the corporation as a close corporation. stock transfer restrictions, enforceability

(4) When it is necessary to impose strict qualifications on who may or may not become a shareholder of the corporation. The enforceability of shareholder qualifications is enhanced if the corporation is organized as a close corporation. If it is desired to limit shareholdership to a specified family or to a certain class of persons, close corporation status may be useful. shareholder qualifications, provisions for

(5) When there is a real danger of corporate deadlock in the foreseeable future. If the corporation is owned or controlled by two persons or by two equal factions, the danger of deadlock among the shareholders or directors usually exists. The deadlock-resolution procedures available to a close corporation (i.e., the provisional appointment of a director or custodian, easy dissolution, etc.) are often useful under these circumstances. deadlock prevention, provisions for

(6) When it is desired to make corporate distributions that are not in proportion to share ownership. If the corporation has, or will in the future have, assets which are to be distributed unequally to the shareholders, a close corporation may be advantageous because such provisions are easier to implement and enforce in a close corporation. Family corporations often need such provisions. unequal distributions, provisions for

(7) When it is desired to control the voting or limit the discretion or power of the board of directors. Such limitations can be either general or on specified matters, such as the issuing of dividends or fixing the compensation of officers. A creditor or investor may require such provisions as a condition of extending credit to or making an investment in the corporation. Article of incorporation or bylaw provisions limiting the statutory discretion of the board of directors are easier to enforce in a close corporation. controlling board of directors, provisions for

(8) When it is necessary to insure the appointment or continuation in office of specified persons, often under specified conditions. Provisions of this nature are useful in attracting qualified persons into the business. Such provisions are more likely to be enforceable in a close corporation. appointment of officers, provisions for

(9) When it is desired to have the corporation managed by outsiders (i.e., nonshareholders) for a specified period or under specified conditions. Such provisions are easier to implement and enforce in a close corporation. outside management, provisions for

5.20 Professional Corporations - A Brief Description

other entities, use of by professionals

It should be noted at the outset that in most states professionals may conduct business in the form of either a limited liability company (see chapter 4, supra) or a limited liability partnership (see sections 3.11-3.13, supra). Some states also permit professionals to conduct business as a "professional association". If one of the objectives of the professionals is to limit the liability of the individual professionals for the malpractice claims of other professionals or employees of the business, these entities may be preferable to a professional corporation in many instances. It should also be noted that the retirement benefits available under the other entities are substantially the same as those available to the shareholders and employees of a professional corporation. Superior medical benefits may be provided to the shareholders of a professional corporation, however.

professional corporations, authority for organizing

The first task in ascertaining the local law with respect to professional corporations is that of locating the authority, statutory or otherwise, under which they may be organized. Both the type and the form of the organizing authority varies greatly from state to state. In some states the authority is found in the general corporation laws, usually in a special section or chapter. Several states have adopted the Professional Corporation Supplement to the Model Business Corporation Act. In other states the authority is found in the laws or rules authorizing or regulating the particular professions involved. For example, in many states the authority regulating professional corporations of attorneys is contained in the rules regulating the conduct of attorneys.

professional corporation, who may form

What persons are permitted to form and conduct business as a professional corporation? Attorneys, physicians, and dentists may form professional corporations in every state. Architects, engineers, accountants, psychologists, chiropractors, veterinarians, and optometrists may incorporate professionally in most states. Such persons as marriage counsellors, nurses, physical therapists, and harbor pilots qualify in some states. In many states the rule followed is that professional corporations may be formed by persons performing licensed services which may not be rendered by a corporation organized under the general corporation laws. Only a close examination of the applicable laws or licensing rules of the state in question will disclose the professions permitted to incorporate.

professional corporations, shareholder qualifications

In most states, the stock of a professional corporation may be owned only by individual persons licensed to perform the professional service rendered by the corporation. In a few states the stock may also be owned by partnerships or other professional corporations authorized to render the same professional service and by persons licensed in the same profession in other states. In all states it is unlawful to transfer shares of a professional corporation to a non-qualifying person or organization. It is a good practice, therefore, to impose transfer restrictions on all stock issued by a professional corporation, prohibiting, among other things, its transfer to non-qualifying persons.

professional corporations, buy-out provisions

If a shareholder of a professional corporation dies or becomes disqualified to practice the profession of the corporation, his or her stock should be purchased by the corporation or by another qualified person. The best practice is to include a buy-out provision in the appropriate corporate documents requiring the remaining shareholders or the corporation to purchase, within the required time period, the shares of stock owned by any deceased or disqualified shareholder at a fixed or determinable price. Buy-out provisions are especially important for professional corporations because many states provide for forced dissolution or forfeiture of the corporate charter if the corporation retains as a shareholder or professional employee any person who has been professionally disqualified. See section 5.17, supra, for further reading on buy-out provisions and stock transfer restrictions.

professional corporations, officers and directors

In most states the directors and officers of a professional corporation must be practitioners of the corporation's profession. Some states permit lay directors (never a majority, however) and officers (usually non-managing), with the proviso that lay directors and officers are to have no authority over professional matters.

Professional corporations may, in most states, render only one type of professional service. The mixing of professional services is usually prohibited except where the services are classified by the licensing authority as the same general service or profession (e.g., architects and engineers in some states), or are closely related to one another (e.g., orthodontists and dentists). While professional corporations are not usually permitted to engage in general business activities, they are allowed to invest their funds in real estate, bonds, stocks, and other traditional forms of investment, and to own and manage property used in rendering the professional service of the corporation.

professional corporations, permitted business activities

Generally, the name of a professional corporation must contain words such as "professional corporation," "professional association," "chartered," "incorporated," or abbreviations of these or similar words. In some states the last name of one or more of the shareholders must appear in the corporate name. Each state, and many times each licensing authority within the state, has its own requirements for the name of a professional corporation. It is important, therefore, to thoroughly examine both the statutory provisions and the applicable licensing regulations of the particular profession before choosing a corporate name. In addition, the usual requirements in choosing a corporate name (not deceptively similar to the name of an existing corporation, etc. - see section 5.05, supra) apply to professional corporations, unless dispensed with by the professional corporation laws. It should be noted that in most states the general corporation laws apply to professional corporations, except where they are inconsistent with the professional corporation laws, in which case the latter usually prevails.

professional corporations, corporate name

applicability of general corporation laws

In most states professional corporations may engage in the normal fundamental corporate acts of amending the articles of incorporation and bylaws, dissolution, merger, and consolidation, provided that the professional purposes and status of the corporation and its shareholders are maintained. If a professional corporation ceases to render professional services, in some states its articles of incorporation may be amended so as to delete the rendering of professional services from its purposes and become a general business corporation (a corporate name change is usually necessary, also). In other states a professional corporation must be dissolved if it ceases to render professional services. A check of the applicable statute, regulation, or rule will indicate the policy followed in a particular state or by a particular profession within the state.

professional corporations, basic corporate acts, cessation of professional services

The professional corporation laws or rules in most states specifically provide that any confidential relationship that exists between a professional person and a client or patient is preserved notwithstanding the use of a corporation as the business form. The same rule undoubtedly is, or would be, followed in states where the statute or rules are silent on the subject. Generally, the existence of a professional corporation has no effect on the laws and rules governing professional relationships and standards of professional conduct.

professional corporation, effect on confidential relationships

Regardless of the corporate form, a professional person is personally liable for his or her negligence and misconduct and for that of those under his or her supervision and control. This rule, with minor variations, is followed in every state. In some states all of the shareholders of a professional corporation are liable for the negligence or misconduct of any shareholder, while in others the shareholders are not liable for negligence or misconduct of other shareholders. In a few states the personal liability of individual shareholders may be limited in amount if financial responsibility in the form of liability insurance or a surety bond is shown by the corporation. The whole issue of the liability of one professional for the professional acts of another professional in same organization is complex and beyond the scope of this book. It should be noted, however, the shareholders of a professional corporation, like shareholders generally, are not personally liable for the general, nonprofessional debts and obligations of the corporation.

professional corporation, effect on personal liability

Qualifying to do business in other states presents a special problem for professional corporations. A professional corporation, unlike a general business corporation, cannot qualify to do business in a foreign state by merely registering as a foreign corporation, although registration is normally required (see section 6.08, infra). Generally, a corporation may render professional services in a foreign state only through persons licensed to render such services in that state, and must comply with the requirements of that state related to corporate purposes, qualifications of shareholders, directors, and officers, and responsibility for professional services. The problems of qualifying in foreign states are compounded by the wide variation among the states as to professional requirements, professions covered, and operating rules.

professional corporation, qualifying in other states

5.21 The Mechanics of Incorporating - A Checklist

the mechanics of incorporating, practical aspects

The incorporation process begins, of course, with the business bargain of the participants. Once the details of the bargain have been discussed and agreed upon, the mechanics of incorporating can be routine. The usual problem, however, is that many of the details of the bargain have not been resolved, or even discussed, when the time arrives to draft the incorporation documents. Many times the participants simply are not aware that such matters as a Subchapter S election, stock transfer restrictions, veto powers, preemptive rights, or employee benefit plans even exist, much less that they should be considered if full advantage is to be taken of doing business in the corporate form. Even if the basic decisions on matters of this type have been made, many of the details needed to properly draft the incorporation documents are often left unresolved.

incorporation, use of checklist

It is important that each participant in a small business corporation be made aware of every significant corporate option. Further, the options should be explained or presented to the participants at a time and in a manner that will enable them to make informed, intelligent decisions. The most practical method of fulfilling this function is to use a checklist or similar document when conferring with the participants that contains every relevant matter that should be considered by the participants. The use of such a checklist will also permit the incorporation documents to be prepared more effectively.

incorporation of business, necessary documents

The documents necessary to organize and incorporate a small business corporation will vary, depending on the type and complexity of the particular business setting. A start-up business with minimum capitalization, a single class of common stock, and participants unconcerned with stock transfer restrictions, buy-out provisions, veto powers, or the tax aspects of incorporating, may require only articles of incorporation, a set of bylaws, minutes of an organizational meeting, and a few stock certificates. An existing business with numerous participants may require much more. The documents that may be needed to organize and incorporate a typical small business corporation include the following:

(1) A preincorporation agreement.
(2) A shareholders' agreement.
(3) Articles of incorporation.
(4) Corporate bylaws.
(5) Minutes of organizational meetings.
(6) Stock certificates.
(7) Debt instruments.
(8) Employment contracts.
(9) A Subchapter S election and consent.
(10) Deeds and other documents transferring assets to the corporation.
(11) Affidavits and other documents needed to comply with the local filing requirements, if any exist.
(12) A banking resolution.
(13) An organizational expense statement.
(14) Documents necessary to qualify the corporation to transact business in other states.
(15) Plans implementing employee benefit programs.
(16) Notices and other documents necessary to comply with state Bulk Sales or Fraudulent Conveyance laws.
(17) Registration statements or other documents necessary to comply with state or federal securities laws.

incorporation of business, use of checklist

In addition to the preparation of the above documents it will usually be necessary to perform certain functions in order to properly organize and incorporate a business. The Checklist and Guide shown below lists the documents and functions customarily required to organize and set up a typical small business corporation. It is suggested that it be used as a reference when interviewing the participants and as a guide in preparing the documents and performing the functions necessary to organize and incorporate the business.

INCORPORATION CHECKLIST AND GUIDE

A. **The desirability of incorporating.** See chapter 1, supra, for guidance and instructions. Incorporation may not be advisable if any of the following circumstances exist:

(1) The business is new or has an unproven earning capacity.

(2) The business is a one-person business.

(3) The nature of the business does not require incorporation.

(4) The financial circumstances of neither the business nor its participants require incorporation.

B. **Preliminary matters.** The following functions should be performed at the outset of the incorporation process:

(1) Obtain the written or verbal authority necessary to incorporate the business. See section 5.13, supra.

(2) Obtain an agreement or understanding with the participants as to the amount and terms of the fees to be charged for organizing and incorporating the business.

(3) Make arrangements for payment of the required filing fees and incorporation or franchise taxes. These fees and taxes are set forth in Appendix I, infra, under the heading of "Fees."

C. **Preincorporation agreement.** See sections 5.03 and 5.13, supra, for guidance and instructions. Use Exhibit 5-B, infra, as a guide in preparing a preincorporation agreement. A preincorporation agreement may be advisable if any of the following circumstances exist:

(1) The business participants are numerous or geographically widespread.

(2) The business participants are not all on friendly terms with one another.

(3) The incorporation process will be extended or delayed.

(4) Incorporation is contingent upon the raising of a certain amount of capital or upon the happening of other events.

(5) Promoters are obtaining stock subscriptions.

D. **Determining the state of incorporation.** See section 5.04, supra, for guidance and instructions. Incorporation in a state other than the home state should be considered in the following instances:

(1) Where the corporation will transact business in at least one other state to the extent that qualification as a foreign corporation in that state will be necessary. See section 6.08, infra, for further reading.

(2) Where the laws of the home state do not permit the corporation to be organized in the desired manner. See section 5.04, supra, for further reading.

E. **The close corporation election.** See section 5.19, supra, for guidance and instructions. In a state that has close corporation laws, it should be determined whether the corporation should be organized as a close corporation under the applicable close corporation code or statute. The conditions under which close corporation status might be advantageous are listed in section 5.19, supra. The close corporation laws, if any, in each state are designated and cited in Appendix I, infra, under the heading of "Close Corporation Laws."

F. **Selecting and clearing a corporate name.** See section 5.05, supra, for guidance and instructions. The name of the corporation should be related to the business of the enterprise and to any trademarks or trade names used in the business and should be adaptable to advertising the business of the corporation. Once a corporate name has been chosen, it may be necessary to perform the following functions before filing the articles of incorporation:

(1) Ascertain whether the desired corporate name complies with the statutory requirements for corporate names in the home state and in each state where the corporation will be transacting significant business. The corporate name requirements in each state are summarized in Appendix I, infra, under the heading of "Corporate Name."

(2) Ascertain whether the desired name is available in the home state and in each state where the corporation will be transacting significant business.

(3) If necessary, reserve the name in the home state and in each state where the corporation will be qualifying as a foreign corporation.

G. **Shareholders' agreement.** See section 5.06, supra, for guidance and instructions and use Exhibit 5-C, infra, as a guide in preparing a shareholders agreement. A shareholders agreement may be necessary under the following circumstances:

(1) Where stock transfer restrictions are to be imposed for any reason. See section 5.17, supra, for further reading on the imposition of stock transfer restrictions.

(2) Where stock buy-out provisions are to be imposed for reasons of either control of the corporate stock or the breaking of deadlocks. See sections 5.15 and 5.17, supra, for further reading on these matters.

(3) Where veto powers are to be imposed involving shareholder voting rights or individual shareholder approval of certain corporate acts. See section 5.15, supra, for further reading on these matters.

(4) Where certain participants are to be guaranteed certain corporate officerships or positions for extended periods. See section 5.15, supra, for further reading on this matter.

(5) Where compensation or dividends in certain amounts are to be guaranteed to certain participants. See section 5.15, supra, for further reading on this matter.

(6) Where the Subchapter S election requires shareholder cooperation. See section 5.18, supra, for further reading on this matter.

(7) Where the corporation will be organized as a close corporation. See section 5.19, supra, for further reading on this matter.

H. **Preparing articles of incorporation.** See section 5.09, supra, for guidance and instructions and use Exhibit 5-G, infra, as a guide in preparing the articles of incorporation. The statute containing the article of incorporation requirements in each state is cited in Appendix I, infra, under the heading of "Articles of Incorporation: Contents." The following matters should be dealt with in the articles of incorporation:

(1) Corporate name. A name meeting the requirements described in paragraph F above should be chosen.

(2) Corporate stock. See section 5.14, supra, for guidance and instructions. If necessary, the following matters should be dealt with in the article provisions dealing with corporate stock:

(a) The authorized classes of stock.

(b) The number of authorized shares of each class of stock.

(c) The par value, if any, of the shares in each class of stock.

(d) The board of directors voting requirements for the issuance of each class of stock.

(e) The preferences, limitations, and voting, dividend, and distribution rights of the shares in each class of stock.

(f) The restrictions, if any, that shall be imposed on the transfer of the shares in each class of stock, and the type, terms, conditions, and valuation methods of such restrictions. See section 5.17, supra, for further reading on stock transfer restrictions.

(g) The classes of stock, if any, that shall be subject to buy-out provisions, and the type, terms, conditions, and valuation methods of such provisions. See section 5.17, supra, for further reading on buy-out provisions.

(h) The classes of stock, if any, that are to be subject to preemptive rights, and the terms, conditions, and extent of such rights. See section 5.12, supra, for further reading on preemptive rights.

(3) Registered office and agent. The address of the registered office of the corporation and the name of the person who shall serve as its registered agent should be determined.

(4) Incorporators. The number of incorporators should be determined and the name and address of each incorporator should be ascertained.

(5) Corporate purpose. If a purpose clause is required or desired, the purpose of the corporation should be described in a manner that will satisfy the state filing officer and give the participants the business flexibility they desire. If the participants wish to limit the field of business of the corporation, self-denying language may be inserted in the purpose clause. See section 5.09, supra, for further reading on this matter.

(6) Board of Directors. See section 5.07, supra, for general information on the board of directors. The statutory board of director requirements in each state are summarized in Appendix I, infra, under the heading of "Board of Directors." The following matters should be dealt with in the article provisions dealing with the board of directors:

(a) The number of directors constituting the initial and subsequent boards.

(b) The qualifications, if any, that are to be required of directors.

(c) Those who shall serve as the initial board of directors.

(d) The shareholder voting requirements for the election of directors and the filling of vacancies on the board of directors, including any provisions for cumulative or class voting. See sections 5.06, 5.07, and 5.15, supra, for further information on these matters.

(e) The shareholder voting requirements for removing directors, both with and without cause, including directors elected through cumulative or class voting. See section 4.15, for further reading on this matter.

(f) If state law permits, whether certain functions normally delegated to the board of directors (e.g., electing officers, declaring dividends, issuing stock, making loans, etc.) shall be retained by the shareholders, and if so retained, the shareholder voting requirements necessary to implement such functions. See section 4.15, supra, for further information.

(g) Whether directors shall be permitted to serve the corporation in other capacities and determine their own compensation as officers and directors, if permitted under state law.

(h) Whether to relieve directors who in good faith rely on the corporate books and records of personal liability for the illegal issuance of dividends and other acts, if permitted by state law.

(i) Whether to validate the acts of interested directors and officers, if permitted under state law.

(j) Whether to indemnify directors and officers for expenses incurred on behalf of the corporation.

(k) The circumstances whereunder or the matters upon which board of director voting requirements of greater than a majority shall be imposed, and the specific voting and quorum requirements that shall be imposed. See section 5.15, supra, for further reading on this matter.

(l) The special procedures, if any, to be implemented in the event of deadlock in the board of directors. See section 5.15, supra, for further reading on the handling of deadlocks.

(7) Veto powers of shareholders. A veto power is the power of a shareholder to prevent the happening of a corporate act or function. The corporate acts or functions, if any, that are to be prohibited without shareholder approval should be determined and the shareholder voting requirements for approval should be specified. See section 5.15, supra, for further reading on veto powers.

(8) Fundamental corporate changes. The shareholder voting requirements for the approval of the extraordinary corporate acts of merger, consolidation, dissolution, and the sale or transfer of substantial corporate assets should be specified, especially if they are to be other than as provided by statute. The statutory voting requirements for these acts in each state are set forth in Appendix I, infra, under the heading of "Acts Requiring Shareholder Approval."

(9) Transacting business in other jurisdictions. If desired, a provision specifically authorizing the corporation to conduct business in other states or countries may be inserted. See section 6.08, infra, for further reading on this matter.

(10) Amending the articles of incorporation. The shareholder voting requirements for amending the articles of incorporation generally should be specified, especially if they are to be other than as provided by statute. The statutory voting requirements for amending the articles of incorporation in each state are set forth in Appendix I, infra. The shareholder voting requirements for amending the article provisions, if any, that specify voting requirements that are higher than the voting requirements for amending the articles of incorporation generally should be specified. See sections 5.15, supra, and 6.07, infra, for further reading on this matter.

(11) Dissenting shareholders' rights of appraisal. The rights of appraisal and sale, if any, that shall be granted to dissenting shareholders, in the event of a merger, consolidation, sale of corporate assets, corporate deadlock, or otherwise, and the conditions or circumstances under which such rights shall be granted. See sections 5.06, supra, and 6.11, infra, for further reading.

(12) Examining the corporate books and records. The rights of shareholders to examine the corporate books and records should be specified, especially if the rights are to be other than as provided by law. See section 5.06, supra, for more information.

(13) Action without meeting. If a state action-without-meeting statute so requires or permits, the types of action that may be taken without a meeting and the procedures to be followed in the taking of such action should be specified. If the right to act without meeting is to be denied or limited, it should be so specified. See sections 5.11, supra, and 6.04, infra, for further reading on this matter.

(14) Bylaws. See section 5.10, supra, for further reading on corporate bylaws. The statutory bylaw requirements in each state are summarized in Appendix I, infra, under the heading of "Bylaws." The following matters should be dealt with in the article provisions, if any, dealing with the corporate bylaws:

(a) Whether the bylaws should be adopted by the shareholders or by the board of directors.

(b) Whether the bylaws may be amended by the shareholders or by the board of directors, or by both, should be specified, along with the voting requirements for amendment, especially if the requirements are to be other than those provided by statute. See sections 5.10 and 5.15, supra, for further reading on these matters.

(c) The provisions, if any, dealing with the internal affairs of the corporation that shall be inserted in the articles of incorporation instead of, or in addition to, the bylaws.

I. Preparing corporate bylaws. See section 5.10, supra, for instructions and guidance and use Exhibit 5-F, infra, as a guide in preparing the corporate bylaws. The bylaws may contain any provision for managing the business and regulating the affairs of the corporation that is not inconsistent with the corporation laws or the articles of incorporation. The following matters should be dealt with in the corporate bylaws:

(1) Shareholder meetings. See sections 5.06 and 5.11, supra, for further reading on shareholder meetings. The following matters related to shareholder meetings should be specified:

(a) The date, location, and quorum requirements for the annual meeting of shareholders.

(b) The notice, quorum, and other requirements for special meetings of shareholders.

(c) The methods of determining who may receive notice of and vote at shareholder meetings, including the date of closing of the stock transfer book, the preparation of voting lists, and the use of proxies.

(d) The shareholder voting requirements, both generally and as to any specified matters.

(e) If desired or if required under local law, provisions granting, denying, or limiting the rights of shareholders to act without meeting may be set forth. See sections 5.11, supra, and 6.04, infra, for further reading on action-without-meeting statutes and see Appendix I, infra, for a summary of the statutory provisions in each state.

(2) The board of directors. See section 5.07, supra, for further reading on the board of directors. The statutory board of director requirements in each state are summarized in Appendix I, infra, under the heading of "Board of Directors." The following matters related to the board of directors should be specified:

(a) Qualifications for directors. The qualifications, if any, that are to be required of directors should be set forth.

(b) Number of directors. The number of directors, or the method of determining the number of directors should be specified.

(c) Term. The term of each director should be specified.

(d) Removal. The methods of removing a director should be specified.

(e) Filling vacancies. The method of filling a vacancy on the board of directors should be set forth.

(f) Meetings. The notice, quorum, and voting requirements for regular and special meetings of the board of directors should be specified. High quorum requirements should accompany high voting requirements.

(g) Action without meeting. If desired or if required under local law, provisions granting, denying, or limiting the rights of the board of directors to act without meeting may be set forth. See sections 5.11, supra, and 6.04, infra, for further reading on action-without-meeting statutes and see Appendix I, infra, for a summary of the statutory provisions in each state.

(h) Compensation. The compensation, if any, of directors should be specified, along with the rights of directors to vote for changes in the amount of their compensation.

(3) Officers. See section 5.08, supra, for further reading on corporate officers. The statutory officer requirements in each state are summarized in Appendix I, infra, under the heading of "Officers." The following matters related to the officers of the corporation should be specified:

(a) Offices. The titles, functions, and duties of each corporate officer should be set forth.

(b) Term of office. Whether the corporate officers shall serve specific terms of office or at the pleasure of the board of directors should be specified, and, if terms are to be served, the term for each office should be specified.

(c) Election of officers. The voting requirements for the election of the various corporate officers should be specified.

(d) Removal. The method of removing a corporate officer should be specified.

(e) Filling vacancies. The method of filling a vacant corporate office should be specified.

(4) Location of corporate offices. The address of the registered office of the corporation and any other offices of the corporation should be listed.

(5) Contracts. The corporate officers who are to be empowered to sign contracts, checks, and other documents on behalf of the corporation should be identified, and any limitations, restrictions, or conditions that are to be imposed or required on the signing of such documents should be specified. See section 5.08, supra, for further reading.

(6) Fiscal year. The period that shall constitute the fiscal (or tax) year of the corporation should be specified. See sections 5.02 and 5.18, supra, for further reading on fiscal year requirements.

(7) Amendment. How and by whom the bylaws may be amended, both generally and for those provisions, if any, that impose higher voting requirements, should be explicitly set forth, even if they are also set forth in the articles of incorporation.

(8) Issuance of stock. The board of director voting requirements for the issuance of stock should be specified and the officers empowered to sign the stock certificates identified. The form of stock certificates to be used by the corporation may also be specified, if desired. See section 5.11, supra, for further reading.

(9) Corporate seal. Whether the corporation shall have an official seal and who shall maintain possession of it should be specified. See section 5.11, supra, for further reading.

(10) Books and records. The books and records that shall constitute the official books and records of the corporation, who shall be responsible for their upkeep, and who shall retain custody of them, should be set forth. See section 5.11, supra, for further reading.

(11) Emergency bylaws. If desired and permitted by state law, the corporation may adopt emergency bylaws. If adopted they should be set forth. See section 5.10 for further reading.

J. **Preparing minutes of organizational meetings.** See section 5.11, supra, for guidance and instruction and use Exhibit 5-E, infra, as a guide in preparing the minutes of the organizational meeting. The statutory organizational meeting requirements in each state are summarized in Appendix I, infra, under the heading of "Organizational Meeting." The following matters should be dealt with in minutes of organizational meetings:

(1) The meeting. The name of the body or persons holding the meeting should be stated. The date and place of the meeting, the name of the person taking the minutes of the meeting, and compliance with the notice requirements, if any, of the meeting should also be set forth.

(2) Election of officers. The names of the persons who were elected and installed as the initial corporate officers, and how and by whom they were elected, should be stated.

(3) Bank. The bank or banks to be used by the corporation should be named and the officers or persons authorized to sign checks and drafts on the corporate accounts should be identified.

(4) Election of directors. If the initial board of directors was not named in the articles of incorporation, the names of the persons who shall serve as the first board of directors of the corporation, and how and by whom they were elected, should be set forth.

(5) Shares of stock. A resolution specifying the number of shares of each class of stock that are to be issued, to whom they are to be issued, the consideration to be received by the corporation for the stock, and allocating the consideration to capital or surplus should be set forth. See section 5.14, supra, for further reading.

(6) Valuation of property or services. If stock is being issued for property or services, a resolution establishing the value that is to be assigned to the property or services received by the corporation in exchange for the stock should be set forth. See section 5.14, supra, for further reading.

(7) Debt obligations. If the corporation is to issue debt instruments in exchange for property or cash, the amounts and terms of the corporate obligations under such instruments should be stated. If a substantial portion of the capitalization of the corporation is to consist of debt, an acceptable debt-to-equity ratio for the corporation should be established. See section 5.14, supra, for further reading.

(8) Leases. If the corporation is to lease any equipment, assets, or property, either from the participants or from others, a resolution establishing the terms and conditions of the leases should be set forth. See section 5.14, supra, for further reading.

(9) Subchapter S election. If such an election is desired, a resolution stating that the corporation shall elect to be taxed under Subchapter S of the Internal Revenue Code and stating when and by whom the election shall be filed should be set forth. See section 5.18, supra, for further reading.

(10) Employment contracts. If the corporation is to enter into employment contracts with any of its officers or employees, a resolution establishing the terms and conditions of such contracts, identifying the officers who shall sign such contracts on behalf of the corporation, and authorizing the officers to sign the contracts on behalf of the corporation should be set forth. See section 5.08, supra, for further reading.

(11) Corporate advisers. If desired, resolutions employing the corporation's attorney, accountant, engineer, and other advisers and establishing the terms of their employment should be set forth.

K. Complying with state and local filing requirements. All states require filings with the state corporation filing official, usually the Secretary of State, and some states require filings at the county or local level as well. A few states require publication of the incorporation. See Appendix I, infra, for a summary of the filing and publication requirements in each state. The proper number of copies of the articles of incorporation, properly signed and, if necessary, verified, should be filed with the state filing official, along with any required affidavits or other documents, and the required filing fees and franchise taxes paid. See section 5.09, supra, for further reading on this matter. The filing fees and taxes required in each state and the name and address of the state filing official in each state are set forth in Appendix I, infra, under the headings of "Fees" and "State Filing Official."

state and local filing requirements, complying with

L. Preparing stock certificates. Stock certificates representing the shares of stock to be issued by the corporation should be prepared and signed. The certificates should contain notices of any applicable transfer or other restrictions. See section 5.11, supra, for further reading on this matter and use Exhibit 5-J, infra, as a guide in preparing stock certificates. The signature requirements for stock certificates in each state are set forth in Appendix I, infra, under the heading of "Stock Certificates."

M. Drafting employment contracts. If necessary, employment contracts for certain corporate officers or employees should be drafted, executed, and approved by a resolution of the board of directors. See sections 5.08 and 5.15, supra, for further reading on employment contracts. Exhibit 5-L, infra, may be used as a guide in the preparation of an employment contract.

N. Banking resolution. Most banks require a board of director resolution, usually on a prescribed form, authorizing the corporation to deposit funds and transact business with the bank. If required, one should be prepared and executed.

O. Organizational expense statement. If the corporation is to amortize its organizational expenses, a statement of election must be prepared and filed with the corporation's first income tax return. To avoid oversight, the statement should be prepared at the time of incorporation or as soon thereafter as all of the expenses are known. See section 5.02, supra, for further reading on this matter and use Exhibit 5-A, infra, as guide in preparing the statement.

P. Qualifying in other states. If the corporation will be transacting significant business in other states, the necessity of qualifying in those states should be examined. If necessary, the corporation should be qualified as a foreign corporation in the appropriate states. See section 6.08, infra, for further reading on qualifying to do business in other states.

Q. Preparing and filing a Subchapter S election. If the corporation is to be taxed under Subchapter S of the Internal Revenue Code, an election and consent must be prepared, signed, and filed with the regional office of the Internal Revenue Service. See section 5.18, supra, for further reading on the Subchapter S election. Use Exhibit 5-K, infra, as a guide in preparing Subchapter S election and consent.

R. Preparing employee benefit plans. If the participants wish to adopt and implement retirement or other employee benefit plans, it may be necessary to draft or procure the appropriate plans and programs and obtain Treasury Department approval of certain plans. See section 6.01, infra, for further reading on this matter.

S. Determining the taxability of the incorporation. If property or assets other than cash are being transferred to the corporation in exchange for stock, a determination should be made as to whether the transfer shall be taxable or tax-free. The appropriate steps to insure the implementation of the determination should be taken. See section 5.02, supra, for further reading on this matter.

T. Qualifying the corporation's stock under Section 1244. A determination should be made as to whether to qualify the corporate stock under Section 1244 of the Internal Revenue Code. If the qualification is desired, the appropriate steps taken to insure the qualification. See section 5.14, supra, for further reading on Section 1244 stock.

U. Complying with Bulk Sales and Fraudulent Conveyance laws. If inventory, merchandise, or other tangible assets are being transferred to the corporation from a predecessor business, it may be necessary to issue notices or take certain actions in order to comply with the applicable state Bulk Sales and/or Fraudulent Conveyance laws. See section 5.13, supra, for further reading on this matter.

V. Complying with securities laws. If required by federal or state securities laws, it may be necessary to either register the corporate stock with the Securities and Exchange Commission or the State Securities Commissioner or insure the application of a registration exemption. See section 5.16, supra, for further reading on this matter.

STATEMENT OF ELECTION

TO AMORTIZE ORGANIZATIONAL EXPENSES

BY

THE ______________________ CORPORATION

Taxpayer's Identification No. _______________

The ______________________ Corporation is a corporation newly organized under the laws of the State of _______________ on _______________, and which commenced the transaction of business on _______________.

The Corporation hereby elects under Section 248 of the Internal Revenue Code to treat the following organizational expenses as deferred expenses to be amortized ratably over a period of 60 months beginning with the month of ___________, 19 _____.

1. Legal fees for the drafting of Articles of Incorporation, Corporate Bylaws, a Shareholders' Agreement, Minutes of Organizational Meetings, and other related documents, in the amount of $ _________, paid by the corporation to ______________________, Attorney at Law, on _______________.

2. Fees for accounting services in setting up the initial books and records of the Corporation in the amount of $ ___________, paid by the corporation to ______________________ on _______________.

3. Incorporation fees, franchise taxes and filing expenses in the total amount of $ ___________, paid by the corporation to the Secretary of State of the State of _______________ on _______________.

4. Fees and expenses in the total amount of $ _______________ paid by the corporation on _______________ to ______________________ for attending the organizational meetings of the Corporation.

5. The following additional fees and expenses were incurred in the process of organizing the Corporation: ____.
   These fees and expenses were paid by the corporation to ______________________________ on _______________.

The total amount of fees and expenses to be amortized by the corporation is $ _________.

Dated this ___________ day of _______________, 19 _______.

THE ______________________ CORPORATION

by ______________________
Secretary - Treasurer

PREINCORPORATION AGREEMENT

THIS AGREEMENT, dated ________________, by and among ________________, the parties.

WHEREAS, the parties are jointly engaged in the business of ____________________, conducted under the name of ____________________, at ____________________; and

WHEREAS, the parties desire, under certain conditions, to organize a corporation under which to conduct their business.

NOW THEREFORE, the parties agree as follows:

1. **Formation of Corporation.** Upon the happening of the events described in Section 8 of the agreement, the parties shall organize a corporation under the Corporation Laws of the State of ____________________, which will hereinafter be referred to as "the Corporation."

2. **Organization of Corporation.** The Corporation shall be organized in accordance with the following requirements:

   a. The name of the Corporation shall be __________________________.

   b. The capitalization of the Corporation shall be $____________.

   c. The Corporation shall issue _________ shares of ________ par value common stock.

   d The incorporators of the Corporation shall be ______________________________.

   e. The initial directors of the Corporation shall be ______________________________.

3. **Insurance of Stock.** The common stock of the Corporation shall be issued as follows:

Name of Shareholder	Number of Shares	Consideration for Shares

4. **Subscription to Stock.** Each party hereby subscribes to and agrees to purchase the shares of stock described in Section 3 of this agreement for the consideration therein described within 10 days of the effective date of the incorporation.

5. **Control of Corporation.** The parties agree to vote their shares and to otherwise act so as to provide as follows:

   a. The initial directors of the Corporation shall continue in office for at least three years.

   b. The Officers of the Corporation shall be ______________________________.

   c. Corporate checks shall be signed by ______________________________.

   d. The Corporation shall employ the following persons at the following positions for the following compensation:

Name	Position	Compensation

6. **Subchapter S Election.** The Corporation shall file an election to be taxed under Subchapter S of the Internal Revenue Code and the parties shall execute the documents necessary for the election.

7. **Transfer of Stock.** The stock of the Corporation shall not be transferable by the shareholders unless it is first offered, for a reasonable period and at a reasonable price, to the Corporation and, if not purchased by the Corporation, then to the other shareholders. The specific periods and prices shall be determined when the Corporation is organized.

8. **Conditions to Formation of Corporation.** The Corporation shall not be formed and Sections 1 through 7 of this agreement shall not become enforceable until the happening of both of the following events:

   a. The above-described business of the parties is operated by the parties as a general partnership for a period sufficient to permit the parties to determine the financial viability of the business.

   b. Each party indicates in writing that he or she wishes to proceed with the incorporation of the business.

9. **Acknowledgement of Partnership Pending Incorporation.** The parties acknowledge that, until the incorporation of the business, they are equal partners in a general partnership doing business under the name of __________________________.

IN WITNESS WHEREOF, the parties have signed this agreement as of the date first above appearing.

______________________	______________________	______________________
Name	Name	Name

SHAREHOLDERS' AGREEMENT

THIS AGREEMENT, dated ____________________, by and between ____________________, the Shareholders, and ____________________, a corporation organized under the laws of the State of ____________________, the Corporation.

WHEREAS, the Shareholders are the holders of all of the issued and outstanding capital stock of the Corporation; and

WHEREAS, the Shareholders desire to enter into an agreement among themselves and with the Corporation regarding the control and management of the Corporation and the voting and disposition of its capital stock.

NOW THEREFORE, the Shareholders agree among themselves and with the Corporation as follows:

1. **Election of Directors.** The Shareholders shall vote their shares of stock in the corporation at all times so that the Board of Directors of the Corporation will consist of the following persons: ____________________.

2. **Removal of Directors.** A director may be removed from office, with or without cause, upon the affirmative vote or written consent of the holders of ________ percent of the issued and outstanding shares of capital stock of the Corporation.

3. **Election of Officers.** The officers of the Corporation and their respective compensation shall be as follows: ____________________ ____________________.

Each officer shall serve as long as he or she holds stock in the Corporation, is active in the business of the Corporation, is reasonably able to perform his or her duties as an officer, and makes the management of the corporate business his or her principal business occupation. In the event of the retirement or disqualification of an officer, a replacement officer shall be chosen by the Board of Directors.

4. **Issuance of Stock or Securities.** The Corporation shall not issue any further stock or securities of any nature or form without the affirmative vote or written consent of the holders of ________ percent of the issued and outstanding shares of capital stock of the Corporation.

5. **Issuance of Dividends.** The Corporation shall cause dividends in cash to be issued on its common stock under the following circumstances: ____________________.

6. **Employment Contract.** The Corporation shall employ ____________________ (the Employee) as ____________________ for a period of ____________________ at an annual salary of $ ____________, payable ____________. In addition, the Employee shall receive the following benefits: ____________________.

The Employee shall perform the following duties to the satisfaction of the Corporation: ____________________.

The Corporation shall enter into an employment contract with the Employee upon the terms described in this Section 6, and the President and the Secretary of the Corporation shall execute the employment contract on behalf of the corporation.

7. **Corporate Acts or Changes.** The affirmative vote or written consent of the holders of ________ percent of the issued and outstanding shares of capital stock of the Corporation shall be necessary for any of the following corporate acts:

   (a) The participation of the Corporation in a merger, consolidation, or share exchange.

   (b) A reduction or increase in the stated capital of the Corporation.

   (c) The sale, lease, or transfer of all or substantially all of the property or assets of the Corporation.

   (d) The dissolution of the Corporation.

   (e) An amendment to the Corporation's articles of incorporation.

8. **Subchapter S Election.** The Corporation shall file the documents necessary to qualify the Corporation as an S corporation under Subchapter S of the Internal Revenue Code and the Shareholders agree to execute the documents necessary to obtain such qualification. The Subchapter S election shall be terminated or revoked only upon the affirmative vote or written consent of the holders of ________ percent of the issued and outstanding shares of capital stock of the Corporation, and the Shareholders shall not execute documents revoking the Subchapter S qualification unless such vote or consent is first obtained. Each shareholder agrees not to transfer his or her shares, other than as provided in this Agreement, voluntarily or by operation of law (including transfers caused by his or her death or legal incapacity), or otherwise cause the Subchapter S election to be terminated or revoked. The Corporation shall not unfairly withhold corporate earnings or distributions from any shareholder.

9. Transfer of Stock. Should any shareholder desire to sell or otherwise transfer any portion of his or her stock in the Corporation during his or her lifetime, the selling shareholder shall give written notice of such desire to the Corporation and to all other shareholders, either in person by written receipt from the deliveree or by registered mail. Thereafter, the Corporation shall have the exclusive right to purchase all (and not part) of such stock at the price and upon the terms specified in Section 11 of this Agreement for a period of thirty days. If the Corporation fails to exercise this right of purchase within such period the other shareholders, in proportion to their respective shareholdings in the Corporation, shall have a similar right for a period of thirty days. Should any shareholder fail to exercise his or her right to purchase all (and not part) of the proportionate share of the stock of the selling shareholder within such period, the remaining shareholders, in proportion to their respective holdings, shall have a right to purchase such shares for a period of ten days. Should both the Corporation and the nonselling shareholders fail to purchase all of the shares sought to be transferred by the selling shareholder, then the selling shareholder may dispose of all of such shares without restriction, except as provided in Section 8 of this agreement relating to the Subchapter S election. All notices of election to purchase the shares sought to be transferred shall be in writing and shall be delivered to the Corporation and to all other shareholders, including the selling shareholder, either in person by written receipt from the deliveree or by registered mail.

10. Purchase of Stock Upon Death of Shareholder. The Corporation shall purchase all (and not part) of the stock of any shareholder upon the death of the shareholder at the price specified in Section 11 of this Agreement. Each shareholder agrees that all of his or her stock in the Corporation shall be promptly transferred to the Corporation without restriction upon the tender by the Corporation to the holder of the shares of the price specified in Section 11. The Corporation shall apply to the ____________________ Insurance Company for a policy of insurance on the life of each shareholder in an amount adequate to purchase all of the stock of the shareholder at the price specified in Section 11. The Corporation shall pay the premiums on such policies and shall be the owner and beneficiary of the policies. The Shareholders shall cooperate in obtaining the issuance of such policies. If the value or anticipated price of the stock of any shareholder changes substantially, the Corporation shall take the steps necessary to increase or decrease the amount of insurance on the life of such shareholder. A schedule showing the amount, premiums, and insurer on all insurance purchased under this Agreement, including any substituted or additional policies whenever purchased, shall be attached to this Agreement and provided to all shareholders.

11. Valuation of Stock; Payment. The value of each share of stock shall be determined by the Shareholders as of the date of this Agreement, which value is $ ____________. The value of each share of stock shall be redetermined by the Shareholders at the end of each fiscal year of the Corporation, which value shall be established by the written consent of the holders of ________ percent of the outstanding shares. Such redetermined value, whenever made, shall be made to appear in an attachment to this Agreement, and notice of such value and the date thereof shall be delivered to each shareholder and to the Corporation within ten days after the establishment thereof.

In the event of a transfer under Sections 9 or 10 of this Agreement, the valuation last established by the Shareholders shall be the purchase price of each share of stock, except that if the Shareholders have been unable to determine a value for each share of stock under this Section for a period exceeding 24 months prior to the transfer or proposed transfer, the purchase price of each share of stock shall be the book value of the stock as determined by dividing book value of the assets of the Corporation by the total number of shares of stock that were outstanding immediately prior to the happening of the event causing the transfer or proposed transfer.

The book value of the assets of the Corporation shall be determined by an independent accountant in accordance with generally accepted accounting practices and shall be made as of the end of the last accounting period of the Corporation prior to the happening of the event causing the transfer or proposed transfer, except that the value of inventories, supplies, and similar tangible assets, and of accounts receivable in the ordinary course of business, shall be as of the date of the happening of the event causing the transfer or proposed transfer. The good will of the Corporation shall not be treated as an asset unless all Shareholders agree in writing to the value thereof for purposes of book value. In the event of a transfer under Section 9 of this Agreement, the event giving rise to the transfer or proposed transfer shall be the delivery of notice of desire to sell or transfer by the selling shareholder.

In the event of a transfer under Section 9 of this Agreement, the purchase price of the stock shall be paid in ________ installments, payable as follows: ____.

Interest at the rate of ________ percent per annum shall be paid on the unpaid portion of the purchase price. Security in the form of ________________ shall be posted by the purchasers to secure the payment of the unpaid installments.

In the event of a transfer under Section 10 of this Agreement, the entire purchase price shall be paid within ____________ days of the death of the shareholder.

12. Endorsements on Stock Certificates. A notice of all transfer and other restrictions imposed by this Agreement shall appear on all certificates representing shares of stock issued by the Corporation.

13. Corporate Deadlock. Should the Shareholders or the Board of Directors of the Corporation become deadlocked and unable to function and remain so deadlocked for a period of ____________ consecutive months, any shareholder or group of shareholders may offer, in writing, to purchase the shares of all other shareholders at the price specified in Section 11 of this Agreement. Should ________ percent or more of the other shareholders refuse or fail to accept such offer within 30 days after delivery thereof to them, the offering shareholder or shareholders shall be entitled to dissolve the Corporation pursuant to the Corporation Laws of the State of ________________, immediately thereafter, notwithstanding the provisions of Section 7 of this Agreement.

14. **Amendment.** This Agreement may be amended from time to time only upon the written consent of the holders of ________ percent of issued and outstanding shares of capital stock of the Corporation.

15. **Binding Effect.** This Agreement shall be binding on the Corporation and all of the Shareholders and their respective assignees, heirs, personal representatives, and successors in interest.

IN WITNESS WHEREOF, the parties have executed this Agreement as of the day and year first above written.

The ______________________________ Corporation ______________________________
Name, Shareholder

by ______________________________
President

____
Name, Shareholder

____
Name, Shareholder

EXHIBIT 5-D

PROXY

The undersigned shareholder hereby appoints ________________________ as the shareholder's general proxy to cast the votes of the shareholder at all general, special, or adjourned meetings of the shareholders of the ________________________ Corporation, a corporation organized under the laws of the State of ________________, from time to time and from year to year, when the undersigned is not present at any such meeting or meetings, or, if present, chooses not to vote in person. This proxy shall be effective for __________ years from the date hereof unless sooner revoked by written notice given to the Secretary of the Corporation.

Dated ______________________________

____
Name, Shareholder

MINUTES OF ORGANIZATIONAL MEETING

OF ______________________________ CORPORATION

The organizational meeting of ________________________, a corporation organized under the laws of the State of ________________, was held by the initial board of directors on ________________, at ____________.

The following directors were present at the meeting: ____.

Also present at the meeting were: ____.

Upon motions duly made and unanimously passed, ____________________ was chosen as the Chairman of the Board of Directors, and ____________________ was chosen as Secretary of the meeting.

The first order of business was the nomination and election of the officers of the Corporation and the fixing of their compensation. The following persons were nominated to the following offices of the Corporation at the following salaries:

Name	Office	Salary

The nomination of the foregoing slate of officers was seconded and they were unanimously elected as the officers of the Corporation at the salaries above listed.

It was reported that Articles of Incorporation for the Corporation had been filed in the office of the Secretary of State of the State of ________________, and that the effective date of the incorporation was ________________. The Secretary was instructed to insert a duplicate original copy of the Articles of Incorporation in the official records of the Corporation.

The Secretary presented a proposed set of bylaws for the corporation that had been prepared by ________________. After discussion and on motion duly made and unanimously adopted, it was RESOLVED that the proposed bylaws be and are adopted as the Bylaws of the Corporation. The Secretary was instructed to insert a copy of the Bylaws in the official records of the Corporation.

It was recognized that ________________________, Attorney at Law, would not be expected to devote his full time to the affairs of the Corporation and that he would be entitled to submit to the Corporation statements for legal services performed from time to time at the request of the Corporation at the rate of $ ________ per hour.

The Secretary presented a form of seal for the Corporation. After discussion and upon motion duly made and unanimously adopted, it was RESOLVED, that the seal, an impression of which is affixed to these minutes, be and is adopted as the official seal of the Corporation.

The Secretary presented a form of stock certificate for use by the Corporation. After discussion and upon motion duly made, and unanimously adopted, it was RESOLVED, that the form of certificate presented at the meeting be and is approved as the form of stock certificate to be used by the Corporation in the issuance of its common stock. It was further RESOLVED that the corporation shall not issue uncertified shares of its common stock.

Upon motion duly made and unanimously adopted, it was RESOLVED that the Corporation elect to be taxed under the provisions of Subchapter S of the Internal Revenue Code. The officers of the Corporation were directed to prepare, execute, and file with the Internal Revenue Service a form 2553 and to otherwise comply with the provisions of Subchapter S so as to qualify the Corporation to be taxed as a small business corporation thereunder.

Upon motion duly made and unanimously adopted, it was RESOLVED that the common stock of the Corporation be issued to the following persons, in the following amounts, for the following consideration, the value of which was determined by the board of directors to be the value shown below.

Name	No. of Shares	Form of Consideration	Value of Consideration

The officers of the Corporation were directed to carry out this resolution by issuing the stock described above upon the receipt by the Corporation of the designated consideration. Upon motion duly made and unanimously adopted, it was further RESOLVED that the consideration received by the Corporation for the issuance of the stock described above be allocated on the books of the Corporation as follows: $ ____________ to capital; $ ____________ to surplus.

Upon motion duly made and unanimously adopted, it was RESOLVED that all certificates representing shares of common stock of the Corporation shall contain the following notice:

> "The shares of stock represented by this certificate are subject to transfer and other restrictions contained in the Articles of Incorporation, the Bylaws, and a Shareholders' Agreement dated ________________, a copy of each of which is filed in the registered office of the corporation. No transfer of the shares represented by this certificate shall be valid unless the requirements of those documents are first complied with to the satisfaction of the Corporation."

Upon motion duly made and unanimously adopted, it was RESOLVED that ________________ be the bank of the Corporation, and that the officers of the Corporation obtain the necessary documents so as to permit the Corporation to transact business and deposit and withdraw funds with the bank.

Upon motion duly made and unanimously adopted, it was RESOLVED that the fiscal year of the Corporation shall begin on ______________ and shall end on ______________.

The Treasurer reported that fees and expenses in the amount of $ __________ were incurred in the process of incorporating and organizing the Corporation. Upon motion duly made and unanimously adopted, it was RESOLVED that the Treasurer be authorized and directed to pay these fees and expenses and that these expenditures be amortized by the Corporation over a period of 60 months in accordance with Section 248 of the Internal Revenue Code.

Upon motion duly made and unanimously adopted, it was RESOLVED that the Corporation ratify and adopt all previous resolutions, actions, and proceedings of the incorporators of the Corporation made and entered into for or on behalf of the Corporation, including the filing of the Articles of Incorporation of the Corporation.

Upon motion duly made and unanimously adopted, it was RESOLVED that an office of the Corporation be established and maintained at ________________, that until further action by the Board of Directors, the meetings of the Board of Directors and shareholders shall be held at such office, and that regular meetings of the Board of Directors be held without notice at the Corporation's office at ________ p.m. on the ________ day of each month.

Upon motion duly made and unanimously adopted, it was RESOLVED that the Officers of the Corporation be and are authorized and directed to qualify the Corporation as a foreign corporation authorized to transact business in the States of ________________, and in connection therewith to appoint all necessary agents or attorneys for service of process and to take all other appropriate action in connection with such qualification.

Upon motion duly made and unanimously adopted, it was RESOLVED that the Corporation shall employ the following persons for the following positions for the periods and for the compensation indicated below:

Name	Position	Period of Employment	Compensation

Upon motion duly made and unanimously adopted, it was further RESOLVED that the Corporation enter into an employment contract with ________________ upon the terms above specified, and that the President and Secretary of the Corporation shall execute the contract on behalf of the Corporation. The Secretary was directed to file a copy of the employment contract with the minutes of this meeting.

There being no further business to come before the meeting, upon motion duly made and unanimously adopted, the meeting was adjourned.

____
Secretary

Approved: ________________________
Director

____
Director

____
Director

BYLAWS OF

______________________ CORPORATION

ARTICLE 1

Corporate Identification

1.01. **Name.** The corporation shall transact business under the name of ______________________.

1.02. **Corporate Offices.** The address of the principal office of the corporation shall be ______________________. The corporation shall maintain offices at ______________________.

1.03. **Seal.** The Board of Directors shall provide for a corporate seal, which shall be circular in form and shall have inscribed thereon the name of the corporation, the state of incorporation, and the words "Corporate Seal."

1.04. **Fiscal Year.** The fiscal year of the corporation shall begin on the ________ day of ____________, and shall end on the ________ day of ____________.

ARTICLE 2

Shareholders

2.01. **Place of Meetings.** Meetings of the shareholders of the corporation shall be held at the principal office of the corporation, unless all shareholders entitled to vote agree in writing to meet elsewhere.

2.02. **Annual Meetings.** The annual meeting of the shareholders shall be held at __________ o'clock on the ______________ day of ______________________ each year. If this day is a legal holiday, then the meeting shall be held on the first following day that is not a legal holiday. A failure to hold the annual meeting shall not impair the ability of the corporation to act or transact business.

2.03. **Special Meetings.** Special meetings of the shareholders may be called by the President or by the Board of Directors, and shall be called by the President upon the signed written request of the holders of ten percent or more of the outstanding shares of the corporation entitled to vote at the meeting. Only business within the purpose or purposes described in the notice of the meeting may be conducted at a special meeting of the shareholders.

2.04. **Action Without Meeting.** Any action required or permitted to be taken at a meeting of the shareholders, may be taken without a meeting if a consent, in writing, setting forth the action so taken is signed by all of the shareholders who would have been entitled to vote on the action had a meeting been held.

2.05. **Notice of Meetings.** Written notice stating the place, day, and hour of the meeting, and, in the case of a special meeting, the purpose or purposes for which the meeting is called, shall be delivered or mailed to each shareholder who is entitled to vote at the meeting with the written or printed signature of the President and Secretary subscribed thereto, not less than ten nor more than sixty days before the date of the meeting. A waiver of the notice of any meeting, in writing, signed by the person entitled to the notice, whether before, at, or after the time stated therein, shall be deemed equivalent of such notice. Attendance by a shareholder, without objection to the notice, whether in person or by proxy, at a shareholders' meeting shall constitute a waiver of notice of the meeting.

2.06. **Closing of Transfer Books.** For the purposes of determining the shareholders who are entitled to notice of or to vote at a meeting of shareholders or an adjournment thereof, or the shareholders who are entitled to receive payment of any dividend, or in order to make a determination of shareholders for any other proper purpose, the Board of Directors of the corporation may provide that the stock transfer books shall be closed for a stated period not to exceed fifty days. If the stock transfer book shall be closed for the purpose of determining shareholders entitled to notice of or to vote at a meeting of shareholders, such books shall be closed for at least ten days immediately preceding such meeting. In lieu of closing the stock transfer books, the Board of Directors may fix in advance a date as the record date for any such determination of shareholders, such date in any case to be not more than fifty days and, in the case of a meeting of shareholders, not less than ten days prior to the date on which the particular action requiring such determination of shareholders, is to be taken. If the stock transfer books are not closed and no record date is fixed for the determination of stockholders entitled to notice of or to vote at a meeting of shareholders, or of shareholders entitled to receive payment of a dividend, the date on which notice of the meeting is mailed or the date on which the resolution the Board of Directors declaring such dividend is adopted, as the case may be, shall be the record date for such determination of shareholders. When a determination of shareholders entitled to vote at any meeting of shareholders has been made as provided in this section, such determination shall apply to any adjournment thereof except where the determination has been made through the closing of the stock transfer books and the stated period of closing has expired.

2.07. **Voting Lists.** The officer or agent having charge of the stock transfer books for shares of the corporation shall make, at least ten days before each meeting of shareholders, a complete list of the shareholders entitled to vote at such meeting, or any adjournment thereof, arranged in alphabetical order with the address of, and the number of shares held by each shareholder, which list, for the period between its compilation and the meeting for which it was compiled, shall be kept on file at the registered office of the corporation and shall be subject to inspection by any shareholder at any time during normal business hours. Such list shall also be produced and kept open at the time and place of the meeting and shall be subject to inspection by any shareholder during the meeting. The original stock transfer book shall be prima facie evidence of the shareholders entitled to examine such list or transfer books or to vote at any meeting of shareholders.

2.08. **Quorum and Voting.** A majority of the outstanding shares of the corporation entitled to vote, when represented in person or by proxy, shall constitute a quorum at a meeting of shareholders. If less than a majority of the outstanding shares are represented at a meeting, a majority of the shares so represented may adjourn the meeting from time to time (but not to exceed sixty days) without further notice. At such adjourned meeting at which a quorum shall be present or represented, any business may be transacted which might have been transacted at the meeting as originally scheduled. The shareholders present at a duly organized meeting may continue to transact business until adjournment, notwithstanding the withdrawal of shareholders sufficient to leave less than a quorum. Unless a greater vote on a particular matter is required by law, by the Articles of Incorporation, or by these Bylaws, a majority vote of the shares present and entitled to vote shall carry any action proposed or voted on at a shareholders' meeting.

2.09. **Proxies.** At all meetings of shareholders, a shareholder may vote by proxy executed in writing by the shareholder or by the shareholder's authorized attorney in fact. Such proxy may be filed with the Secretary of the corporation before or at the time of the meeting. No proxy shall be valid after eleven months from the date of its execution, unless otherwise provided in the proxy.

2.10. **Voting of Shares by Certain Holders.** Shares standing in the name of another corporation may be voted by such officer, agent, or proxy as the bylaws of such corporation may prescribe, or, in the absence of such provisions, as the Board of Directors of such corporation may determine, provided, however, that no shares held by another corporation, the election of whose directors is controlled by this corporation, shall be entitled to vote.

Shares held by an administrator, executor, guardian, or conservator may be voted by such person, either in person or by proxy, without a transfer of such shares into such person's name. Shares standing in the name of a trustee may be voted by the trustee, either in person or by proxy, but a trustee shall not be entitled to vote shares so held without a transfer of such shares into the trustee's name.

Shares standing in the name of a receiver may be voted by the receiver, and shares held by or under the control of a receiver may be voted by the receiver without the transfer thereof into the receiver's name if the authority to do so is contained in an appropriate order of the court by whom the receiver was appointed.

A shareholder whose shares are pledged shall be entitled to vote such shares until the shares have been transferred into the name of the pledgee, and thereafter the pledgee shall be entitled to vote the shares so transferred.

Shares of its own stock belonging to the corporation or held by it in a fiduciary capacity shall not be voted, directly or indirectly, at any meeting, and shall not be counted in determining the total number of outstanding shares at any given time.

ARTICLE 3

Board of Directors

3.01. **General Powers.** The business and affairs of the corporation shall be managed by its Board of Directors, except as otherwise provided by law or by the Articles of Incorporation.

3.02. **Number, Tenure, and Qualifications.** The number of directors of the corporation shall be ________. The number of directors may be changed only as provided in the Articles of Incorporation. Each director shall hold office until the next annual meeting of the shareholders and until his or her successor shall have been elected and qualified. Directors need not be residents of any particular state or shareholders of the corporation.

3.03. **Regular Meetings.** A meeting of the Board of Directors shall be held without notice other than this provision immediately after, and at the same place as, the annual meeting of shareholders. The Board of Directors may provide, by resolution, the time and place for the holding of regular meetings without other notice than such resolution.

3.04. Special Meetings; Notice. Special meetings of the Board of Directors may be called by or at the request of the President or any two directors. The person or persons authorized to call special meetings of the Board of Directors may fix any place, wherever located, as the place for holding a special meeting of the Board of Directors called by them. Written notice of a special meeting shall be given to each director at least two days prior to a special meeting, except that if the written notice is mailed to a director or is given by telegram at least four days prior notice must be given, which notice shall be deemed given when mailed or telegraphed. Any director may waive notice of any meeting. The attendance of a director at a meeting shall constitute a waiver of notice of such meeting, except where a director attends a meeting for the express purpose of objecting to the transaction of any business because the meeting is not lawfully called or convened. Neither the business to be transacted nor the purpose of any regular or special meeting of the Board of Directors need be specified in the notice or waiver of notice of such meeting.

3.05. Action Without Meeting. Any action required or permitted to be taken at any meeting of the Board of Directors, or any committee thereof, may be taken without a meeting if a written consent setting forth the action so taken is signed by all of the directors that would have been entitled to vote on the action had a meeting been held.

3.06. Quorum. A majority of the Board of Directors shall constitute a quorum for the transaction of business at any meeting of the Board of Directors, but if less than such majority be present at a meeting, a majority of the directors present may adjourn the meeting from time to time without further notice. The directors present at a meeting may continue to transact business until adjournment not withstanding the withdrawal of directors sufficient to leave less than a quorum.

3.07. Voting Requirements. Except as otherwise provided by law, in the Articles of Incorporation, or in these Bylaws, a majority vote of the directors present at a meeting at which a quorum is present shall be required for an act or resolution under consideration to constitute an act or resolution of the Board of Directors.

3.08. Vacancies. Any vacancy occurring in the Board of Directors shall be filled by an election held by the shareholders who elected the director whose death or departure created the vacancy. A director elected to fill a vacancy shall be elected for the unexpired term of the director's predecessor in office. Any directorship to be filled by reason of an increase in the number of directors shall be filled by election at an annual meeting of shareholders or at a special meeting of shareholders called for that purpose. A director chosen to fill a vacancy resulting from an increase in the number of directors shall hold office until the director's successor shall have been elected and qualified.

3.09. Compensation. By resolution of the Board of Directors the directors may be paid their expenses, if any, for attendance at any meeting of the Board of Directors, and, if such compensation is approved by a majority vote of the shareholders entitled to vote, may be paid a fixed sum for attendance at any meeting of the Board of Directors or a stated salary as director. No payment shall preclude any director from serving the corporation in any other capacity and receiving compensation therefor.

3.10. Presumption of Assent. A director of the corporation who is present at a meeting of the Board of Directors at which action on any corporate matter is taken shall be presumed to have assented to the action taken unless the dissent of the director shall be entered in the minutes of the meeting or unless the director shall file a written dissent to such action before adjournment thereof or shall forward such dissent by registered mail to the Secretary of the corporation immediately after the adjournment of the meeting. Such right to dissent shall not apply to a director who voted in favor of the action dissented to.

3.11. Removal of Directors. At a special meeting of the shareholders called expressly for that purpose, Directors may be removed in the manner provided in this section. One or more directors or the entire Board of Directors may be removed, with or without cause, by a vote of the holders of a majority of the shares then entitled to vote at an election of directors. No director may be removed if the votes cast against a director's removal would be sufficient to elect the director if cumulatively voted at an election of the entire Board of Directors. A director shall be entitled to receive notice of and a hearing with respect to his or her removal for cause.

3.12. Standards of Conduct. A director shall discharge his or her duties as a director, including his or her duties as a member of a committee, in good faith, with the care an ordinarily prudent person in a like position would exercise under similar circumstances; and in a manner that he or she reasonably believes to be in the best interests of the corporation.

In discharging his or her duties a director is entitled to rely on information, opinions, reports, or statements, including financial statements and other financial data, if prepared or presented by:

(1) one or more officers or employees of the corporation whom the director reasonably believes to be reliable and competent in the matters presented;

(2) legal counsel, public accountants, or other persons as to matters the director reasonably believes are within the person's professional or expert competence; or

(3) a committee of the board of directors of which the director is not a member if the director reasonably believes the committee merits confidence.

A director is not acting in good faith if the director has knowledge concerning the matter in question that makes otherwise permissible reliance unwarranted.

A director is not liable for any action taken as a director, or any failure to take any action, if he or she performed the duties of office in compliance with this section.

ARTICLE 4

Officers

4.01. **Number, Election and Tenure.** The officers of the corporation shall be a President, a Vice President, a Secretary, and a Treasurer, each of whom shall be elected by the Board of Directors. Such other officers and assistant officers as may be deemed necessary may be elected or appointed by the Board of Directors. All officers of the corporation shall serve at the pleasure of the Board of Directors for the compensation fixed under Section 4.09 of these Bylaws. Any two or more offices may be held by the same person, except as otherwise provided by law.

4.02. **Removal.** Any officer or agent elected or appointed by the Board of Directors may be removed, with or without cause, by the Board of Directors whenever in its judgment the best interests of the corporation would be served thereby, but such removal shall be without prejudice to the contract rights, if any, of the person so removed.

4.03. **Vacancies.** Whenever a vacancy shall occur in any office by reason of death, resignation, increase in number of offices of the corporation, or otherwise, the vacancy shall be filled by the Board of Directors, and the officer so elected shall hold office as provided in Section 4.01 of these Bylaws.

4.04. **President.** The President shall be the principal executive officer of the corporation, and, subject to the control of the Board of Directors, shall have general control of the business, affairs, and property of the corporation, and control over its agents, officers, and employees. The President shall, when present, preside at all meetings of the shareholders and of the Board of Directors, and shall perform such other duties and exercise such other powers as from time to time may be assigned to the President by these Bylaws or by the Board of Directors.

4.05. **Vice President.** The Vice President shall perform all duties incumbent upon the President during the absence or disability of the President, and shall perform such other duties as from time to time may be assigned to the Vice President by these Bylaws or by the Board of Directors.

4.06. **The Secretary.** The Secretary shall: (a) keep the minutes of the shareholders' meetings and of the Board of Directors' meetings in one or more books provided for that purpose; (b) see that all notices are duly given in accordance with the provisions of these bylaws as required by law; (c) be the custodian of the corporate records and of the seal of the corporation and see that the seal of the corporation is affixed to all documents, the execution of which on behalf of the corporation under its seal, is duly authorized; (d) keep a register of the address of each shareholder, which shall be furnished to the secretary by such shareholder; (e) sign with the President, or the Vice President, certificates for shares of the corporation, the issuance of which shall have been authorized by a resolution of the Board of Directors; (f) have general charge of the stock transfer books of the corporation; and (g) perform all duties incident to the office of secretary and such other duties as from time to time may be assigned to the Secretary by the President or the Board of Directors.

4.07. **The Treasurer.** If required by the Board of Directors, the Treasurer shall give a bond for the faithful discharge of his or her duties in such sum and with such surety or sureties as the Board of Directors shall determine. The Treasurer shall: (a) have charge and custody of and be responsible for all funds and securities of the corporation; (b) receive and give receipts for monies due and payable to the corporation from any source whatsoever; (c) deposit all monies received in the name of the corporation in the banks or other depositories as shall be selected in accordance with the provisions of Article 5 of these Bylaws; and (d) perform the duties as from time to time may be assigned to the Treasurer by the President or the Board of Directors.

4.08. **Assistant Secretaries and Treasurers.** One or more Assistant Secretaries or Assistant Treasurers may be appointed by the Board of Directors. Such persons shall have such duties as from time to time may be assigned to them by the Board of Directors, the President, or the Secretary or Treasurer, as the case may be.

4.09. **Compensation.** The compensation of the officers shall be fixed or approved from time to time by the Board of Directors and no officer shall be prevented from receiving such compensation by reason of the fact that the officer is also a director of the corporation.

ARTICLE 5

Contracts, Loans, Checks, Deposits, and Official Books and Records

5.01. **Contracts.** The Board of Directors may authorize any officer or agent to enter into any contract or execute and deliver any instrument in the name of and on behalf of the corporation, and such authority may be general or confined to specific matters.

5.02. **Loans.** No loans shall be contracted on behalf of the corporation and no evidence of indebtedness shall be issued in its name unless authorized by a resolution of the Board of Directors. The Board of Directors shall have the following power with respect to the lending of funds:

(a). **Loans of Funds, Generally.** To lend money in furtherance of any of the purposes of the Corporation; to invest and reinvest the funds of the Corporation from time to time; and to take and hold any property as security for the payment of funds so loaned or invested.

(b). **Loans to Employees and Directors.** If approved by the holders of a majority of the voting shares, to lend money and use its credit to assist any employee or director of the Corporation, if the Board of Directors determines that such loan or assistance may benefit the Corporation.

5.03. **Checks, Drafts, Etc.** All checks, drafts, or other orders for the payment of money, notes, or other evidence of indebtedness issued in the name of the corporation shall be signed by such officer or agent of the corporation and in such manner as shall from time to time be determined by a resolution of the Board of Directors.

5.04. **Deposits.** All funds of the corporation not otherwise employed shall be deposited from time to time to the credit of the corporation in such banks or other depositories as the Board of Directors may by resolution select.

5.05. **Official Books and Records.** The official books and records of the corporation shall consist of the minute book, the stock book, the stock transfer book, and the books and records of account. The Secretary shall be responsible for their upkeep and safekeeping. Any shareholder, either in person or by representative, shall have the right to inspect and make copies or extracts of the official books and records at any reasonable time for any lawful purpose.

ARTICLE 6

Capital Stock

6.01. **Certificates for Shares.** Certificates representing shares of the corporation shall be in such form as shall be determined by the Board of Directors. Such certificates shall be signed by the President or the Vice President and by the Secretary or an Assistant Secretary. All certificates for shares shall be consecutively numbered or otherwise identified. The name and address of the person to whom the shares represented thereby are issued, with the number of shares and the date of issue, shall be entered on the stock transfer books of the corporation. All certificates surrendered to the corporation for transfer shall be cancelled and no new certificates shall be issued until the former certificate for a like number of shares shall have been surrendered and cancelled, except that in case of a lost, destroyed, or mutilated certificate a new one may be issued therefor upon such terms and indemnity to the corporation as the Board of Directors may prescribe.

6.02. **Consideration for Shares.** The consideration for the issuance of shares may be paid, in whole or in part, in money, in other property, tangible or intangible, or in labor or services actually performed for the Corporation. When payment of the consideration for which shares are to be issued shall have been received by the Corporation, such shares shall be deemed to be fully paid and nonassessable. Neither promissory notes nor future services shall constitute payment or part payment for the issuance of shares of the Corporation. In the absence of fraud in the transaction, the judgment of the Board of Directors as to the value of the consideration received for shares shall be conclusive. No certificate shall be issued for any share until the share is fully paid.

6.03. **Issuance of Shares.** Shares of capital stock of the corporation shall not be issued except on a majority vote of the Board of Directors. The vote of each director shall appear in the written minutes of each Board of Directors' meeting in which the issuance of shares was approved.

6.04. **Dividends.** The holders of the capital stock of the Corporation shall be entitled to receive, when and as declared by the Board of Directors, solely out of unreserved and unrestricted earned surplus, dividends payable either in cash, in property, or in shares of capital stock. No dividends shall be paid upon the capital stock in any medium if the source out of which it is proposed to pay the dividend is due to or arises from unrealized appreciation in value or from a revaluation of assets, or if the Corporation is, or is thereby rendered, incapable of paying its debts as they become due in the usual course of its business.

6.05. **Uncertified Shares.** Shares of the capital stock of the Corporation shall not be issued without a certificate.

ARTICLE 7

Amendments

7.01. **Amendment.** These Bylaws may be amended or repealed, and new bylaws may be adopted, by the holders of a majority of the voting shares at any annual or special meeting or by a majority vote of the Board of Directors at any regular or special meeting, except that the shareholders in amending or repealing a particular bylaw may provide that the Board of Directors may not amend or repeal that bylaw.

ARTICLES OF INCORPORATION

OF

______________________ CORPORATION

The undersigned persons, acting as the incorporators of a corporation organized under the Corporation Laws of the State of ________________, adopt the following Articles of Incorporation:

ARTICLE 1

Name

1.01. Name. The name of the Corporation is ____________________.

ARTICLE 2

Registered Office and Agent

2.01. Registered Office. The street address of the initial registered office of the Corporation is ____________________.

2.02. Registered Agent. The name of the initial registered agent of the Corporation at the above office is ______________.

ARTICLE 3

Capital Stock

3.01. Number of Authorized Shares and Par Value. The aggregate number of shares that the Corporation shall have authority to issue is __________ shares of common stock, which stock shall be without par value.

3.02. Preemptive Rights of Shareholders. The Corporation elects to have preemptive rights. The shareholders of the corporation shall have a preemptive right to purchase, at equitable prices, terms, and conditions fixed by the Board of Directors, the shares of capital stock of the Corporation or securities convertible into or carrying options or warrants to purchase such shares, as may be issued from time to time, after the issuance of the first __________ shares of capital stock. This preemptive right shall apply to all shares issued by the Corporation after the first __________ shares, including shares presently or subsequently authorized, shares held in the treasury of the Corporation, and shares issued for services or property. Shares issued to employees of the Corporation under a plan approved by the holders of ________ percent of the issued and outstanding voting shares of the Corporation shall not be subject to preemptive rights.

3.03. Cumulative Voting. All shareholders are entitled to cumulate their votes for directors. At each election for directors, every shareholder shall have the right to vote, in person or by proxy, the number of shares held by the shareholder for as many persons as there are directors to be elected and for whose election the shareholder has the right to vote, or to cumulate such votes by giving one candidate as many votes as there are directors to be elected multiplied by the number of shares held by the shareholder, or by distributing the votes on the same principle among any number of candidates.

3.04. Classes of Stock. The capital stock of the Corporation shall not be divided into classes.

3.05. Issuance of Stock. Shares of capital stock of the corporation shall not be issued except on the affirmative vote or written consent of at least ________ percent of the directors, which vote or consent shall appear in the written minutes of the Board of Directors' meeting in which the issuance was authorized.

3.06. Restriction on Transfer of Stock. No shareholder shall pledge, mortgage, sell, or otherwise transfer all or any portion of the shareholder's stock unless it shall first be offered to the corporation at a price no greater than a bona fide offer by any third person, which offer shall be open to the corporation for a period of thirty days. In the event that any of the said stock is not purchased by the corporation during such period, it shall be offered to the remaining shareholders of the same class of stock in the same proportion as their respective stock interests in said class of stock, for a like price and for a similar period of time. Should any of the remaining shareholders decline to purchase his or her proportionate share of the stock during that period, that stock shall be offered to the then remaining shareholders for a like price and for a similar period of time. In the event that any of said stock is not purchased by the corporation or the shareholders, the remaining stock may then be sold by the shareholder without restriction. Notice of this restriction shall appear on all stock certificates issued by the corporation.

ARTICLE 4

Incorporators

4.01. The name and address of each incorporator of the Corporation is:

ARTICLE 5

Directors

5.01. **Number of Directors.** The Board of Directors of the Corporation shall consist of ____________ members, who need not be residents of any particular state or shareholders of the Corporation. The number of directors may be increased or decreased from time to time by amendment of this Section of these Articles of Incorporation, but no decrease shall have the effect of shortening the term of any incumbent director. The affirmative vote of the holders of ________ percent of the issued and outstanding voting shares of the Corporation shall be required to amend this Section of these Articles of Incorporation.

5.02. **Names and Addresses of Initial Directors.** The names and addresses of the persons who are to serve as the initial Board of Directors of the Corporation until the first annual meeting of shareholders and until their successors shall have been elected and qualified, are:

5.03. **Transactions with Directors.** Any contract or other transaction between the Corporation and a director, or between the Corporation and any firm, organization or corporation of which a director is a member, employee, shareholder, director, or officer, or in which the director has an interest, shall be valid for all purposes, if the fact of such interest was disclosed or known to the Board of Directors and if the Board of Directors authorizes or ratifies the contract or transaction or if the contract or transaction was disclosed to and ratified by the shareholders, or if the contract or transaction is fair to the corporation. This section shall not be construed to invalidate any contract or other transaction that would otherwise be valid under applicable law.

5.04. **Indemnification.** The corporation, acting through its Board of Directors, shall have the authority to indemnify or advance expenses to any director, officer, employee, or agent of the corporation, when the said director, officer, employee, or agent has incurred expenses or liabilities (including attorneys' fees), which, in the absolute discretion of the Board of Directors, are considered to have been incurred on behalf of the Corporation. The rights set forth in this Section shall be in addition to any rights for indemnification provided by applicable law.

The Corporation may purchase and maintain insurance on behalf of any person who is or was a director, officer, employee, or agent of the Corporation, or who is or was serving at the request of the Corporation as a director, officer, employee, or agent of another corporation, partnership, joint venture, trust, or other enterprise against any liability asserted against and incurred by that person in any such capacity or arising out of that person's status as such, whether or not the Corporation could indemnify that person against such liability under the provisions of this Section.

5.05. **Removal of Directors.** One or more of the directors or the entire Board of Directors may be removed, with or without cause, by a vote of the holders of a majority of the shares then entitled to vote for the election of directors. No director may be removed if the votes cast against the director's removal would be sufficient to elect the director if cumulatively voted at an election of the entire Board of Directors. A director shall be entitled to receive notice of, and a hearing with respect to, his or her removal for cause.

ARTICLE 6

Purposes, Foreign Business, and Duration

6.01. **Purposes.** The purpose or purposes for which the Corporation is organized are to engage in the business of ___________________, and to do everything necessary, proper, advisable, or convenient for the accomplishment of the foregoing purposes, and to do all things incidental to them or connected with them that are not forbidden by law or by these Articles of Incorporation.

6.02. **Conducting Business in Other Jurisdictions.** The Corporation may conduct business and otherwise carry out its purposes and exercise its powers in any state, territory, district, or possession of the United States, or in any foreign country, to the full extent permitted by the laws of the state, territory, district, or possession of the United States, or by the foreign country; and it may limit its purpose or purposes in any state, territory, district, or possession of the United States, or foreign country.

6.03. **Period of Duration.** The period of duration of the Corporation shall be ___________________ .

ARTICLE 7

Amendment and Fundamental Changes

7.01. **Amendment.** These Articles of Incorporation may be amended only by the written consent or affirmative vote of the holders of a majority of the issued and outstanding voting shares, except that any section of these Articles of Incorporation that provide for a greater vote of the shareholders may be amended only upon the written consent or affirmative vote of the shareholders provided for in that section.

7.02. **Fundamental Changes.** The affirmative vote or written consent of the holders of ________ percent of the issued and outstanding voting shares of the Corporation shall be necessary for the following corporate acts:

(a) The adoption by the Corporation of a plan of merger, consolidation, or share exchange.

(b) The sale, lease, exchange, or transfer by the Corporation of all or substantially all of its property or assets other than in the regular course of business.

(c) The voluntary dissolution of the Corporation by its Board of Directors and shareholders.

7.03. **Bylaws.** The initial Bylaws shall be adopted by the Board of Directors. The power to alter, amend, or repeal the Bylaws or to adopt new Bylaws shall be vested in the shareholders and the Board of Directors, except that the shareholders in amending or repealing a particular bylaw may provide that the Board of Directors may not amend or repeal that bylaw. The Bylaws may contain any provision for the regulation and management of the affairs of the Corporation that is not inconsistent with the law or these Articles of Incorporation.

IN WITNESS WHEREOF, the incorporators, by their signatures below, affirm under penalty of perjury the truth of the matters set forth above.

______________________________	______________________________
Name, Incorporator	Name, Incorporator

NOTICE OF SPECIAL MEETING OF SHAREHOLDERS

TO: All Shareholders of ________________________ Corporation.

You and each of you are hereby notified that, pursuant to Article ________, Section ________ of the Bylaws, a special meeting of the shareholders of ________________________ Corporation will be held at ________ o'clock on ________________________ at the office of the Corporation located at ________________________, for the purpose of voting on proposed amendments to the Articles of Incorporation of the Corporation. Amendments have been proposed and recommended by the Board of Directors to Article ________ of the Articles of Incorporation. A copy of the proposed amendments is attached to this notice.

This notice was deposited, postage prepaid, in the United States mail on ____________________.

____
Secretary

NOTICE OF SPECIAL MEETING OF THE

BOARD OF DIRECTORS OF ____________________

TO: All Directors of ________________________ Corporation.

You and each of you are hereby notified that, pursuant to Article ________, Section ________ of the Bylaws, a special meeting of the Board of Directors of ________________________ Corporation will be held on ________________________ at ________ o'clock at the office of the Corporation located at ________________________, for the purpose of electing a president of the Corporation and the transaction of any other lawful business.

This notice was deposited, postage prepaid, in the United States mail on ____________________.

____
Secretary

WAIVER OF NOTICE OF ORGANIZATIONAL MEETING OF DIRECTORS

The undersigned, constituting all of the Directors of ________________________ Corporation, do hereby severally waive notice of the time and place of the organizational meeting of the Board of Directors of ________________________ Corporation, and consent to the holding of the meeting at ________________________, on ____________________ at ________ o'clock, and further consent to the transaction of any and all business that may come before the meeting.

Dated ____________________

____
Director

____
Director

____
Director

MEMORANDUM OF SHAREHOLDER ACTION WITHOUT MEETING

The undersigned, constituting all of the shareholders of the Speculation Real Estate Company, hereby unanimously consent to the following action of the shareholders taken in lieu of a meeting of the shareholders:

RESOLVED that the corporation shall sell its landscaping business, complete with all fixtures, accounts, and personal and real property of any nature, tangible and intangible, to Landscapes, Inc., a California Corporation, on or before January 10, 1993, for the price of $30,500, payable in three equal installments on January 10, 1993, April 1, 1993, and June 1, 1993.

This memorandum is prepared and the above action is approved pursuant to Section 2.04 of the Bylaws, and pursuant to section 603 of the California Corporation Code.

IN WITNESS WHEREOF, the shareholders have signed this memorandum on the dates indicated below, effective this 8th day of January, 1993.

______________	__________	______________	__________
Shareholder	Date	Shareholder	Date
______________	__________	______________	__________
Shareholder	Date	Shareholder	Date

MEMORANDUM OF BOARD OF DIRECTOR ACTION WITHOUT A MEETING

Pursuant to Section 3.04 of the Bylaws and Section 1701.54 of the Ohio General Corporation Code, the following action is taken and approved by the Board of Directors of the Jones Hardware Corporation by unanimous written consent as if a meeting had been properly called and held and all the directors were present at the meeting and voted in favor of such action:

RESOLVED that the Corporation issue one thousand (1,000) shares of its common stock to John J. Jones upon the receipt from Mr. Jones of the sum of ten thousand dollars ($10,000).

IN WITNESS WHEREOF, the following Directors, constituting the entire Board of Directors of the Jones Hardware Corporation, have signed this memorandum on the dates indicated below, effective this 10th day of January, 1993.

______________	__________	______________	__________
Director	Date	Director	Date
______________	__________	______________	__________
Director	Date	Director	Date

INCORPORATED UNDER THE LAWS OF

THE STATE OF COLORADO

No. 26

Shares 200

THE SMITH ENTERPRISE CORPORATION

Capital Stock No Par Value

This Certifies that SAMUEL S. SMITH is the owner of Two Hundred (200) Shares of the Capital Stock of THE SMITH ENTERPRISE CORPORATION Fully paid and non-assessable transferable only on the books of the Corporation by the holder hereof in person or by Attorney upon surrender of this Certificate properly endorsed.

In Witness Whereof, the said Corporation has caused this Certificate to be signed by its duly authorized officers and to be sealed with the Seal of the Corporation this Tenth day of March A.D. 19 99

SECRETARY

PRESIDENT

SHARES 200 EACH.

© GOES 53

NOTICE OF STOCK TRANSFER RESTRICTIONS

The shares of stock represented by this certificate are subject to transfer and other restrictions as set forth in the Articles of Incorporation of the Corporation and in a Shareholders' Agreement dated ________________, copies of which are filed with the Corporation at its registered office. No transfer or other disposition of the shares represented by this certificate shall be valid or recognized by the Corporation unless the requirements set forth in those documents are first complied with to the satisfaction of the Corporation.

Form **2553**
(Rev. September 1996)
Department of the Treasury
Internal Revenue Service

Election by a Small Business Corporation

(Under section 1362 of the Internal Revenue Code)
▶ For Paperwork Reduction Act Notice, see page 1 of instructions.
▶ See separate instructions.

OMB No. 1545-0146

Notes: 1. *This election to be an S corporation can be accepted only if all the tests are met under* **Who May Elect** *on page 1 of the instructions; all signatures in Parts I and III are originals (no photocopies); and the exact name and address of the corporation and other required form information are provided.*

2. *Do not file* **Form 1120S,** *U.S. Income Tax Return for an S Corporation, for any tax year before the year the election takes effect.*

3. *If the corporation was in existence before the effective date of this election, see* **Taxes an S Corporation May Owe** *on page 1 of the instructions.*

Part I Election Information

Please Type or Print	Name of corporation (see instructions)	A Employer identification number
	Number, street, and room or suite no. (If a P.O. box, see instructions.)	B Date incorporated
	City or town, state, and ZIP code	C State of incorporation

D Election is to be effective for tax year beginning (month, day, year) . . . . ▶ / /

E Name and title of officer or legal representative who the IRS may call for more information | F Telephone number of officer or legal representative ( )

G If the corporation changed its name or address after applying for the EIN shown in A above, check this box . . . . ▶ ☐

H If this election takes effect for the first tax year the corporation exists, enter month, day, and year of the earliest of the following: (1) date the corporation first had shareholders, (2) date the corporation first had assets, or (3) date the corporation began doing business . . . . ▶ / /

I Selected tax year: Annual return will be filed for tax year ending (month and day) ▶ ....

If the tax year ends on any date other than December 31, except for an automatic 52-53-week tax year ending with reference to the month of December, you **must** complete Part II on the back. If the date you enter is the ending date of an automatic 52-53-week tax year, write "52-53-week year" to the right of the date. See Temporary Regulations section 1.441-2T(e)(3).

J Name and address of each shareholder; shareholder's spouse having a community property interest in the corporation's stock; and each tenant in common, joint tenant, and tenant by the entirety. (A husband and wife (and their estates) are counted as one shareholder in determining the number of shareholders without regard to the manner in which the stock is owned.)	K Shareholders' Consent Statement. Under penalties of perjury, we declare that we consent to the election of the above-named corporation to be an S corporation under section 1362(a) and that we have examined this consent statement, including accompanying schedules and statements, and to the best of our knowledge and belief, it is true, correct, and complete. We understand our consent is binding and may not be withdrawn after the corporation has made a valid election. (Shareholders sign and date below.)		L Stock owned		M Social security number or employer identification number (see instructions)	N Shareholder's tax year ends (month and day)
	Signature	Date	Number of shares	Dates acquired		

Under penalties of perjury, I declare that I have examined this election, including accompanying schedules and statements, and to the best of my knowledge and belief, it is true, correct, and complete.

Signature of officer ▶ Title ▶ Date ▶

See Parts II and III on back. Cat. No. 18629R Form **2553** (Rev. 9-96)

2553 (Rev 9-96) Page **2**

Part II Selection of Fiscal Tax Year (All corporations using this part must complete item O and item P, Q, or R.)

O Check the applicable box to indicate whether the corporation is:

1. ☐ A new corporation adopting the tax year entered in item I, Part I.
2. ☐ An existing corporation retaining the tax year entered in item I, Part I.
3. ☐ An existing corporation changing to the tax year entered in item I, Part I.

P Complete item P if the corporation is using the expeditious approval provisions of Rev. Proc. 87-32, 1987-2 C.B. 396, to request **(1)** a natural business year (as defined in section 4.01(1) of Rev. Proc. 87-32) or **(2)** a year that satisfies the ownership tax year test in section 4.01(2) of Rev. Proc. 87-32. Check the applicable box below to indicate the representation statement the corporation is making as required under section 4 of Rev. Proc. 87-32.

1. Natural Business Year ▶ ☐ I represent that the corporation is retaining or changing to a tax year that coincides with its natural business year as defined in section 4.01(1) of Rev. Proc. 87-32 and as verified by its satisfaction of the requirements of section 4.02(1) of Rev. Proc. 87-32. In addition, if the corporation is changing to a natural business year as defined in section 4.01(1), I further represent that such tax year results in less deferral of income to the owners than the corporation's present tax year. I also represent that the corporation is not described in section 3.01(2) of Rev. Proc. 87-32. **(See instructions for additional information that must be attached.)**

2. Ownership Tax Year ▶ ☐ I represent that shareholders holding more than half of the shares of the stock (as of the first day of the tax year to which the request relates) of the corporation have the same tax year or are concurrently changing to the tax year that the corporation adopts, retains, or changes to per item I, Part I. I also represent that the corporation is not described in section 3.01(2) of Rev. Proc. 87-32.

Note: *If you do not use item P and the corporation wants a fiscal tax year, complete either item Q or R below. Item Q is used to request a fiscal tax year based on a business purpose and to make a back-up section 444 election. Item R is used to make a regular section 444 election.*

Q Business Purpose—To request a fiscal tax year based on a business purpose, you must check box Q1 and pay a user fee. See instructions for details. You may also check box Q2 and/or box Q3.

1. Check here ▶ ☐ if the fiscal year entered in item I, Part I, is requested under the provisions of section 6.03 of Rev. Proc. 87-32. Attach to Form 2553 a statement showing the business purpose for the requested fiscal year. See instructions for additional information that must be attached.

2. Check here ▶ ☐ to show that the corporation intends to make a back-up section 444 election in the event the corporation's business purpose request is not approved by the IRS. (See instructions for more information.)

3. Check here ▶ ☐ to show that the corporation agrees to adopt or change to a tax year ending December 31 if necessary for the IRS to accept this election for S corporation status in the event (1) the corporation's business purpose request is not approved and the corporation makes a back-up section 444 election, but is ultimately not qualified to make a section 444 election, or (2) the corporation's business purpose request is not approved and the corporation did not make a back-up section 444 election.

R Section 444 Election—To make a section 444 election, you must check box R1 and you may also check box R2.

1. Check here ▶ ☐ to show the corporation will make, if qualified, a section 444 election to have the fiscal tax year shown in item I, Part I. To make the election, you must complete **Form 8716,** Election To Have a Tax Year Other Than a Required Tax Year, and either attach it to Form 2553 or file it separately.

2. Check here ▶ ☐ to show that the corporation agrees to adopt or change to a tax year ending December 31 if necessary for the IRS to accept this election for S corporation status in the event the corporation is ultimately not qualified to make a section 444 election.

Part III Qualified Subchapter S Trust (QSST) Election Under Section 1361(d)(2)*

Income beneficiary's name and address	Social security number
Trust's name and address	Employer identification number

Date on which stock of the corporation was transferred to the trust (month, day, year) . . . . ▶ / /

In order for the trust named above to be a QSST and thus a qualifying shareholder of the S corporation for which this Form 2553 is filed, I hereby make the election under section 1361(d)(2). Under penalties of perjury, I certify that the trust meets the definitional requirements of section 1361(d)(3) and that all other information provided in Part III is true, correct, and complete.

Signature of income beneficiary or signature and title of legal representative or other qualified person making the election | Date

*Use Part III to make the QSST election only if stock of the corporation has been transferred to the trust on or before the date on which the corporation makes its election to be an S corporation. The QSST election must be made and filed separately if stock of the corporation is transferred to the trust after the date on which the corporation makes the S election.

*U.S. Government Printing Office: 1996 — 405-455/40162

EMPLOYMENT CONTRACT

THIS AGREEMENT, dated ____________________, between ____________________, a corporation created under the laws of the State of ____________________, (the Corporation), and ____________________, of ____________________ (the Employee).

The Corporation and the Employee agree as follows:

1. The Corporation hereby employs the Employee and the Employee hereby enters the employ of the Corporation as ____________________ at ________________ for a term beginning ________________ and ending ________________, unless sooner terminated under Section 6 of this agreement.

2. During the period of this agreement, including all extensions and renewals, the Employee agrees to devote all of his working and professional time and efforts to the interests of the Corporation and to perform his duties in an efficient, trustworthy, and competent manner. Following the termination of this agreement for any reason, the Employee agrees not to engage in the management of a ____________________ business for a period of ____________ years within ____________ miles of any significant place of business of the Corporation.

3. The duties of the Employee shall be as follows: ____.

4. For the services rendered under this agreement, the Employee shall be compensated by the Corporation as follows:

An annual salary of $ ____________, payable in equal monthly installments.

The following death, disability, retirement, profit-sharing, and other benefits: ____________________________.

The following other compensation: ____.

5. It is expressly understood and agreed as follows:

(a) All inventions, patents, copyrights, developments and ideas and concepts developed by the Employee during the course of his employment under this agreement shall be the exclusive property of the Corporation.

(b) The Employee shall have no right, either during or after employment under this agreement, to use, sell, copy, transfer, or otherwise make use of, either for himself or for any persons other than the Corporation, any of the confidential business information and trade secrets of the Corporation.

6. Should the Employee, during any period covered by this agreement, fail to perform his duties by reason of illness, injury, or other incapacity, and should such nonperformance continue for a period of ____________ consecutive months, the Corporation shall have the right to terminate this agreement upon 30 days prior written notice mailed or delivered to the Employee at the following address: ____________________. In the event of termination under this Section 6, the Employee shall be entitled to termination benefits payable at the effective date of the termination equal to his then monthly fixed salary under Section 4 of this agreement times the number of whole months this agreement has been in effect divided by 12.

7. If this agreement is terminated by the Corporation prior to its expiration, other than under Section 6 hereof, the Corporation shall pay to the Employee liquidated damages in the amount provided under this Section 7 in full satisfaction of all claims, liabilities, and damages owing or owed to the Employee by the Corporation as a result of such termination. The amount of the liquidated damages shall be determined as follows: ____.

8. The Corporation shall not merge into or otherwise combine with another corporation, or sell or transfer all or substantially all of its assets to another entity during the term of this agreement unless such other corporation or entity shall assume this agreement and upon such assumption the Employee and the other corporation or entity shall become obligated to perform the terms and conditions of this agreement.

9. Upon the expiration of the term of this agreement as specified in Section 1 hereof, this agreement may be renewed for successive one-year periods upon the consent of both parties, under the terms and conditions contained in this agreement, except that upon renewal the compensation of the employee under Section 4 may be revised as negotiated and agreed upon by the parties at the time of renewal.

IN WITNESS WHEREOF, the parties have caused this agreement to be executed on the date first above appearing.

____
The Employee

The ____________________ Corporation

By ____________________
President

CHAPTER SIX

OPERATING A SMALL BUSINESS CORPORATION

6.01 Employee Compensation - Current, Fringe and Deferred

employee compensation, forms of

The compensation of an employee of a small business corporation typically consists of current compensation plus various fringe and deferred compensation benefits. Discussed in this section are the salary, bonus, and other current compensation payments that may be made to corporate employees, and the various fringe and retirement benefits and other deferred compensation that may be paid to corporate employees. Because of its impact on all forms of employee compensation, the effect of stock ownership by an employee on the amount and form of his or her deductible compensation is discussed throughout this section.

shareholder-employee, deductible compensation, limitations

A disadvantage of the corporate form of doing business is the limitation imposed on the amount of currently deductible compensation for personal services that a corporation may pay to an employee who is also a shareholder of the corporation (i.e., a shareholder-employee). A corporation may deduct as an ordinary and necessary business expense "a reasonable allowance for personal services actually rendered" by a shareholder-employee. See 26 U.S.C. 162(a)(1). Compensation in excess of this amount is permitted, but the excessive amounts are not deductible by the corporation and are treated and taxed as dividends, which means that the excessive funds are effectively taxed twice (see section 5.02, supra, for an illustration). It should be noted that the statutory limitation applies not just to current compensation, but to all forms of compensation, including fringe and deferred compensation, and it is the total amount of shareholder-employee compensation that must meet the statutory requirement of reasonableness.

nonshareholder-employee, deductibility of compensation

It should be noted that the limitation on the amount of deductible compensation applies only to shareholder-employees and not to other employees of a corporation. Nonshareholder-employees, because they are not owners of the business and cannot be deemed to have received constructive dividends, are assumed to have contracted for their compensation in arms-length negotiations and the amount of their deductible compensation is not usually limited. Exceptions to this rule are occasionally made for family members or close associates of shareholder-employees. Because the income and deductions of an S corporation are assessed only at the shareholder level whether or not dividends are issued, the deductible compensation limitation for shareholder-employees does not apply to S corporations.

deductible compensation limitation, general rules

As indicated above, to be deductible by the corporation, the compensation paid to a shareholder-employee must be - (1) solely for services actually rendered to the corporation, and (2) reasonable in amount. See 26 U.S.C. 162(a)(1). Both of these conditions must be satisfied in order for a shareholder-employee's compensation to be deductible by the corporation. In determining whether the compensation paid to a shareholder-employee was solely for services actually rendered to the corporation, much consideration is given to the issue of whether the compensation had the appearance of a dividend. Factors such as the percentage relationship between shareholdings and the amount of compensation and when the compensation was paid are considered. If the compensation was paid at the end of the year and was directly proportional to shareholdings, it is likely to be deemed a dividend.

shareholder-employee, reasonableness of compensation

The key issue in determining whether the compensation paid to a shareholder-employee is totally deductible by the corporation is usually whether the compensation was reasonable in amount. The objective test in determining the reasonableness of a shareholder-employee's compensation is whether the amount paid was more than what "would ordinarily be paid for like services by like enterprises under like circumstances." See Treasury Reg. 1.162-7(b)(3). In applying this test, factors such as the employee's qualifications and responsibilities, the amount of the corporation's earnings, the amounts paid to the same employee in prior years, and the amounts paid to similar employees in the same company and in other companies are considered. See Hammond Lead Products, Inc. v. Comm., 425 F. 2nd 31, 33 (CA 7, 1970).

shareholder-employee, compensation for past services, deductibility

It is common for the participants of a small business corporation to forgo compensation in the early years of the business in order to conserve working capital. The amount, and sometimes the existence, of their compensation in the early years of the business is often contingent upon whether the business earns enough to pay its other expenses. Later, when the business prospers, the participants often wish to pay themselves the compensation they failed to receive during the early years. Such arrangements are generally permitted on the proposition that compensation paid for services rendered by a participant in prior years is currently deductible by the corporation. See Auburn & Assoc. v. U.S., 336 F. Supp. 457, 462 (WDPA, 1971). The prior services must have been rendered to the present corporation, however, and not to a predecessor entity. See Young v. Comm., 650 F. 2nd 1083 (CA 9, 1981). The compensation for prior services may be in addition to compensation for current services. The best practice in such situations is for the board of directors of the corporation to adopt a resolution approving the payment of compensation for services rendered in prior years before the compensation is paid to the participant.

contingent compensation, deductibility

Contingent compensation arrangements are common in small business corporations. Under such arrangements an employee's compensation may be contingent upon corporate profits, sales, or other relevant criterion. Generally, a greater amount of compensation may be deducted by the corporation under a contingent compensation arrangement than under a straight salary arrangement, provided that the compensation is "paid pursuant to a free bargain between the employer and the individual made before the services are rendered." See Treasury Reg. 1.162-7(b)(2),(3). The same general rule applies to shareholder-employees, even in the absence of arms-length bargaining.

shareholder-employee, deductibility of bonuses

Bonuses paid to shareholder-employees, especially the year-end variety, are frequently challenged by the I.R.S.. Such bonuses are often treated as dividends by the I.R.S., even if the amount of compensation is reasonable, on the theory that the shareholder-employees, as the owners of the business, will receive the excess funds in any event and that their only incentive for awarding the bonuses is to avoid issuing dividends. The deductibility of bonuses are enhanced if they are not paid at the year's end, if they are paid pursuant to a written agreement entered into in advance, and if the paying of bonuses is a custom in that particular business.

shareholder-employee, compensation, deductibility, burden of proof

The issue of the deductibility of payments made to shareholder-employees normally arises when the I.R.S. disallows all or part of the deductions claimed by the corporation for such payments. The corporation then has the burden of showing that the amounts deducted constituted reasonable compensation and were for services actually rendered to the corporation.

employee benefit plans, general requirements

An advantage of the corporate form of doing business is the availability of superior tax-qualified retirement and fringe benefits to corporate employees. The tax-qualified fringe benefits that may be paid to corporate employees include group life insurance benefits, health and accident insurance benefits, and some eight other miscellaneous lesser benefits, all of which are described below in this section. To be tax-qualified (i.e., not taxable to the employee yet deductible by the corporation), a benefit must be offered in the form of a plan adopted by the corporation in accordance with the requirements of the Treasury Regulations. Generally, a plan must be in writing, it must be maintained for the exclusive benefit of the employees, and it must be established for an indefinite period of time. In addition, the employees' rights under the plan must be legally enforceable, and the employees must be provided with reasonable notification of the benefits available under the plan.

group life insurance benefits, general aspects

A corporation may adopt a group life insurance plan providing up to $50,000 of group term life insurance on the life of each of its employees. The cost of the insurance is deductible by the corporation and is not includible in the gross income of the employees. See 26 U.S.C. 79. This fringe benefit is available to all corporate employees (including shareholder-employees) except 2-percent shareholders of S corporations (see section 4.18, supra). For income tax purposes the deductible cost of the insurance is determined from a table of such costs in the Treasury Regulations, and not from the actual premiums paid by the corporation. See 26 U.S.C. 79(c) and Treasury Reg. 1.79-3(d)(2). An employee is permitted to have insurance coverage under such a plan in excess of $50,000, but the cost of the excess coverage is taxable to the employee. If a corporation wishes to adopt an employee group life insurance plan, the plan should be formally adopted by the board of directors and notice of the adoption of the plan (and of the benefits available thereunder) should be given to all employees.

employee health and accident plans, general aspects

A corporation may also adopt a tax-qualified employee health and accident plan. Under an employee health and accident plan, the corporation may pay the premiums on health and accident insurance policies, contribute to trust funds set up to provide health and accident benefits, or reimburse employees for their actual health and accident expenses. See 26 U.S.C. 105(b), 106. Health and accident benefits for spouses and dependents of employees are includible under such plans, as are benefits for retired employees. See Treasury Reg. 1.106-1 and Revenue Ruling 62-199, 1962-2 C.B. 38. Contributions by corporate employers to such plans are currently deductible by the corporation and are not taxable to the employees if the plan satisfies the statutory requirements. See 26 U.S.C. 106. This fringe benefit is available to all corporate employees, except 2-percent shareholders of S corporations (see section 5.18, supra).

health and accident plans, how to adopt

A specific health and accident plan is required, and the plan should be in writing. However, a program, policy, or custom may constitute a plan as long as notice of the plan is given to all employees. See Treasury Reg. 1.105-5. The best practice, especially if the corporation has a high percentage of shareholder-employees, is for the board of directors to adopt a specific employee health and accident benefit plan meeting the nondiscriminatory requirements described below and include the plan in the corporate bylaws.

employee benefit plans, non-discriminatory requirements

Employee group life insurance plans and employee health and accident plans, like all employee benefit plans, must meet certain nondiscriminatory requirements as to eligibility and benefits if the benefits are to be tax-free to highly compensated employees. If at least 80 percent of the employees who are not highly compensated employees are covered under a health plan or a group-term life insurance plan during the plan year, such plan is deemed to have met the eligibility and benefit nondiscrimination requirements. There are other nondiscrimination criteria that are applicable if the 80 percent participation requirement cannot be met. A highly compensated employee is one who earns more than $75,000 (this figure is adjusted for cost of living increases) per year, owns five percent or more of the employer, or who meets certain other earning and ownership criteria. See 26 U.S.C. 414(q).

other corporate fringe benefits

Other currently deductible fringe benefits that may be provided by a corporation to its employees (including shareholder-employees) without constituting taxable income to the employees, include:

employee death benefits

(1) Death benefit payments of up to $5,000 per employee. See 26 U.S.C. 101(b)(2).

meals and lodging

(2) The value of meals furnished to the employee and the employee's dependents, if furnished on the business premises, and lodging, if the employee is required to accept lodging on the business premises as a condition of employment. See 26 U.S.C. 119. This benefit is not available to employees who are 2-percent shareholder of S corporations (see section 5.18, supra).

employee moving expenses

(3) Moving expenses incurred by an employee and his or her dependents as a result of employment, including the following:

(a) the expenses of moving household goods and personal effects from the former residence to the new, and

(b) the expenses of traveling from the former residence to the new, including the costs of lodging. See 26 U.S.C. 217.

group legal services plans

(4) Legal services, and employer contributions therefor, that are provided under a qualified group legal services plan. See 26 U.S.C. 120.

entertainment expenses

(5) 50 percent of non-lavish entertainment expenses directly related to or associated with the active conduct of trade or business, including expenditures for food and beverages under circumstances conducive to business discussions. See 26 U.S.C. 274(a), (n).

travel expenses

(6) Travel expenses, including the costs of non-extravagant meals and lodging, incurred in the course of company business. See 26 U.S.C. 162(a)(2). Limitations are imposed on deductions for foreign travel. See 26 U.S.C. 274(c).

business gifts

(7) Business gifts not exceeding $25. See 26 U.S.C. 274(b).

employee business expenses, deductibility

An employee who incurs a nonreimbursable business expense is not entitled to a tax deduction for that expense unless the employee is required to bear the expense as a condition of employment. If the corporation has a policy of not reimbursing its employees for otherwise deductible business expenses, the adoption by its board of directors of a resolution stating that its employees are expected to bear the cost of such expenses as a condition of their employment will better enable its employees to deduct such expenses from their gross income. A similar provision in an employment contract will serve the same purpose for an individual employee. See Revenue Ruling 57-502, 1957-2 C.B. 118.

deductible business expenses, record keeping

If a corporation reimburses its employees for deductible business expenses, it is important that both the employee and the corporation keep adequate records substantiating the expenses. Record keeping includes both a record of the expenditures and documentary evidence (receipts, bills, etc.) supporting the record. The record should include the amount of the expense, the time and place of the expense, the business purpose of the expenditure, and the business relationship of the persons involved. See 26 U.S.C. 274(d). A similar record should be kept by employees who are not reimbursed for such expenses.

employee stock ownership programs, advantages of

Many corporations use employee stock ownership programs as incentives to attract and retain competent employees. Such programs not only provide extra compensation at reduced tax rates to key employees without straining the corporation's cash flow, they can also provide the corporation with needed capital and valuable tax deductions. Because there is an ascertainable market for their stock, publicly-held corporations enjoy distinct advantages under these programs.

employee stock ownership programs, disadvantages of for small business corporations

The disadvantages of employee stock ownership programs for small business corporations are - (1) the stock seldom has a readily-ascertainable market value, and (2) the stock is usually subjected to transfer restrictions and buy-out provisions that restrict its value to the recipients. While these factors limit both the attractiveness of the stock as an employment incentive and the tax advantages of such programs, many small business corporations, because of their size and flexibility, are able to offer their employees a more realistic chance of "growing with the company" through such programs than larger corporations.

employee stock bonus plans, description

A corporation has three basic methods of making its stock available to its employees. These methods are - (1) employee stock bonus plans, (2) stock option plans, and (3) stock purchase agreements. There are substantial differences in both the operational and tax aspects of each method. Under an employee stock bonus plan, the corporation distributes stock to its employees, usually as additional compensation for personal services, in amounts customarily geared to company profits, individual performance, length of service, or some other business-related factor. The plan may be company-wide or it may be limited to certain departments, divisions, or even individuals within the company. The plan may be limited to stock bonuses, or it may provide for the payment of both cash and stock in various proportions.

Generally, the distribution of stock by a corporation to an employee under an employee stock bonus plan results in taxable income to the employee equal to the fair market value of the stock at the time of distribution. See Treasury Reg. 1.61-2(d)(4). The corporation is entitled to a deduction against income in the year of distribution equal to the amount of income taxable to the employee, assuming, in the case of a shareholder-employee, that the employee's total compensation, including the stock bonus, is both reasonable in amount and solely for services rendered. If the distributed stock is subject to transfer restrictions, its value for income tax purposes is usually the price determined by the pricing mechanism contained in the agreement or documents containing the transfer restrictions, unless the I.R.S. establishes a different value. See 26 U.S.C. 83(d)(1). employee stock bonus plans, tax treatment

Under a stock option plan, an employee is given the right, called an option, to purchase stock of the corporation at a fixed or determinable price, usually within a specified period of time. Typically an employee will purchase the stock by exercising the option, hold the stock at least long enough to qualify for favorable tax treatment, and then dispose of the stock at a substantial gain. There are three types of stock option plans that may be implemented by a corporation. These are - (1) incentive stock options, (2) employee stock purchase plans, and (3) nonqualified stock option plans. employee stock option plans, general aspects

Incentive stock options and employee stock purchase plans qualify for favorable tax treatment (usually a tax deferral for the employee), while nonqualified stock option plans do not. An incentive stock option plan must be approved by the shareholders and must satisfy the requirements of 26 U.S.C. 422(b). Because employee stock purchase plans are available only to corporate employees owning less than five percent of the stock in the corporation, they are seldom used by small business corporations. See 26 U.S.C. 423. Because they are not subject to tax law limitations as to price, time of exercise, and employee eligibility, nonqualified stock options are more flexible than incentive stock options. Any employee, or class of employees, may be granted nonqualified stock options at any price and for any period of time. employee stock option plans, types of plans

Stock purchase agreements (which should not be confused with employee stock purchase plans described in the preceding paragraph) differ from stock options in that under a stock purchase agreement an employee has a contractual obligation to purchase stock rather than an option to do so. Under a stock purchase agreement an employee is normally obligated to purchase a fixed number of shares within a certain period of time at a fixed or determinable price. Because stock purchase agreements are not tax-qualified, they are not subject to restrictions as to price or availability and may be made available at any desired price to individual employees or to various classes of employees. stock purchase agreements, description

The term "deferred compensation" normally includes all compensation, regardless of its form, paid or delivered to an employee, or the employee's designee, in the tax years following the rendition of the service giving rise to the compensation. For tax purposes, deferred compensation plans are divided into two categories: (1) tax-qualified employee benefit plans, and (2) nonqualified (i.e., not tax-qualified) deferred compensation plans. deferred compensation, definition

It should be understood that the subject of deferred compensation for corporate employees is complex and highly technical in nature. Only a brief outline of the subject is given below, the purpose of which is to acquaint the reader with the various types of plans that are available to corporate employees. The advise of an experienced tax or investment adviser should be sought before adopting a deferred compensation plan. deferred compensation, scope of section

Nonqualified deferred compensation plans do not receive special tax treatment and are not subject to employee discrimination requirements. Such plans may be established for any one or more groups or classes of employees, including shareholder employees, or for a single employee. Qualified deferred compensation plans, on the other hand, must meet specific statutory requirements as to employee discrimination and applicability. The major practical difference between the two categories of deferred compensation is that only qualified plans may be contemporaneously funded without the employee being assessed reportable income in the year of the funding. While nonqualified plans have the advantage of flexibility, because they cannot be contemporaneously funded without the incurrence of an immediate employee tax liability, they are seldom used by small business corporations. deferred compensation, qualified v. nonqualified

qualified employee benefit plans, general aspects

The great majority of deferred compensation plans adopted by small business corporations are qualified employee benefit plans. While such plans are generally subject to a vast array of federal statutory and regulatory requirements, they enjoy the enormous advantage of providing employees with a funded source for their deferred compensation, while providing both employees and employers with significant tax advantages over nonqualified plans. The funding advantage is particularly important to nonshareholder employees of small business corporations because the size and longevity of such corporations are often insufficient to lend long-term credibility to unfunded plans.

qualified employee benefit plans, tax advantages

The tax advantages of qualified employee benefit plans over nonqualified plans are as follows:

(1) The employer is entitled to a deduction against income in the year of contribution, regardless of when the compensation is distributed to the employee.

(2) The employee, even if he or she has a vested right to the compensation, is not taxed on the deferred compensation until it is distributed to the employee.

(3) The income and gain accrued on funds contributed to the plan are not taxed to the employee until the funds are distributed to the employee.

(4) If stock of the employer corporation is distributed as a benefit under such a plan, the tax on any increase in value of the stock may be postponed until the stock is sold by the recipient.

(5) Benefits attributable to employer contributions under such plans, up to a limit of $100,000, can be paid to an employee's beneficiary without being subjected to the federal estate tax.

types of qualified employee benefit plans

There are seven kinds of qualified deferred compensation employee benefit plans available to employees of small business corporations, including S corporations. These include: (1) pension plans, (2) annuity plans, (3) profit-sharing plans, (4) stock bonus plans, (5) employee stock ownership plans, (6) simplified employee pension plans, and (7) 401(k) plans.

defined contribution plan, definition

defined benefit plan, definition

To avoid confusion in reading and interpreting the tax laws related to these plans, it should be noted that the Internal Revenue Code divides all qualified deferred compensation plans into two categories: defined contribution plans and defined benefit plans. A defined contribution plan is a plan that requires an individual account for each participating employee and provides benefits based solely on the amount contributed to the employee's account, together with any income, expenses, gains or losses attributable to the account. See 26 U.S.C. 414(i). A defined benefit plan is any plan other than a defined contribution plan. See 26 U.S.C. 414(j).

defined contribution plan vs. defined benefit plans

Under a defined contribution plan the controlling factor is the annual amount contributed to the plan, regardless of the amount of benefits that might later accrue from the contribution. Under a defined benefit plan, on the other hand, the controlling factor is the benefit, and the amount contributed is adjusted so as to produce the desired benefit. Limits are imposed on the amount of annual benefits that may be provided under a defined benefit plan, whereas in a defined contribution plan limits are imposed on the amount of annual contributions. Defined benefit plans are subject to benefit accrual and minimum funding requirements not imposed on defined contribution plans. Profit-sharing plans and stock bonus plans, for example, are defined contribution plans, while annuity plans and most pension plans are defined benefit plans.

pension plans, description

defined benefit plans, benefit limits

Under a pension plan a certain level of benefits must be paid to an employee upon retirement, usually for the remainder of the employee's life. The employer's annual contributions to the plan are actuarially computed so as to produce the desired benefit at the time the employee retires or otherwise qualifies for the benefits. The annual benefits under such plans, as with all defined benefit plans, cannot exceed the lesser of $90,000 or 100 percent of the employee's average annual compensation for the employee's high three years. See 26 U.S.C. 415(b)(1). The $90,000 limit is adjusted annually for cost of living changes, and in 1998 the limit had increased to $130,000. The employer's contributions under a pension plan are mandatory and are not dependent upon profits.

An annuity plan is a type of defined benefit pension plan whereunder the employer purchases retirement annuities instead of depositing the contributions into a pension trust. See 26 U.S.C. 404(a)(2) and Treasury Reg. 1.404(a)-3(a). The benefit limits under annuity plans are those for defined benefit plans generally: the lesser of $90,000 or 100 percent of the employee's average annual compensation for the employee's high three years, with the $90,000 cap adjusted annually for cost of living changes. The cap, as adjusted, was $130,000 in 1998.

annuity plans, description, benefit limits

Under a profit-sharing plan employer contributions are made only out of current or accumulated profits. If the employer has no profits for a certain year, no contributions are required. If contributions are made they are normally allocated to employees on the basis of a percentage of their compensation. Profit-sharing plans are defined contribution plans with no definitely determinable benefits provided to employees. Under such plans, as with all defined contribution plans, limits are imposed on the annual amounts that may be contributed to an employee's account under the plan. Contributions above these limits are not tax sheltered. The contribution limit for a single profit-sharing plan is 15 percent of compensation. See 26 U.S.C. 404(a)(3). However, any number of defined contribution plans may be adopted by an employer, and the overall contribution limit for all defined contribution plans applicable to a particular employee is the lesser of $30,000 or 25 percent of the employee's annual compensation. See 26 U.S.C. 415(c)(1). The $30,000 contribution limit on defined contribution plans will not be indexed (i.e., adjusted annually for inflation) until the contribution limit on defined benefit plans, as adjusted for inflation, exceeds $120,000.

profit-sharing plans, description, contribution limits

defined contribution plans, contribution limits

A qualified deferred compensation stock bonus plan is similar to a profit-sharing plan except that the benefits are paid in the form of stock of the employer corporation rather than cash. Under such plans, which should not be confused with employee stock bonus plans (see supra, this section), the employer's contributions are not necessarily dependent upon profits. A stock bonus plan is a defined contribution plan and the contribution limits described in the preceding paragraph apply.

qualified stock bonus plans, general aspects

An employee stock ownership plan (an ESOP) is a defined contribution stock bonus plan (or a stock bonus and money purchase plan) whereunder the trustee of the plan is permitted to borrow funds from either the corporation or certain shareholder-officers. See 26 U.S.C. 4975(e). Under an ESOP a corporation may establish a retirement plan for its employees and fund the plan with its own stock. If the plan meets the general requirements for all qualified employee benefit plans (see infra, this section) and certain special rules for ESOPs, the employer corporation can deduct the fair market value of its stock contributions to the plan against current income. See 26 U.S.C. 404(a)(9).

employee stock ownership plans, general aspects

A simplified employee pension plan (SEP) permits an employer to provide substantial tax-sheltered retirement benefits to its employees without incurring the expenses of adopting and maintaining a complex retirement plan. Under a SEP the employer simply contributes to an individual retirement account (IRA) for each participating employee, who then enjoys a tax-deferred accumulation of benefits in the same manner as a traditional plan. Like traditional plans, the employer is entitled to an immediate income tax deduction for the amount contributed and the participant is not taxed on the contributions until the funds are withdrawn from the participant's IRA. The contribution limits for a SEP are the lesser of $22,500 or 15 percent of a participant's annual compensation. However, the amounts contributed, if any, to a SEP in any particular year are discretionary with the employer, who may not discriminate among employees and must contribute the same compensation percentage for each employee.

SEP description, contribution limits

The advantages of a SEP over a traditional plan are simplicity of adoption and administration. For most employers a SEP may be adopted by completing a simple one-page form (Form 5305-SEP) at any time before the due date of the employer's income tax return for the year the SEP is started. Once adopted, the administration of a SEP is also simple. No reports or tax returns are required of the employer, who need only make contributions to the participants' IRAs and furnish each participant with a copy of Form 5305-SEP. Because each SEP participant is responsible for maintaining his or her own IRA, the employer has no fiduciary responsibility to maintain the IRAs once the contributions are made. The participant's SEP IRAs are subject to the same withdrawal and other restrictions that are applicable to IRAs generally. Employers with 25 or fewer employees may also provide elective deferral SEPs similar to 401(k) plans, provided that at least 50 percent of the employees elect to make such deferrals. See 26 U.S.C. 408(k)(6).

SEP, advantages of over traditional plans

elective deferral SEPs

SEP, disadvantages of for employer

The down side of SEPs from the employer's standpoint are the liberal participation and vesting requirements. All employees of age 21 or more, including part-time employees, who have performed services for the employer during at least three of the preceding five years and who have received compensation totaling at least $300 (as indexed) during the current year must be allowed to participate in the plan. See 26 U.S.C. 408(k)(2). All SEP contributions are subject to an immediate 100 percent vesting requirement. See 26 U.S.C. 408(k)(4). This means that the employer cannot prevent a participant from withdrawing the SEP contributions at any time. All things considered, however, a SEP can be an inexpensive and simple method of providing for the retirement needs of the owners and employees of a small business.

section 401(k) plan, general aspects

Section 401(k) plans, which are also referred to as "salary reduction" or "salary deferral" plans, permit an employee to defer the receipt of current cash compensation and have the deferral contributed on the employee's behalf to a qualified plan. If all tax law requirements are met, the employee is not taxed on the deferred amount (or on earnings on the deferred amounts) until distributions are made under the plan. See 26 U.S.C. 401(k). The maximum amount that an employee may elect to defer under all 401(k) plans is $7,000 per year. The $7,000 cap is adjusted annually for inflation. Several special nondiscriminatory rules are applicable to 401(k) plans.

qualified employee benefit plans, combinations of plans, benefit limits

Many small business corporations adopt both a defined benefit plan and a defined contribution plan in providing for the retirement needs of their employees. A pension plan supplemented by a profit-sharing plan is probably the most common example. Statutory limits are imposed on the combined benefits that an employee may be granted under such an arrangement. These limitations are determined by computing for each plan the fraction of the statutory limit to which an employee is entitled under the plan and adding the fractions. The statutory limits as to the sum of the fractions are 1.25 as applied only to maximum dollar limits and 1.4 as applied to percentage of compensation limits. See 26 U.S.C. 415(e). In other words, if an employee earns more than the maximum statutory dollar limitation, the applicable fraction is 1.25; otherwise the applicable fraction is 1.4. If a plan is "top heavy," the 1.25 fractional dollar limitation may be reduced to 1.0. See 26 U.S.C. 416(h).

qualified employee benefit plans, non-discrimination and eligibility requirements

All qualified employee benefit plans must meet certain requirements as to employee eligibility and participation, vesting, funding, and benefit distribution in order to retain their tax-sheltered status. For most plans a trust must be created solely for the benefit of the employees and their beneficiaries. See 26 U.S.C. 401(a)(1). A plan may not discriminate, either as to participation or benefits, in favor of officers, shareholders, or highly compensated employees. See 26 U.S.C. 401(a)(4), 410. Generally, a plan must benefit at least 70 percent of all employees who are not highly compensated employees, although other nondiscriminatory tests are permitted. See 26 U.S.C. 410(b). A minimum age of 21 is required for participation, and an employee meeting the age requirement must be allowed to participate after one year of employment. See 26 U.S.C. 410(a)(1).

qualified employee benefit plans, vesting requirements

top heavy plan, definition

key employee, definition

Generally, qualified employee benefit plans may delay the vesting of employee benefits resulting from employer contributions for up to five years or provide for incremental vesting over periods of up to seven years. See 26 U.S.C. 411. If a plan is "top heavy," more stringent vesting requirements are imposed. See 26 U.S.C. 416(b). Generally, a plan is "top heavy" if 60 percent or more of the benefits or contributions under the plan are on the account of key employees. See 26 U.S.C. 416(g). "Key employees" include corporate officers, the ten largest shareholders, persons holding five percent of more of the stock in the corporation, and persons holding one percent or more of the corporate stock whose annual compensation from the corporation exceeds $150,000 (as indexed for cost of living changes).

qualified employee benefit plans, distribution requirements

The distribution of benefits under a qualified plan must normally begin when the participant attains the age of 70 1/2 years, unless an earlier age is specified in the plan. The benefits must be distributed to an employee or the employee's beneficiary within certain periods, or periodically over the employee's life expectancy. Different rules apply to distributions to key employees under top heavy plans.

There are no specific statutory requirements as to whom a corporation must appoint as the trustee of a qualified employee benefit plan that does not include shareholder-employees. However, a qualified plan that includes shareholder-employees must appoint a bank or other person certified by the Treasury Secretary as the trustee of the plan. See 26 U.S.C. 401(d)(1). If the plan so provides, the trustee of a corporate-sponsored plan may, within certain limits, make loans to plan participants. See 26 U.S.C. 4975(d)(1). In general, the trustee of a qualified plan has fiduciary responsibilities and must invest the funds of the pension trust in a prudent manner. See 29 U.S.C. 1104(a).

qualified employee benefit plans, trustee, loans to employees

It is permissible for a qualified employee benefit plan to exclude an employee from coverage under the plan if the whole of the employee's compensation constitutes "wages" taken into account for social security benefits. It is also permissible to provide a different rate of benefits with respect to compensation paid in excess of the amount taken into account for purposes of determining social security benefits. See 26 U.S.C. 401(a)(5). This is the so-called integration with social security feature of qualified plans. Integration with social security has the effect of reducing contributions for and benefits of lower-paid employees under qualified plans. There are several permissible methods of integrating qualified plans with social security, and different rules are applicable to different types of plans. See Treasury Reg. 1.401-3(e)(1).

qualified employee benefit plans, integration with social security

6.02 Dividends, Redemptions and Other Distributions

distributions to shareholders, forms of

A dividend is a shareholder's pro rata share of any fund or property set apart by the corporation from its earnings and profits for distribution to its shareholders. A redemption is the repurchase or buying back by a corporation of previously issued shares of its own stock. Other distributions by a corporation to its shareholders include stock splits, stock dividends, and (for tax purposes) a return of capital.

dividends, circumstances when issued

Because funds distributed to shareholders as dividends are effectively taxed twice (see section 5.02, supra), small business corporations typically distribute most of their profits in the form of compensation for personal services. Occasionally, however, it becomes either necessary or advantageous for a small business corporation to distribute funds in the form of dividends. A common reason for such distributions is the fulfillment of contractual or legal obligations to minority or outside shareholders. An outside shareholder may be an investor in the business, the spouse, legatee or personal representative of a deceased participant, a former participant who is no longer active in the corporate business but who retains stock in the corporation, or an outsider who has acquired stock in the corporation. Knowledgeable minority or outside shareholders in small business corporations often insure themselves a portion of the corporate profits through agreements calling for the distribution of dividends in certain amounts. Fiduciary obligations to minority shareholders can also mandate the issuance of dividends as a means of distributing a fair share of the corporate profits to them. An S corporation, the dividends of which are not subject to double taxation, may elect to distribute funds to its shareholders in the form of dividends to compensate inactive or family-member shareholders in lower income brackets.

dividends, issuance of for tax purposes

If the business of a corporation is profitable, the limitations placed on the amount of deductible compensation for personal services that may be paid to shareholder-employees could render it impossible for the corporation to distribute a sufficient portion of its earnings to its participants in the form of compensation to avoid the penalties imposed by the personal holding company tax or the accumulated earnings tax (see section 5.02, supra). In such instances the corporation may be forced to distribute its excess income in the form of dividends in order to avoid substantial tax penalties. In this situation, the amount of taxes saved by issuing dividends exceeds the additional tax liability created by their issuance.

dividends, form of, when issued

Dividends may be issued in the form of cash, property, or shares of stock in the corporation. Cash is the most common form of dividend, of course, but property of almost any sort may be used with equal legality, provided that it is physically and legally possible to divide the property among the shareholders. A distiller once caused a spectacular rise in the price of its stock by allegedly spreading a rumor of an impending dividend to be paid in liquor. See Park & Tilford v. Schulte, 160 F. 2nd 984 (CA 2, 1947). If the funds (or other properties) are legally available, dividends may be declared and paid at any time or upon any intervals of time. The practice, followed by many publicly-held corporations, of issuing quarterly dividends is not legally required.

dividends, legal sources of funds for

The corporation laws of every state regulate, in one way or another, the source of corporate dividends. Many corporation laws require that dividends be paid out of some form of surplus, usually unreserved and unrestricted earned surplus. Many states also permit the issuance of so-called "nimble dividends," usually out of current profits. In other states dividends may not be paid if the payment thereof would either render the corporation unable to pay its debts as they become due or cause the corporation's total assets to be less than its total liabilities plus the amounts needed to redeem any outstanding preferred securities. Because the issuance of dividends is so closely regulated by statute, because the statutory requirements vary from state to state, and because personal liability for the unlawful issuance of dividends is usually imposed on directors voting therefor, it is important that the local corporation laws be carefully checked and complied with before dividends are issued.

The existence of certain types of surpluses are often directly related to the accounting and bookkeeping practices of a corporation. The rate or method of depreciation applied to the corporation's capital assets, for example, can have a direct bearing on the amount of funds available for distribution as dividends. Whether the buildings, fixtures, and equipment of the corporation are carried on the corporate books at cost or at market value can also significantly affect the amount of surplus available. The allocation of funds received as consideration for shares of stock, especially no par value stock, may also affect the amount of surplus available. While a discussion of corporate accounting is beyond the scope of this handbook, the reader should be aware of the effects of accounting and bookkeeping procedures on the availability of funds for distribution as dividends. And, it should be noted, the accounting and bookkeeping methods used by a corporation may be changed by the board of directors so as to create additional surplus, although shareholder approval may be required if the stated capital is reduced.

dividends, available funds, accounting practices

In addition to the state corporation laws, the issuance of dividends may be governed by a corporation's articles of incorporation and by a corporation's contracts with creditors or shareholders. It is not unusual for the articles of incorporation of a small business corporation to impose restrictions on the issuance of dividends beyond those imposed by the corporation laws. Such restrictions, if reasonable, are generally permissible and must be complied with before dividends may lawfully be issued. Similarly, article provisions requiring the issuance of dividends under certain conditions are sometimes inserted to protect the interests of minority or outside shareholders (see infra, this section).

issuance of dividends, methods of controlling

A creditor who deems the statutory standards for dividend regulation insufficient to protect its interest in a corporation, may contractually require the corporation to impose additional restrictions on the declaration and payment of dividends. Typically, such restrictions preclude the corporation from declaring dividends or purchasing its own stock unless its working capital, total assets, or total surplus exceed the amounts specified in the contract. On the other hand, an equity investor in a corporation may, as a condition of the investment, contractually require the corporation to issue dividends under certain conditions (see infra, this section).

issuance of dividends, contracts for

Dividends are ordinarily declared by the board of directors in the form of a resolution, although no specific procedure is statutorily required in most states and the distribution of money or property by a corporation to its shareholders may constitute a dividend even though the transaction was not formally designated as such by the board of directors. The best practice is for the board of directors to formally meet, consider the financial status of the corporation as represented by the corporate books and accounts, and declare the desired dividend to be paid on a specified date to the shareholders of record as of a certain earlier date. It is important that the board of directors be presented with sufficient financial information upon which to base a dividend declaration. Balance sheets and profit and loss statements prepared by either the corporate officers or the corporation's accountant are customarily used. The reason for this requirement is that the corporation laws of many states relieve directors from personal liability for the declaration of improper or illegal dividends if they rely in good faith on financial information presented to them by corporate officers or agents.

dividends, legal requirements

declaration of dividends, procedure

The record date for the determination of shareholders entitled to receive dividends is governed by statute in many states. In any event, this date should be no earlier than the date of the director's meeting (or the date of the director action if a formal meeting is not held and an action-without-meeting statute is relied upon). The best practice is to make the record date a future date so that shareholders who wish to have stock transferred prior to the record date will have an opportunity to do so. See Exhibit 6-A at the end of this chapter for a sample board of director resolution for the declaration and payment of dividends.

shareholders entitled to dividends, determination

The board of directors is normally given wide discretion over the issuance of dividends. As indicated above, they may exercise their discretion initially in selecting the accounting and bookkeeping methods of the corporation, thereby controlling, to a considerable extent, the amount of funds available for dividend distribution. Once the funds are available, the directors again have considerable discretion in determining whether the funds should be distributed as dividends or retained in the business.

issuance of dividends, director discretion

issuance of dividends, typical conflicts

Conflicts between active corporate participants and outside shareholders may arise over the issuance, or nonissuance, of dividends. It is normally in the best interests of the active participants to use corporate profits to pay salaries (especially their own) and finance expansion of the business. It is seldom in their interest to issue substantial dividends. On the other hand, it is almost always in the interest of outside shareholders to have substantial dividends declared and paid. Because they cannot normally sell their stock for a reasonable price on the open market and because the value of their stock is usually established by the active participants, dividends are often the only return that outside shareholders have on their investment in the corporation. Not surprisingly, the active participants of a corporation have been known to refrain from issuing dividends for extended periods in attempts to squeeze out minority shareholders. See section 6.05, infra, for further reading on squeeze outs.

actions to compel issuance of dividends

When dividends are intentionally withheld, especially as a squeeze-out tactic, a minority shareholder may seek to compel the corporation to issue dividends. In such cases, relief is likely to be granted if it can be shown that the directors (who are usually the active participants or their designees) acted fraudulently or in bad faith in refusing to issue dividends. See Belk v. Belk's Department Store, Inc. v., 250 N.C. 99, 108 S.E. 2nd 131 (1959). Relief may also be granted if it is shown that the active participants, acting through the board of directors or otherwise, breached their fiduciary obligation to the minority or outside shareholders by the unreasonable withholding of dividends. See Smith v. Atlantic Properties, Inc., 422 N.E. 2nd 798 (Mass. Apps. 1981).

outside shareholders, methods of insuring dividends

Rather than rely upon the costly and uncertain results of litigation, it is a far better practice for outside shareholders to require, as a condition of their investment in the company, that dividends be declared and paid under conditions that insure them a fair return on their investment. This may be accomplished, either through article of incorporation provision or by contract, by requiring dividends to be issued when the surplus reaches certain levels or by limiting salaries and other payments to the active participants until dividends in specified amounts are issued.

stock dividends, general aspects

The corporation laws of every state permit a corporation, under specified conditions, to issue dividends composed of its own shares (i.e., stock dividends). Stock dividends are not frequently issued by small business corporations, and when they are issued it is usually for tax reasons. Stock dividends do not normally constitute income when received by a shareholder, although the per-share capitalized basis of a shareholder's stock is diluted because the purchase price or other basis of the stock must then include the stock received as a dividend in addition to the stock previously acquired. If the stock received as a dividend is not common stock, special tax rules may be applicable. See 26 U.S.C. 306.

stock dividends, general requirements

When stock dividends are issued the following special statutory requirements must normally be complied with: (1) the corporation must have a sufficient surplus to permit the required transfer to stated capital, (2) the amount of surplus transferred to stated capital must be disclosed to the shareholders when the dividend is paid, and (3) to avoid the dilution of one class of stock in favor of another, no dividend payable in shares of one class of stock may be paid to the holders of another class of stock unless authorized by either the articles of incorporation or the written consent or majority vote of the shareholders of the class of stock to be distributed. The specific restrictions and requirements related to the issuance of stock dividends vary, so the corporation laws of the local state should be checked and complied with.

stock splits, general aspects

Stock splits are similar to, and are often confused with, stock dividends. The difference is that when a stock dividend is issued a transfer from surplus to stated capital must be made on the books of the corporation, usually in the amount of the par value of the stock issued as a dividend or in the amount of the reasonable value of the stock if it has no par value. A stock split, like a stock dividend, involves the issuance of a certain number of shares for each share currently held. However, no transfer to stated capital is required for a stock split. In practice, a stock dividend is normally declared when the amount of stock distributed is small compared to the amount of stock outstanding (a distribution, say, of one share per 100 shares held). If the ratio is high (a distribution, say, of one share per two shares held), the transaction is normally a stock split. Another practical difference between a stock split and a stock dividend is that if the stock has a par value a stock split will normally require a reduction in the par value of the stock, which usually requires an amendment to the articles of incorporation.

The redemption by a corporation of its own stock is similar in some respects to a dividend distribution. The primary difference is that a dividend payment involves only a distribution of money or property by the corporation, while a stock redemption involves the exchange of all or a portion of a shareholder's stock in return for money or property. Like the issuance of stock, the redemption of stock normally requires board of director approval. stock redemptions, general aspects

The corporation laws of most states, usually expressly but sometimes by implication, permit a corporation to purchase or otherwise acquire shares of its own stock under certain conditions. It is a common practice to include a similar power in the articles of incorporation, subject, of course, to any applicable statutory limitations. It is also important to insure that the fiduciary obligations of the controlling shareholders to the minority are not violated in any redemption transaction. See Donahue v. Rudd Electrotype Co., 367 Mass. 578, 328 N.E. 2nd 505 (1975). stock redemptions, general aspects

As in the case of stock dividends, the funds available for stock redemptions are restricted by statute in most states, and the applicable statutes must be strictly followed in order to prevent personal liability from being imposed on the directors and the participating shareholders. Most corporation laws require a corporation to purchase its own stock only out of unreserved and unrestricted surplus with certain exceptions, such as purchases for the purposes of eliminating fractional shares, consolidating indebtedness, redeeming the stock of legally-entitled dissenting shareholders, and retiring redeemable stock. Most corporation laws also preclude any redemption when the corporation is insolvent or would be rendered insolvent by the proposed redemption. The redemption of its own stock by a corporation is a matter largely regulated by statute, and the applicable provisions of the local corporation laws should be ascertained and complied with. stock redemptions, general requirements

Shares of its own stock reacquired by a corporation can normally be held by the corporation as treasury stock, be restored to unissued status, or be eliminated from authorized shares. The latter two options may require article of incorporation amendment and filings with the Secretary of State to become effective. The holding of shares as treasury stock usually operates to restrict the surplus of the corporation. Again, the matter is largely statutory and the applicable statutes should be checked in this regard. reacquired stock, disposition of by corporation

It is a common practice for shareholders of small business corporations to enter into buy-out agreements with the corporation providing for the purchase or redemption of all or a portion of a shareholder's stock under certain conditions (see section 5.17, supra). The tax rules applicable to such redemptions are obviously important to both the shareholder and the corporation. A brief description of the applicable tax rules is set forth below. stock redemptions, buy-out agreements

The general tax rule governing stock redemptions by a corporation is that the transaction will be treated as a distribution of property by the corporation unless the transaction can be properly characterized as a sale or exchange of stock. See 26 U.S.C. 302(a). It is almost always in the interest of a shareholder to have a stock redemption transaction treated as a sale or exchange of stock. The difference between the two treatments is that most distributions of property are taxed to the shareholder as ordinary income, while in a sale or exchange of stock the shareholder is taxed at capital gain rates only on the gain realized in the transaction. The tax rules applicable to corporate distributions are discussed below in this section. stock redemptions, tax treatment

The following rules apply in determining whether the redemption of stock by a corporation will be taxed as a corporate distribution or as a sale or exchange of stock:

(1) If the redemption results in the complete termination of a shareholder's equity interest in the corporation, the transaction will be deemed a sale or exchange of stock and not a distribution. See 26 U.S.C. 302(b)(3). While the shareholder may remain a creditor of the corporation after the transaction, care must be taken to insure that his or her equity in the corporation is terminated by the transaction. If the shareholder retains a constructive interest in the corporation through stock owned by a family member or by means of a partnership, trust, estate, or corporation in which the shareholder or a family member has an interest, the shareholder's interest in the corporation will not be deemed to have been completely terminated by the redemption transaction. See 26 U.S.C. 302(c), 318(a). If a shareholder is issued debentures or other debt obligations of the corporation in return for his or her stock, care must be taken to insure that the debt instruments are not the substantial equivalent of equity. See Treasury Reg. 1.302-4(d). complete redemption of shareholder's interest, requirements

substantially disproportionate stock redemption, requirements

(2) If the redemption transaction results in a substantially disproportionate redemption of a shareholder's stock holdings in the corporation, the transaction will be deemed a sale or exchange of stock and not a distribution, even if the shareholder's equity interest in the corporation is not completely terminated by the transaction. See 26 U.S.C. 302(b)(2). For a redemption transaction to result in a substantially disproportionate redemption, the following specific requirements must be satisfied: (a) the shareholder's relative voting and common stock-holding interest in the corporation must be reduced by a factor of more than 20 percent by the transaction, (b) the shareholder must hold less than 50 percent of all voting stock in the corporation after the transaction, and (c) the redemption must not be part of a series of redemptions the result of which is to render the instant redemption transaction not substantially disproportionate. See 26 U.S.C. 302(b)(2)(B),(C),(D). As in the case of a complete termination, the statutory requirements may not be circumvented through family, corporate, partnership, trust, or other constructive holdings. See 26 U.S.C. 302(c)(1), 318(b)(1).

stock redemption in partial liquidation, requirements

(3) If the redemption is of the stock of an individual shareholder in partial liquidation of the corporation, the transaction will be deemed a sale or exchange of stock and not a distribution. See 26 U.S.C. 302(b)(4). For purposes of this rule, stock held by a partnership, estate, or trust is treated as being held proportionally by its partners or beneficiaries. See 26 U.S.C. 302(e)(5). The requirements that must be met in order for a partial liquidation to occur are discussed in section 7.03, infra.

stock redemption not equivalent to dividend, requirements

(4) If the redemption transaction is not essentially the equivalent of a dividend it will be treated as a sale or exchange of stock even if the redemption transaction fails to qualify under the three rules described above. See 26 U.S.C. 302(b)(1). In practice, however, it is difficult for shareholders of small business corporations to qualify under this rule. All pro-rata redemptions are normally treated as distributions regardless of other circumstances, especially if the corporation has only a single class of stock. See Treasury Reg. 1.302-2(b). The Supreme Court has ruled that the business purposes of the redemption and the absence of tax-avoidance purposes are irrelevant, and that the only test is whether the redemption is essentially the equivalent of a dividend (i.e., having the same effect on the control and rights to assets of the corporation as a distribution without any redemption of stock). See U.S. v. Davis, 397 U.S. 301, 25 L. Ed. 2nd 323, 90 S. Ct. 1041 (1970). Again, the constructive stock-ownership tests described in the preceding rules are applied.

redemption of stock of deceased shareholder, requirements

(5) The redemption of the stock of a deceased shareholder is deemed a sale or exchange of stock to the extent of the amount of the decedent's death taxes and expenses under the circumstances described below, regardless of any other tax rules. See 26 U.S.C. 303(a). For this rule to apply, the value of all of the corporation's stock in the decedent's gross estate must exceed 35 percent of the value of the decedent's adjusted gross estate. See 26 U.S.C. 303(b)(2)(A). Special rules apply if stock of two or more corporations is included in the estate. See 26 U.S.C. 303(b)(2)(B). The amount of the redemption included under this rule may not exceed the sum of the estate, inheritance, and other death taxes, plus the funeral and other administrative expenses allowable as deductions under the federal estate tax laws. See 26 U.S.C. 303(a). This redemption rule is available only to personal representatives, heirs, and legatees of deceased shareholders who bear the financial burden of such expenses, and not to their transferees or purchasers. See 26 U.S.C. 303(b)(3) and Treasury Reg. 1.303-2(f). It is not necessary, however, that the redemption proceeds be needed or used to pay such expenses. For this rule to apply the redemption must be effected after the death of the shareholder and within 90 days after the end of the three-year period for assessing federal estate taxes. See 26 U.S.C. 303(b)(1).

stock purchases from corporate shareholders, redemption rules

(6) If the same person or persons control two or more corporations and if one of the controlled corporations purchases the stock of one of the other controlled corporations, the transaction will be deemed a redemption of stock and the rules described above apply. See 26 U.S.C. 304(a)(1). Also, the acquisition by a subsidiary corporation of the stock of its parent corporation from a shareholder of the parent is deemed a redemption transaction. See 26 U.S.C. 304(a)(2). Special rules, too lengthy to list here, are applicable to these transactions. See 26 U.S.C. 304(b),(c).

The tax aspects of the various forms of corporate distributions (i.e., dividends, certain stock redemptions, etc.) are important to the participants of many small business corporations. For federal income tax purposes, distributions by a corporation to its shareholders, other than as compensation for personal services, are classified as (1) dividends, (2) return of capital, or (3) gain, including capital gain. Dividends (whether cash or property) are taxed as ordinary income to the shareholder and are not deductible by the corporation. Distributions in the form of a return of capital are neither taxable to the shareholder nor deductible by the corporation. Gain is taxable to the shareholder and is not deductible by the corporation. It should be noted that special rules apply when the shareholder is another corporation. See 26 U.S.C. 301. corporate distributions, tax treatment

Practically every distribution by a corporation to its shareholders, other than as compensation for personal services or for the redemption of stock, is deemed for tax purposes to be a dividend to the extent of the corporation's current or accumulated earnings and profits. See 26 U.S.C. 316(a). A corporation's accumulated earnings and profits normally approximates its earned surplus or its taxable income, although special tax rules may vary the amount. See 26 U.S.C. 312. corporate distributions, treated as dividends

A distribution by a corporation is considered to be a return of capital to a shareholder to the extent that it exceeds the shareholder's proportionate share of the corporate earnings and profits and does not exceed the adjusted basis of his or her stock, which is normally its purchase price. If the distribution exceeds the adjusted basis of the shareholder's stock, the excess will be taxed as a gain to the shareholder. See 26 U.S.C. 301(c). corporate distributions, return of capital

If property (as opposed to cash) is distributed to a shareholder, the amount of the distribution is deemed for tax purposes to be the lesser of the fair market value of the property or the adjusted basis of the property in the hands of the corporation immediately prior to the distribution increased by any gain on the distribution realized by the corporation. See 26 U.S.C. 301. Generally, gain (but not loss) is recognized by a corporation on a nonliquidating distribution of appreciated property. Gain is recognized to the extent that the fair market value of the property exceeds its adjusted basis. See 26 U.S.C. 311. distributions of property, valuation, tax treatment

The distribution of stock by a corporation to its shareholders, whether as a dividend or in a stock split, is not usually a taxable transaction. See 26 U.S.C. 305(a). There are, however, five exceptions to this rule, and stock distributions are taxable transactions in the following instances: stock distributions, tax treatment

(1) Where the shareholders have the option of receiving stock or cash or other property of the corporation. See 26 U.S.C. 305(b)(1). It should be noted that this rule applies to all shareholders receiving the stock, even if only one shareholder is given such an option. See Treasury Reg. 1.305-2.

(2) Where the distribution of a stock dividend has the effect of increasing the relative interest of some shareholders in the assets or earnings of the corporation and, as part of the same series of events, other shareholders receive cash or other property. See 26 U.S.C. 305(b)(2). This rule normally applies to cases where a corporation has more than one class of common stock and issues stock dividends to one class and money or property dividends to the other class or classes.

(3) Where preferred stock is distributed to some of the holders of common stock and common stock is distributed to the others. See 26 U.S.C. 305(b)(3). Under this rule the distribution is taxable to all shareholders.

(4) Where the stock is distributed to the holders of preferred stock. See 26 U.S.C. 305(b)(4).

(5) Where the stock distributed is preferred stock convertible into other stock, unless it can be established that the distribution will not result in a disproportionate distribution. See 26 U.S.C. 305(b)(5).

6.03 Required Governmental Reports and Returns

small business corporations, handling reporting requirements

Once a corporation has been organized and has commenced the transaction of business, it is usually required to prepare and file a variety of federal, state, and local reports and returns. In large corporations separate departments are often created to handle the corporate reporting requirements, especially those related to federal and state taxes. Most small business corporations rely on accountants, tax consultants, lawyers, or external auditors to supply the expertise needed to cope with their reporting requirements.

purpose of section

The purpose of this section is to assist the participants of a typical small business corporation in dealing with the various federal, state, and local reporting requirements by providing them with a guide as to the type and number of reports and returns that may be required. No attempt is made to give technical guidance on the completion or filing of any forms, reports, or returns.

small business corporations, federal reports and returns

The federal reports and returns that a typical small business corporation may have to prepare and file include the following:

(1) Reports dealing with federal withholding taxes. Included here are personal income taxes of employees and the employees' portion of social security and medicare taxes. These are the so-called "trust fund" taxes, the nonpayment of which may result in personal liability for responsible corporate officers (see section 6.06, infra). The employer's portion of social security and medicare taxes must also be reported and paid. The federal withholding tax reports must be filed quarterly, usually on a Form 941. A W-2 Form must be given to each corporate employee not later than January 31 and transmitted to the Internal Revenue by the last day of February of each year. The required forms are provided by the local office of the Internal Revenue Service upon request. An Employer's Annual Federal Unemployment Tax Return must be filed by January 31 of each year using a Form 940 or 940-EZ.

(2) Annual corporate income tax returns. These must be filed by all C corporations subject to the federal corporate income tax, regardless of whether the corporation had taxable income during the tax year. See 26 U.S.C. 6012(a)(2). The return, which is on Form 1120, must be filed on or before the 15th day of the third month following the close of the corporation's fiscal year. Thus, if the corporation's fiscal year ends on December 31st, the return must be filed by March 15th.

(3) Informational income tax returns for S corporations. If the corporation is an S corporation it must file an informational income tax return on Form 1120S by the 15th day of the third month following the close of the corporation's fiscal year. See 26 U.S.C. 6037. If the corporation's tax year is the calendar year, the return is due on March 15th.

(4) Information at the source returns. If the corporation, in the course of its trade or business, makes payments of $600 or more during the tax year to any person in the form of otherwise unreported rents, salaries, wages, premiums, annuities, compensation, remunerations, emoluments, or other fixed or determinable gains, profits, or income, then information at the source returns must be filed with the I.R.S. showing such payments. See 26 U.S.C. 6041.

(5) Dividend payment returns. If the corporation pays dividends of $10 or more during the tax year, a return must be filed showing such payments. See 26 U.S.C. 6042.

(6) Interest payment returns. If the corporation pays interest of $10 or more during the tax year it must file a return showing such payments. See 26 U.S.C. 6049.

(7) Other informational returns. The corporation may have to file other informational income tax returns if an employee receives either stock dividends from the corporation or allowances excludable from income. See 26 U.S.C. 6011 and Treasury Reg. 31.6011(a).

(8) Qualified employee benefit plan reports. Periodic reports and returns must be filed with the Internal Revenue Service and the Department of Labor showing the contributions made to and the status of any qualified employee benefit plans maintained by the corporation for the benefit of its employees. See 26 U.S.C. 6057, 6058 and 29 U.S.C. 1201 et. seq. If an outside trustee, such as a bank, administers the plans, the reporting responsibilities should be coordinated with the trustee.

(9) Liquidation, dissolution, termination, or contraction returns. A return must be filed within 30 days after the adoption by the corporation of a plan calling for its dissolution or liquidation, in whole or in part. See 26 U.S.C. 6043.

(10) Securities and Exchange Commission reports. If the corporation has raised capital through a public offering of its stock, or if it has assets in excess of one million dollars and a class of equity securities held by 500 or more persons, it is subject to the annual and quarterly reporting requirements of the Securities Exchange Act of 1934. See 15 U.S.C. 78L(g).

A typical small business corporation may have to comply with the following state and local reporting requirements: small business corporations, state and local reports and returns

(1) Annual or periodic corporate franchise reports and fees. See the heading "Periodic Reports" in Appendix I, infra, for the reporting requirements in each state.

(2) State (and sometimes local) corporate income tax returns. If the state or locality imposes an income tax on corporations, an annual return must normally be filed.

(3) State (and sometimes local) withholding and unemployment taxes. Most states require employers, including corporations, to withhold the income and unemployment taxes of their employees and to file periodic reports thereon.

(4) Sales and use tax returns. If the corporation is engaged in retail sales and if the state or locality imposes a sales or use tax, the corporation will probably be required to collect the tax and periodically forward the collected funds, along with a tax return, to the taxing authority. A sales tax license from each taxing authority is usually required, also.

(5) Real property tax reports. If the corporation owns real property, state and local taxes on the property must normally be periodically paid. Usually a tax notice is sent by the local taxing authority and a tax return is not required.

(6) Personal property tax reports. State or local personal property taxes are often assessed on all or certain types of personal property owned or leased by the corporation either during the previous year or as of a certain date. Separate inventory taxes are assessed in some states. Some form of annual or periodic return is usually required for most types of personal property taxes.

(7) Occupational tax reports. In some states or localities an occupational or "head" tax is imposed, taxing the privilege of working in that state or locality. The employer is normally required to collect the tax and file periodic reports with the taxing authority.

(8) Stock transfer tax reports. These are usually required in states where a tax is imposed on the transfer of stock.

6.04 Handling Corporate Meetings

small business corporations, necessity of meetings

Because the participants of most small business corporations function as the shareholders, directors, and officers of the corporation, and because they often work in close contact with one another, formal corporate meetings tend to be viewed as a waste of time. In some quarters at least, requests for formal meetings are viewed as a sign of either distrust or impending corporate trickery. Fortunately, under ordinary circumstances most meetings and other formal transactions required or contemplated by the corporation laws may be either dispensed with or held on paper only. It is important, however, that certain ritual meetings and transactions called for in the corporation laws be at least nominally complied with. Otherwise, the existence of the corporation and its capacity to conduct business may be subject to attack either by creditors or by its own shareholders, should financial difficulties or internal disputes later arise.

corporate meeting, types of

This section deals with all corporate meetings except organizational meetings, which are dealt with in sections 5.07 and 5.21, supra. Corporate meetings include meetings of incorporators, shareholders, and the board of directors and committees thereof. It is important to understand that directors and shareholders must, for most purposes, act as a body and not individually, and that to act as a body it is necessary, in the absence of a statute to the contrary, to hold a meeting.

action-without-meeting statutes, general requirements

Every state has a statute giving sanction to action taken by shareholders or directors without a meeting if a written consent describing the action taken is prepared and signed by all or a specified number of the persons who would have been entitled to vote on the matter had a meeting been held. Several states have similar statutes that are applicable to incorporators. The handling of corporate meetings is greatly facilitated by these statutes. The statute in the local state should be checked before proceeding, however, because the scope of action-without-meeting statutes vary. Most action-without-meeting statutes cover all types of meetings (except, in some states, organizational meetings), including annual meetings of shareholders and other formal meetings specified in the corporation laws. See section 5.11, supra, for further reading on action-without-meeting statutes. The action-without-meeting statutes in each state are summarized in Appendix I, infra, under the heading of "Action Without Meeting."

annual meeting of shareholders, necessity of

In most states the only corporate meeting specifically required by statute is the annual meeting of shareholders. The time and place of this meeting is usually required by statute to be set forth in the bylaws. However, a failure to hold such a meeting does not invalidate corporate acts or otherwise impair the ability of the corporation to transact business. If a shareholder desires such a meeting, it must be held, and most corporation laws provide methods of enforcing this right, including court proceedings. Even if the annual meeting of shareholders is not held, certain functions required to be fulfilled at the meeting (such as the election of directors) must be accomplished if the corporation is to continue to function effectively.

annual meeting of shareholders, how to handle informally

In a typical small business corporation involving only a few shareholders, all or most of whom are directly involved in the management of the corporate business and all of whom are on friendly terms, the simplest and easiest method of handling the annual meeting of shareholders is under an action-without-meeting statute. Under such a statute it is only necessary to prepare a consent or memorandum describing the action taken (normally the election or reelection of directors and perhaps a few other corporate housekeeping items), include a waiver of any statutorily required notice, state in the memorandum that the action constitutes the annual meeting of shareholders, obtain the signatures of all of the shareholders in their shareholder capacity, and file the memorandum in the corporate minute book. See section 5.11 and Exhibit 5-I, supra, for guidance in the preparation of such a memorandum.

directors' meetings, requirements, how to handle

Directors' meetings are not specifically regulated by statute in most states. Most corporation laws simply provide that the board of directors or any committee thereof may meet at regular or special meetings at such times and places and upon such notice as the bylaws may prescribe. However, certain important corporate functions (see section 5.07, supra, for a list) must be performed by the board of directors if the corporation is to transact business in a lawful manner, and these functions must be carried out whether or not the directors actually meet. Again, in a typical small business corporation with few directors all of whom are on friendly terms, the simplest method of handling board of director functions is by a memorandum under an action-without-meeting statute in the manner described above.

formal corporate meetings, requirements

If, for whatever reason, the corporate participants are not on friendly terms, or if there are shareholders who are not active in the corporate business, or if for any other reason corporate meetings cannot be held informally, it may be necessary to hold one or more formal corporate meetings. In such instances it is important to comply with the bylaw, article of incorporation, and statutory requirements as to notice, quorum, voting, and other requirements of the particular meeting sought to be held.

When holding a formal shareholders' meeting, whether annual or special, the following matters should be complied with:

shareholders' meetings, notice requirements

(1) Notice of the meeting. The state corporation laws and the corporate bylaws normally designate the shareholders who are entitled to receive notice of meetings and the periods of time within which the notices must be sent. Usually shareholders of record as of a certain fixed period prior to the meeting are entitled to notice. The notice is especially important for special meetings of shareholders because normally only the matters described in the notice may be considered at the meeting. Any lawful business may normally be considered at an annual meeting. See Exhibit 5-H at the end of chapter 5, supra, for a sample notice of shareholders' meetings. See section 5.11, supra, for further reading on the preparation of the minutes of a shareholders' meeting.

shareholders' meetings, quorum requirements

(2) Quorum requirements. The articles of incorporation or bylaws usually contain the quorum requirements; otherwise the minimum quorum requirements in the state corporation laws govern.

shareholders' meetings, voting requirements

(3) Voting requirements. The articles of incorporation normally contain the voting requirements and limitations for each class of stock. The state corporation laws usually govern the requirements of proxies. It is important to note that different matters considered at a shareholders' meeting may carry different voting requirements. For example, cumulative voting requirements may apply to the election or removal of directors, the approval of bylaw amendments may require only a simple majority vote, and article of incorporation amendments may require a very high or unanimous vote.

directors' meetings, legal aspects

Formal directors' meetings are generally easier to handle than shareholder meetings, mainly because fewer persons are involved in most instances. The corporate bylaws normally specify when, where, and upon what notice regular or special meetings of the board of directors, or committees thereof, may be held. Quorum requirements for directors' meetings are also usually contained in the bylaws, although the state corporation laws may impose certain minimum requirements.

directors' meetings, notice requirements

Notices of regular meetings of the board of directors are not usually required. In most states notices of special meetings need not specify the purpose of the meeting, although it is a good practice to do so and doing so does not normally limit the business that may be conducted at the meeting. See Exhibit 5-H at the end of chapter 5, supra, for a sample of such a notice.

directors' meetings, general aspects

Most corporation laws provide that the attendance of a director at a meeting constitutes a waiver of notice of the meeting unless the director attends the meeting for the sole purpose of objecting to the transaction of any business because the meeting was not lawfully convened. In most states, it should be noted, a directors' meeting is lawfully convened if the directors can hear each other's voices at the same time by telephonic devices or otherwise, unless such meetings are precluded by the articles of incorporation or bylaws. See the heading of "Action Without Meeting" in Appendix I, infra, for a description of the telephonic meeting requirements in each state. See section 5.11, supra, for guidance in the preparation of minutes of directors' meetings, and see section 5.07, supra, for general reading on board of director functions.

6.05 Handling Internal Disputes

participant disputes, general aspects

The creation of a corporation is, of course, no guarantee that disputes will not arise among the business participants. While a properly devised corporate management and control structure will provide a means of resolving most participant disputes stemming from financial or business differences, it is impossible to provide for the resolution of all participant disputes, especially those rooted in personal distrust and animosity. It is disputes of this nature that are most likely to result in corporate power struggles and attempted squeeze-outs.

power struggles, equal shareholders, consequences

Serious power struggles between shareholders, or groups of shareholders, owning or controlling equal or nearly equal blocks of shares in the corporation are the most difficult internal disputes to deal with. If the competing factions are determined in their efforts to gain control of the corporation, or at least prevent the other faction from gaining control, there is little that can be done from a legal standpoint to resolve the dispute other than follow the procedures, if any, contained in the corporate management and control structure. These procedures normally call for either the dissolution of the corporation or for the purchase of the stock of one faction by the other under certain conditions. See section 5.15, supra, for further reading on the corporate management and control structure.

power struggles, equal shareholders, typical results

Unfortunately, it often happens that one or both of the competing factions either does not wish to follow the required dispute-settling procedures, or is financially or otherwise unable to do so. The result, more often than not, is corporate deadlock, paralyzing the corporation and preventing it from carrying out the functions for which it was formed. The best result that can be hoped for in such situations is some type of workable compromise to keep the corporation functioning long enough to find a suitable buyer, if that is feasible under the circumstances. Most likely, the eventual result of an even-sided power struggle will be the dissolution and liquidation of the corporation, matters which are discussed in section 7.03, infra.

squeeze-out, definition, general aspects

Most disputes in small business corporations are between the holders of unequal amounts of stock; that is between majority and minority shareholders. The most common form of such a dispute is the so-called "squeeze-out" (or "freeze-out," as some authorities call it). A squeeze-out is the attempt by majority shareholders to eliminate or reduce to insignificance the interests and corporate powers of some or all of the minority shareholders, usually without the payment of fair value to the minority shareholders for their interests in the corporation. In small business corporations the active participants are usually the majority shareholders, and the minority shareholders are usually outside shareholders, former participants, the heirs, legatees or transferees of former participants, or active participants not on friendly terms with the other active participants.

squeeze-outs, typical causes

Squeeze-out attempts against minority shareholders often originate from disputes over corporate policy wherein a minority shareholder has used his or her veto power to effectively block the efforts of the majority to implement their desired policy. In other cases squeeze-outs are brought about by the desire of the majority to either eliminate the interest of the minority shareholders for financial reasons or acquire the minority's interest in the corporation for less than fair value.

squeeze-outs, forms of, techniques

In practice, squeeze-outs are usually implemented through one or more of the following techniques:

(1) The payment of high salaries and bonuses to the majority participants, while either discharging or reducing the compensation of those being squeezed out. If those being squeezed out are not employees of the corporation, the majority will refuse to issue dividends, thus denying the minority any return on their investment in the corporation.

(2) The issuance of large amounts of new stock to the majority shareholders, usually either for services or at grossly inadequate prices. This technique serves to further dilute the interests of those being squeezed out and to enhance the interests of the majority, sometimes to the point where they can override veto powers and implement such extraordinary corporate acts as merger, dissolution, and the sale or transfer of assets.

(3) The majority participants may cause the corporation to sell or transfer its assets, usually at inadequate prices, either to themselves or to entities that they control.

(4) The formation of a new corporation by the majority participants and the transfer of all or most of the business or assets of the old corporation to the new, often with the dissolution of the old corporation.

(5) The merger or consolidation of the corporation with another corporation owned by the majority participants under terms that are unfair to the minority.

(6) The draining off of corporate earnings in the form of unreasonably high rents on property owned by the majority or exorbitant payments under contracts between the corporation and entities owned or controlled by the majority.

(7) The purchase of the stock of those being squeezed out at unfairly low prices without disclosing to the sellers inside or unknown information that would increase the price of their stock.

(8) If the business or assets of the corporation so lend themselves, the dissolving of the corporation by the majority and the dividing up of the assets in a manner that permits the majority to form a new corporation and continue the business, excluding those being squeezed out.

Many of the squeeze-out techniques described above can be prevented, or at least made more difficult, by the insertion of veto powers and other control devices when the corporation is organized (see section 5.15, supra). It often happens, however, that when the corporation is being organized the participants, who are then on friendly terms and do not anticipate serious disputes, do not wish to impose such restrictions on the corporation and its majority participants. In practice it is often difficult, especially at the outset, for an equal participant in, say, a three-person business to envision himself or herself as a minority participant, even though in actuality the participant is only one vote away from becoming such in any dispute. squeeze-outs, when to prevent

Probably the most common device used in small business corporations to protect the interests of minority shareholders is preemptive rights, which are discussed in section 5.12, supra. While minority shareholders are certainly better off with preemptive rights than without them, the protection afforded by such rights can often be circumvented or evaded by sophisticated squeezers, especially if the state corporation laws are relied upon as the source of such rights. To circumvent statutory preemptive rights, the majority participants may issue additional stock when they know the minority does not have the funds available with which to exercise its preemptive right by purchasing the stock. Or the majority may issue the additional stock in such quantities or at such a price that the minority either cannot or will not purchase it, often because the minority is reluctant to "throw good money after bad" in such situations. Sometimes statutory preemptive rights can be evaded by issuing stock for property or for the repayment for "loans" the majority have made to the corporation. squeeze-outs, effect of preemptive rights

Clearly, the insertion of strongly protected veto powers and control devices in the corporate management and control structure is the best protection for minority shareholders. If preemptive rights are to be relied on, the extent and scope of such rights should be explicitly set forth in the articles of incorporation. In the absence of such devices or provisions, minority shareholders normally have only one recourse against determined squeezers: the courts, many of which recognize and protect the rights of minority shareholders in small business corporations. squeeze-outs, effect of veto powers

It has been held that, in the absence of a legitimate business purpose, majority shareholders may not dilute the interests of the minority by issuing additional stock, especially in great numbers at low prices, even if the minority is protected by preemptive rights which they are in a position to exercise. See Katzowitz v. Sidler, 24 N.Y. 2nd 512, 301 N.Y.S. 2nd 470, 249 N.E. 2nd 359 (1969). It has also been held that in the absence of a legitimate business reason to the contrary, minority participants have the right not to have to purchase additional stock in order to maintain their relative position in the corporation. See Bennett v. Breuil Petroleum Corp., 34 Del. Ch. 6, 99 A. 2nd 236 (1953). dilution of stock, when prohibited, cases squeeze-outs, prohibited techniques, cases

On squeezing techniques other than the issuance of stock, many courts have protected the interests of minority participants and shareholders by imposing fiduciary duties on those in control of small business corporations. See Annotation: Duties and Liabilities - Acquiring Stock of Minority Shareholders, 7 A.L.R. 3rd 500. For example, the payment of excessive fees and salaries to majority participants justified the awarding of damages to a minority participant in Newton v. Hornblower, Inc., 224 Kan. 506, 582 P. 2nd 1136 (1978). The sale of corporate assets for inadequate consideration by the majority created a cause of action for a minority shareholder in Pupecki v. James Madison Corp., 376 Mass. 212, 382 N.E. 2nd 1030 (1978). The controlling shareholders were not permitted to unreasonably deny employment to a minority shareholder in Wilkes v. Springside Nursing Home, Inc., 370 Mass. 842, 353 N.E. 2nd 657 (1976). It was held that a majority shareholder could not cause a merger for the sole purpose of eliminating the interests of minority shareholders in Singer v. Magnavox Co. 380 A. 2nd 969 (Del., 1977). And, it should be noted, in the proper situation the courts may impose a fiduciary duty on minority shareholders to protect and preserve the interests of the majority. See Helms v. Duckworth, 249 F. 2nd 482 (CADC, 1957).

squeeze-outs, difficulty of preventing

It should also be understood that many courts are reluctant to interfere with the internal affairs of corporations by imposing fiduciary duties on those in control. See Bellows v. Porter, 201 F. 2nd 429 (CA 8, 1953), and Clagett v. Davis, 131 N.E. 2nd 459 (Ohio Com. Pleas, 1953). Even in states where fiduciary duties protecting minority interests are recognized, the burden of a complaining shareholder is great. Not only must such a shareholder show the wrong imposed on himself, he or she must in most cases show that no legitimate business purpose was served by the action complained of. Litigation should be the last resort of an aggrieved minority shareholder.

squeeze-outs, remedies, personal actions

Should a wronged shareholder resort to litigation, there are at least three possible types of actions that may be resorted to for relief. A person who has been personally wronged as a shareholder, may, in his or her individual capacity, sue the shareholders perpetrating the alleged wrong and, in most cases, the corporation. This is the most common type of action brought by minority shareholders being squeezed out of small business corporations for the reason that it is usually the minority shareholder (as opposed to the corporation) that is damaged by the alleged wrong.

squeeze-outs, remedies, derivative actions

If the corporation is damaged by the actions of the controlling participants or shareholders, a minority shareholder may bring a shareholder's derivative action against the wrong-doers to enforce a corporate right. One advantage of a derivative action is that a successful plaintiff can normally recover the expenses of maintaining the action, including attorney's fees. The detriments of such an action are that certain prerequisites must usually be met in order to bring the action. These include a prior demand on the corporation and, in some cases, the other shareholders, unless such a demand would be futile, the posting of security, and a requirement of share ownership by the plaintiff when the alleged wrong occurred. In practice it is often difficult to determine whether a particular action is derivative or personal to the shareholder. See Gordon v. Elliman, 306 N.Y. 456, 119 N.E. 2nd 331 (1954).

squeeze-outs, remedies, securities laws

The third possible type of action available to an aggrieved shareholder, in some instances at least, is an action under section 10(b) of the Securities Exchange Act of 1934 (15 U.S.C. 78j(b)) and its implementing rule, Rule 10b-5 (17 C.F.R. 240.10b-5). Under this statute and rule it is unlawful for any person to use the mails or interstate commerce to employ any manipulative or deceptive device or contrivance in connection with the purchase or sale of a security. This statute and rule have been held to give private rights to aggrieved buyers and sellers of securities. See Glick v. Campagna, 613 F. 2nd 31 (CA3, 1979). This type of action is particularly useful in situations where large amounts of stock are distributed at prices lower than its true value. See Rekant v. Desser, 425 F. 2nd 872 (CA 5, 1970).

abandoning shareholder, illustration

A problem often encountered by the participants of small business corporations is that of the abandoning shareholder. Suppose that A, B and C are equal participants of and employed by Corporation X. Suppose further that a few months or years after the formation of Corporation X, A becomes disenchanted with the business and leaves the employ of the corporation, refusing, however, to return his stock. If the corporation later prospers and increases greatly in value, must B and C share the fruits of that prosperity with A? If the corporation has been properly organized the answer is no. Otherwise, much depends on the circumstances of A's departure, his previous contributions to the business, and the subsequent actions of B and C.

abandoning shareholder, how to handle

If corporation X was properly organized, each participant, upon leaving the employ of the corporation, would have been contractually bound, either through an employment contract or a shareholders' agreement, to return his or her stock to either the corporation or the other shareholders at a fixed or determinable price. Assuming that either the corporation or B and C were financially and otherwise able to fulfill their obligations to A and repurchase the stock, the problem would have been solved by the purchase of A's stock in this manner, either voluntarily or pursuant to an action for specific performance brought by B and C.

abandoning shareholder, remedies of other shareholders

If, as often happens, there was nothing requiring A to return his stock upon leaving the employ of the corporation, B and C could, depending on the actions of A, encounter real problems. If A has really abandoned the business and has no further interest in it (which is unlikely if the corporation later prospers), B and C can probably dissolve the corporation, pay or attempt to pay A for his stock, and form another corporation to carry on the business. They would be well-advised to implement this rather costly procedure soon after A departs and before the corporation prospers. If, as is more likely, A retains an investor's interest in the corporation and has sufficient stock or veto powers to prevent its dissolution, B and C may be forced to either purchase A's stock at a premium or share their prosperity with him. There is some authority, however, permitting B and C, without dissolving X, to form a new corporation and carry on the business thereunder without A, provided that A is justly compensated for his stock in X and has in fact contributed little or nothing to either the capitalization or growth of X. See Carr v. O'Brien Co., 386 Pa. 196, 125 A. 2nd 607 (1956).

removal of directors, general aspects

Disputes and power struggles in small business corporations frequently take the form of attempts to remove directors from office. Provisions dealing with the removal of directors may be found in the bylaws, the articles of incorporation, and in the state corporation laws, all of which should be checked before attempting to remove a director. Most corporation laws provide that a director may be removed, with or without cause, by the shareholders, often by majority vote. Provisions are usually made for the protection of directors elected through cumulative or class voting by imposing the same voting requirements for the removal of a director as were required for his or her election. In many states different voting requirements for the removal of directors may be set forth in the articles of incorporation or bylaws. It should be noted that even in the absence of statute, the shareholders empowered to elect directors have the inherent common law power to remove them for cause, subject to adequate notice. See Auer v. Dressel, 306 N.Y. 427, 118 N.E. 2nd 590, 48 A.L.R. 2nd 604 (1954).

employees, disputes with corporation, typical causes

Another common source of unrest and litigation in small business corporations are disputes between the corporation and current or former employees of the corporation related to one or more of the following matters: (1) the use of inventions, patents, developments, and ideas produced by the employee during the course of his or her employment by the corporation, (2) the use by the employee of the corporation's confidential business information and trade secrets during or following employment, and (3) competing by the employee with the corporation after the termination of employment. The best practice, of course, is to explicitly deal with these matters in an employment contract or other agreement between the employee and the corporation, the provisions of which are normally binding on the parties. If, as is often the case, there is nothing in writing dealing with these matters, and the existing law on the subject must be resorted to for guidance.

employee work product, protection of

The personal use by an employee or former employee of the inventions, patents, developments, and ideas that the employee produced during the course of his or her employment by the corporation (i.e., the employee's work product) is prohibited if so provided in a valid employment contract or other agreement. See Consolidated Vultee Aircraft Corp. v. Garbell, 204 F. 2nd 946 (CA9, 1953). In the absence of such an agreement, however, the law on the subject is not clear. Generally, the mere existence of an employer-employee relationship does not give the employer an exclusive "shop right" to the inventions and other work products of the employee. However, implications drawn from the circumstances of employment (the use of the employer's property, an implied consent to the employer's exclusive use, etc.) are often held to create exclusive rights in the employer. See Annotation: Employee's Invention-Shop Right Rule, 61 A.L.R. 2nd 356 (1958).

corporate trade secrets, protection

The right of an employer to prevent an employee from making use of the employer's confidential business information and trade secrets, either during or after employment, is beyond question if that right is specified in an employment contract or other valid agreement. In the absence of such an agreement, however, the law is not clear as to exactly what information is protected from disclosure and use by the employee or former employee. While the courts consistently hold that "trade secrets" may not be disclosed or used by former or present employees, the type of information that constitutes a trade secret is not clear. Such items as customer lists, production processes, advertising methods, and skills acquired during employment may or may not be entitled to protection depending on the particular situation and jurisdiction. See Allen Mfg. Co. v. Loika, 145 Conn. 509, 144 A. 2nd 306 (1958), Annotation: Customer List as Trade Secret-Factors, 28 A.L.R. 3rd 7 (1969), and Annotation: Skills Acquired in Employment-Use, 30 A.L.R. 3rd 631 (1970).

employee, competing with corporation, prevention

The law is clear that a former employee is not prohibited from competing against a former employer in the absence of a valid agreement not to do so. It is also well settled in most states that a covenant not to compete, if reasonable, is enforceable if entered into as a part of a transaction involving employment, property, or business. See Annotation: Covenant Not To Compete, 1 A.L.R. 3rd 778 (1965). Generally, covenants not to compete are easier to enforce if entered into in connection with a business transaction (like the sale of a business) than if entered into in connection with employment. In a few states covenants not to compete are unenforceable if an employer-employee relationship existed between the parties. In any event, to be enforceable a covenant not to compete must be reasonable as to duration, territory, and types of activities prohibited. See Annotation: Employee-Restrictive Covenant-Time, 41 A.L.R. 2d 15 (1955); Annotation: Sale-Covenant as to Competition-Time, 45 A.L.R. 2d 77 (1956); Annotation: Employee-Restrictive Covenant-Area, 43 A.L.R. 2d 94 (1955); and Annotation: Sale-Covenant as to Competition-Area, 46 A.L.R. 2d 119 (1956).

6.06 Personal Liability of Corporate Participants

participant liability, general aspects

In large corporations substantially different roles are played by the shareholders, the directors, and the officers. Whether personal liability for corporate acts exists in such corporations often depends on whether the person involved was acting as an officer, director, or shareholder at the time of the alleged wrong. Because the participants of small business corporations typically occupy the three roles simultaneously, coaction between shareholders, directors, and officers occurs in practically all corporate activities, including those giving rise to personal liability. Often it is this disregard of corporate formality that creates the personal liability. It only follows, therefore, that in imposing personal liability on the participants of a small business corporation, a court is likely to ignore the traditional corporate roles and look at the essence of the action complained of and the individuals who caused it.

participant liability, to whom liable, sources of liability

Personal liability may be imposed on the participant of a small business corporation for the benefit of (1) the corporation itself, (2) one or more of the shareholders of the corporation, (3) creditors of the corporation, or (4) governmental entities. Personal liability may be imposed by the direct or indirect application of state or federal statutes, under common law doctrines, or by a combination of statutory and common law rules.

participant liability, typical causes

The personal liability of a corporate participant may result from (1) intentional wrongful acts perpetrated by the corporate participant in the course of conducting corporate affairs, acting either singly or in concert, (2) the negligence of a participant or his or her failure to act, (3) the breach by a participant of a duty, trust, or obligation imposed by reason of the participant's position in the corporation, (4) the faulty organization of the corporation, or (5) the abuse or disregard of the corporate entity by a participant. The remedy most often imposed against corporate participants for wrongful or negligent conduct is monetary damages, although injunctive relief, including removal from office, may be obtained in the proper case.

corporate opportunity doctrine, general aspects

A participant in a small business corporation has a fiduciary obligation not to divert a corporate business opportunity to his or her personal gain. See Tovrea Land & Cattle Co. v. Linsenmeyer, 100 Ariz. 107, 412 P. 2nd 47 (1966). Called the "corporate opportunity doctrine," this rule of law applies to any transaction or series of transactions wherein a corporate participant or employee diverts to his or her personal gain a business opportunity that properly belongs to the corporation. See generally, Note, Corporate Opportunity, 74 Harvard Law Review 765. For example, a corporate participant may not secretly use information belonging to the corporation (see Essex Trust Co. v. Enwright, 214 Mass. 507, 102 N.E. 441 (1913)), or enter into a business reasonably incident to the corporate business (see Kerrigan v. Unity Savings Assn., 58 Ill. 2nd 20, 317 N.E. 2nd 39 (1974)), or receive secret commissions on corporate transactions (see Flynn v. Zimmerman, 23 Ill. App. 2nd 467, 163 N.E. 2nd 568 (1960)), or purchase mining claims in the same area as the corporation's claims (see Schildberg Rock Products Co. v. Brooks, 258 Iowa 759, 140 N.W. 2nd 132 (1966)).

corporate opportunity doctrine, applicability

Under the corporate opportunity doctrine, a corporate participant or employee who sets up a competing company and diverts corporate accounts to the competing company may be liable in damages to the corporation. See General Auto. Mfg. Co. v. Singer, 19 Wis. 2nd 528, 120 N.W. 2nd 659 (1963), and Raines v. Toney, 228 Ark. 1170, 313 S.W. 2nd 802 (1958). Corporate participants or employees may also be liable to the corporation if they acquire for themselves property or assets essential to the corporation's business. See Knutsen v. Frushour, 92 Idaho 37, 436 P. 2nd 521 (1968). Some states have statutory standards of conduct for directors and officers of corporations (they usually impose the "prudent man" standard) and the courts often apply these standards in corporate opportunity doctrine cases.

corporate opportunity doctrine, when not applicable

Of course, not every business opportunity presented to a corporate participant or employee belongs to the corporation. The corporate opportunity doctrine has been held not to apply in the following situations:

(1) When the corporation has, in good faith, considered and rejected the business opportunity or has failed to avail itself of it. See Diedrick v. Helm, 217 Minn. 483, 14 N.W. 2nd 913, 153 A.L.R. 649 (1944). The corporate action is likely to be closely scrutinized, however, if the person seeking the opportunity also dominates the rejecting corporation. See Guth v. Loft, Inc., 23 Del. Ch. 255, 5 A. 2nd 503 (1930).

(2) When the corporation is insolvent or financially unable to avail itself of the opportunity. See Canion v. Texas Cycle Supply, Inc., 537 S.W. 2nd 510 (Tex. Civil Apps. 1976). While a participant is not obligated to use or loan his or her personal funds to assist the corporation in availing itself of a business opportunity (see Hart v. Bell, 222 Minn. 69, 23 N.W. 2nd 375 (1946)), the financial inability of the corporation may not be relied upon by those whose wrongful actions have created the inability. See Daloisio v. Peninsula Land Co., 43 N.J. Super. 79, 127 A. 2nd 885 (1956).

(3) When the opportunity in question is presented to a participant or employee in his or her individual capacity and is one which the corporation, because of its line of business, has no legitimate business interest other than a general investment interest. See Johnston v. Green, 35 Del. Ch. 479, 121 A. 2nd 919 (1956).

corporate opportunity doctrine, remedies

The proper remedy for the wrongful appropriation of a corporate business opportunity is an action by the corporation against the participant either directly for damages or to impress a constructive trust upon the monies or profits resulting from the opportunity. If, as is often the case with small business corporations, those in control of the corporation are also the alleged wrongdoers, the action may be brought derivatively by a minority or outside shareholder. Injunctive relief may also be granted to prevent the continued wrongful appropriation of the opportunity, especially if trade secrets are being exploited or if the offender is violating a covenant not to compete. See Associated Coal Sales Corp. v. Hughes, 53 A.D. 2nd 838, 385 N.Y.S. 2nd 559 (1976).

corporate opportunity doctrine, effect of ratification or resignation

The general ratification by a corporation or its shareholders of the acts of its officers and directors does not relieve an officer or director of liability for the wrongful appropriation of a corporate opportunity in the absence of a full and frank disclosure of the entire transaction. See Lutherland v. Dahlen, 357 Pa. 143, 53 A. 2nd 143 (1947) and Melgard v. Moscow Idaho Seed Co., 73 Idaho 265, 251 P. 2nd 546 (1952). The fact that a person resigns his or her position with the corporation does not permit such a person to convert to his or her own use a corporate opportunity acquired while serving as an officer or director. See Byrne v. Barrett, 268 N.Y. 199, 197 N.E. 217, 100 A.L.R. 680 (1935).

participant liability, contracts with corporation

Related somewhat to the corporate opportunity doctrine is the situation where a participant, or an entity that he or she controls, enters into a contract with the corporation that is either unfair to the corporation or not properly authorized by the corporation. This matter is dealt with in section 5.07, supra, and the reader is referred to that section for further reading. While the usual relief in such cases is the avoidance of the contract complained of, if the corporation has been damaged by the contract, the corporation or its successor in interest may recover damages from the persons involved. See Talbot v. James, 259 S.C. 73, 190 S.E. 2nd 759 (1972).

participant liability to corporation for negligence

Corporate participants, especially in their roles as directors, may be held personally liable to the corporation for negligence or lack of diligence in the performance of their duties. If, for example, through the neglect of their duties as directors, corporate assets are unlawfully diverted to other directors, to officers, or to outsiders, the negligent directors may be held personally accountable to the corporation for such losses through a shareholder's derivative action. See Heit v. Bixby, 276 F. Supp. 217 (EDMO, 1967).

participant liability to corporation, statutory

In addition to common law liability, statutory liability to the corporation for certain specific acts is also imposed on corporate participants, usually in their roles as directors, by the corporation laws of most states. These statutes generally provide that directors who vote for or assent to certain corporate acts may be held jointly and severally liable to the corporation for any losses incurred by the corporation because of such acts. The specified acts typically include -

(1) the issuance of a dividend or other distribution of assets contrary to the provisions of either the corporation laws or the articles of incorporation;

(2) the unlawful redemption by the corporation of its own shares;

(3) the distribution of corporate assets during the liquidation of the corporation without making provision for the payment of all corporate debts; and

(4) the making or guaranteeing of a corporate loan to a director of the corporation.

participant liability, statutory, defenses

The statutes described above often provide that a director who complies with the statutory standard of conduct for directors may be relieved of liability. These statutes may also provide that a director held liable thereunder shall be entitled to contribution from all other directors who voted to approve the wrongful action and from any shareholders who knowingly received unlawfully distributed dividends or assets. The specific statutory liabilities, the extent of the liabilities, and the defenses available to such directors vary from state to state, and the applicable statute of the state in question should be checked.

participant liability to shareholders, typical causes

A controlling shareholder of a small business corporation may be personally liable to a minority shareholder for the following acts:

(1) the breach of a fiduciary duty imposed on controlling shareholders for the protection of minority shareholders,

(2) a failure to exercise good faith or ordinary diligence in the operation of the corporation,

(3) an illegal issuance of dividends or the unlawful distribution of corporate assets, or

(4) a violation of a federal or state securities law or regulation.

participant liability, shareholder's derivative action

Some courts are reluctant to hold shareholders of a corporation personally liable to other shareholders of the same corporation. In such jurisdictions a complaining shareholder may have to seek relief derivatively through the corporation by means of a shareholder's derivative action (see section 6.05, supra).

controlling shareholder, fiduciary duty, personal liability

There is a substantial body of law, some of which is statutory in some states, the gist of which is that the controlling shareholders of a small business corporation must deal fairly, honestly and openly with minority or outside shareholders. Fiduciary duties are imposed on the controlling shareholders to insure the implementation of these standards. A violation of these duties may render a controlling shareholder personally liable to a minority shareholder. Fiduciary duties are most likely to be imposed in situations where a controlling shareholder is either personally dealing with the corporation, attempting to sell his or her corporate stock, or attempting to squeeze-out a minority interest. See section 5.06 and 6.05, supra, for further reading on the fiduciary obligations of controlling shareholders.

participant liability, insider trading

In addition to the fiduciary obligations discussed previously in this section and in sections 5.06 and 6.05, supra, a controlling or majority shareholder may be personally liable to a minority shareholder for the violation of fiduciary duties related to insider trading. Such violations usually consist of the use of inside information not disseminated to outside shareholders as the basis for buying or selling shares of the corporate stock. See Annotation: Duties and Liabilities in Acquiring Minority Shareholder's Stock, 7 A.L.R. 3rd 500 (1966).

participant liability, bad faith or negligence

The general rule is that a controlling shareholder who fails to exercise good faith or ordinary diligence in the management of the corporation may be personally liable to nonparticipating shareholders for resulting losses, even if the shareholder has not personally been involved in any wrong-doing and has not benefitted from the actions complained of. See Zweifach v. Scranton Lace Co., 156 F. Supp. 384 (MDPA, 1957) and Sternberg v. Blaine, 179 Ark. 448, 17 S.W. 2nd 286 (1929). The corporation laws of some states render directors personally liable to nonparticipating shareholders for the issuance of illegal dividends, for the unlawful distribution of corporate assets, and for the unlawful redemption of stock. This liability is normally in addition to the liability of the participating directors to the corporation itself.

participant liability to corporate creditors, general aspects

The participants of small business corporations may be personally liable to creditors of the corporation when - (1) they have acted illegally or improperly in depleting the assets of the corporation, (2) the corporation was defectively formed or has become defunct, or (3) they have disregarded the corporate entity and have acted individually with regard to the matters giving rise to the liability. Of course, a participant who has personally guaranteed a corporate obligation is contractually liable to the creditor for the obligation. Also, participants who commit personal torts in the course of their corporate activities may be personally liable to the injured parties, which liability is usually in addition to that of the corporation under the doctrine of respondent superior.

participant liability, depletion of corporate assets

Probably the most common cause of personal liability of corporate participants to creditors of the corporation is the depletion of corporate assets through intentional acts of the participants to the extent that the corporation is rendered insolvent. Such acts may take the form of the payment of excessive compensation to themselves (see Glenmore Distilleries Co. v. Seideman, 267 F. Supp. 915 (EDNY, 1967)), the payment of corporate debts owed to themselves in preference to debts owed to other creditors (see section 7.01, infra, and Cooper v. Miss. Land Co., 220 So. 2nd 302 (Miss., 1969)), the redemption of stock owned by the controlling participants (see Burton Mill & Cabinet Works, Inc. v. Truemper, 422 S.W. 2nd 825 (Tex. Civ. Apps., 1967)), and distributing corporate assets to shareholders without first providing for the payment of all corporate debts (see Hoover v. Galbraith, 7 Cal. 2nd 519, 498 P. 2nd 981 (1972)). The liability of corporate participants for these acts may be statutory, under the common law, or a combination of both.

participant liability, mismanagement of corporation

A more difficult question is the liability of a participant to corporate creditors for mismanagement, negligence, or lack of diligence in running the corporation that results in the depletion of corporate assets and insolvency. The majority rule seems to be that participants may be held personally liable to corporate creditors on such grounds, especially if the conduct of the participant is found to constitute gross or culpable negligence. See Devereux v. Berger, 264 Md. 20, 284 A. 2nd 605 (1971). Many courts, however, follow the minority rule precluding liability on such grounds. See Speer v. Dighton Grain, Inc., 229 Kan. 272, 624 P. 2nd 952 (1981).

participant liability, defective incorporation

If a corporation is defectively formed, personal liability to the creditors of the corporation may be imposed on participating officers and directors (and on certain shareholders and incorporators in some states). Generally, however, if a good faith effort was made to correctly form the corporation and if the defect complained of did not prejudice the creditor, a court will find that a de facto or de jure corporation existed and will not impose personal liability on the participants. Much, of course, depends on the particular defect complained of and the extent of the noncompliance. The most common defects are failures to comply with the statutorily-required conditions precedent to doing business, such as the local filing of the articles of incorporation, the filing of certain affidavits, and the election of the required directors and officers. The extent of such liability and the particular persons liable usually depends on the specific language of the statute creating the liability.

participant liability, defunct corporation

A difficulty frequently encountered by small business corporations is the forfeiture of its charter because of a failure to pay the required annual or periodic state franchise fees or file the required reports with the Secretary of State or other state filing official. If a corporation was declared defunct and no attempt was made to reinstate the corporation, personal liability to creditors of the defunct corporation may be imposed on those purporting to transact corporate business. See Borbein, Young & Co. v. Cirese, 401 S.W. 2nd 940 (Mo. Apps., 1966). However, if the corporation subsequently pays the fees and files the required reports and is reinstated by the Secretary of State, many courts have ruled that the corporation was a de facto corporation during the period of forfeiture, thus relieving the participants of personal liability. See U.S. v. Standard Beauty Supply Stores, Inc., 561 F. 2nd 774 (CA 9, 1977). Other courts, however, have ruled to the contrary. See Moore v. Rommel, 223 Ark. 989, 350 S.W. 2nd 190 (1961).

Personal liability to corporate creditors is often imposed on the participants of a small business corporation under the doctrine of "piercing the corporate veil." Some courts, in imposing this doctrine, refer to the corporation as the "alter ego" of its participants or controlling shareholders. In imposing this doctrine the courts disregard the corporate entity when its recognition would result in the perpetration of a fraud or other unjust or undesirable consequences inconsistent with the purposes of corporations. See Norman v. Del Elia, 111 Ariz. 480, 533 P. 2nd 537 (1975). participant liability, piercing corporate veil

A court is most likely to pierce the corporate veil and impose personal liability on a corporate participant where it is shown that one or more of the following conditions existed: doctrine of piercing corporate veil, when imposed

(1) the corporation was under-capitalized or inadequately financed,

(2) separate books and records for the corporation were not kept,

(3) the finances and obligations of the corporation were not kept separately from those of its individual participants,

(4) the corporation was used to promote fraud or illegalities,

(5) the required corporate formalities were not followed, or

(6) the corporation was a mere sham. See Briggs Transportation Co. v. Starr Sales Co., Inc., 262 N.W. 2nd 805, 810 (Iowa, 1978).

While the doctrine of piercing the corporate veil may be applied to any corporation, it is most often applied to one-person and family corporations because the acts and circumstances giving rise to its application are most often found in those corporations. In Valley Mechanical Contractors v. Gonzales, 894 S.W. 2d 832 (Tex. App., 1995), a creditor of a corporate participant was permitted to pierce the corporate veil and collect a debt owed by the participant from corporate funds upon a showing that the corporation was the participant's "alter ego." While the doctrine is usually applied in cases seeking to impose liability for corporate debts on the participants, it may also be invoked for purposes of bankruptcy, taxation, and labor, unemployment and workmen's compensation laws. The doctrine also applies to subsidiary corporations who may be liable under this doctrine for debts owed by the parent corporation. piercing corporate veil doctrine, applicability

A corporate liability that is frequently imposed personally on the participants of a small business corporation is the liability for the payment of taxes withheld by a corporation from the salaries and wages of its employees. These are the so-called "trust fund taxes," which includes the employees' income taxes, social security and medicare taxes, and unemployment contributions. Any person responsible for the collection of these taxes may be personally liable for the 100 percent penalty imposed for their nonpayment. See 26 U.S.C. 6671, 6672. The courts have held that any person so connected with the business as to exercise control over its financial affairs may be personally liable for the payment of the 100 percent penalty. See Koegel v. U.S., 437 F. Supp. 176 (SDNY, 1977). Criminal penalties may also be imposed on those responsible for the payment of such taxes. See 26 U.S.C. 7202. participant liability for trust fund taxes

6.07 Amending the Articles of Incorporation

amendment of corporation laws, effect on corporate charter

The corporation laws of practically every state, and sometimes the constitution, provide that the state may amend or repeal the corporation laws and promulgate regulations thereunder. Most corporation laws further provide that the statutory changes and regulations shall be binding on any corporation formed under the corporation laws. Since it is generally held that the state corporation laws are effectively a part of a corporation's charter (see Kreicker v. Naylor Pipe Co., 374 Ill. 364, 29 N.E. 2nd 502, 506 (1940), affirmed w/o opinion in 312 U.S. 659), it follows that amendments to the state corporation laws, and, to a lesser extent changes in the regulations issued thereunder, constitute amendments to the corporate charter and, if applicable, to the articles of incorporation of corporations formed prior to the amendment.

amendment of corporation laws, limitations

While a state may not destroy or impair vested property rights by changing the corporation laws, it can promote the administration of corporate affairs and protect shareholders, creditors, and the public by such changes. See Phillips Petroleum Co. v. Jenkins, 297 U.S. 629, 56 S. Ct. 611, 80 L. Ed. 943 (1936). Amendments of the latter sort most often occur when a state changes its corporation laws so as to require different shareholder voting requirements for certain corporate acts or require or regulate certain corporate features, such as preemptive rights. Statutory amendments of this sort may effectively amend nonconforming provisions in the articles of incorporation of pre-existing corporations.

amending articles of incorporation, general aspects

The most common method of changing the articles of incorporation, of course, is through amendment by the corporation, and the corporation laws of every state provide procedures for such amendments. Some states give corporations broad general powers of amendment, while other states are much more specific as to exactly what provisions may be amended and how such amendments may be effected. Generally, however, the articles of incorporation may be amended so as to include any provision that may be included in original articles at the time of the amendment. Because the amendment process is entirely statutory and because the requirements vary from state to state, the applicable statutes should be examined before proceeding.

amending articles of incorporation, requirements

It is common for the corporation laws of a particular state to impose, often in separate code sections, different requirements for various types of article amendments. For example, different procedural and shareholder voting requirements may be required for amendments related to merger or dissolution than, say, for amendments changing the corporate purpose or name. It is also common to require class voting by shareholders for article amendments that specifically affect a particular class of shareholders, whether by changing the aggregate number of authorized shares of that class, changing its par value, or changing any of its rights, preferences, or privileges.

articles of incorporation, provisions

Well-drafted articles of incorporation should themselves contain provisions dealing with their amendment. Such provisions are normally permissible, provided that the minimum statutory shareholder voting requirements are complied with. Article provisions dealing with amendments are often inserted as a means of implementing the management and control structure of the corporation, usually to prevent the repeal or circumvention of veto powers and high shareholder voting requirements by subsequent article amendment. See section 5.15, supra, for further reading on the importance of article amendment requirements in the corporate management and control structure.

amending articles of incorporation, procedure

The procedure for amending articles of incorporation is normally a three-step process. The steps are: (1) the initiation process, which normally consists of a board of director resolution; (2) the approval process, which consists of a vote of the shareholders; and (3) the filing process, which is the filing of articles of amendment with the Secretary of State or other state filing official. If there are only a few shareholders and if the state has an action-without-meeting statute, it is usually possible to carry out the first two steps of the amendment process informally under that statute. See section 6.04, supra, for further reading on corporate meeting requirements.

Typically, the first step in amending the articles of incorporation is for the board of directors to adopt a resolution setting forth the proposed amendment and directing that it be submitted to a vote of the shareholders at either an annual or a special meeting. See Exhibit 6-B at the end of this chapter for a sample resolution. The corporation laws of many states permit shareholders to propose article amendments by petition to the board of directors. Normally the holders of a specified number of shares (often 10 percent) are required to join in the petition. amending articles, how to initiate

Regardless of whether a proposed amendment is initiated by director or shareholder action, most corporation laws require that written notice of the proposed amendment be given to the shareholders. Notice of a proposed article amendment may be waived by the shareholders in most states. The required voting procedures, if any, are usually statutory, and the applicable sections of the state corporation code should be checked in this regard. The shareholder voting majority needed for the approval of an amendment is normally specified in the applicable statute or article of incorporation provision. As indicated above, it is common to impose different voting requirements for amendments to different provisions of the articles. The statutory shareholder voting requirements for amending the articles of incorporation in each state are summarized in Appendix I, infra, under the heading of "Articles of Incorporation: Amendment." amending articles, notice and voting requirements

Once a proposed article amendment has been approved by the shareholders, most states require articles of amendment to be filed with the Secretary of State or other state filing official. The articles of amendment must usually contain certain specific provisions, such as the name of the corporation, the amendment as approved by the shareholders, the date of the approval of the amendment by the shareholders, the shareholder voting requirements and results, and any changes in the stated capital of the corporation. The articles of amendment must normally be verified by two corporate officers and are deemed effective either upon filing with the Secretary of State or upon the issuance of a certificate of amendment by the Secretary of State. Articles of amendment are usually subject to the same state and local filing requirements as original articles of incorporation, and the payment of certain fees is required upon filing. Matters related to articles of amendment are statutory, and the specific statutory requirements should be ascertained and complied with. See Exhibit 6-D at the end of this chapter for sample articles of amendment. The fees for amending the articles of incorporation in each state are set forth in Appendix I, infra, under the heading of "Fees." articles of amendment, requirements, fees

If a corporation has qualified to transact business in states other than the state of incorporation, additional amendment requirements must be complied with if the certificate of authorization in the foreign state is to remain in effect. Most states require foreign corporations to file copies or statements of article amendments with the Secretary of State or other state filing official within a specified period (usually 30 days) after their enactment in the home state. In addition, if the article amendments effect a change in the name of the corporation or in its purposes, an amended certificate of authority may have to be applied for and obtained in the foreign state. If the article amendments result in a merger or consolidation, additional filings may be necessary in the foreign state. In any event, the specific statutory requirements of the foreign state must be ascertained and complied with if the corporation's certificate of authorization in that state is to remain in effect. See section 6.08, infra, for further reading on qualifying to do business in foreign states. amending articles, foreign corporation

If the articles of incorporation have been amended several times, it may be difficult to ascertain their current status from the files of the Secretary of State or other state filing official. To correct this problem most states provide for the filing of what are called "restated articles of incorporation." Restated articles of incorporation are merely a copy or current composite of the articles of incorporation containing all previous amendments. Restating the articles of incorporation is a function of the board of directors in most states, and shareholder approval is not usually required unless the restatement includes an amendment that requires shareholder approval. Again, the matter is statutory and the applicable statute should be ascertained and complied with. A fee is usually assessed for filing restated articles of incorporation with the state filing official. restated articles of incorporation

changing registered agent or office

The corporation laws of most states provide that unless the articles of incorporation provide otherwise, certain ministerial or clerical amendments to the articles may be made by the board of directors without shareholder approval. Included here are amendments that delete the names and addresses of the initial directors and registered agent, change the required portion of the corporate name (i.e., changing "Corporation" to "Corp.," etc.), and any other changes expressly permitted by statute to be made without shareholder approval. It should be noted that the address of a corporation's registered office and the name and address of its registered agent may also be changed without shareholder approval. Such matters are usually dealt with in a separate statutory provision requiring only the filing of a statement with the state filing official showing the desired change and, in most states, the payment of a fee. Again, the specific statute should checked and complied with.

6.08 Doing Business in Other States

corporation, doing business, local vs. foreign

If all of the offices, plants, and outlets of a business are located in the home state and if all of its sales and other transactions occur in the home state, then the business is unquestionably local and the corporation will have no need to qualify to do business in other states, even if it solicits sales in other states through the mail or by telephone. Conversely, if a corporation has permanent facilities or substantial offices or outlets in a foreign state, it must qualify to do business as a foreign corporation in that state. But what about the construction company that occasionally takes a project in a neighboring state? Or the manufacturing or marketing company that sells or distributes its products through employees or agents stationed in other states? Or the trucking company that regularly travels to and accepts contracts in other states? Must these companies qualify to do business in the other states? And what are the consequences if they should qualify and don't?

doing business in foreign state, what constitutes

Unfortunately, it is impossible to definitively state exactly what does and what does not constitute the transaction of business within a state for purposes of compelling the qualification of a foreign corporation. A century of litigation and legislation on the issue, however, has produced some guidelines. First of all, not every business activity by a corporation within a foreign state constitutes the transaction of business for the purpose of requiring qualification. The corporation laws of most states contain a nonexclusive list of certain activities that do not constitute the transaction of business for purposes of qualification. Although the listed activities vary somewhat from state to state, they generally include most of the following:

doing business, activities not constituting

(1) defending, maintaining, or settling a lawsuit or other proceeding;

(2) maintaining a bank account;

(3) maintaining a stock transfer or similar office;

(4) the taking or giving of mortgages, security interests, and other evidences of indebtedness, and the enforcement of same;

(5) effecting sales through independent contractors;

(6) soliciting or procuring orders, either by mail or through agents or employees, that must be accepted in another state before they are binding;

(7) transacting business solely in interstate commerce;

(8) isolated business transactions lasting less than 30 days and not constituting a repeated transaction;

(9) holding board of director or shareholder meetings and similar internal corporate activities; and

(10) owning, without more, real or personal property.

doing business, how to determine

The corporation laws of some states do not contain a list of activities that do not require qualification. And, it should be noted, even in states with such a list, the enumerated activities are not all inclusive and do not necessarily include every permitted activity. Examining the reported cases in a jurisdiction will probably shed some light on the subject, but don't expect to find a definitive answer for every conceivable activity. For practical purposes, the list of permitted activities shown above is probably the best guide available on the subject, even in states whose statutes do not contain such a list. The existence of a list of permitted activities in a state in indicated in Appendix I, infra, under the heading of "Foreign Corporations."

doing business, interstate commerce vs. intrastate commerce

A corporation is not required to qualify in a foreign state if it is engaged only in interstate commerce in the foreign state. See Eli Lilly Co. v. Sav-on-Drugs, 366 U.S. 276,278, 81 S. Ct. 1316, 6 L. Ed. 2nd 288 (1961). However, if a corporation is engaged in intrastate commerce as well as interstate commerce within a foreign state, it can be compelled to qualify. See Railway Express Agency, Inc. v. Virginia, 282 U.S. 440, 51 S. Ct. 201, 75 L. Ed. 450 (1931). The tough question, of course, is what constitutes intrastate commerce? Unfortunately, there is no easy answer to this question, a conclusion attested to by a series of Supreme Court cases on the subject. A good rule of thumb, however, is that if the activity within the state is purely sales, it is probably interstate commerce, but if there are related activities (e.g., service, installation, repair, etc.), the activity is probably intrastate as well. See Holby, Doing Business: Defining State Control Over Foreign Corporations, 32 Vanderbilt Law Review 1105, 1117.

doing business, different purposes, degree of activity

It should be understood that a corporation may be deemed to be "doing business" in a foreign state for purposes other than compelling qualification as a foreign corporation. A corporation may also be "doing business" for purposes of state taxation and service of process under a long arm statute. Each purpose requires a different degree of business involvement within the foreign state. It is generally held that the transaction of business for purposes of compelling qualification as a foreign corporation requires a greater degree of business activity than the other two purposes. Therefore, reported cases involving the other two purposes are not necessarily relevant to the issue of compelling qualification as a foreign corporation.

foreign corporation, failure to qualify, penalties

If a corporation transacts sufficient intrastate business within a foreign state to warrant qualification and does not obtain a certificate of authorization from that state, certain penalties may be imposed. The penalties, which vary greatly from state to state, may include fines of up to $10,000 for the corporation and up to $1,000 for corporate directors, officers or agents, denial of access to local courts, a tolling of the statute of limitations on claims against the corporation, liability for all fees accruing during the period of noncompliance plus penalties, and the invalidation of corporate contracts. Some states excuse certain penalties if the foreign corporation later qualifies and pays the required fees and taxes. The penalties that may be assessed in each state are listed in Appendix I, infra, under the heading of "Foreign Corporations."

foreign corporation, whether to qualify, factors

If there is a question as to whether a corporation should qualify in a foreign state, the safe approach is to qualify and avoid the possible penalties. However, the safe approach is not always the practical approach, because qualification invariably includes burdens. While a foreign corporation, once it receives a certificate of authority, is entitled to the same rights and privileges as a domestic corporation, it is also subject to the same duties and liabilities. In practice this means the filing of annual or periodic reports, the paying of corporate filing fees and franchise taxes, and exposure to other applicable taxes in the foreign state, including sales and income taxes. In addition, by qualifying the corporation will become subject to any limitations or restrictions placed on domestic corporations by that state. All of these factors should be considered when deciding whether a corporation should qualify in a foreign state.

foreign corporation, liability for state taxes

While a foreign corporation may be legally liable for income or sales taxes in a foreign state whether or not it obtains a certificate of authority in that state, as a practical matter the taxing authorities often rely on the Secretary of State or other state filing official for information or notice that a foreign corporation is doing business in the state. See 15 U.S.C. 381 for the federal statutory restrictions on the powers of states to impose income taxes on foreign corporations.

qualifying in foreign state, authority for

If it is decided to qualify a corporation in a foreign state, the first step is for the corporation to authorize itself to do so. To accomplish this there should be - (1) an article of incorporation provision empowering the corporation to transact business in other states, and (2) a board of director resolution authorizing the corporate officers to proceed and directing them to execute the necessary documents and pay the required fees. See Exhibit 6-C at the end of this chapter for a sample resolution.

qualifying in foreign states, article provisions

Properly drafted articles of incorporation should contain a provision empowering the corporation to transact business in other states. Occasionally, usually as a control device, the articles will specifically limit the conduct of corporate business to a certain state or states. Frequently, the articles contain nothing on the subject. While an article provision empowering the corporation to transact business in other states is probably not legally required in most states because that power is usually set forth in the "powers" section of the corporation laws, the best practice is to include such a provision in the articles.

certificate of authority, application requirements

Once the proper internal authority to qualify the corporation in the foreign state has been obtained, the next step is to apply for qualification in the foreign state. To accomplish this the necessary forms must be obtained, usually from the office of the Secretary of State or other state filing official in the foreign state. Most states require a foreign corporation to obtain a certificate of authority from the state filing official in order to qualify as a foreign corporation. A few states impose other methods of qualification. The name and address of the state filing official in each state and the type of qualification required are set forth in Appendix I, infra.

The information requested in the application for qualification varies somewhat from state to state, but the following information is generally required:

(1) The name of the corporation and its state of incorporation.

(2) The corporate name to be used in the foreign state. If the corporate name does not contain one of the words required by the foreign state (usually "corporation," "company," etc., see section 5.05, supra), a word must be selected for use with the corporate name in the foreign state.

(3) The date of incorporation and the period of duration of the corporation.

(4) The address of the principal office of the corporation in its home state.

(5) The name of the proposed registered agent and the address of the proposed registered office of the corporation in the foreign state.

(6) The proposed purposes of the corporation in transacting business in the foreign state.

(7) The names and addresses of the officers and directors of the corporation.

(8) The number of shares of stock that the corporation is authorized to issue, itemized by class and series, if any, and the number of such shares that have been issued.

(9) Estimates of the value of all property owned or to be owned by the corporation and of the gross amount of business conducted or to be conducted annually by the corporation and estimates of the value or amounts thereof that will be held or conducted in the foreign state.

certificate of authority, filing requirements

Many states require the filing of copies of a foreign corporation's articles of incorporation, usually certified by the home state filing official, often in lieu of some of the requirements listed above. Other states require statements of good standing from the corporation's home state. The states vary as to the requirements of local agents, some requiring the agents to be local residents or attorneys and others permitting corporations or local public officials to serve. There are miscellaneous other requirements in some states too numerous to mention here.

certificate of authority, name requirements

The most common filing problem of corporations seeking to qualify in a foreign state is that of the corporate name. Most states impose the following requirements on the name of a foreign corporation: (1) it must contain one of the required words ("corporation," "company," etc. or abbreviations thereof), (2) it must not be deceptively similar to (or it must be distinguishable from) the name of any other corporation or other covered entity, and (3) it must not contain any words indicating or implying that it is organized for any purpose not contained in its articles of incorporation.

foreign corporation, name change, when required

Difficulties may arise under (1) and (3) above in connection with either required or prohibited words when the requirements of the foreign state differ from those of the home state. The only solution, normally, is to change the corporate name in the foreign state, either by adding a suffix such as "Inc." or "Co.," or by deleting or changing one or more of the substantive words in the name so as to comply with the foreign state requirements. If this is not acceptable to the corporation, the alternatives are to refrain from qualifying in the foreign state or seek review of the decision of the filing official, if review is provided under the law of the foreign state. See Annotation: Corporations - Protection of Name, 26 A.L.R. 3rd 994 (1969).

foreign corporation, name rejected, remedies

If the foreign state filing official rules that the proposed corporate name is deceptively similar to (or is not distinguishable from) the name of another corporation or entity, the alternatives are -

(1) appeal or seek judicial review of the official's decision as and if provided under local law,

(2) adopt a fictitious name for use in the foreign state (a board of director resolution adopting the fictitious name is often required),

(3) obtain the written consent of the holder of the established name (one of more words may still have to be added to make the names distinguishable), or

(4) obtain a court decree establishing the prior right of the corporation to the use of the desired name.

certificate of authority, effect of issuance

When an application has been approved by the state filing official in the foreign state, and when the required fees and taxes have been paid, a certificate of authority (or a similar document) will be issued authorizing the corporation to transact business in the foreign state for the purposes stated in the application. The certificate normally remains in effect as long as the corporation remains in good standing in the foreign state.

foreign corporation, article amendments

In addition to filing annual or periodic reports and paying the required fees and taxes, a qualifying corporation must keep the foreign state apprised of all amendments to its articles of incorporation in the home state made after the issuance of the certificate of authority. Time limits (usually 30 days) are customarily imposed for filing copies or statements of article amendments in the foreign state. See section 6.07, supra, for further reading on this matter.

certificate of withdrawal, requirements

It is not unusual for a corporation to discontinue the transaction of business in a foreign state after having received a certificate of authority from that state. In such a case the corporation is normally required to obtain a certificate of withdrawal from the foreign state. A failure to obtain this certificate could subject the corporation or its participants to liability for fees and penalties imposed by the foreign state. A certificate of withdrawal must be applied for from the foreign state filing official, usually on a prescribed form which seeks information concerning future service of process, the payment of previously assessed fees and taxes in the foreign state, and the payment of creditors in the foreign state. Again, the requirements vary from state to state, so the specific statutory and administrative requirements of the particular state should be checked before proceeding.

certificate of revocation, when issued

If a corporation fails to comply with the statutory or administrative requirements of a foreign state, a certificate of revocation may be issued by the foreign state revoking the authority of the corporation to transact business in the foreign state. The most common causes for certificates of revocation are the failure to file the required annual or periodic reports and the failure to pay the required fees and taxes assessed by the foreign state. Other grounds include the failure to maintain a registered agent in the foreign state, a failure to notify the foreign state of a change in the location of either the main office of the corporation or its local registered office, and a failure to file amendments to the corporation's articles of incorporation.

certificate of revocation, notice, penalties

Most states send a written notice to a foreign corporation prior to the issuance of a certificate of revocation, giving the corporation a certain period (20 to 90 days, depending on the state) in which to correct the deficiencies. When a certificate of revocation is issued, the authority of the corporation to transact business in that state is terminated, and the transaction of any further business by the corporation in that state may subject the corporation and its officers or directors to the penalties imposed on nonqualifying foreign corporations.

6.09 Raising Capital - Refinancing a Business

small business corporations, typical needs for capital

Most small business corporations need additional capital at one time or another. For a successful corporation, the need for capital is usually a matter of expedience. For a struggling corporation, however, it can be a matter of survival. The need may be occasioned by a slump in sales or business, by the necessity of purchasing equipment, machinery, or inventory, by a desire to expand the business into other fields or markets, by the death, disability, or retirement of a key participant and the obligation to purchase his or her stock in the corporation, or by any number of other causes. Whatever the cause, once the need has arisen the primary concern of the participants is how and where to raise the needed capital in the form best suited to their particular business and personal situations.

capital, form of

Capital may be provided to a small business corporation in the form of either debt or equity, or in a combination of each. Other methods used to raise capital include the retention of earnings, sales of assets not needed in the business, sales and leasebacks of assets, credit purchases, and trade credit. These methods are self-explanatory in most respects and will not be discussed in this section. These methods of raising capital may be used in lieu of or in addition to debt or equity financing.

debt financing, general aspects

The big advantage of debt financing, whether long-term or short, is that it permits the infusion of capital without changing either the relative ownership interests of the corporate participants or the management and control structure of the corporation. Because the interest and other expenses of debt financing are deductible by the corporation, debt financing may also be advantageous from a tax standpoint. The disadvantage of debt financing is that it is expensive. Interest charges, loan origination and discount fees, and principal repayments must all be paid out of current profits. More often than not, especially with financially-troubled corporations, debt capital cannot be obtained from commercial lenders without the personal guarantees of individual participants. Another problem, especially if the debt capital is obtained directly or indirectly from one or more of the participants, is that of maintaining an acceptable corporate debt-to-equity ratio. See section 5.14, supra, for further reading on the debt-to-equity ratio.

equity financing, general aspects

The great advantage of equity financing is that the capital infusion does not strain the cash flow of the corporation. The disadvantages of equity financing are: (1) it may dilute or change the ownership positions of the original corporate participants, both in the corporation generally and relative to each other, (2) it usually necessitates changes in the management and control structure of the corporation, and (3) it is almost always less advantageous taxwise to the corporation. Especially where capital is needed for expansion purposes and must be obtained from outside sources, the issue in equity financing is whether it is better for the existing participants to own a larger percentage of a smaller business or a lesser percentage of a larger business.

availability of financing, factors

The availability of any source of financing often depends on the purpose for which the funds are needed (it is much easier, say, to raise capital to expand a profitable business than to rescue an unprofitable one from bankruptcy). Another important factor in the raising of capital is the earnings record of the corporation, the existence of which, it should be noted, is a big advantage of an existing business over a start-up business. The net worth of the corporation is an equally important factor in the search for capital. The financial statements of individual corporate participants are also important, especially if debt financing is desired.

form of capital, typical choices

The first task of a corporation in need of capital is to determine the type of capital most advantageous to its particular needs. Assuming that the alternative sources of capital described in the second paragraph of this section have been exhausted, the choices are usually between - (1) short-term debt financing, (2) long-term debt financing, (3) a private sale of corporate stock, and (4) a public sale of corporate stock. Each of these sources of capital, except the last, is discussed separately below. While a discussion of the requirements for a public sale of stock is beyond the scope of this handbook, the reader will find the discussion of federal and state securities laws in section 5.16, supra, helpful.

short-term, debt, availability, requirements

Short-term debt financing is usually preferable for a corporation with temporary cash-flow difficulties, but whose long-term business prospects appear sound. Short-term debt financing, which is normally obtained in the form of loans or line-of-credit cash advances, is most often obtained from commercial banks or finance companies. Finance companies, or similarly-named institutions, generally require less collateral than commercial banks, but charge higher rates of interest. Unless a corporation is well-established, security is likely to be required for this type of financing. The personal guarantees of individual corporate participants may also be required, especially if the corporation is relatively new or has insufficient security for the amount of capital desired. Short-term debt may be obtained in the form of accounts receivable financing, inventory loans, or loans secured by security interests on personal property, assignments of title, conditional sales contracts, or warehouse or trust receipts. Corporations with seasonal credit needs may be eligible for short term (12 months or less) loans or lines of credit of up to $500,000 from the Small Business Administration.

long-term debt, sources of, form of

Long-term debt financing may be obtained from commercial banks, from insurance companies and other institutional lenders, from government-sponsored sources, and from private individuals. Long-term debt is customarily in the form of notes (usually secured by real estate or equipment), bonds, or debentures. The personal guarantees of individual corporate participants may or may not be required depending on the form of the debt (notes are more likely to require a personal guarantee than bonds or debentures), the financial status of the corporation, and the amount of capital required.

long-term debt, commercial banks

Commercial banks are the most common source of long-term debt financing for small business corporations. Notes secured by real estate, equipment, or other tangibles are the usual form of long-term debt given by commercial banks. The personal guarantees of individual corporate participants are often required. It generally takes less time to obtain long-term credit from a commercial bank than from institutional or government-sponsored lenders, and the initiation and ancillary costs are usually less than with institutional lenders.

long-term debt, institutional sources

Insurance companies and other institutional lenders occasionally provide long-term loans to established small business corporations, usually for expansion or modernization purposes. Loans of this type usually range from $250,000 upwards into the millions of dollars, and corporate assets of at least a million dollars are normally required. Institutional lenders are often interested in obtaining options to convert a portion of their debt to equity as a hedge against inflation. The required form of debt is likely to be bonds or debentures, sometimes accompanied by options, warrants, or conversion rights.

Institutional loans are usually unsecured, and a broad analysis of the corporate business is typically required prior to approval. Marketing and engineering reports are frequently required, and in-depth studies are often made on such matters as the corporation's competitive position, its inventory position, and the adequacy of its depreciation, depletion, and obsolescence charges. Conditions are frequently imposed limiting such matters as the issuance of dividends, the impairment of capital, the sale of business assets, and the redemption of stock during the term of the loan. Obviously, much expense is involved in obtaining this type of financing, and the size of the loan should be large enough to warrant the expense.

long-term debt, S.B.A. loans

If a corporation is unable to obtain financing from commercial or institutional sources, it may be eligible for assistance from the Small Business Administration (S.B.A.). The S.B.A. annually makes over 25,000 loans totaling over three billion dollars to small businesses. Financing aids offered by the S.B.A. include contract loans, disaster loans, economic opportunity loans, development company loans, small business energy loans, and several other special types of loans. The interest rates are generally competitive with or lower than those of commercial lenders. Certain qualifications must be met, however, before a small business corporation can obtain an S.B.A. loan. Current information as to the availability of and qualifications for the various S.B.A. loans may be obtained from the local office of the S.B.A.

debt financing, Government loan guarantee programs

In addition to direct loans to small businesses, the Federal Government also sponsors loan guarantee programs whereby loans to small businesses by conventional lenders are guaranteed by the Government. Federal loan guarantees to small businesses may be available under the following programs:

(1) The Business and Industrial Loan Program of the Farmers Home Administration. Under this program preferences are given to businesses creating jobs in rural areas.

(2) The Business Development Program of the Economic Development Administration in the Commerce Department. Under this program preferences are given to businesses located in urban areas with high unemployment or depressed economies.

(3) The Business Loan Program of the Small Business Administration.

To obtain the current status of any desired loan guarantee program and the current requirements and qualifications thereunder, the best practice is to contact the nearest office of the sponsoring agency.

Small Business Investment Companies (S.B.I.C.s) and Minority Small Business Investment Companies (M.S.B.I.C.s) formed under the Small Business Investment Act of 1958 are licensed by the S.B.A. to provide long-term venture and growth capital for qualifying small businesses. S.B.I.C.s and M.S.B.I.C.s can furnish capital to small businesses through three methods: (1) direct loans of from 5 to 20 years in duration, (2) the purchase of convertible debentures issued by small business corporations, and (3) the direct purchase of stock (usually from dissident shareholders). To qualify for an S.B.I.C. loan a business must be independently owned and operated, not dominant in its field, have a net worth of less than six million dollars, and have an average net income of less than two million dollars. debt financing, S.B.I.C. sources

If equity financing is desired by a small business corporation, it must be decided whether to sell the corporation's stock privately or publicly. Unless the individual corporate participants or the corporate officers personally know of persons interested in purchasing stock of the corporation in the quantities required to raise the needed capital, it will probably be necessary to obtain an underwriter to dispose of the stock, regardless of whether the sale of stock is private or public. To sell the stock privately it must be sold under one or more of the registration exemptions under the Securities Act of 1933. Several of these exemptions, it should be noted, present attractive opportunities for small business corporations in search of capital. These registration exemptions are discussed in section 5.16, supra. equity financing, private sale of stock, requirements

The private sale of stock has the advantage of being less expensive to consummate, but it is more likely to result in control and management concessions by the original participants than a public sale. A public sale of stock may require the registration of the stock with the Securities and Exchange Commission, a time-consuming and expensive undertaking that is beyond the scope of this handbook. equity financing, public sale of stock

6.10 Restructuring a Business - Multiple Corporations

small businesses, causes of change

A characteristic of small business enterprises is that they seldom endure without change. The death, disability, or disenchantment of a single participant may cause substantial changes in the nature and structure of a business. And even if the original business participants remain, their personal desires and goals tend to change with time, and these changes are often reflected in the economic or structural makeup of the business. New business opportunities, changes in the general business climate, the opening of new markets and the closing of old, and technological developments may also result in substantial changes in the nature and structure of a business. And, of course, changes in a business usually mean changes in the form, nature, or structure of the corporation through which it is conducted.

Structural changes in a small business corporation are most likely to be necessitated by the following developments or events:

small business corporations, structural changes, typical causes

(1) Changes in the external operation of a business, such as the acquisition of substantial assets, the development of other business lines, or the expansion of an existing business into other fields.

(2) Internal management changes in an existing business, such as the division of a business into separate geographical areas or into separate lines or departments.

(3) Personal desires of the business participants unrelated to the operation of the business, such as the parceling of business assets into separate corporations for purposes of estate planning or the settling of disputes.

small business corporations, structural changes

Probably the most common cause of structural change in small business corporations is the acquisition or development of another business. Typically, the new business is related to the principal business of the corporation. A real estate sales company, for example, may organize its own leasing, management, or property development business, or a successful restaurant may set up or purchase a catering service. A related business is often developed or acquired because the principal business cannot be run successfully without it. Other times a related business is developed or acquired because it can be profitably run in conjunction with the principal business. Or a related business may be acquired or developed to provide a market or outlet for the products or services of the principal business, either generally or during off-peak or slow periods. Also, a corporation with excess funds may purchase a new business or acquire a substantial asset, such as a valuable tract of real estate or a patent, for purposes of investment or future development.

small businesses, consequences of growth

Even if another business is not acquired or developed, it is not unusual for a successful business to grow, structurally, financially, and geographically. The construction company that 15 years ago was paving driveways in Tucson is now building airports in Michigan. The delivery company that 20 years ago had two trucks in Hoboken now has a fleet of trucks and a half-dozen airplanes and makes deliveries in every major city. In each case the business grew in ways not fully anticipated by the original participants, often beyond their wildest dreams. What was originally a tightly-controlled and well-organized small business corporation has outgrown its structure and has become difficult to manage efficiently. Departments or lines of business not contemplated when the corporation was organized have been forced into a corporate structure that cannot effectively accommodate them. Frequently it is difficult to distinguish the profitable lines of the business from the unprofitable, and the corporation is often unable to take advantage of favorable aspects of the tax laws.

restructuring of corporation, legal issues

Regardless of how or why a new business is developed or acquired, or for whatever purpose the principal business is sought to be restructured, the basic legal questions to be answered in connection with any proposed restructuring are:

(1) Shall the separate businesses or the separate departments or lines of the same business be divided into separate corporations or into separate "divisions" within the same corporation?

(2) If multiple corporations are to be formed, shall their relationship be vertical (i.e., subsidiary corporations whose stock is owned by a parent corporation) or horizontal (i.e., corporations whose stock is owned by the same shareholders, often called brother-sister corporations)?

The factors that should be considered in determining whether and how to restructure a business into multiple corporations are - multiple corporation, use of, factors

(1) the tax factor,
(2) the geographical factor,
(3) the operational or management factor,
(4) the risk or limited liability factor,
(5) the after-acquired-property factor,
(6) the prestige or public relations factor, and
(7) the estate planning or asset distribution factor.

A good rule of thumb is that multiple corporations should not be formed for tax purposes alone. The principal reason for this rule is that for most federal income tax purposes multiple corporations are treated as a single corporation if they constitute a "controlled group" of corporations. See 26 U.S.C. 1551, 1552. And even if the group of corporations does not qualify as a controlled group, if they are, in fact, owned or controlled, directly or indirectly, by the same interests, their income, deductions, credits, and allocations may be reallocated by the Internal Revenue Service so as to prevent the evasion of taxes. See 26 U.S.C. 482 and Wisconsin Big Boy Corp. v. Comm., 452 F. 2nd 137 (CA 7, 1971). multiple corporations, tax factors

For income tax purposes, it does not normally matter whether a controlled group of corporations is organized vertically (i.e., parent-subsidiary corporations), horizontally (i.e., brother-sister corporations), or in some combination of the two. See 26 U.S.C. 1563(a). Generally, a parent-subsidiary relationship is considered to exist between two corporations if one corporation owns or controls 80 percent of more of the stock of the other. A brother-sister relationship is generally deemed to exist if five or fewer persons own or control 80 percent of more of the stock of two or more corporations. See 26 U.S.C. 1563(a)(1),(2) (this statute also imposes certain other specific requirements, and it should be reviewed before proceeding). Certain types of stock (usually preferred and treasury) are excluded for purposes of determining the applicable ownership percentages, and constructive stock ownership rules are applied. See 26 U.S.C. 1563(c),(d). multiple corporations, vertical vs. horizontal, definitions

A significant tax disadvantage of multiple corporations, especially in the brother-sister form, is that if there are losses in some corporations and not in others, the losses of one corporation may not be offset against the profits of another. If the corporations are in the parent-subsidiary form, the losses and profits can often be combined in a consolidated tax return. The establishment of multiple corporations may also increase the risk of the imposition of the accumulated earnings tax on the more profitable corporations. Finally, if the transfer of funds between profitable and nonprofitable corporations is not justifiable on business grounds, unfavorable tax consequences may result. multiple corporations, tax disadvantages

Certain substantial tax benefits, however, can be achieved by the creation of multiple corporations. These include: multiple corporations, tax advantages

(1) Beneficial Subchapter S elections. By using multiple corporations it may be possible to adopt the Subchapter S election to certain unprofitable aspects of the business and pass the losses directly to the shareholders. Also, the use of multiple corporations may permit a Subchapter S election for a certain portion of the business when the business as a whole could not qualify, either because of the number of shareholders or the type of income. While an S corporation can be a parent corporation, it may not be a subsidiary corporation unless it is a "qualified Subchapter S subsidiary," so the multiple corporations may have to be of the brother-sister type in order to take advantage of the Subchapter S election. See section 5.18, supra, for further reading on S corporations and the Subchapter S election.

(2) Beneficial use of Section 1244 stock. If a certain line or portion of the business seems doomed to eventual financial failure, the use of multiple corporations may permit this portion of the business to be separately incorporated with stock that qualifies under Section 1244 of the Internal Revenue Code, thus permitting the shareholders to treat the loss as an ordinary loss. Also, the use of separate corporations qualifying under Section 1244 may permit the losses to be incurred in different tax years. Again, the multiple corporations must be in the brother-sister form to qualify. See section 5.14, supra, for further reading on Section 1244 stock.

(3) Beneficial tax treatment in the event of sale. If it is anticipated that certain assets, aspects, or portions of the business may later be sold, the creation of multiple corporations (especially at the outset) may provide a more useful and flexible method of achieving favorable tax treatment at the time of the sale. See section 7.02, infra, for further reading on the selling of a business.

(4) The various corporations can adopt different tax years, employ different methods of accounting, and qualify for tax elections that might not otherwise be available.

multiple corporations, geographical factor

The geographical factor is often closely tied to the necessity of qualifying the corporation to do business in other states (which is discussed in section 6.08, supra). If business is conducted in several states to the extent that qualification as a foreign corporation is necessary, it may be advantageous to form a separate corporation, usually a subsidiary, to conduct all of the business within a particular state. In so doing, the principal corporation will not have to qualify in the foreign states and will most likely not be subject to either local taxes or service of process in those states.

same, typical considerations

If a business is already divided into several corporations in the home state, the formation of a single corporation to conduct business in a foreign state could preclude the necessity and expense of qualifying several corporations in that state. On the other hand, if business is conducted in several states and if consideration is being given to dividing the business into multiple corporations in such a way that each of them would transact business in the foreign states, the geographical factor would work against the creation of multiple corporations because of the necessity and expense of qualifying each corporation in the foreign states.

multiple corporations, geographical factor, practical aspects

Of course, the necessity of qualifying in foreign states is only one aspect of the geographical factor. The other aspects include the practical advantages and disadvantages of consolidating the various business functions and activities in a certain geographical area under central, and usually local, management. In this regard, much depends on both the amount of business conducted in the geographical area and the size and remoteness of the area.

multiple corporations, operational factor

The operational or management factor becomes important in situations where the business is divided into several branches, each of which is large enough to warrant some degree of autonomy. The separate branches may constitute either separate functions of the principal business (e.g., manufacturing, advertising, sales, etc.) or separate lines of the overall business (e.g., commercial construction, residential construction, highway construction, etc.). The creation of separate corporations for each branch of the business in these situations tends to promote management morale and employee incentive by making it easier to isolate each branch of the business and reward the employees of the profitable branches through profit-sharing and other incentive-type programs. The creation of multiple corporations also makes it easier to isolate, and either reorganize or dispose of, the unprofitable lines or aspects of the business. The usual corporate relationship used in the situations described in this paragraph is that of parent-subsidiary, although brother-sister corporations can often be effectively used for separate lines of the business.

multiple corporations, disadvantages

The disadvantages of multiple corporations in such situations are those of multiple corporations generally: the increased expense of maintaining separate books and records and holding separate meetings, the increased difficulty of coordinating overall business policy and controlling the overall business operation, and possible tax disadvantages.

The risk or limited liability factor may be important in situations where a certain phase or line of business is hazardous or involves risks not faced by the rest of the business. If one phase of the business involves an operation or procedure that is especially hazardous, such as the use or transportation of explosives, poisons, toxins, or radio-active materials, it may be advantageous to transact that phase of the business through a separate corporation and thereby protect the principal business and its assets from the financial risks imposed by the hazardous operation. Such an arrangement may be especially advantageous if liability insurance for the dangerous operation is either unavailable or prohibitively expensive. It is not uncommon, for example, for a taxi business to form a separate corporation for each taxicab. The formation of a separate corporation may also be advantageous in the situation where a new business venture or product is being instituted that may fail or incur heavy liabilities. multiple corporations, risk factor

Either type of corporate relationship (i.e., parent-subsidiary or brother-sister) is normally satisfactory for the purpose of limiting the risk or liability of the principal business. Care must be taken, however, to insure that the corporation formed to carry on the hazardous or risky business is adequately capitalized and will not expose its shareholders to the claims of its creditors, either under the doctrine of piercing the corporate veil or otherwise See section 6.06, supra, for further reading on shareholder liability. multiple corporations, risk factor, legal aspects

A factor related somewhat to the limited liability factor is the after-acquired-property factor. Commercial lenders often require small business corporations to subject property or assets later acquired by the corporation to the security provisions of mortgages or security agreements. The formation of separate corporations to hold later-acquired business assets and property can lend financial flexibility to a business by preventing such assets and properties from being encumbered by the after-acquired-property clauses in the earlier debt instruments of the principal corporation. Brother-sister corporations are normally preferable in these situations, especially if the underlying debts have not been personally guaranteed by individual business participants. multiple corporations, after-acquired property factor

The public relations or prestige factor normally comes into play in situations where the good will or prestige of the principal business, or that of certain of its products, may be endangered by the addition of another product, service or function to the business. For example, if a company produces a high-quality, expensive product that is well known, the marketability of that product might be endangered by the addition of a cheaper, less-expensive product. Similarly, if a successful company wishes to develop and market a new product or service that might prove unsuccessful, it may wish to protect the prestige of the principal company should the product or service prove to be a failure. In either situation, the formation of a separate corporation with a distinctive name would shield the principal corporation from public association with the new product, service, or function. Brother-sister corporations are usually preferable in these situations for practical reasons, but parent-subsidiary corporations are equally acceptable from a legal standpoint. multiple corporations, prestige factor

The estate-planning and asset-distribution factor is most likely to be important in one-person and family businesses. Multiple corporations are often used by the participants of these businesses to facilitate the distribution of particular corporate or business assets to specific persons. Suppose, for example, that a corporation owns an office building that the principal participant wishes to convey to a certain son or daughter upon his death. Rather than conveying the building to himself during his lifetime or liquidating the corporation upon his death, the simplest method might be to create a separate corporation to hold the office building and then provide in his will or trust that upon his death the stock in the new corporation be distributed to the son or daughter. For practical reasons, brother-sister corporations are normally preferable in these situations. multiple corporations, estate planning factor

If it is decided to form separate corporations in connection with the restructuring of a business, the question of whether to form parent-subsidiary or brother-sister corporations should be addressed. Many times the purpose for which the separate corporation is being formed dictates the type of corporations to be formed. For example, if one of the reasons for forming a separate corporation is to take advantage of a beneficial Subchapter S election, the corporations must be of the brother-sister type because an S corporation may not be a subsidiary corporation and may not own 80 percent or more of the stock of another active corporation. multiple corporations, form of, factors

multiple corporations, tax considerations

While the issue of the type of corporations to form may occasionally be resolved by the practicalities of the situation or the personal desires of the participants, more often than not the decision on the matter will be tax-related. The principal tax considerations in determining the type of corporations to be formed are - (1) the total tax liability of the entire business enterprise after the restructuring, and (2) capitalizing the new corporation (or corporations) without exposing either the principal corporation or its shareholders to additional tax liabilities. The first consideration was discussed briefly earlier in this section and the second consideration is discussed briefly below. The reader is advised that both of these considerations are often complex and involved, and that the advice of tax counsel should be obtained.

capitalizing subsidiary corporation, tax aspects

Whenever a new corporation is formed in the course of restructuring a business, it is important to capitalize the new corporation in such a manner as to protect both the principal corporation and its shareholders from additional tax liabilities. To this end, a subsidiary corporation can normally be formed and capitalized tax-free, if desired, by complying with the requirements of 26 U.S.C. 351. Under certain circumstances, however, especially if the basis of the assets being transferred to the new corporation is low, a fully or partially taxable incorporation may be advantageous. See section 5.02, supra, for further reading on the taxability of an incorporation.

capitalizing brother-sister corporations, tax aspects

The tax risk of capitalizing a new corporation is usually more acute in the case of a brother-sister corporation, especially if the principal corporation has substantial accumulated earnings and profits. The overriding risk is that the transfer of assets to the new corporation, or the transfer of stock of the new corporation to the shareholders of the principal corporation, may be viewed by the Internal Revenue Service as a bail out by the principal corporation of its accumulated earnings and profits. Such a happening would have the effect of exposing the shareholders to a dividend tax liability at ordinary income rates on money they did not actually receive, and of capitalizing the new corporation with funds or assets that have been effectively taxed twice.

6.11 Acquiring Another Business

As indicated in the previous section, it is not unusual for a successful or well-capitalized small business corporation to seek to expand by acquiring another business. It is assumed in this section that the business being acquired is a going business, as opposed, say, to a start-up or inactive business, the acquisition of which would be relatively simple. It should be noted that the discussion in this section is from the viewpoint of the purchasing corporation. For a discussion of the sale of a business from the viewpoint of the seller (there are significant differences), see section 7.02, infra.

scope of section

A corporation may purchase another business through any of the following methods:

methods of acquiring business

(1) The asset-purchase method, whereby the assets of the acquired business are purchased in exchange for cash, property, or securities of the purchasing corporation.

(2) The stock-purchase method, whereby the stock or other indicia of ownership of the acquired business is purchased in exchange for cash, property, or securities of the purchasing corporation.

(3) The merger method, whereby the acquired business is merged with the purchasing corporation.

methods of acquisition, general aspects

In an asset purchase the purchaser contracts with the management of the acquired business, while in a stock purchase the purchaser contracts with the individual owners or shareholders of the acquired business. While it may be technically possible for the acquired business in a stock purchase to be a limited partnership or other entity with tangible evidences of ownership, in practice a business acquired in a stock purchase is nearly always a corporation. In both an asset purchase and a stock purchase the ownership interest of the sellers is terminated by the sale, while in a merger the ownership interest of the sellers survives the transaction, although in a different form. For purposes of this section, a "merger" includes a merger, share exchange or consolidation under the applicable state corporation laws. A merger, it should be noted, differs from a consolidation in that in a merger one of the two merging corporations survives the merger and retains its corporate existence, while in a consolidation both corporations cease to exist and a new corporation emerges. In a share exchange, the purchasing corporation acquires, pursuant to a plan, all of the stock of the selling corporation in exchange for cash, property, or securities of the purchasing corporation. See section 7.02, infra, for further reading on mergers, share exchanges and consolidations.

merger vs. consolidation

share exchange, definition

selecting method of acquisition, factors

In determining the method of acquisition best suited to a purchasing corporation, the following factors should be considered:

(1) The proposed use of the acquired business and its compatibility with the principal business of the purchasing corporation.

(2) The nature of the assets and liabilities of the business being acquired.

(3) The form of legal entity of the acquired business (i.e., corporation, partnership, etc.).

(4) The number of shareholders or owners of the business being acquired and their relationship with one another.

(5) The nature and size of the business being acquired and the risk of there being unknown or undisclosed liabilities.

(6) The existence in the acquired business of nonassignable debt obligations, contracts, leases, franchises, licenses, and the like.

(7) The tax considerations of the acquisition.

acquired business, role after acquisition

It is important for a purchasing corporation to determine in advance the role to be played by the acquired business in the overall business structure of the enterprise after the acquisition. In this regard, the compatibility of the two businesses should be examined and a determination made as to whether the business enterprise after the acquisition will function more effectively as a single corporation or as multiple corporations (see section 6.10, supra). A determination, for example, that an acquired business will function more effectively as a separate corporation will favor a stock purchase.

acquired business, nature of assets

The nature of the assets and liabilities of the business being acquired often dictates the method of sale. If its principal assets are land, patents, leases, or other tangible assets easy to transfer and incorporate into the existing business, an asset purchase is likely to be favored. Conversely, if its principal assets are either intangible (e.g., good will in its various forms) or difficult to transfer separately, a stock purchase or merger is likely to be favored. Also, it often happens that the business being acquired has assets or liabilities that are not wanted by the purchaser. Examples of unwanted assets or liabilities are unfavorable leases, sales contracts or collective bargaining agreements, and expensive employee retirement or benefit programs. Large unsecured debts or liabilities may also be unwanted by the purchaser, especially if the terms or interest rates are unfavorable. The existence of problem assets or liabilities favors an asset purchase wherein the problem assets or liabilities need not be purchased or assumed.

acquired business, unwanted assets and liabilities

acquired business, form of entity

The form of entity of an acquired business is important because unless the business is a corporation or possibly a limited liability company, it may be difficult to employ any method of acquisition other than an asset purchase. If the business to be acquired is not a corporation and if the purchasing corporation wishes to effect either a merger or a stock purchase, it may be feasible to incorporate the acquired business just prior to acquisition, most likely in a tax-free incorporation under 26 U.S.C. 351 (see section 5.02, supra).

acquired business, number and relationship of owners

The number of owners of an acquired business and their relationships with one another is particularly important if the business is a corporation. The number of shareholders is often the deciding factor in determining whether to purchase the assets or the stock of the corporation being acquired. If its shareholders are too numerous or geographically widespread, it may be impossible to purchase all of the stock of the acquired corporation at a uniform and reasonable price.

acquired business, dissenting shareholders, appraisal rights

The relationship of the shareholders of the acquired corporation with one another is important because of the appraisal and redemption rights of dissenting shareholders and because of the requirement of shareholder approval of mergers and sales of assets in most states. If high shareholder voting requirements are imposed by either a state statute or the articles of incorporation of the acquired corporation, a proposed merger or sale of assets may be vetoed by a few dissenting shareholders. And even if a merger or sale of assets is approved by the shareholders, if dissenting shareholders with appraisal and redemption rights are too numerous, it may render the acquisition in either of these forms financially unacceptable to the purchasing corporation.

acquired business, undisclosed liabilities

In either a stock purchase or a merger the purchasing or surviving corporation is liable for the debts and other liabilities of the acquired corporation. The prevailing risk to the purchasing corporation in a stock purchase, and to a lesser extent in a merger, is the possible existence of undisclosed or unknown liabilities of the acquired business which the purchasing corporation will later have to assume and pay. Particularly if the acquired business is sizeable or has questionable record-keeping practices, it is virtually impossible at any given moment to accurately determine in dollars and cents its outstanding debts and liabilities. For example, the acquired business may have unknowingly breached a warranty, become liable for an uninsured tort of an employee, or incurred a tax liability, the demand for any of which has yet to be delivered to management. Such uncertainties can be guarded against to some extent by extracting personal warranties from the principals of the acquired business and by establishing escrows for a few years, but the long-term risk remains on the purchasing corporation in a stock purchase.

acquired business, nonassignable assets

Sometimes a major asset of an acquired business is the existence of a license, franchise, contract, or similar asset that is, by its terms, nonassignable. In such situations the continued existence of the acquired business in its present form must be perpetuated if the asset is to survive the acquisition. If the business is not a corporation, its continued existence is virtually impossible. If the business is a corporation, a stock purchase will normally perpetuate its existence sufficiently to preserve the asset, although much obviously depends on the specific language of the document creating the asset. Again depending on the particular phraseology of the document creating the asset, a merger wherein the acquired business is the surviving corporation may also suffice to preserve the asset. A reverse triangular merger may be useful in this situation (see section 7.02, infra).

It is common for an acquired business to have debt obligations that the purchasing corporation wishes to assume, but which by their terms are nonassignable and become due and payable upon the transfer of assets, merger, or other extraordinary action by the acquired business. Such debt obligations normally consist of mortgages or security agreements that contain "due on sale" clauses, but they may also consist of debentures, bonds, and even redemption and other rights of preferred shareholders. Whatever their form, care must be taken so as not to accelerate the debt obligation by the proposed acquisition. A stock purchase is normally the form of acquisition best suited to this type of situation, but even then it may be necessary to obtain the consent of the obligation holder prior to the acquisition. A merger wherein the acquired business is the surviving corporation may also suffice. acquired business, nonassignable debts

While federal income tax considerations are seldom the principal reason for acquiring another business, they frequently delineate the form of the acquisition. Unless the purchasing corporation pays for the acquired business with appreciated property, it will incur no direct present tax liability from the acquisition transaction. Therefore, the paramount tax considerations for a purchasing corporation are the indirect and future considerations, which include the following: acquiring business, tax considerations

(1) The tax treatment of the cost of the assets acquired. This consideration applies to an asset purchase and to a stock purchase qualified under 26 U.S.C. 338 (which is discussed 3 paragraphs below). It is usually to the benefit of a purchasing corporation to assign as much of the purchase price as possible to depreciable or amortizable assets such as buildings, equipment, machinery, patents, leaseholds, covenants not to compete, and other assets with limited lives, and to noncapital items such as inventory and accounts receivable. Such assignments will have the effect of reducing the income taxes payable on the future operation of the acquired business. Similarly, it is usually in the best interest of a purchasing corporation to assign as little of the purchase price as possible to nondepreciable capital assets such as land, securities, goodwill, and trademarks. If the parties by agreement allocate the purchase price among the purchased assets, their allocation will usually be honored by the Internal Revenue Service. If no allocation is made by the parties, the I.R.S. may establish the allocation, which might be quite different from what the parties intended. The parties are not allowed to allocate the purchase price among the assets in a stock purchase qualified under 26 U.S.C. 338 because the allocations are made in the manner set forth in the Treasury Regulations. See 26 U.S.C. 338(b)(3). acquired assets, allocation of purchase price; allocation of purchase price, section 338 election

(2) The availability after acquisition of the beneficial tax attributes of the acquired business. Such tax features as investment tax credit carryovers, capital loss carryovers, foreign tax credit carryovers, beneficial tax elections and accounting methods, and convenient fiscal years may be valuable to the purchasing corporation. It is important to acquire the business through a method that preserves these beneficial tax attributes. The tax form of the sale (see infra, this section) often determines the transferability of the beneficial tax attributes of the acquired business. Generally, the beneficial tax attributes of an acquired business are preserved in a stock purchase and in a tax-free reorganization, but are not preserved in an asset purchase. preserving tax attributes of acquired business; acquisition of business, form of consideration

It should be understood that in a taxable transaction (as opposed to a tax-free reorganization) it makes no difference, for federal income tax purposes, whether the purchasing corporation pays for the acquired business with cash, property, its own securities, or securities of its parent corporation. If property or stock is used, it must be valued at its fair market value, which may present a problem for a small business corporation whose stock has no public market. The best practice is for the parties to the transaction to agree on a value for the stock or property for purposes of the acquisition. Obviously, it is to the future tax advantage of a purchasing corporation to value the stock or property as high as possible. acquisition of business, form of consideration

The reader should be aware that under Section 338 of the Internal Revenue Code, a purchasing corporation may elect to have a qualifying stock purchase treated as an asset purchase for tax purposes. See 26 U.S.C. 338(a). Under Section 338 the acquired corporation (it's called the "target corporation" in the I.R.C.) is treated as having sold all of its assets in a single transaction on the acquisition date. Thereafter, the corporation is treated as a new corporation that purchased the assets on the day after the acquisition date. stock purchase, section 338 election

section 338 election, general aspects

Qualifying under Section 338 is usually advantageous in the situation where the assets of the acquired business have a low tax basis and the purchaser wishes to step-up the basis of the acquired assets by allocating the purchase price to them, rather than to the acquired stock. Accordingly, Section 338 is useful to the purchaser who, for whatever reason, is purchasing the seller's stock to get its assets. However, because it is treated as an asset purchase, most of the beneficial tax attributes of the acquired business are not carried over to the purchaser in a transaction qualified under Section 338.

section 338 election, requirements

To qualify under Section 338 at least 80 percent of the seller's total voting stock and at least 80 percent of its total shares must be purchased in a transaction or series of transactions during a 12-month period. See 26 U.S.C. 338(d)(3). The purchaser must make the election to qualify the transaction under Section 338 not later than the 15th day of the 9th month after the acquisition date. See 26 U.S.C. 338(g). The acquired corporation need not be liquidated to obtain this tax treatment.

acquisition of business, tax form

For federal income tax purposes, the acquisition of a business may take any of four basic forms - (1) a currently taxable sale, (2) a deferred payment sale, (3) an installment sale, or (4) a tax-free reorganization, with or without boot. These taxable forms of acquisition should not be confused with the three basic methods of acquiring a business discussed previously in this section (i.e., asset purchase, stock purchase, and merger). The tax form of an acquisition is usually determined by the form and time of payment of the consideration given for the acquired business. Any of the three methods of acquisition, except possibly a merger, may take any of the four basic tax forms, depending on the form of the consideration and when it is paid.

currently taxable sale, tax treatment

The best example of a currently taxable sale is a transaction wherein the assets or stock of a business are sold for cash payable at closing. In such a sale the purchaser must allocate the entire purchase price to the assets or stock acquired. In a currently taxable asset purchase the purchasing corporation inherits none of the tax attributes of the seller, while in a currently taxable stock purchase the tax attributes of the seller may continue, provided that the business is not liquidated or substantially changed, and the purchase is not qualified under Section 338. See 26 U.S.C. 381(a)(1), 382(a).

deferred payment sale, tax treatment

A deferred payment sale is, for tax purposes, any sale, other than an installment sale or a reorganization, wherein the purchasing corporation becomes obligated to make payments in the future. The tax consequences to the purchasing corporation of a deferred payment sale are generally the same as a currently taxable sale (see previous paragraph). The only notable variations concern the establishment of the tax basis of acquired assets when the purchaser's future obligations are contingent and the requirement, if any, to treat a portion of the future consideration as interest. See respectively, Treasury Regs. 1.453-6, 1.1001-1, and 26 U.S.C. 483.

installment sale, tax provisions

The installment sale provisions of 26 U.S.C. 453 are, unless elected out by the seller, applicable to any sale of either stock or assets (other than inventory) whenever at least one payment is to be received after the close of the tax year in which the sale occurs. See 26 U.S.C. 453(b)(1), (d). Because installment sales are generally entered into for the tax purposes of the seller, the discussion of this form of sale is set forth in section 7.02, infra. Generally, the tax consequences to the purchasing corporation of an installment sale are the same as those in a deferred payment sale (see previous paragraph).

tax-free reorganizations, types

For federal income tax purposes there are three types of tax-free reorganizations applicable to acquisitions by small business corporations. See 26 U.S.C. 368 (a)(1). These are:

A reorganization, description

(1) The A reorganization, which is a merger, consolidation, or share exchange under an applicable state statute wherein the shareholders of the acquired business retain a continuing interest in the surviving corporation or its parent. Only the merger method of acquisition (which includes a consolidation or share exchange - see above) will qualify as an A reorganization. See section 7.02, infra, for further reading on corporate mergers, share exchanges, and consolidations.

B reorganization, description

(2) The B reorganization, which is the acquisition by the purchasing corporation of at least 80 percent of the total combined voting power of all classes of voting stock, and at least 80 percent of the total number of shares of all classes of stock, in the acquired corporation in exchange for voting stock of the purchasing corporation or its parent. No other consideration may be given, and the acquisition must take place in a single transaction or in a series of transactions within a short period of time (usually one year). See Treasury Reg. 1.368-2(c). Only a stock purchase or, in some states, a share exchange will qualify as a B reorganization, which is strictly a stock-for-stock transaction with no boot permitted.

C reorganization, description

(3) The C reorganization, which is the acquisition of substantially all of the assets of the acquired business in exchange for voting stock of the purchasing corporation or its parent, plus boot, in the form of cash or the assumption of liabilities of the seller, in an amount not exceeding 20 percent of the market value of the assets acquired. The C reorganization is essentially a stock-for-assets transaction, and the acquisition must be an asset purchase to qualify.

tax-free reorganizations, requirements

There are other types of reorganizations under 26 U.S.C. 368(a)(1), but they are not generally applicable to small business corporations and are not discussed here. It should be noted that in addition to a literal compliance with the statutory requirements, to qualify as a tax-free reorganization the transaction giving rise to the reorganization must have a valid business purpose and not be a sham used only to avoid taxes. See Gregory v. Helvering, 293 U.S. 465, 79 L. Ed. 596, 55 S. Ct. 266 (1935). Also, it is important that the seller acquire a legitimate ownership interest in the purchasing corporation in order to preserve the tax-free status of the reorganization. See Pinellas Ice & Cold Storage Co. v. Comm., 287 U.S. 462, 77 L. Ed. 428, 53 S.Ct. 257 (1933).

tax-free reorganization, tax treatment of boot

The acquisition of a business through an A, B, or C reorganization is nontaxable to both the buyer and the seller, unless "boot" is given in an A or C reorganization, in which case the boot is taxable to the seller. The purchasing corporation, in an A, B, or C reorganization, acquires the stock or property of the acquired business at the same tax basis that it had in the hands of the seller prior to the acquisition, unless boot is given in a C reorganization, in which case the purchaser's basis may be stepped up to the extent of any gain recognized by the seller. It is important in a B or C reorganization that the purchasing corporation not pay the legal or accounting bills of the seller, as this may be counted as boot and could cause the transaction to lose its tax-free status. See Revenue Ruling 73-54, 1973-1 C.B. 187. The purchasing corporation inherits most of the beneficial tax attributes of the acquired business in an A, B, or C reorganization.

The foregoing paragraphs give only the basic concepts of tax-free reorganizations and are intended to make the reader aware of such reorganizations and their applicability to small business corporations. Expert tax guidance should be obtained before attempting to carry out a tax-free reorganization.

Returning to the three methods of acquiring another business described earlier in this section: an asset purchase, a stock purchase, and a merger. It should be remembered that for purposes of this section a "merger".includes a merger, share exchange, or consolidation under applicable state law. The advantages and disadvantages to the purchasing corporation of each method of acquiring another business are listed below.

The advantages of an asset purchase to the purchasing corporation are:

asset purchase, advantages

(1) The purchaser is not usually responsible for the general liabilities of the seller. However, if the purchaser is a "mere continuation" of the seller, a court may impose the seller's general liabilities on the purchaser. See Plaza Express Co. v. Middle States Motor Freight, Inc., 40 Ill. App. 2nd 117, 189 N.E. 2nd 382 (1963).

(2) It is easier to determine and control the liabilities, including tax liabilities, being assumed by the purchaser.

(3) The parties to the transaction can, within reasonable limits, allocate the purchase price among the assets being acquired, tangible and intangible, so as to gain the maximum tax advantage.

(4) Unwanted or problem assets of the acquired business need not be purchased.

(5) There is no need to negotiate with minority shareholders or owners of the acquired business for the purchase of their interests.

(6) Representations and warranties of the seller survive the transaction and are enforceable thereafter by the purchasing corporation.

(7) Restrictions under state laws as to mergers involving foreign corporations are avoided.

(8) A business that is not a corporation may be acquired.

asset purchase, disadvantages

The disadvantages of an asset purchase to the purchasing corporation are:

(1) If the assets are numerous, the mechanics of the acquisition can be cumbersome and expensive because of the necessity of transferring each asset separately from the seller to the purchaser.

(2) Minority shareholders of the acquired business may be entitled to appraisal rights, which may be expensive if numerous.

de facto merger, effect

(3) If a statute or article of incorporation provision of the seller so provides, the sale may require the approval of the seller's shareholders, and high or unanimous shareholder voting requirements may permit minority shareholders to veto the sale. Also, if the acquisition constitutes a de facto merger under state law, minority shareholders of the purchaser may be entitled to appraisal and other rights. See Rath v. Rath Packing Co., 257 Iowa 1277, 136 N.W. 2nd 410 (1965).

(4) Most of the beneficial tax attributes of the acquired business will not be preserved, unless the transaction qualifies as a C reorganization.

(5) Sales and property taxes must normally be contended with and paid.

(6) Nonassignable assets (licenses, franchises, etc.) of the seller are not usually perpetuated and nonassignable debts of the seller may be accelerated by the acquisition.

(7) Bulk Transfer laws (Article 6 of the U.C.C.) must often be complied with.

(8) The integration or transfer of pension plans, stock options, employment contracts, and labor contracts are difficult to achieve.

(9) In a taxable transaction there will be a step-down in the tax basis of the acquired assets if their market value is less than the seller's tax basis.

(10) The seller's identity as a business will be lost, although if the seller is a corporation it may technically remain in existence, often as a shell or holding company.

(11) The acquired assets may be subjected to after-acquired property clauses in the purchaser's debt instruments.

The advantages of a stock purchase to the purchasing corporation are:

stock purchase, advantages

(1) It is mechanically the simplest method of acquiring a business if the acquired business has relatively few shareholders. However, if liquidation or integration into the purchaser's business is planned, specific assets may later have to be transferred.

(2) There are no appraisal rights of minority shareholders to contend with.

(3) Statutory or article of incorporation restrictions upon the seller with respect to mergers and sales of assets may be avoided.

(4) It is the method most likely to preserve and perpetuate nonassignable assets and debts of the seller.

(5) It is usually not necessary to comply with Bulk Transfer laws.

(6) It retains the corporate and business identity of the acquired business and the attendant benefits, including the seller's beneficial tax attributes.

(7) The acquired stock is not likely to be subjected to after-acquired-property clauses in the purchaser's debt instruments.

The disadvantages of a stock purchase to the purchasing corporation are:

stock purchase, disadvantages

(1) The risk of unknown or undisclosed liabilities of the acquired business that the purchasing corporation may later have to pay is greater. A thorough examination into the entire business operation of the seller is usually necessary. Personal warranties from the seller's principals, along with escrows, can be used to guard against liabilities of this type.

(2) The purchaser must assume the seller's tax basis in the assets and property acquired, regardless of the purchase price, unless the transaction is qualified under 26 U.S.C. 338.

(3) It may be difficult to purchase all of the stock of the acquired business at a reasonable and uniform price if the acquired business has numerous or geographically widespread shareholders.

(4) Restrictions imposed on the transfer of the seller's stock, coupled with veto powers or high shareholder voting requirements, may permit minority shareholders of the seller to block the proposed sale.

(5) In most instances, the acquired business must be a corporation.

merger, advantages

The advantages of a merger to the purchasing corporation are:

(1) The mechanics of the transaction are relatively simple (see section 7.02, infra).

(2) Because the transfer is by operation of law, separate conveyances of assets are not normally needed and local sales and transfer taxes are usually avoided.

(3) The perpetuation of nonassignable assets and debts can sometimes be accomplished, especially if the acquired business is the surviving corporation in the merger. Much depends, however, on the specific language of the instrument creating the asset or debt.

(4) Great flexibility is permitted as to the types of securities that may be issued to the shareholders of the acquired business.

merger, disadvantages

The disadvantages of a merger to the purchasing corporation are:

(1) All liabilities of the acquired business are assumed, whether or not they are known or disclosed.

(2) Appraisal rights of dissenting shareholders of both corporations may have to be dealt with.

(3) The shareholders of both corporations must normally approve the merger, and high or unanimous shareholder voting requirements in either corporation can render the merger impossible.

(4) Notice and other time-consuming requirements of state law must be complied with.

(5) The identity of the non-surviving corporation (usually the acquired business) will be lost.

(6) The acquired business must be a corporation or one that can easily be incorporated.

(7) The corporation laws of some states restrict mergers involving foreign corporations, especially if the foreign corporation is to be the surviving corporation.

EXHIBIT 6-A

BOARD OF DIRECTOR

RESOLUTION DECLARING CASH DIVIDEND

WHEREAS, it appeared from the reports furnished the Board of Directors by the officers of the Corporation, and by its accountant, that the Corporation has a surplus of funds that may lawfully be used for the payment of dividends, and that a cash dividend on the outstanding shares of Class A preferred stock and common stock of the corporation should be declared and issued.

Upon a motion duly made and unanimously adopted, it was RESOLVED by the Board of Directors that a dividend of $ __________ per share be declared and paid on the Class A preferred stock of the Corporation and a dividend of $ __________ per share be declared and paid on the common stock of the Corporation out of unreserved and unrestricted earned surplus to the holders of stock as shown by the records of the Corporation on ________________, distributable on ________________, and that the Treasurer be directed to mail checks for the payment of such dividends to the shareholders of record.

EXHIBIT 6-B

BOARD OF DIRECTOR RESOLUTION

RECOMMENDING AN AMENDMENT TO THE ARTICLES OF INCORPORATION

Upon a motion duly made and unanimously adopted, it was RESOLVED by the Board of Directors that Article 3, Section 3.01 of the Articles of Incorporation of the Corporation should be amended to provide as follows:

> Number of Authorized Shares and Par Value. The total number of shares that the Corporation shall have authority to issue is 10,000 shares of common stock, which stock shall be without par value.

It was FURTHER RESOLVED that the adoption of this amendment by the shareholders be recommended by the Board of Directors and that this amendment be submitted to a vote of the shareholders at a special meeting of shareholders called for the purpose of considering this amendment, which meeting shall be held on ________________, pursuant to notice as provided in the Bylaws.

EXHIBIT 6-C

BOARD OF DIRECTOR

RESOLUTION TO QUALIFY THE CORPORATION

TO TRANSACT BUSINESS IN FOREIGN STATES

Upon a motion duly made and unanimously adopted, it was RESOLVED by the Board of Directors that, pursuant to Article 6, Section 6.02 of the Articles of Incorporation, the Corporation qualify as a foreign corporation to transact business in the States of Pennsylvania and New York, and that the officers of the Corporation be and hereby are empowered and authorized to execute the necessary documents and pay the required fees and taxes in order to qualify the Corporation as a foreign corporation in such states.

ARTICLES OF AMENDMENT

TO THE

ARTICLES OF INCORPORATION

OF

______________________ CORPORATION

Pursuant to Sections ____________ of the Corporation Code of the State of ________________ the following Articles of Amendment to its Articles of Incorporation are adopted by the ________________________ Corporation:

First: The name of the Corporation is ________________________.

Second: The following amendments to the Articles of Incorporation were adopted by the shareholders of the Corporation on ________________, in the manner prescribed by the Corporation Code of the State of ________________, and pursuant to Article ____________ of the Articles of Incorporation:

Article 3, Section 3.01 is amended to provide as follows: Number of Authorized Shares and Par Value. The total number of shares that the Corporation shall have authority to issue is 10,000 shares of common stock, which stock shall be without par value.

Third: The number of shares of common stock of the Corporation outstanding at the time of the adoption of the above amendment was __________; and the number of shares entitled to vote on the amendment was __________.

Fourth: The number of shares of common stock that voted for the above amendment was __________; and the number of shares of common stock that voted against the above amendment was __________.

Fifth: The designation, number of shares, and voting results of each class of stock of the Corporation entitled to vote on the above amendment as a class were as follows:

Class	Number of Shares	Shares Voting For	Shares Voting Against

Sixth: Any exchange, reclassification, or cancellation of issued shares provided for in the amendment shall be effected in the following manner: None.

Seventh: The manner in which the above amendment effects a change in the amount of stated capital of the Corporation, and amount of stated capital as changed by such amendment, are as follows: Increased by $5,000.00.

Dated: ____________________

The ________________________ Corporation

By ________________________

President

and

____

Secretary

Subscribed and sworn to before me this __________ day of ________________, 19 _____, by ____________________, President, and ____________________, Secretary, of the ________________, Corporation, a corporation organized under the laws of the State of ________________.

____

Notary Public

CHAPTER SEVEN

TERMINATING A SMALL BUSINESS CORPORATION

7.01 The Alternatives Available to a Failing Business

business failure, typical causes, factors

Unfortunately, not every small business enterprise prospers. Many flounder in the waters of free enterprise. Statistically, more flounder than prosper. The most common causes of failure in small business enterprises include inadequate capitalization, poor management, dissention among the participants, an overly-competitive market, a depressed economy, inflation, the loss of a key employee, labor problems, and changes in the laws or regulations governing the business.

business failure, applicability of alternatives

For the participants of many small business enterprises there comes a time when the failure of the business must be dealt with. While business failure is never easy to deal with, the losses can be minimized if the failure is dealt with on a rational basis. It should be understood that regardless of the cause of a particular business failure, there are alternatives available to the participants of a failing small business corporation. The practicable alternatives that are typically available are listed below. The applicability of a particular alternative to the participants of a small business corporation normally depends largely on three factors: (1) whether the corporation has significant assets, (2) whether the corporation has a potential future earning capacity, and (3) whether and to what extent the participants are personally liable for the corporate debts.

business failure, practicable alternatives

The practicable alternatives available to the participants of a typical small business corporation whose business has failed beyond the point of a currently feasible recapitalization include the following:

abandonment of corporation, general aspects

(1) Abandonment of the corporation. Under this alternative the participants simply abandon the corporation without formal or judicial procedures, leaving the corporate assets, if any, to the creditors. In most instances of abandonment, the corporation will ultimately be dissolved for failure to file reports and pay the required fees and taxes, either by operation or law or by petition of the Attorney General (see section 7.03, infra). This alternative is best suited to the situation where the corporation is hopelessly insolvent with all of its assets pledged to creditors or encumbered by statutory or judicial liens. The abandonment alternative is most frequently used by lightly-capitalized corporations with no significant assets and only a few participants. The overriding danger in this alternative is that the corporate creditors will attempt to hold the participants personally liable for the corporate debts. (See section 6.06, supra, for further reading on the liability of corporate participants for corporate debts.) The main advantage of abandonment is that the participants are spared the legal and other expenses of liquidating or otherwise officially winding up the corporation. It is not uncommon under this alternative for the participants to make informal arrangements permitting certain creditors (usually those to whom they are personally liable) to satisfy at least a portion of their claims against what remains of the corporate assets.

creditors' composition, general aspects

(2) A creditors' composition. Under this alternative an agreement is reached between the corporation and its creditors whereby the creditors typically agree either to take less that the full amount on their claims in return for immediate payment or extend the time for payment of their claims in return for a promise by the corporation to pay the claims in full within a certain period, either from the proceeds of the sale of certain assets or otherwise. More often than not the individual corporate participants are also parties to the agreement, usually because they have either personally guaranteed certain of the corporate debts or are otherwise exposed to personal liability for all or certain of the debts.

creditors' composition, advantages and disadvantages

A creditors' composition is best employed either in lieu of liquidation where the corporation has significant assets and is being dissolved or otherwise terminated, or where the corporation has a potential future earning capacity and the participants desire to continue the business but need temporary relief from the creditors to do so. A creditors' composition has the advantage of being less expensive than a judicial liquidation or a bankruptcy proceeding, and it permits the corporation to remain in business, if that is desired. Its disadvantages are that it is practicable only in situations where the creditors are not numerous and are largely unsecured and that it may be superseded at any time by a bankruptcy or state insolvency proceeding. See generally, Williamson, The Attorney's Handbook on Small Business Reorganization Under Chapter 11, 5th Ed., 1998, sec. 2.03, The Nonbankruptcy Alternatives, and 15A Am. Jur. 2nd, Composition With Creditors, secs. 1-10.

assignment for benefit of creditors, general aspects

(3) Assignment for benefit of creditors. This is a proceeding under either the common law or a state statute whereby the debtor conveys substantially all of its property to a trustee, who is empowered to distribute the property to the creditors of the debtor in fulfillment of their claims. Statutes in many states regulate the form of such assignments, although assignments under the common law are also valid unless the statutory proceeding is exclusive. A creditor must assent to the assignment, however, in order for it to be bound by it. The power to authorize an assignment for benefit of creditors rests with the board of directors of the corporation unless otherwise provided by statute.

assignment for benefit of creditors, advantages and disadvantages

This alternative has the advantages of being less expensive than either a judicial liquidation or a bankruptcy proceeding, and it avoids the stigma of bankruptcy and permits the corporation to continue to exist, although devoid of most of its assets. Its disadvantages are that it requires the cooperation of all significant corporate creditors to be effective and that it may be superseded at any time by a bankruptcy proceeding (such an assignment may itself constitute grounds for relief in an involuntary bankruptcy proceeding, see 11 U.S.C. 303(h)(2)). This alternative is most effective in the situation where there are relatively few creditors, where the corporation has assets, such as accounts receivable or claims against others, that will be sufficient in time to satisfy most of the creditors, but not as their claims become due, or where it is desired to preserve at least the shell of the corporation. It can be a useful alternative when the participants are potentially liable for significant corporate debts.

Chapter 11 reorganization, general aspects

(4) A voluntary proceeding under Chapter 11 of the Bankruptcy Code. Under this alternative the corporation, usually pursuant to a board of director resolution, must file a voluntary petition in the United States Bankruptcy Court seeking to reorganize or liquidate under Chapter 11 of the Bankruptcy Code. The filing of such a petition automatically stays the commencement or continuation of most actions and proceedings against the corporation. See 11 U.S.C. 362(a). Upon the filing of the petition, the bankruptcy court acquires jurisdiction over the corporation and all of its assets, wherever located, but the corporation remains in possession of its property with the powers and duties of a trustee, unless it is shown that a trustee should be appointed. See 11 U.S.C. 1107. The debtor has 120 days in which to file a reorganization or liquidation plan, which must, among other things, designate claims into classes, specify the treatment of each class of claims, and provide an adequate means of executing the plan whereunder each class of creditors will receive at least as much as they would receive if the corporation was liquidated under Chapter 7. See 11 U.S.C. 1121(a), 1129(a)(7). The corporation must also file a disclosure statement adequately disclosing its financial condition and assets. See 11 U.S.C. 1125. The proposed reorganization plan must be accepted by two-thirds in amount or one-half in number of the creditors of at least one class of claims impaired by the plan. See 11 U.S.C. 1126, 1129(a)(10). After acceptance by the creditors, the plan must be confirmed by the court to become effective, which means, among other things, that the plan must be found to be feasible and not likely to result in liquidation or further reorganization. See 11 U.S.C. 1129.

A chapter 11 proceeding is expensive and usually requires an extended period during which to carry out the reorganization. However, it has the great advantages of not requiring the consent of every significant creditor, of protecting the corporation from dissatisfied creditors during the period of the reorganization, of being enforceable against every creditor, and of permitting the corporation to remain in business. This alternative is usually feasible only for a corporation with substantial assets and a promising future earning capacity that needs relief from its creditors in order to get back on its feet. See generally, Williamson, The Attorney's Handbook on Small Business Reorganization under Chapter 11, 5th edition, 1998.

chapter 11 proceeding, advantages and disadvantages

(5) A voluntary proceeding under Chapter 7 of the Bankruptcy Code. Under this alternative the corporation must file a petition in the United States Bankruptcy Court seeking liquidation under Chapter 7 of the Bankruptcy Code. A trustee in bankruptcy is then elected or appointed to collect the corporate assets, liquidate them, and distribute the proceeds to the corporate creditors in accordance with the priorities set forth in the Bankruptcy Code. See 11 U.S.C. 702, 726. Because a Chapter 7 proceeding can be expensive and because it seldom results in benefits to either the corporation or its participants, this alternative is seldom advisable for a small business corporation. However, a chapter 7 proceeding may be advisable for one or more of the corporate participants if they are liable for significant corporate debts. If liquidation of the corporation is desired by the participants, it is usually more feasible to liquidate it under the state corporation laws (see section 7.03, infra).

chapter 7 liquidation, general aspects

(6) Sale of the corporation or its business. This alternative is viable only if a purchaser can be found. This usually means that the corporation, despite its current financial difficulties, must have either a promise of substantial future earnings, if properly recapitalized or reorganized, or assets that may be valuable in the future. The sale may be in the form of a sale of the corporate assets, a sale or exchange of stock, or a merger with another corporation. See section 7.02, infra, for further reading on the sale of a small business.

sale of corporation, when practicable

(7) Voluntary dissolution and liquidation. This alternative is best suited to the situation where the value of the corporate assets exceeds the value of the claims against the corporation, or where there are corporate assets that are of value only to the participants, who wish to lawfully and safely purchase them from the corporation. See section 7.03, infra, for further reading on the dissolution and liquidation of small business corporations.

dissolution and liquidation, when practicable

An issue that frequently arises in connection with a failing small business corporation is the right of an insolvent corporation to prefer creditors. The law on this issue varies from state to state, depending on the type of creditor, the wording of the applicable statutes, if any, and the local case law. It should be noted that several states have statutes, either in the corporation laws, the insolvency laws, or the fraudulent conveyance laws, dealing with the preference of creditors. These statutes, which should always be examined, may or may not be applicable to a particular situation depending on the wording of the statute and the facts of the situation at hand.

preference of creditors, general aspects

In the absence of statute, most courts adhere, in varying degrees, to the so-called "trust fund" theory, whereunder the assets of an insolvent corporation are deemed to constitute a trust for the benefit of its creditors. See 19 Am. Jur. 2nd, Corporations, sec. 1021. In applying this doctrine, however, most courts have concluded that it is permissible, in the absence of fraud, for an insolvent corporation that is still active and transacting business to prefer one general creditor over another. See Land Red-E-Mixed Concrete Co. v. Cash Whitman, Inc., 425 S.W. 2nd 919, 922 (Mo., 1968). On the other hand, if the insolvent corporation is no longer active or transacting business, the courts usually deny the corporation the right to prefer one general creditor over another. See Delia v. Comm., 362 F. 2nd 400, 402 (CA 6, 1966).

preference of creditors, common law rules

preference of participants as creditors

Even in states that permit a preference of creditors, it is generally held that the participants of an insolvent corporation may not prefer their own antecedent claims to those of other corporate creditors. See Kirk v. H.G.P. Corp., 208 Kan. 777, 494 P. 2nd 1087 (1972), and Cooper v. Miss. Land Co., 220 So. 2nd 302 (Miss., 1969). It is generally permissible in the absence of fraud, however, for an insolvent corporation to give preference to the claim of a corporate participant in exchange for a contemporaneous loan or other valuable consideration advanced in good faith to the corporation. See 19 Am. Jur. 2nd, Corporations, sec. 1578. A tougher question is whether an insolvent corporation may give preference to claims for which a corporate participant is personally liable. The general rule seems to be that if the corporation is permitted under state law to prefer its general creditors, it may, in the absence of fraud, equally prefer a general creditor for whose claim a participant is personally liable. See Bank of Commerce v. Rosemary & Thyme, Inc., 218 Va. 781, 239 S.E. 2nd 909 (1978).

preference of participants' creditors

preference of creditors, factors

In practice, the issue of a preference of creditors by an insolvent corporation is seldom clearly and concisely presented. The issues of fact are usually in dispute and the issues of law clouded in uncertainty. Typically, much depends on such factors as when the corporation became insolvent, whether and when the various creditors knew of the insolvency, whether the corporation was still active at the time of the preference, how the preference was given, the nature of the preference, the wording and applicability of a particular statute, and the elusive factors of fraud and good faith. See generally, 19 Am. Jur. 2nd, Corporations, secs. 1572-1581.

insolvent corporation, creditors' remedies

Another matter that frequently arises in connection with a failing small business corporation is that of the rights of its creditors to collect their claims, either from the corporate assets or from third parties, including the corporate participants. The remedies of the creditors of an insolvent corporation vary depending on the status of the law in the local state. Generally, however, the following remedies are available to the creditors of an insolvent corporation who are unable to collect their claims from the corporation:

rights of creditors against participants

(1) **Personal actions against corporate participants for legal misconduct in operating the corporation.** Under the proper circumstances personal actions may be filed for common law misconduct in managing the corporation, for illegally distributing corporate assets, or under the doctrine of piercing the corporate veil. See section 6.06, supra, for further reading on the personal liability of corporate participants.

right of creditors to accounting

(2) **An action against the corporation and its participants for an accounting.** This remedy is best suited to the situation where the corporation had substantial assets when the creditor supplied the goods, funds, or services to the corporation that have since disappeared without an adequate explanation. See generally, 1 Am. Jur. 2nd, Accounts and Accounting, secs. 50-64.

rights of creditors, fraudulent transfers

(3) **An action to set aside fraudulent transfers and subject corporate assets in the hands of others to the claims of corporate creditors.** This remedy is viable in the situation where the corporate participants have distributed substantial corporate assets to themselves or to others without first satisfying corporate creditors. If a creditor has obtained a judgment against the corporation, an attachment proceeding against specific corporate assets may be an appropriate form of this remedy. If specific corporate assets cannot be located, if assets have been converted to cash, or if the creditor does not have a lien or security interest that attaches to the assets sought to be recovered, it may be necessary to obtain a judgment against the corporation in order to bring such an action. In states prohibiting a preference of general creditors by an insolvent corporation, it may be necessary to bring such an action in the name of all corporate creditors in order that the proceeds may be ratably distributed to them. See generally, 19 Am. Jur. 2nd, Corporations, sec. 1583.

(4) An action against other creditors to set aside unlawful preferential transfers. This type of action is useful where an unlawful preference has been made that was not necessarily fraudulent, or where fraud cannot be proven. The action may be brought against general creditors or against corporate participants who are also creditors of the corporation. Much depends on what constitutes a preferential transfer in the particular jurisdiction. Again, if state law so requires it may be necessary to bring the action in the names of all persons who were creditors at the time of the alleged preferential transfer so that the proceeds of the action can be ratably distributed to them. See generally, 19 Am. Jur. 2nd, Corporations, sec. 1584.

rights of creditors, preferential transfers

(5) An action to appoint a receiver and involuntarily liquidate the corporation. This proceeding is governed by the corporation laws in most states, and the relevant statutory provisions should be examined. An unsatisfied judgment against the corporation and a showing of corporate insolvency must usually be shown in order to maintain such a proceeding. This proceeding is viable only if the corporation has significant assets that can be located and liquidated. See section 7.03, infra, for further reading on involuntary liquidation proceedings.

rights of creditors, involuntary liquidation

(6) An involuntary proceeding to liquidate the corporation under Chapter 7 of the Bankruptcy Code. An involuntary Chapter 7 bankruptcy proceeding may be commenced by three or more creditors whose claims total $10,000 or more, unless there are fewer than 12 creditors, in which case a single creditor meeting the $10,000 claim limit may commence the proceeding. See 11 U.S.C. 303(b). An order for relief under Chapter 7 may be entered if it is shown that the corporation is generally not paying its debts as they become due. See 11 U.S.C. 303(h). In a Chapter 7 proceeding, a trustee is elected or appointed to collect the corporate assets, liquidate them, and pay the creditors in accordance with the priorities set forth in the Bankruptcy Code. It is important to note that a bankruptcy trustee may set aside - (1) preferential transfers made to ordinary creditors within 90 days of the date of the filing of the bankruptcy proceeding, (2) preferential transfers to insiders made within one year of the date of filing, and (3) fraudulent transfers made within one year of the date of filing. See 11 U.S.C. 547(b), 548(a). If a creditor has reason to believe that substantial assets have been transferred in such a manner that the transfers are avoidable in bankruptcy, an involuntary Chapter 7 proceeding may be a viable remedy.

rights of creditors, involuntary chapter 7 liquidation

voidable transfers, bankruptcy trustee

7.02 Selling a Business

sale of business, general aspects

It is not unusual for the results of a lifetime of work to ride on the successful sale of a small business. If the business has prospered, its successful sale can turn years of deprivation and toil into a prosperous retirement or sound financial future, spiced with fond memories of nursing the business to prosperity. If the sale is brought about by a disenchantment with the business or by disagreement or deadlock among its participants, the success of the sale is still important. Whatever the reason for the sale, and whether all or a portion of a business is being sold, it is important that the sale be conducted in such a manner as to command the highest possible selling price. It is also important that the consideration from the sale be paid in a manner suited to the needs and wishes of the sellers and that the taxes payable by reason of the sale be kept to a minimum. If only a portion of the business is being sold, it is important that it be sold in a manner that will enable the sellers to successfully conduct the remaining portion of the business.

sale of business, professional assistance

Because the sale of a business is an important event, and because the sale is usually a complicated transaction, it is important to employ professional assistance in effecting the sale. A professional appraiser may be needed to determine the value of the business and its assets. An accountant will almost surely be needed to assist in the tax-planning and other financial aspects of the sale. An attorney will be needed to plan the legal aspects of the sale, to draft or examine the legal documents needed to consummate the sale, and to negotiate with the prospective purchasers, if necessary.

Many of the matters discussed or referred to in this section are dealt with in section 6.11, supra, entitled "Acquiring Another Business." Rather than repeat in this section the matters covered in section 6.11, references to that section will be made throughout this section. The reader should be familiar with section 6.11 before reading this section.

sale of business, basic functions

From the viewpoint of the seller, the legal aspects of the sale of a business consists of three basic functions: (1) determining the value of the business, (2) determining the method of sale, and (3) determining the method of payment. Included in each function is the matter of federal income tax considerations. While the functions are obviously interrelated (the selling price is often affected by the method of sale or payment, the method of sale may affect the method of payment, etc.), each element should be considered separately and thoroughly if the best possible sale is to be effected. A wrong choice on any of the three elements may ruin an otherwise satisfactory sale.

determination of value, importance

Determining the value of a small business is not usually considered to be a "legal" matter. However, a few matters related to valuation warrant discussion, mainly because the corporation's attorney is often involved in negotiations with prospective purchasers and should be familiar with the valuation process. The valuation process is important because only when a realistic estimate of the fair market value of a business has been obtained will it be possible to intelligently decide whether to sell the business and at what price.

purpose of valuation

The first matter to consider is the purpose of the valuation. In practice, value is often determined differently for different purposes. For example, the same property is likely to be valued differently for purposes of insurance coverage, security for a loan, and the imposition of taxes. In the situation where a business is being sold, the purpose of the valuation should be for sale to outsiders. Therefore, the value to be determined should be that which a willing buyer would pay to a willing seller under like circumstances: in other words, the fair market value of the business. Such personal or internal notions of value as book value and values determined under shareholder agreements should be largely disregarded when the sale of the business to outsiders is being contemplated.

value of business, stock sale vs. asset sale

The stock of most small business corporations has no market value independent of a transfer of an interest in the corporation's assets. Even if a few shares of stock have been sold independently, the value of the stock in such sales is not usually an accurate indicator of the value of the same stock in a sale involving substantially all of the corporation's stock. Because the value of a small business corporation's stock is normally dependent on the value of its assets, it makes little difference in determining its fair market value whether a stock sale or an asset sale is contemplated.

valuation of business, tangible factors

good will, what constitutes

Three tangible factors and one intangible factor are generally given the greatest consideration in appraising or valuing a small business corporation. The tangible factors are - (1) corporate earnings, past and potential, (2) the net corporate assets (assets minus liabilities), and (3) projected net profitability (the dividend paying capacity in larger corporations). The intangible factor is good will, which includes such considerations as the location of the business, the existence of trade or brand names, and a record of successful and reputable operation over an extended period. It should be noted that while this section deals primarily with the sale of a small business corporation, the same principles are applicable to the sale of a limited liability company, a partnership, or a sole proprietorship.

valuation of business, intangible factors

In valuing a business, there may be other intangibles to consider, some of which may detract from the value of the business. Included here are such matters as the importance of key employees to the success of the business and the chances of their departure, the trend or economic outlook for the particular trade or industry of the business, the existence of potential future liabilities, whether from the nature of the business or otherwise, and the general economic condition and outlook for the area where the business is located. The economic outlook, both for the trade or industry of the business and for the area or section of the country where the business is located, is particularly important. It is difficult to sell a business whose main product is becoming technologically obsolete or whose sales are depressed because of a general economic depression in the local area. On the other hand, if the company's product is technologically new and on the rise or if sales are on the rise because of a boom in the local economy, the price of the business is likely to be enhanced.

valuation of business, method of appraisal

The best indicators of fair market value for most small business corporations are recent sales of comparable businesses in the area. No two businesses are exactly alike, however, and it is always necessary to realistically compare the business being sold with the comparable in order to accurately value the business from the sale. In comparing the two businesses, the tangible and intangible factors described above should be specifically compared and distinguished. The value of a small business corporation may also be estimated by the so-called "income approach," wherein the income from the business is capitalized to determine the fair market value of the business. See section 5.17, supra, for an assessment of the capitalization of earnings method of valuation as applied to small business corporations.

As discussed in section 6.11, supra, there are three basic methods of selling a small business corporation: (1) an asset sale, (2) a stock sale, and (3) a merger. In an asset sale, the assets of the selling corporation are sold by the corporation in exchange for cash, property or securities of the purchaser. In a stock sale, the stock of the selling corporation is sold by the stockholders in exchange for cash, property, or securities of the purchaser. In a merger, the selling corporation is merged or consolidated in one form or another with the purchasing corporation. See section 6.11, supra, for further reading on each type of sale.

selecting method of sale, factors

Determining the method of sale best suited to the sellers is usually the most important legal function in the sale of a small business corporation. In determining the method of sale to be used, the following factors should be considered:

(1) the extent, if any, of the personal liabilities of the individual shareholders for unsecured corporate debts and obligations,

(2) the degree of support for the sale by the various shareholders or groups of shareholders,

(3) whether all or a portion of the business is being sold,

(4) the nature of the corporation (i.e., whether it is a collapsible corporation, a personal holding company, an S corporation, etc.), and

(5) the tax aspects of the sale.

personal liability of shareholders, method of sale

If all or some of the individual shareholders are personally liable for sizeable unsecured corporate debts or liabilities, those shareholders are likely to favor a stock sale or merger wherein the debts will be assumed by the purchaser. The assumption of corporate debts by a purchaser usually has the practical effect of reducing the cash price paid for the business, which in turn reduces the price of the corporate stock for all of the shareholders and spreads the cost of the assumption of corporate liabilities among all of the shareholders, whether or not they are personally liable for any of the corporate debts.

minority opposition to sale, method of sale

If the sale of a business is favored by its controlling shareholders but opposed by a sizeable minority of shareholders, those in control are likely to favor a method of sale that cannot be voted down or vetoed by the minority. If either state law or the articles of incorporation impose shareholder voting requirements that will permit the dissenters to block a merger or an asset sale, then that method of sale will not be favored by the majority. Also, if applicable state law or the articles of incorporation give dissenting shareholders rights of appraisal and redemption in the event of either a merger or an asset sale, a sale by either of these methods could be rendered financially unattractive to the controlling shareholders because of the effect of such rights on the selling price of the corporation. Unless precluded by stock transfer restrictions or veto powers, a stock sale may be possible regardless of the voting rights of the minority if the purchaser is interested only in purchasing control of the corporation and not complete ownership.

sale of portion of business, method of sale

If only a portion of the business is being sold, an asset sale is usually required unless the portion being sold can be separately spun off and incorporated prior to sale. If a stock sale is desired and if the portion of the business being sold can be separately incorporated prior to sale without the imposition of taxes, the stock of the separate corporation should be issued to the shareholders of the principal corporation and not by the principal corporation itself. If an asset sale with installment payments is contemplated, it may be advantageous to qualify the separate corporation under Subchapter S of the Internal Revenue Code so as to avoid the double tax that may otherwise result (see infra, this section).

collapsible corporation, method of sale

personal holding company, method of sale

S corporation, method of sale

If the corporation being sold is a collapsible corporation (see section 5.02, supra), a stock sale may result in ordinary income being charged to the shareholders. An asset sale or merger may be preferable in such a case. If the corporation is a personal holding company, or will be rendered such by the sale, the retention of the proceeds of the sale by the corporation (as in an asset sale) could subject it to penalty tax provisions (see section 5.02, supra). Unless a timely liquidation is planned, this factor works against an asset sale. If the corporation is an S corporation, if the sale is an asset sale, if the sales price is to be paid in installments extending over several years, and if more than 25 percent of the funds paid to the corporation in any corporate tax year constitutes interest (i.e., passive investment income), the corporation may lose its Subchapter S status and a portion of the interest may be taxed at the highest corporate rates. See 26 U.S.C. 1362, 1375(a) and section 5.18, supra.

tax basis of assets and stock, method of sale

type of assets, method of sale

Most sales of small business corporations are taxable transactions (as opposed to tax-free reorganizations). In a taxable transaction the tax aspects of the sale often play a direct, and sometimes deciding, role in determining the method of sale best suited to the sellers. In determining the tax aspects of a sale, a primary consideration is the tax basis of the assets in the hands of the corporation as compared to the tax basis of the corporate stock in the hands of the shareholders. If the stock has a low tax basis (as it usually does in small business corporations) and the corporate assets have a high tax basis, an asset sale would ordinarily be preferable to the seller. Another factor to consider is the type of assets to be transferred. If the assets being sold are primarily noncapital assets upon which any gain would be taxed as ordinary income, a stock sale may be preferable to the seller. But if the assets are primarily capital assets upon which any gain would be taxed as a capital gain, an asset sale may be preferable to the seller, depending, of course on the tax basis of the assets in the hands of the corporation.

asset sale, allocation of purchase price, priorities

In an asset sale the parties to the sale are usually permitted to allocate the purchase price among the assets being transferred. If gain will be realized from the sale, it will ordinarily be to the tax advantage of the seller to allocate the purchase price in accordance with the following priorities:

(1) First, to capital assets and Section 1231 assets, because any gain will be taxed as a capital gain. Section 1231 assets include depreciable personal property and real estate, either of which must be used in a trade or business and held by the business for more than one year. See 26 U.S.C. 1231(b)(1). Generally, net gains realized from the sale of Section 1231 assets are treated as capital gains, while net losses are treated as ordinary losses.

capital assets, section 1231 assets, tax treatment

(2) Second, to depreciable and other assets upon which a capital gain subject to recapture provisions will be realized. Included here are Section 1245 assets upon which depreciation has been deducted, real estate that is subject to accelerated depreciation, and property upon which an investment tax credit has been allowed. Any gain realized from the sale of these assets will be taxed as ordinary income to the extent of the depreciation or tax credits previously taken. In general, Section 1245 property is depreciable personal property (excluding buildings) used as an integral part of manufacturing, production, or the furnishing of services. See 26 U.S.C. 1245(a)(3).

assets subject to depreciation recapture, tax treatment

(3) Third, to noncapital assets and covenants not to compete. The entire amount of any gain realized from these assets will be taxed as ordinary income. Noncapital assets include inventory, raw materials, work in progress, and accounts receivable.

noncapital assets, covenant not to compete, tax treatment

It should be noted that if loss will be realized from the sale of assets, the order of the above priorities should be reversed. In other words, if a net taxable loss will be realized from the sale, it will normally be to the tax advantage of the seller to allocate the purchase price in the reverse order from that shown above.

sale with tax loss, allocation priorities

Another tax consideration of the seller in selecting the method of sale is the avoidance of a double tax; that is, a tax imposed at both the corporate and the shareholder levels. A double tax is imposed in an asset sale when the corporation is taxed on the gain realized on the sale of its assets and the proceeds of the sale are then distributed to the shareholders in the form of taxable dividends. A double tax is especially difficult to avoid in situations where an asset sale is employed and extended payments are to be made to the seller in the years after the sale.

sale of business, double tax

It may be possible to avoid a double tax in an asset sale with extended payments by qualifying the selling corporation under Subchapter S of the Internal Revenue Code and not liquidating the corporation until all or most of the payments have been received. Such an arrangement will avoid the double tax as long as the corporation's passive investment income (i.e., the interest on the payments) does not exceed 25 percent of its gross receipts. Also, if an asset sale qualifies as an installment sale and if the selling corporation is liquidated under 26 U.S.C. 331 (see section 7.03, infra), the installment obligations may be distributed to the shareholders without the imposition of an immediate tax (the shareholders will be charged with income as the payments are received, not when the obligations are distributed). See 26 U.S.C. 453(h). If a double tax cannot be avoided by any of the means described above, an asset sale should not be used.

double tax, how to avoid

The merger method of sale is not frequently used by small business corporations, mainly because they are usually purchased by other small business corporations whose stock has little or no market value. On occasion, however, a merger is appropriate, usually because either the stock of the purchasing corporation is publicly traded or the purchasing corporation will provide employment for all or most of the shareholders of the selling corporation. The merger method of sale has the advantage of being the most flexible method of sale, especially if a tax-free transfer is contemplated. Almost any type of security, including debt instruments, may be issued by the surviving corporation to the shareholders of the merging corporation, and cash or property may also be used as consideration. Because the transfer is by operation of law, there is normally no need to prepare legal documents for the separate conveyance of assets or stock. Finally, because the transaction is not technically a sale, local sales and transfer taxes are usually avoided.

merger, use of by small business corporations

merger method, advantages of

merger, share exchange, and consolidation, definitions

Mergers, share exchanges, and consolidations are statutory proceedings wherein two or more corporations are united with one another. In a merger, one corporation is absorbed into another. The former is called the merging corporation and the latter is called the surviving corporation. Legally, the merging corporation ceases to exist after the merger, while the surviving corporation continues to exist, but in an altered form. In a share exchange the purchasing corporation acquires, pursuant to a plan, all of the stock of the selling corporation in exchange for cash, property, or securities of the purchasing corporation. In a consolidation the two corporations are absorbed into a newly created third corporation. Because each of these proceedings involve basically the same procedures, the procedures described below for a merger are also applicable to a share exchange and a consolidation.

merger, requirements, appraisal rights

Because a merger is a statutory proceeding, it is important that all of the requirements of the applicable statute are strictly complied with. The first step is to check the appropriate statute to insure that the corporations are permitted to merge in the desired manner. In this regard some state statutes restrict mergers involving foreign corporations, usually by requiring the surviving corporation to be a domestic corporation. Another matter that should be checked, both in the corporation laws and the articles of incorporation of both corporations, is the appraisal rights of dissenting shareholders. In most states the shareholders of either corporation who vote against the merger and who file objections with the corporation have the right to have their stock appraised and purchased, usually under judicial supervision. It should be understood that appraisal rights of dissenting shareholders are measured differently in different states, depending on the wording of the statute and the judicial construction of the appraisal rights created therein. Some courts have held that dissenting shareholders are entitled to their pro rata share of the entire value of the corporation, while other courts have held that dissenting shareholders are entitled only to the market value of their minority holdings and permit corporations to apply "minority interest" and "marketability" discounts in valuing the stock of dissenting minority shareholders. See respectively, Cavalier Oil Corp. v. Harnett, 564 A.2d 1137 (Del., 1989), and Armstrong v. Marathon Oil Co., 32 Ohio St. 3d 397, 513 NE 2d 776 (1987).

merger, how to implement

Although the specifics may vary somewhat from state to state, the following steps must normally be taken to effect a merger:

merger agreement, contents

(1) Negotiation of the basic merger agreement. This agreement (the merger agreement) should contain the terms and conditions of the merger, the procedures for implementing the agreement, and the specifics necessary to perfect the surviving corporation and meet the statutory requirements. These negotiations are usually carried out by the ranking officers of both corporations and their attorneys.

merger agreement, director action

(2) Approval of the merger agreement by the board of directors of each corporation. The approval should be in the form of a resolution that also sets the time and place of a special shareholders' meeting called for the purpose of voting on the merger agreement.

merger agreement, shareholder action

(3) Approval of the merger agreement by the shareholders of each corporation. The shareholder voting requirements of the applicable statute or article of incorporation provision must be met by each corporation if the merger is to be effected. A shareholders' meeting may not be required if a written consent to the merger is signed by the number of shareholders required under the local action-without-meeting statute (see section 6.04, supra, and Appendix I, infra).

articles of merger, signing of

(4) Preparation and signing of the articles of merger. Once the merger agreement has been approved by the shareholders of each corporation, the articles of merger should be prepared and signed by the appropriate officers of each corporation.

(5) Filing the articles of merger (including a certification of shareholder approval of the merger) and other required documents. In most states these documents must be filed with the state filing official. The specific filing requirements vary considerably from state to state, and the applicable statutes and regulations should be carefully checked. If either corporation is subject to the proxy rules of the Securities Act of 1934 (see 15 U.S.C. 78L, 78n), or if new securities are being issued, filings with the Securities and Exchange Commission or the state securities commissioner may be necessary. In some states a notice of the merger may have to be published in a local newspaper. Also, any required fees or franchise taxes must be paid. The merger usually becomes effective when the articles of merger are filed with the state filing official unless a different date is set forth in the merger agreement. articles of merger, filing requirements merger, when effective

(6) Exchange of securities by assenting shareholders and payments to dissenting shareholders. The assenting shareholders of the merging corporation exchange their stock for securities of the surviving corporation, cash, or other property, as called for in the merger agreement. The dissenting shareholders of either corporation are paid for their stock in accordance to their rights of dissent and appraisal under the applicable statutory or article of incorporation provisions. merger, exchange of securities, payment

There are two unique types of mergers that add flexibility to the merger method of sale. Both types are permitted under the corporation laws of most states and under the tax-free reorganization provisions of the Internal Revenue Code. These are the so-called triangular mergers: specifically, the forward triangular merger and the reverse triangular merger. In a forward triangular merger the acquired (i.e., the selling) corporation is merged into a subsidiary of the acquiring corporation, with the subsidiary surviving the merger, and the shareholders of the acquired corporation receive securities of the parent corporation in exchange for their stock. In a reverse triangular merger a subsidiary of the acquiring corporation merges into the acquired corporation, with the shareholders of the acquired corporation again exchanging their stock for securities of the parent corporation, which then controls the acquired corporation (which survives the merger). Triangular mergers are useful when it is desired to avoid approval and appraisal rights of the parent corporation's shareholders (because its subsidiary is technically performing the merger, its shareholders have no such rights), when it is desired to protect the parent corporation from liabilities of the acquired corporation, and when the acquired corporation has nonassignable assets or debts that must be preserved in the merger. types of mergers forward triangular merger reverse triangular merger triangular mergers, use of

If a merger is to qualify as a tax-free reorganization (an A reorganization, see section 6.11, supra), care must be taken to preserve the tax-free status of the transaction. While nonvoting stock and debt securities may be issued by the surviving corporation in an A reorganization, debt securities may be treated as boot and thus be taxable, often at ordinary income rates if they take on the appearance of dividends. See 26 U.S.C. 356(a)(2), 302(b)(1). Generally, at least 50 percent of the premerger equity must be retained by the sellers, and debt, cash, or other boot in excess of 50 percent will render the whole transaction taxable. See Revenue Ruling 66-224, 1966-2 C.B. 114. As in all tax-free reorganizations, care must be taken so as not to lose the tax-free status under the step transaction doctrine. This doctrine provides that in a series of transactions the net effect of all of the steps will be considered, rather than each step separately, in determining tax status. Finally, if preferred stock is to be issued in the reorganization, the pitfalls of 26 U.S.C. 306 must be avoided if the sellers are to avoid tax liability. A reorganization preserving tax-free status step transaction doctrine, effect

From the standpoint of the seller, the method of payment is always an important aspect of the sale. A high selling price for the corporation can be misleading if most of the consideration consists of unmarketable securities or future payment obligations by a corporation that may not survive. A high selling price is equally meaningless if a large share of the proceeds is eaten up by taxes. There are two elements in the method of payment: the form of the payment (usually cash, securities, or property) and the time of payment. It is important to devise both a form and a time of payment that will insure the sellers the eventual receipt of their bargain with the best possible tax treatment. sale of business, method of payment, importance

tax-free reorganization, type of consideration

tax-free reorganization, time of payment

One of the first matters to be resolved in any sale is whether the transaction is to be taxable or tax-free. In a tax-free sale the form of consideration available to the seller is limited to securities of the purchasing corporation or its parent. While some boot is permitted in A and C reorganizations, it is taxable. The time of payment of the consideration in a tax-free transaction is important only insofar as it does not cause the tax-free status of the sale to be lost. The consideration is normally delivered to the sellers upon the consummation of the sale, but occasionally contingencies in the sale may delay the completion of payment in its final form. Complete payment in its final form may be delayed for up to five years under the proper conditions without losing the tax-free status of the sale. See Revenue Procedure 79-14, 1979-1 C.B. 496. As a practical matter, tax-free sales of small business corporations are rare. They are usually limited to situations where the stock of the purchasing corporation or its parent is publicly traded and has a market value, or where the purchasing corporation agrees to provide employment and a meaningful management role in the purchasing corporation for all or most of the shareholders of the selling corporation.

taxable sale, form of consideration

like-kind transfer, tax treatment

Because most sales of small business corporations are taxable transactions, the usual objective is to obtain a form and time of payment that best serves the financial and tax interests of the seller. In this regard it should be noted that in most taxable transactions the form of the consideration makes little difference taxwise (although it is obviously important for other purposes). The seller may receive cash, securities, property, or practically any type or form of consideration without altering the tax aspects of the sale. Any property or securities given as consideration must be valued at their fair market value for purposes of the sale (see section 6.11, supra). If the parties agree on a value of the property or securities for purposes of the sale, it is always in the best interest of the seller to set the value as low as possible. An exception to the rule that the form of consideration does not affect the tax liability of the sale is when like-kind property is received in an asset sale, in which case a portion of the sale may be tax-free. See 26 U.S.C. 1031.

taxable sale, time of payment, tax aspects

The time of payment of the consideration to the sellers in taxable sales may be categorized for tax purposes as - (1) currently taxable sales, (2) deferred payment sales, and (3) installment sales. See section 6.11, supra, for a definition of each type of sale. In a currently taxable sale and in most deferred payment sales, the seller will realize all of the taxable gain or deductible loss in the year of the sale. If the purchaser's future payment obligations in a deferred payment sale are contingent, the seller may be able to delay the taxability of the future payments until they are actually received. See Revenue Ruling 58-402, 1958-2 C.B. 15.

installment sales, general aspects

installment obligations, distribution in liquidation tax aspects

Installment sales are popular with sellers of small business corporations. An installment sale may be either an asset sale or a stock sale. The principal reason for the popularity of installment sales is that they permit the seller to spread most of the gain realized on the sale over the period of payment, and thereby reduce both the initial and the overall tax liability. To qualify as an installment sale at least one payment must be received after the tax year in which the sale is made. See 26 U.S.C. 453(b). The installment sale provisions automatically apply to any such sale unless elected out by the seller. If the sale does not include inventory or personal property regularly sold on the installment plan (sales of which are excluded from installment sales, see 26 U.S.C. 453(b)(2)), the seller will recognize gain in any tax year in proportion to the portion of the proceeds received in that year. See 26 U.S.C. 453(c). If an asset sale qualifies as an installment sale and if the selling corporation is liquidated under 26 U.S.C. 331 (see section 7.03, infra), the installment obligations may be distributed to the shareholders without the imposition of an immediate tax (the shareholders will be charged with income as the payments are received, not when the obligations are distributed). See 26 U.S.C. 453(h).

installment sales, recapture provisions, interest payments

A disadvantage of an installment sale to the seller is that depreciation recapture is deemed to be received first, and investment tax credit recapture is deemed to be received in the year of sale, even if no payments are received in that year. See Treasury Regs. 1.1245-6(d), 1.1250-1(c)(6) and 26 U.S.C. 453(i). It should be noted that if an installment sale is to be used it is important to provide for the payment of interest on the purchaser's future payment obligations. Otherwise, the future payments may be immediately taxable to the seller or an interest rate may be imputed by the Internal Revenue Service.

7.03 Dissolution and Liquidation

The dissolution of a corporation terminates its existence as a body politic. A corporation may be dissolved voluntarily, usually with the consent of its shareholders, or involuntarily by the state or by a court. Because it terminates the legal existence of the corporation, dissolution is deemed an extraordinary corporate act requiring the approval of a specified percentage of its shareholders if voluntary, or a judicial finding of specified conditions or grounds if involuntary. The corporation laws of the state of incorporation govern all dissolution proceedings.

dissolution of corporation, general aspects

There are three basic types or methods of corporate dissolution: (1) Voluntary dissolution, which may occur upon the initiative of the incorporators, the board of directors, or, in many states, the shareholders, and requires the approval of a specified percentage of the shareholders. (2) Administrative dissolution, which occurs either by operation of law or upon the initiative of the state filing official, usually for a failure to file required reports or pay required fees or taxes. (3) Judicial dissolution, which may occur upon the initiative of the state, a shareholder, a creditor, or the corporation itself, and requires specified findings by a designated court.

corporate dissolution, basic types of

Although it often accompanies dissolution and is usually covered in the same sections of the state corporation laws as dissolution, liquidation is a separate transaction. The liquidation of a corporation is the winding up of its business, the payment of its creditors, and the distribution of the remainder of its assets to its shareholders in the redemption or cancellation of their stock. There can be dissolution without liquidation (e.g., when a corporation has no assets), and there can be liquidation without dissolution (e.g., when a corporation is to be recapitalized to begin a new business). Unlike dissolution, liquidation is normally a taxable transaction, and, if the value of a corporation's assets exceeds it liabilities, federal income tax considerations often play a dominant role in determining when and how a corporation is liquidated.

liquidation of corporation, general aspects

A corporation may be voluntarily dissolved at any time after it has been formed, even if it has not issued any stock or conducted any business. In most states, a corporation that has not commenced doing business and that either has not issued stock or has no shares of stock outstanding may be voluntarily dissolved by the incorporators or, in some states, by the initial board of directors. A majority vote of the designated body (i.e., the incorporators or the initial board of directors) is usually required. In either event, the voluntary dissolution of a corporation that has not started doing business is relatively simple and the procedures therefor are usually explicitly set forth in the dissolution section of the state corporation laws.

voluntary dissolution before start of business, requirements

Most voluntary dissolutions occur after the corporation has started doing business. The voluntary dissolution of a corporation that has started doing business may be initiated by the board of directors or, in many states, by one or more of the shareholders. There are two types of shareholder-initiated voluntary dissolutions. One type usually requires the unanimous written consent of all of the shareholders and is specifically provided for in the corporation laws of many states. In a few states unanimity is not always required and the consent of shareholders without voting rights is not required in some states. The other type of shareholder-initiated voluntary dissolution is the so-called easy dissolution or dissolution at will, where dissolution may occur upon the demand of one or a specified number or percentage of the shareholders. Dissolutions of this type are often provided for in a close corporation code or statute. An article of incorporation provision authorizing dissolution in this manner is usually required. See section 5.19, supra, for further reading on close corporations. It should be noted that once dissolution has been initiated, the dissolution procedures in a shareholder-initiated dissolution are substantially the same as those described below for a board of director initiated dissolution.

voluntary dissolution, types of

shareholder-initiated dissolution, types of

board of director initiated dissolution, requirements

In a dissolution at the initiative of the board of directors, the board must pass a resolution recommending that the corporation be dissolved and directing that the dissolution resolution be presented to the shareholders at an annual or special meeting. In many states the board of director resolution is not required to recommend resolution if a conflict of interest or other special conditions exist. If shareholder approval can be obtained informally under an action-without-meeting statute (which may be difficult if there is shareholder opposition to the dissolution), there will be no need for a shareholders' meeting. Otherwise, appropriate written notice of the meeting and of its purpose must be given to each shareholder of record. The proposed resolution must then be approved by the percentage of shareholders required by either the state corporation laws or the articles of incorporation, whichever is applicable. If more than one class of stock is outstanding, class voting is normally required, in which case the dissolution resolution must be approved by each class of shareholders. In a few states all shareholders are entitled to vote on dissolution, whether or not they have voting rights. The shareholder voting requirements for voluntary dissolution in each state are set forth in Appendix I, infra, under the heading of "Acts Requiring Shareholder Approval."

statement of intent to dissolve, necessity of

In many states when a proposed dissolution resolution is approved by the required number of shareholders the appropriate corporate officers are required to execute and file with the state filing official a statement of intent to dissolve the corporation. The matters required to be set forth in the statement of intent to dissolve, if one is required, are usually simple and explicitly set forth in the applicable statute. In some states a notice of an intent to dissolve must be published or sent to creditors. In other states the preparation and filing of a statement of intent to dissolve is not required. In those states the first formal action after the adoption and shareholder approval of a dissolution resolution is the preparation and filing of articles of dissolution (see below).

filing statement of intent to dissolve, effect of

In the states where the filing of a statement of intent to dissolve is required, the liquidation of the corporation and the winding up of its affairs must take place before articles of dissolution are filed. Once a statement of intent to dissolve has been filed, or its publication commenced, the corporation must cease all normal business activity and remain in business only for purposes of liquidating its assets, discharging its liabilities, and generally winding up its affairs. Articles of dissolution may be filed with the state filing official only when these activities have been completed. When the articles of dissolution are accepted for filing, the state filing official normally issues a certificate of dissolution terminating the existence of the corporation for all purposes except the disposition of pending lawsuits and other proceedings.

filing articles of dissolution, effect of

In the states where the filing of a statement of intent to dissolve is not required, the liquidation and winding up activities may take place after the articles of dissolution are filed with the state filing official. In these states, after the effective date of the articles of dissolution a corporation continues to exist but may not carry on any business except business that is necessary to wind up its affairs and liquidate its assets. The effective date of the articles of dissolution is the date that they are accepted for filing by the state filing official unless a later effective date (usually 90 days or less after the date of filing) is set forth in the articles of dissolution.

articles of dissolution, contents

The matters required to be set forth in the articles of dissolution are usually explicitly set forth in the dissolution section of the state corporation laws. The matters typically required are: (1) the name of the corporation, (2) the date the dissolution was authorized, and (3) the shareholder voting requirements and results if the dissolution was approved by the shareholders. In states where a statement of intent to dissolve is required to be filed, the articles of dissolution must also include the date of filing of the statement of intent to dissolve and statements indicating that all corporate debts and lawsuits have been paid, resolved, or accounted for and that all of the remaining corporate assets have been lawfully distributed to the shareholders.

revocation of dissolution, procedure

The corporation laws of most states provide for the revocation of a voluntary dissolution. In the states where the filing of a statement of intent to dissolve is required, a dissolution can be revoked after the statement of intent to dissolve is filed, but not after the articles of dissolution are filed. In most of these states, a revocation of dissolution must be approved by all of the shareholders and is effected by filing a statement of revocation containing prescribed information with the state filing official. In the states where dissolution is commenced by the filing of articles of dissolution, a dissolution can normally be revoked within a specified period (usually 120 days) after the effective date of the dissolution. In these states a revocation of a dissolution may be authorized in the same manner as the dissolution itself, and is effected by the filing of articles of revocation of dissolution containing prescribed information with the state filing official.

expiration of period of existence, dissolution

While the articles of incorporation of most small business corporations provide for perpetual existence, occasionally the articles will provide for a limited period of corporate existence. If the period of existence set forth in the articles expires without having been extended through amendment, the corporation ceases to exist and, in the absence of a modifying statute, is automatically dissolved as a matter of law without further action by the courts, the state, or the shareholders or directors of the corporation. See 19 Am. Jur. 2d, Corporations, sec. 1590. The general rule is that a corporation exists after the termination of its period of existence only for the purpose of winding up its affairs. However, if it continues to transact business after that date it is liable as a de facto corporation for its debts and contracts. Statutes in some states govern the status and conduct of corporations whose period of existence has expired. The corporation laws of several states provide for the administrative dissolution of a corporation whose period of existence has expired.

administrative or involuntary dissolution by state

The corporation laws of every state provide for the involuntary or administrative dissolution of corporations by the state upon specified grounds. The grounds usually include - (1) procurement of articles of incorporation by fraud, (2) the abuse by the corporation of its legal authority, (3) the failure to appoint and maintain a registered agent and office, and (4) the failure to file annual or periodic reports and pay the required fees and franchise taxes. In some states the grounds include such matters as insolvency, restraint of trade, unfair competition, persistent violations of state laws, and that its continued existence is not in the public interest. Most states provide for some form of notice of the alleged violations, and if the violations are not corrected within a specified period after the notice, an action to dissolve the corporation is filed, usually by the Attorney General.

involuntary dissolution for failure to pay fees or file reports

defunct corporations, reinstatement

In most states dissolution for failure to pay fees and franchise taxes or file reports with the Secretary of State is administrative rather than judicial. Corporations dissolved for these purposes are referred to as defunct corporations. Many states provide for the renewal or reinstatement of defunct corporations upon the payment of all delinquent fees, taxes, and penalties and the filing of current reports. The use of the corporate name is not usually protected during the defunct period, however, and if another corporation adopts or reserves the name during the defunct period, the defunct corporation must change its name prior to reinstatement. Judicial review of a refusal by the Secretary of State to reinstate a defunct corporation is usually provided for in the corporation laws.

involuntary dissolution by shareholders, grounds for

The corporation laws of most states provide for the involuntary dissolution of a corporation by the action of one or more of its shareholders, usually when it is established that certain conditions or grounds exist. Even in the absence of statute, or if the applicable statute does not list specific grounds for involuntary dissolution, the courts will often order the dissolution of a corporation upon the suit of a shareholder if the appropriate conditions or grounds are alleged and established. The specific conditions or grounds for involuntary dissolution vary somewhat from state to state, depending on the wording of the applicable statute and the local case law, but they usually include the following:

(1) A deadlock by the board of directors in managing the corporation which the shareholders have been unable to break and which will result in irreparable injury to the corporation.

(2) Illegal, oppressive, or fraudulent acts or conduct by the board of directors or those in control of the corporation.

(3) A deadlock for an extended period (usually two years or more) by the shareholders in their attempts to elect directors that is resulting in injury to the corporation or its shareholders.

(4) The wasting or misapplication of corporate assets by those in control of the corporation.

(5) Abandonment of the corporate business by the board of directors or those in control of the corporation.

(6) The persistent commission of illegal or ultra-vires acts by those in control of the corporation.

involuntary dissolution by shareholders, procedure

In most states a complaining or aggrieved shareholder must file a civil action in the appropriate court seeking the involuntary dissolution and liquidation of the corporation. The complaint must allege one or more of the statutorily or judicially imposed conditions or grounds for involuntary dissolution by a shareholder. Often a temporary injunction is sought to prevent further wrong-doing during the pendency of the case. Usually a single shareholder may bring such an action, but in some states the action must be brought by the holders of a certain percentage of the outstanding stock. If the shareholder's allegations are sustained by the court, the court will normally appoint a receiver to supervise the liquidation of the corporation and, upon completion of liquidation, enter a decree of dissolution. Should the shareholder and the corporation resolve their differences prior to the entry of the decree, the corporate property may be returned to the corporation and the judicial proceeding discontinued. Such proceedings are governed by the corporation laws in most states and the appropriate sections thereof should be checked and complied with.

involuntary dissolution by shareholders, judicial discretion, factors

In deciding whether to involuntarily dissolve a small business corporation upon the complaint of a shareholder, the courts must balance the interests of the complaining shareholder against those of the corporation and the other shareholders. See Leibert v. Clapp, 13 N.Y. 2nd 313, 247 N.Y.S. 2nd 102, 196 N.E. 2nd 540 (1963). Just because it is established that one or more of the grounds for involuntary dissolution exist does not necessarily mean that the corporation will be ordered dissolved by the court. See Thisted v. Tower Management Corp., 147 Mont. 1, 409 P. 2nd 813 (1966). Because dissolution is such a drastic remedy, many courts are reluctant to grant such relief unless it is established that dissolution is in the best interest of all parties or that the equities of the case clearly favor the complaining shareholder. Factors typically considered by the courts in such actions include the profitability of the corporation, the degree or extent of the unlawful conduct complained of, whether the plaintiff has been free of misconduct, and whether remedies other than dissolution are feasible. It should be noted that statutes in several states specifically authorize remedies in lieu of dissolution, including an election to purchase the complaining shareholder's stock by the corporation or the other shareholders.

involuntary dissolution by creditors, requirements, procedure

The creditors of a corporation are also entitled to involuntarily dissolve the corporation under certain circumstances. In most states the following two conditions must exist to permit the involuntary dissolution of a corporation by its creditors: (1) the creditor must have a claim against the corporation that has either been admitted in writing by the corporation as being due and owing or reduced to judgment with an unsatisfied execution returned, and (2) it must be established that the corporation is insolvent. In such cases the normal practice is for the creditor to file a civil action in the appropriate court seeking to involuntarily dissolve and liquidate the corporation under the supervision of the court. Involuntary dissolution actions by creditors are often brought in conjunction with actions to set aside illegal preferences or fraudulent conveyances of corporate assets. See section 7.01, supra, for further reading on preferential and fraudulent transfers.

methods of liquidating corporation

As indicated earlier in this section, liquidation is a proceeding that is separate from dissolution. There are three methods of liquidating a small business corporation: (1) judicial liquidation, (2) nonjudicial liquidation, and (3) bankruptcy liquidation under Chapter 7 or Chapter 11 of the Bankruptcy Code. It should be noted that a small business corporation may also be liquidated under an assignment for the benefit of creditors, under a creditors' composition, and informally by its participants. These methods, most of which are not sanctioned by statute, are discussed in section 7.01, supra. Judicial and nonjudicial liquidations are discussed below in this section. Brief descriptions of Chapter 7 and Chapter 11 bankruptcy proceedings are set forth in section 7.01, supra.

judicial liquidation, general aspects

Judicial liquidations are provided for in the corporation laws of practically every state. Such liquidations are most frequently used in involuntary dissolution proceedings brought by the state, minority shareholders, or creditors of the corporation. The applicable statute normally authorizes the court to appoint receivers, issue injunctions, and take other actions necessary to preserve corporate assets and carry on or wind up the corporate business during the pendency of the proceeding. The court is also empowered to pay the expenses of the proceeding, including the fees of receivers and attorneys, out of the corporate assets. The notification of creditors and the filing of claims by them is also covered by statute in most states. Some statutes also establish priorities for the payment of claims and expenses, and the balance of the corporate assets after the payment of claims and expenses must be distributed to the shareholders in accordance with their rights and interests.

nonjudicial liquidation, general aspects

Nonjudicial liquidation is more flexible and considerably less expensive than judicial liquidation, and, in the absence of dispute, is the usual method of liquidating a small business corporation. A nonjudicial liquidation is a voluntary proceeding carried out under the provisions of the state corporation laws governing voluntary dissolutions. Liquidation proceedings are usually carried out during dissolution proceedings, although dissolution is not usually a legal prerequisite, and in most states a corporation can be liquidated without being dissolved. Typically, the only state statutory requirements for nonjudicial liquidation are that the debts and obligations of the corporation be paid or provided for and that the remainder of the corporate assets be distributed, in cash or in kind, to the shareholders according to their respective rights and interests. Corporate management is usually responsible for carrying out a nonjudicial liquidation, and personal liability is usually imposed on directors who authorize illegal liquidation distributions.

liquidation, importance of tax considerations

In most nonjudicial liquidations of small business corporations the paramount concerns of the participants and shareholders are not the requirements of the state corporation laws, but those of the Internal Revenue Code. Even if the decision to liquidate is not tax-oriented, the form of the liquidation is almost certain to be dictated by tax considerations, unless the corporate assets do not exceed its liabilities to creditors. Further, because the Internal Revenue Code does not distinguish between judicial and nonjudicial liquidations, the form of a judicial liquidation may also be governed by tax considerations.

liquidation, tax consequences to corporation

For corporate liquidations occurring after July 31, 1986, a corporation recognizes gain or loss upon the distribution of its property in a complete liquidation in the same manner as if the distributed property was sold to the distributee at its fair market value. See 26 U.S.C. 336(a). There is an exception to this rule for liquidations of certain subsidiary corporations. See 26 U.S.C. 337. Generally, a corporation recognizes no gain or loss from distributions in liquidation, even if completely depreciated property is distributed. See 26 U.S.C. 336(a). The principal exceptions to this rule relate to the distribution of installment obligations and property subject to depreciation recapture. See 26 U.S.C. 336(b), 453B.

liquidation, tax treatment of gain or loss, general rule

Distributions in the complete liquidation of a corporation are usually treated as full payment in exchange for stock. See 26 U.S.C. 331(a). The shareholder's gain or loss from a distribution in complete liquidation is determined by comparing the amount of money (or the fair market value of any property) distributed to the shareholder with the cost or other basis of the shareholder's stock. In most cases the redemption of stock by a liquidating corporation results in a capital gain or loss to the shareholder because the stock is ordinarily a capital asset. For tax purposes, there need not be a formal surrender of the shares of stock by the shareholder or cancellation of the stock by the corporation. As long as the distribution is in complete liquidation of the corporation, it is treated for income tax purposes as being received in exchange for stock. This rule applies to the entire liquidating distribution, even if a portion of the distribution consists of undistributed corporate earnings, which, had they been distributed earlier, would have been dividend income.

adoption of liquidation plan, importance

In most corporate liquidations the overriding danger, taxwise, is that the liquidation distributions will be treated for tax purposes as distributions of property (i.e., as dividends) and not as sales or exchanges of stock. To this end, the best practice in any nonjudicial liquidation where the value of the corporation's assets exceeds the amount of its liabilities is to formally adopt a plan of liquidation. To do so will reduce the risk of the Internal Revenue Service treating the liquidation as simply a distribution of property or a redemption of stock (see section 6.02, supra). The plan of liquidation should be first adopted by a resolution of the board of directors and then approved or ratified by the shareholders, both of which can usually often be accomplished informally under action-without-meeting statutes.

partial liquidation, what constitutes

Of course, not all corporate liquidations are complete or total liquidations. Partial liquidations are often made by small business corporations. A partial liquidation occurs when a corporation, in the course of winding up a portion of its business, distributes some of its assets to its shareholders in return for the redemption or cancellation of a portion of its outstanding shares of stock. For tax purposes and otherwise, it is often difficult to distinguish a partial liquidation transaction from a redemption transaction. It should be noted that The Internal Revenue Code deals with partial liquidations under the section of the Code dealing with stock redemptions (26 U.S.C. 302) and not in the sections dealing with corporate liquidations.

partial liquidations, general aspects

As in a complete liquidation, the overriding danger, taxwise, in a partial liquidation is that the transaction will be treated as a corporate distribution and not as a sale or exchange of stock, thus denying the shareholders the benefit of capital gains tax treatment. It is important, therefore, that distributions in partial liquidation to individual shareholders meet the statutory requirements so as to qualify the distributions for capital gain recognition. As in complete liquidations, partial liquidations by collapsible corporations do not qualify for capital gain recognition. See 26 U.S.C. 341(a)(2). Also, partial liquidation tax treatment is not available to shareholders who are corporations. See 26 U.S.C. 302(b)(4)(A).

distribution in partial liquidation, tax treatment

partial liquidation, applicability of stock redemption rules

For income tax purposes, a distribution in partial liquidation of a corporation occurs if - (1) the distribution is not essentially the substantial equivalent of a dividend, as determined at the corporate level, and (2) the distribution is pursuant to a plan and occurs either in the tax year in which the plan is adopted or in the next tax year. See 26 U.S.C. 302(e)(1). A distribution in partial liquidation is deemed not essentially the equivalent of a dividend if it is attributable to the cessation by the corporation of the conduct of a qualified trade or business or if it consists of the assets of a qualified trade or business, and if immediately after the distribution the corporation is actively engaged in the conduct of a qualified trade or business. See 26 U.S.C. 302(e)(2). A qualified trade or business is defined as any trade or business actively conducted for a 5-year period immediately preceding the distribution and not acquired in a taxable transaction by the corporation during that period. See 26 U.S.C. 302(e)(3). Thus, distributions to an individual shareholder in the partial liquidation of the corporation will be accorded capital gains tax treatment if, in connection with the distribution, there is a genuine contraction of the corporate business, the distribution is made pursuant to a plan adopted by the corporation, and the distribution occurs within one tax year after the adoption of the plan. The substantial equivalency test may also be satisfied under the rules applicable to the taxation of stock redemptions, which are discussed in section 6.02, supra.

reincorporation of business, tax treatment

A problem that may arise in connection with the liquidation of a corporation is that of reincorporation, which is an attempt by the shareholders of a liquidated corporation to continue the corporate business in a new or different corporation. Generally, if a liquidation is preceded or followed by a transfer to another corporation of all or a portion of the assets of the liquidating corporation, the assets or funds distributed to the shareholders may be treated as dividends (and taxed as ordinary income) or the liquidation transaction may be treated as a corporate reorganization in which the distribution to the shareholders constitutes taxable boot. See Treasury Reg. 1.331-1(c). A new corporation resulting from a reincorporation will not be recognized for tax purposes if it is shown that the liquidation-reincorporation transaction was a sham to avoid the payment of taxes or that the transaction falls into one of the specific forms of corporate reorganizations recognized in the Internal Revenue Code. See Moffatt v. Commissioner, 363 F. 2nd 262 (CA 9, 1966) and Commissioner v. Berghash, 361 F. 2nd 257 (CA 2, 1966).

APPENDIX I

SUMMARIES OF STATE BUSINESS ORGANIZATION LAWS

CONTENTS

NOTE: The primary purpose of the information set forth in the state law summaries contained in this Appendix is to give a general summary of the law on a particular matter and to direct the reader to the appropriate statute. The information shown is generally current to January 1, 1999 and is believed by the author to be accurate. However, no warranties of accuracy are made and the reader should check the information before relying on it.

SUMMARY OF ALABAMA BUSINESS ORGANIZATION LAWS

PARTNERSHIP LAWS.

General Partnerships: Uniform Partnership Act (1996) adopted. CA 10-8A-101
Limited Partnerships: Alabama Limited Partnership Act of 1997. CA 10-9B-101 et seq.
Limited Liability Partnerships: Provided for. CA 10-8A-1001 et seq. Special provisions for professional LLPs. CA 10-8A-1010.
Name Registration: Registration of trade name with Secretary of State permitted but not required. CA 8-12-6 et seq.

LIMITED LIABILITY COMPANY LAWS. Alabama Limited Liability Company Act. CA 10-12-1 et seq.

Formation of LLC: One or more persons may form an LLC by filing articles of organization with Probate Judge of county of LLC's initial registered office. See CA 10-12-10 for article of organization content requirements.
General LLC Requirements: May have one or more members. May conduct any lawful business. Special requirements are applicable to professional LLCs (see CA 10-12-45).
Management of LLC: Vested in members unless otherwise provided in articles of organization.
New or Substituted Members: Admitted to LLC only with consent of all members unless otherwise provided in operating agreement.
Conversion Statutes: Merger and consolidation statute. CA 10-12-54 et seq. No partnership conversion statute.

CORPORATION LAWS. Alabama Business Corporation Act (based on Revised Model Business Corporation Act). CA 10-2B-1.01 et seq.

Corporate Name: Must contain the word "corporation" or "incorporated" or an abbreviation thereof and must not be the same as or deceptively similar to the registered name of any other corporation. Corporate name must be registered with Secretary of State and may be reserved for 120 days by written, telephone or electronic application to Secretary of State. CA 10-2B-4.01, 4.02.
Incorporators: One or more individuals or entities. CA 10-2B-2.01.
Articles of Incorporation:
- **Contents:** See CA 10-2B-2.02 for required and optional article of incorporation content requirements.
- **Filing and Recording:** The original and two copies of the articles of incorporation must be filed with the probate judge of the county of the corporation's registered office and the filing fee paid. Corporate existence begins when the articles of incorporation are accepted for filing by the probate judge. CA 10-2B-1.22, 1.25.
- **Amendment:** Requires a majority of the votes entitled to be cast unless a statute, the articles of incorporation, or the board of directors require a greater vote. The board of directors can make certain amendments without shareholder approval. CA 10-2B-10.01, .02, .03.

Organizational Meeting: Held after incorporation by the initial board of directors. CA 10-2B-2.05.
Bylaws: Initial bylaws adopted by board of directors unless that right is reserved to shareholders in articles of incorporation. May be amended by the board of directors or shareholders unless that power is reserved exclusively to the shareholders in articles of incorporation. CA 10-2B-2.06, 10.20.
Action Without Meeting: Shareholders may act without meeting if a written consent to the action is signed by all shareholders entitled to vote. See CA 10-2B-7.04. Unless the articles of incorporation or bylaws provide otherwise, the board of directors may meet via conference telephone or similar equipment and may act without meeting if all directors sign written consent to action. CA 10-2B-8.20, 8.21.
Stock Certificates: Must be signed by two officers designated in bylaws or by board of directors. Shares may be issued without a certificate unless prohibited by articles of incorporation. CA 10-2B-6.25, 6.26.
Consideration For Stock: May consist of money, labor done or services actually received. CA 10-2B-6.21.
Stock Transfer Restrictions: May be imposed by the articles of incorporation, bylaws or a shareholders' agreement. A restriction must be conspicuously noted on the stock certificate to be enforceable against a person without knowledge of the restriction. CA 10-2B-6.27.
Cumulative Voting: Not permitted unless provided for in the articles of incorporation. CA 10-2B-7.28.
Preemptive Rights: Exists unless denied or limited in the articles of incorporation. CA 10-2B-6.30.
Acts Requiring Shareholder Approval: Unless the articles of incorporation require a greater vote, a two-thirds vote of the shares entitled to vote is required for a merger or consolidation, for the sale or transfer of all or substantially all of the corporate assets not in the usual course of business, and for voluntary dissolution. CA 10-2B-11.03, 12.02, 14.02. Shareholder approval is also required to amend the articles of incorporation (see above).
Board of Directors: May consist of one or more natural persons of age 19 or more with the number of directors specified in the articles of incorporation or bylaws. CA 10-2B-8.02, 8.03.
Officers: Those specified in bylaws. No specified officers required. The same person may hold any number of offices. CA 10-2B-8.40.
Foreign Corporations: Must obtain a certificate of authority from the Secretary of State to transact business in Alabama. The penalties for transacting business without a certificate of authority include nonaccess to state courts and voidability of contracts. CA 10-2B-15.01, 15.02.
Close Corporation Laws: Has Close Corporation Code. CA 10-2A-300 et seq. A close corporation must have 30 or fewer shareholders.
Periodic Reports: Domestic and authorized foreign corporations must file an annual report on prescribed forms with the Department of Revenue by March 15 of each year and pay an annual report fee to remain in good standing. CA 10-2B-16.22. Domestic corporations must file an ad valorem stock tax report by the third Monday in January each year, unless the corporation pays the tax. CA 40-14-70, 72, 73.

STATE FILING OFFICIAL. (For limited purposes) Secretary of State, P.O. Box 5616, Montgomery, AL 36103-5616 (205-242-7200).

Fees:
- Filing Articles of Incorporation - $75
- Application for Certificate of Authority - $175
- Franchise Tax (domestic corp.) - $10 per $1000 of capital ($50 minimum).
- Filing LLC Articles of Organization - $75
- Filing LLP Registration Application - $75
- LLP Annual Fee - $70
- Name Reservation - $10
- Amending Articles of Incorporation - $10 ($20 if name change).
- Corp. Annual Report - $10
- Other Corp. Fees - See CA 10-2B-1.22.
- Other LLC Fees - See CA 10-12-60
- Filing Application for Registration of Foreign LLC - $75
- Registration of Foreign LLP - $40

SUMMARY OF ALASKA BUSINESS ORGANIZATION LAWS

PARTNERSHIP LAWS.

General Partnerships: Uniform Partnership Act adopted. AS 32.05.010 et seq.
Limited Partnerships: Revised Uniform Limited Partnership Act adopted. AS 32.11.010 et seq.
Limited Liability Partnerships: Provided for. See AS 32.05.405 et seq. $1,000,000 of liability insurance or qualifying assets required.
Name Registration: Not required.

LIMITED LIABILITY COMPANY LAWS. Alaska Limited Liability Act. AS 10.50.010 et seq.

Formation of LLC: One or more persons may form LLC by filing articles of organization with state filing official. See AS 10.50.075 for article of organization content requirements.
General LLC Requirements: May have one or more members. May conduct any lawful business.
Management of LLC: Reserved to members unless otherwise provided in articles of organization.
New or Substituted Members: Admission to LLC requires written consent of all members unless operating agreement provides otherwise.
Conversion Statutes: Merger and consolidation statute. AS 10.50.500 et seq. Partnership conversion statute. AS 10.50.570.

CORPORATION LAWS. Alaska Corporations Code (based in part on Model Business Corporation Act). AS 10.06.005 et seq.

Corporate Name: Must contain the word "corporation," "company," "incorporated," "limited," or an abbreviation thereof, and may not be the same as or deceptively similar to the name of any other corporation or registered name. Availability of name may be checked by telephone with state filing official. Name may be reserved for 120 days. AS 10.06.105, 110, 115.

Incorporators: One or more natural persons of age 18 or more. AS 10.06.205.

Articles of Incorporation:

Contents: See AS 10.06.208, 210 for required and optional article of incorporation content requirements.

Filing and Recording: An original and one copy of the articles of incorporation and a codified statement of activities must be filed with the state filing official and the filing fee paid. AS 10.06.213, 215. Corporate existence begins when the articles of incorporation are accepted for filing. AS 10.06.218.

Amendment: Requires a majority vote of the shares entitled to vote, unless a statute or the articles of incorporation require a greater vote. The board of directors may make certain minor amendments without shareholder approval. AS 10.06.504, 508, 990(5).

Organizational Meeting: Held after incorporation by the incorporators or by the initial board of directors, if named in the articles of incorporation. AS 10.06.223.

Bylaws: Initial bylaws adopted by incorporators or initial board of directors. May be amended by the shareholders and by the board of directors unless otherwise provided in the articles of incorporation. AS 10.06.223, 225, 228.

Action Without Meeting: Unless prohibited by the articles of incorporation or bylaws, the shareholders may act without meeting if a written consent to the action is signed by all shareholders entitled to vote on the matter. Unless prohibited by the articles of incorporation or bylaws, the board of directors may meet via conference telephone or similar communications equipment, and may act without meeting if all directors sign a written consent to the action. AS 10.06.423, 475.

Stock Certificates: Must be signed by president or vice president and by secretary or assistant secretary. Shares may be issued without a certificate unless the articles of incorporation or bylaws provide otherwise. AS 10.06.348, 349, 353.

Consideration For Stock: May consist of money, tangible or intangible property, or services actually performed for the corporation. May not consist of future services or promissory notes. AS 10.06.338.

Stock Transfer Restrictions: May be set forth in the articles of incorporation or in a shareholders' agreement. AS 10.06.210, 424.

Cumulative Voting: Permitted unless denied in the articles of incorporation. AS 10.06.420.

Preemptive Rights: Exists (with exceptions) unless limited or denied in the articles of incorporation. AS 10.06.428.

Acts Requiring Shareholder Approval: Unless the articles of incorporation require a greater vote, a two-thirds vote of all shares is required for a merger, consolidation or share exchange and for the sale or disposition of all or substantially all of the corporate assets not in the usual course of business. The affirmative vote of two-thirds of the shares entitled to vote is required for voluntary dissolution, unless the articles of incorporation require a greater vote.. AS 10.06.546, 570, 605, 990(5). Shareholder approval is also required for most amendments to the articles of incorporation (see above).

Board of Directors: May consist of one or more persons, with number specified in bylaws or articles of incorporation. AS 10.06.453.

Officers: Must have president, secretary, and treasurer. The bylaws may provide for other officers. The same person may hold any two or more offices except the offices of president and secretary. If there is only one shareholder the same person may hold all offices. AS 10.06.483.

Foreign Corporations: Must obtain a certificate of authority from the state filing official to transact business in Alaska. The statute contains a nonexclusive list of activities that do not constitute transacting business in the state. The penalties for transacting business without a certificate of authority include nonaccess to state courts, a penalty of up to $10,000 per year, and liability for all fees and penalties that would haven been assessed had a certificate of authority been issued. AS 10.06.705, 710, 713, 718.

Close Corporation Laws: None.

Periodic Reports: Domestic and authorized foreign corporations must file a biennial report with the state filing official by February 1 of the appropriate year and pay a biennial report fee to remain in good standing. AS 10.06.805, 808, 811.

STATE FILING OFFICIAL. Department of Commerce and Economic Development, Corporations Section (Telephone: 907-465-2530).

Fees:
Filing Articles of Incorporation - $250
Amending Articles of Incorporation - $25
Filing LLC Articles of Organization - $250
Amending LLC Articles of Organization - $25
Filing LLP Registration Document - $250
Name Reservation - $25
Biennial Report - $100 for Alaska Corp., LLC or LLP
- $200 for Foreign Corp.
Application of Foreign Corp. for Certificate of Authority - $350
Other Fees - Contact state filing official.

SUMMARY OF ARIZONA BUSINESS ORGANIZATION LAWS

PARTNERSHIP LAWS.

General Partnerships: Revised Uniform Partnership Act adopted. ARS 29-1001 et seq.
Limited Partnerships: Revised Uniform Limited Partnership Act adopted. ARS 29-301 et seq. (see 29-367 for LLP provision.)
Limited Liability Partnerships: Registered LLPs provided for. ARS 29-1101 et seq. (see ARS 29-1103A for publication requirement.)
Name Registration: Must file a fictitious name certificate with the county recorder of each county where the partnership has a place of business if the partnership name does not contain the surnames of all partners and is not formed for the practice of law. ARS 29-102, 103.

LIMITED LIABILITY COMPANY LAWS. Arizona Limited Liability Company Act. ARS 29-601 et seq.

Formation of LLC: One or more natural persons may sign and file two copies of articles of organization with state filing official. See ARS 29-632 for article of organization content requirements. See ARS 29-635C for publication requirement.
General LLC Requirements: May have one or more members. May conduct any lawful business except banking or insurance. Special requirements are applicable to professional LLCs (see ARS 29-841 to 847).
Management of LLC: Vested in members unless vested in managers by articles of organization.
New or Substituted Members: Admission to LLC requires consent of all members unless otherwise provided in operating agreement.
Conversion Statutes: Merger or consolidation statute. ARS 29-751 et seq. No partnership conversion statute.

CORPORATION LAWS. General Corporation Law (based on Revised Model Business Corporation Act). ARS 10-120 et seq.

Corporate Name: Must contain the word "corporation," "company," "incorporated," or "limited," or an abbreviation thereof and may not include the word "bank," "deposit," "trust," or "trust company" unless the corporation is engaged in that activity. Must be distinguishable from the name of any other registered entity or name. Name may be reserved for 120 days. ARS 10-401, 402.
Incorporators: One or more individuals or entities. ARS 10-201.
Articles of Incorporation:
- **Contents:** See ARS 10-202 for content requirements for articles of incorporation and certificate of disclosure.
- **Filing and Recording:** Two copies of the articles of incorporation and certificate of disclosure must be filed with the state filing official and the filing fee paid. Corporate existence begins when the articles of incorporation are accepted for filing. ARS 10-120, 202. Must publish articles of incorporation within 60 days after filing and file affidavit of publication. ARS 10-203D.
- **Amendment:** Requires a majority of the votes entitled to be cast unless a statute, the articles of incorporation, or the board of directors require a greater vote. The board of directors can make certain amendments without shareholder approval. ARS 10-1002, 1003.

Organizational Meeting: Held after incorporation by the initial board of directors. ARS 10-205.
Bylaws: Initial bylaws adopted by board of directors. May be amended by the shareholders and by the board of directors unless that power is reserved to the shareholders in the articles of incorporation. ARS 10-206, 1020.
Action Without Meeting: The shareholders may act without meeting if all shareholders entitled to vote sign a written consent to the action. ARS 10-704. Unless the articles of incorporation or bylaws provide otherwise, the board of directors may meet via conference telephone and may act without meeting if each director signs a written consent to the action. ARS 10-820, 821.
Stock Certificates: Must be signed by officer(s) designed in bylaws or by board of directors. Shares may be issued without a certificate ARS 10-625, 626.
Consideration For Stock: May consist of any tangible or intangible property or benefit to corporation, including cash, services performed, or other securities of the corporation. May not consist of future services or promissory notes. ARS 10-621.
Stock Transfer Restrictions: Must be conspicuously noted on the stock certificate to be enforceable against all transferees. ARS 10-627.
Cumulative Voting: Must be permitted. Art. 14 sec. 10 of Constitution, ARS 10-728.
Preemptive Rights: Do not exist unless provided for in the articles of incorporation. ARS 10-630.
Acts Requiring Shareholder Approval: Unless a statute, the articles of incorporation, or the board of directors require a greater vote, a majority of the votes entitled to be cast is required for a merger, consolidation or share exchange, for the sale or disposition of all or substantially all of the corporate assets not in the usual course of business, for voluntary dissolution, and for most amendments to the articles of incorporation. ARS 10-1103, 1202, 1402, 1003.
Board of Directors: May consist of one or more individuals, with number specified in the articles of incorporation or bylaws. ARS 10-803.
Officers: Those provided for in bylaws. The same person may simultaneously hold more than one office. ARS 10-840.
Foreign Corporations: Must be authorized by the state filing official to transact business in Arizona. The statute contains a nonexclusive list of activities that do not constitute transacting business in the state. The penalties for transacting business without authorization include nonaccess to state courts, liability for all unpaid fees and penalties, and a penalty of up to $1,000. ARS 10-1501, 1502.
Close Corporation Laws: Has Close Corporation Code. ARS 10-1801 et seq. The name of a close corporation must include words "Arizona Close Corporation" or an abbreviation thereof and the number of original investors (i.e., owners) may not exceed ten.
Periodic Reports: Domestic and authorized foreign corporations must file an annual report and a certificate of disclosure with the state filing official by the 15th day of the 4th month after the end of the corporation's fiscal year and pay an annual report fee to remain in good standing. ARS 10-1622.

STATE FILING OFFICIAL. Arizona Corporation Commission, 1210 West Washington Street, Phoenix, AZ 85005 (Telephone: 602-542-3076).

Fees:
- Filing Articles of Incorporation - $60
- Filing LLC Articles of Organization - $50
- Application by Foreign LLC for Authority - $150
- Application by Foreign Corp. for Authority - $175
- Name Reservation - $10
- Amending Articles of Incorporation - $25
- Annual Report of Corp. - $45
- Filing LLP Statement of Qualification - Unknown
- Other Corp. Fees - See ARS 10-122.
- Other LLC Fees - See ARS 29-851.

SUMMARY OF ARKANSAS BUSINESS ORGANIZATION LAWS

PARTNERSHIP LAWS.

General Partnerships: Uniform Partnership Act adopted. ACA 4-42-101 et seq.
Limited Partnerships: Revised Uniform Limited Partnership Act adopted. ACA 4-43-101 et seq.
Limited Liability Partnerships: Provided for. ACA 4-42-703.
Name Registration: Must file a fictitious name certificate with the clerk of each county where business is conducted if the partnership name does not contain the names of all partners. ACA 4-7-203.

LIMITED LIABILITY COMPANY LAWS.
Small Business Entity Tax Pass Through Act of 1993. ACA 4-32-101 et seq.

Formation of LLC: One or more persons may form LLC by filing articles of organization with Secretary of State. See ACA 4-32-202 for article of organization content requirements.
General LLC Requirements: May have one or more members. May conduct any lawful business including the rendering of professional services, but professional is personally liable for own acts. See ACA 4-32-106, 308.
Management of LLC: Vested in members unless articles of organization or operating agreement provides for managers.
New or Substituted Members: Admitted to LLC only with consent of all members unless operating agreement provides otherwise.
Conversion Statutes: Merger and Consolidation statute. ACA 4-32-1201 et seq. No partnership conversion statute.

CORPORATION LAWS.
Arkansas Business Corporation Act (based on Revised Model Business Corporation Act). ACA 4-27-101 et seq.

Corporate Name: Must contain the word "corporation," "incorporated," "company," or "limited," or an abbreviation thereof. Must be distinguishable upon the records of the Secretary of State from the names of other corporations. A notification form may be filed with the Secretary of State to check the availability of a corporate name. Name may be reserved for 120 days. ACA 4-27-401, 402.
Incorporators: One or more individuals or entities. ACA 4-27-201.
Articles of Incorporation:
- **Contents:** See ACA 4-27-202 for required and optional article of incorporation content requirements.
- **Filing and Recording:** An original and one copy of the articles of incorporation must be filed with the Secretary of State and the filing fee paid. Corporate existence begins when the articles of incorporation are accepted for filing. ACA 4-27-120, 203.
- **Amendment:** Requires a majority of the votes entitled to be cast unless a statute, the articles of incorporation, or the board of directors require a greater vote. The board of directors can make certain minor amendments without shareholder approval. ACA 4-27-1002, 1003.

Organizational Meeting: Held after incorporation by the initial board of directors if named in the articles of incorporation. Otherwise held after incorporation by the incorporators, who may act without meeting if all incorporators sign a written consent to the action. ACA 4-27-205.
Bylaws: Initial bylaws adopted by the incorporators or the board of directors. May be amended by the shareholders and by the board of directors unless that power is reserved to the shareholders in the articles of incorporation. A shareholder amendment may preclude board of director amendment. ACA 27-206, 1020.
Action Without Meeting: Shareholders may act without meeting if a written consent to the action is signed by shareholders sufficient to carry the action at a meeting, except that consents to increase capital stock or bonded indebtedness must be signed by all shareholders. ACA 4-27-704. Unless the articles of incorporation or bylaws provide otherwise, the board of directors may meet via conference telephone or similar communications equipment and may act without meeting if all directors sign a written consent to the action. ACA 4-27-820, 821.
Stock Certificates: Must be signed by two officers designated in the bylaws or by the board of directors. Shares may be issued without a certificate unless the articles of incorporation or bylaws provide otherwise. ACA 4-27-625, 626.
Consideration For Stock: May consist of money paid, labor done, or property received. May not consist of future services or promissory notes. ACA 4-27-621.
Stock Transfer Restrictions: May be imposed by the articles of incorporation, bylaws or a shareholder agreement. A restriction must be conspicuously noted on the stock certificate to be valid against a person without notice of the restriction. ACA 4-27-627.
Cumulative Voting: Not permitted unless provided for in the articles of incorporation and prior notice is given. ACA 4-27-728.
Preemptive Rights: Do not exist unless contained in the articles of incorporation. ACA 4-27-630.
Acts Requiring Shareholder Approval: Unless a statute, the articles of incorporation, or the board of directors require a greater vote, a majority of the votes entitled to be cast is required for a merger or share exchange, for the sale or disposition of all or substantially all of the corporate assets not in the usual course of business, for voluntary dissolution, and for most amendments to the articles of incorporation (see above). See ACA 4-27-1103, 1202, 1402, 1003.
Board of Directors: May consist of one or more individuals, with number specified in the articles of incorporation or bylaws. ACA 4-27-803.
Officers: Those described in the bylaws or appointed by the board of directors in accordance with the bylaws. No specific officers required. The same person may simultaneously hold more than one office in the corporation. ACA 4-27-840.
Foreign Corporations: Must obtain a certificate of authority from the Secretary of State to transact business in Arkansas. The statute contains a nonexclusive list of activities that do not constitute transacting business in the state. The penalties for transacting business without a certificate of authority include nonaccess to state courts and a civil penalty of $100 to $5,000. ACA 4-27-1501, 1502.
Close Corporation Laws: None, except that a corporation with 50 or fewer shareholders may, in its articles of incorporation, dispense with or limit the authority of its board of directors. ACA 4-27-801.
Periodic Reports: Domestic and authorized foreign corporations must file an annual franchise tax report with the Secretary of State by April 1 of each year and pay an annual franchise tax to remain in good standing. ACA 4-27-1622, 26-54-102.

STATE FILING OFFICIAL.
Secretary of State, Corporation Division, State Capital, Little Rock, AR 72203 (Telephone: 501-682-1010).

Fees:
- Filing Articles of Incorporation - $50
- Application for Certificate of Authority - $300
- Filing LLC Articles of Organization - $50
- Filing LLP Registration - $50
- Name Reservation - $25
- Amending Articles of Incorporation - $50
- Amending LLC Articles of Organization - $25
- Other Corp. Fees - See ACA 4-27-122.
- Other LLC Fees - See ACA 4-32-1301

SUMMARY OF CALIFORNIA BUSINESS ORGANIZATION LAWS

PARTNERSHIP LAWS.

General Partnerships: Uniform Partnership Act of 1994. Corp. C. 16100 et seq.

Limited Partnerships: Revised Uniform Limited Partnership Act adopted. Corp. C. 15611-15723.

Limited Liability Partnerships: Registered limited liability partnerships recognized. Corp. C. 16951, et seq.

Name Registration: Must file a fictitious name statement with the clerk of the county of the partnership's principal place of business if the partnership name does not contain the names of all partners. Must publish the statement and file proof of publication with the county clerk. Bus. & Prof. C. 17900, 17915, 17917.

LIMITED LIABILITY COMPANY LAWS. Beverly-Killea Limited Liability Company Act. Corp. C. 17000 et seq.

Formation of LLC: One or more persons may file articles of organization with Secretary of State. See Corp. C. 17051 for article of organization content requirements.

General LLC Requirements: Must have two or more members. Must specify period of existence in articles of organization. May conduct any lawful business except banking, insurance or trust company business.

Management of LLC: Vested in members unless vested in managers in articles of organization. Corp C. 17150

New or Substituted Members: Admission requires consent of all members unless operating agreement or articles provide otherwise.

Conversion Statutes: Merger statute. Corp. C. 17550 et seq. No partnership conversion statute.

CORPORATION LAWS. General Corporation Law (Model Business Corporation Acts not adopted). Corp. C. 100 et seq.

Corporate Name: A close corporation name must contain the word "corporation," "incorporated," or "limited," or an abbreviation thereof. No word requirements for other corporations. May not be misleading or the same as or deceptively similar to the name of any other corporation. A name may be reserved for 60 days. Name availability may be checked with Secretary of State by telephone. Corp C. 201, 202.

Incorporators: One or more natural persons, partnerships, associations, or corporations. Corp. C. 200.

Articles of Incorporation:

Contents: See Corp. C. 202-204 for required and optional article of incorporation content requirements.

Filing and Recording: An original copy of the articles of incorporation must be filed with the Secretary of State and the filing fee and minimum franchise tax paid. Corporate existence begins when the articles of incorporation are accepted for filing. Corp. C. 110, 200.

Amendment: Requires a majority vote of the outstanding shares entitled to vote, unless a statute or the articles of incorporation require a greater vote. The board of directors can make certain amendments without shareholder approval. Corp. C. 903, 902.

Organizational Meeting: Held by the initial board of directors if named in the articles; otherwise held by the incorporators. Corp. C. 210.

Bylaws: Initial bylaws adopted by the board of directors or the incorporators. May be amended by the shareholders and the board of directors, unless the articles of incorporation or bylaws reserve that power to the shareholders. Corp. C. 210, 211.

Action Without Meeting: Unless the articles of incorporation provide otherwise, the shareholders may act without meeting if a written consent to the action is signed by shareholders sufficient to carry the action at a meeting and notice is given to nonconsenting shareholders, except that the election of directors requires a unanimous written consent. Corp. C. 603. The board of directors may act without meeting if all directors sign a written consent to the action, and, unless otherwise provided in the articles of incorporation or bylaws, may meet via electronic communications equipment whereby all members can concurrently hear each other. Corp. C. 307.

Stock Certificates: Must be signed by chairman or vice chairman of board, president, or vice president, and by the chief financial officer, the secretary, or the assistant of either. Shares may be issued without a certificate. Corp. C. 416.

Consideration For Stock: May consist of money, labor or services performed, or property received. May not consist of future services or promissory notes, unless collateralized by property other than the shares being issued. Corp. C. 409.

Stock Transfer Restrictions: May be imposed by the articles of incorporation, bylaws, or a shareholders' agreement. A restriction must be noted on the stock certificate to be enforceable against a person without knowledge of the restriction. Corp. C. 204(b), 212(b), 300, 418, 421.

Cumulative Voting: Must be permitted (except for listed corporations) if prior notice of an intent to cumulate votes is given. Corp. C. 708.

Preemptive Rights: Do not exist unless contained in the articles of incorporation. Corp. C. 406.

Acts Requiring Shareholder Approval: Unless a statute or the articles of incorporation require a greater vote, a majority vote of the shares entitled to vote is required for the sale or transfer of all or substantially all of the corporate assets not in the usual course of business, for a merger, for voluntary dissolution, and for most amendments to the articles of incorporation. Corp. C. 152, 1001, 1103, 1900, 903.

Board of Directors: Must consist of at least three natural persons, except that there need not be more directors than shareholders. The number of directors must be specified in the bylaws or the articles of incorporation. Corp. C. 164, 212.

Officers: Must have president (or chairman of board), secretary, and chief financial officer. The bylaws may provide for other officers. The same person may hold any number of offices unless the articles of incorporation or bylaws provide otherwise. Corp. C. 312.

Foreign Corporations: Must obtain a certificate of qualification from the Secretary of State to transact intrastate business in California. The penalties for transacting intrastate business without a certificate of qualification include nonaccess to state courts, a $20.00 per day penalty, and fines of $500 to $1,000. Corp. C. 2105, 2203, 2258.

Close Corporation Laws: Has close corporation statute whereunder a corporation with 35 or fewer shareholders may elect to be a close corporation by so stating in its articles of incorporation. Corp. C. 158. The following Corp. Code sections deal with close corporations: 186 (shareholder agreements), 202(a) (corporate name), 204 (articles of incorporation), 300 (management), 418 (stock certificates), 421 (stock transfer restrictions), 706, and 1111 (voting trusts), 1201 (reorganization), 1800 (involuntary dissolution), and 1904 (voluntary dissolution).

Periodic Reports: Domestic and authorized foreign corporations must file an annual report with the Secretary of State and pay an annual report fee and an annual franchise tax to remain in good standing. Corp. C. 1502, Rev. & Tax C. 23151, 23153.

STATE FILING OFFICIAL. Secretary of State, 1230 "J" Street, Sacramento, CA 95814 (Telephone: 916-653-6814).

Fees: Filing Articles of Incorporation - $100 plus minimum franchise tax. Other Fees - See Gov't. C. 12180 et seq.
Filing LLC Articles of Organization - $70. Amending Articles of Incorporation - $30. Name Reservation - $10.
Filing LLP Registration Statement - $70

SUMMARY OF COLORADO BUSINESS ORGANIZATION LAWS

PARTNERSHIP LAWS.

General Partnerships: Colorado Uniform Partnership Act (1997). CRS 7-64-101 et seq.
Limited Partnerships: Revised Uniform Limited Partnership Act adopted. CRS 7-62-101 et seq.
Limited Liability Partnerships: Registered LLPs for general & limited partnerships provided for. CRS 7-64-1001 et seq.
Name Registration: Must register with Department of Revenue if partnership name does not contain partners' names. CRS 24-35-301.

LIMITED LIABILITY COMPANY LAWS. Colorado Limited Liability Company Act. CRS 7-80-101 et seq.

Formation of LLC: One or more natural persons of age 18 or more may form LLC by filing articles of organization with Secretary of State. See CRS 7-80-204 for the article of organization content requirements.
General LLC Requirements: May have one or more members. May conduct any lawful business.
Management of LLC: Vested in members unless vested in managers in articles of organization.
New or Substituted Members: Admitted to LLC only on written consent of all members.
Conversion Statutes: Partnership conversion and merger statutes. CRS 7-80-1001 et seq. CRS 7-90-201 et seq.

CORPORATION LAWS. Colorado Business Corporation Act (based on Revised Model Business Corporation Act). CRS 7-101-101 et seq.

Corporate Name: Must contain the word "corporation," "company," "incorporated," or "limited," or an abbreviation thereof. May not be the same as or deceptively similar to the name of any other corporation, limited liability company, or limited partnership. Name may be reserved for 120 days. Availability of name may be checked with Secretary of State by telephone. CRS 7-104-101, 102.
Incorporators: One or more individuals of age 18 or more or entities. CRS 7-102-101.
Articles of Incorporation:
Contents: See CRS 7-102-102 for required and optional article of incorporation content requirements.
Filing and Recording: An original and one copy of the articles of incorporation must be filed with the Secretary of State and the filing fee paid. Corporate existence begins when the articles of incorporation are filed with the Secretary of State. CRS 7-101-201, 7-102-103.
Amendment: Requires a majority of the votes entitled to be cast unless a statute, the board of directors or the articles of incorporation require a greater vote. The board of directors may make ministerial amendments without shareholder approval. CRS 7-110-102, 103.
Organizational Meeting: Held after incorporation by incorporators or initial board of directors in or out of state. CRS 7-102-105.
Bylaws: Initial bylaws adopted by incorporators or initial board of directors. May be amended by shareholders and by the board of directors unless the articles of incorporation provide otherwise. CRS 7-102-106, 7-110-201.
Action Without Meeting: Unless the articles of incorporation provide otherwise, the shareholders may act without meeting if all shareholders entitled to vote consent to the action in writing. CRS 7-107-105. Unless otherwise provided in the bylaws, the board of directors may meet via audio communications and may act without meeting if all directors consent to the action in writing. CRS 7-108-201, 202. Incorporators may conduct organizational meeting by written consent. CRS 7-102-105(2).
Stock Certificates: Must be signed by officer(s) designated in bylaws or by board of directors. Shares may be issued without a certificate unless otherwise provided in bylaws. CRS 7-106-206, 207.
Consideration For Stock: May consist of any property or benefit to corporation, including cash, secured promissory notes, services performed, and other securities of corporation. May not consist of future services or unsecured promissory notes. CRS 7-4-104, 105.
Stock Transfer Restrictions: May be imposed by the articles of incorporation, bylaws or a shareholders' agreement. A restriction must be conspicuously noted on the stock certificate to be enforceable against a person without knowledge of the restriction. CRS 7-106-208.
Cumulative Voting: Must be permitted unless denied in the articles of incorporation. CRS 7-102-102(3).
Preemptive Rights: Do not exist unless provided for in articles of incorporation for corporations formed after 6-30-94. CRS 7-106-301(1).
Acts Requiring Shareholder Approval: Unless a statute, the articles of incorporation or the board of directors require a greater vote, a majority of the votes entitled to be cast is required for a merger or share exchange, for the sale or disposition of all or substantially all of the corporate assets not in the usual course of business, for voluntary dissolution, and for most amendments to the articles of incorporation (see above). CRS 7-111-103, 7-112-102, 7-114-102, 7-110-103.
Board of Directors: May consist of one or more persons of age 18 or more with number of directors specified in bylaws. CRS 7-108-102, 103.
Officers: Those described in the bylaws or appointed by the board of directors in accordance with the bylaws. No specific officers required. The same person may simultaneously hold more than one office in the corporation. Officers must be age 18 or more. CRS 7-108-301.
Foreign Corporations: Must file application for authority to transact business in Colorado with Secretary of State. The statute contains a nonexclusive list of activities that do not constitute transacting business in the state. The penalties for transacting business without authority include nonaccess to state courts, liability for all fees, taxes, and penalties that would have been imposed had a certificate of authority been issued, corporate civil penalties of up to $5,000, and personal civil penalties of up to $1,000. CRS 7-115-101, 102.
Close Corporation Laws: None.
Periodic Reports: Domestic and authorized foreign corporations must file a biennial report on forms furnished by, and within the time prescribed by, the Secretary of State and pay a biennial report fee to remain in good standing. CRS 7-116-107.

STATE FILING OFFICIAL. Secretary of State, 1560 Broadway, Suite 200, Denver, CO 80202 (Telephone: 303-894-2251).

Fees:
Filing Articles of Incorporation - $50
Application for Certificate of Authority - $75
Filing LLC Articles of Organization - $50
Filing LLP Registration Statement - $50
Name Reservation - $10
Amending Articles of Incorporation - $25
Amending LLC Articles of Organization - $25
Biennial Report - $25 for Colo. Corp. or LLC
- $100 for Foreign Corp. or LLC
Other Fees - Contact Secretary of State.

SUMMARY OF CONNECTICUT BUSINESS ORGANIZATION LAWS

PARTNERSHIP LAWS.

General Partnerships: Uniform Partnership Act (1994) adopted. CGS 34-300 et seq.

Limited Partnerships: Revised Uniform Limited Partnership Act adopted. CGS 34-9 et seq.

Limited Liability Partnerships: Registered limited liability partnerships provided for. CGS 34-406 et seq.

Name Registration: A fictitious name certificate must be filed with the town clerk in each town where business is conducted if the partnership name does not contain at least one of the partner's names. CGS 35-1.

LIMITED LIABILITY COMPANY LAWS. Connecticut Limited Liability Company Act: CGS 34-100 et seq.

Formation of LLC: One or more persons may form LLC by filing articles of organization with Secretary of State. See CGS 34-121 for article of organization content requirements.

General LLC Requirements: Must have two or more members. May conduct any lawful business except banking business. Special requirements are imposed on professional LLCs (CGS 34-119(b)).

Management of LLC: Vested in members unless vested in managers by articles of incorporation.

New or Substituted Members: Majority in interest of members must consent unless operating agreement provides otherwise.

Conversion Statutes: Partnership conversion statute. CGS 34-199, 200. Merger or consolidation statute. CGS 34-193 et seq.

CORPORATION LAWS. Connecticut Business Corporation Act. CGS 33-601 et seq. (Revised Model Business Corporation Act adopted).

Corporate Name: Must contain the word "corporation," "company," "incorporated," "limited," "Societa per Azioni," or an abbreviation thereof. Must be distinguishable on the records of the Secretary of State from the name of any other registered entity. Name may be reserved for 120 days. No informal name clearance procedure. CGS 33-655, 656.

Incorporators: One or more persons. CGS 33-635.

Certificate of Incorporation:

Contents: See CGS 33-636 for required and optional certificate of incorporation content requirements.

Filing and Recording: The certificate of incorporation must be filed with the Secretary of State and the filing fee and initial franchise tax paid. Corporate existence begins when the Secretary of State approves the certificate of incorporation. CGS 33-608, 637.

Amendment: Requires majority vote of the shares entitled to vote, unless certificate of incorporation requires greater vote. Board of directors can make certain amendments without shareholder approval. (2/3rds vote required in corps. formed prior to 1-1-97). CGS 33-797, 798.

Organizational Meeting: Held after incorporation by initial directors or incorporators, who may act without meeting if each incorporator signs a written consent to the action. CGS 33-639.

Bylaws: Initial bylaws adopted by initial board of directors or incorporators. May be amended by the shareholders and, if the certificate of incorporation so provides, by the board of directors. CGS 33-640, 806.

Action Without Meeting: The board of directors may act without meeting if all directors sign a written consent to the action. CGS 33-749. The shareholders may act without meeting if a written consent to the action is signed by all shareholders entitled to vote, or, if the certificate of incorporation so provides, by shareholders sufficient to carry the action at a meeting, if notice is given to nonconsenting shareholders entitled to vote. CGS 33-698.

Stock Certificates: Must be signed by two officers designated for that purpose in bylaws or by board of directors. Shares may be issued without a certificate. CGS 33-676, 677.

Consideration For Stock: May consist of tangible or intangible property or benefit to the corp., including cash, promissory notes, services performed or to be performed or other securities of the corp. CGS 33-672(a).

Stock Transfer Restrictions: May be contained in certificate of incorporation, bylaws or in a shareholders' agreement. CGS 33-678.

Cumulative Voting: Not permitted unless provided for in the certificate of incorporation. CGS 33-712.

Preemptive Rights: Do not exist unless granted in certificate of incorporation. Exists in corps. formed prior to 1-1-97 unless denied in certificate of incorporation. CGS 33-683.

Acts Requiring Shareholder Approval: Unless the certificate of incorporation or board of directors requires a greater vote, a majority vote of the shares entitled to vote is required for a merger or consolidation for the sale or disposition of all or substantially all of the corporate assets not in the usual course of business, and for voluntary dissolution. CGS 33-817, 831, 881.

Board of Directors: May consist of one or more individuals with number specified in certificate of incorporation or bylaws. CGS 33-737.

Officers: Those provided for in the bylaws. The same person may hold more than one office. CGS 33-763.

Foreign Corporations: Must obtain a certificate of authority from the Secretary of State to transact business in Connecticut. The statute contains a nonexclusive list of activities that do not constitute transacting business in the state. The penalties for transacting business without a certificate of authority include nonaccess to state courts, a penalty of $2,000 per year, and liability for all fees, taxes, and penalties that would have been assessed had a certificate of authority been issued. CGS 33-920, 921.

Close Corporation Laws: Corp. may be managed under a shareholders' agreement that complies with CGS 33-717.

Periodic Reports: All domestic and authorized foreign corporations must file a biennial report with the Secretary of State and pay a biennial report fee and an annual franchise tax to remain in good standing. The first report is due 30 days after the organizational meeting. Subsequent reports are due on dates established by the Secretary of State. CGS 33-953.

STATE FILING OFFICIAL. Secretary of State, 30 Trinity Street, Hartford, CT 06106 (Telephone: 203-566-8570).

Fees:

Filing Certificate of Incorporation - $50 plus initial franchise tax.	Franchise Tax - Based on capitalization ($150 minimum).
Application for Certificate of Authority - $50 filing fee plus $250 license fee.	Amending Certificate of Incorporation - $50
Filing LLC Articles of Organization - $60	Other Corp. Fees - See CGS 33-617, 618
Filing LLP Certificate - $60	Other LLC Fees - See CGS 34-112
Name Reservation - $30	Other LLP Fees - See CGS 34-413

SUMMARY OF DELAWARE BUSINESS ORGANIZATION LAWS

PARTNERSHIP LAWS.

General Partnerships: Uniform Partnership Act adopted. DCA 6-1501 et seq.
Limited Partnerships: Revised Uniform Limited Partnership Act adopted. DCA 6-17-101 et seq.
Limited Liability Partnerships: Provided for. DCA 6-1544 et seq. (Must provide $1,000,000 of liability insurance or security deposit).
Name Registration: Must file a fictitious name certificate with the office of the Prothonotary of each county where business is conducted if the partnership name does not contain the surname of each partner. DCA 6-3101.

LIMITED LIABILITY COMPANY LAWS. Delaware Limited Liability Company Act. DCA 6-18-101 et seq.

Formation of LLC: One or more persons may form LLC by filing a certificate of formation with the Secretary of State. See DCA 6-18-201 for certificate of formation content requirements.
General LLC Requirements: May have one or more members. May conduct any lawful business except banking or insurance.
Management of LLC: Vested in members unless otherwise provided in LLC Agreement.
New or Substituted Members: Admission to LLC requires consent of all members unless otherwise provided in LLC Agreement.
Conversion Statutes: Merger and consolidated statute. DCA 6-18-209. No partnership conversion statute.

CORPORATION LAWS. General Corporation Law of Delaware (Model Business Corporation Acts not adopted). DCA 8-101 et seq.

Corporate Name: Must contain one of the following words: association, company, corporation, club, foundation, fund, incorporated, institute, society, union, syndicate, or limited, or the abbreviation co., corp., ltd., or inc. Name must be distinguishable on the records of the Secretary of State from the names of other corporations and limited partnerships. Name may be reserved for 30 days by formal application. Name may be informally reserved for 30 days without fee upon verbal or written request to Secretary of State. DCA 8-102(a)(1).
Incorporators: One or more persons, partnerships, associations, or corporations of any state. DCA 8-101.
Certificate of Incorporation:
Contents: See DCA 8-102(a), (b) for required and optional certificate of incorporation content requirements.
Filing and Recording: An original copy of the certificate of incorporation must be filed with the Secretary of State and the filing fee paid. A certified copy of the certificate of incorporation must be recorded in the recorder's office in the county of the corporation's registered office. DCA 8-103. Corporate existence begins when the certificate of incorporation is accepted for filing. DCA 8-106.
Amendment: Requires a majority vote of the outstanding shares entitled to vote, unless the certificate of incorporation requires a greater vote. DCA 8-242, 102(b)(4).
Organizational Meeting: Held by incorporators or by initial board of directors if named in certificate of incorporation. The incorporators or directors may act without meeting if they all sign a written consent to the action. DCA 8-108.
Bylaws: Initial bylaws adopted by incorporators or by initial board of directors if named in certificate of incorporation. May be amended by the shareholders and, if stock has not been issued or if so provided in the certificate of incorporation, by the board of directors. DCA 8-109.
Action Without Meeting: Unless otherwise provided in the certificate of incorporation, the shareholders may act without meeting if a written consent to the action is signed by shareholders sufficient to carry the action at a meeting and notice is given to nonconsenting shareholders. DCA 8-228. Unless restricted by the certificate of incorporation or bylaws, the board of directors may act without meeting if all directors sign a written consent to the action and may meet via conference telephone or similar communications equipment. DCA 8-141(f), (i).
Stock Certificates: Must be signed by chairman or vice chairman of board, president, or vice president, and by secretary or treasurer or assistant of either. Shares may be issued without a certificate, but a shareholder is entitled to a certificate upon demand. DCA 8-158.
Consideration For Stock: May consist of cash, services rendered, personal property, or real property or leases thereof. DCA 8-152.
Stock Transfer Restrictions: May be imposed by the certificate of incorporation, bylaws, or a shareholders' agreement. A restriction must be conspicuously noted on the stock certificate to be enforceable against a person without knowledge of the restriction. DCA 8-202.
Cumulative Voting: Not permitted unless provided for in the certificate of incorporation. DCA 8-214.
Preemptive Rights: Do not exist unless contained in the certificate of incorporation. DCA 8-102(b)(3).
Acts Requiring Shareholder Approval: Unless the certificate of incorporation requires a greater vote, a majority vote of the shares entitled to vote is required for a merger or consolidation, for the sale or disposition of all or substantially all of the corporate assets, for voluntary dissolution, and to amend the certificate of incorporation. DCA 8-251, 271, 275, 242, 102(b)(4).
Board of Directors: May consist of one or more persons, with number specified in the certificate of incorporation or bylaws. DCA 8-141(b).
Officers: Those specified in the bylaws or appointed by the board of directors in accordance with the bylaws. The same person may hold any two or more offices unless the certificate of incorporation or bylaws provide otherwise. DCA 8-142.
Foreign Corporations: Must obtain a certificate of authority from the Secretary of State before transacting business in Delaware. The statute contains a list of activities that do not constitute doing business in the state. The penalties for transacting business without a certificate of authority include nonaccess to state courts, corporate fines of $200 to $500 per offense, and agent fines of $100 to $500. DCA 8-371, 373, 378.
Close Corporation Laws: Has Close Corporation Code. DCA 8-342 to 356. Certificate of incorporation must state that corp. is a close corporation, that all issued stock will be held by thirty or fewer persons, and that a "public offering" of stock will not be made.
Periodic Reports: Delaware corporations must file an annual franchise tax report with the Secretary of State by March 1 of each year and pay annual franchise tax to remain in good standing. Foreign corporations must file an annual report by June 30 of each year and pay an annual filing fee to remain in good standing. DCA 8-374, 502.

STATE FILING OFFICIAL. Secretary of State, Corporations Department, P.O. Box 898, Dover, DE 19901 (Telephone: 302-739-3073).

Fees:
Filing Certificate of Incorporation - $50 + capitalization tax ($15 minimum).
Amending Certificate of Incorporation - $30 (more if capitalization is increased).
Filing LLC Certificate of Formation - $50
Filing LLP Registration Application - $100 per partner
Name Reservation - $10
Application for Certificate of Authority - $80
Annual Filing Fee (Foreign Corp.) - $50
Other Corp. Fees - See DCA 8-391.

SUMMARY OF DISTRICT OF COLUMBIA BUSINESS ORGANIZATION LAWS

PARTNERSHIP LAWS.

General Partnerships: Uniform Partnership Act of 1996. DCC 41-151.1 et seq.
Limited Partnerships: Revised Uniform Limited Partnership Act adopted. DCC 41-401 et seq.
Limited Liability Partnerships: Registered LLPs for general & limited partnerships provided for. DCC 41-160.1 et seq.
Name Registration: Not required.

LIMITED LIABILITY COMPANY LAWS. Limited Liability Company Act. DCC 29-1301 et seq.

Formation of LLC: One or more persons may form LLC by filing articles of organization with Mayor. See DCC 29-1306 for article of organization content requirements.
General LLC Requirements: Must have two or more members. May conduct any lawful business. Special provisions for professional LLCs (DCC 29-1314(c)).
Management of LLC: Vested in members unless otherwise provided in articles of organization.
New or Substituted Members: Admission to LLC requires consent of all members unless otherwise provided in articles of organization or operating agreement.
Conversion Statutes: Partnership conversion statute. DCC 29-1313. Merger statute. DCC 29-1340.

CORPORATION LAWS. District of Columbia Business Corporation Act (based on Model Business Corporation Act). DCC 29-301 et seq.

Corporate Name: Must contain the word "corporation," "company," "incorporated," "limited," or an abbreviation thereof. May not be the same as or deceptively similar to the name of any other domestic or authorized foreign corporation. Name may not indicate that the corporation is organized under an act of Congress. Name may be reserved for 60 days. No procedure for checking availability of name. DCC 29-308, 309.
Incorporators: One or more natural persons of age 18 or more. DCC 29-346.
Articles of Incorporation:

Contents: See DCC 29-347 for required and optional article of incorporation content requirements.
Filing and Recording: Two original copies of the articles of incorporation must be filed with the district filing official and the filing and license fees paid. Corporate existence begins when a certificate of incorporation is issued by the district filing official. DCC 29-348, 349.
Amendment: Requires a two-thirds vote of the outstanding shares entitled to vote, unless the articles of incorporation require a greater vote. DCC 29-354, 399.36.

Organizational Meeting: Held in the United States by the initial board of directors after incorporation. DCC 29-351.
Minimum Capitalization Requirement: $1,000. DCC 29-347, 350.
Bylaws: Initial bylaws adopted by the board of directors unless that power is reserved to the shareholders in the articles of incorporation. May be amended by the board of directors unless that power is reserved to the shareholders in the articles of incorporation. DCC 29-324, 351.
Action Without Meeting: The shareholders and the board of directors may act without meeting if all shareholders entitled to vote or all directors, as the case may be, sign a written consent to the action and the consent is filed with the corporate minutes. DCC 29-399.37.
Stock Certificates: Must be signed by the president or the vice president. Shares may be issued without a certificate. DCC 29-320.
Consideration For Stock: May consist of money, tangible or intangible property, or labor or services actually performed for the corporation. May not consist of promissory notes or future services. DCC 29-317.
Stock Transfer Restrictions: Must be noted on the stock certificate. DCC 29-320.
Cumulative Voting: Not permitted unless provided for in the articles of incorporation. DCC 29-327.
Preemptive Rights: Exist unless limited or denied in the articles of incorporation. DCC 29-323.
Acts Requiring Shareholder Approval: Unless the articles of incorporation require a greater vote, a two-thirds vote of all shares is required for merger or consolidation. DCCE 29-367, 399.36. Unless the articles of incorporation require a greater vote, a two-thirds vote of the shares entitled to vote is required for the sale or disposition of all or substantially all of the corporate assets not in the usual course of business, for voluntary dissolution, and to amend the articles of incorporation. DCC 29-375, 378, 354, 399.36.
Board of Directors: May consist of one or more persons with the number of directors fixed in the bylaws. DCC 29-333.
Officers: Must have president. Other officers may be provided for in bylaws. The same person may hold any number of offices. DCC 29-343.
Foreign Corporations: Must obtain a certificate of authority from the district filing official before transacting business in the district. The statute lists certain activities for which a certificate of authority is not required. The penalties for transacting business without a certificate of authority include nonaccess to courts, liability for all fees and charges that would have been assessed had a certificate of authority been issued, a penalty of up to $500, and a criminal fine of up to $500. DCC 29-399, 399.20
Close Corporation Laws: Has close corporation code. DCC 29-399.54 et seq.
Periodic Reports: Domestic and authorized foreign corporations must file an annual report with the district filing officer by April 15 of each year and pay an annual report fee to remain in good standing. DCC 29-398, 399.13.

DISTRICT FILING OFFICIAL. Mayor. Filing functions delegated to Corporation Division, Department of Consumer & Regulatory Affairs, 614 "H" Street, Washington, DC 20001 (Telephone: 202-727-7278).

Fees: Filing Articles of Incorporation - $100 plus license fee based on capitalization ($20 minimum).
Amending Articles of Incorporation - $100
Application for Certificate of Authority - $150
Other Corp. Fees - See DCC 29-399.22.
Filing LLP Statement of Qualification - $150
Filing LLC Articles of Organization - $100
Corp. Annual Report Fee - $100
Name Reservation - $25
Other LLC & LLP Fees - Call District Filing Official

SUMMARY OF FLORIDA BUSINESS ORGANIZATION LAWS

PARTNERSHIP LAWS.

General Partnerships: Revised Uniform Partnership Act of 1995. FSA 620.8101 et seq.

Limited Partnerships: Revised Uniform Limited Partnership Act adopted. FSA 620.101 et seq.

Limited Liability Partnerships: Registered LLPs for general & limited partnerships provided for. FSA 620.78 et seq. LLPs must carry liability insurance of at least $100,000 per partner. FSA 620.7851.

Name Registration: Must register partnership name with state filing official if it does not contain partners' names. FSA 865.09.

LIMITED LIABILITY COMPANY LAWS. Florida Limited Liability Company Act. FSA 608.401 et seq.

Formation of LLC: Two or more persons may form LLC by filing articles of organization with Department of State. See FSA 608.407 for article of organization content requirements.

General LLC Requirements: Must have two or more members. May conduct any lawful business. May adopt "regulations" to govern LLC activities. Professional LLCs must comply with requirements of FSA 621.01 et seq.

Management of LLC: Vested in members unless otherwise provided in articles of organization.

New or Substituted Members: Requires consent of all members unless otherwise provided in articles of organization or regulations.

Conversion Statutes: None in LLC Act.

CORPORATION LAWS. Corporation Law of Florida (based on Revised Model Business Corporation Act). FSA 607.0101 et seq.

Corporate Name: Must contain the word "corporation," "company," or "incorporated," or an abbreviation thereof and must be distinguishable from the filed or registered names of all other entities. Name may be reserved for 120 days. No advance or informal name clearance procedure. FSA 607.0401, 0402.

Incorporators: One or more individuals or entities. FSA 607.0201.

Articles of Incorporation:

Contents: See FSA 607.0202 for required and optional article of incorporation content requirements.

Filing and Recording: An original and one copy of the articles of incorporation must be filed with the state filing official and the filing fee paid. Corporate existence begins when the articles of incorporation are accepted for filing. FSA 607.0120, 0203.

Amendment: Requires a majority of votes entitled to be cast unless a statute, the articles of incorporation, or the board of directors require a greater vote. The board of directors may make ministerial amendments without shareholder approval. FSA 607.1002, 1003.

Organizational Meeting: Held after incorporation by the initial board of directors if named in the articles of incorporation. Otherwise held after incorporation by the incorporators, who may act without meeting if all incorporators sign a written consent to the action. FSA 607.0205.

Bylaws: Initial bylaws adopted by the incorporators or the board of directors, unless that power is reserved to the shareholders in the articles of incorporation. May be amended by the shareholders and by the board of directors unless that power is reserved to the shareholders in the articles of incorporation, or unless a shareholder amendment precludes subsequent board of director amendment. FSA 607.0206, 1020.

Action Without Meeting: Unless otherwise provided in the articles of incorporation, the shareholders may act without meeting if a written consent to the action is signed by shareholders sufficient to carry the action at a meeting and notice is given to nonconsenting shareholders. FSA 607.0704. Unless the articles of incorporation or bylaws provide otherwise, the board of directors may meet via conference telephone or similar equipment, and may act without meeting if all directors sign a written consent to the action. FSA 607.0820, 0821.

Stock Certificates: Must be signed by the officer or officers designated in the bylaws or by the board of directors. Shares may be issued without a certificate unless the articles of incorporation or bylaws provide otherwise. FSA 607.0625, 0626.

Consideration For Stock: May consist of any tangible or intangible property or benefit to the corporation, including cash, promissory notes, services performed or to be performed, and other securities of the corporation. Shares issued for promissory notes or future services may be placed in escrow or otherwise restricted pending payment of note or performance of services. FSA 607.0621.

Stock Transfer Restrictions: May be imposed by the articles of incorporation, bylaws, or a shareholders agreement. A restriction must be conspicuously noted on the stock certificate to be enforceable against a person without knowledge of the restriction. FSA 607.0627.

Cumulative Voting: Not permitted unless provided for in the articles of incorporation. FSA 607.0728.

Preemptive Rights: Do not exist unless contained in the articles of incorporation. FSA 607.0630.

Acts Requiring Shareholder Approval: Unless the articles of incorporation, a statute, or the board of directors require a greater vote, a majority of the votes entitled to be cast is required for a merger or share exchange, for the sale or transfer of all or substantially all of the corporate assets not in the usual course of business, for voluntary dissolution, and for most amendments to the articles of incorporation (see above). FSA 607.1103, 1202, 1402, 1003.

Board of Directors: May consist of one or more individuals, with the number of directors specified in the bylaws or articles of incorporation. A corporation with 100 or fewer shareholders may dispense with or limit the authority of the board of directors. FSA 607.0803, 0801.

Officers: Those described in the bylaws or appointed by the board of directors in accordance with the bylaws. No specific officers required. The same person may simultaneously hold more than one office in the corporation. FSA 607.08401.

Foreign Corporations: Must obtain a certificate of authority from the state filing official before transacting business in Florida. The statute contains a nonexclusive list of activities that do not constitute transacting business in the state. The penalties for transacting business without a certificate of authority include nonaccess to state courts, liability for all fees, taxes and penalties that would have been imposed had a certificate of authority been issued, and a civil penalty of $500 to $1000 per year. FSA 607.1501, 1502.

Close Corporation Laws: A corporation with 100 or fewer shareholders may be managed under a shareholders' agreement. FSA 607.0732.

Periodic Reports: All domestic and authorized foreign corporations must file an annual report with state filing official by April 30 of each year and pay an annual report fee to remain in good standing. FSA 607.1622, 0122(19).

STATE FILING OFFICIAL. Department of State, Div. of Corporations, P.O. Box 6327, Tallahassee, FL 32314 (Telephone: 904-488-9000).

Fees:

Filing Articles of Incorporation - $35	Amending Articles of Incorporation - $35	Name Reservation - $35
Application for Certificate of Authority - $35	Corp. Annual Report - $61.25 + $88.75 supp. fee	Other Corp. Fees - see FSA 607.0122.
Filing LLC Articles of Organization - $250	Filing LLC Annual Report - $100	Other LLC Fees - See FSA 608.452
Filing LLP Statement of Registration - $100 per partner ($10,000 max.)		

SUMMARY OF GEORGIA BUSINESS ORGANIZATION LAWS

PARTNERSHIP LAWS.

General Partnerships: Uniform Partnership Act adopted. GCA 14-8-1 et seq.

Limited Partnerships: Revised Uniform Limited Partnership Act adopted. GCA 14-9-101 et seq.

Limited Liability Partnerships: LLPs for general & limited partnerships provided for. GCA 14-8-2(6.1), 62-64.

Name Registration: Must file a fictitious name statement with the clerk of the superior court in the county where the partnership's principal business is conducted if the partnership name does not contain the names of all partners. GCA 10-1-490.

LIMITED LIABILITY COMPANY LAWS. Georgia Limited Liability Company Act. GCA 14-11-100 et seq.

Formation of LLC: One or more persons may form an LLC by filing articles of organization with Secretary of State. See GCA 14-11-204 for article of organization content requirements.

General LLC Requirements: May have one or more members. May conduct any lawful business which a corporation or partnership may conduct, including the rendering of professional services.

Management of LLC: Vested in members unless vested in manager(s) by articles of organization or written operating agreement.

New or Substituted Members: Admitted to LLC only consent of all members unless otherwise provided in articles of organization or operating agreement.

Conversion Statutes: Partnership and corporation conversion statute. GCA 14-11-212. Merger statute. 14-11-901 et seq.

CORPORATION LAWS. Georgia Business Corporation Code (based on Revised Model Business Corporation Act). GCA 14-2-101 et seq.

Corporate Name: Must contain the word "corporation," "company," "incorporation," or "limited," or an abbreviation thereof. May not exceed 80 characters (including spaces and punctuation) in length and must be distinguishable on the records of the Secretary of State from the name of any other corporation, limited partnership, or professional association. Name may be reserved for 90 days. Availability of name may be checked with state filing official without fee by letter or telephone. GCA 14-2-401, 402.

Incorporators: One or more individuals or entities. GCA 14-2-201.

Articles of Incorporation:

Contents: See GCA 14-2-202 for required and optional article of incorporation content requirements.

Filing and Recording: A notice of incorporation must be published for two consecutive weeks in a local newspaper. Publication agreement and two copies of the articles of incorporation must be filed with the state filing official and the filing fee paid. Corporate existence begins when articles of incorporation are filed. GCA 14-2-201.1, 120, 203.

Amendment: Requires a majority of the votes entitled to be cast, unless a statute, the articles of incorporation, or the board of directors require a greater vote. The board of directors can make ministerial amendments without shareholder approval. GCA 14-2-1003, 1002.

Organizational Meeting: Held after incorporation by the initial board of directors if named in the articles of incorporation. Otherwise held after incorporation by the incorporators, who may act without meeting if they all sign a written consent to the action. GCA 14-2-205.

Bylaws: Initial bylaws adopted by board of directors or incorporators. May be amended by the shareholders and by the board of directors unless the articles reserve that power to the shareholders. Shareholder amendments can prohibit board of director amendment. GCA 14-2-206,1020.

Action Without Meeting: The shareholders may act without meeting if a written consent to the action is signed by all shareholders entitled to vote or, if the articles of incorporation so provide, by shareholders sufficient to carry the action at a meeting and the required notice is given. Unless the articles of incorporation or bylaws provide otherwise, the board of directors may meet via conference telephone or similar communications equipment and may act without meeting if a written consent to the action is signed by all directors. GCA 14-2-704, 820, 821.

Stock Certificates: Must be signed by the officers designated in the bylaws or by the board of directors. Stock may be issued without a certificate unless the articles of incorporation or bylaws provide otherwise. GCA 14-2-625, 626.

Consideration For Stock: May consist of any tangible or intangible property or benefit to the corporation, including cash, promissory notes, services performed or to be performed, and other securities of the corporation. Shares issued for promissory notes or future services may be placed in escrow or otherwise restricted pending payment of note or performance of services. GCA 14-2-621.

Stock Transfer Restrictions: May be imposed by the articles of incorporation, bylaws or a shareholders agreement. A restriction must be conspicuously noted on the stock certificate to be enforceable against a person without knowledge of the restriction. GCA 14-2-627.

Cumulative Voting: Not permitted unless provided for in the articles of incorporation and 48-hour prior notice is given. GCA 14-2-728.

Preemptive Rights: Do not exist unless contained in the articles of incorporation, except that in corporations formed prior to July 1, 1989 and in close corporations they exist unless they are denied or limited in the articles of incorporation. GCA 14-2-630.

Acts Requiring Shareholder Approval: Unless a statute, the articles of incorporation, or the board of directors require a greater vote, a majority of the votes entitled to be cast is required for a merger or share exchange, for the sale or disposition of all or substantially all of the corporate assets not in the usual course of business, for voluntary dissolution, and for most amendments to the articles of incorporation (see above). GCA 14-2-1103, 1202, 1402, 1003.

Board of Directors: May consist of one or more individuals with the number of directors specified in the articles of incorporation or bylaws. The board of directors may be eliminated in a shareholders' agreement under GCA 14-2-731(c). GCA 14-2-803.

Officers: Those specified in bylaws or appointed by board of directors. The same person may hold more than one office. GCA 14-2-840.

Foreign Corporations: Must obtain a certificate of authority from the Secretary of State before transacting business in Georgia. The statute contains a nonexclusive list of activities that do not constitute transacting business in the state. The penalties for transacting business without a certificate of authority include nonaccess to state courts and a $500 per year civil penalty. GCA 14-2-1501, 1502.

Close Corporation Laws: Has Georgia Close Corporation Code. GCA 14-2-901 to 950. A statutory close corporation must have 50 or fewer shareholders. Any corporation may be managed by its shareholders under a unanimous shareholders' agreement. GCA 14-2-731(c).

Periodic Reports: Domestic and authorized foreign corporations must file an annual report with the Secretary of State by April 1 of each year and pay an annual registration fee and an annual license tax to remain in good standing. GCA 14-2-1622, 48-13-73 to 78.

STATE FILING OFFICIAL. Secretary of State, Corporation Division, 2 Martin Luther King, Jr. Dr., Suite 315 West Tower, Atlanta, GA 30334 (Telephone: 404-656-2817).

Fees:

Filing Articles of Incorporation - $60	Amending Articles of Incorporation - $20	Application for Certificate of Authority - $170
Filing LLC Articles of Organization - $75	Filing LLP Election - $60	Publishing Intent to Incorporate - $40
	Other LLC Fees - See GCA 14-11-1101.	Other Corp. Fees - See GCA 14-2-122.

SUMMARY OF HAWAII BUSINESS ORGANIZATION LAWS

PARTNERSHIP LAWS.

General Partnerships: Uniform Partnership Act adopted. HRS 425-101 et seq.

Limited Partnerships: Revised Uniform Limited Partnership Act adopted. HRS 425D-101 et seq.

Limited Liability Partnerships: Provided for. HRS 425-151 et seq. (Liability insurance or deposit required. HRS 425-172).

Name Registration: Must register partnership name with the state filing official and file an annual statement. HRS 425-1 et seq.

LIMITED LIABILITY COMPANY LAWS. Uniform Limited Liability Company Act. HRS 428-101 et seq.

Formation of LLC: One or more persons may organize an LLC by filing articles of organization with the State Filing Official. See HRS 428-203 for the article of organization content requirements.

General LLC Requirements: May have one or more members. May conduct any lawful business except banking, insurance, and the professions listed in HRS 428-111(a)(3).

Management of LLC: Must designate whether member or manager managed in articles of organization. See HRS 428-404 for specifics.

New or Substituted Members: Requires consent of all members unless operating agreement provides otherwise. HRS 428-501.

Conversion Statutes: Partnership conversion statute. HRS 428-902, 903. Merger statute. HRS 428-904 to 908.

CORPORATION LAWS. Hawaii Business Corporations Act (based on Model Business Corporation Act). HRS 415-2 et seq.

Corporate Name: Must contain the word "corporation," "incorporated," or "limited" or an abbreviation thereof. May not be the same as or substantially identical to the name of any other corporation or partnership. May reserve name for 120 days by application. HRS 415-8, 9.

Incorporators: One or more individuals. HRS 415-53.

Articles of Incorporation:

Contents: Must set forth (1) name of corporation, (2) number of shares that are authorized to be issued in each class, (3) address of corporation's initial or principal office, (4) number of directors on initial board and name and address of each, and (5) name, title, and address of each officer. May set forth period of duration, limitations on purposes of corporation, rights and preferences of each class of shares, preemptive rights provisions, names of share subscribers, subscription price of shares and amounts paid by subscribers, lawful bylaw provisions, and lawful provisions regarding the management of the corporation, the powers of the corporation and its directors and shareholders, and the par value of stock. HRS 415-54.

Filing and Recording: The articles of incorporation must be signed by the incorporators if the corporation has not been organized or by two officers if it has been organized. The articles of incorporation must be filed with the state filing official and the filing fee paid. HRS 415-55. Corporate existence begins when the articles of incorporation are accepted for filing. HRS 415-56.

Amendment: Requires a majority vote of the shares entitled to vote unless the articles of incorporation require a greater vote, (a two-thirds vote is required for corporations incorporated before July 1, 1987). HRS 415-59, 143.

Organizational Meeting: Held after incorporation by the initial board of directors. HRS 415-57.

Bylaws: Initial bylaws adopted by the board of directors. May be amended by the board of directors, unless the articles of incorporation reserve that power to the shareholders. Board of director amendments may be changed or repealed by the shareholders. HRS 415-27.

Action Without Meeting: The shareholders may act without meeting if all shareholders entitled to vote sign a written consent to the action. HRS 415-145. Unless the articles or bylaws provide otherwise, the board of directors may meet via conference telephone or similar communications equipment and may act without meeting if all directors sign a written consent to the action. HRS 415-43, 44.

Stock Certificates: Must be signed by chairman or vice chairman of board, president, or vice president, and by secretary, treasurer or assistant of either. Shares may be issued without a certificate unless the articles of incorporation provide otherwise. HRS 415-23.

Consideration For Stock: May consist of any tangible or intangible property or benefit to the corporation, including cash, promissory notes, services performed, future services, and other securities of the corporation. If shares are issued for promissory notes or future services, a written report thereof must be made to all shareholders. HRS 415-19.

Stock Transfer Restrictions: No statutory provisions.

Cumulative Voting: Must be permitted if a shareholder gives 48-hour prior notice of intent to cumulate. HRS 415-33.

Preemptive Rights: Exists unless denied or limited in the articles of incorporation. HRS 415-26.

Acts Requiring Shareholder Approval: Unless the articles of incorporation require a greater vote, the affirmative vote of a majority of the shares entitled to vote is required for a merger or consolidation, for the sale or disposition of all or substantially all of the corporate assets not in the usual course of business, for voluntary dissolution, and to amend the articles of incorporation. Different voting requirements apply to corporations formed prior to July 1, 1987. HRS 415-73, 79, 84, 59, 143.

Board of Directors: Must have three or more directors except that there need not be more directors than shareholders. The number of directors may be specified in the articles of incorporation or bylaws. At least one director must be Hawaii resident. HRS 415-35, 36.

Officers: Must have president, vice president, secretary and treasurer. The same person may simultaneously hold any two or more offices. If there are two or more directors there must be two or more officers. HRS 415-50.

Foreign Corporations: Must obtain a certificate of authority from the state filing official before transacting business in Hawaii. The statute contains a nonexclusive list of activities that do not constitute transacting business in the state. The penalties for transacting business without a certificate of authority include nonaccess to state courts and liability for all fees, taxes, and penalties that would have been assessed had a certificate of authority been issued. HRS 415-106, 124.

Close Corporation Laws: None. A 50% shareholder may be exempted from unemployment insurance coverage. HRS 383-7.

Periodic Reports: Domestic and authorized foreign corporations must file an annual report with the state filing official and pay annual fee to remain in good standing. Report due March 31 for domestic corporations and June 30 for foreign corporations. HRS 415-125, 126, 131.

STATE FILING OFFICIAL. Director, Dept. of Commerce & Consumer Affairs, 1010 Richards St., Honolulu, HI 96813 (808-586-2727).

Fees:

Filing Articles of Incorporation - $100	Name Reservation - $20	Other Corp. Fees - See HRS 415-127, 128, 129.
Amending Articles of Incorporation - $50	Corp. Annual Report - $25	Other LLP Fees - See HRS 425-169.
Filing LLC Articles of Organization - $100	Filing LLP Annual Report - $50	Other LLC Fees - See HRS 428-1301.
Filing LLP Certificate - $100 per partner ($5,000 max.)		

SUMMARY OF IDAHO BUSINESS ORGANIZATION LAWS

PARTNERSHIP LAWS.

General Partnerships: Uniform Partnership Act adopted. IC 53-301 et seq. (IC 53-3-101 et seq. effective 1-1-2001.)
Limited Partnerships: Revised Uniform Limited Partnership Act adopted. IC 53-201 et seq.
Limited Liability Partnerships: Registered limited liability partnerships provided for. IC 53-302, 343A-343C.
Name Registration: Must file a fictitious name certificate with the county recorder in each county where business is conducted if the partnership name does not contain the names of all partners. IC 53-501 et seq.

LIMITED LIABILITY COMPANY LAWS. Idaho Limited Liability Company Act. IC 53-601 et seq.

Formation of LLC: One or more persons may form an LLC by filing articles of organization with the Secretary of State. See IC 53-608 for the article of organization content requirements.
General LLC Requirements: May have one or more members. May conduct any lawful business. Special requirements for professional LLCs (IC 53-605(2), 608(7), 615). Must file annual report.
Management of LLC: Vested in members unless vested in manager(s) in operating agreement. IC 53-621.
New or Substituted Members: Requires written consent of all members unless otherwise provided in operating agreement.
Conversion Statutes: Merger or consolidation statute. IC 53-661 et seq. No partnership conversion statute.

CORPORATION LAWS. Idaho Business Corporation Act (based on Revised Model Business Corporation Act). IC 30-1-101 et seq.

Corporate Name: Must contain the word "corporation," "company" (which may not be preceded by the word "and"), "incorporated," or "limited" or an abbreviation thereof and may not be the same as or deceptively similar to the name of any other corporation or registered entity. Name may be reserved for four months by application. IC 30-1-401, 402.
Incorporators: One or more persons. IC 30-1-201.
Articles of Incorporation:
- **Contents:** See IC 30-1-202 for required and optional article of incorporation content requirements.
- **Filing and Recording:** The articles of incorporation must be filed with the Secretary of State and the filing fee paid. Corporate existence begins when the articles are filed. IC 30-1-120, 203.
- **Amendment:** Unless corporation laws, the articles of incorporation or the board of directors require a greater vote, a majority of the votes entitled to be cast is required. IC 30-1-1003.

Organizational Meeting: Held after incorporation by initial board of directors, if named in articles, otherwise by incorporators. IC 30-1-205.
Bylaws: Initial bylaws adopted by the board of directors or incorporators. May be amended by the board of directors, unless power reserved to shareholders in articles of incorporation. Board of director amendments may be changed or repealed by shareholders. IC 30-1-1020.
Action Without Meeting: The shareholders may act without meeting if all shareholders entitled to vote sign a written consent to the action. IC 30-1-704. Unless the articles of incorporation or bylaws provide otherwise, the board of directors may act without meeting if all directors sign a written consent to the action. IC 30-1-821.
Stock Certificates: Must be signed by 2 officers designated in bylaws or by board of directors. Shares may be issued without a certificate. IC 30-1-625, 626.
Consideration For Stock: May consist of tangible or intangible property, including cash, promissory notes, services performed or other securities of the corp. IC 30-1-621.
Stock Transfer Restrictions: May be contained in the articles of incorporation, bylaws, or a shareholders' agreement. A restriction must be conspicuously noted on the stock certificate to be enforceable against a person without knowledge of the restriction. IC 30-1-627.
Cumulative Voting: Denied unless permitted in the articles of incorporation. IC 30-1-728.
Preemptive Rights: Do not exist unless granted in the articles of incorporation. IC 30-1-630.
Acts Requiring Shareholder Approval: Unless corporation laws, board of directors, or articles of incorporation require a greater vote, a majority of the votes entitled to be cast is required for a merger, for the sale or disposition of substantially all of the corporate assets not in the usual course of business, for voluntary dissolution, and to amend the articles of incorporation. IC 30-1-1103, 1202, 1402, 1003.
Board of Directors: May consist of one or more individuals. The number of directors must be specified in the articles of incorporation or the bylaws. IC 30-1-803.
Officers: Those provided for in the bylaws. The same person may hold more than one office. IC 30-1-840.
Foreign Corporations: Must obtain a certificate of authority from the Secretary of State before transacting business in Idaho. The statute contains a nonexclusive list of activities that do not constitute transacting business in the state. The penalties for transacting business without a certificate of authority include nonaccess to state courts and liability for all fees, taxes and penalties that would have been assessed had a certificate of authority been issued. IC 30-1-1501, 1502.
Close Corporation Laws: Shareholders may operate corp. under a shareholders' agreement that complies with IC 30-1-732.
Periodic Reports: Domestic and authorized foreign corporations must file an annual report on prescribed forms with the Secretary of State between July 1 and November 30 of each year and pay an annual income or franchise tax to remain in good standing. IC 30-1-1622.

STATE FILING OFFICIAL. Secretary of State, State House, Room 203, Boise, ID 83720 (Telephone: 208-334-2300).

Fees:
- Filing Articles of Incorporation - $100
- Amending Articles of Incorporation - $30
- Filing LLC Articles of Organization - $100 if typed - $120 if not typed or has attachments
- Filing LLP Application - $100 if typed - $120 if not typed or has attachments
- Application for Certificate of Authority - $100
- Name Reservation - $20
- Annual Report - No Fee
- Other Corp. Fees - See IC 30-1-122.
- Other LLC Fees - IC 53-665

SUMMARY OF ILLINOIS BUSINESS ORGANIZATION LAWS

PARTNERSHIP LAWS.

General Partnerships: Uniform Partnership Act adopted. 805 ILCS 205/1 et seq.

Limited Partnerships: Revised Uniform Limited Partnership Act adopted. 805 ILCS 210/110 et seq.

Limited Liability Partnerships: Register limited liability partnerships provided for. 805 ILCS 205/8.1 et seq.

Name Registration: Must file a fictitious name certificate with the county clerk of the county of the partnership's place of business if partnership name does not contain the names of all partners. Within 10 days after filing, notice of the certificate must be published in a local newspaper for three consecutive weeks and proof of publication must be filed with the county clerk. 805 ILCS 405/1.

LIMITED LIABILITY COMPANY LAWS. Limited Liability Company Act. 805 ILCS 180/1-1 et seq.

Formation of LLC: One or more persons may form an LLC by filing articles of organization with the Secretary of State. See 805 ILCS 180/5-5 for the article of organization content requirements.

General LLC Requirements: May have one or more members. May conduct any lawful business except banking, insurance or dentistry or medical practice (unless all members and managers are licensed).

Management of LLC: Vested in members unless vested in managers by articles of organization.

New or Substituted Members: Requires consent of all members unless otherwise provided in articles of organization or operating agreement.

Conversion Statutes: Partnership merger statute. 805 ILCS 205/7.1.

CORPORATION LAWS. Business Corporation Act of 1983 (Model Business Corporation Acts not adopted). 805 ILCS 5/1.01 et seq.

Corporate Name: Must contain the word "corporation," "company," "incorporated," or "limited" or an abbreviation thereof, and must be distinguishable on the records of the Secretary of State from any other corporate name. Name may be reserved for 90 days. Availability of name may be checked with Secretary of State by telephone or letter. 805 ILCS 5/4.05, 4.10.

Incorporators: One or more corporations or natural persons of age 18 or more. 805 ILCS 5/2.05.

Articles of Incorporation:

Contents: See 805 ILCS 5/2.10 for required and optional article of incorporation content requirements.

Filing and Recording: Two copies of articles of incorporation must be filed with Secretary of State and a filing fee paid. Certificate of incorporation must be recorded within 15 days in recorder's office in county of corporation's registered office. 805 ILCS 5/2.10, 1.10. Corporate existence begins when certificate of incorporation is issued by Secretary of State. 805 ILCS 5/2.15.

Amendment: Requires a two-thirds vote of the outstanding shares entitled to vote unless the articles of incorporation specify a different vote of not less than a majority. 805 ILCS 5/10.20. The board of directors acting alone can make ministerial amendments. 805 ILCS 5/10.15.

Organizational Meeting: Held after incorporation by initial board of directors if named in articles of incorporation. Otherwise held after incorporation by incorporators, who may act without meeting if all incorporators sign a written consent to the action. 805 ILCS 5/2.20, 2.05.

Bylaws: Initial bylaws adopted by the board of directors or the shareholders. May be amended by the shareholders and by the board of directors unless that power is reserved to the shareholders in the articles of incorporation. A shareholder amendment can prohibit its subsequent amendment by the board of directors. 805 ILCS 5/2.20, 2.25.

Action Without Meeting: Unless the articles of incorporation provide otherwise, the shareholders may act without meeting if a written consent to the action is signed by all shareholders entitled to vote or by the holders of shares sufficient to carry the action at a meeting. 805 ILCS 5/7.10. Unless prohibited by the articles of incorporation or bylaws, the board of directors may meet via conference telephone or similar communications equipment and may act without meeting if all directors sign a written consent to the action. 805 ILCS 5/8.15, 8.45.

Stock Certificates: Must be signed by the appropriate corporate officers. Shares may be issued without a certificate unless the articles of incorporation or bylaws provide otherwise. 805 ILCS 5/6.35.

Consideration For Stock: May consist of money, tangible or intangible property, or labor or services actually performed. 805 ILCS 5/6.30.

Stock Transfer Restrictions: May be contained in the articles of incorporation, bylaws, or a shareholder agreement. A restriction must be conspicuously noted on the stock certificate to be enforceable against a person without knowledge of the restriction. 805 ILCS 5/6.55.

Cumulative Voting: Permitted unless denied or limited in the articles of incorporation. 805 ILCS 5/7.40.

Preemptive Rights: Do not exist unless contained in the articles of incorporation. 805 ILCS 5/6.50.

Acts Requiring Shareholder Approval: Unless the articles of incorporation require a different vote of not less than a majority, a two-thirds vote of the outstanding shares entitled to vote is required for a merger or consolidation, the sale or disposition of all or substantially all of the corporate assets not in the usual course of business, for voluntary dissolution, and for most amendments to the articles of incorporation (see above). 805 ILCS 5/11.20, 11.60, 12.15, 10.20.

Board of Directors: May consist of one or more persons, with the number of directors specified in the bylaws. 805 ILCS 5/8.10.

Officers: Those specified in the bylaws. No specific officers required. The same person may hold any two or more offices in the corporation if the bylaws so provide. An Illinois judge may not be an officer. 805 ILCS 5/8.50, 37-160.11.

Foreign Corporations: Must obtain a certificate of authority from the Secretary of State before transacting business in Illinois. The penalties for transacting business without a certificate include nonaccess to state courts, liability for all fees, taxes and penalties that would have been imposed had a certificate been issued, and a penalty of 10% of the accrued charges or $200 plus $5 per month of violation, whichever is greater. 805 ILCS 5/13.05, 13.70.

Close Corporation Laws: Has Close Corporation Code 805 ILCS 5/2A.05 to 2A.60. No limit imposed on number of shareholders in close corp. Any corporation may be managed under a unanimous shareholders' agreement. 805 ILCS 5/7.71.

Periodic Reports: Domestic and authorized foreign corporations must file annual report on prescribed forms with the Secretary of State within 60 days after 1st day of anniversary month and pay annual fee and franchise tax to remain in good standing. 805 ILCS 5/14.05, 14.10.

STATE FILING OFFICIAL. Secretary of State, Dept. of Business Services, Michael J. Howlett Bldg., Springfield, IL 62756 (Telephone: 217-782-7880).

Fees: Filing Articles of Incorporation - $75 | Amending Articles of Incorporation - $25 | Application for Certificate of Authority - $75
Corp. Name Reservation - $25 | Annual Report of Corp. - $25 | Other Corp. Fees - See 805 ILCS 5/15.10.
Filing LLC Articles of Organization - $400 | LLC Annual report - $200 | Other LLC Fees - See 805 ILCS 180/50.10.
LLP Application - $100 per partner ($5,000 max.)

SUMMARY OF INDIANA BUSINESS ORGANIZATION LAWS

PARTNERSHIP LAWS.

General Partnerships: Uniform Partnership Act adopted. IC 23-4-1-1 et seq.

Limited Partnerships: Revised Uniform Limited Partnership Act adopted. IC 23-16-1-1 et seq.

Limited Liability Partnerships: Limited liability partnerships provided for. IC 23-4-1-44 et seq.

Name Registration: Must file a fictitious name certificate with the recorder of each county where a place of business is located if the partnership name does not contain the surnames of all partners. IC 23-15-1-1.

LIMITED LIABILITY COMPANY LAWS. Indiana Business Flexibility Act. IC 23-18-1-1 et seq.

Formation of LLC: One or more persons may form an LLC by filing articles of organization with the Secretary of State. See IC 23-18-2-4 for the article of organization content requirements.

General LLC Requirements: May have one or more members. May conduct any lawful business.

Management of LLC: Vested in members unless managers are provided for in articles of organization.

New or Substituted Members: Requires written consent of all members unless otherwise provided in operating agreement.

Conversion Statutes: Merger statute. IC 23-18-7-1 et seq. No partnership conversion statute.

CORPORATION LAWS. Indiana Business Corporation Law (based on Revised Model Business Corporation Act). IC 23-1-17-1 et seq.

Corporate Name: Must contain the word "corporation," "incorporated," "company," or "limited" or an abbreviation thereof, and must be distinguishable on the records of the Secretary of State from the name of any other corporation. Name may be reserved for a renewable period of 120 days. IC 23-1-23-1, 2.

Incorporators: One or more individuals or entities. IC 23-1-21-1.

Articles of Incorporation:

Contents: See IC 23-1-21-2 for required and optional article of incorporation content requirements.

Filing and Recording: An original and one copy of the articles of incorporation must be filed with the Secretary of State and the filing fee paid. Corporate existence begins when the articles of incorporation are accepted for filing. IC 23-1-18-1, 23-1-21-3.

Amendment: Requires a majority of the votes entitled to be cast unless a statute, the articles of incorporation, or the board of directors require a greater vote. The board of directors can make certain minor amendments without shareholder approval. IC 23-1-38-2, 3.

Organizational Meeting: Held after incorporation by initial board of directors if named in articles of incorporation. Otherwise held after the incorporation by incorporators, who may act without meeting if all incorporators sign a written consent to the action. IC 23-1-21-5.

Bylaws: Initial bylaws adopted by the incorporators or board of directors. IC 23-1-21-6. May be amended only by the board of directors unless the articles of incorporation provide otherwise. IC 23-1-39-1.

Action Without Meeting: Shareholders may act without meeting if all shareholders entitled to vote sign a written consent to the action. IC 23-1-29-4. Unless the articles of incorporation or bylaws provide otherwise, the board of directors may meet via conference telephone or similar communications equipment and may act without meeting if all directors sign a written consent to the action. IC 23-1-34-1, 2.

Stock Certificates: Must be signed by two officers (one officer if the corporation has only one officer) designated in bylaws or by board of directors. Shares may be issued without a certificate unless otherwise provided in articles of incorporation or bylaws. IC 23-1-26-6, 7.

Consideration For Stock: May consist of any tangible or intangible property or benefit to the corporation, including cash, promissory notes, services performed or to be performed, and other securities of the corporation. Shares issued for promissory notes or future services may be placed in escrow or otherwise restricted pending payment of note or performance of services. IC 23-1-26-2(b). If stock is issued for promissory notes or future services, a written report to the shareholders must be made. IC 23-1-53-2(b).

Stock Transfer Restrictions: May be imposed by the articles of incorporation, bylaws, or a shareholders' agreement. A restriction must be conspicuously noted on the stock certificate to be enforceable against a person without notice of the restriction. IC 23-1-26-8.

Cumulative Voting: Not permitted unless provided for in the articles of incorporation and 48-hour prior notice is given. IC 23-1-30-9.

Preemptive Rights: Do not exist unless contained in the articles of incorporation. IC 23-1-27-1.

Acts Requiring Shareholder Approval: Unless a statute, the articles of incorporation, or the board of directors require a greater vote, a majority of the votes entitled to be cast is required for a merger or share exchange, for the sale or disposition of all or substantially all of the corporate assets not in the usual course of business, for voluntary dissolution, and for most amendments to the articles of incorporation (see above). IC 23-1-40-3, 23-1-41-2, 23-1-45-2, 23-1-38-3.

Board of Directors: May consist of one or more individuals, with number specified in articles of incorporation or bylaws. IC 23-1-33-3.

Officers: Those described in the bylaws or appointed by the board of directors in accordance with the bylaws. No specific officers required, but must have at least one officer. The same person may simultaneously hold more than one office in the corporation. IC 23-1-36-1.

Foreign Corporations: Must obtain a certificate of authority from the Secretary of State before transacting business in Indiana. The statute contains a nonexclusive list of activities that do not constitute transacting business in the state. The penalties for transacting business without a certificate of authority include nonaccess to state courts and a civil penalty of up to $10,000. IC 23-1-49-1, 2.

Close Corporation Laws: Has no close corporation code. A corporation with 50 or fewer shareholders may dispense with or limit the authority of the board of directors and is subject to a special rule on demands for shareholders' meeting. IC 23-1-33-1(c), 23-1-29-2(b).

Periodic Reports: Domestic and authorized foreign corporations must file an annual report with the Secretary of State on prescribed forms by the end of its anniversary calendar quarter and pay an annual report fee to remain in good standing. IC 23-1-53-3.

STATE FILING OFFICIAL. Secretary of State, Corporation Division, 302 West Washington, Room E-018, Indianapolis, IN 46204 (317-232-6576).

Fees:

Filing Articles of Incorporation - $90	Name Reservation - $20	Application for Certificate of Authority - $90
Amending Articles of Incorporation - $30	Biennial Report of Corp. or LLC - $30	Other Corp. Fees - See IC 23-1-18-3.
Filing LLC Articles of Organization - $90	LLP Registration Fee - $90	Other LLC Fees - See IC 23-18-12-3.

SUMMARY OF IOWA BUSINESS ORGANIZATION LAWS

PARTNERSHIP LAWS.

General Partnerships: Uniform Partnership Act adopted. CI 486.1 et seq.

Limited Partnerships: Revised Uniform Limited Partnership Act adopted. CI 487.101 et seq.

Limited Liability Partnerships: Registered limited liability partnerships provided for. CI 486.44 et seq.

Name Registration: Must file a fictitious name statement with the recorder of each county where business is conducted if the partnership name does not contain the surnames of all partners. CI 547.1.

LIMITED LIABILITY COMPANY LAWS. Iowa Limited Liability Company Act. CI 490A.100 et seq.

Formation of LLC: One or more persons may form an LLC by filing articles of organization with the Secretary of State. See CI 490A.303 for the article of organization content requirements.

General LLC Requirements: May have one or more members. May conduct any lawful business. There are special requirements for professional LLCs (CI 490A.1501 et seq.).

Management of LLC: Vested in members unless otherwise provided in articles of organization or operating agreement.

New or Substituted Members: Admission to LLC requires written consent of all members unless otherwise provided in articles of organization or operating agreement. CI 490A-306.

Conversion Statutes: Merger statute. CI 490A.1201 et seq. Partnership conversion statute. CI 490A-304.

CORPORATION LAWS. Iowa Business Corporation Act (based on Revised Model Business Corporation Act). CI 490.101 et seq.

Corporate Name: Must include the word "corporation," "company," "incorporated," or "limited" or a listed abbreviation thereof, and must be distinguishable on the records of the Secretary of State from the names of other corporations. Name may be reserved for 120 days. The availability of a name may be informally checked with the Secretary of State without fee. CI 490.401, 402.

Incorporators: One or more individuals or entities. CI 490.201.

Articles of Incorporation:

Contents: See CI 490.202 for required and optional article of incorporation content requirements.

Filing and Recording: A signed copy of the articles of incorporation must be filed with the Secretary of State and the filing fee paid. Corporate existence begins when the articles of incorporation are accepted for filing. CI 490.120, 203.

Amendment: Requires a majority of the votes entitled to be cast unless a statute, the articles of incorporation, or the board of directors require a greater vote. The board of directors may make certain minor amendments without shareholder approval, unless the articles of incorporation provide otherwise. CI 490.1002, 1003.

Organizational Meeting: Held after incorporation by the initial board of directors if named in the articles of incorporation. Otherwise held after incorporation by the incorporators, who may act without meeting if all incorporators sign a written consent to the action. CI 490.205.

Bylaws: Initial bylaws adopted by the board of directors or the incorporators. May be amended by the shareholders and by the board of directors unless that power is reserved to the shareholders in the articles of incorporation or unless a shareholder amendment prohibits its subsequent amendment by the board of directors. CI 490.206, 1020.

Action Without Meeting: Unless the articles of incorporation provide otherwise, shareholders may act without meeting if the holders of 90% of the shares entitled to vote sign a written consent to the action. CI 490.704. Unless the articles of incorporation or bylaws provide otherwise, the board of directors may meet via conference telephone or similar communications equipment and may act without meeting if all directors sign a written consent to the action. CI 490.820, 821.

Stock Certificates: Must be signed by two officers designated in the bylaws or by the board of directors. Shares may be issued without a certificate unless the articles of incorporation or bylaws provide otherwise. CI 490.625, 626.

Consideration For Stock: May consist of any tangible or intangible property or benefit to the corporation, including cash, promissory notes, services performed or to be performed or other securities of the corporation. Shares issued for promissory notes or future services or benefits may be restricted or placed in escrow until payment or performance has been received. CI 490.621.

Stock Transfer Restrictions: May be imposed by the articles of incorporation, bylaws, or a shareholders' agreement. A restriction must be conspicuously noted on the stock certificate to be enforceable against a person without notice of the restriction. CI 490.627.

Cumulative Voting: Permitted only if provided for in the articles of incorporation and prior notice is given. CI 490.728.

Preemptive Rights: Do not exist unless provided for in the articles of incorporation. CI 490.630.

Acts Requiring Shareholder Approval: Unless a statute, the articles of incorporation, or the board of directors require a greater vote, a majority of the votes entitled to be cast is required for a merger or share exchange, for the sale of all of the corporate assets not in the usual course of business, for voluntary dissolution, and for most amendments to the articles of incorporation. CI 490.1103, 1202, 1402, 1003.

Board of Directors: May consist of one or more individuals, with the number specified in the articles of incorporation or bylaws. CI 490.803.

Officers: Those described in the bylaws or appointed by the board of directors in accordance with the bylaws. No specific officers required. The same person may simultaneously hold more than one office in the corporation. CI 490.840.

Foreign Corporations: Must obtain a certificate of authority from the Secretary of State before transacting business in Iowa. The statute contains a nonexclusive list of activities that do not constitute transacting business in the state. The penalties for transacting business without a certificate of authority include nonaccess to state courts and a civil penalty of up to $1000. CI 490.1501, 1502.

Close Corporation Laws: Has no close corporation code. A corporation with 50 or fewer shareholders may in its articles of incorporation dispense with or limit the authority of the board of directors. CI 490.801.

Periodic Reports: Domestic and authorized foreign corporations must file a biennial report with the Secretary of State and pay a biennial report fee to remain in good standing. CI 490.1622.

STATE FILING OFFICIAL. Secretary of State, Corp. Division, Hoover Bldg., Des Moines, IA 50319 (Telephone: 515-281-5204).

Fees:
- Filing Articles of Incorporation - $50
- Amending Articles of Incorporation - $50
- Filing LLC Articles of Organization - $50
- Filing LLP Registration - $100
- Name Reservation - $10
- Application for Certificate of Authority - $100
- Other LLC Fees - See CI 490A-124.
- Other Corp. Fees - See CI 490.122.

SUMMARY OF KANSAS BUSINESS ORGANIZATION LAWS

PARTNERSHIP LAWS.

General Partnerships: Uniform Partnership Act adopted. KSA 56-301 et seq.
Limited Partnerships: Revised Uniform Limited Partnership Act adopted. KSA 56-la101 et seq.
Limited Liability Partnerships: Registered limited liability partnerships provided for. KSA 56-345.
Name Registration: Not required.

LIMITED LIABILITY COMPANY LAWS. Kansas Limited Liability Company Act. KSA 17-7601 et seq.

Formation of LLC: Any person may form an LLC by filing articles of organization with the Secretary of State. See KSA 17-7607 for the article of organization content requirements.
General LLC Requirements: Must have two or more members. May conduct any lawful business. Must qualify as limited liability agricultural company to own or lease agricultural land. KSA 17-5904.
Management of LLC: Vested in members unless otherwise provided in articles of organization or operating agreement.
New or Substituted Members: Requires consent of all members unless operating agreement provides otherwise. KSA 17-7618.
Conversion Statutes: Merger or consolidation statute. KSA 17-7650. Partnership conversion statute. KSA 17-7654.

CORPORATION LAWS. Kansas General Corporate Code (Model Business Corporation Acts not adopted). KSA 17-6001 et seq.

Corporate Name: Must contain one of the following words: association, church, college, company (or co.), corporation (or corp.), club, foundation, fund, incorporated (or inc.), institute, society, union, syndicate, or limited (or ltd.). Must be distinguishable on the records of the Secretary of State from the name of any other corporation, partnership, or limited liability company. Name may be reserved for 120 days and availability of name may be checked with Secretary of State by letter or telephone. KSA 17-6002(a)(1), 7402.
Incorporators: One or more persons, partnerships, corporations or associations. KSA 17-6001(a).
Articles of Incorporation:
Contents: See KSA 17-6002 for required and optional article of incorporation content requirements.
Filing and Recording: An original and one copy of the articles of incorporation must be filed with the Secretary of State and the filing fee and franchise tax paid. A certified copy of the articles of incorporation must be recorded with the register of deeds in the county of the corporation's registered office. Corporate existence begins when the articles of incorporation are accepted for filing if they are duly recorded with the register of deeds. Documents may be filed by fax. KSA 17-6003, 6006, 6003a.
Amendment: Requires a majority vote of the outstanding shares entitled to vote, unless the articles of incorporation require a greater vote. KSA 17-6602, 6002(4).
Organizational Meeting: Held after incorporation by the incorporators or by the initial board of directors if named in the articles of incorporation. The incorporators or directors may act without meeting if they all sign a written consent to the action. KSA 17-6008.
Bylaws: Initial bylaws adopted by the incorporators or the board of directors. May be amended by the shareholders and, if so provided in the articles of incorporation, by the board of directors. KSA 17-6009.
Action Without Meeting: Unless restricted by the articles of incorporation or bylaws, the board of directors may act without meeting if all directors sign a written consent to the action and may meet via conference telephone or similar communications equipment. KSA 17-6301. Shareholders may act without meeting if all shareholders entitled to vote sign a written consent to the action. KSA 17-6518.
Stock Certificates: Must be signed by chairman or vice chairman of board, president, or vice president, and by treasurer, secretary, or assistant thereof. Shares may be issued without a certificate, but a shareholder is entitled to a certificate upon demand. KSA 17-6408.
Consideration For Stock: May consist of cash, services rendered, real or personal property, or leases of real property. KSA 17-6402.
Stock Transfer Restrictions: May be imposed by the articles of incorporation, bylaws, or a shareholders' agreement. A restriction must be conspicuously noted on the stock certificate to be enforceable against a person without knowledge of the restriction. KSA 17-6426.
Cumulative Voting: Not permitted unless provided for in the articles of incorporation. KSA 17-6504.
Preemptive Rights: Do not exist unless contained in the articles of incorporation. KSA 17-6407.
Acts Requiring Shareholder Approval: Unless the articles of incorporation require a greater vote, a majority vote of the outstanding shares entitled to vote is required for a merger or consolidation, for the sale or disposition of all or substantially all of the corporate assets, for voluntary dissolution, and to amend the articles of incorporation. KSA 17-6701, 6801, 6804, 6602, 6002(4).
Board of Directors: May consist of one or more persons with the number specified in the articles of incorporation or bylaws. KSA 17-6301.
Officers: Those described or provided for in the bylaws. No specific officers required. Any number of offices may be held by the same person unless the articles of incorporation or bylaws provide otherwise. KSA 17-6302.
Foreign Corporations: Must obtain certificate of authority from Secretary of State to do business in Kansas (see KSA 17-7303 for definition of "doing business in Kansas"). The penalties for doing business without certificate of authority include nonaccess to state courts and liability for all fees, taxes and penalties that would have accrued had a certificate of authority been issued. KSA 17-7301, 7307, 7505.
Close Corporation Laws: Has Close Corporation Code. KSA 17-7201-7216. A statutory close corporation must have 30 or fewer shareholders and it must make no public offering of its stock.
Periodic Reports: Domestic and foreign corporations doing business in Kansas must file an annual report with the Secretary of State by the due date of its federal income tax return and pay an annual franchise tax to remain in good standing. KSA 17-7503, 7505.

STATE FILING OFFICIAL. Secretary of State, State Capitol, Topeka, KS 66612 (Telephone: 913-296-2236).

Fees: Filing Articles of Incorporation - $75 Application for Certificate of Authority - $75 + $20 for certificate. Name Reservation - $20
Amending Articles of Incorporation - $20
Other Corp. Fees - See KSA 17-7502 et seq.
Filing LLC Articles of Organization - $150
Other LLC Fees - See KSA 17-7646 et seq.
Filing LLP Registration Application - $75 per partner.

SUMMARY OF KENTUCKY BUSINESS ORGANIZATION LAWS

PARTNERSHIP LAWS

General Partnerships: Uniform Partnership Act adopted. KRS 362.150 et seq.

Limited Partnerships: Revised Uniform Limited Partnership Act adopted. KRS 362.401 et seq.

Limited Liability Partnerships: Registered limited liability partnerships provided for. KRS 362.555 et seq.

Name Registration: If partnership name does not contain the real name of at least one partner, an assumed name certificate must be filed with the Secretary of State with a copy provided for each county where partnership business is conducted. KRS 365.015.

LIMITED LIABILITY COMPANY LAWS. Kentucky Limited Liability Company Act. KRS 275.001 et seq.

Formation of LLC: One or more persons may form an LLC by filing articles of organization with Secretary of State. See KRS 275.025 for article of organization content requirements.

General LLC Requirements: Must have two or more members. May conduct any lawful business, including rendering professional services.

Management of LLC: Vested in members unless vested in manager(s) by articles of organization.

New or Substituted Members: Admission to LLC requires written consent of all members unless otherwise provided in operating agreement.

Conversion Statutes: Partnership conversion statute. KRS 275.370. Merger statute. KRS 275.345 et seq.

CORPORATION LAWS. Kentucky Business Corporation Act (based on Revised Model Business Corporation Act). KRS chap. 271B.

Corporate Name: Must contain the word "corporation," "incorporated," "company," or "limited," or an abbreviation thereof and must be distinguishable from the names of other corporations, registered partnerships, and fictitious names on file. Name may be reserved for 120 days and name availability may be checked with Secretary of State by telephone. KRS 271B.4-010, 4-020.

Incorporators: One or more individuals or entities. KRS 271B.2-010.

Articles of Incorporation:

Contents: See KRS 271B.2-020 for required and optional article of incorporation content requirements.

Filing and Recording: An original and two copies of the articles of incorporation must be filed with the Secretary of State and the filing fee and incorporation tax paid. One filed copy must be recorded with the clerk of the county of the corporation's registered office. Corporate existence begins when the articles of incorporation are accepted for filing. KRS 271B.1-200(9), (10), 271B.2-030, 136.060.

Amendment: Requires a majority of the votes entitled to be cast unless a statute, the board of directors or the articles of incorporation require a greater vote. The board of directors may make some minor amendments without shareholder approval. KRS 271B.10-020, 030.

Organizational Meeting: Held after incorporation by the initial board of directors if named in the articles of incorporation. Otherwise held after incorporation by the incorporators, who may act without meeting if all incorporators sign a written consent thereto. KRS 271B.2-050.

Bylaws: Initial bylaws adopted by the incorporators or board of directors. May be amended by the shareholders and by the board of directors unless that power is reserved to the shareholders in the articles of incorporation or unless a shareholder amendment precludes its subsequent amendment by the board of directors. KRS 271B.2-060, 10-200.

Action Without Meeting: Unless the articles of incorporation provide otherwise, shareholders may act without meeting if all shareholders entitled to vote sign a written consent to the action, or if the articles of incorporation so provide and except for the election of directors, if 80% of the shareholders entitled to vote sign a written consent to the action and the required notice is given. KRS 271B.7-040. Unless the articles of incorporation or bylaws provide otherwise, the board of directors may meet via conference telephone or similar communications equipment and may act without meeting if all directors sign a written consent to the action. KRS 271B.8-200, 210.

Stock Certificates: Must be signed by two officers designated in the bylaws or by the board of directors. Shares may be issued without a certificate unless the articles of incorporation or bylaws provide otherwise. KRS 271B.6-250, 260.

Consideration For Stock: May consist of money paid, labor done, or property actually received. KRS 271B.6-210

Stock Transfer Restrictions: May be imposed by the articles of incorporation, bylaws or a shareholders' agreement. A restriction must be conspicuously noted on the stock certificate to be enforceable against a person without knowledge of the restriction. KRS 271B.6-270.

Cumulative Voting: Must be permitted. KRS 271B.7-280.

Preemptive Rights: Do not exist (for corps. formed after January 1, 1989) unless contained in the articles of incorporation. KRS 271B.6-300.

Acts Requiring Shareholder Approval: Unless a statute, the articles of incorporation or the board of directors require a greater vote, a majority of the votes entitled to be cast is required for a merger or share exchange, for the sale or disposition of all or substantially all of the corporate assets not in the usual course of business, for voluntary dissolution, and for most amendments to the articles of incorporation (see above). KRS 271B.11-030, 12-020, 14-020, 10.030.

Board of Directors: May consist of one or more individuals, with number specified in bylaws or articles of incorporation. KRS 271B.8-030.

Officers: Those described in the bylaws or appointed by the board of directors in accordance with the bylaws. No specific officers required. The same person may simultaneously hold more than one office in the corporation. KRS 271B.8-400.

Foreign Corporations: Must obtain a certificate of authority from the Secretary of State before transacting business in Kentucky. The statute contains a nonexclusive list of activities that do not constitute transacting business in the state. The penalties for transacting business without a certificate of authority include nonaccess to state courts and a civil penalty of $2 per day not to exceed $500 per year. KRS 271B.15-010, 020.

Close Corporation Laws: Has no Close Corporation Code. A corporation with 50 or fewer shareholders may in its articles of incorporation dispense with or limit the authority of the board of directors. KRS 271B.8-010.

Periodic Reports: Domestic and authorized foreign corporations must file an annual report with the Secretary of State by June 30 of each year and pay annual report fee and an annual license tax to remain in good standing. KRS 271B.16-220, 136.070.

STATE FILING OFFICIAL. Secretary of State, New Capitol Building, Frankfurt, KY 40601 (Telephone: 502-564-7330).

Fees: Filing Articles of Incorporation - $40 plus an incorporation tax based on capitalization ($10 minimum). Annual Report of Corp. or LLC - $15

Application for Certificate of Authority - $90. Amending Articles of Incorporation - $40 Other Corp. Fees - See KRS 271B.1-220.

Filing LLC Articles of Organization - $40 Corp. or LLC Name Reservation - $15 Other LLC Fees - See KRS 275-055.

Filing LLP Registration Statement - $200

SUMMARY OF LOUISIANA BUSINESS ORGANIZATION LAWS

PARTNERSHIP LAWS.

General Partnerships: Uniform Partnership Act not adopted. See LSA-CC 2801 et seq. for general partnership laws.

Limited Partnerships: Uniform Limited Partnership Acts not adopted. See LSA-CC 2837 et seq. for limited partnership laws.

Limited Liability Partnerships: Registered limited liability partnerships provided for. LSA-RS 9:3431 et seq.

Name Registration: Must register a partnership agreement with the Secretary of State. LSA-RS 9-3402. Must file a fictitious name certificate with the register of conveyances or the clerk of the court if the partnership name does not contain the names of all partners. LSA-RS 51-281.

LIMITED LIABILITY COMPANY LAWS. Limited Liability Company Law. LSA-RS 12:1301 et seq.

Formation of LLC: One or more persons may organize an LLC by filing articles of organization and initial report with the Secretary of State. See LSA-RS 12:1305 for the article of organization and initial report content requirements.

General LLC Requirements: May have one or more members. May conduct any lawful business except banking, insurance underwriting, or operating homesteads or building and loan associations.

Management of LLC: Vested in members unless otherwise provided in articles of organization.

New or Substituted Members: Admission to LLC requires written consent of all members unless otherwise provided in articles of organization or operating agreement.

Conversion Statutes: Merger or consolidation statute. LSA-RS 12:1357 et seq. No partnership conversion statute.

CORPORATION LAWS. Business Corporation Law (Model Business Corporation Acts not adopted). LSA-RS 12-1 et seq.

Corporate Name: Must contain the word "corporation," "incorporated," "limited," or "company" (not preceded by "and") or an abbreviation thereof, and must not be deceptively similar to the name of any other corporation, limited liability company, or trade name. Name may be reserved for 60 days. Availability of name may be checked with Secretary of State by letter or telephone. LSA-RS 12-23.

Incorporators: One or more natural or artificial persons capable of contracting. LSA-RS 12-21.

Articles of Incorporation:

Contents: See LSA-RS 12-24 for required and optional article of incorporation content requirements.

Filing and Recording: The articles of incorporation must be filed with the Secretary of State, together with an initial report and the registered agent's affidavit of acceptance. Within 30 days thereafter a copy of the certificate of incorporation must be filed with the recorder of mortgages in the parish of the corporation's registered office. Corporate existence begins when a certificate of incorporation is issued by the Secretary of State. LSA-RS 12-25, 101.

Amendment: Requires a two-thirds vote of the shares present and entitled to vote unless the articles of incorporation require a different vote of not less than a majority. LSA-RS 12-31.

Organizational Meeting: No statutory provisions.

Minimum Capitalization Requirement: No statutory requirement, but may be required in the articles of incorporation. LSA-RS 12-26.

Bylaws: May be adopted and amended by the board of directors, subject to the power of the shareholders to change or repeal them, unless the articles of incorporation provide otherwise. LSA-RS 12-28.

Action Without Meeting: Shareholders may act without meeting if all shareholders entitled to vote sign a written consent to the action or, if the articles so provide, if the consent is signed by shareholders sufficient to carry the action at a meeting and prompt notice is given to all shareholders. LSA-RS 12-76. Unless otherwise provided in the articles of incorporation or bylaws, the board of directors may act without meeting if all directors sign a written consent to the action, and may meet via conference telephone or similar communications equipment if the bylaws so provide. LSA-RS 12-81.

Stock Certificates: Must be signed by the president and the secretary or by the officers specified in the articles of incorporation or bylaws. LSA-RS 12-57. No provisions for issuing shares without a certificate.

Consideration For Stock: May consist of cash, property, or services actually rendered, but not notes or uncertified checks. LSA-RS 12-52.

Stock Transfer Restrictions: May be contained in the articles of incorporation, the bylaws, or a shareholders' agreement. Must be set forth, summarized, or referred to on the stock certificate to be enforceable. LSA-RS 12-24(c)(5), 28, 29, 57.

Cumulative Voting: Not permitted unless provided for in the articles of incorporation. LSA-RS 12-75.

Preemptive Rights: Do not exist unless contained in the articles of incorporation. LSA-RS 12-72.

Acts Requiring Shareholder Approval: Unless the articles of incorporation require a different vote of not less than a majority, a two-thirds vote of the voting shares is required for a merger, consolidation or share exchange, for the sale or disposition of all or substantially all of the assets of a solvent corporation, and to amend the articles of incorporation. LSA-RS 12-112, 121, 31. Unless the articles of incorporation require a greater vote, a majority vote of the voting shares is required for voluntary dissolution. LSA-RS 12-142.

Board of Directors: Must consist of three or more directors, except that there need not be more directors than shareholders. The number of directors is the number listed in the initial report unless the articles of incorporation or bylaws specify a different number. LSA-RS 12-81.

Officers: Must have president, secretary, and treasurer. The bylaws may provide for a vice president and other officers. The same person may hold any two offices, but may not sign certificates and other instruments in a dual capacity. LSA-RS 12-82.

Foreign Corporations: Must obtain a certificate of authority from the Secretary of State to transact business in Louisiana. The statute contains a nonexclusive list of activities that do not constitute transacting business in the state. The penalties for transacting business without a certificate of authority include nonaccess to state courts and liability for all fees, taxes, and penalties that would have been assessed had a certificate of authority been issued. LSA-RS 12-301, 302, 314.

Close Corporation Laws: None.

Periodic Reports: Domestic and authorized foreign corporations must file an annual report with the Secretary of State by the anniversary date of its incorporation and pay an annual report fee and an annual franchise tax to remain in good standing. LSA-RS 12-102, 309, 47-601, 609.

STATE FILING OFFICIAL. Secretary of State, 3851 Essen Lane, Baton Rouge, LA 70809 (Telephone: 504-925-4704).

Fees:
Filing Articles of Incorporation - $50
Amending Articles of Incorporation - $50
Filing LLC Articles of Organization - $60
Filing LLP Registration Application - $100
Application for Certificate of Authority - $50
Name Reservation - $5
Annual Report - $12
Other Corp. Fees - See LSA-RS 12-171.
Other LLC Fees - See LSA-RS 12:1364.

SUMMARY OF MAINE BUSINESS ORGANIZATION LAWS

PARTNERSHIP LAWS.

General Partnerships: Uniform Partnership Act adopted. MRSA 31-281 et seq.
Limited Partnerships: Revised Uniform Limited Partnership Act adopted. MRSA 31-401 et seq.
Limited Liability Partnerships: Maine Limited Liability Partnership Act. MRSA 31-801 et seq.
Name Registration: Mercantile partnership must file name certificate with city clerk. MRSA 31-1.

LIMITED LIABILITY COMPANY LAWS. Maine Limited Liability Company Act. MRSA 31-601 et seq.

Formation of LLC: One or more persons may form an LLC by filing articles of organization with the Secretary of State. See MRSA 31-622 for the article of organization content requirements.
General LLC Requirements: May have one or more members. May conduct any lawful business.
Management of LLC: Vested in members unless vested in manager(s) by articles of organization.
New or Substituted Members: Consent of all members required unless operating agreement or articles of organization provide otherwise.
Conversion Statutes: Merger or consolidation statute. MRSA 31-741 et seq. No partnership conversion statute.

CORPORATION LAWS. Maine Business Corporation Act (based on Model Business Corporation Act). MRSA 13A-101 et seq.

Corporate Name: No required words. May not be the same as or deceptively similar to the name of any other corporation or any registered trade or service mark. May reserve name for 10 days or for 120 days. Secretary of State will conduct a preliminary name search upon request. MRSA 13A-301, 302.
Incorporators: One or more natural persons or corporations. MRSA 13A-402.
Articles of Incorporation:
Contents: See MRSA 13A-403, 404 for required and optional article of incorporation content requirements.
Filing and Recording: An original signed copy of the articles of incorporation must be filed with the Secretary of State and the filing fee and organization tax paid. Corporate existence begins when the articles of incorporation are accepted for filing. MRSA 13A-405, 406.
Amendment: Requires a majority vote of the outstanding shares entitled to vote unless the articles of incorporation require a greater vote. The board of directors or the clerk may make certain minor amendments without shareholder approval. MRSA 13A-805, 804.
Organizational Meeting: Held after incorporation by the incorporators or by the initial board of directors if named in the articles of incorporation. MRSA 13A-407.
Bylaws: Unless articles of incorporation provide otherwise, initial bylaws must be adopted by initial board of directors or by incorporators if initial directors not named in articles. May be amended by board of directors and by shareholders unless articles of incorporation provide otherwise. Board of directors may not amend a shareholder-adopted bylaw for two years. MRSA 13A-601.
Action Without Meeting: The shareholders may act without meeting if all shareholders entitled to vote sign a written consent to the action. MRSA 13A-620. Unless the articles of incorporation or bylaws provide otherwise, the board of directors may meet via conference telephone or similar communications equipment and may act without meeting if all directors sign a written consent to the action. MRSA 13A-708, 711.
Stock Certificates: Must be signed by any two of the following: president, vice president, clerk, secretary, assistant secretary, or two other officers designated in the bylaws. MRSA 13A-511. No provisions for issuing shares without a certificate.
Consideration For Stock: May consist of money, tangible or intangible property, or labor or services actually performed for the corporation. May not consist of promissory notes or future services. MRSA 13A-507.
Stock Transfer Restrictions: May be contained in the articles of incorporation, bylaws, or a shareholders' agreement. A restriction must be conspicuously noted on the stock certificate to be enforceable against a person without knowledge of the restriction. MRSA 13A-616.
Cumulative Voting: Not permitted unless provided for in the articles of incorporation and prior notice is given. MRSA 13A-622.
Preemptive Rights: Exist (with exceptions) unless denied or limited in the articles of incorporation. MRSA 13A-623.
Acts Requiring Shareholder Approval: Unless the articles of incorporation require a greater vote, a majority vote of the shares entitled to vote is required for a merger or consolidation, for the sale of all or substantially all of the corporate assets not in the usual course of business, and for most amendments to the articles of incorporation. MRSA 13A-902, 1003, 805. Unless the articles of incorporation require a greater vote, a two-thirds vote of the shares entitled to vote is required for a voluntary dissolution. MRSA 13A-1103.
Board of Directors: Must consist of three or more directors, except that there need not be more directors than shareholders. The number of directors must be specified in the articles of incorporation. MRSA 13A-703.
Officers: Must have president, treasurer, and clerk. May have a vice president and other officers if provided for in the bylaws or appointed by the board of directors. The same person may hold any two or more offices in the corporation. MRSA 13A-714.
Foreign Corporations: Must be authorized by the Secretary of State to do business in Maine. The statute contains a nonexclusive list of activities that do not constitute doing business in the state. The penalties for doing business without authorization include nonaccess to state courts and liability for all fees, penalties and taxes that would have been imposed if authority to do business had been granted plus a $25 per day penalty. MRSA 13A-1201, 1214.
Close Corporation Laws: Has no close corporation code. A corporation with 20 or fewer shareholders may, in its articles of incorporation, dispense with the board of directors and permit the shareholders to manage the corporation. MRSA 13A-701.
Periodic Reports: Domestic and authorized foreign corporations must file an annual report with the Secretary of State by a date specified by the Secretary of State and pay an annual report fee to remain in good standing. MRSA 13A-1301.

STATE FILING OFFICIAL. Secretary of State, Corporation Bureau, State House Station 101, Augusta, ME 04333 (207-287-3676).

Fees: Filing Articles of Incorporation - $75 plus organization tax based on capitalization ($30 minimum).

Amending Articles of Incorporation - $35	Name Reservation - $20	Other Corp. Fees - See MRSA 13A-1401.
Filing LLC Articles of Organization - $250	Corp. or LLC Annual Report - $60	Other LLC Fees - See MRSA 31-751.
Filing LLP Certificate - $250	Other LLP Fees - See MRSA 31-871.	

SUMMARY OF MARYLAND BUSINESS ORGANIZATION LAWS

PARTNERSHIP LAWS.

General Partnerships: Maryland Revised Uniform Partnership Act adopted. ACM - C&A 9A-101 et seq.
Limited Partnerships: Revised Uniform Limited Partnership Act adopted. ACM - C&A 10-101 et seq.
Limited Liability Partnerships: Registered LLPs for general & limited partnerships provided for. ACM - C&A 9A-1001 et seq.
Name Registration: Must file a certificate with the state filing official (see below) if the partnership is engaged in the mercantile, trading or manufacturing business or if the partnership name does not contain the names of all partners. ACM - C&A 1-406.

LIMITED LIABILITY COMPANY LAWS. Maryland Limited Liability Company Act. ACM - C&A 4A-101 et seq.

Formation of LLC: A person may form an LLC by filing articles of organization with the state filing official. See ACM - C&A 4A-204 for the article of organization content requirements.
General LLC Requirements: May have one or more members. May conduct any lawful business except insurance. Professional LLCs authorized for listed professionals.
Management of LLC: Controlled by operating agreement. ACM - C&A 4A-402.
New or Substituted Members: Admission to LLC requires consent of all members unless otherwise provided in the operating agreement.
Conversion Statutes: Merger statute. ACM - C&A 4A-701 et seq. Partnership and Sole Proprietorship conversion statutes. ACM - C&A 4A-211, 212.

CORPORATION LAWS. General Corporation Law (Model Business Corporation Acts not adopted). ACM - C&A 2-101 et seq.

Corporate Name: Must contain the word "corporation," "company," "incorporation," or "limited" or an abbreviation thereof. May not be same as or misleadingly similar to the name of any other corporation, limited partnership, or limited liability company. Name may be reserved for 30 days. Availability of name may be checked with state filing official by letter or telephone. ACM - C&A 2-106, 107.
Incorporators: One or more individuals of age 18 or more. ACM - C&A 2-102.
Articles of Incorporation:
Contents: See ACM - C&A 2-104, 105 for required and optional article of incorporation content requirements.
Filing and Recording: The articles of incorporation must be filed with, and the filing fee and the organization and capitalization fee paid to, the state filing official, who transmits them to the clerk of the court in the county of the corporation's principal office. Corporate existence begins when the articles of incorporation are accepted for filing. ACM - C&A 2-102.
Amendment: Requires a two-thirds vote of all shares entitled to vote unless the articles of incorporation require a different vote of not less than a majority. The board of directors may make certain amendments without shareholder approval. ACM - C&A 2-604, 605, 104.
Organizational Meeting: Held after incorporation by the initial board of directors. ACM - C&A 2-109.
Bylaws: Initial bylaws adopted by initial board of directors. May be amended by shareholders. May also be amended by board of directors if articles of incorporation or bylaws so provide. ACM - C&A 2-109.
Action Without Meeting: The shareholders and the board of directors may act without meeting if all shareholders or directors, as the case may be, sign a written consent to the action. ACM - C&A 2-408, 505. Unless restricted by the articles of incorporation or bylaws, the board of directors may meet via conference telephone or similar communications equipment. ACM - C&A 2-409(d).
Stock Certificates: Must be signed by chairman of board, president, or vice president and by secretary, treasurer, or assistant of either. Shares may be issued without a certificate unless the articles of incorporation or bylaws provide otherwise. ACM - C&A 2-212, 210.
Consideration For Stock: May consist of money, tangible or intangible property, labor or services actually performed for the corporation, promissory notes, or contracts for future labor or services. ACM - C&A 2-206.
Stock Transfer Restrictions: May be contained in the articles and must be noted on the stock certificate. ACM - C&A 2-104(b)(2), 211(d).
Cumulative Voting: Permitted if authorized in the articles of incorporation. ACM - C&A 2-104(b)(7), 2-404(c).
Preemptive Rights: Do not exist unless contained in the articles of incorporation. ACM - C&A 2-205.
Acts Requiring Shareholder Approval: Unless the articles of incorporation provide for a different vote of not less than a majority, a two-thirds vote of all shares entitled to vote is required for a merger, consolidation, or share exchange, for the sale or transfer of all or substantially all of the corporate assets not in the usual course of business, for voluntary dissolution, and for most amendments to the articles of incorporation (see above). ACM - C&A 3-105, 3-403, 2-604, 2-102.
Board of Directors: Must consist of three or more directors, except that there need not be more directors than shareholders. The number of directors may be specified in the articles of incorporation or bylaws. ACM - C&A 2-402, 403.
Officers: Must have president, secretary, and treasurer. The bylaws may provide for other officers and may provide that the same person may hold any two or more offices except the offices of president and vice president. ACM - C&A 2-412, 415.
Foreign Corporations: Must qualify with the state filing official to do intrastate business in Maryland. Unless qualified to do intrastate business, must register with state filing official before doing interstate or foreign business by certifying name and address of local registered agent. Statute contains lists of activities that do not constitute doing intrastate business and that do not constitute doing interstate or foreign business. Penalties for failing to register or qualify include nonaccess to state courts, a $200 corporate fine, and individual fines of up to $1,000 for agents of foreign corporations (also a misdemeanor offense). ACM - C&A 7-103, 104, 202, 203, 301, 302.
Close Corporation Laws: Has Close Corporation Code (ACM - C&A 4-101 et seq.). No limit on number of shareholders in close corp.
Periodic Reports: Domestic and qualifying foreign corporations must file an annual report on prescribed forms with the state filing official by April 15 of each year and pay annual report fee to remain in good standing. ACM - C&A 1-203, ACM T&P 11-101.

STATE FILING OFFICIAL. Department of Assessments and Taxation, 301 West Preston Street, Baltimore, MD 21201 (Telephone: 410-225-1184).

Fees:
Filing Articles of Incorporation - $20
Corp. Organization and Capitalization Fee - Based on Capitalization ($20 minimum).
Amending Articles of Incorporation - $20
Qualification of Foreign Corporation - $50
Annual Report of Corp. - $100
Filing LLC Articles of Organization - $50
Filing LLP Certificate - $50
Name Reservation - $7
Other Fees - See ACM - C&A 1-203.

SUMMARY OF MASSACHUSETTS BUSINESS ORGANIZATION LAWS

PARTNERSHIP LAWS.

General Partnerships: Uniform Partnership Act adopted. MGLA chap. 108A.

Limited Partnerships: Revised Uniform Limited Partnership Act adopted. MGLA chap. 109.

Limited Liability Partnerships: Provided for. MGLA 108A-45 et seq.

Name Registration: If the partnership name does not contain the true surname of at least one partner, a fictitious name certificate must be filed with the clerk of every city or town where a partnership office is maintained. MGLA 110-5, 6.

LIMITED LIABILITY COMPANY LAWS. Massachusetts Limited Liability Company Act. MGLA chap. 156C.

Formation of LLC: One or more persons may form an LLC by filing a Certificate of Organization with the state filing official. See MGLA 156C-12 for the Certificate of Organization content requirements.

General LLC Requirements: May carry on any lawful business, trade, profession, purpose or activity. Must have two or more members. Special requirements for professional LLCs.

Management of LLC: Vested in members unless otherwise provided in operating agreement.

New or Substituted Members: Admission to LLC requires consent of all members unless operating agreement provides otherwise.

Conversion Statutes: Merger statute. MGLA 156C-59. No partnership conversion statute.

CORPORATION LAWS. Business Corporation Law (Model Business Corporation Acts not adopted). MGLA chap. 156B.

Corporate Name: Any name which, in state filing official's judgment, indicates incorporation, except the name or trade name of any other corporation, firm, association, or person carrying on business in the state. Availability of name may be checked with state filing official by telephone. Name may be reserved for 30 days upon written request. MGLA 156B-11.

Incorporators: One or more individuals of age 18 or more or other entities. MGLA 156B-12.

Articles of Organization: (Must use forms supplied by state filing official.)

- **Contents:** See MGLA 156B-13 for required and optional article of incorporation content requirements.
- **Filing and Recording:** The articles of incorporation must be filed with the state filing official and the incorporation fee paid. Corporate existence begins when articles of incorporation are accepted for filing. MGLA 156B-6, 12.
- **Amendment:** Unless the articles of organization or bylaws provide for a different vote of not less than a majority, a two-thirds vote of the outstanding shares entitled to vote is required, except that a majority vote of the outstanding shares entitled to vote is required for certain minor amendments. MGLA 156B-70, 71, 8.

Organizational Meeting: Held by the incorporators, who may act without meeting if all incorporators sign a written consent to the action. MGLA 156B-12.

Bylaws: Initial bylaws adopted by the incorporators. May be amended by the shareholders and, if so provided in the articles of organization, by the board of directors. The shareholders may amend or repeal any bylaw adopted by the board of directors. MGLA 156B-12, 17.

Action Without Meeting: Shareholders may act without meeting if all shareholders entitled to vote sign a written consent to the action. Unless the articles or bylaws provide otherwise, the board of directors may act without meeting if all directors sign a written consent to the action, and may meet via conference telephone or similar communications equipment. MGLA 156B-43, 59.

Stock Certificates: Must be signed by chairman of board, president, or vice president and by treasurer or assistant treasurer. Unless prohibited by the articles of organization or bylaws, shares may be issued without a certificate. MGLA 156B-27.

Consideration For Stock: May consist of cash, tangible or intangible property, services, debts, notes, or expenses. MGLA 156B-18.

Stock Transfer Restrictions: May be contained in the articles of organization, bylaws, or a shareholders' agreement. Must be set forth or conspicuously noted on the stock certificate. MGLA 156B-27.

Cumulative Voting: No statutory provisions.

Preemptive Rights: Do not exist unless contained in the articles of organization or in a shareholder-adopted bylaw. MGLA 156B-20.

Acts Requiring Shareholder Approval: Unless the articles of organization or bylaws require a different vote of not less than a majority, a two-thirds vote of the outstanding shares entitled to vote is required for the sale or transfer of all or substantially all of the corporate assets (if the articles of incorporation so provide), for a merger or consolidation, for voluntary dissolution, and for most amendments to the articles of organization (see above). MGLA 156B-75, 78, 100, 71, 8.

Board of Directors: Must have at least three directors except that there need not be more directors than shareholders. The number of directors must be specified in the bylaws. MGLA 156B-47.

Officers: Must have president, treasurer and clerk. The bylaws may provide for other officers. Unless the bylaws provide otherwise, the treasurer and clerk must be elected by the shareholders and the president must be a director and must be elected by the directors. The clerk must be a state resident unless the corporation has a registered agent. MGLA 156B-48.

Foreign Corporations: Must file a certificate with the state filing official within ten days after the commencement of doing business in the state and pay a filing fee. The statute contains a list of activities that do not constitute doing business in state. The penalties for doing business without filing a certificate include nonaccess to state courts and fines of up to $500 per year. MGLA 181-3, 4, 9.

Close Corporation Laws: None. Shareholders of "close corporation" have fiduciary obligations to each other. 402 Mass. 650, 524 N.E. 2d 849.

Periodic Reports: Domestic and registered foreign corporations must file an annual report with the state filing official by the 15th day of the third month after the end of its fiscal year and pay an annual filing fee to remain in good standing. MGLA 156B-109, 181-4.

STATE FILING OFFICIAL. Secretary of Commonwealth, Corporations Div., 1 Ashburton Place, 17th Fl., Boston, MA 02108 (617-727-9640).

Fees:

Filing Corp. Articles of Organization - $200 minimum	Name Reservation - $15	LLC & LLP Annual Report - $500
Amending Articles of Organization - $100 minimum	Corp. Annual Report - $85	Other Fees - Contact state filing official.
Filing LLC Certificate of Organization - $500		
Filing LLP Registration Statement - $500		

SUMMARY OF MICHIGAN BUSINESS ORGANIZATION LAWS

PARTNERSHIP LAWS.

General Partnerships: Uniform Partnership Act adopted. MSA 20.1 et seq.

Limited Partnerships: Revised Uniform Limited Partnership Act adopted. MSA 20.1101 et seq.

Limited Liability Partnerships: Registered limited liability partnerships provided for. MSA 20.44 et seq.

Name Registration: Must file partnership certificate with the county clerk in county of partnership's place of business. Must also file fictitious name certificate with county clerk if the partnership name does not contain the names of all partners. MSA 20.111, 19.821.

LIMITED LIABILITY COMPANY LAWS. Michigan Limited Liability Company Act. MSA 21.198(4101) et seq.

Formation of LLC: One or more persons may form LLC by filing articles of organization with state filing official. See MSA 21.198(4203) for article of organization content requirements.

General LLC Requirements: May have one or more members. May conduct any lawful business, but professional LLCs are subject to special requirements (see MSA 21.198(4901) et seq.).

Management of LLC: Reserved to members unless articles of organization provide for managers. MSA 21.198(4401).

New or Substituted Members: Admitted to LLC only with consent of all members unless operating agreement provides otherwise.

Conversion Statutes: Merger statute. MSA 21.198(4701) et seq. Partnership conversion statute. MSA 21.198(4707).

CORPORATION LAWS. Business Corporation Act (Model Acts not adopted). MSA 21.200(101) et seq. (MCL 450.1101 et seq.)

Corporate Name: Must contain the word "corporation," "company," "incorporated," or "limited" or a listed abbreviation thereof. Must be distinguishable from the name of any other corporation or limited partnership. Name may be reserved for four months. No informal procedure for checking availability of name. MSA 21.200(211), (212), (215).

Incorporators: One or more individuals or entities. MSA 21.200 (201).

Articles of Incorporation:

Contents: See MSA 21.200(202), (209) for required and optional article of incorporation content requirements.

Filing and Recording: An original copy of the articles of incorporation must be filed with the state filing official and the filing fee paid. Corporate existence begins when the articles of incorporation are accepted for filing. MSA 21.200(131), (221).

Amendment: Requires a majority vote of the outstanding shares entitled to vote, unless the articles of incorporation require a greater vote. MSA 21.200(611), (455).

Organizational Meeting: Held by the incorporators before or after incorporation. MSA 21.200(223).

Bylaws: Initial bylaws adopted by the incorporators, board of directors or shareholders. May be amended by the shareholders and by the board of directors unless the articles of incorporation or bylaws reserve that power to the shareholders or prohibit the board of directors from amending certain bylaws. MSA 21.200(231).

Action Without Meeting: Shareholders may act without meeting if all shareholders entitled to vote sign a written consent to the action, or, if the articles of incorporation so provide, if a written consent is signed by shareholders sufficient to carry the matter at a meeting and notice is given to other shareholders. MSA 21.200(407). Unless prohibited by the articles of incorporation or bylaws, the board of directors may meet via conference telephone or similar communications equipment and may act without meeting if all directors sign a written consent to the action. MSA 21.200(521), (525).

Stock Certificates: Must be signed by chairman or vice chairman of board, president or vice president or by another corporate officer. Shares may be issued without a certificate unless the articles of incorporation or bylaws provide otherwise. MSA 21.200(331), (336).

Consideration For Stock: May consist of any tangible or intangible property or benefit to the corporation, including cash, promissory notes, services rendered or to be rendered or other securities of the corporation. MSA 21.200(314).

Stock Transfer Restrictions: May be imposed by articles of incorporation, bylaws or shareholders' agreement. A restriction must be conspicuously noted on stock certificate to be enforceable against persons without knowledge of the restriction. MSA 21.200(472), (473).

Cumulative Voting: Not permitted unless provided for in the articles of incorporation. MSA 21.200(451)

Preemptive Rights: Do not exist unless contained in the articles of incorporation or in an agreement between one or more shareholders and the corporation. MSA 21.200(343).

Acts Requiring Shareholder Approval: Unless the articles of incorporation require a greater vote, a majority vote of the shares entitled to vote is required for a merger or share exchange, for the sale or transfer of all or substantially all of the corporate assets not in the usual course of business, for voluntary dissolution, and to amend the articles of incorporation. MSA 21.200(703a), (753), (804), (611), (455).

Board of Directors: May consist of one or more members, with the number of directors fixed in the bylaws or articles of incorporation. A corporation may, in its articles of incorporation, dispense with or limit the authority of the board of directors. MSA 21.200(505), (463).

Officers: Must have president, secretary and treasurer. Other officers may be provided for in the bylaws or appointed by the board of directors. The same person may hold any two or more offices in the corporation, but may not sign documents in a dual capacity. MSA 21.200(531).

Foreign Corporations: Must obtain a certificate of authority from the state filing official before doing business in Michigan. The statute contains a nonexclusive list of activities that do not constitute transacting business in the state. The penalties for doing business without a certificate of authority include nonaccess to state courts and liability for all fees, taxes and penalties that would have been imposed had a certificate of authority been issued. MSA 21.200(1003), (1011), (1012), (1051).

Close Corporation Laws: Shareholders may manage corp. under a shareholders' agreement that complies with MSA 21.200(488).

Periodic Reports: Domestic and authorized foreign corporations must file an annual report on specified forms with the state filing official by May 15 of each year and pay an annual report fee to remain in good standing. MSA 21.200(911).

STATE FILING OFFICIAL. Department of Commerce, Corporations & Securities Div., P.O. Box 30222, Lansing, MI 48909 (517-373-1820).

Fees: Filing Articles of Incorporation - $10 plus a fee based on capitalization ($50 minimum, see MSA 21.200(1062)). Name Reservation - $10
Amending Articles of Incorporation - $10 (more if capitalization is increased). Corp. Annual Report - $15
Filing LLC Articles of Organization - $50 Other Corp. Fees - See MSA 21.200(1060).
Filing LLP Registration Statement - $100 Other LLC Fees - See MSA 21.198(5101).

SUMMARY OF MINNESOTA BUSINESS ORGANIZATION LAWS

PARTNERSHIP LAWS.

General Partnerships: Uniform Partnership Act of 1994. MS 323A.1-01 et seq.

Limited Partnerships: Revised Uniform Limited Partnership Act adopted. MS 322A.01 et seq.

Limited Liability Partnerships: Provided for. MS 323A.10-01 et seq. Limited Partnership may be LLP. MS 322A.88.

Name Registration: Must file a fictitious name certificate with the Secretary of State and publish in a newspaper in the county where the partnership's principal office is located if the partnership name does not contain the names of all partners. MS 333.01 et seq.

LIMITED LIABILITY COMPANY LAWS. Minnesota Limited Liability Company Act. MS 322B.01 et seq.

Formation of LLC: One or more natural persons may form an LLC by filing articles of organization with the Secretary of State. See MS 322B.115 for the article of organization content requirements.

General LLC Requirements: May have one or more members. May conduct any lawful business.

Management of LLC: Managed by governors and managers unless members sign Member Control Agreement.

New or Substituted Members: Membership interests freely assignable unless articles of organization provide otherwise.

Conversion Statutes: Merger, exchange, or transfer statute. MS 322B.70 et seq. No partnership conversion statute.

CORPORATION LAWS. Minnesota Business Corporation Act (Model Business Corporation Acts not adopted). MS 302A.001 et seq.

Corporate Name: Must contain the word "corporation," "incorporated," "limited," or "company" (not preceded by "and") or an abbreviation thereof. Must be distinguishable on the records of the Secretary of State from the names of other corporations, limited partnerships, and limited liability companies. Name may be reserved for a renewable 12-month period. MS 302A.115, 117.

Incorporators: One or more natural persons of age or more. MS 302A.105.

Articles of Incorporation:

Contents: See MS 302A.111 for required and optional article of incorporation content requirements.

Filing and Recording: The articles of incorporation must be filed with the Secretary of State and the incorporation and filing fees paid. Corporate existence begins when the articles of incorporation are accepted for filing. MSA 302A.151, 153.

Amendment: Requires a majority vote of the shares present and entitled to vote, unless the articles of incorporation require a greater vote. Different voting requirements exist for close corporations and for cumulative voting amendments. MS 302A.135, 437, 215.

Organizational Meeting: Held after incorporation by incorporators or by initial directors if named in articles. MS 302A.171.

Bylaws: Initial bylaws adopted by the incorporators or board of directors. May be amended by the board of directors unless that power is reserved to the shareholders in the articles of incorporation. Shareholders may amend bylaws adopted by the board of directors. MS 302A.181.

Action Without Meeting: Shareholders may act without meeting if all shareholders entitled to vote sign a written consent to the action. MS 302A.441. The board of directors may act without meeting if all directors sign a written consent to the action, or, on matters not requiring shareholder approval and if the articles of incorporation so provide, if the consent is signed by the number of directors needed to carry the matter at a meeting and written notice is immediately given to the other directors. MS 302A.239. The board of directors and, if authorized by the bylaws, the shareholders may meet via electronic audio communications. MS 302A.231, 436.

Stock Certificates: Must be signed by the agent or officer authorized to do so in the articles of incorporation or bylaws. Shares may be issued without a certificate unless prohibited by the articles of incorporation or bylaws. MS 302A.417.

Consideration For Stock: May consist of any consideration including money, tangible or intangible property, or other benefit received by corporation or to be received under written agreement, unless the articles of incorporation provide otherwise. MS 302A.405.

Stock Transfer Restrictions: May be contained in the articles of incorporation, bylaws, or a shareholders' resolution or agreement. Must be conspicuously noted on the stock certificate to be enforceable against a person without knowledge of the restriction. MS 302A.429.

Cumulative Voting: Permitted unless denied in the articles of incorporation. Prior written notice is required. MS 302A.215.

Preemptive Rights: Exist (with exceptions) unless denied in the articles of incorporation. MS 302A.413.

Acts Requiring Shareholder Approval: Unless the articles of incorporation require a greater vote, a majority vote of the shares entitled to vote is required for a merger or share exchange, for the sale or disposition of all or substantially all of the corporate assets not in the usual course of business, for voluntary dissolution, and to amend the articles of incorporation. MS 302A.613, 661, 721, 135, 437.

Board of Directors: May consist of one or more natural persons. The number of directors must be specified in bylaws or articles of incorporation. Subject to shareholder control agreement or unanimous shareholder action. MS 302A.201, 203, 205, 457.

Officers: Must have chief executive officer and chief financial officer. Specific offices and titles may be specified in the bylaws or the articles of incorporation. The same person may hold any or all offices in the corporation. MS 302A.301, 311, 315.

Foreign Corporations: Must obtain a certificate of authority from the Secretary of State to transact business in Minnesota. The statute contains a list of activities that do not constitute transacting business in the state. The penalties for transacting business without a certificate of authority include nonaccess to state courts and civil penalties of up to $1,000 plus $100 per month of violation. MS 303.03, 303.20.

Close Corporation Laws: Does not have Close Corporation Code, but the Business Corporation Act contains several provisions dealing with close corporations (i.e., corporations with 35 or fewer shareholders), including provisions for a shareholder control agreement. See MS 302A.011(6a), 135, 201, 436, 457, 751.

Periodic Reports: Domestic and authorized foreign corporations must file an annual report with the Commissioner of Revenue or the Secretary of State by May 15 of each year and pay an annual license fee to remain in good standing. MS 289A.18, 302A.821, 303.07, 303.14.

STATE FILING OFFICIAL. Secretary of State, 180 State Office Bldg., St. Paul, MN 55155 (Telephone: 612-296-2803).

Fees:
- Filing Articles of Incorporation - $135 ($35 filing fee + $100 incorporation fee).
- Name Reservation - $35
- Amending Articles of Incorporation - $35
- Annual Corp. License Fee - Based on Minnesota income ($40 minimum).
- Application for Certificate of Authority - $250
- Filing LLP Statement of Qualification - $135
- Filing LLC Articles of Organization - $135

SUMMARY OF MISSISSIPPI BUSINESS ORGANIZATION LAWS

PARTNERSHIP LAWS.

General Partnerships: Uniform Partnership Act adopted. MCA 79-12-1 et seq.
Limited Partnerships: Revised Uniform Limited Partnership Act adopted. MCA 79-14-101 et seq.
Limited Liability Partnerships: Limited liability partnerships provided for. MCA 79-12-87 et seq.
Name Registration: Not required.

LIMITED LIABILITY COMPANY LAWS. Mississippi Limited Liability Company Act. MCA 79-29-101 et seq.

Formation of LLC: Any person may form an LLC by filing a Certificate of Formation with the Secretary of State. See MCA 79-29-201 for the Certificate of Formation content requirements.
General LLC Requirements: May have one or more members. May conduct any lawful business. Special requirements apply to professional LLCs (MCA 79-29-901 et seq.).
Management of LLC: Vested in members unless otherwise provided in the certificate of formation.
New or Substituted Members: Requires consent of all members unless otherwise provided in certificate of formation or LLC agreement.
Conversion Statutes: None in LLC Act.

CORPORATION LAWS. Mississippi Business Corporation Act (based on Revised Model Business Corp. Act). MCA 79-4-1.01 et seq.

Corporate Name: Must contain the word "corporation," "incorporated," "company," or "limited" or a listed abbreviation thereof. Must be distinguishable on records of Secretary of State from names of other corporations. Name may be reserved for 180 days. MCA 79-4-4.01, 4.02.
Incorporators: One or more individuals or entities. MCA 79-4-2.01.
Articles of Incorporation:
Contents: See MCA 79-4-2.02 for required and optional article of incorporation content requirements.
Filing and Recording: A signed copy of the articles of incorporation must be filed with the Secretary of State and the filing fee paid. Corporate existence begins when the articles of incorporation are accepted for filing. MCA 79-4-1.20, 2.03.
Amendment: Requires a majority of the votes entitled to be cast unless a statute, the board of directors, or the articles of incorporation require a greater vote. The board of directors may make minor amendments without shareholder approval. MCA 79-4-10.02, 10.03.
Organizational Meeting: Held after incorporation by the initial board of directors if named in the articles of incorporation. Otherwise held after incorporation by the incorporators, who may act without meeting if they all sign a written consent to the action. MCA 79-4-2.05.
Bylaws: Initial bylaws adopted by the incorporators or board of directors. May be amended by the shareholders and by the board of directors unless that power is reserved to the shareholders in articles of incorporation. A shareholder amendment may preclude its subsequent amendment by the board of directors. MCA 79-4-2.06, 10.20.
Action Without Meeting: Shareholders may act without meeting if all shareholders entitled to vote sign a written consent to the action. MCA 79-4-7.04. Unless the articles of incorporation or bylaws provide otherwise, the board of directors may meet via conference telephone or similar communications equipment and may act without meeting if all directors sign a written consent to the action. MCA 79-4-8.20, 8.21.
Stock Certificates: Must be signed by two officers designated in the bylaws or by the board of directors. Shares may be issued without a certificate unless the articles of incorporation or bylaws provide otherwise. MCA 79-4-6.25, 6.26.
Consideration For Stock: May consist of any tangible or intangible property or benefit to the corporation, including cash, promissory notes, services performed or to be performed, and other securities of the corporation. Shares issued for promissory notes or future services may be placed in escrow or otherwise restricted pending payment of note or performance of services. MCA 79-4-6.21.
Stock Transfer Restrictions: May be imposed by the articles of incorporation, bylaws or a shareholders' agreement. A restriction must be conspicuously noted on the stock certificate to be enforceable against a person without knowledge of the restriction. MCA 79-4-6.27.
Cumulative Voting: Permitted unless denied in the articles of incorporation. MCA 79-4-7.28.
Preemptive Rights: Do not exist unless contained in the articles of incorporation. MCA 79-4-6.30.
Acts Requiring Shareholder Approval: Unless a statute, the articles of incorporation, or the board of directors require a greater vote, a majority of the votes entitled to be cast is required for a merger or share exchange, for the sale or disposition of all or substantially all of the corporate assets not in the usual course of business, for voluntary dissolution, and for most amendments to the articles of incorporation (see above). MCA 79-4-11.03, 12.02, 14.02, 10.03.
Board of Directors: May consist of one or more individuals with the number specified in bylaws or articles of incorporation. MCA 79-4-8.03.
Officers: Those described in the bylaws or appointed by the board of directors in accordance with the bylaws. No specific officers required. The same person may simultaneously hold more than one office in the corporation. MCA 79-4-8.40.
Foreign Corporations: Must obtain a certificate of authority from the Secretary of State before transacting business in Mississippi. The statute contains a list of activities that do not constitute transacting business in the state. The penalties for transacting business without a certificate of authority include nonaccess to state courts and civil penalties of $10 per day up to $1,000 per year. MCA 79-4-15.01, 15.02.
Close Corporation Laws: A unanimous shareholder agreement may dispense with or limit the authority of the board of directors and provide for management of the corporation by the shareholders. MCA 79-4-7.32, 8.01.
Periodic Reports: Each domestic and authorized foreign corporation must file an annual report with the Secretary of State by the 60th day after the anniversary date of its incorporation or authorization and pay an annual report fee and a franchise tax to remain in good standing. MCA 79-4-16.22, 27-13-5, 7.

STATE FILING OFFICIAL. Secretary of State, 202 North Congress, P.O. Box 136, Jackson, MS 39205-0136 (Telephone: 601-359-1333).

Fees:
Filing Articles of Incorporation - $50
Amending Articles of Incorporation - $50
Filing LLP Certificate of Registration - $250
Filing LLC Certificate of Formation - $50
Annual Report - $25
Application for Certificate of Authority - $500
Name Reservation - $25
Other Corp. Fees - See MCA 79-4-1.22.
Other LLP Fees - See MCA 79-12-111.
Other LLC Fees - See MCA 79-29-1203.

SUMMARY OF MISSOURI BUSINESS ORGANIZATION LAWS

PARTNERSHIP LAWS.

General Partnerships: Uniform Partnership Act adopted. VAMS 358.010 et seq.

Limited Partnerships: Revised Uniform Limited Partnership Act adopted. VAMS 359.011 et seq.

Limited Liability Partnerships: Registered limited liability partnerships provided for. VAMS 358.440 et seq.

Name Registration: Must register the partnership name with the Secretary of State within five days after starting business if the partnership name does not contain the names of all partners. VAMS 417.210.

LIMITED LIABILITY COMPANY LAWS. Missouri Limited Liability Company Act. VAMS 347.010 et seq.

Formation of LLC: One or more persons may form an LLC by filing articles of organization with the Secretary of State. See VAMS 347.039 for the article of organization content requirements.

General LLC Requirements: May have one or more members. May conduct any lawful business.

Management of LLC: Vested in members unless vested in managers by articles of organization. VAMS 347.079.

New or Substituted Members: Requires written consent of all members unless otherwise provided in the operating agreement.

Conversion Statutes: Partnership conversion statute. VAMS 347.125. Merger or consolidation statute. VAMS 347.127 et seq.

CORPORATION LAWS. General Business and Corporation Law of Missouri (Model Acts not adopted). VAMS 351.010 et seq.

Corporate Name: Must contain the word "company," "corporation," "incorporated," or "limited" or end with an abbreviation thereof and must be distinguishable from the name of any other corporation or registered entity. Name may be reserved for 60 days. Availability of name may be checked with the Secretary of State without fee by letter or telephone. VAMS 351.110, 115.

Incorporators: One or more natural persons of age 18 or more. VAMS 351.050.

Articles of Incorporation:

Contents: See VAMS 351.055 for required and optional article of incorporation content requirements.

Filing and Recording: An original and one copy of the articles of incorporation must be filed with the Secretary of State and the filing fee paid. Corporate existence begins when the articles of incorporation are accepted for filing. VAMS 351.060, 075.

Amendment: Requires a majority vote of the outstanding shares entitled to vote for all amendments except those affecting cumulative voting, unless the articles of incorporation or a shareholder-adopted bylaw require a greater vote. Nonvoting shares are entitled to vote on certain amendments. VAMS 351.090, 093, 270.

Organizational Meeting: Held by the initial board of directors if named in the articles of incorporation. Otherwise held first by the incorporators and then by the initial board of directors. The incorporators may act by unanimous written consent. VAMS 351.080.

Bylaws: Initial bylaws adopted by the initial board of directors, if named in articles of incorporation, or by the incorporators. May be amended only by the shareholders unless the articles of incorporation permit amendment by the board of directors. VAMS 351.080, 290.

Action Without Meeting: The shareholders and the board of directors may act without meeting if all shareholders entitled to vote or all directors, as the case may be, sign a written consent to the action. The board of directors may meet via conference telephone or similar communications equipment unless otherwise provided in the articles of incorporation or bylaws. VAMS 351.273, 340, 335.

Stock Certificates: Must be signed by the president or vice president and by the secretary, treasurer, or an assistant secretary or treasurer. VAMS 351.295. No provisions for issuing shares without a certificate.

Consideration For Stock: May consist of money paid, labor done, or property actually received. VAMS 351.160, 165.

Stock Transfer Restrictions: No statutory provisions.

Cumulative Voting: Permitted unless denied in the articles of incorporation or bylaws. VAMS 351.245.

Preemptive Rights: Exists unless denied or limited in the articles of incorporation. VAMS 351.305.

Acts Requiring Shareholder Approval: Unless the articles of incorporation or a shareholder-adopted bylaw require a greater vote, a two-thirds vote of the outstanding shares entitled to vote is required for a merger or consolidation, for the sale of all or substantially all of the corporate assets not in the usual course of business, and (unless the board of directors requires a greater vote) for voluntary dissolution. VAMS 351.425, 400, 464, 270. Shareholder approval is also required to amend the articles of incorporation (see above).

Board of Directors: Must consist of three or more directors unless the articles of incorporation specify fewer. The number of directors must be specified in the articles of incorporation or, if the articles of incorporation so provide, in the bylaws. VAMS 351.315, 055.

Officers: Must have president and secretary. The bylaws may provide for other officers and agents. Unless the articles of incorporation or bylaws provide otherwise, the same person may hold any two or more offices in the corporation. VAMS 351.360.

Foreign Corporations: Must obtain a certificate of authority from the Secretary of State to transact business in Missouri. The statute contains a nonexclusive list of activities that do not constitute transacting business in the state. The penalties for transacting business without a certificate of authority include nonaccess to state courts and a fine of not less than $1,000. VAMS 351.571, 574.

Close Corporation Laws: Has Close Corporation Code. VAMS 351.750 et seq. To be statutory close corporation, the articles of incorporation must contain a statement to that effect and there must be 50 or fewer shareholders.

Periodic Reports: Domestic and authorized foreign corporations must file an annual registration report and franchise tax return with the Secretary of State by the 15th day of the 4th month after the close of its fiscal year and pay a registration fee and franchise tax to remain in good standing. VAMS 351.120, 147.020.

STATE FILING OFFICIAL. Secretary of State, Jefferson City, MO 65101 (Telephone: 314-340-7490).

Fees:
- Filing Articles of Incorporation - $3 plus a fee based on capitalization ($50 minimum).
- Name Reservation - $20
- Amending Articles of Incorporation - $20
- Application for Certificate of Authority - $150
- Other Corp. Fees - See VAMS 351.658.
- Filing LLC Articles of Organization - $100
- Annual Registration Fee - $40
- Other LLC Fees - See VAMS 347.179.
- Filing LLP Application - $25 per partner ($100 max.)

SUMMARY OF MONTANA BUSINESS ORGANIZATION LAWS

PARTNERSHIP LAWS.

General Partnerships: Uniform Partnership Act adopted. MCA 35-10-101 et seq.
Limited Partnerships: Revised Uniform Limited Partnership Act adopted. MCA 35-12-501 et seq.
Limited Liability Partnerships: Registered limited liability partnerships provided for. MCA 35-10-701 et seq.
Name Registration: Must register partnership name with Secretary of State if it does not contain the names of all partners. MCA 30-13-202.

LIMITED LIABILITY COMPANY LAWS. Montana Limited Liability Company Act. MCA 35-8-101.

Formation of LLC: One or more persons may form an LLC by filing articles of organization with the Secretary of State. See MCA 35-8-202 for the article of organization content requirements.
General LLC Requirements: May have one or more members. May conduct any lawful business except banking and insurance. Special requirements for professional LLCs (MCA 35-8-1301 to 1307).
Management of LLC: Vested in members unless vested in manager(s) in articles of organization.
New or Substituted Members: Consent of all members required unless otherwise provided in articles of organization or operating agreement.
Conversion Statutes: None in LLC Act.

CORPORATION LAWS. Montana Business Corporation Act (based on Revised Model Business Corporation Act). MCA 35-1-112 et seq.

Corporate Name: Must contain the word "corporation," "incorporated," "company," or "limited" or a listed abbreviation thereof. Must be distinguishable on the records of the Secretary of State from the names of other corporations and registered businesses. Name may be reserved for 120 days. Availability of name may be checked with Secretary of State by letter or telephone. MCA 35-1-308, 309.
Incorporators: One or more individuals or entities. MCA 35-1-215.
Articles of Incorporation:
Contents: See MCA 35-1-216 for required and optional article of incorporation content requirements.
Filing and Recording: A signed copy of the articles of incorporation must be filed with the Secretary of State and the filing and license fees paid. Corporate existence begins when the articles of incorporation are accepted for filing. MCA 35-1-217, 220.
Amendment: Requires a majority of the votes entitled to be cast, unless a statute, the board of directors, or the articles of incorporation require a greater vote. The board of directors can make certain minor amendments without shareholder approval. MCA 35-1-226, 227.
Organizational Meeting: Held after incorporation by the initial board of directors if named in articles of incorporation. Otherwise held after incorporation by the incorporators, who may act without meeting if each incorporator signs a written consent to the action. MCA 35-1-222.
Bylaws: Initial bylaws adopted by incorporators or board of directors. May be amended by the shareholders and the board of directors unless the articles of incorporation reserve that power to the shareholders. A shareholder amendment can preclude its further amendment by the board of directors. MCA 35-1-234, 236.
Action Without Meeting: Shareholders may act without meeting if all shareholders entitled to vote sign a written consent to the action. MCA 35-1-519. Unless the articles of incorporation or bylaws provide otherwise, the board of directors may meet via conference telephone or similar communications equipment and may act without meeting if all directors sign a written consent to the action. MCA 35-1-431, 432.
Stock Certificates: Must be signed by two officers designated in bylaws or by the board of directors. Shares may be issued without a certificate unless the articles of incorporation or bylaws provide otherwise. MCA 35-1-626, 627.
Consideration For Stock: May consist of any tangible or intangible property or benefit to the corporation, including cash, promissory notes, services performed or to be performed, and other securities of the corporation. Shares issued for promissory notes or future services may be placed in escrow or otherwise restricted pending payment of note or performance of services. MCA 35-1-623.
Stock Transfer Restrictions: May be imposed by the articles of incorporation, bylaws or a shareholder agreement. A restriction must be conspicuously noted on the stock certificate to be enforceable against a person without knowledge of the restriction. MCA 35-1-628.
Cumulative Voting: Permitted unless denied in the original articles of incorporation or in a special amendment thereto. MCA 35-1-531.
Preemptive Rights: Do not exist unless contained in the articles of incorporation. MCA 35-1-535.
Acts Requiring Shareholder Approval: Unless a statute, the articles of incorporation, or the board of directors require a greater vote, or unless the articles of incorporation require a majority vote, two-thirds of the votes entitled to be cast is required for a merger or share exchange, for the sale or disposition of all or substantially all of the corporate assets not in the usual course of business, and for voluntary dissolution. MCA 35-1-815, 823, 932. Shareholder approval is also required for most amendments to the articles of incorporation (see above).
Board of Directors: May consist of one or more individuals, with the number specified in articles of incorporation or bylaws. MCA 35-1-419.
Officers: Those described in the bylaws or appointed by the board of directors in accordance with the bylaws. No specific officers required. The same person may simultaneously hold more than one office in the corporation. MCA 35-1-441.
Foreign Corporations: Must obtain a certificate of authority from the Secretary of State before transacting business in Montana. The statute contains a nonexclusive list of activities that do not constitute transacting business in the state. The penalties for transacting business without a certificate of authority include nonaccess to state courts and a civil penalty of $5 per day up to $1,000 per year. MCA 35-1-1026, 1027.
Close Corporation Laws: Has Montana Close Corporation Act. MCA 35-9-101 et seq. A statutory close corporation must have 25 or fewer shareholders.
Periodic Reports: Domestic and authorized foreign corporations must file an annual report with the Secretary of State by April 15 of each year and file a state license tax return by the 15th day of the fifth month after close of the corporation's tax year. MCA 35-1-1104, 15-31-121.

STATE FILING OFFICIAL. Secretary of State, State Capitol, Helena, MT 59620 (Telephone: 406-444-3665).

Fees: Filing Articles of Incorporation - $20 plus license fee based on capitalization ($50 for first 50,000 shares). Name Reservation - $10
Amending Articles of Incorporation - $15 Corp. or LLC Annual Report - $10 Filing LLP Application for Registration - $70
Filing LLC Articles of Organization - $70 ($20 filing fee + $50 license fee) Other Fees - Contact Secretary of State

SUMMARY OF NEBRASKA BUSINESS ORGANIZATION LAWS

PARTNERSHIP LAWS.

General Partnerships: Uniform Partnership Act adopted. RRS 67-301 et seq.
Limited Partnerships: Revised Uniform Limited Partnership Act adopted. RRS 67-233 et seq.
Limited Liability Partnerships: Registered LLPs provided for. RRS 67-344 et seq.
Name Registration: All partnerships must record and publish a certificate with the county clerk of the county of the partnership's place of business. RRS 67-101 et seq. A trade name may be recorded with the Secretary of State if desired. RRS 87-210.

LIMITED LIABILITY COMPANY LAWS. Limited Liability Company Act. RRS 21-2601 et seq.

Formation of LLC: One or more persons may form an LLC by filing articles of organization with the Secretary of State. See RRS 21-2606 for the article of incorporation content requirements.
General LLC Requirements: Must have two or more members. May conduct any lawful business except banking and insurance. Special rules exist for farm or ranching LLCs and professional LLCs.
Management of LLC: Vested in members unless otherwise provided in the articles of organization.
New or Substituted Members: Admission to LLC requires majority vote of members. RRS 21-2621.
Conversion Statutes: Merger statute. RRS 21-2652. No partnership conversion statute.

CORPORATION LAWS. Business Corporation Act (based on Revised Model Business Corporation Act). RRS 21-2001 et seq.

Corporate Name: Must contain the word "corporation," "company," "incorporated," or "limited," or an abbreviation thereof. Must be distinguishable from the names of all other corporations and registered trade names. Name may be reserved for 120 days. Availability of name may be checked with Secretary of State by telephone. RRS 21-2028, 2029.
Incorporators: One or more individuals or entities. RRS 21-2017.
Articles of Incorporation:
Contents: See RRS 21-2018 for required and optional article of incorporation content requirements.
Filing and Recording: An original and one copy of the articles of incorporation must be filed with the Secretary of State and the filing and recording fees paid. Corporate existence begins when the articles of incorporation are filed. RRS 21-2003, 2019.
Amendment: Requires two-thirds of the votes entitled to be cast unless a statute, the articles of incorporation, or the board of directors require a greater vote. Board of directors can make ministerial amendments without shareholder approval. RRS 21-20,117, 20,118.
Organizational Meeting: Held after incorporation by the initial board of directors if named in articles of incorporation. Otherwise held by the incorporators, who may act without meeting if all incorporators sign a written consent to the action. RRS 21-2021.
Bylaws: Initial bylaws adopted by the incorporators or board of directors. May be amended by the shareholders and by the board of directors unless that power is reserved to the shareholders in the articles of incorporation. A shareholder amendment may preclude its subsequent amendment by the board of directors. RRS 21-2022, 20,125.
Action Without Meeting: Shareholders may act without meeting if all shareholders entitled to vote sign a written consent to the action. RRS 21-2054. Unless the articles of incorporation or bylaws provide otherwise, the board of directors may act without meeting if all directors sign a written consent to the action. RRS 21-2089.
Stock Certificates: Must be signed by two officers designated in the bylaws or by board of directors. RRS 21-2044. Shares may be issued without a certificate unless otherwise provided in the articles of incorporation or bylaws. RRS 21-2045.
Consideration For Stock: May consist of money, promissory notes, tangible or intangible property, or labor or services performed or to be performed for the corporation. RRS 21-2040.
Stock Transfer Restrictions: May be imposed by the articles of incorporation, bylaws or a shareholders' agreement. A restriction must be conspicuously noted on the stock certificate to be enforceable against a person without knowledge of the restriction. RRS 21-2046.
Cumulative Voting: Must be permitted. RRS 21-2066.
Preemptive Rights: Do not exist unless provided for in the articles of incorporation. RRS 21-2048.
Acts Requiring Shareholder Approval: Unless a statute, the articles of incorporation, or the board of directors require a greater vote, a two-thirds majority of all votes entitled to be cast is required for a merger, consolidation or share exchange, for the sale or transfer of all or substantially all of the corporate assets not in the usual course of business, for a voluntary dissolution, and for most amendments to the articles of incorporation. RRS 21-20,118, 20,130, 20,136, 20,152.
Board of Directors: May consist of one or more individuals with the number specified in the articles of incorporation or bylaws. RRS 21-2080.
Officers: Those specified in the bylaws. The same person may hold more than one office. RRS 21-2097.
Foreign Corporations: Must obtain a certificate of authority from the Secretary of State to transact business in Nebraska. The statute contains a nonexclusive list of activities that do not constitute transacting business in the state. The penalties for transacting business without a certificate of authority include nonaccess to state courts and civil penalties of $500 per day up to $10,000 per year. RRS 21-20,168, 20,169.
Close Corporation Laws: Shareholders may manage corporation under unanimous shareholders' agreement. RRS 21-2069.
Periodic Reports: Domestic and authorized foreign corporations must file an annual report with the Secretary of State by April 15 of each year and pay an annual occupation tax to remain in good standing. RRS 21-20,188.

STATE FILING OFFICIAL. Secretary of State, Corporations Division, 2300 State Capitol Building, Lincoln, NE 68509 (Telephone: 402-471-2554).

Fees:
Filing Articles of Incorporation - Fee based on capitalization ($60 minimum).
Amending Articles of Incorporation - $25
Name Reservation - $25
Application for Certificate of Authority - $130
Filing LLC Articles of Organization - $10 plus recording fee of $3 per page.
Filing LLP Registration Application - $250 plus recording fee of $3 per page.
Recording Fee - $5 per page for corp. documents.
Other Corp. Fees - See RRS 21-2005.
Other LLC Fees - See RRS 21-2634.
Other LLP Fees - See RRS 67-344.
Other fees generally - See RRS 33-101.

SUMMARY OF NEVADA BUSINESS ORGANIZATION LAWS

PARTNERSHIP LAWS.

General Partnerships: Uniform Partnership Act adopted. NRS 87.010 et seq.

Limited Partnerships: Revised Uniform Limited Partnership Act adopted. NRS 88.315 et seq.

Limited Liability Partnerships: Registered limited liability partnerships provided for. NRS 87.440 et seq.

Name Registration: Must file a fictitious name certificate with the county clerk of each county where business is conducted if the partnership name does not contain the names of all partners. NRS 602.010 et seq.

LIMITED LIABILITY COMPANY LAWS. Nevada Limited Liability Company Act. NRS 86.011 et seq.

Formation of LLC: One or more persons may form an LLC by filing articles of incorporation and a certificate of acceptance of appointment by the LLC's resident agent with the Secretary of State. See NRS 86.161 for article of organization content requirements.

General LLC Requirements: May have one or more members. May conduct any lawful business except insurance.

Management of LLC: Vested in members in proportion to contributed capital unless otherwise provided in articles of organization or operating agreement. NRS 86.291.

New or Substituted Members: Admission to LLC requires approval of majority in interest of other members unless otherwise provided in articles of organization or operating agreement. NRS 86.351.

Conversion Statutes: None in LLC Act.

CORPORATION LAWS. Private Corporations Law (Model Business Corporation Acts not adopted). NRS 78.010 et seq.

Corporate Name: No required words except that the name of a natural person must be combined with the word "Incorporated," "Limited," "Company," "Corporation," or a similar word or an abbreviation thereof. Name must be distinguishable from the names of all other organized or registered entities. Name may be reserved for 90 days. Availability of name may be checked informally with Secretary of State. NRS 78.035, 039, 040.

Incorporators: One or more persons. NRS 78.030.

Articles of Incorporation:

Contents: See NRS 78.035 and 78.037 for required and optional article of incorporation content requirements.

Filing and Recording: The articles of incorporation and an acceptance of appointment signed by the resident agent must be filed with Secretary of State and the filing fee paid. Corporate existence begins when the articles of incorporation are filed. NRS 78.030, 050.

Amendment: Requires a majority vote of the shares entitled to vote, unless the articles require a greater vote. NRS 78.390.

Organizational Meeting: No statutory provisions. Presumably held by initial board of directors.

Bylaws: May be adopted by the board of directors or the shareholders. May be amended by the board of directors unless the articles of incorporation provide otherwise. NRS 78.120.

Action Without Meeting: Unless the articles of incorporation or bylaws provide otherwise, shareholders may meet via conference telephone or similar equipment and may act without meeting if a written consent to the action is signed by shareholders sufficient to carry the action at a meeting. NRS 78.320. Unless the articles of incorporation or bylaws provide otherwise, the board of directors may meet via conference telephone or similar equipment and may act without meeting if all directors sign a duly filed written consent to the action. NRS 78.315.

Stock Certificates: Must be signed by the officers designated by the corporation. Shares may be issued without a certificate if the articles of incorporation or bylaws so provide. NRS 78-235.

Consideration For Stock: May consist of any tangible or intangible property or benefit to the corporation, including cash, promissory notes, services performed or to be performed, and other securities of the corporation. Shares issued for promissory notes or future services may be placed in escrow or otherwise restricted pending payment of note or performance of services. NRS 78.211.

Stock Transfer Restrictions: May be imposed by the articles of incorporation, bylaws or a shareholders' agreement. The restriction must be conspicuously noted on the stock certificate to be enforceable against a person without knowledge of the restriction. NRS 78.242.

Cumulative Voting: Not permitted unless provided for in the articles of incorporation and prior notice is given. NRS 78.360.

Preemptive Rights: Do not exist unless contained in the articles of incorporation for corporations formed on or after October 1, 1991. Exist unless denied in the articles of incorporation for corporations formed prior to October 1, 1991. NRS 78.267, 265.

Acts Requiring Shareholder Approval: Unless a statute, the articles of incorporation, or the board of directors require a greater vote, a majority vote of the shares entitled to vote is required for a merger or share exchange. NRS 78.453. Unless the articles of incorporation require a greater vote, a majority vote of the shares entitled to vote is required for the sale or transfer of all corporate assets, for voluntary dissolution, and to amend the articles of incorporation. NRS 78.565, 580, 390.

Board of Directors: May consist of one or more individuals of age 18 or more, with number specified in bylaws or articles. NRS 78.115.

Officers: Must have president, secretary and treasurer. May have other officers. One person may hold any two or more offices. NRS 78.130.

Foreign Corporations: Must qualify with the Secretary of State before doing business in Nevada. The statute contains a list of activities that do not constitute doing business in the state. The penalties for doing business without qualifying include nonaccess to state courts, a corporate fine of $500 or more, and individual fines of $500 or more. NRS 80.010, 015, 210.

Close Corporation Laws: Has Close Corporation Code (NRS 78A.010 et seq) whereunder a statutory close corporation must have 30 or fewer shareholders and make no public offering of its stock.

Periodic Reports: Domestic and authorized foreign corporations must file an annual report with the Secretary of State by the last day of its anniversary month and pay an annual fee to remain in good standing. NRS 78.150, 760, 80.110.

STATE FILING OFFICIAL. Secretary of State, Capitol Complex, Carson City, NV 89701 (Telephone: 702-687-5203).

Fees: Filing Articles of Incorporation - Fee based on capitalization ($125 minimum).

Amending Articles of Incorporation - $75	Name Reservation - $20	Other Corp. Fees - See NRS 78.150, 78.755 et seq.
Filing LLC Articles of Organization - $125	Corp. Annual Fee - $85	Other LLC Fees - See NRS 88.561.
Filing LLP Certificate of Registration - $125		Other LLP Fees - See NRS 87.550.

SUMMARY OF NEW HAMPSHIRE BUSINESS ORGANIZATION LAWS

PARTNERSHIP LAWS.

General Partnerships: Uniform Partnership Act adopted. RSA chap. 304-A.

Limited Partnerships: Revised Uniform Limited Partnership Act adopted. RSA chap. 304-B.

Limited Liability Partnerships: Registered LLPs provided for. RSA 304-A:44 et seq.

Name Registration: Must file a trade name certificate with the Secretary of State if the partnership name does not contain the names of all partners. RSA 349:1, 5. Must also file a certificate upon the addition or withdrawal of a partner. RSA 349:2.

LIMITED LIABILITY COMPANY LAWS. Limited Liability Company Law. RSA 304-C:1 et seq.

Formation of LLC: One or more persons may form an LLC by filing a certificate of formation and a securities registration statement with the Secretary of State. See RSA 304-C:12 for the certificate of formation content requirements.

General LLC Requirements: May have one or more members. May conduct any lawful business except banking, railroad construction, insurance or trust businesses. Professional LLCs must be formed under Professional LLC Law (RSA 304-D:1 et seq.).

Management of LLC: Vested in members unless otherwise provided in LLC agreement.

New or Substituted Members: Admission to LLC requires approval of all members unless otherwise provided in LLC agreement.

Conversion Statutes: Merger statute. RSA 304-C:18 et seq. Conversion statute. RSA 304-C:17-a et seq.

CORPORATION LAWS. New Hampshire Business Corporation Act (based on Revised Model Business Corporation Act). RSA chap. 293-A.

Corporate Name: Must contain the word "corporation," "incorporated," or "limited," or an abbreviation thereof. May not be the same as or deceptively similar to the name of any other corporation or other registered entity. Name may be reserved for 120 days. Availability of name may be checked informally with Secretary of State. RSA 293-A:4.01, 4.02.

Incorporators: One or more individuals or entities. RSA 293-A:2.01.

Articles of Incorporation:

Contents: See RSA 293-A:2.02 for required and optional article of incorporation content requirements.

Filing and Recording: Two original copies of the articles of incorporation must be filed with the Secretary of State and the filing and license fees paid. Corporate existence begins when the articles of incorporation are filed. A statement concerning the registration of the corporation's stock must also be filed. RSA 293-A:1.20, 2.03, 421-B:13.

Amendment: Requires majority of votes entitled to be cast, unless a statute, the board of directors, a shareholder-adopted bylaw, or the articles of incorporation require a greater vote. The board of directors can make ministerial amendments. RSA 293-A:10.02, 10.03.

Organizational Meeting: Held after incorporation by initial board of directors if named in articles of incorporation. Otherwise held after incorporation by incorporators, who may act without meeting if all incorporators sign a written consent to the action. RSA 293-A:2.05.

Bylaws: Initial bylaws adopted by the incorporators or board of directors. May be amended by the shareholders and by the board of directors unless that power is reserved to the shareholders in the articles of incorporation or as to a particular amendment. RSA 293-A:2.06, 10.20.

Action Without Meeting: Shareholders may act without meeting if all shareholders entitled to vote sign a written consent to the action. RSA 293-A:7.04. Unless the articles or bylaws provide otherwise, the board of directors may meet via communications equipment whereby they can simultaneously hear each other and may act without meeting if all directors sign a written consent to the action. RSA 293-A:8.20, 8.21.

Stock Certificates: Must be signed by two officers designated in bylaws or by the board of directors. Shares may be issued without a certificate unless the articles of incorporation or bylaws provide otherwise. RSA 293-A:6.25, 6.26.

Consideration For Stock: May consist of any tangible or intangible property or benefit to the corporation, including cash, promissory notes, services performed or to be performed, and other securities of the corporation. RSA 293-A:6.21.

Stock Transfer Restrictions: May be imposed by the articles of incorporation, bylaws or a shareholders' agreement. A restriction must be conspicuously noted on the stock certificate to be enforceable against a person without knowledge of the restriction. RSA 293-A:6.27.

Cumulative Voting: Not permitted unless provided for in the articles of incorporation and prior notice is given. RSA 293-A:7.28.

Preemptive Rights: Do not exist unless provided in the articles of incorporation. RSA 293-A:6.30.

Acts Requiring Shareholder Approval: Unless a statute, the articles of incorporation, or the board of directors require a greater vote, a majority of all votes entitled to be cast is required for a merger or share exchange, for the sale of all of the corporate assets not in the usual course of business, for voluntary dissolution, and for most amendments to the articles of incorporation. RSA 293-A:11.03, 12.02, 14.02, 10.03.

Board of Directors: May consist of one or more individuals with the number of directors specified in the bylaws or articles of incorporation. May be dispensed with or have authority limited in the articles of incorporation or in a shareholders' agreement. RSA 293-A:8.01, 8.03.

Officers: Those described in the bylaws or appointed by the board of directors in accordance with the bylaws. No specific officers required. The same person may simultaneously hold more than one office. RSA 293-A:8.40.

Foreign Corporations: Must obtain a certificate of authority from the Secretary of State to transact business in New Hampshire. The statute contains a nonexclusive list of activities that do not constitute transacting business in the state. The penalties for transacting business without a certificate of authority include nonaccess to state courts and liability for all fees, taxes and penalties that would have been assessed had a certificate of authority been issued. RSA 293A-15.01, 15.02.

Close Corporation Laws: The shareholders may operate a corporation under a unanimous shareholders agreement. RSA 293-A:7.32.

Periodic Reports: Domestic and authorized foreign corporations must file an annual report on prescribed forms with the Secretary of State by April 1 of each year and pay an annual report fee and an annual franchise fee to remain in good standing. RSA 203-A:16.22, 1.22.

STATE FILING OFFICIAL. Secretary of State, Corporations Division, State House Annex, Concord, NH 03301 (Telephone: 603-271-3244).

Fees: Filing Articles of Incorporation - $35 filing fee, plus $50 stock registration fee, plus license fee based on capitalization ($75 minimum).

Amending Articles of Incorporation - $35 | Corp. or LLC Annual Report Fee - $100 | Other Corp. Fees - See RSA 293-A:1.22.

Application for Certificate of Authority - $35 plus $200 license fee. | Other LLC Fees - See RSA 304-C:81.

Filing LLC Certificate of Formation - $35 | Name Reservation - $15 | Other LLP Fees - See RSA 304-A:51.

Filing LLP Registration Statement - $100

SUMMARY OF NEW JERSEY BUSINESS ORGANIZATION LAWS

PARTNERSHIP LAWS.

General Partnerships: Uniform Partnership Act adopted. NJSA 42:1-1 et seq.

Limited Partnerships: Revised Uniform Limited Partnership Act adopted. NJSA 42:2A-1 et seq.

Limited Liability Partnerships: Registered limited liability partnerships provided for. NJSA 42:1-44 et seq.

Name Registration: If partnership name does not contain the names of all partners a fictitious name certificate must be filed with the county clerk in each county where business is conducted. A nonresident partner must designate the county clerk as agent for service of process. Must file a statement with the Secretary of State if the partnership name contains the words "and company" or "& Co." NJSA 56:1-1, 2.

LIMITED LIABILITY COMPANY LAWS. New Jersey Limited Liability Company Act. NJSA 42:2B-1 et seq.

Formation of LLC: One or more persons may form an LLC by filing a certificate of formation with the Secretary of State. See NJSA 42:2B-11 for the certificate of formation content requirements.

General LLC Requirements: Must have two or more members. May conduct any lawful business.

Management of LLC: Vested in members unless otherwise provided in operating agreement.

New or Substituted Members: Admission to LLC requires consent of all members unless otherwise provided in operating agreement.

Conversion Statutes: Merger or consolidation statute. NJSA 42:2B-20. No partnership conversion statute.

CORPORATION LAWS. New Jersey Business Corporation Act (Model Business Corporation Acts not adopted). NJSA 14A:1-1 et seq.

Corporate Name: Must contain the word "corporation," "company," or "incorporated" or an abbreviation thereof or the abbreviation "Ltd." and must be distinguishable on records of Secretary of State from the reserved or existing name of any other corporation or limited partnership. May not contain the words "blind" or "handicapped" or similar words unless approved by the Attorney General. Name may be reserved for 120 days. A certificate of availability of name is issued by the Secretary of State upon a written request. NJSA 14A:2-2, 2.2, 3.

Incorporators: One or more individuals or corporations. NJSA 14A:2-6.

Certificate of Incorporation:

Contents: See NJSA 14A:2-7 for required and optional certificate of incorporation content requirements.

Filing and Recording: The certificate of incorporation must be filed with the Secretary of State and the filing fee paid. Corporate existence begins when the certificate of incorporation is accepted for filing. NJSA 14A:2-7.

Amendment: Requires a majority vote of the shares entitled to vote unless the certificate of incorporation requires a greater vote. The board of directors may make certain minor amendments without shareholder approval. NJSA 14A:9-2.

Organizational Meeting: Held after incorporation by the initial board of directors. NJSA 14A:2-8.

Bylaws: Initial bylaws adopted by board of directors. May be amended by the shareholders and by the board of directors unless the certificate of incorporation reserves that power to the shareholders. Shareholder amendments may prohibit board of director amendment. NJSA 14A:2-9.

Action Without Meeting: Shareholders may act without meeting if a written consent to the action is signed by all shareholders entitled to vote, or, unless otherwise provided in the certificate of incorporation and except for the election of directors, by shareholders sufficient to carry the action at a meeting if the notice requirements are complied with. NJSA 14A:5-6. Unless otherwise provided in the certificate of incorporation or bylaws, the board of directors may act without meeting if all directors sign a written consent to the action and may meet via conference telephone or similar communications equipment. NJSA 14A:6-7.1, 10.

Stock Certificates: Must be signed by chairman or vice chairman of board, president or vice president and may be countersigned by the treasurer, secretary, or assistant thereof. Shares may be issued without a certificate. NJSA 14A:7-11.

Consideration For Stock: May consist of money, real property, tangible or intangible personal property, secured or unsecured obligations, or labor or services performed or to be performed for the corporation. NJSA 14A:7-5.

Stock Transfer Restrictions: May be imposed by certificate of incorporation, bylaws, employee benefit plan, or shareholders' agreement. Must be conspicuously noted on stock certificate to be enforceable against a person without knowledge of the restriction. NJSA 14A:7-12.

Cumulative Voting: Not permitted unless provided for in the certificate of incorporation. NJSA 14A:5-24.

Preemptive Rights: Do not exist unless contained in the certificate of incorporation. NJSA 14A:5-29.

Acts Requiring Shareholder Approval: Unless the certificate of incorporation requires a greater vote, a majority of the votes cast is required for a merger, consolidation, or share exchange, for the sale or disposition of all or substantially all of the corporate assets not in the usual course of business, for voluntary dissolution, and for most amendments to the certificate of incorporation (see above). NJSA 14A:10-3, 10-11, 10-13, 12-4, 9-2, 5-12.

Board of Directors: May consist of one or more persons with the number of directors specified in the certificate of incorporation or bylaws. A corporation may, in its certificate of incorporation, dispense with or limit the authority of the board of directors. NJSA 14A:6-2, 5-21(2).

Officers: Must have president, secretary, and treasurer. The bylaws may provide for other officers. The same person may hold any two or more offices, but may not execute certain instruments in more than one capacity. NJSA 14A:6-15.

Foreign Corporations: Must obtain a certificate of authority from the Secretary of State to transact business in New Jersey. The statute contains a nonexclusive list of activities that do not constitute transacting business in the state. The penalties for transacting business without a certificate of authority include nonaccess to state courts, a reinstatement fee of $200, and liability for all fees, taxes and penalties that would have been imposed had a certificate of authority been issued. NJSA 14A:13-3, 11, 2(3).

Close Corporation Laws: Corp. may be managed by shareholders under cert. of incorporation provision complying with NJSA 14A:5-21.

Periodic Reports: Domestic and authorized foreign corporations must file an annual report on prescribed forms with the Secretary of State by a prescribed date and pay an annual report fee and an annual franchise tax to remain in good standing NJSA 14A:4-5, 15-2, 3, 54:10A-2.

STATE FILING OFFICIAL. Secretary of State, 820 Bear Tavern Road, West Trenton, NJ 08625 (Telephone: 609-984-1900).

Fees:

Filing Certificate of Incorporation - $100
Amending Certificate of Incorporation - $50
Filing LLC Certificate of Formation - $100
Filing LLP Certificate of Registration - $100

Name Reservation - $50
Corp. Annual Report - $40
LLC Annual Report - $50

Other Corp. Fees - See NJSA 14A:15-2, 3.
Other LLC Fees - See NJSA 42:2B-65.
Other LLP Fees - See NJSA 42:1-48.

SUMMARY OF NEW MEXICO BUSINESS ORGANIZATION LAWS

PARTNERSHIP LAWS.

General Partnerships: Uniform Partnership Act (1994). NMS 54-1A-101 et seq.
Limited Partnerships: Revised Uniform Limited Partnership Act adopted. NMS 54-2-1 et seq.
Limited Liability Partnerships: Provided for. NMS 54-1-44 et seq. ($500,000 of liability insurance or security deposit required.)
Name Registration: Not required, but may register trade name with Secretary of State. NMS 57-3-2.

LIMITED LIABILITY COMPANY LAWS. Limited Liability Company Act. NMS 53-19-1 et seq.

Formation of LLC: One or more persons may form an LLC by filing articles of organization with the State Filing Official. See NMS 53-19-8 for the article of organization content requirements.
General LLC Requirements: May have one or more members. May conduct any lawful business.
Management of LLC: Vested in members unless vested in managers in articles of organization.
New or Substituted Members: Admission to LLC requires written consent of all members unless otherwise provided in the articles of organization or operating agreement.
Conversion Statutes: Partnership conversion statute. NMS 53-19-60, 61. Merger or consolidation statute. NMS 53-19-62 et seq.

CORPORATION LAWS. Business Corporation Act (based on Model Business Corporation Act). NMS 53-11-1 et seq.

Corporate Name: Must contain the separate word "corporation," "company," " incorporated," or "limited" or an abbreviation thereof and may not be the same as or confusedly similar to the existing or reserved name of any other corporation. Name may be reserved for 120 days. Separate name clearance procedure not available. NMS 53-11-7, 8.
Incorporators: One or more persons or a corporation. NMS 53-12-1.
Articles of Incorporation:
- **Contents:** See NMS 53-12-2 for required and optional article of incorporation content requirements.
- **Filing and Recording:** Two original copies of the articles of incorporation, together with the registered agent's affidavit of acceptance of appointment, must be filed with the state filing official and the filing fee and franchise tax paid. Corporate existence begins when the articles of incorporation are accepted for filing. NMS 53-12-3, 4.
- **Amendment:** Requires a majority vote of the shares entitled to vote unless the articles of incorporation require a greater vote. NMS 53-13-2, 53-18-6.

Organizational Meeting: Held after incorporation by the initial board of directors. NMS 53-12-5.
Bylaws: Initial bylaws adopted by the board of directors. May be amended by board of directors unless that power is reserved to the shareholders in the articles of incorporation. NMS 53-11-27.
Action Without Meeting: Shareholders may act without meeting if all shareholders entitled to vote sign a written consent to the action. NMS 53-18-8. Unless provided otherwise in the articles of incorporation or bylaws, the board of directors may act without meeting if all directors sign a written consent to the action and may meet via conference telephone or similar communications equipment. NMS 53-11-43, 42.
Stock Certificates: Must be signed by chairman or vice chairman of board, president or vice president and by treasurer, secretary, or assistant of either. Shares may be issued without a certificate unless the articles of incorporation or bylaws provide otherwise. NMS 53-11-23.
Consideration For Stock: May consist of money, tangible or intangible property, or labor or services actually performed for the corporation. May not consist of promissory notes or future services. NMS 53-11-19.
Stock Transfer Restrictions: May be set forth in the articles of incorporation. NMS 53-12-2.
Cumulative Voting: Not permitted unless provided for in the articles of incorporation. NMS 53-11-33.
Preemptive Rights: Exist unless denied or limited in the articles of incorporation. NMS 53-11-26.
Acts Requiring Shareholder Approval: Unless the articles of incorporation require a greater vote, a majority vote of the shares entitled to vote is required for a merger, consolidation, or share exchange, for the sale of all or substantially all of the corporate assets not in the usual course of business, for voluntary dissolution, and to amend the articles of incorporation. NMS 53-14-3, 53-15-2, 53-16-3, 53-13-2, 53-18-6.
Board of Directors: May consist of one or more directors with the number of directors specified in the articles of incorporation or bylaws. NMS 53-11-36. Each director must file an affidavit with the corporation consenting to serve on the board. NMS 53-12-6.
Officers: Those specified or provided for in the bylaws. The number of officers must be sufficient to sign corporate instruments and stock certificates. NMS 53-11-48.
Foreign Corporations: Must obtain a certificate of authority from the state filing official to transact business in New Mexico. The statute contains a nonexclusive list of activities that do not constitute transacting business in the state. The penalties for transacting business without a certificate of authority include nonaccess to state courts, liability for all fees, taxes and penalties that would have been imposed had a certificate of authority been issued, and a civil penalty of $200 per offense. NMS 53-17-1, 20.
Close Corporation Laws: None.
Periodic Reports: Domestic and authorized foreign corporations must file an annual report with the state filing official by the 15th day of the third month after the end of corporation's tax year and pay an annual report fee and an annual franchise tax to remain in good standing. The first report is due 30 days after the issuance of the certificate of incorporation. NMS 53-5-2, 53-2-1, 7-2A-5.1.

STATE FILING OFFICIAL. State Corporation Commission, P.O. Drawer 1269, Santa Fe, NM 87504-1269 (Telephone: 505-827-4500).

Fees:
Filing Articles of Incorporation - $100 to $1,000 depending on capitalization.
Amending Articles of Incorporation - $100 (more if capitalization is increased).
Filing LLC Articles of Organization - $50
Filing LLP Registration - $50

Corp. Name Reservation - $25
Other Corp. Fees - See NMS 53-2-1.
Other LLC Fees - See NMS 53-19-63.

SUMMARY OF NEW YORK BUSINESS ORGANIZATION LAWS

PARTNERSHIP LAWS.

General Partnerships: Uniform Partnership Act adopted. PL 1 to 82.

Limited Partnerships: Revised Uniform Limited Partnership Act adopted. PL 121-101 et seq.

Limited Liability Partnerships: Registered limited liability partnerships provided for. PL 121-1500 et seq.

Name Registration: All general partnerships (except law firms) must file a fictitious name certificate with the county clerk in each county where business is conducted. GBL 130.

LIMITED LIABILITY COMPANY LAWS. Limited Liability Company Law (LLCL).

Formation of LLC: One or more persons may form an LLC by filing articles of organization with the state filing official. See LLCL 203(e) for the article of organization content requirements.

General LLC Requirements: May have one or more members. May conduct any lawful business unless prohibited by another statute. Professional LLCs must comply with special provisions (LLCL 1201 et seq.).

Management of LLC: Vested in members unless articles of organization provide for managers. LLCL 401.

New or Substituted Members: Admission to LLC requires vote or written consent of majority in interest of members, unless the operating agreement provides otherwise. LLCL 602, 604.

Conversion Statutes: Partnership conversion statute. LLCL 1006, 1007. Merger or consolidation statute. LLCL 1001-1005.

CORPORATION LAWS. New York Business Corporation Law (BCL). (Model Business Corporation Acts not adopted).

Corporate Name: Must contain the word "corporation," "incorporated," or "limited" or an abbreviation thereof and must not be confusedly or deceptively similar to the name of any other corporation. The statute contains a list of forbidden names. Name may be reserved for a renewable 60-day period. Written requests concerning the availability of a name are accepted by the state filing official. BCL 301, 302, 303.

Incorporators: One or more natural persons of age 18 or more. BCL 401.

Certificate of Incorporation:

Contents: See BCL 402 for required optional certificate of incorporation content requirements.

Filing and Recording: Certificate of incorporation must be filed with state filing official (who sends copy to county clerk) and filing fee and organization tax paid. Corporate existence begins when the certificate of incorporation is filed. BCL 104, 104-A, 402, 403, TL 180.

Amendment: Requires majority vote of the outstanding shares entitled to vote unless the certificate of incorporation requires a greater vote. The board of directors may make certain minor amendments without shareholder approval. BCL 803, 616.

Organizational Meeting: Held by the incorporators after incorporation. The incorporators may act without meeting if each incorporator or his or her attorney-in-fact signs a written consent to the action. BCL 404.

Bylaws: Initial bylaws adopted by the incorporators. May be amended by the shareholders and, if so provided in the certificate of incorporation or in an original or a shareholder-adopted bylaw, by the board of directors. The shareholders may change director amendments. BCL 601.

Action Without Meeting: Shareholders may act without meeting if a written consent to the action is signed by all shareholders entitled to vote. BCL 615. Unless otherwise provided in the certificate of incorporation or bylaws, the board of directors may act without meeting if all directors sign a written consent to the action, and may meet via conference telephone or similar communications equipment. BCL 708.

Stock Certificates: Must be signed by chairman or vice chairman of board, president or vice president, and by secretary, treasurer, or assistant of either. Shares may be issued without a certificate unless the certificate of incorporation or bylaws provide otherwise. BCL 508.

Consideration For Stock: May consist of money, tangible or intangible property, or labor or services actually performed for the corporation. May not consist of obligation of subscriber for future services. BCL 504.

Stock Transfer Restrictions: May be set forth in the certificate of incorporation and in the bylaws. BCL 402, 508(d).

Cumulative Voting: Not permitted unless provided for in the certificate of incorporation. BCL 618.

Preemptive Rights: Do not exist unless contained in the certificate of incorporation. BCL 505.

Acts Requiring Shareholder Approval: Unless the certificate of incorporation requires a greater vote, a two-thirds vote of the outstanding shares entitled to vote is required for a merger, consolidation, or share exchange, for the sale or transfer of all or substantially all of the corporate assets not in the usual course of business, and for voluntary dissolution. BCL 903, 913, 909, 1001, 616. Shareholder approval is also required for most amendments to the certificate of incorporation (see above).

Board of Directors: May consist of one or more persons of age 18 or more, with the number of directors specified in the bylaws or by shareholder action (if no number is specified, there is one). BCL 701, 702.

Officers: May have president, vice president, secretary, and treasurer. The bylaws may provide for other officers. The same person may hold any two or more offices. Sole shareholder may hold all offices. BCL 715.

Foreign Corporations: Must be authorized by the state filing official to do business in New York. The statute contains a nonexclusive list of activities that do not constitute doing business in the state. The penalties for doing business without authorization include nonaccess to state courts and liability for all fees, taxes and penalties that would have been imposed had authority to do business been obtained. The Attorney General may seek injunctive relief. BCL 1301, 1303, 1312, TL 181.

Close Corporation Laws: Has no close corporation code. However, the 10 largest shareholders of every corporation, except those with publicly-traded stock, are personally liable for corporate debts for unpaid wages or salaries owed to employees. BCL 630.

Periodic Reports: Domestic and authorized foreign corporations must file an annual statement with the state filing official and an annual franchise tax report with the State Tax Commission within 2 1/2 months after the end of the corporation's tax year and pay an annual franchise tax to remain in good standing. BCL 408, TL 208, 209, 210.

STATE FILING OFFICIAL. Department of State, 162 Washington Avenue, Albany, NY 12210 (Telephone: 518-474-4750).

Fees:

Filing Certificate of Incorporation - $125 plus organization tax based on capitalization ($10 minimum). — Name Reservation - $20

Amending Certificate of Incorporation - $60 (more if capitalization increased). — Other Corp. Fees - See BCL 104-A

Filing LLC Articles of Organization - $200 — Other LLC Fees - LLCL 1101

Filing LLP Registration - $200

SUMMARY OF NORTH CAROLINA BUSINESS ORGANIZATION LAWS

PARTNERSHIP LAWS.

General Partnerships: Uniform Partnership Act adopted. GS 59-31 et seq.

Limited Partnerships: Revised Uniform Limited Partnership Act adopted. GS 59-101 et seq.

Limited Liability Partnerships: Registered limited liability partnerships provided for. GS 59-84.2, 84.3.

Name Registration: Must file a fictitious name certificate with the register of deeds in each county where business is conducted if the partnership name does not contain the names of all partners (law firms excepted). GS 59-84.1, 66-68.

LIMITED LIABILITY COMPANY LAWS. North Carolina Limited Liability Company Act. GS 57C-1-01 et seq.

Formation of LLC: One or more persons may form an LLC by filing articles of organization with the Secretary of State. See GS 57C-2-21 for the article of organization content requirements.

General LLC Requirements: May have one or more members. May engage in any lawful business. Professional LLCs must comply with Professional Corporation Act (GS 57C-2-01(c)).

Management of LLC: Reserved to managers (all members are deemed to be managers unless the articles of organization provide otherwise).

New or Substituted Members: Requires consent of all members unless operating agreement or articles of organization provide otherwise.

Conversion Statutes: None in LLC Act.

CORPORATION LAWS. North Carolina Business Corporation Act (based on Revised Model Business Corporation Act). GS 55-1-1 et seq.

Corporate Name: Must contain the word "corporation," "incorporated," "company," or "limited" or an abbreviation thereof and must be distinguishable from the actual, reserved or fictitious name of any other corporation. Name may be reserved for 120 days. GS 55-4-01, 02.

Incorporators: One or more individuals or entities. GS 55-2-01.

Articles of Incorporation:

Contents: See GS 55-2-02 for required and optional article of incorporation content requirements..

Filing and Recording: An original and one copy of the articles of incorporation must be filed with the Secretary of State and the filing fee paid. Corporate existence begins when the articles of incorporation are accepted for filing. GS 55-1-20, 55-2-03.

Amendment: Requires majority of votes entitled to be cast, unless a statute, the board of directors, a shareholder-adopted bylaw, or the articles of incorporation require a greater vote. The board of directors may make certain ministerial amendments. GS 55-10-02, 03.

Organizational Meeting: Held after incorporation by initial board of directors if named in articles of incorporation. Otherwise held after incorporation by incorporators, who may act without meeting if all incorporators sign a written consent to the action. GS 55-2-05.

Bylaws: Initial bylaws adopted by the incorporators or board of directors. May be amended by the shareholders and by the board of directors unless that power is reserved to the shareholders in the articles of incorporation. A shareholder amendment may preclude its subsequent amendment by the board of directors. GS 55-2-06, 55-10-20.

Action Without Meeting: Shareholders may act without meeting if all shareholders entitled to vote sign a written consent to the action. GS 55-7-04. Unless the articles of incorporation or bylaws provide otherwise, the board of directors may meet via conference telephone or similar communications equipment and may act without meeting if all directors sign a written consent to the action. GS 55-8-20, 21.

Stock Certificates: Must be signed by two officers designated in bylaws or by the board of directors. Shares may be issued without a certificate unless the articles of incorporation or bylaws provide otherwise. GS 55-6-25, 26.

Consideration For Stock: May consist of any tangible or intangible property or benefit to the corporation, including cash, promissory notes, services performed or to be performed, and other securities of the corporation. Shares issued for promissory notes or future services may be placed in escrow or otherwise restricted pending payment of note or performance of services. GS 55-6-21.

Stock Transfer Restrictions: May be imposed by the articles of incorporation, bylaws or a shareholders' agreement. A restriction must be conspicuously noted on the stock certificate to be enforceable against a person without knowledge of the restriction. GS 55-6-27.

Cumulative Voting: Not permitted unless provided for in the articles of incorporation and prior notice is given (must be permitted in corporations formed prior to July 1, 1990). GS 55-7-28.

Preemptive Rights: Do not exist unless contained in the articles of incorporation (exist for corps. formed before July 1, 1990). GS 55-6-30.

Acts Requiring Shareholder Approval: Unless a statute, the articles of incorporation, a bylaw adopted by the shareholders, or the board of directors require a greater vote, a majority of the votes entitled to be cast is required for a merger or share exchange, for the sale or disposition of all or substantially all of the corporate assets not in the usual course of business, for voluntary dissolution, and for most amendments to the articles of incorporation (see above). GS 55-11-03, 55-12-02, 55-14-02, 55-10-03.

Board of Directors: May consist of one or more individuals with number specified in bylaws or articles of incorporation. GS 55-8-03.

Officers: Those described in the bylaws or appointed by the board of directors in accordance with the bylaws. No specific officers required. The same person may simultaneously hold more than one office, but may not act in a dual capacity where two officers are required. GS 55-8-40.

Foreign Corporations: Must obtain a certificate of authority from the Secretary of State before transacting business in North Carolina. The statute contains a nonexclusive list of activities that do not constitute transacting business in the state. The penalties for transacting business without a certificate of authority include nonaccess to state courts, liability for all fees, taxes and penalties that would have been imposed had a certificate of authority been issued, and a civil penalty of $10 per day not to exceed $1000 per year. GS 55-15-01, 02.

Close Corporation Laws: Shareholders may manage corporation under unanimous shareholders' agreement. GS 55-7-31, 55-8-01.

Periodic Reports: Each domestic and authorized foreign corporation must file an annual report with the Secretary of State by the 60th day after the end of its anniversary month and pay an annual report fee to remain in good standing. Such corporations must also file a a franchise tax report with the Secretary of Revenue and pay an annual franchise tax. GS 55-16-22, 55-1-22, 105-122.

STATE FILING OFFICIAL. Secretary of State, 300 North Salisbury Street, Raleigh, NC 27611 (Telephone: 919-733-5140).

Fees:
- Filing Articles of Incorporation - $125
- Application For Certificate of Authority - $250
- Filing LLC Articles of Organization - $125
- Filing LLP Registration Application - $100
- Amending Articles of Incorporation - $50
- Annual Report of Corp. - $20
- Name Reservation - $10
- Other Corp. Fees - See GS 55-1-22.
- Other LLC Fees - See GS 57C-1-22.

SUMMARY OF NORTH DAKOTA BUSINESS ORGANIZATION LAWS

PARTNERSHIP LAWS.

General Partnerships: Uniform Partnership Act repealed. CC 45-13-01 et seq.

Limited Partnerships: Revised Uniform Limited Partnership Act adopted. CC 45-10.1-01 et seq.

Limited Liability Partnerships: Limited liability partnerships provided for. CC 45-22-01 et seq.

Name Registration: Must file a fictitious name certificate with the Secretary of State if the partnership name does not contain the names of all partners. CC 45-11-01.

LIMITED LIABILITY COMPANY LAWS. North Dakota Limited Liability Company Act. CC 10-32-01 et seq.

Formation of LLC: One or more individuals of age 18 or more may form an LLC by filing articles of organization with the Secretary of State. See CC 10-32-07 for the article of organization content requirements.

General LLC Requirements: Must have two or more members unless articles of organization authorize 1-member LLC. May conduct any lawful business. Must qualify under CC 10-06-1.01 et seq. to conduct farming or ranching business.

Management of LLC: Vested in board of governors unless members have member-control agreement. CC 10-32-69.

New or Substituted Members: Admission to LLC requires written consent of all members unless articles of organization provide otherwise.

Conversion Statutes: Merger or exchange statute. CC 10-32-100 et seq. No partnership conversion statute.

CORPORATION LAWS. North Dakota Business Corporation Act (Model Business Corporation Acts not adopted). CC 10-19.1-01 et seq.

Corporate Name: Must contain the word "corporation," "incorporated," "limited," or "company" or an abbreviation thereof and may not be the same as or deceptively similar to the existing or reserved name of any other corporation or other registered entity or trade name. Name may be reserved for 12 months. CC 10-19.1-13, 14.

Incorporators: One or more individuals of age 18 or more. CC 10-19.1-09.

Articles of Incorporation:

Contents: See CC 10-19.1-10 for required and optional article of incorporation content requirements.

Filing and Recording: An original copy of the articles of incorporation and the registered agent's consent to serve must be filed with the Secretary of State and the filing fee and license fee paid. Corporate existence begins when the Secretary of State issues a certificate of incorporation. CC 10-19.1-11, 12, 15.

Amendment: Requires a majority vote of shares present and entitled to vote, unless the articles of incorporation require a greater vote. CC 10-19.1-19, 74.

Note: A corporation must qualify as a "farming or ranching corporation" to engage in the business of farming or ranching. CC 10-06-1.01 et seq.

Organizational Meeting: Held after incorporation by the incorporators or by the initial board of directors if named in articles of incorporation. May take written action in lieu of meeting. CC 10-19.1-30.

Bylaws: Initial bylaws adopted by the incorporators or the initial board of directors. May be amended by the shareholders and by the board of directors, unless that power is reserved to the shareholders in the articles of incorporation. CC 10-19.1-31.

Action Without Meeting: Shareholders may act without meeting if all shareholders entitled to vote sign a written consent to the action. NDCC 10-19.1-75. The board of directors may meet via communications equipment whereby they can simultaneously hear each other and may act without meeting if a written consent to the action is signed by all directors, or, if the articles of incorporation so provide, by directors sufficient to carry the action at a meeting and immediate notice is given to all directors. CC 10-19.1-43, 47.

Stock Certificates: Must be signed by president or vice president and by secretary or assistant secretary. Shares may not be issued without a certificate. CC 10-19.1-66.

Consideration For Stock: May consist of money, tangible or intangible property, or labor or services actually performed for the corporation. May not consist of promissory notes or future services. CC 10-19.1-63.

Stock Transfer Restrictions: May be imposed by the articles of incorporation, bylaws or a shareholders' resolution or agreement, and must be conspicuously noted on the stock certificate to be enforceable against a person without knowledge of the restriction. CC 10-19.1-70.

Cumulative Voting: Must be permitted. CC 10-19.1-10(2), 39.

Preemptive Rights: Exist unless denied or limited in the articles of incorporation or by the board of directors. CC 10-19.1-65.

Acts Requiring Shareholder Approval: Unless the articles of incorporation require a greater vote, a majority vote of all shares entitled to vote is required for a merger or share exchange, for the sale or transfer of all or substantially all of the corporate assets not in the usual course of business, for voluntary dissolution, and to amend the articles of incorporation. CC 10-19.1-98, 104, 107, 19, 74.

Board of Directors: May consist of one or more individuals with number specified in articles of incorporation or bylaws. CC 10-19.1-33, 34.

Officers: Must have president, vice president, secretary and treasurer. The bylaws may provide for other officers. The same person may hold any two or more offices and may sign documents in a dual capacity. CC 10-19.1-52, 55.

Foreign Corporations: Must obtain a certificate of authority from the Secretary of State to transact business in North Dakota. The statute contains nonexclusive list of activities that do not constitute transacting business in the state. The penalties for transacting business without a certificate of authority include nonaccess to state courts and liability for all fees and penalties that would have been imposed had a certificate of authority been issued. CC 10-22-01, 19.

Close Corporation Laws: None.

Periodic Reports: Domestic and authorized foreign corporations must file an annual report with the Secretary of State by August 1 (April 1 for foreign corporations) of each year and pay an annual report fee and an annual license fee to remain in good standing. CC 10-23-01 to 07.

STATE FILING OFFICIAL. Secretary of State, Capitol Building, Bismarck, ND 58501 (Telephone: 701-328-4284).

Fees: Filing Articles of Incorporation - $30 plus license fee (see below) plus $10 for registered agent's consent.

Amending Articles of Incorporation - $20 License Fee - Based on capitalization ($50 minimum). Other Corp. Fees - See CC 10-19.1-147.

Filing LLC Articles of Organization - $125 Annual Report - $25 Other LLC Fees - See CC 10-32-150.

Filing LLP Registration - $25-$250 depending on no. of partners Name Reservation - $10 Other LLP Fees - See CC 45-22-22.

SUMMARY OF OHIO BUSINESS ORGANIZATION LAWS

PARTNERSHIP LAWS.

General Partnerships: Uniform Partnership Act adopted. RC 1775.01 et seq.

Limited Partnerships: Revised Uniform Limited Partnership Act adopted. RC 1782.01 et seq.

Limited Liability Partnerships: Registered Limited Liability Partnerships provided for. RC 1775.61 et seq.

Name Registration: Must file a fictitious name certificate with the county recorder in the county of the partnership's principal office and in each county where real estate is owned if the partnership name does not contain the names of all partners. RC 1777.02.

LIMITED LIABILITY COMPANY LAWS. Limited Liability Company Law. RC 1705.01 et seq.

Formation of LLC: One or more persons may form an LLC by filing articles of organization with the Secretary of State. See RC 1705.04 for article of organization content requirements.

General LLC Requirements: May have one or more members. May conduct any lawful business not precluded by statute. Special requirements for professional LLCs (RC 1705.04(C)).

Management of LLC: Vested in members in proportion to capital contributions unless otherwise provided in written operating agreement.

New or Substituted Members: Admission to LLC requires consent of all members unless written operating agreement provides otherwise.

Conversion Statutes: Merger and consolidation statute. RC 1705.36 et seq. No partnership conversion statute.

CORPORATION LAWS. General Corporation Law (Model Business Corporation Acts not adopted). RC 1701.01 et seq.

Corporate Name: Must contain the word "Company," "Corporation," or "Incorporated" or a listed abbreviation thereof and must be distinguishable on the records of the Secretary of State from the name of any other corporation or registered trade name. Name may be reserved for 60 days. Availability of name may be checked with state filing official by telephone. RC 1701.04, 05.

Incorporators: One or more individuals, corporations, or other entities. RC 1701.04.

Articles of Incorporation:

- **Contents:** See RC 1701.04 for required and optional article of incorporation content requirements.
- **Filing and Recording:** The articles of incorporation, together with the agent's acceptance of appointment, must be filed with the state filing official and the filing fees paid. Corporate existence begins when articles of incorporation are accepted for filing. RC 1701.04, 07.
- **Amendment:** Requires a two-thirds vote of shares entitled to vote unless the articles of incorporation require a different vote of not less than a majority. The board of directors may make certain minor amendments without shareholder approval. RC 1701.70, 71.

Organizational Meeting: Held after incorporation by the shareholders. RC 1701.10.

Minimum Capitalization Requirement: No statutory requirement, but may be specified in the articles of incorporation. RC 1701.04, 12.

Regulations and Bylaws: Initial regulations adopted by the shareholders. May be amended by a two-thirds vote of the shareholders unless the articles of incorporation or regulations require a different vote of not less than a majority. RC 1701.11. The board of directors may adopt bylaws for their own use that are not inconsistent with the articles of incorporation or the regulations. RC 1701.59.

Action Without Meeting: Unless the articles of incorporation or regulations provide otherwise, the shareholders and the board of directors may act without meeting if all of the shareholders entitled to vote or all of the directors, as the case may be, sign a written consent to the action. RC 1701.54. Unless otherwise provided in the articles of incorporation, regulations, or bylaws, the board of directors may meet via conference telephone or similar communications equipment. RC 1701.61.

Stock Certificates: Must be signed by chairman of board, president or vice president, and by secretary, treasurer, or assistant thereof. Shares may be issued without a certificate unless otherwise provided in the articles of incorporation or regulations. RC 1701.24.

Consideration For Stock: May consist of money or property actually transferred to the corporation or services actually rendered to the corporation. May not consist of notes or obligations of the subscriber or promises of future services. RC 1701.18.

Stock Transfer Restrictions: May be contained in the regulations, articles of incorporation, or a written agreement. A restriction must appear or be noted on the stock certificate to be enforceable against a transferee. RC 1701.04, 11, 25.

Cumulative Voting: Permitted unless denied in an amendment to the articles of incorporation. Prior notice is required. RC 1701.55, 69.

Preemptive Rights: Exist unless denied or limited in articles of incorporation or released by vote of affected shareholders. RC 1701.15.

Acts Requiring Shareholder Approval: Unless the articles of incorporation or regulations specify a different vote of not less than a majority, a two-thirds vote of the shares entitled to vote is required for a merger or consolidation, for the sale or transfer of all or substantially all of the corporate assets not in the usual course of business, and for voluntary dissolution. RC 1701.78, 76, 86. Shareholder approval is also required for most amendments to the articles of incorporation and to amend the regulations (see above).

Board of Directors: Must consist of at least three directors except that there need not be more directors than shareholders. The number of directors may be specified in the articles of incorporation or regulations. RC 1701.56.

Officers: Must have president, secretary, and treasurer. May have other officers. The same person may hold any two or more offices, but may not sign legal documents in a dual capacity. RC 1701.64.

Foreign Corporations: Must obtain a license from the Secretary of State before transacting business in Ohio. The statute contains a list of exempt corporations. The penalties for transacting business without a license include nonaccess to state courts, liability for all fees, taxes and penalties that would have been assessed had a license been issued, and a $250 to $10,000 penalty. RC 1703.02, 03, 28, 29.

Close Corporation Laws: Has close corporation statute (RC 1701.591) whereunder a close corporation may be operated under a close corporation agreement, which must be agreed to in writing by all shareholders, set forth in the articles of incorporation, regulations, or in a written agreement, and include a statement that the corporation is to be governed by RC 1701.591.

Periodic Reports: Domestic and licensed foreign corporations must file an annual report with the state treasurer on prescribed forms by March 31 of each year and pay an annual franchise tax to remain in good standing. RC 5733.01 et seq., 1703.07.

STATE FILING OFFICIAL. Secretary of State, Corporations Div., 30 E. Broad St., 14th Fl., Columbus, OH 43266-0418 (614-466-3910).

Fees:

- Filing Articles of Incorporation - Fee based on capitalization ($85 minimum).
- Amending Articles of Incorporation - $35 (more if capitalization is increased).
- Filing LLC Articles of Organization - $85
- Filing LLP Registration Application - $85
- Annual Report - $10
- Name Reservation - $5
- Other Fees - See RC 111.16.

SUMMARY OF OKLAHOMA BUSINESS ORGANIZATION LAWS

PARTNERSHIP LAWS.

General Partnerships: Oklahoma Revised Uniform Partnership Act. 54 OSA 1-101 et seq.

Limited Partnerships: Revised Uniform Limited Partnership Act adopted. 54 OSA 301 et seq.

Limited Liability Partnerships: Provided for. 54 OSA 1-1001 et seq.

Name Registration: If the partnership name does not contain the names of all partners, a fictitious name certificate must be filed with the county clerk in the county of the partnership's principal place of business and published once in a county newspaper. 54 OSA 81 et seq.

LIMITED LIABILITY COMPANY LAWS. Oklahoma Limited Liability Company Act. 18 OSA 2000 et seq.

Formation of LLC: One or more persons may form an LLC by filing articles of organization with the Secretary of State. See 18 OSA 2005 for the article of organization content requirements.

General LLC Requirements: May have one or more members. May conduct any lawful business except banking and insurance. Special limitations imposed on farming and ranching LLCs (18 OSA 955).

Management of LLC: Vested in manager(s) unless articles of organization or operating agreement provide otherwise. 18 OSA 2013.

New or Substituted Members: Admission to LLC requires written consent of all members unless articles of organization or operating agreement provide otherwise. 18 OSA 2035.

Conversion Statutes: Merger statute. 18 OSA 2054.

CORPORATION LAWS. Oklahoma General Corporation Act (Model Business Corporation Acts not adopted). 18 OSA 1001 et seq.

Corporate Name: Must contain the word "association," "company," "corporation," "club," "foundation," "fund," "incorporated," "institute," "society," "union," "syndicate," "or "limited," or the abbreviation "co.," "corp.," "inc.," or "ltd." Must be distinguishable on the records of the Secretary of State from the names of other corporations, limited partnerships and trade names. Name may be reserved for 60 days. Availability of name may be checked with Secretary of State by telephone. 18 OSA 1006(A), 1139.

Incorporators: One or more persons, partnerships, associations or corporations. 18 OSA 1005.

Certificate of Incorporation:

- **Contents:** See 18 OSA 1006 for the required and optional certificate of incorporation content requirements.
- **Filing and Recording:** An original and one copy of the certificate of incorporation must be filed with Secretary of State and the filing fee and franchise tax paid. Corporate existence begins when the certificate of incorporation is accepted for filing. 18 OSA 1007, 1010.
- **Amendment:** Requires majority vote of outstanding shares entitled to vote, unless the certificate of incorporation requires a greater vote. 18 OSA 1077, 1006(B)(4).

Note: Only qualifying domestic corporations may engage in the business of farming or ranching. 18 OSA 951 et seq. With only limited exceptions, no corporation may own real estate in the state that is located outside of an incorporated city or town. 18 OSA 1020.

Organizational Meeting: Held after incorporation by the incorporators or by the initial board of directors if named in certificate of incorporation. Incorporators or directors may act without meeting if they all sign a written consent to the action. 18 OSA 1012.

Bylaws: Initial bylaws adopted by incorporators or board of directors. May be amended by the shareholders and, if so provided in the certificate of incorporation, by the board of directors. 18 OSA 1013.

Action Without Meeting: Unless otherwise provided in the certificate of incorporation, shareholders may act without meeting if a written consent to the action is signed by shareholders sufficient to carry the matter at a meeting and notice is given to nonconsenting shareholders. Unanimous shareholder consent is required for listed corporations unless otherwise provided in the certificate of incorporation. 18 OSA 1073. Unless otherwise restricted by the certificate of incorporation or bylaws, the board of directors may meet via conference telephone or similar communications equipment, and may act without meeting if all directors sign a written consent to the action. 18 OSA 1027(F).

Stock Certificates: Must be signed by chairman or vice chairman of board, president, or vice president and by treasurer or secretary or assistant thereof. Shares may be issued without a certificate but a shareholder is entitled to certificate upon demand. 18 OSA 1039.

Consideration For Stock: May consist of cash, services rendered, real or personal property, or leases of real property. 18 OSA 1033.

Stock Transfer Restrictions: May be contained in the certificate of incorporation, bylaws, or a shareholders' agreement. A restriction must be conspicuously noted on the stock certificate to be enforceable against a person without knowledge of the restriction. 18 OSA 1055.

Cumulative Voting: Not permitted unless provided for in the certificate of incorporation. 18 OSA 1059.

Preemptive Rights: Do not exist unless contained in the certificate of incorporation. 18 OSA 1006(B)(3), 1038, 1042.

Acts Requiring Shareholder Approval: Unless the certificate of incorporation requires a greater vote, a majority vote of the outstanding shares entitled to vote is required for a merger, consolidation or share exchange, for the sale or transfer of all or substantially all of the corporate assets, for voluntary dissolution, and to amend the certificate of incorporation. 18 OSA 1006(B)(4), 1081, 1092, 1096, 1077.

Board of Directors: May consist of one or more members, with number specified in bylaws or certificate of incorporation. 18 OSA 1027.

Officers: Those specified in the bylaws or appointed by the board of directors in accordance with the bylaws. The same person may hold any number of offices in the corporation unless otherwise provided in the certificate of incorporation or bylaws. 18 OSA 1028.

Foreign Corporations: Must qualify with the Secretary of State to do business in Oklahoma. The statute contains a list of activities that do not require qualification. The penalties for doing business in the state without qualifying include nonaccess to state courts, corporate fines of $200 to $500 per offense, and personal fines for agents of $100 to $500 per offense. 18 OSA 1130, 1132, 1134, 1137.

Close Corporation Laws: None.

Periodic Reports: Domestic and qualifying foreign corporations must file a franchise tax report with the Oklahoma Tax Commission between July 1 and August 31 of each year and pay an annual franchise tax to remain in good standing. 68 OSA 1210.

STATE FILING OFFICIAL. Secretary of State, State Capitol Building, Oklahoma City, OK 73105 (Telephone: 405-521-3911).

Fees:
- Filing Certificate of Incorporation - Fee based on capitalization ($50 minimum).
- Annual Franchise Tax - $10 to $20,000 (based on capitalization).
- Filing LLP Statement of Qualification - $100
- Filing LLC Articles of Organization - $100
- Name Reservation - $10
- Amending Certificate of Incorporation - $50
- Other Corp. Fees - See 18 OSA 1142.
- Other LLC Fees - See 18 OSA 2055.

SUMMARY OF OREGON BUSINESS ORGANIZATION LAWS

PARTNERSHIP LAWS.

General Partnerships: Uniform Partnership Act adopted. ORS 67.005 et seq.

Limited Partnerships: Revised Uniform Limited Partnership Act adopted. ORS 70.005 et seq.

Limited Liability Partnerships: Registered LLPs provided for. ORS 67.500 et seq.

Name Registration: Must register partnership name with Secretary of State if it does not contain the names of all partners. ORS 648.010.

LIMITED LIABILITY COMPANY LAWS. Oregon Limited Liability Company Act. ORS 63.001 et seq.

Formation of LLC: One or more individuals of age 18 or more may form LLC by filing articles of organization with state filing official. See ORS 63.047 for the article of organization content requirements.

General LLC Requirements: May have one or more members. May conduct any lawful business. ORS 63.074. Special rules apply to LLCs who render professional services. ORS 63.076.

Management of LLC: Vested in members unless articles of organization provide for managers. ORS 63.130.

New or Substituted Members: Admission to LLC requires consent of all members unless articles of organization or operating agreement provide otherwise. ORS 63.255.

Conversion Statutes: Merger statute. ORS 63.481 et seq. No partnership conversion statute.

CORPORATION LAWS. Oregon Business Corporation Act (based on Revised Model Business Corporation Act). ORS 60.001 et seq.

Corporate Name: Must contain the word "corporation," "incorporated," "company," or "limited" or an abbreviation thereof. May not include the word "cooperative." Must be distinguishable on records of Secretary of State from the names of other corporations, limited partnerships, and other entities. Name may be reserved for 120 days. Informal name clearance available from Secretary of State. ORS 60.094, 097.

Incorporators: One or more natural persons of age 18 or more, corporations, or other entities. ORS 60.044.

Articles of Incorporation:

Contents: See ORS 60.047 for required and optional article of incorporation content requirements.

Filing and Recording: A signed copy of the articles of incorporation must be filed with the Secretary of State and the filing fee paid. Corporate existence begins when the articles of incorporation are accepted for filing. ORS 60.004, 051, 054.

Amendment: Requires a majority of the votes entitled to be cast unless a statute, the board of directors, or the articles of incorporation require a greater vote. The board of directors may make ministerial amendments without shareholder approval. ORS 60.434, 437.

Organizational Meeting: Held after incorporation by the initial board of directors if named in articles of incorporation. Otherwise held after incorporation by the incorporators, who may act without meeting if all incorporators sign a written consent to the action. ORS 60.057.

Bylaws: Initial bylaws adopted by incorporators or board of directors. May be amended by shareholders and by board of directors unless the articles reserve that power to the shareholders. A shareholder amendment may prohibit board of director amendment. ORS 60.061, 461.

Action Without Meeting: Shareholders may act without meeting if all shareholders entitled to vote sign a written consent to the action. ORS 60.211. Unless the articles of incorporation or bylaws provide otherwise, the board of directors may meet via conference telephone or similar communications equipment and may act without meeting if all directors sign a written consent to the action. ORS 60.341. Unless otherwise provided in the articles of incorporation or bylaws, the bylaws or a board of director resolution may permit the shareholders to meet via conference telephone or similar communications equipment. ORS 60.222.

Stock Certificates: Must be signed by two officers designated in bylaws or by the board of directors. Shares may be issued without a certificate unless the articles of incorporation or bylaws provide otherwise. ORS 60.161, 164.

Consideration For Stock: May consist of any tangible or intangible property or benefit to the corporation, including cash, promissory notes, services performed or to be performed, and other securities of the corporation. Shares issued for promissory notes or future services may be placed in escrow or otherwise restricted pending payment of note or performance of services. ORS 60.147.

Stock Transfer Restrictions: May be contained in the articles of incorporation, bylaws, or a shareholders' agreement. A restriction must be conspicuously noted on the stock certificate to be enforceable against a person without knowledge of the restriction. ORS 60.167.

Cumulative Voting: Permitted only if provided for in the articles of incorporation. ORS 60.251.

Preemptive Rights: Do not exist unless contained in the articles of incorporation for corps. formed after June 15, 1987. ORS 60.174.

Acts Requiring Shareholder Approval: Unless a statute, the articles of incorporation, or the board of directors require a greater vote, a majority of the votes entitled to be cast is required for a merger or share exchange, for the sale or disposition of all or substantially all of the corporate assets not in the usual course of business, for voluntary dissolution, and for most amendments to the articles of incorporation (see above). ORS 60.487, 534, 627, 437.

Board of Directors: May consist of one or more individuals with the number specified in articles of incorporation or bylaws. ORS 60.307.

Officers: Must have president and secretary. May also have those described in the bylaws or appointed by the board of directors in accordance with the bylaws. The same person may simultaneously hold more than one office in the corporation. ORS 60.371.

Foreign Corporations: Must obtain authorization from the Secretary of State to transact business in Oregon. Statute contains a list of activities that do not constitute transacting business in the state. The penalties for transacting business without authorization include nonaccess to state courts and liability for all fees that would have been imposed had authorization been granted. ORS 60.701, 704.

Close Corporation Laws: None.

Periodic Reports: Domestic and authorized foreign corporations must file an annual report on prescribed forms with the Secretary of State by the anniversary date of its incorporation or qualification and pay an annual report fee to remain in good standing. ORS 60.787.

STATE FILING OFFICIAL. Secretary of State, Corporations Division, 158 12th Street, N.E., Salem, OR 97310 (Telephone: 503-986-2200).

Fees:

Filing Articles of Incorporation - $50	Amending Articles of Incorporation - $10	Other Corp. Fees - See ORS 60.007.
Filing LLP Registration Application - $40	Name Reservation - $10	Other LLP Fees - See ORS 67.525.
Filing LLC Articles of Organization - $40	Annual Report of Corp. or LLC - $30 domestic - $220 foreign	Other LLC Fees - See ORS 63.007.

SUMMARY OF PENNSYLVANIA BUSINESS ORGANIZATION LAWS

PARTNERSHIP LAWS.

General Partnerships: Uniform Partnership Act adopted. 15 PCS 8301 et seq.

Limited Partnerships: Revised Uniform Limited Partnership Act adopted. 15 PCS 8501 et seq.

Limited Liability Partnerships: Registered LLPs for general & limited partnerships provided for. 15 PCS 8201 et seq. (LLPs must carry liability insurance or post deposit. 15 PCS 8206.)

Name Registration: Must register partnership name with state filing official if it does not contain the partners' names. 54 PCS 303.

LIMITED LIABILITY COMPANY LAWS. Limited Liability Company Law. 15 PCS 8901 et seq.

Formation of LLC: One or more persons may form an LLC by filing a certificate of organization with the state filing official. See 15 PCS 8913 for the certificate of organization content requirements.

General LLC Requirements: May have one or more members. May conduct any business that a general partnership may conduct. Special requirements for professional LLCs (15 PCS 8995 et seq.).

Management of LLC: Vested in members unless vested in manager(s) by certificate of organization. 15 PCS 8941.

New or Substituted Members: Requires written consent of all members unless otherwise provided in operating agreement.

Conversion Statutes: Merger and consolidation statute. 15 PCS 8956 et seq. No partnership conversion statute.

CORPORATION LAWS. Business Corporation Law of 1988 (Model Business Corporation Acts not adopted). 15 PCS 1101 et seq.

Corporate Name: Must contain the word "corporation," "company," "incorporated," or "limited" or an abbreviation thereof, or the word "association, "fund" or "syndicate." Must not be confusedly similar to the existing or reserved name of any other corporation, limited partnership, or registered association. Name may be reserved for 120 days. 15 PCS 1303, 1305.

Incorporators: One or more corporations or natural persons of full age. 15 PCS 1302.

Articles of Incorporation:

Contents: See 15 PCS 1306 for required and optional article of incorporation content requirements.

Filing and Recording: The articles of incorporation and a docketing statement must be filed with the state filing official and the filing fee paid. A notice of the filing of the articles of incorporation must be published once in each of two local newspapers. Corporate existence begins when the articles of incorporation are accepted for filing. 15 PCS 134, 1307, 1308, 1309.

Amendment: Requires a majority of the votes cast by the shareholders entitled to vote unless the articles of incorporation or a statute require a greater vote. The board of directors can make certain minor amendments without shareholder approval. 15 PCS 1914.

Organizational Meeting: Held after incorporation by the initial board of directors if named in the articles of incorporation; otherwise held after incorporation by the incorporators, who may act by written consent or proxy. 15 PCS 1310.

Bylaws: Initial bylaws adopted at organizational meeting by initial board of directors or incorporators (deemed adopted by shareholders). May be amended by the shareholders and, if so provided in the bylaws and with certain exceptions, by the board of directors. 15 PCS 1310, 1504.

Action Without Meeting: Unless prohibited by the bylaws, the shareholders may act without meeting if a written consent to the action is signed by all shareholders entitled to vote or, if the bylaws so provide, by shareholders sufficient to carry the action at a meeting if written notice is given to nonconsenting shareholders entitled to vote. 15 PCS 1766. Unless prohibited by the bylaws, the board of directors may act without meeting if all directors sign a written consent to the action. 15 PCS 1727. Unless otherwise provided in the bylaws, the shareholders, the board of directors, and the incorporators may meet via conference telephone or similar communications equipment. 15 PCS 1708.

Stock Certificates: May be signed in such manner as the corporation may determine. Shares may be issued without a certificate if the articles of incorporation so provide (close corporations excepted). 15 PCS 1528.

Consideration For Stock: Unless the bylaws provide otherwise, may consist of money, obligations, services performed or to be performed, other securities or obligations of the issuing corporation, or other tangible or intangible property. 15 PCS 1524.

Stock Transfer Restrictions: May be contained in the bylaws, articles of incorporation, or a shareholders' agreement. A restriction must be conspicuously noted on the stock certificate to be enforceable against a person without knowledge of the restriction. 15 PCS 1529, 1306.

Cumulative Voting: Permitted unless denied in the articles of incorporation. 15 PCS 1758.

Preemptive Rights: Do not exist unless contained in the articles of incorporation. 15 PCS 1530.

Acts Requiring Shareholder Approval: Unless a different vote is required by the articles of incorporation, a majority of the votes cast by the shareholders entitled to vote is required for a merger, consolidation or share exchange, for the sale or transfer of all or substantially all of the corporate assets not in the usual course of business, and for voluntary dissolution. 15 PCS 1924, 1931, 1932, 1974, 1306(b). Shareholder approval is also required for most amendments to the articles of incorporation and for certain amendments to the bylaws (see above).

Board of Directors: May consist of one or more natural persons of full age, with the number of directors specified in the bylaws or the articles of incorporation. The functions of the board of directors may be delegated to others in a shareholder-adopted bylaw. 15 PCS 1721-1723.

Officers: Must have president, secretary and treasurer, or persons who act as such regardless of title. May have other officers. All officers must be natural persons of full age, except that the treasurer may be a corporation. The same person may hold two or more offices. 15 PCS 1732.

Foreign Corporations: Must obtain a certificate of authority from the state filing official to transact business in Pennsylvania. The statute contains a nonexclusive list of activities that do not constitute transacting business in the state. The penalties for transacting business without a certificate of authority include nonaccess to state courts and liability for all taxes and fees that would have been imposed had a certificate of authority been issued. 15 PCS 4121, 4122, 4141.

Close Corporation Laws: Has Close Corporation Code. 15 PCS 2301 to 2337. The articles of incorporation must state that the corporation is a statutory close corporation and that there will be no "public offering" of its shares. No limit on the number of shareholders.

Periodic Reports: Domestic and authorized foreign corporations must file an annual report with the Department of Revenue by the 15th day of the third month after the close of its fiscal year and pay a corporate income tax and a capital stock tax. PSA 72-7403, 7602.

STATE FILING OFFICIAL. Dept. of State, Corporation Bureau, 308 North Office Building, Harrisburg, PA 17120 (Phone: 717-787-1057).

Fees:

Filing Articles of Incorporation - $100	Amending Articles of Incorporation - $52	Other Fees - See 15 PCS 153.
Filing LLC Certificate of Organization - $100	Filing LLP Statement of Registration - $200/partner	Name Reservation - $52

SUMMARY OF RHODE ISLAND BUSINESS ORGANIZATION LAWS

PARTNERSHIP LAWS.

General Partnerships: Uniform Partnership Act adopted. GL 7-12-1 et seq.

Limited Partnerships: Revised Uniform Limited Partnership Act adopted. GL 7-13-1 et seq.

Limited Liability Partnerships: Provided for. GL 7-12-56 et seq. Financial responsibility required for professional LLPs.

Name Registration: Must file a fictitious name certificate with the clerk of the town or city where business is conducted if the partnership name does not contain the real surname of at least one partner. GL 6-1-1.

LIMITED LIABILITY COMPANY LAWS. Rhode Island Limited Liability Company Act. GL 7-16-1 et seq.

Formation of LLC: One or more persons may form an LLC by filing articles of organization with the Secretary of State. See GL 7-16-6 for the article of organization content requirements.

General LLC Requirements: May have one or more members. May conduct any business that a limited partnership may conduct except the provision of professional services.

Management of LLC: Vested in members unless otherwise provided in articles of organization or a written operating agreement. GL 7-16-14.

New or Substituted Members: Admission to LLC requires consent of all members unless otherwise provided in a written operating agreement. GL 7-16-36.

Conversion Statutes: Merger or consolidation statute. GL 7-16-59 et seq. No partnership conversion statute.

CORPORATION LAWS. Rhode Island Business Corporation Act (based on Model Business Corporation Act). GL 7-1.1-1 et seq.

Corporate Name: Must contain the word "corporation," "company," "incorporated," or "limited," or an abbreviation thereof and must not be the same as or deceptively similar to the existing or reserved name of any other corporation or limited partnership. Name may be reserved for 120 days. No formal procedure for determining availability of name, but may write or telephone Secretary of State. GL 7-1.1-7, 8.

Incorporators: One or more persons. GL 7-1.1-47.

Articles of Incorporation:

Contents: See GL 7-1.1-48 for required and optional article of incorporation content requirements.

Filing and Recording: Two original copies of the articles of incorporation must be filed with the Secretary of State and the filing and license fees paid. Corporate existence begins when the Secretary of State issues a certificate of incorporation. GL 7-1.1-49, 50.

Amendment: Requires majority vote of shares entitled to vote unless the articles of incorporation require a greater vote. GL 7-1.1-54, 30.1.

Organizational Meeting: Held after incorporation by the initial board of directors. GL 7-1.1-52.

Bylaws: Initial bylaws adopted by incorporators or board of directors. May be amended by the shareholders and, unless otherwise provided in the articles of incorporation, by the board of directors. Any board of director amendment may be changed by the shareholders. GL 7-1.1-25.

Action Without Meeting: The shareholders may act without meeting if all shareholders entitled to vote sign a written consent to the action or, with certain exceptions, if the consent is signed by shareholders sufficient to carry the action at a meeting and prompt notice of the action is given to the nonconsenting shareholders entitled to vote. GL 7-1.1-30.3. Unless otherwise provided in the articles of incorporation or bylaws, the board of directors may meet via conference telephone or similar communications equipment and may act without meeting if all directors sign a written consent to the action. GL 7-1.1-39, 39.1.

Stock Certificates: Must be signed by the officers designated in the bylaws, or by the chairman or vice chairman of the board, the president, or a vice president, and by the treasurer, secretary, or an assistant thereof. Shares may be issued without a certificate. GL 7-1.1-21.

Consideration For Stock: May consist of money, tangible or intangible property, or labor or services actually performed for the corporation. May not consist of promissory notes or future services. GL 7-1.1-18

Stock Transfer Restrictions: May be contained in the articles of incorporation, bylaws or a shareholders' agreement. A restriction must be conspicuously noted on the stock certificate to be enforceable against a person without knowledge of the restriction. GL 7-1.1-21.1.

Cumulative Voting: Not permitted unless provided for in the articles of incorporation. GL 7-1.1-31(d).

Preemptive Rights: Exist unless denied or limited in the articles of incorporation. GL 7-1.1-24.

Acts Requiring Shareholder Approval: Unless the articles of incorporation require a greater vote, a majority vote of the shares entitled to vote is required for a merger or consolidation, for the sale or transfer of all or substantially all of the corporate assets not in the usual course of business, for voluntary dissolution, and to amend the articles of incorporation. GL 7-1.1-67, 72, 77, 54, 30.1.

Board of Directors: May consist of one or more directors, with the number specified in the articles of incorporation or bylaws. GL 7-1.1-34.

Officers: Must have president, secretary and treasurer. The bylaws may provide for other officers. The same person may hold any two or more offices in the corporation. GL 7-1.1-44.

Foreign Corporations: Must obtain a certificate of authority from the Secretary of State before transacting business in Rhode Island. The statute contains a nonexclusive list of activities that do not constitute transacting business in the state. The penalties for transacting business without a certificate of authority include nonaccess to state courts and liability for all fees, taxes and penalties that would have been imposed had a certificate of authority been issued. GL 7-1.1-99, 117.

Close Corporation Laws: Has a close corporation statute (GL 7-1.1-51) whereunder a statutory close corporation may be formed by providing a heading in the articles of incorporation declaring the corporation to be a close corporation pursuant to GL 7-1.1-51. Unanimous shareholder approval is required. No limit to the number of shareholders in a statutory close corporation.

Periodic Reports: Domestic and authorized foreign corporations must file an annual report with the Secretary of State by March 1 of each year and pay an annual filing fee and an annual franchise tax to remain in good standing. GL 7-1.1-118, 119, 44-12-1 et seq.

STATE FILING OFFICIAL. Secretary of State, State House, Providence, RI 02903 (Telephone: 401-277-3040).

Fees:

Filing Articles of Incorporation - $70 plus a license fee based on capitalization ($80 minimum).
Amending Articles of Incorporation - $50 (more if capitalization increased).
Filing LLP Registration Application - $100/partner ($2,500 max.)
Filing LLC Articles of Organization - $150

Name Reservation - $50
Annual Report - $50
Other Corp. Fees - See GL 7-1.1-121 to 124.
Other LLC Fees - See GL 7-16-65.

SUMMARY OF SOUTH CAROLINA BUSINESS ORGANIZATION LAWS

PARTNERSHIP LAWS.

General Partnerships: Uniform Partnership Act adopted. CL 33-41-10 et seq.

Limited Partnerships: Revised Uniform Limited Partnership Act adopted. CL 33-42-10 et seq.

Limited Liability Partnerships: Registered limited liability partnerships recognized. CL 33-41-1110 et seq.

Name Registration: A partnership carrying on a mercantile or industrial business must file a fictitious name certificate with the clerk of the county court in the county of its principal place of business if the partnership name does not contain the names of all partners. CL 39-13-10.

LIMITED LIABILITY COMPANY LAWS. South Carolina Limited Liability Company Act. CL 33-44-101 et seq.

Formation of LLC: One or more persons may organize an LLC by filing articles of organization with the Secretary of State. See CL 33-44-203 for the article of organization content requirements.

General LLC Requirements: May have one or more members. May conduct any lawful business.

Management of LLC: Must specify whether LLC is to be manager-managed in articles of organization.

New or Substituted Members: Admission to LLC requires consent of all members unless operating agreement provides otherwise.

Conversion Statutes: Merger statute. CL 33-44-904 et seq. Partnership conversion statute. CL 33-44-902, 903.

CORPORATION LAWS. S.C. Business Corporation Act of 1988 (based on Revised Model Business Corporation Act). CL 33-1-101 et seq.

Corporate Name: Must contain the word "corporation," "company," "incorporated" or "limited" or an abbreviation thereof and must be distinguishable on records of Secretary of State from the existing or reserved name of any other corporation or other registered entity. Name may be reserved for 120 days. Availability of name may be checked informally with Secretary of State by telephone. CL 33-4-101, 102.

Incorporators: Any individual or entity. CL 33-2-101.

Articles of Incorporation:

Contents: See CL 33-2-102 for required and optional article of incorporation content requirements.

Filing and Recording: An original and one copy of the articles of incorporation, together with an attorney's certificate of statutory compliance and an initial tax report, must be filed with the Secretary of State and the filing fee, filing tax and initial license tax paid. Corporate existence begins when the articles of incorporation are accepted for filing. CL 33-1-200, 33-2-102, 103.

Amendment: Requires two-thirds of the votes entitled to be cast unless a statute or the board of directors require a greater vote or unless the articles of incorporation require a different vote of not less than a majority. The board of directors can make certain minor amendments without shareholder approval. CL 33-10-102, 103.

Organizational Meeting: Held after incorporation by the initial board of directors if named in articles of incorporation. Otherwise held after incorporation by the incorporators, who may act without meeting if all incorporators sign a written consent to the action. CL 33-2-105.

Bylaws: Initial bylaws adopted by the incorporators or board of directors. May be amended by the shareholders and by the board of directors unless that power is reserved to the shareholders in the articles of incorporation or unless a shareholder amendment prohibits its subsequent amendment by the board of directors. CL 33-2-106, 33-10-200.

Action Without Meeting: Shareholders may act without meeting if all shareholders entitled to vote sign a written consent to the action. CL 33-7-104. Unless the articles of incorporation or bylaws provide otherwise, the board of directors may meet via conference telephone or similar communications equipment and may act without meeting if all directors sign a written consent to the action. CL 33-8-200, 210.

Stock Certificates: Must be signed by two officers designated in the bylaws or by the board of directors. Shares may be issued without a certificate unless the articles of incorporation, bylaws, or a shareholders' agreement provide otherwise. CL 33-6-250, 260.

Consideration For Stock: May consist of any tangible or intangible property or benefit to the corporation, including cash, promissory notes, services performed or to be performed, and other securities of the corporation. Shares issued for promissory notes or future services may be placed in escrow or otherwise restricted pending payment of note or performance of services. CL 33-6-210.

Stock Transfer Restrictions: May be imposed by the articles of incorporation, bylaws or a shareholders' agreement. A restriction must be conspicuously noted on the stock certificate to be enforceable against a person without knowledge of the restriction. CL 33-6-270.

Cumulative Voting: Permitted unless denied in the articles of incorporation. Shareholder must give prior notice. CL 33-7-280.

Preemptive Rights: Exist (with exceptions) unless limited or denied in the articles of incorporation. CL 33-6-300.

Acts Requiring Shareholder Approval: Unless a statute or the board of directors require a greater vote or unless the articles of incorporation require a different vote of not less than a majority, two-thirds of the votes entitled to be cast is required for a merger or share exchange, for the sale or transfer of all or substantially all of the corporate assets not in the usual course of business, for voluntary dissolution, and for most amendments to the articles of incorporation (see above). CL 33-11-103, 33-12-102, 33-14-102, 33-10-103.

Board of Directors: May consist of one or more individuals with the number of directors specified in the articles of incorporation or bylaws. May be dispensed with or have authority limited in the articles of incorporation or in a unanimous shareholder agreement. CL 33-8-101, 103.

Officers: Those described in the bylaws or appointed by the board of directors in accordance with the bylaws. No specific officers required. The same person may simultaneously hold more than one office in the corporation. CL 33-8-400.

Foreign Corporations: Must obtain a certificate of authority from the Secretary of State before transacting business in South Carolina. The statute contains a nonexclusive list of activities that do not constitute transacting business in the state. The penalties for transacting business without a certificate of authority include nonaccess to state courts and civil penalties of $10 per day up to $1,000 per year. CL 33-15-101, 102.

Close Corporation Laws: Has South Carolina Close Corporation Supplement. CL 33-18-101 et seq. No limit on number of shareholders.

Periodic Reports: Domestic and authorized foreign corporations must file annual report with Dept. of Revenue & Taxation by the 15th day of the third month after the end of their fiscal year and pay an annual license tax to remain in good standing. CL 33-16-220, 12-19-20, 70.

STATE FILING OFFICIAL. Secretary of State, Wade Hampton Office Building, P.O. Box 11350, Columbia, SC 29211 (Telephone: 803-734-2158).

Fees: Filing Articles of Incorporation - $100 filing fee plus $25 tax; Amending Articles of Incorporation - $10 plus $100 filing tax.
Filing LLC Articles of Organization - $110; Name Reservation - $10; Other Corp. Fees - See CL 33-1-220.
Filing LLP Registration Application - $100; Other LLC Fees - See CL 33-44-1204.

SUMMARY OF SOUTH DAKOTA BUSINESS ORGANIZATION LAWS

GENERAL PARTNERSHIP LAWS.

General Partnerships: Uniform Partnership Act adopted. CL 48-1-1 et seq.
Limited Partnerships: Revised Uniform Limited Partnership Act adopted. CL 48-7-101 et seq.
Limited Liability Partnerships: Registered LLPs for general & limited partnerships provided for. CL 48-2-15 et seq., 48-7-108 et seq.
Name Registration: Must file a fictitious name certificate with the register of deeds in each county where a partnership business is maintained if the partnership name does not contain the surname of each partner. CL 37-11-1.

LIMITED LIABILITY COMPANY LAWS. Uniform Limited Liability Company Act. CL 47-34A-101 et seq.

Formation of LLC: One or more persons may organize an LLC by filing articles of organization and first annual report with Secretary of State. See CL 47-34A-203 for article of organization content requirements.
General LLC Requirements: May have one or more members. May conduct any lawful business (see CL 47-34A-112).
Management of LLC: Must specify in articles of organization whether LLC is to be manager-managed.
New or Substituted Members: Admission to LLC requires consent of all members unless otherwise provided in operating agreement.
Conversion Statutes: Merger statute. CL 47-34A-904 et seq. Partnership conversion statute. CL 47-34A-902, 903.

CORPORATION LAWS. South Dakota Business Corporation Act (based on Model Business Corporation Act). CL 47-2-1 et seq.

Corporate Name: Must contain the word "corporation," "incorporated," "company," or "limited," or an abbreviation thereof and may not be the same as or deceptively similar to the name of any other corporation or limited partnership. Name may be reserved for 120 days. No formal name clearance procedure. CL 47-2-36, 38, 40, 41.
Incorporators: One or more natural persons of age of majority. CL 47-2-4.
Articles of Incorporation:
Contents: See CL 47-2-5 for required and optional article of incorporation content requirements.
Filing and Recording: An original and one copy of the articles of incorporation must be filed with Secretary of State and the filing fee paid. Corporate existence begins when the Secretary of State issues a certificate of incorporation. CL 47-2-6, 7.
Amendment: Requires majority vote of shares entitled to vote unless articles of incorporation require a greater vote. CL 47-2-13, 47-4-22.
Note: Corporations or LLCs may not engage in the business of farming, except for family farm corporations, authorized farm corporations, and certain other specified corporations. CL 47-9A-1 et seq.
Organizational Meeting: Held after incorporation by the initial board of directors. CL 47-2-48.
Minimum Capitalization Requirement: $1,000. CL 47-3-40.
Bylaws: Initial bylaws adopted by the board of directors May be amended by the board of directors unless that power is reserved to the shareholders in the articles of incorporation. CL 47-2-49.
Action Without Meeting: The shareholders may act without meeting if all shareholders entitled to vote sign a written consent to the action. CL 47-4-4. Unless otherwise provided in the articles of incorporation or bylaws, the board of directors may meet via conference telephone or similar communications equipment and may act without meeting if all directors sign a written consent to the action. CL 47-5-9, 11.
Stock Certificates: Must be signed by president or vice president and by secretary or assistant secretary. Shares may be issued without a certificate unless otherwise provided in the articles of incorporation or bylaws. CL 47-3-12, 12.1.
Consideration For Stock: May consist of money, tangible or intangible property, or labor or services actually performed for the corporation. CL 47-3-26. May not consist of promissory notes or future services. CL 47-3-28.
Stock Transfer Restrictions: May be included in the articles of incorporation. CL 47-2-5(9).
Cumulative Voting: Must be permitted. CL 47-4-17, 47-5-6.
Preemptive Rights: Exists unless denied or limited in the articles of incorporation. CL 47-3-47.
Acts Requiring Shareholder Approval: Unless the articles of incorporation require a greater vote, a majority vote of the shares entitled to vote is required for a merger, consolidation, or share exchange, for the sale of all or substantially all of the corporate assets not in the usual course of business, for voluntary dissolution, and to amend the articles of incorporation. CL 47-6-4, 47-6-21, 47-7-4.1, 47-2-13, 47-4-22.
Board of Directors: May consist of one or more persons with number specified in bylaws or articles of incorporation. CL 47-5-4.
Officers: Those described in the bylaws or appointed by the board of directors in accordance with the bylaws. No specific officers required. The same person may simultaneously hold more than one office in the corporation. CL 47-5-24.1.
Foreign Corporations: Must obtain a certificate of authority from the Secretary of State before transacting business in South Dakota. The statute contains a nonexclusive list of activities that do not constitute transacting business in the state. The penalties for transacting business without a certificate of authority include nonaccess to state courts and liability for all fees, taxes and penalties that would have been assessed had a certificate of authority been issued. CL 47-8-1, 1.1, 30, 32..
Close Corporation Laws: None.
Periodic Reports: Domestic and authorized foreign corporations must file an annual report with the Secretary of State by the first day of the second month after the anniversary month and pay an annual fee to remain in good standing. CL 47-9-1, 3.

STATE FILING OFFICIAL. Secretary of State, State Capitol, Pierre, SD 57501 (Telephone: 605-773-3537).

Fees: Filing Articles of Incorporation - Fee based on capitalization ($90 minimum). Amending Articles of Incorporation - $20
Filing LLC Articles of Organization and Annual Report - $90 minimum (based on capitalization, CL 47-34A-211, 212).
Filing LLP Registration Statement - $90 Corp. Annual Report - $25 Other Corp. Fees - See CL 47-9-7.
Name Reservation - $15 Other LLC Fees - See CL 47-34A-1206.

SUMMARY OF TENNESSEE BUSINESS ORGANIZATION LAWS

PARTNERSHIP LAWS.

General Partnerships: Uniform Partnership Act adopted. TCA 61-1-101 et seq.

Limited Partnerships: Revised Uniform Limited Partnership Act adopted. TCA 61-2-101 et seq.

Limited Liability Partnerships: Registered limited liability partnerships provided for. TCA 61-1-143 et seq.

Name Registration: Not required.

LIMITED LIABILITY COMPANY LAWS. Tennessee Limited Liability Company Act. TCA 48-201-101 et seq.

Formation of LLC: One or more individuals may form an LLC by filing articles of organization with the Secretary of State. See TCA 48-205-101 for the article of organization content requirements.

General LLC Requirements: Must have two or more members. May conduct any lawful business. Special requirements are applicable to professional LLCs (TCA-48-248-101 et seq.).

Management of LLC: Must elect member-management or board-of-governor-management in articles of organization.

New or Substituted Members: Admission to LLC requires unanimous consent of members unless otherwise provided in articles of organization or operating agreement. TCA 48-218-102.

Conversion Statutes: Partnership conversion statute. TCA 48-204-101 et seq. Merger statute. TCA 48-244-101 et seq.

CORPORATION LAWS. Tennessee Business Corporation Act (based on Revised Model Business Corporation Act). TCA 48-11-101 et seq.

Corporate Name: Must contain the word "corporation," "incorporated," or "company," or an abbreviation thereof. Must be distinguishable on the records of the Secretary of State from the real, assumed or reserved name of any other corporation or limited partnership. Name may be reserved for 4 months. TCA 48-14-101, 102.

Incorporators: One or more individuals or entities. TCA 48-12-101.

Charter:

- **Contents:** See TCA 48-12-102 for required and optional charter content requirements.
- **Filing and Recording:** An original and one copy of the charter must be filed with Secretary of State and the filing fee paid. A copy of the charter must also be filed with the county register in the county of the corporation's principal office. Corporate existence begins when the charter is accepted for filing by the Secretary of State. TCA 48-11-301, 303, 48-12-103.
- **Amendment:** Requires a majority of the votes entitled to be cast unless a statute, the board of directors, or the charter require a greater vote. The board of directors may make ministerial amendments without shareholder approval. TCA 48-20-102, 103.

Organizational Meeting: Held after incorporation by the initial board of directors if named in charter. Otherwise held after incorporation by the incorporators, who may act without meeting if all incorporators sign a written consent to the action. TCA 48-12-105.

Bylaws: Initial bylaws adopted by the incorporators or board of directors. May be amended by the shareholders and by the board of directors, unless that power is reserved to the shareholders in the charter or unless a shareholder amendment prohibits its subsequent amendment by the board of directors. TCA 48-12-106, 48-20-201.

Action Without Meeting: The shareholders may act without meeting if all shareholders entitled to vote sign a written consent to the action. TCA 48-17-104. Unless the charter or the bylaws provide otherwise, the board of directors may meet via conference telephone or similar communications equipment and may act without meeting if all directors sign a written consent to the action. TCA 48-18-201, 202.

Stock Certificates: Must be signed by two officers designated in the bylaws or by the board of directors. Shares may be issued without a certificate unless the charter or bylaws provide otherwise. TCA 48-16-206, 207.

Consideration For Stock: May consist of any tangible or intangible property or benefit to the corporation, including cash, promissory notes, services performed or to be performed, and other securities of the corporation. Shares issued for promissory notes or future services may be placed in escrow or otherwise restricted pending payment of note or performance of services. TCA 48-16-202.

Stock Transfer Restrictions: May be contained in the charter, the bylaws or a shareholders' agreement. A restriction must be conspicuously noted on the stock certificate to be enforceable against a person without knowledge of the restriction. TCA 48-16-208.

Cumulative Voting: Not permitted unless provided for in the charter and prior notice is given. TCA 48-17-209.

Preemptive Rights: Do not exist unless contained in the charter. TCA 48-16-301.

Acts Requiring Shareholder Approval: Unless the charter, a statute, or the board of directors require a greater vote, a majority of the votes entitled to be cast is required for merger or share exchange, sale or disposition of all or substantially all of the corporate assets not in the usual course of business, voluntary dissolution, and most charter amendments. TCA 48-21-103, 48-22-102, 48-24-102, 48-20-103.

Board of Directors: May consist of one or more individuals with the number of directors specified in the bylaws or charter. TCA 48-18-103.

Officers: Must have president and secretary. Other officers may be provided for in the bylaws or appointed by the board of directors. The same person may simultaneously hold more than one office, except the offices of president and secretary. TCA 48-18-401.

Foreign Corporations: Must obtain a certificate of authority from the Secretary of State before transacting business in Tennessee. The statute contains a nonexclusive list of activities that do not constitute transacting business in the state. The penalties for transacting business without a certificate of authority include nonaccess to state courts and liability for treble the amount of the fees, taxes, penalties, and interest that would have been imposed had a certificate of authority been issued. TCA 48-25-101, 102.

Close Corporation Laws: A corporation may be managed by its shareholders under a shareholders' agreement. A corporation with 50 or fewer shareholders may in its charter dispense with or limit the authority of the board of directors. TCA 48-17-302, 48-18-101(c).

Periodic Reports: Domestic and authorized foreign corporations must file an annual report with the Secretary of State by the first day of the fourth month after the close of the corporation's fiscal year and pay an annual report fee to remain in good standing. TCA 48-26-203. Such corporations must also pay an annual franchise tax and an excise tax. TCA 67-4-903 et seq, 67-4-806 et seq.

STATE FILING OFFICIAL. Secretary of State, 1800 James K. Polk Building, Nashville, TN 37219-5040 (Telephone: 615-741-2286).

Fees: Filing Charter - $100 Amending Charter - $20 Name Reservation - $20 Annual Report of corp.- $20
Filing LLC Articles of Organization - $50/member ($300 min., $3,000 max.) Other Corp. Fees - See TCA 48-11-303
Filing LLP Registration Application - $50/partner ($250 min., $2,500 max.) Other LLP Fees - See TCA 61-1-148.
Other LLC Fees - See TCA 48-247-103.

SUMMARY OF TEXAS BUSINESS ORGANIZATION LAWS

PARTNERSHIP LAWS.

General Partnerships: Uniform Partnership Act adopted. VACS 6132b-1.01 et seq.

Limited Partnerships: Revised Uniform Limited Partnership Act adopted. VACS 6132a-1.

Limited Liability Partnerships: Registered LLPs provided for. VACS 6132b-3.08. LLPs must carry $100,000 of liability insurance or provide $100,000 deposit.

Name Registration: Must file a fictitious name certificate with the county clerk of each county where a business premises is maintained if the partnership name does not contain the name of each partner. Bus. & Comm. C. 36.10.

LIMITED LIABILITY COMPANY LAWS. Texas Limited Liability Company Act. VACS 1528n.

Formation of LLC: One or more natural persons of age 18 or more may form an LLC by filing articles of organization with the Secretary of State. See VACS 1528n §3.02 for the article of organization content requirements.

General LLC Requirements: May have one or more members. May conduct any lawful business. Special requirements for professional LLCs (see VACS 1528n §11.01 et seq.).

Management of LLC: Vested in manager(s) unless reserved to members in articles of organization or regulations. VACS 1528n §2.12.

New or Substituted Members: Requires written consent of all members unless otherwise provided in regulations. VACS 1528n § 4.01, 4.07.

Conversion Statutes: Merger statute. VACS 1528n §10.01 et seq. Conversion Statute. VACS 1528n §10.08 et seq.

CORPORATION LAWS. Texas Business Corporation Act (Model Business Corporation Acts not adopted). BCA 1.01 et seq.

Corporate Name: Must contain the word "corporation," "company," or "incorporated," or an abbreviation thereof. May not contain the word "lottery." May not be the same as or deceptively similar to the existing or reserved name of any other corporation. Name may be reserved for 120 days. Informal name clearance provided by Secretary of State via telephone or letter. BCA 2.05, 2.06.

Incorporators: Any natural person of age 18 or more or any corporation, estate, or other entity. BCA 3.01.

Articles of Incorporation:

Contents: See BCA 3.02 for required and optional article of incorporation content requirements.

Filing and Recording: An original and one copy of the articles of incorporation must be filed with the state filing official and the filing fee paid. Corporate existence begins when a certificate of incorporation is issued by the state filing official. BCA 3.03, 3.04.

Amendment: Requires a two-thirds vote of the shares entitled to vote unless the articles of incorporation or bylaws require a different vote of not less than a majority. All shareholders may vote on certain matters requiring class voting. BCA 4.02, 4.03, 2.28B.

Organizational Meeting: Held after incorporation by the initial board of directors. BCA 3.06.

Minimum Capitalization Requirement: $1,000. BCA 3.05.

Bylaws: Initial bylaws adopted by the board of directors. May be amended by the board of directors and by the shareholders unless otherwise provided in the articles of incorporation or in a shareholder-adopted bylaw. BCA 2.23.

Action Without Meeting: The shareholders may act without meeting if a written consent to the action is signed by all shareholders entitled to vote or, if so provided in the articles of incorporation, by shareholders sufficient to carry the action at a meeting. BCA 9.10A. Unless otherwise provided in the articles of incorporation or bylaws, the board of directors may act without meeting if all directors sign a written consent to the action. BCA 9.10B. The shareholders and the board of directors may meet via conference telephone or similar communications equipment, unless otherwise provided in the articles of incorporation or bylaws. BCA 9.10C.

Stock Certificates: Must be signed by the officer or officers designated in the bylaws. Shares may be issued without a certificate unless otherwise provided in the articles of incorporation or bylaws. BCA 2.19.

Consideration For Stock: May consist of any tangible or intangible benefit to the corporation, including cash, promissory notes, services performed or to be performed, or other securities of the corporation. BCA 2.16.

Stock Transfer Restrictions: May be imposed by the articles of incorporation, bylaws or a shareholders' agreement. A restriction must be conspicuously noted on the stock certificate to be enforceable against a person without knowledge of the restriction. BCA 2.22.

Cumulative Voting: Not permitted unless provided for in the articles of incorporation and prior written notice is given. BCA 2.28, 2.29.

Preemptive Rights: Exist unless limited or denied in the articles of incorporation and a notice of the limitation or denial is set forth on the stock certificate. BCA 2.19, 2.22-1.

Acts Requiring Shareholder Approval: Unless the articles of incorporation or bylaws require a different vote of not less than a majority or unless the board of directors requires a greater vote in the case of a merger or share exchange, a two-thirds vote of the shares entitled to vote is required for a merger or share exchange, for the sale or transfer of all or substantially all of the corporate assets not in the usual course of business, for voluntary dissolution, and for most amendments to the articles of incorporation (see above). BCA 5.03, 5.09, 6.03, 4.02, 2.28B.

Board of Directors: May consist of one or more persons with the number specified in the bylaws or articles of incorporation. BCA 2.32.

Officers: Must have a president and a secretary. May have other officers. The same person may hold any two or more offices. BCA 2.42.

Foreign Corporations: Must obtain a certificate of authority from the Secretary of State before transacting business in Texas. The statute contains a nonexclusive list of activities that do not constitute transacting business in the state. The penalties for transacting business without a certificate of authority include nonaccess to state courts, liability for all fees, taxes and penalties that would have been imposed had a certificate of authority been obtained, and fines of $100 to $5,000 for each month of violation. BCA 8.01, 8.18.

Close Corporation Laws: Has Texas Close Corporation Law. BCA 12.01 et seq. No shareholder limit for close corporation. BCA 3.02(A)(9).

Periodic Reports: Domestic and authorized foreign corporations must file an annual franchise tax report on prescribed forms with the Comptroller of Public Accounts by May 16 of each year and pay an annual franchise tax to remain in good standing. Tax C. 171.002, 202.

STATE FILING OFFICIAL. Secretary of State, Corp. Div., Sam Houston Bldg., 6th Fl., P.O. Box 12697, Austin, TX 78711 (512-463-5555).

Fees:

Filing Articles of Incorporation - $300	Initial Franchise Tax Deposit - $100	Other Corp. Fees - See BCA 10.01.
Filing LLC Articles of Organization - $200	Amending Articles of Incorporation - $150	Other LLC Fees - See VACS 1528n §9.01.
Filing LLP Registration Application - $200 per partner	Name Reservation - $40	

SUMMARY OF UTAH BUSINESS ORGANIZATION LAWS

PARTNERSHIP LAWS.

General Partnerships: Uniform Partnership Act adopted. UCA 48-1-1 et seq.

Limited Partnerships: Revised Uniform Limited Partnership Act adopted. UCA 48-2a-101 et seq.

Limited Liability Partnerships: Utah Limited Liability Partnership Act. UCA 48-1-41 et seq.

Name Registration: Must file certificate with state filing official if partnership name does not contain each partner's name. UCA 42-2-5.

LIMITED LIABILITY COMPANY LAWS. Utah Limited Liability Company Act. UCA 48-2b-101 et seq.

Formation of LLC: An LLC may be organized by filing articles of organization with the state filing official. See UCA 48-2b-116 for the article of organization content requirements.

General LLC Requirements: May have one or more members. May conduct any lawful business. Special requirements for prof. LLCs.

Management of LLC: Vested in members in proportion to their interests in LLC profits unless otherwise provided in the articles of organization. UCA 48-2b-125.

New or Substituted Members: Requires written consent of all members unless otherwise provided in operating agreement. UCA 48-2b-122.

Conversion Statutes: None in LLC Act.

CORPORATION LAWS. Utah Revised Business Corporation Act (based on Revised Model Business Corp. Act). UCA 16-10a-101 et seq.

Corporate Name: Must contain the word "corporation," "company," or "incorporated," or an abbreviation thereof, and must be distinguishable on the records of the state filing official from the names of other corporations, limited liability companies, and partnerships. Name may be reserved for 120 days. UCA 16-10a-401, 402.

Incorporators: One or more persons. Natural persons must be age 18 or more. UCA 16-10a-201.

Articles of Incorporation:

Contents: See UCA 16-10a-202 for required and optional article of incorporation content requirements.

Filing and Recording: An original and one copy of the articles of incorporation, including the registered agent's signed acceptance of appointment, must be filed with the state filing official and the filing fee paid. Corporate existence begins when articles of incorporation are accepted for filing. UCA 16-10a-120, 202, 203.

Amendment: Requires a majority of the votes entitled to be cast, unless a statute, the articles of incorporation, the bylaws (if authorized by the articles of incorporation), or the board of directors require a greater vote. The board of directors may make certain minor amendments without shareholder approval. UCA 16-10a-1002, 1003.

Organizational Meeting: Held after incorporation by initial board of directors if named in articles of incorporation. Otherwise held after incorporation by incorporators, who may act without meeting if all incorporators sign a written consent to the action. UCA 16-10a-205.

Bylaws: Initial bylaws adopted by the incorporators or the board of directors. May be amended by the shareholders and by the board of directors, unless the articles of incorporation, the bylaws, or a statute reserve that power to the shareholders. UCA 16-10a-206, 1020.

Action Without Meeting: The shareholders may act without meeting if written consents to the action are signed by shareholders sufficient to carry the action at a meeting and notice is given to nonconsenting shareholders (election of directors requires unanimous written consent). UCA 16-10a-704. The board of directors may act without meeting if all directors sign a written consent to the action. UCA 16-10a-821. The shareholders and the board of directors may meet via conference telephone or similar communications equipment. UCA 16-10a-708, 820.

Stock Certificates: Must be signed by two officers designated in bylaws or by the board of directors. Shares may be issued without a certificate unless the articles of incorporation or bylaws provide otherwise. UCA 16-10a-625, 626.

Consideration For Stock: May consist of any tangible or intangible property or benefit to the corporation, including cash, promissory notes, services performed or to be performed, and other securities of the corporation. Shares issued for promissory notes or future services may be placed in escrow or otherwise restricted pending payment of note or performance of services. UCA 16-10a-621.

Stock Transfer Restrictions: May be imposed by the articles of incorporation, bylaws or a shareholders' agreement. A restriction must be conspicuously noted on the stock certificate to be enforceable against a person without knowledge of the restriction. UCA 16-10a-627.

Cumulative Voting: Not permitted unless provided for in the articles of incorporation. UCA 16-10a-728.

Preemptive Rights: Do not exist unless contained in the articles of incorporation. UCA 16-10a-630.

Acts Requiring Shareholder Approval: Unless a statute, the articles of incorporation, the bylaws, or the board of directors require a greater vote, a majority of all of the votes entitled to be cast is required for a merger or share exchange, for the sale or transfer of all or substantially all of the corporate assets not in the usual course of business, and for voluntary dissolution. UCA 16-10a-1103, 1202, 1402. Shareholder approval is also required for most amendments to the articles of incorporation (see above).

Board of Directors: Must consist of three or more individuals, except that there need not be more directors than shareholders entitled to vote. The number of directors must be specified in the bylaws. UCA 16-10a-803.

Officers: Those described in the bylaws or appointed by the board of directors in accordance with the bylaws. No specific officers required. The same person may simultaneously hold more than one office in the corporation. UCA 16-10a-830.

Foreign Corporations: Must obtain authority from the state filing official to do business in Utah. The statute contains a nonexclusive list of activities that do not constitute doing business in the state. The penalties for doing business without authority include nonaccess to state courts, corporate penalties of $100 per day up to $5,000 per year, and officer penalties of up to $1,000. UCA 16-10a-1501, 1502.

Close Corporation Laws: Shareholders may manage corporation under unanimous shareholder agreement. UCA 16-10a-732, 801(b).

Periodic Reports: Domestic and authorized foreign corporations must file an annual report with the state filing official and pay an annual report fee to remain in good standing. UCA 16-10a-1607. Such corporations must also pay an annual franchise tax. UCA 59-7-102, 123.

STATE FILING OFFICIAL. Dept. of Commerce, Corp. Div., 160 East 300 South, 2nd Fl., Salt Lake City, UT 84145-0801 (801-530-4849).

Fees:
- Filing Articles of Incorporation - $50
- Filing LLC Articles of Organization - $50
- Filing LLP Application Statement - $20
- Amending Articles of Incorporation - $25
- Other Fees - Contact state filing official.
- Name Reservation - $20
- Annual Report - $15

SUMMARY OF VERMONT BUSINESS ORGANIZATION LAWS

PARTNERSHIP LAWS.

General Partnerships: Uniform Partnership Act adopted. 11 VSA 3201 et seq.

Limited Partnerships: Revised Uniform Limited Partnership Act adopted. 11 VSA 3401 et seq.

Limited Liability Partnerships: Registered LLPs provided for. 11 VSA 3291 et seq.

Name Registration: Within 10 days after commencing business a partnership must file a return listing specified information with the Secretary of State. 11 VSA 1621.

LIMITED LIABILITY COMPANY LAWS. Uniform Limited Liability Company Act. 11 VSA 3001 et seq.

Formation of LLC: One or more persons may organize an LLC by filing articles of organization with the State Filing Official. See VSA 3023 for the article of organization content requirements.

General LLC Requirements: May have one or more members. May conduct any lawful business.

Management of LLC: Must state in articles of organization whether the LLC is to be manager-managed.

New or Substituted Members: Admission requires consent of all members unless operating agreement provides otherwise.

Conversion Statutes: Partnership conversion statute. 11 VSA 3122, 3123. Merger Statute. 11 VSA 3124 et seq.

CORPORATION LAWS. Vermont Business Corporation Act (based on Revised Model Business Corporation Act). 11A VSA 1.01 et seq.

Corporate Name: Must contain the word "corporation," "company," "incorporated," or "limited," or an abbreviation thereof. May not be the same as or deceptively similar to the name of any other corporation or registered name. May not contain the word "cooperative" unless it is organized as such. Name may be reserved for 120 days. No formal name clearance procedure. 11A VSA 4.01, 4.02.

Incorporators: One or more natural persons of age of majority. 11A VSA 2.01.

Articles of Incorporation:

Contents: See 11A VSA 2.02 for required and optional article of incorporation content requirements.

Filing and Recording: Two copies of the articles of incorporation must be filed with the Secretary of State and the filing fee paid. Corporate existence begins when a certificate of incorporation is issued by the Secretary of State. 11A VSA 1.20, 2.03.

Amendment: Requires a majority of the votes entitled to be cast unless a statute, the articles of incorporation, or the board of directors require a greater vote. The board of directors can make ministerial amendments without shareholder approval. 11A VSA 10.02, 10.03.

Organizational Meeting: Held after incorporation by initial board of directors if named in articles of incorporation. Otherwise held after incorporation by the incorporators, who may act without meeting if all incorporators sign a written consent to the action. 11A VSA 2.05.

Bylaws: Initial bylaws adopted by board of directors or incorporators. May be amended by board of directors or by shareholders unless power to amend is reserved to shareholders in articles of incorporation or unless shareholder amendment prohibits board of director amendment. 11A VSA 2.06, 10.20.

Action Without Meeting: Unless precluded by the articles of incorporation, shareholders may act without meeting if all shareholders entitled to vote on the action sign a written consent to the action or, if the articles of incorporation so provide, if the holders of a majority of the shares entitled to vote on the action sign a written consent to the action and prior notice of the action is given to each shareholder. 11A VSA 7.04. Unless precluded by the articles of incorporation or bylaws, the board of directors may act without meeting if all directors sign a written consent to the action. 11A VSA 8.21.

Stock Certificates: Must be signed by two officers designated in the bylaws or by the board of directors. Shares may be issued without a certificate unless the articles of incorporation or bylaws provide otherwise. 11A VSA 6.25, 6.26.

Consideration For Stock: May consist of money, tangible or intangible property, labor or services performed, or other securities of the corporation. May not consist of future services. 11A VSA 6.21.

Stock Transfer Restrictions: May be imposed by the articles of incorporation, bylaws or a shareholders' agreement. A restriction must be conspicuously noted on the stock certificate to be enforceable against a person without knowledge of the restriction. 11A VSA 6.27.

Cumulative Voting: Not permitted unless provided for in the articles of incorporation and 48 hours prior notice is given. 11A VSA 7.28.

Preemptive Rights: Do not exist unless provided for in the articles of incorporation. 11A VSA 6.30.

Acts Requiring Shareholder Approval: Unless a statute, the articles of incorporation, or the board of directors require a greater vote, a majority of the votes entitled to be cast is required for a merger or share exchange, for the sale or transfer of all or substantially all of the corporate assets not in the usual course of business, for voluntary dissolution, and for most amendments to the articles of incorporation. 11A VSA 11.03, 12.02, 14.02, 10.03.

Board of Directors: Must consist of three or more directors, except that there need not be more directors than shareholders. The number of directors may be specified in the bylaws or articles of incorporation. 11A VSA 8.03.

Officers: Must have president, secretary, and such other officers as the bylaws may provide. The same persons may hold any two or more offices except the offices of president and secretary (professional corporations excepted). 11A VSA 8.40.

Foreign Corporations: Must obtain a certificate of authority from the Secretary of State to transact business in Vermont. The penalties for transacting business without a certificate of authority include nonaccess to state courts and liability for all fees, taxes and penalties that would have been imposed had a certificate been issued, and a civil penalty of $50 per day not to exceed $1,000 per year. 11A VSA 15.01, 15.02.

Close Corporation Laws: Has Close Corporation Code whereunder a corporation with 35 or fewer shareholders may elect to be a close corporation. 11A VSA 20.01 et seq.

Periodic Reports: Domestic and authorized foreign corporations must file an annual report with the Secretary of State on prescribed forms and pay an annual fee within 2 1/2 months after the close of the corporation's fiscal year to remain in good standing. 11A VSA 16.22.

STATE FILING OFFICIAL. Secretary of State, Corporations Div., State House, Montpelier, VT 05602 (Telephone: 802-828-2386).

Fees:

Filing Articles of Incorporation - $75	Name Reservation - $25	Other Corp. Fees - See 11A VSA 1.22.
Amending Articles of Incorporation - $25		Other LLP Fees - See 11 VSA 3310.
Filing LLC Articles of Organization - $75		Other LLC Fees - See 11 VSA 3013.
Filing LLP Statement of Qualification - $75 ($100 for foreign LLP)		

SUMMARY OF VIRGINIA BUSINESS ORGANIZATION LAWS

PARTNERSHIP LAWS.

General Partnerships: Virginia Uniform Partnership Act (1996). CV 50-73.79 et seq.

Limited Partnerships: Revised Uniform Limited Partnership Act adopted. CV 50-73.1 et seq.

Limited Liability Partnerships: Registered LLPs for general & limited partnerships provided for. CV 50-73.132 et seq.

Name Registration: Every partnership must file a registration certificate where deeds are recorded for its place of business. CV 50-74. An assumed name certificate must be filed in the same office if the partnership name does not contain the names of all partners. CV 59.1-69.

LIMITED LIABILITY COMPANY LAWS. Virginia Limited Liability Company Act. CV 13.1-1000 et seq.

Formation of LLC: One or more persons may form an LLC by filing articles of organization with the state filing official. See CV 13.1-1011 for article of organization content requirements.

General LLC Requirements: May have one or more members. May conduct any lawful business.

Management of LLC: Vested in members in proportion to their capital contributions unless otherwise provided in the articles of organization or an operating agreement. CV 13.1-1022.

New or Substituted Members: Admission to LLC requires consent of all members unless otherwise provided in articles of organization or operating agreement. CV 13.1-1038.1, 1040.

Conversion Statutes: Partnership conversion statute. CV 13.1-1010.1, 1010.2. Merger statute. CV 13.1-1070 et seq.

CORPORATION LAWS. Virginia Stock Corporation Act (based on Revised Model Business Corporation Act). CV 13.1-601 et seq.

Corporate Name: Must contain the word "corporation," "company," "incorporated," or "limited," or a listed abbreviation thereof and must be distinguishable on the records of the state filing official from the names of other corporations. Name may be reserved for 120 days. Availability of name may be checked with state filing official by telephone. CV 13.1-630, 631.

Incorporators: One or more individuals or entities. CV 13.1-618.

Articles of Incorporation:

Contents: See CV 13.1-619 for required and optional article of incorporation content requirements.

Filing and Recording: A signed copy of the articles of incorporation must be filed with the state filing official and the filing fee and charter fee paid. Corporate existence begins when the state filing official issues a certificate of incorporation. CV 13.1-604, 618, 621.

Amendment: Requires two-thirds of all votes entitled to be cast, unless the articles of incorporation require a different vote of not less than a majority or unless the board of directors or a statute require a greater vote. The board of directors may make certain minor amendments without shareholder approval. CV 13.1-706, 707.

Organizational Meeting: Held after incorporation by the initial board of directors if named in articles of incorporation. Otherwise held after incorporation by the incorporators, who may act without meeting if all incorporators sign a written consent to the action. CV 13.1-623.

Bylaws: Initial bylaws adopted by incorporators or board of directors. Can be amended by the shareholders and by the board of directors unless the articles reserve that power to the shareholders. Shareholder amendments can prohibit board of director amendment. CV 13.1-624, 714.

Action Without Meeting: Shareholders may act without meeting if all shareholders entitled to vote sign a written consent to the action. CV 13.1-657. Unless the articles of incorporation or bylaws provide otherwise, the board of directors may meet via conference telephone or similar communications equipment and may act without meeting if all directors sign a written consent to the action. CV 13.1-684, 685.

Stock Certificates: Must be signed by two officers designated in the bylaws or by the board of directors. Shares may be issued without a certificate unless the articles of incorporation or bylaws provide otherwise. CV 13.1-647, 648.

Consideration For Stock: May consist of any tangible or intangible property or benefit to the corporation, including cash, promissory notes, services performed or to be performed, and other securities of the corporation. Shares issued for promissory notes or future services may be placed in escrow or otherwise restricted pending payment of note or performance of services. CV 13.1-643.

Stock Transfer Restrictions: May be contained in the articles of incorporation, bylaws or a shareholders' agreement. A restriction must be conspicuously noted on the stock certificate to be enforceable against a person without knowledge of the restriction. CV 13.1-649.

Cumulative Voting: Not permitted unless provided for in the articles of incorporation and prior notice is given. CV 13.1-669.

Preemptive Rights: Exist unless limited or denied in the articles of incorporation. CV 13.1-651.

Acts Requiring Shareholder Approval: Unless the articles of incorporation require a different vote of not less than a majority or unless the board of directors or a statute require a greater vote, two-thirds of all votes entitled to be cast is required for a merger or share exchange, for the sale of all or substantially all of the corporate assets not in the usual course of business, for voluntary dissolution, and for most amendments to the articles of incorporation (see above). CV 13.1-718, 724, 740, 707.

Board of Directors: May consist of one or more individuals, with the number of directors specified in the bylaws or articles of incorporation. No director may be named or elected without his or her prior consent. The board of directors may be dispensed with or have its authority limited in a shareholders' agreement or in the articles of incorporation. CV 13.1-673, 675.

Officers: Those provided for in bylaws or by board of directors. The same person may hold any two or more offices. CV 13.1-693.

Foreign Corporations: Must obtain a certificate of authority from the state filing official to transact business in Virginia. The statute contains a nonexclusive list of activities that do not constitute transacting business in the state. The penalties for transacting business without a certificate of authority include nonaccess to state courts and corporate and personal penalties of $500 to $5000. CV 13.1-757, 758, 613.

Close Corporation Laws: A corp. with 300 or fewer shareholders may be managed by shareholder's agreement under CV 13.1-671.1.

Periodic Reports: Domestic and authorized foreign corporations must file an annual report with the state filing official by April 1 of each year (after the year of incorporation) and pay an annual registration fee to remain in good standing. CV 13.1-775, 775.1.

STATE FILING OFFICIAL. State Corporation Commission, Jefferson Building, Richmond, VA 23219 (Telephone: 804-371-9672).

Fees:
- Filing Articles of Incorporation - $25
- Amending Articles of Incorporation - $25
- Other LLC Fees - See CV 13.1-1005.
- Charter Fee - $50 to $2,500 depending on capitalization.
- Name Reservation - $10
- Other LLP Fees - See CV 50-73.83.
- Filing LLC Articles of Organization - $100
- Other Corp. Fees - See CV 13.1-615.1, 616.
- Filing LLP Registration Statement - $100

SUMMARY OF WASHINGTON BUSINESS ORGANIZATION LAWS

PARTNERSHIP LAWS.

General Partnerships: Revised Partnership Act. RCW 25.05.005 et seq.

Limited Partnerships: Revised Uniform Limited Partnership Act adopted. RCW 25.10.010 et seq.

Limited Liability Partnerships: Limited liability partnerships provided for. RCW 25.05.500 et seq.

Name Registration: Must file a fictitious name certificate with the Department of Licensing if the partnership name does not contain the surname of each general partner. RCW 19.80.010.

LIMITED LIABILITY COMPANY LAWS. Washington Limited Liability Company Act. RCW 25.15.005 et seq.

Formation of LLC: One or more persons may form an LLC by filing a certificate of formation with the Secretary of State. See RCW 25.15.070 for the certificate of formation content requirements.

General LLC Requirements: May have one or more members. May conduct any lawful business except banking and insurance. Special rules for professional LLCs (RCW 25.15.045).

Management of LLC: Vested in members unless vested in manager(s) by certificate of formation. RCW 25.15.150.

New or Substituted Members: Admission to LLC requires consent of all members unless otherwise provided in LLC agreement.

Conversion Statutes: Merger statute. RCW 25.15.395 et seq. No partnership conversion statute.

CORPORATION LAWS. Washington Business Corporation Act (based on Revised Model Business Corp. Act). RCW 23B.01.010 et seq.

Corporate Name: Must contain the word "corporation," "incorporated," "company," or "limited" or a listed abbreviation thereof, and must be distinguishable from the names of other corporations and registered entities. Name may be reserved for 180 days. RCW 23B.04.010, 020.

Incorporators: One or more individuals or entities. RCW 23B.02.010.

Articles of Incorporation:

Contents: See RCW 23B.02.020 for required and optional article of incorporation content requirements.

Filing and Recording: An original and one copy of the articles of incorporation must be filed with the Secretary of State and the filing fee and initial license fee paid. Corporate existence begins when the articles of incorporation are filed. RCW 23B.01.200, 220, 23B.02.030.

Amendment: Requires two-thirds of all votes entitled to be cast, unless a statute or the board of directors require a greater vote or unless the articles of incorporation require a different vote of not less than a majority. The board of directors may make certain minor amendments without shareholder approval, unless the articles of incorporation provide otherwise. RCW 23B.10.020, 030.

Organizational Meeting: Held after incorporation by initial board of directors if named in articles of incorporation. Otherwise held after incorporation by the incorporators, who may act without meeting if all incorporators sign a written consent to the action. RCW 23B.02.050.

Bylaws: Initial bylaws adopted by incorporators or board of directors. May be amended by the shareholders and the board of directors unless the articles reserve that power to the shareholders. Shareholder amendments can prohibit board of director amendment. RCW 23B.02.060, 10.200.

Action Without Meeting: Shareholders may act without meeting if all shareholders entitled to vote sign a written consent to the action, and, if the bylaws or articles of incorporation so provide, may meet via conference telephone or similar communications equipment. RCW 23B.07.040, 080. Unless the articles of incorporation or bylaws provide otherwise, the board of directors may meet via conference telephone or similar communications equipment and may act without meeting if all directors sign a written consent to the action. RCW 23B.08.200, 210.

Stock Certificates: Must be signed by two officers designated in the bylaws or by the board of directors. Shares may be issued without a certificate unless the articles of incorporation or bylaws provide otherwise. RCW 23B.06.250, 260.

Consideration For Stock: May consist of any tangible or intangible property or benefit to the corporation, including cash, promissory notes, services performed or to be performed, and other securities of the corporation. Shares issued for promissory notes or future services may be placed in escrow or otherwise restricted pending payment of note or performance of services. RCW 23B.06.210.

Stock Transfer Restrictions: May be imposed by the articles of incorporation, bylaws or a shareholders' agreement. A restriction must be conspicuously noted on the stock certificate to be enforceable against a person without knowledge of the restriction. RCW 23B.06.270.

Cumulative Voting: Permitted unless denied in the articles of incorporation. RCW 23B.07.280.

Preemptive Rights: Exist unless denied or limited in the articles of incorporation. RCW 23B.06.300.

Acts Requiring Shareholder Approval: Unless a statute or the board of directors requires a greater vote or the articles of incorporation require a different vote of not less than a majority, two-thirds of the votes entitled to be cast is required for a merger or share exchange, for the sale or disposition of all or substantially all of the corporate assets not in the usual course of business, for voluntary dissolution, and for most amendments to the articles of incorporation (see above). RCW 23B.11.030, 12.020, 14.020, 10.030.

Board of Directors: May consist of one or more individuals with the number of directors specified in the articles of incorporation or bylaws. Articles of incorporation or shareholders agreement may dispense with or limit authority of board of directors. RCW 23B.08.010, 030, .07.320.

Officers: Those described in the bylaws or appointed by the board of directors in accordance with the bylaws. No specific officers required. The same person may simultaneously hold more than one office in the corporation. RCW 23B.08.400.

Foreign Corporations: Must obtain a certificate of authority from the Secretary of State before transacting business in Washington. The statute contains a nonexclusive list of activities that do not constitute transacting business in the state. The penalties for transacting business without a certificate of authority include nonaccess to state courts and liability for all fees and penalties that would have been imposed had a certificate of authority been issued. RCW 23B.15.010, 020.

Close Corporation Laws: May manage corporation under unanimous shareholders agreement. RCW 23B.07.320.

Periodic Reports: Domestic and authorized foreign corporations must file an initial and an annual report with the Secretary of State and pay an annual report fee and an annual license fee to remain in good standing. The initial report is due 120 days from the date of incorporation. Annual reports are due when the annual license fee is due (Secretary of State sends notice). RCW 23B.16.220, 01.220, 530.

STATE FILING OFFICIAL. Secretary of State, Corporation Div., P.O. Box 40234, Olympia, WA 98504-0234 (Telephone: 360-753-7115).

Fees: Filing Articles of Incorporation - $175 (includes initial license fee). Other LLC Fees - See RCW 25.15.
Filing LLC Certificate of Formation - $175 Name Reservation - $20 Other LLP Fees - See RCW 25.05.
Filing LLP Registration Application - $175 Other Corp. Fees - See RCW 23B.01.220, 500-570.

SUMMARY OF WEST VIRGINIA BUSINESS ORGANIZATION LAWS

PARTNERSHIP LAWS.

General Partnerships: Uniform Partnership Act adopted. WVC 47B-1-1 et seq.
Limited Partnerships: Revised Uniform Limited Partnership Act adopted. WVC 47-9-1 et seq.
Limited Liability Partnerships: Registered LLPs provided for. WVC 47B-10-1 et seq.
Name Registration: Must file a fictitious name certificate with the clerk of the county commission in the county of the partnership's principal place of business if the partnership name does not contain the names of all partners. WVC 47-8-2.

LIMITED LIABILITY COMPANY LAWS. Uniform Limited Liability Company Act adopted. WVC 31B-1-101 et seq.

Formation of LLC: One or more persons may organize an LLC by filing articles of organization with the Secretary of State. See WVC 31B-2-203 for the article of organization content requirements.
General LLC Requirements: May have one or more members. May be organized for any lawful purpose.
Management of LLC: Must state in articles of organization whether LLC is to be manager-managed.
New or Substituted Members: Admission to LLC requires consent of all members unless operating agreement provides otherwise.
Conversion Statutes: Partnership conversion statute. WVC 31B-9-902, 903. Merger statute. WVC 31B-9-904 et seq.

CORPORATION LAWS. West Virginia Corporation Act (based on Model Business Corporation Act). WVC 31-1-1 et seq.

Corporate Name: Must contain the word "corporation," "company," "incorporated," or "limited" or an abbreviation thereof and may not be the same as or deceptively similar to the name of any other corporation. Name may be reserved for 120 days. Availability of name may be checked with Secretary of State without charge by letter or telephone. WVC 31-1-11, 12.
Incorporators: One or more persons or a corporation. WVC 31-1-26.
Articles of Incorporation:
Contents: See WVC 31-1-27 for required and optional article of incorporation content requirements.
Filing and Recording: Two original copies of the articles of incorporation must be filed with the Secretary of State and the filing fee and initial license tax paid. Within 6 months the certificate of incorporation must be recorded with the clerk of the county commission in the county of the corporation's principal office. Corporate existence begins when the Secretary of State issues a certificate of incorporation. WVC 31-1-28, 29.
Amendment: Requires a majority vote of the shares entitled to vote unless the articles require a greater vote. WVC 31-1-107, 71.
Organizational Meeting: Held after incorporation by the initial board of directors. WVC 31-1-30.
Bylaws: Initial bylaws adopted by the board of directors. May be amended by the board of directors, subject to repeal or change by the shareholders, unless that power is reserved to the shareholders in the articles of incorporation. WVC 31-1-17.
Action Without Meeting: The shareholders may act without meeting if all shareholders entitled to vote sign a written consent to the action. Unless otherwise provided in the articles of incorporation or bylaws, the board of directors may act without meeting if all directors sign a written consent to the action. If the articles of incorporation or bylaws so provide, the shareholders and the board of directors may meet via conference telephone or similar communications equipment. WVC 31-1-73.
Stock Certificates: Must be signed by the president or the vice president and by the secretary or the assistant secretary. Shares may not be issued without a certificate. WVC 31-1-87.
Consideration For Stock: May consist of money, tangible or intangible property, or labor or services actually performed for the corporation. May not consist of promissory notes or future services. WVC 31-1-82.
Stock Transfer Restrictions: May be included in the articles of incorporation. WVC 31-1-27(b)(5).
Cumulative Voting: Must be permitted. WVC 31-1-93.
Preemptive Rights: Exist unless limited or denied in the articles of incorporation. WVC 31-1-27(b)(4).
Acts Requiring Shareholder Approval: Unless the articles of incorporation require a greater vote, a majority vote of the outstanding shares entitled to vote is required for a merger or consolidation, for the sale or transfer of all or substantially all of the corporate assets not in the usual course of business, for voluntary dissolution, and to amend the articles of incorporation. WVC 31-1-117, 121, 126, 107, 71.
Board of Directors: May consist of one or more persons. The number of directors must be specified in the articles of incorporation or bylaws. The board of directors may be dispensed with or have its authority limited in the articles of incorporation. WVC 31-1-21, 95.
Officers: Must have president, secretary and treasurer. The bylaws may provide for other officers. The same person may hold any two or more offices in the corporation except the offices of president and secretary. WVC 31-1-104.
Foreign Corporations: Must obtain a certificate of authority from the Secretary of State before transacting business in West Virginia. The statute contains a nonexclusive list of activities that do not constitute transacting business in the state. The penalties for transacting business without a certificate of authority include nonaccess to state courts and liability for all fees, taxes and penalties that would have been assessed had a certificate of authority been issued. WVC 31-1-49, 66.
Close Corporation Laws: None.
Periodic Reports: Domestic and authorized foreign corporations must file an annual report on prescribed forms with the State Tax Commissioner by July 1 of each year and pay an annual license tax to remain in good standing. WVC 11-12C-2, 4.

STATE FILING OFFICIAL. Secretary of State, State Capitol Building, Charleston, WV 25305 (Telephone: 304-558-6000).

Fees:
Filing Articles of Incorporation - $50
Filing LLC Articles of Organization - $100
Filing LLP Registration Statement - $500
Amending Articles of Incorporation - $25
Other Corp., LLC & LLP Fees - See WVC 59-1-2.

SUMMARY OF WISCONSIN BUSINESS ORGANIZATION LAWS

PARTNERSHIP LAWS.

General Partnerships: Uniform Partnership Act adopted. WSA 178.01 et seq.

Limited Partnerships: Revised Uniform Partnership Act adopted. WSA 179.01 et seq.

Limited Liability Partnerships: Registered LLPs provided for. WSA 178.40 et seq.

Name Registration: Not Required.

LIMITED LIABILITY COMPANY LAWS. Wisconsin Limited Liability Company Act. WSA 183.0102 et seq.

Formation of LLC: One or more persons may form an LLC by filing articles of organization with the State Filing Official. See WSA 183.0202 for the article of organization content requirements.

General LLC Requirements: May have one or more members. May conduct any lawful business.

Management of LLC: Vested in members unless vested in manager(s) by articles of organization. WSA 183.0401.

New or Substituted Members: Consent of all members required unless operating agreement provides otherwise. WSA 183.0706, .0801.

Conversion Statutes: None in LLC Act.

CORPORATION LAWS. Wisconsin Business Corporation Law (based on Revised Model Business Corporation Act). WSA 180.0101 et seq.

Corporate Name: Must contain the word "corporation," "incorporated," "company," or "limited" or a listed abbreviation thereof, and must be distinguishable on the records of the Secretary of State from the name of any other corporation or other registered entity. Name may be reserved for 120 days. Availability of name may be checked with Secretary of State by telephone. WSA 180.0401, .0402.

Incorporators: One or more individuals or entities. WSA 180.0201.

Articles of Incorporation:

Contents: See WSA 180.0202 for required and optional article of incorporation content requirements.

Filing and Recording: An original and one copy of the articles of incorporation must be filed with the Secretary of State and the filing fee paid. Corporate existence begins when the articles of incorporation are accepted for filing. WSA 180.0120, .0203.

Amendment: Requires a majority of the votes entitled to be cast unless a statute, the articles of incorporation, a bylaw adopted under authority of the articles of incorporation, or the board of directors require a greater vote. The board of directors can make ministerial amendments without shareholder approval, unless the articles of incorporation provide otherwise. WSA 180.1002, .1003.

Organizational Meeting: Held after incorporation by initial board of directors if named in articles of incorporation. Otherwise held after incorporation by the incorporators, who may act without meeting if all incorporators sign a written consent to the action. WSA 180.0205.

Bylaws: Initial bylaws adopted by incorporators, shareholders, or board of directors. May be amended by the shareholders and by the board of directors unless the articles of incorporation, a statute, or a shareholder amendment provide otherwise. WSA 180.0206, .1020.

Action Without Meeting: Shareholders may act without meeting if a written consent to the action is signed by all shareholders or (except when cumulative voting is permitted) by shareholders sufficient to carry the action at a meeting if the articles of incorporation so provide and if notice is given to nonconsenting shareholders. WSA 180.0704. Unless the articles of incorporation or bylaws provide otherwise, the board of directors may meet via conference telephone or similar communications equipment or by fax and may act without meeting if all directors sign a written consent to the action. WSA 180.0820, .0821.

Stock Certificates: Must be signed by two officers designated in the bylaws or by the board of directors. Shares may be issued without a certificate unless the articles of incorporation or bylaws provide otherwise. WSA 180.0625, .0626.

Consideration For Stock: May consist of any tangible or intangible property or benefit to the corporation, including cash, promissory notes, services performed or to be performed, and other securities of the corporation. Shares issued for promissory notes or future services may be placed in escrow or otherwise restricted pending payment of note or performance of services. WSA 180.0621.

Stock Transfer Restrictions: May be imposed by the articles of incorporation, bylaws or a shareholders' agreement. A restriction must be conspicuously noted on the stock certificate to be enforceable against a person without knowledge of the restriction. WSA 180.0627.

Cumulative Voting: Not permitted unless provided for in the articles of incorporation and prior notice is given. WSA 180.0728.

Preemptive Rights: Do not exist unless contained in the articles of incorporation for corps. formed after January 1, 1991. WSA 180.0630.

Acts Requiring Shareholder Approval: Unless the articles of incorporation, a statute, or a bylaw adopted under authority of the articles of incorporation require a greater vote, a majority of the votes entitled to be cast is required for a merger or share exchange, for the sale or transfer of all or substantially all of the corporate assets not in the usual course of business, and for voluntary dissolution. WSA 180.1103, .1202, .1402. Shareholder approval is also required for most amendments to the articles of incorporation (see above).

Board of Directors: May consist of one or more natural persons, with the number specified in the articles or bylaws. WSA 180.0803.

Officers: Those described in the bylaws or appointed by the board of directors in accordance with the bylaws. No specific officers required. The same person may simultaneously hold more than one office in the corporation. WSA 180.0840.

Foreign Corporations: Must obtain a certificate of authority from the Secretary of State before transacting business in Wisconsin. The statute contains a nonexclusive list of activities that do not constitute transacting business in the state. The penalties for transacting business without a certificate include nonaccess to state courts, liability for all fees, taxes and penalties that would have been imposed had a certificate of authority been issued, and a civil penalty of the lesser of \$5,000 or 50% of the accrued fees, taxes and penalties. WSA 180.1501, .1502.

Close Corporation Laws: Has Close Corporation Code (WSA 180.1801-.1837) whereunder a corporation with 50 or fewer shareholders may elect to be a statutory close corporation by so providing in its articles of incorporation.

Periodic Reports: Domestic and authorized foreign corporations must file an annual report on prescribed forms with the Secretary of State by the last day of the quarter of its anniversary month and pay an annual report fee to remain in good standing. WSA 180.1622.

STATE FILING OFFICIAL. Secretary of State, Corporation Division, P.O. Box 7846, Madison, WI 53707 (Telephone: 608-266-3590).

Fees:

Filing Articles of Incorporation - \$90 to \$10,000 depending on capitalization.

Name Reservation - \$15 written, \$30 telephone

Amending Articles of Incorporation - \$40 (more if capitalization increased).

Other Corp. fees - See WSA 180.0122.

Filing LLC Articles of Organization - \$130

Other LLC Fees - See WSA 183.0114.

Filing LLP Registration Statement - \$100

Other LLP Fees - See WSA 178.48.

SUMMARY OF WYOMING BUSINESS ORGANIZATION LAWS

PARTNERSHIP LAWS.

General Partnerships: Uniform Partnership Act adopted. WSA 17-21-101 et seq.

Limited Partnerships: Revised Uniform Limited Partnership Act adopted. WSA 17-14-201 et seq.

Limited Liability Partnerships: Registered LLPs provided for. WSA 17-21-1101 et seq.

Name Registration: Not required. A trade name may be registered under WSA 40-2-103.

LIMITED LIABILITY COMPANY LAWS. Wyoming Limited Liability Company Act. WSA 17-15-101 et seq.

Formation of LLC: A person may form an LLC by filing articles of organization with the Secretary of State. See WSA 17-15-107(a) for the article of organization content requirements.

General LLC Requirements: Must have two or more members. May conduct any lawful business except banking and insurance. LLC may elect to be "flexible LLC" under WSA 17-15-144.

Management of LLC: Vested in members unless otherwise provided in articles of organization. WSA 17-15-116.

New or Substituted Members: Admission to LLC requires written consent of all members. WSA 17-15-122.

Conversion Statutes: Merger statute. WSA 17-15-139 et seq. No partnership conversion statute.

CORPORATION LAWS. Wyoming Business Corporation Act (based on Revised Model Business Corporation Act). WSA 17-16-101 et seq.

Corporate Name: No required words. May not be the same as or deceptively similar to the existing or reserved name of any other corporation, limited partnership, limited liability company, trade name, or trademark. Name may be reserved for 120 days. Availability of name may be checked by telephone with the Secretary of State without fee. WSA 17-16-401, 402.

Incorporators: One or more individuals or entities. WSA 17-16-201.

Articles of Incorporation:

Contents: See WSA 17-16-202 for required and optional article of incorporation content requirements.

Filing and Recording: An original and one copy of the signed articles of incorporation, together with a consent to appointment signed by the registered agent, must be filed with the Secretary of State and the filing fee paid. Corporate existence begins when the articles of incorporation are accepted for filing. WSA 17-16-120, 202, 203.

Amendment: Requires a majority of the votes entitled to be cast unless a statute, the board of directors, or the articles of incorporation require a greater vote. The board of directors can make minor amendments without shareholder approval. WSA 17-16-1002, 1003.

Organizational Meeting: Held after incorporation by initial board of directors if named in articles of incorporation. Otherwise held after incorporation by the incorporators, who may act without meeting if each incorporator signs a written consent to the action. WSA 17-16-205.

Bylaws: Initial bylaws adopted by incorporators or board of directors. May be amended by the shareholders and by the board of directors unless the articles reserve that power to the shareholders. Shareholder amendments can prohibit director amendment. WSA 17-16-206, 1020.

Action Without Meeting: Shareholders may act without meeting if all shareholders entitled to vote sign a written consent to the action. WSA 17-16-704. Unless the articles of incorporation or bylaws provide otherwise, the board of directors may meet via conference telephone or similar communications equipment and may act without meeting if all directors sign a written consent to the action. WSA 17-16-820, 821.

Stock Certificates: Must be signed by two officers designated in the bylaws or by the board of directors. Shares may be issued without a certificate unless the articles of incorporation or bylaws provide otherwise. WSA 17-16-625, 626.

Consideration For Stock: May consist of any tangible or intangible property or benefit to the corporation, including cash, promissory notes, services performed or to be performed, and other securities of the corporation. Shares issued for promissory notes or future services may be placed in escrow or otherwise restricted pending payment of note or performance of services. WSA 17-16-621.

Stock Transfer Restrictions: May be imposed by the articles of incorporation, bylaws or a shareholders' agreement. A restriction must be conspicuously noted on the stock certificate to be enforceable against a person without knowledge of the restriction. WSA 17-16-627.

Cumulative Voting: Not permitted unless provided for in the articles of incorporation and prior notice is given. WSA 17-16-728.

Preemptive Rights: Do not exist unless contained in the articles of incorporation. WSA 17-16-630.

Acts Requiring Shareholder Approval: Unless a statute, the articles of incorporation or the board of directors require a greater vote, a majority of the votes entitled to be cast is required for a merger or share exchange, for the sale or disposition of all or substantially all of the corporate assets not in the usual course of business, for voluntary dissolution, and for most amendments to the articles of incorporation (see above). WSA 17-16-1103, 1202, 1402, 1003.

Board of Directors: May consist of one or more individuals, with the number of directors specified in the bylaws or articles of incorporation. A corporation with 50 or fewer shareholders may dispense with or limit the authority of the board of directors. WSA 17-16-803, 801.

Officers: Those described in the bylaws or appointed by the board of directors in accordance with the bylaws. No specific officers required. The same person may simultaneously hold more than one office in the corporation. WSA 17-16-840.

Foreign Corporations: Must obtain a certificate of authority from the Secretary of State before transacting business in Wyoming. The statute contains a nonexclusive list of activities that do not constitute transacting business in the state. The penalties for transacting business without a certificate include nonaccess to state courts, liability for all fees and taxes that would have accrued had a certificate of authority been issued plus 18%, and a penalty of $1,000. WSA 17-16-1501, 1502.

Close Corporation Laws: Has Wyoming Close Corporation Supplement (WSA 17-17-101 et seq.) whereunder a corporation with 35 or fewer shareholders may elect to be a statutory close corporation.

Periodic Reports: Domestic and authorized foreign corporations must file an annual report with the Secretary of State by the first day of its registration month and pay an annual license tax to remain in good standing. WSA 17-16-1630.

STATE FILING OFFICIAL. Secretary of State, Corp. Division, State Capitol Building, Cheyenne, WY 82002 (Telephone: 307-777-7311).

Fees: Filing Articles of Incorporation - $100; Amending Articles of Incorporation - $25; Name Reservation - $30; Filing LLP Registration - $100; Other Corp. Fees - Contact Secretary of State.; Filing LLC Articles of Organization - $100 to $25,000 (based on capitalization); Other LLC Fees - See WSA 17-15-132.

SUBJECT INDEX

For All Chapters

SUBJECT INDEX
For All Chapters

SUBJECT INDEX
For All Chapters

SUBJECT INDEX
For All Chapters

SUBJECT INDEX
For All Chapters